OBSERV

HANDBOOK

2003

EDITOR
RAJIV GUPTA

NINETY-FIFTH YEAR OF PUBLICATION

© THE ROYAL ASTRONOMICAL SOCIETY OF CANADA
136 DUPONT STREET, TORONTO ON M5R 1V2
2002

ISSN 0080-4193
ISBN 0-9689141-2-8

PRINTED IN CANADA
BY THE UNIVERSITY OF TORONTO PRESS

CANADIAN PUBLICATIONS MAIL REGISTRATION NO. 09818
CANADA POST PUBLICATION AGREEMENT NO. 40069313
U.S. PERIODICALS REGISTRATION NO. 010-751

CONTENTS

**Key to
Marginal
Chapter
Symbols**

Basic
Data

Time

Optics
and
Observing

The Sky
Month
by Month

The
Sun

The
Moon

Planets
and
Satellites

Asteroids

Meteors,
Comets,
and Dust

Stars

Nebulae
and
Galaxies

THE OBSERVER'S HANDBOOK

The *Observer's Handbook* is one of Canada's oldest scientific publications. Created by C.A. Chant, Professor of Astronomy at the University of Toronto, it first appeared nearly a century ago as *The Canadian Astronomical Handbook for 1907*, a small (13 × 17 cm), 108-page publication. A second edition covered the year 1908, but for the following two years most of the information that would have appeared was published instead in installments in the *Journal of the RASC*. The Council of the Society decided to return to a separate publication for 1911 with a new name—the *Observer's Handbook*—and it has been published annually ever since.

Each year some 12 000 copies of the Handbook are distributed to many countries throughout the world, to amateur and professional astronomers, to educators at school and university levels, and to many observatories, planetaria, and libraries. The Handbook is the main source of income for the Royal Astronomical Society of Canada. Since the first edition in 1907, the various editors, assistant editors, editorial assistants (see p. 7), and contributors (see the inside front cover) have voluntarily contributed their time and expertise to produce this unique book.

EDITORS OF THE OBSERVER'S HANDBOOK

		Position	Editions	President RASC
C.A. Chant	(1865–1956)	Editor	1907–1957	1903–1907
Frank Hogg	(1904–1951)	Assistant Editor	1939–1951	1940–1942
Ruth Northcott	(1913–1969)	Assistant Editor	1952–1957	1962–1964
		Editor	1958–1970	
John Percy	(1941–	Editor	1971–1981	1978–1980
Roy Bishop	(1939–	Editor	1982–2000	1984–1986
Rajiv Gupta	(1958–	Editor	2001–	2002–

The *Observer's Handbook* is intended to be "a companion which the observer would wish always to have in his pocket or on the table before him."

C.A. Chant, Toronto, 1906

"We believe that the *Observer's Handbook* is a truly significant contribution that Canadian astronomy in general and our Society in particular has been making to the dissemination of astronomical knowledge for half a century. I trust that it will still occupy the same position of respect after the first hundred years."

Ruth Northcott, Ottawa, 1964

"The more one knows, the more one can benefit from the Handbook. It inspires all who leaf through its pages to learn and question what the tables, graphs and data mean, perhaps to speculate on the mysteries of the Universe, and above all, to get out and look beyond our world. You have in your hands a key to the Universe—a key which will fit many doors. Please use it well and treasure it."

Peter Broughton, Toronto, 1992
Author of *Looking Up, A History of the RASC*

"The *Observer's Handbook* is the single most useful publication for the observational astronomer. Its combination of authoritative data, informative diagrams, and concise text is unique. Anyone interested in astronomy, beginner or expert, amateur or professional, student or teacher, will find the *Observer's Handbook* indispensable. Its international reputation for quality is a credit both to its many contributors and to Canadian astronomy."

Roy Bishop, Halifax, 2000

HOW TO USE THIS HANDBOOK

This Handbook is a concise, high-density compilation of information that is of interest to observers. By reading the following points, you will allow yourself to reap maximum benefit from it.

(1) The Handbook is composed of various *sections*. Related sections are grouped into chapters, as listed in the CONTENTS. Chapter titles are given in large dark-grey boxes and section titles against light background shades, both of which extend to the edge of the page. The section title and chapter title are given in headers at the top of the pages. In addition, staggered marginal symbols (see p. iii for a key) mark the edges of the pages in each chapter. These various identifiers are meant to facilitate the quick location of desired material.

(2) References to other sections are given in SMALL CAPITAL TYPE, and this type is generally reserved for this purpose. Internet email addresses and websites are also given in a **distinctive font**.

(3) The INDEX at the back contains a short listing of keywords.

(4) Long tables are broken into blocks, usually with the shading of blocks of rows, to make the location of entries easier. Every table has a shaded header with the titles of the various columns given in bold type. Detailed explanation of the meaning of the columns is usually given in accompanying text.

(5) SI symbols and abbreviations are used throughout. See pp. 29 and 32 in the section SOME ASTRONOMICAL AND PHYSICAL DATA for the most common abbreviations. The letter "m" is used to denote both minutes of right ascension and metres; the meaning will be clear from the context. Minutes of time are usually abbreviated "min."

(6) The time scale Universal Time is generally used. Times of day are usually given in the 24-hour clock, using numerals separated by colons. The section TIME AND TIME SCALES on pp. 35–40 explains the various time scales used in astronomy.

(7) The section TERMINOLOGY AND SYMBOLS on p. 19 lists Greek letters (and other symbols) and defines some basic terms.

(8) The section TEACHING AND THE OBSERVER'S HANDBOOK on pp. 16–18 gives an overview of the contents of this Handbook.

(9) The website of the Handbook is **www.rasc.ca/handbook**. Resources related to the Handbook are given at this site, and any updates and corrections will also be posted there.

Cover photo

Meteor watching is one of the most popular pastimes of stargazers, whether they are serious observers or beginners. In 2001, the Leonid shower provided a spectacular display, with hourly rates for North American observers approaching or exceeding 1000 on the night of Nov. 17.

This unusual photo of a Leonid fireball was taken by Barry Burgess in St. Croix, Nova Scotia, using a 35-mm f/2 camera lens. It was a 6-minute exposure at 8h UT on Nov. 18, taken on Fuji Superia 400 film using a homemade barn-door tracker. Remarkably, the fireball happened to lie behind a stray cloud, which it illuminated as it passed under Saturn and toward Aldebaran.

For information on meteors, fireballs, and meteorites, see pp. 221–231 in this Handbook.

EDITOR'S COMMENTS

With regret, I announce the retirement of Joseph Veverka, who provided the SATELLITES OF THE SOLAR SYSTEM table for 24 editions, from 1979 to 2002. During that time the number of known natural satellites mushroomed from 35 to 91 and the table grew from a single page to four. On behalf of almost a quarter century of Handbook readers, I thank Professor Veverka for keeping us up-to-date on this important aspect of the solar system.

I welcome the following new contributors: Randy Attwood, who takes over the VOYAGES IN OUR SOLAR SYSTEM section from Roy Bishop; Philip D. Nicholson, who takes over the NATURAL SATELLITES OF THE PLANETS section; and Allan Rahill, who provides a new section, WEATHER RESOURCES ON THE INTERNET. This edition also contains one other new section, POLAR ALIGNMENT, provided by the editor, and the section 2003 TRANSIT OF MERCURY, by Fred Espenak, treats one of the astronomical highlights of the year.

In addition, the following enhancements appear in the current edition:

(1) An introduction has been added to NATURAL SATELLITES OF THE PLANETS.

(2) The TIME section has been updated and expanded.

(3) New, more accurate satellite-based maps have replaced the former surface-based maps in FREQUENCY OF NIGHTTIME CLOUD COVER.

(4) Librated lunar graphics have been added to THE SKY MONTH BY MONTH.

(5) A diagram giving total solar eclipses from 2001–2025 has been added to ECLIPSE PATTERNS.

(6) The TIDES AND THE EARTH-MOON SYSTEM section has been updated and expanded.

(7) The treatment of Mars in PLANETS FOR 2003 has been revised, and a new map of Mars, by Daniel Troiani, accompanies this expanded coverage.

The editorial team introduced last year continues to work very well, and I thank my most capable assistants (listed at the top right of this page) for their countless hours of work on this edition.

Dr. Rajiv Gupta
Department of Mathematics
University of British Columbia
Vancouver BC V6T 1Z2, Canada
gupta@interchange.ubc.ca
Vancouver, 2002 Aug. 15

THE OBSERVER'S HANDBOOK

EDITOR
 Rajiv Gupta
COPY EDITOR
 Betty Robinson
PROOFREADER
 James Edgar

In addition to the 40 contributors listed on the inside front cover, several other individuals and organizations played a role in the production of this Handbook.

Much of the data contained in this Handbook comes from the publications *Astronomical Phenomena for the Year 2003* and *The Astronomical Almanac 2003,* both prepared jointly by the U.S. Naval Observatory's Nautical Almanac Office and Her Majesty's Nautical Almanac Office. Also, the Institut de Mécanique Céleste et de Calcul des Ephémérides in Paris provided ephemerides for Jupiter's Galilean satellites.

The following individuals provided suggestions that led to major enhancements in this edition: Roger Fell and Denis Grey (librated lunar graphics) and Patrice Scattolin (weather resources on the Internet).

In addition, assistance, corrections, or suggestions for improvement were received from Jay Anderson, Brent Archinal, Friedemann Bauer, Roy Bishop, Milan Brkanovic, Alan Dyer, Leo Enright, Bill Greer, Dave Hare, Alister Ling, Joe Morris, Lee Paulsel, Vance Petriew, Ray Shapp, and Daniel Troiani

AN INVITATION FOR MEMBERSHIP IN
THE ROYAL ASTRONOMICAL SOCIETY OF CANADA

The beginnings of the Royal Astronomical Society of Canada go back to the mid-1800s. Then, in 1890, the Society was incorporated within the province of Ontario, received its Royal Charter from King Edward VII in 1903, and was federally incorporated in 1968. The National Office of the Society (containing the business office and library) is located at 136 Dupont St., Toronto ON M5R 1V2; telephone: (416) 924-7973 or (888) 924-7272 from within Canada; email: rasc@rasc.ca; website: www.rasc.ca.

The RASC consists of two employees, Executive Secretary Bonnie Bird and Membership and Publications Coordinator Isaac McGillis, plus more than 4500 members. RASC members are from many countries and all walks of life. Members receive the *Observer's Handbook* (published in September for the next calendar year) and the bimonthly *Journal of the RASC,* which contains review articles, research papers on historical and contemporary topics, education notes, general notes of astronomical interest, book reviews, news items concerning the Society and its Centres, informal articles, and letters. Also included is *SkyNews,* Canada's popular bimonthly astronomy magazine.

Membership fees are $44 per year, or $27.50 for persons under 21 years of age. Life membership is $880. (For members outside of Canada, these figures are to be read as U.S. dollars, to cover higher mailing costs.) An applicant may affiliate with one of the Centres of the Society across Canada or join the Society directly as an unattached member (some Centres levy a surcharge above the regular membership fee).

Mailing addresses, telephone numbers, and email addresses of the 26 RASC Centres, listed in the order that the stars rise, are given below. Each Centre's website may be accessed by appending the Centre's name, with punctuation marks and spaces omitted, to the base URL www.rasc.ca, for example, www.rasc.ca/stjohns (for the Centre Francophone de Montréal, append montrealf), or by clicking a link at this base URL.

St. John's: c/o 206 Frecker Dr., St John's NF A1E 5H9; (709) 364-4953; randy@morgan.ucs.mun.ca

Charlottetown: 38 Mt Edward Rd., Charlottetown PE C1A 5S2; (902) 894-9613; cperryphoto@pei.sympatico.ca

Halifax: PO Box 31011, Halifax NS B3K 5T9; (902) 420-5633; halifax@rasc.ca

Moncton: c/o Dr. Francis LeBlanc, Département de physique et d'astronomie, Université de Moncton, Moncton NB E1A 3E9; (506) 858-3781; leblanfn@umoncton.ca

Québec: 2000 boul. Montmorency, Québec QC G1J 5E7; (418) 660-2815; srac_quebec@hotmail.com

Montréal: (Centre Francophone) CP 206, Station St-Michel, Montréal QC H2A 3L9; (514) 728-4422; scattol@videotron.ca

Montreal: PO Box 1752, Station B, Montreal QC H3B 3L3; (514) 845-2612; mbratton@generation.net

Ottawa: PO Box 33012, 1974 Baseline Rd., Ottawa ON K2C 0E0; (613) 830-3381; contact@ottawa.rasc.ca

Kingston: PO Box 1793, Kingston ON K7L 5J6; (613) 377-6028; rascexec@cliff.path.queensu.ca

Niagara: PO Box 4040, St. Catharines ON L2R 7S3; (905) 935-9355; rascniag@vaxxine.com

Toronto: c/o Ontario Science Centre, 770 Don Mills Rd., Don Mills ON M3C 1T3; (416) 724-7827; nason@tvo.org

Hamilton: PO Box 1223, Waterdown ON L0R 2H0; (905) 544-1747; mark.kaye@sympatico.ca

Kitchener-Waterloo: c/o Peter Daniel, 36 Talbot St., Apt. 101, Kitchener ON N2M 2A9; (519) 823-5769; peekr@golden.net

London: PO Box 842, Station B, London ON N6A 4Z3; (519) 472-1437; pjedicke@fanshawec.on.ca

Sarnia: c/o Jim Selinger, 160 George St., Sarnia ON N7T 7V4; (519) 337-6815; jselinge@mnsi.net

Windsor: c/o Frank J. Shepley, 671 Inman Sideroad, RR #2, Ruthven ON N0P 2G0; (519) 839-5934; fshepley@wincom.net

Thunder Bay: 286 Trinity Cres., Thunder Bay ON P7C 5V6; (807) 475-3406; bronsont@air.on.ca

Winnipeg: PO Box 2694, Winnipeg MB R3C 4B3; (204) 988-0627; Scott_Young@ManitobaMuseum.MB.ca

Regina: PO Box 20014, Cornwall Centre, Regina SK S4P 4J7; (306) 751-0128; info@ras.sk.ca

Saskatoon: PO Box 317, RPO University, Saskatoon SK S7N 4J8; (306) 249-1091; dicksonl@sasktel.net

Edmonton: c/o Edmonton Space & Sciences Centre, 11211-142 St., Edmonton AB T5M 4A1; (780) 477-8881; president@edmontonrasc.com

Calgary: c/o Calgary Science Centre, P.O. Box 2100, Station M, Loc.#73, Calgary AB T2P 2M5; (403) 255-3811; dechesne@telusplanet.net

Okanagan: PO Box 20119 TCM, Kelowna BC V1Y 9H2; (250) 861-3074; guy.m@shaw.ca

Prince George: 7365 Tedford Rd., Prince George BC V2N 6S2; (250) 964-3600; pgcentre@yahoo.com

Vancouver: c/o Gordon Southam Observatory, 1100 Chestnut St., Vancouver BC V6J 3J9; (604) 437-3103; craig.breckenridge@shaw.ca

Victoria: 764 Mapleton Place, Victoria BC V8Z 6W2; (250) 479-5187; David_Lee@telus.net

REPORTING OF ASTRONOMICAL DISCOVERIES

To report a possible significant discovery (e.g. a new comet, nova, or supernova), a message should be sent to the International Astronomical Union's Central Bureau for Astronomical Telegrams. Send electronic mail to **cbat@cfa.harvard.edu**. Messages are monitored at all times. If this preferred method of communication is unavailable, a telephone call may be made to (617) 495-7244 or -7440 or -7444, but telephone calls are discouraged and these numbers will not be answered at all times. Also, a follow-up letter should be sent to the Central Bureau at 60 Garden St., Cambridge MA 02138, USA. Inexperienced observers should have their observation checked before contacting the Central Bureau.

For any new object, specify the date and time of observation, RA and Dec (with epoch), magnitude, and some physical description. For photographic and CCD discoveries, confirmation with a second image is highly desirable. In the case of a new comet, the rate of motion in RA and Dec should also be indicated.

Reports may instead be filled out at **cfa-www.harvard.edu/iau/cbat.html**. Recent IAU circulars and subscription information are also available at this URL.

VISITING HOURS AT SOME CANADIAN OBSERVATORIES AND PLANETARIA

BY MARY LOU WHITEHORNE

OBSERVATORIES

ASTROLab du Mont-Mégantic, Notre-Dame-des-Bois QC J0B 2E0. An interpretation centre, located near the Mount-Mégantic Observatory (1.6-m telescope), with two public observatories, two exhibition halls, a new multimedia show, observing nights with 25-cm, 35-cm, 40-cm, and 61-cm telescopes, is open daily and nightly to the public during the summer (May–Sep.) and on weekends during spring and fall. Open year round for groups. Inquire for updates about the schedule and for reservations (required for observation). (819) 888-2941 or (866) 888-2941; astrolab@interlinx.qc.ca; astrolab.qc.ca

Burke-Gaffney Observatory, Saint Mary's University, Halifax NS B3H 3C3. Public tours on many Sat. evenings, weather permitting. General: (902) 496-8257; Mon. evening or daytime group tours: (902) 420-5633; bgo@ap.stmarys.ca; apwww.stmarys.ca/bgo

Canada-France-Hawaii Telescope (CFHT), Mauna Kea, Hawaii. RASC members visiting the "Big Island" of Hawaii may arrange daytime group tours of the CFHT installations by contacting, at least one month in advance, the Canada-France-Hawaii Telescope Corporation, either by letter: CFHT Corp., PO Box 1597, Kamuela HI 96743, USA; or by telephone: (808) 885-7944. www.cfht.hawaii.edu

Climenhaga Observatory, Dept. of Physics and Astronomy, University of Victoria, Victoria BC V8W 3P6. Public viewing for groups from Apr. until Aug. Appointments: (250) 721-7750; astrowww.phys.uvic.ca/events

David Dunlap Observatory (DDO), PO Box 360, Richmond Hill ON L4C 4Y6. Thur. mornings Oct.–Apr.; Sat. evenings, Apr.–Sep.; Fri. evenings, Jul.-Aug. info@astro.utoronto.ca; ddo.astro.utoronto.ca

Dominion Radio Astrophysical Observatory, Penticton BC V2A 6K3. Conducted tours: Sun., Jul. and Aug. only, 2 p.m. – 5 p.m.; Visitors' Centre: open every day Apr. 1 – Oct. 15, 10 a.m. – 5 p.m. Open weekdays only Oct. 16 – Mar. 14. (250) 490-4355; www.drao.nrc.ca

Gordon MacMillan Southam Observatory, 1100 Chestnut St., Vancouver BC V6J 3J9. Open Fri. and Sat., 7 p.m. – 11 p.m., weather and volunteer staff permitting. Free admission. New 0.5-m reflecting telescope and 15-cm telescope. Call (604) 738-2855 first to see if the facility is open. Information: (604) 738-STAR; ddodge@hrmacmillanspacecentre.com; www.hrmacmillanspacecentre.com

Haliburton Forest Observatory, RR1, Haliburton ON K0M 1S0. Private 60 000-acre dark sky site. Two 250-mm and one 300-mm SCTs, hydrogen-alpha refractor, binoculars, giant outdoor planisphere. Preregister for Tues. and Sat. nights; call for other hours and fees. School group rates. Accommodations. Register at (705) 754-2198. kovacs_is@canada.com; www.haliburtonforest.com

Helen Sawyer Hogg Observatory, Canada Science & Technology Museum, PO Box 9724, Stn. T, 1867 St. Laurent Blvd., Ottawa ON K1G 5A3. 380-mm refractor (from the Dominion Observatory) and Starlab Planetarium. "Discover the Universe" public visits by appointment only and group tours Mon. to Thurs. from Oct. to May, rain or shine. Reservations: (613) 991-9219; www.science-tech.nmstc.ca

Hume Cronyn Observatory, Department of Physics and Astronomy, The University of Western Ontario, London ON N6A 3K7. Summer Open Houses (slide show and viewing with a 250-mm refractor) Sat. in Jun., Jul., and Aug., 8:30 p.m. – 11 p.m. A winter public program is available to groups and individuals by appointment. (519) 661-3183; phobos.astro.uwo.ca

Ken Odaisky Memorial Observatory, Sudbury Astronomy Club, Suite M250, 800 Lasalle Blvd., Sudbury ON P3A 4V4. Free private and group tours through the observatory, housing a 150-mm refractor, Apr. through Oct. Reservations: Eldon Phillips, (705) 673-7339; hhealy@sympatico.ca; ww2.isys.ca/astroclub

Prince George Centre RASC Observatory, c/o 3330 22nd Ave., Prince George BC V2N 1P8. 610-mm Cassegrain telescope. Public viewing Fridays 8 p.m. – midnight from Mar.–May and Aug.–Oct. Group tours available. (250) 964-3600; www.pgweb.com/~astronomical

Science North Solar Observatory, 100 Ramsey Lake Road, Sudbury ON P3E 5S9. Space exhibits open daily, evening star parties twice monthly, travelling portable planetarium. Open every day except Dec. 24, 25, 26, and Jan. 1. (705) 522-3701; events schedule: sciencenorth.ca/plan/calendarofevents/index.html; sciencenorth.ca

University of British Columbia Observatory, 2219 Main Mall (Geophysics & Astronomy Bldg.), Vancouver BC. Free public observing on clear Sat. evenings. (604) 822-6186; tours: (604) 822-3853; www.astro.ubc.ca

University of Saskatchewan Observatory, c/o Dept. of Physics & Engineering Physics, 116 Science Place, Saskatoon SK S7N 5E2. Public viewing on Saturday evenings. (306) 966-6429; physics.usask.ca/observatory

York University Observatory, Dept. of Physics and Astronomy, 4700 Keele St., Toronto ON M3J 1P3. Tours run all year, daytime or evening, by appointment. Wed. evening is Public Viewing, rain or shine, no appointment necessary. Use Steeles Ave. entrance; observatory is in the Petrie Science Building. Hours vary, depending on the season. (416) 736-2100, ext. 77773; www.astro.yorku.ca/observatory

PLANETARIA

Calgary Science Centre, 701-11 Street SW. Mailing address: PO Box 2100, Station M, #73, Calgary AB T2P 2M5. Features Discovery Dome, with Canada's only Digistar projector and Super-70-mm dome movies. Program and sky information: (403) 268-8300; discover@home.com; www.calgaryscience.ca

Centre of the Universe, Herzberg Institute of Astrophysics (National Research Council of Canada), 5071 West Saanich Road, Victoria BC V9E 2E7. Exhibits, theatre, Starlab Planetarium, programs, hands-on tours of 1.8-m Plaskett telescope, 400-mm telescope. Apr.–Oct., open daily, 10 a.m. – 6 p.m. Nov.–Mar., open Tues.–Sun., 10 a.m. – 6 p.m. Public viewing Sat., 6 p.m. – 11 p.m., Apr.–Oct.; and Wed. and Sun., 6 p.m. – 11 p.m., Jul. and Aug. Closed over Christmas. Information and program bookings: (250) 363-8262; www.hia.nrc.ca/cu

Doran Planetarium, Laurentian University, Ramsey Lake Road, Sudbury ON P3E 2C6. Shows in English and French. Information: (705) 675-1151; group reservations: ext. 2227; plegault@nickel.laurentian.ca; www.laurentian.ca/physics/planetarium/planetarium.html

H.R. MacMillan Space Centre, 1100 Chestnut St., Vancouver BC V6J 3J9. Open daily Jul. and Aug.; otherwise open Tues.–Sun. and holidays (except Christmas) from 10 a.m. – 5 p.m. Star Theatre, motion simulator ride, exhibit gallery, live demonstrations, overnight adventure programs, space camps. (604) 738-STAR; lkomori@hrmacmillanspacecentre.com; www.hrmacmillanspacecentre.com

The Lockhart Planetarium, 394 University College, 220 Dysart Road, The University of Manitoba, Winnipeg MB R3T 2M8. Group reservations and public show schedule: (204) 474-9785; www.umanitoba.ca/faculties/science/astronomy

Manitoba Planetarium, 190 Rupert Ave. at Main St., Winnipeg MB R3B 0N2. Victoria Day to Labour Day: shows daily; rest of year: Tues.–Sun. and holidays, closed Mon. The Planetarium is part of the Manitoba Museum of Man and Nature, which includes a Science Centre as well as a Starlab mobile planetarium program. The Museum Shop carries science books for all ages. Reception: (204) 956-2830; Gift Shop (204) 988-0615; planetarium show times: (204) 943-3139; info@manitobamuseum.mb.ca; www.manitobamuseum.mb.ca

Odyssium, Edmonton's space and science centre. Coronation Park, 11211 – 142 Street, Edmonton, AB T5M 4A1. Features Margaret Zeidler Star Theatre, IMAX®, public observatory, 5 permanent galleries, feature exhibitions, Odyssium Gift Shop featuring telescopes. Advance ticket sales and program information: (780) 451-3344; recorded astronomy information: (780) 451-3344; Gift Shop: (780) 452-9100; info@odyssium.com; www.odyssium.com

Ontario Science Centre, 770 Don Mills Road, Toronto ON M3C 1T3. Open every day except Dec. 25. Live planetarium shows daily. (416) 696-3127; www.osc.on.ca

Planétarium de Montréal, 1000 St. Jacques St. W., Montreal QC H3C 1G7. Multimedia presentations in French and English every open day. (514) 872-4530; info@planetarium.montreal.qc.ca; www.planetarium.montreal.qc.ca

Royal Ontario Museum, Education Department, 100 Queen's Park, Toronto ON M5S 2C6. Operates three mobile planetariums for "Travelling Stars" educational programs both at the Museum and in the community. Topics from grades K–13 cover basic astronomy to the astronomy of ancient civilizations, complementing the Ontario school curriculum, and are presented by trained astronomy teachers. (416) 586-5801; schoolv@rom.on.ca; www.rom.on.ca/schools

Solar Wind Portable Planetarium, Toronto, Ontario. Offers curriculum-based presentations. Information: Cathy McWatters, (416) 221-7375; solar.wind@pathcom.com

W. J. McCallion Planetarium, Department of Physics and Astronomy, McMaster University, 1280 Main Street West, Hamilton ON L8S 4M1. (905) 525-9140, ext. 27777; pinks.physics.mcmaster.ca/GSC/planetarium

The Night Sky with its beautiful stars
and its message of our place in the Universe
is a precious treasure of all humanity,
on which we rely for our knowledge and understanding
of our origins and destiny.†

†The International Astronomical Union, Exposition on Adverse Environmental Impacts on Astronomy, Paris, 1992 (*I.A.U. Information Bulletin 69,* January, p. 10, 1993).

RECOMMENDED READING AND ATLASES

Astronomy, a nontechnical monthly magazine for amateur astronomers (Canada and U.S.: (888) 350-2413; www.astronomy.com).

The Backyard Astronomer's Guide, by Terence Dickinson and Alan Dyer. Firefly Books (Canada: (800) 387-6192, United States: (800) 387-5085), 1991. The best guide to equipment and techniques for amateur astronomers, by two experienced observers.

Catalogue of the Astronomical Society of the Pacific ((415) 337-1100; www.astrosociety.org), an excellent source of astronomical educational resources such as books, slides, videos, globes, posters, software, teacher's classroom activity guides, and more.

Catalogue of Sky Publishing Corporation, a good source of books, atlases, globes, slide sets, software, and posters ((800) 253-0245; www.skyandtelescope.com).

Exploring the Night Sky, by Terence Dickinson. Firefly Books (see above), 1987. A guide to stargazing, recommended for children.

The Guide To Amateur Astronomy (2nd edition), by Jack Newton and Philip Teece. Cambridge University Press, Cambridge, 1995. A valuable introduction to many diverse aspects of amateur astronomy.

Nightwatch (3rd ed.), by Terence Dickinson. Firefly Books (see above), 1998. An excellent, introductory observing guide.

SkyNews, the (bimonthly) Canadian magazine of astronomy & stargazing. Send $24 Cdn ($24 U.S. for U.S. addresses) to: SkyNews, RR 1, Cedar Valley ON L0G 1E0; by credit card call (866) 759-0005 (preferred).

Starlight Nights, by Leslie Peltier (1900–1980), 1965. Sky Publishing Corporation. Anyone who enjoys the night sky should read this book.

Sky & Telescope, a monthly magazine widely read by both amateur and professional astronomers ((800) 253-0245; www.skyandtelescope.com).

Atlas of the Moon, by Antonín Rükl. Kalmbach Books, Waukesha, 1992, or Hamlyn Publishing, London, 1991. A first-rate lunar atlas for amateur astronomers.

Bright Star Atlas 2000.0, by Wil Tirion. Introductory atlas containing 9000 stars to magnitude 6.5 and 600 clusters, nebulae and galaxies on 10 charts.

Sky Atlas 2000.0 (2nd ed.), by Wil Tirion and Roger Sinnott, 1998. Large format and well done. Contains 81 000 stars to magnitude 8.5 and 2700 clusters, nebulae and galaxies on 26 charts; laminated version available.

Uranometria 2000.0 Deep Sky Atlas, by Wil Tirion, Barry Rappaport, and Will Remaklus. A new edition of the popular atlas, with stellar data from the HIPPARCOS satellite. Contains more than 280 000 stars to magnitude 9.75 and 30 000 clusters, nebulae, and galaxies on 220 double-page charts.

Millennium Star Atlas, by Roger Sinnott and Michael Perryman. A comprehensive atlas based on data from the HIPPARCOS satellite. Three volumes, each covering 8 hours in RA. Contains more than 1 000 000 stars to magnitude 11 and more than 10 000 clusters, nebulae and galaxies on 1548 charts.

Computer-based Planetarium Programs: Several are available, for example, *Desktop Universe, ECU* (Earth Centered Universe), *Redshift 3, Starry Night, TheSky,* and *Voyager II,* For more information, see the catalogues listed above or do an Internet search at, for example, www.google.com.

Visit www.rasc.ca/handbook/books.html for links to booksellers who carry these books and atlases. Many of these items are also available from Sky Publishing Corp., 49 Bay State Rd., Cambridge MA 02138-1200, USA; (800) 253-0245, www.skyandtelescope.com.

SELECTED LISTING OF INTERNET RESOURCES

The World Wide Web is an important source of astronomical information. A selection of websites together with a reference to a page number in this Handbook (if any) is given below. A listing of all websites mentioned in this Handbook, with URL links to the various sites, is available at:

www.rasc.ca/handbook/websites.html

URL	Description
www.aavso.org	American Association of Variable Star Observers (p. 259)
www.amsmeteors.org	American Meteor Society (pp. 222, 225)
www.lpl.arizona.edu/alpo/	Association of Lunar and Planetary Observers (p. 189)
astrolab.qc.ca	ASTROLab du mont Mégantic (p. 10)
adc.gsfc.nasa.gov	Astronomical Data Center (ADC), maintained by NASA; includes access to most catalogues
www.astrosociety.org	Astronomical Society of the Pacific
www.astronomy.com	*Astronomy* magazine
www.astronomynow.com	*Astronomy Now,* Britain's "Sky & Telescope"
www.cfht.hawaii.edu	Canada-France-Hawaii Telescope (p. 10)
www.space.gc.ca	Canadian Space Agency
www.cleardarksky.com/csk	Clear Sky Clock, by Attila Danko (p. 67)
www.spacedaily.com	Clipping service related to space news
www.cmc.ec.gc.ca/cmc/htmls/clds_vis_e.html	Cloud forecasts for North America (p. 65)
physics.nist.gov/constants	CODATA recommended constants (p. 29)
ddo.astro.utoronto.ca	David Dunlap Observatory (p. 10)
www.drao.nrc.ca	Dominion Radio Astrophysical Observatory (p. 10)
www.mreclipse.com	Eclipse photography and safety (p. 143)
www.glyphweb.com/esky	The Electronic Sky, a general astronomy site
www.hia.nrc.ca	Herzberg Institute of Astrophysics
heritage.stsci.edu	Hubble Heritage Site, emphasizing compelling HST images distilled from scientific data
cfa-www.harvard.edu/iau/cbat.html	International Astronomical Union Central Bureau (p. 9)
www.darksky.org	International Dark-Sky Association (p. 70)
www.imo.net	International Meteor Organization (pp. 221–225)
www.lunar-occultations.com/iota	International Occultation Timing Association (pp. 158, 217)
www.jpl.nasa.gov	Jet Propulsion Laboratory site, many activities for adults and kids
www.kennedyspacecenter.com	Kennedy Space Centre
miac.uqac.uquebec.ca	Meteorites and Impacts Advisory Committee, Canadian Space Agency (p. 225)

URL	Description
gdcinfo.agg.nrcan.gc.ca	Meteorite impact craters (p. 228)
umbra.nascom.nasa.gov/eclipse	NASA eclipse bulletins (p. 142)
sunearth.gsfc.nasa.gov/eclipse	NASA eclipse site (pp. 135–143)
nedwww.ipac.caltech.edu	NASA/IPAC Database, an extensive listing of extragalactic data (p. 286)
spaceflight.nasa.gov	NASA space flight site giving current information on Space Shuttle missions and ISS activities
www.namnmeteors.org	North American Meteor Network (pp. 222, 225)
www.rasc.ca/handbook	*Observer's Handbook* website (p. 6)
planetary.org	Planetary Society—contains over 2000 pages of information about space exploration
www.starlab.com	Project STAR (p. 18)
www.odxa.on.ca/meteor.html	Radio detection of meteors (p. 224)
www.rasc.ca	Royal Astronomical Society of Canada (p. 8)
occsec.wellington.net.nz	Royal Astronomical Society of New Zealand occultations section (p. 159)
www.saguaroastro.org	Saguaro Astronomy Club, includes observing list database (p. 73)
www.heavens-above.com	Satellite tracking information, including International Space Station and Space Shuttle
www.cmc.ec.gc.ca/cmc/htmls/seeing_e.html	Seeing forecasts (p. 67)
simbad.u-strasbg.fr/simbad	SIMBAD database—an extensive listing
www.skyandtelescope.com	*Sky & Telescope* and Sky Publishing (p. 13)
www.cmc.ec.gc.ca/cmc/htmls/transparence_e.html	Sky transparency forecasts (p. 66)
www.skynewsmagazine.com	*SkyNews*—Canada's astronomy magazine (p. 18)
www.stsci.edu	Space Telescope Science Institute; includes access to the Digitized Sky Survey
www.seds.org	Students for the Exploration and Development of Space—includes much useful data
www.weatheroffice.ec.gc.ca/radar/index_e.html	Weather radar images (Canada) (p. 65)
www.intellicast.com	Weather radar images (U.S.) (p. 65)

TEACHING AND THE OBSERVER'S HANDBOOK
By John R. Percy

You are holding in your hand a valuable resource for teaching astronomy. Every user of this Handbook, whether amateur or professional astronomer or teacher in any setting, at any level, can contribute to education in astronomy. Partnerships and coalitions between scientists and educators are especially effective and enjoyable.

As a result of curriculum renewal in Canada, the United States, and other countries, astronomy is now taught in many elementary and secondary schools; see *JRASC, 92,* 38, February 1998. The Canadian astronomical community, including the RASC, has now embarked on a major education and public outreach initiative; see www.casca.ca/ecass/issues/winter2000.

The Night Sky

Teachers should make sure that their students are aware of what can be seen in the night sky, even though "the stars come out at night, but the students don't." THE SKY MONTH BY MONTH section of this Handbook (pp. 74–99) provides an excellent guide. Star charts can be found in many books and magazines (see p. 13) as well as in the section MAPS OF THE NIGHT SKY (pp. 293–300). (Study the first page of this section to get the most out of these maps.) Make sketches, including the horizon and compass points, to record the appearance and changes of the sky.

Night and Day, Seasons, and the Phases of the Moon

These basic astronomical concepts are misunderstood by most people, as many surveys have found. One of the common misconceptions about the seasons is that it is hottest in the summer because of the shape of Earth's orbit—we are closest to the Sun in the summer. But does this explain why the seasons are reversed in the Southern Hemisphere? Even those who "know" that the seasons are due to "the tilt of Earth's axis" may think that, because of the tilt, the hemispheres are closer to the Sun during their respective summers.

Other misconceptions relate to a lack of understanding of the scale of the solar system. Assuming a high speed that we are familiar with, say that of a commercial jet plane, how long would it take to travel to the Moon? To the Sun? If a beach ball represents the Sun, the solar system fits in your town, but the next nearest star is another beach ball on the opposite side of Earth! The sections PRINCIPAL ELEMENTS OF THE SOLAR SYSTEM (pp. 20–21), THE BRIGHTEST STARS (pp. 241–250), and THE NEAREST STARS (pp. 251–255) are useful references for constructing such models.

Here is a useful hands-on activity: Choose a day when the Sun and Moon are both visible in the sky (in the afternoon when the Moon is near first quarter or in the morning when the Moon is near last quarter; see THE SKY MONTH BY MONTH section). Hold a ball in your hand so that the Sun shines on it, and extend it toward the Moon. You will see the ball and the Moon illuminated by the Sun in the *same* way—a clear demonstration that the Moon is a spherical, nonluminous body floating in space.

These concepts are so basic that it is worth teaching them correctly, that is, monitoring the students' preconceptions through interviews and discussions, and being absolutely sure that they understand the concepts and can explain them from their understanding—not just from memorization.

The Sun

(1) Track the path of the Sun in the sky during one day and over successive days and weeks. This may be done safely and simply by using the shadow of a pole (or a

student). Sunrise/sunset data and the changing position of the Sun in the heavens are given in THE SUN chapter of this Handbook (pp. 108–110 and p. 101, respectively).

(2) Project an image of the Sun on a sheet of white cardboard, using binoculars or a small telescope. Observe sunspots, and watch the Sun rotate from day to day. Practise setting up such a demonstration ahead of time. Once you get the hang of it, it can be set up very quickly. **Warning:** Never observe the Sun directly, especially not by looking through binoculars or a telescope. Permanent eye damage could result. When projecting a solar image, use a barrier to prevent anyone from looking directly into the light beam. See the sections FILTERS (pp. 54–57) and VIEWING A SOLAR ECLIPSE—A WARNING (p. 157) in this Handbook.

The Moon

(1) Keep a "Moon journal" as a class project: Observe and record where the Moon is, what shape it is, and when it rises and sets. Note how these variables change over several days and weeks. (Don't forget that the Moon is often visible in daytime.)

(2) Draw the general appearance of the Moon's surface as seen with your naked eye. Many features, including the regions of the Apollo landing sites, can be identified using the MAP OF MOON on pp. 114–115. A film or video of one of the Apollo missions is worth showing to a class.

(3) Eclipses: a three-dimensional model, to the correct scale, is a great aid in explaining eclipses and why there is not an eclipse every two weeks. See the ECLIPSES DURING 2003 section in this Handbook (pp. 134–154) for information on eclipses that may be visible from your locality this year.

(4) If ocean tides occur in your area, correlate the times and the range of the tide with the Moon's position in your sky, its phases, and distances. Lunar phases, perigees, and apogees are tabulated in THE SKY MONTH BY MONTH section, and an overview of tides appears in the TIDES AND THE EARTH–MOON SYSTEM article in this Handbook (pp. 173–177).

The Planets

(1) Nothing can stimulate student interest like direct experience, so observe the planets when they are visible. See THE SKY MONTH BY MONTH and PLANETS sections (pp. 178–198 for the latter) for the visibility of the planets during the year.

(2) Develop an awareness of Earth as a planet. Study photographs of Earth from space. For a hands-on experience, place an Earth globe in sunlight with its north pole oriented northward. Then rotate and tilt the globe so your locality is at the "top" of the globe (the globe will then be oriented the same way in space as is planet Earth). The regions on Earth where the Sun is rising or setting at that moment will be apparent. Note which pole is experiencing 24 hours of daylight. Slowly turn the globe eastward about its axis to show a sped-up day/night progression.

(3) Use slides, films, videos, and posters to capture the excitement of planetary exploration (see the catalogues in RECOMMENDED READING AND ATLASES on p. 13).

Comets and Asteroids

These are interesting topics, especially as it now appears that collisions between these objects and Earth may explain the extinctions of species such as dinosaurs. Use the section METEORITE IMPACT CRATERS OF NORTH AMERICA (pp. 228–231) to have students locate nearby impact craters on geographical maps. See THE BRIGHTEST ASTEROIDS (p. 215) for a finder chart to locate a bright asteroid in the night sky (only binoculars are needed). There is a classic demonstration of "Creating a Comet" (out of dry ice and sand) described at www.noao.edu/education/crecipe.html.

Is a Telescope Necessary?

Binoculars and telescopes can be useful but are not essential; much interesting astronomy can be done with the unaided eye. However, binoculars are often available and should be used when helpful. See the section BINOCULARS (pp. 50–53) for a guide to their selection and use. The inexpensive, make-it-yourself *Project STAR* telescopes are highly recommended. See TELESCOPE PARAMETERS (p. 45) and TELESCOPE EXIT PUPILS (pp. 46–49) for a summary of some quantitative aspects of telescopes.

Resources

In addition to the list of reading material below, you may be able to make use of the following:

(1) See the VISITING HOURS AT SOME CANADIAN OBSERVATORIES AND PLANETARIA article in this Handbook (pp. 10–12). Take your students to visit one of these.

(2) The Royal Astronomical Society of Canada is the largest organization of amateur astronomers in Canada. Their 25 centres across Canada (see the section An Invitation for Membership in the Royal Astronomical Society of Canada on pp. 8–9) present a wide variety of activities that might be interesting to you and your students. A member of the RASC might be willing to visit your class and demonstrate a telescope. The Astronomical Society of the Pacific's Project ASTRO Manual can facilitate such visits. See www.astrosociety.org/education/astro/project_astro.html.

Astro Adventures: An Activity-Based Astronomy Curriculum, by Dennis Schatz and D. Cooper. Pacific Science Center, 200 2nd Ave. N., Seattle WA 93109-4895, USA.

Astronomical Society of the Pacific, 390 Ashton Ave., San Francisco CA 94112, USA. In addition to their excellent astronomical slides and other such material (send for their catalogue), the ASP publishes a free quarterly teachers' newsletter; download current and back issues from www.astrosociety.org/education/publications/tnl/tnl.html.

Astronomy Adventures (Ranger Rick's NatureScope). National Wildlife Federation, 1412 16th St. NW, Washington DC, USA. Excellent, fun activities for younger children in schools and youth groups.

Project SPICA: A Teacher Resource to Enhance Astronomy Education, edited by N. Butcher Ball et al. Kendall/Hunt Publishing Co. 1994. An excellent compilation of activities and resources for teaching grades 3–12.

Project STAR Textbook. Kendall/Hunt Publishing Co. 1993. See also www.learner.org/teacherslab/pup.

Project STAR Hands-on Science Materials: Learning Technologies, Inc., 40 Cameron Ave., Somerville MA 02144, USA.; (800) 537-8703; www.starlab.com. Unique, high-quality, low-cost materials for introducing students (and teachers) to astronomy.

SkyNews, RR 1, Cedar Valley ON L0G 1E0; (866) 759-0005; www.skynewsmagazine.com. Bimonthly. General astronomy from a Canadian perspective. Free with membership to the RASC.

The Universe at Your Fingertips, and More Universe at Your Fingertips, edited by Andrew Fraknoi et al. Astronomical Society of the Pacific, 390 Ashton Ave., San Francisco CA 94112, USA. Another excellent collection of teaching activities and resources for grades 3–12. See also www.astrosociety.org/education/activities/astroacts.html.

TERMINOLOGY AND SYMBOLS

COORDINATE SYSTEMS

Astronomical positions are usually measured in a system based on the *celestial poles* and *celestial equator,* the intersections of Earth's rotation axis and equatorial plane, respectively, and the infinite sphere of the sky. *Right ascension* (RA or α) is measured in hours (h), minutes (m), and seconds (s) of time, eastward along the celestial equator from the vernal equinox (see below). *Declination* (Dec or δ) is measured in degrees (°), minutes ('), and seconds (″) of arc, northward (N or +) or southward (S or −) from the celestial equator toward the north or south celestial pole.

Positions can also be measured in a system based on the *ecliptic*, the intersection of Earth's orbital plane and the infinite sphere of the sky. The Sun appears to move eastward along the ecliptic during the year. *Longitude* is measured eastward along the ecliptic from the vernal equinox; *latitude* is measured at right angles to the ecliptic, northward or southward toward the north or south ecliptic pole. The *vernal equinox* is one of the two intersections of the ecliptic and the celestial equator; it is the one at which the Sun crosses the celestial equator moving from south to north.

An object is *in conjunction with the Sun* if it has the same longitude as the Sun and *at opposition* if its longitude differs from that of the Sun by 180°. Mercury and Venus are at *superior conjunction* when they are more distant than the Sun and at *inferior conjunction* when they are nearer than the Sun (see the diagram on p. 179).

Two *nonsolar* objects are in conjunction if they have the same RA. Generally, but not always, close mutual approaches correspond to conjunctions. Following Jean Meeus, we use the term *quasi-conjunction* to denote separations less than 5° that do not correspond to a conjunction.

If an object crosses the ecliptic moving northward, it is at the *ascending node* of its orbit; if it crosses the ecliptic moving southward, it is at the *descending node.*

Elongation is the geocentric angle between a planet and the Sun, or between a satellite and its primary, measured in the plane formed by Earth and the other two bodies.

SYMBOLS

Sun, Moon, and Planets

⊙	Sun	☾	Last Quarter	⊕	Earth	♅ Uranus
🌑	New Moon	☾	Moon generally	♂	Mars	♆ Neptune
☺	Full Moon	☿	Mercury	♃	Jupiter	♇ Pluto
☽	First Quarter	♀	Venus	♄	Saturn	

Signs of the Zodiac

♈	Aries	0°	♌	Leo	120°	♐	Sagittarius	240°
♉	Taurus	30°	♍	Virgo	150°	♑	Capricornus	270°
♊	Gemini	60°	♎	Libra	180°	♒	Aquarius	300°
♋	Cancer	90°	♏	Scorpius	210°	♓	Pisces	330°

The Greek Alphabet

A, α	alpha	H, η	eta	N, ν nu	T, τ tau
B, β	beta	$\Theta, \theta, \vartheta$	theta	Ξ, ξ xi	Y, υ upsilon
Γ, γ	gamma	I, ι	iota	O, o omicron	Φ, ϕ phi
Δ, δ	delta	K, κ	kappa	Π, π pi	X, χ chi
E, ε	epsilon	Λ, λ	lambda	P, ρ rho	Ψ, ψ psi
Z, ζ	zeta	M, μ	mu	Σ, σ sigma	Ω, ω omega

BASIC DATA

PRINCIPAL ELEMENTS OF THE SOLAR SYSTEM

PHYSICAL ELEMENTS

Object	Equat. Diam. km	Oblate- ness	Mass Earth=1	Den- sity t/m³	Grav- ity* Earth=1	Escape Speed* km/s	Rot'n. Period d	Incl.† °	Albedo
Sun	1 392 000	0	332 946.0	1.41	27.9	617.5	25–35‡	—	—
Mercury	4 879	0	0.055 274	5.43	0.38	4.2	58.646	0.0	0.11
Venus	12 104	0	0.815 005	5.24	0.90	10.4	243.019	177.4	0.65
Earth	12 756	1/298	1.000 000	5.52	1.00	11.2	0.9973	23.4	0.37
Moon	3 475	0	0.012 300	3.34	0.17	2.4	27.3217	6.7	0.12
Mars	6 794	1/154	0.107 447	3.94	0.38	5.0	1.0260	25.2	0.15
Jupiter	142 980††	1/15.4	317.833	1.33	2.53	59.5	0.4101‡‡	3.1	0.52
Saturn	120 540††	1/10.2	95.159	0.70	1.06	35.5	0.4440	25.3	0.47
Uranus[A]	51 120††	1/43.6	14.500	1.30	0.90	21.3	0.7183	97.9	0.51
Neptune[B]	49 530††	1/58.5	17.204	1.76	1.14	23.5	0.6712	28.3	0.41
Pluto[C]	2 300	0?	0.002 5	1.1	0.08	1.3	6.3872	123.	0.3

*At the equator. †Inclination of equator to orbital plane. ‡Depending on latitude. ††At 1 atmosphere (101.325 kPa).
‡‡For the most rapidly rotating part, the equatorial region.
[A]Discovered by William Herschel, 1781 Mar. 3. [B]Discovered by Johann G. Grille, 1846 Sep. 23.
[C]Discovered by Clyde Tombaugh, 1930 Feb. 18.

OSCULATING ORBITAL ELEMENTS, 2003

The tables at the right give the orbital elements of the planets and 30 largest main-belt asteroids, the latter provided by Dr. Brian Marsden. At any given time or "epoch," 6 basic quantities determine each body's elliptical orbit, for example:

(1) the mean distance from the Sun, a, equal to the semimajor axis of the ellipse;
(2) the eccentricity e of the ellipse;
(3) the inclination i of the orbital plane to the ecliptic;
(4) the longitude Ω of the ascending node of the orbital plane on the ecliptic;
(5) the longitude $\tilde{\omega}$ of perihelion;
(6) the body's mean longitude L at the given epoch.

The date of the ecliptic and equinox used to measure the last 4 quantities must also be specified, and may be different from the given epoch. Other, equivalent parameters may be substituted: the distance q of perihelion in place of a; the argument of perihelion, $\omega = \tilde{\omega} - \Omega$, in place of $\tilde{\omega}$; or the mean anomaly, $M = L - \tilde{\omega}$, or time T of perihelion in place of L. Once 6 fundamental quantities are known, all other attributes of the orbit of the body, such as the sidereal period P and synodic period S, can be derived.

If the body followed a perfectly elliptical orbit as predicted by classical orbital mechanics, then for a fixed ecliptic and equinox the first 5 quantities above would be constant over time. However, because of perturbations caused by the gravitational influence of other bodies, the orbits are not perfectly elliptical; hence the orbital elements depend on the epoch. The given *osculating* elements can be used to determine an elliptical orbit that is a close approximation to the actual path of the body for times near the given epoch. Two epochs, corresponding to Jan. 1 and Jul. 20, are provided for the planets; the elements for these epochs can be linearly interpolated to other epochs in 2003 for precision of a few arcseconds (typically 1″ or 2″). For the asteroids one epoch, corresponding to Jun. 10, is given, with resulting precision of about 1′.

HELIOCENTRIC OSCULATING ORBITAL ELEMENTS, 2003
REFERRED TO THE MEAN ECLIPTIC AND EQUINOX OF J2000.0

Planet	Epoch Julian Date 245	Mean Distance a AU	Eccentricity e	Inclination i °	Long. of Asc. Node Ω °	Long. of Perihelion $\tilde{\omega}$ °	Long. at Epoch L °	Sidereal Period P a	Synodic Period* S d
Elements are for epochs 2003 Jan. 1 and 2003 Jul. 20 respectively.									
Mercury	2640.5	0.387 098	0.205 626	7.0048	48.3272	77.4636	55.4074	0.2409	115.88
	2840.5	0.387 097	0.205 637	7.0047	48.3265	77.4619	153.8771	0.2409	115.88
Venus	2640.5	0.723 332	0.006 748	3.3947	76.6702	131.547	137.1098	0.6152	583.90
	2840.5	0.723 330	0.006 735	3.3947	76.6695	131.568	97.5392	0.6152	583.89
Earth†	2640.5	1.000 016	0.016 725	0.0005	183.7	103.0496	100.2021	1.0001	—
	2840.5	0.999 998	0.016 715	0.0005	182.3	102.9374	297.3221	1.0000	—
Mars	2640.5	1.523 631	0.093 529	1.8494	49.5467	336.0845	209.5165	1.8808	780.03
	2840.5	1.523 704	0.093 559	1.8493	49.5450	336.0524	314.3286	1.8809	779.96
Jupiter	2640.5	5.202 511	0.048 922	1.3038	100.5112	14.9341	125.3473	11.8612	398.90
	2840.5	5.202 063	0.048 951	1.3038	100.5111	14.8377	141.9702	11.8597	398.90
Saturn	2640.5	9.584 306	0.057 715	2.4856	113.6268	93.3550	86.8737	29.6686	378.01
	2840.5	9.581 213	0.057 436	2.4857	113.6260	93.7747	93.5640	29.6542	378.01
Uranus	2640.5	19.134 09	0.049 523	0.7718	73.8546	168.9078	326.1885	83.6989	369.68
	2840.5	19.130 18	0.049 912	0.7718	73.8518	169.3623	328.4840	83.6732	369.68
Neptune	2640.5	29.943 29	0.010 274	1.7710	131.7866	68.365	311.4960	163.8534	367.51
	2840.5	29.947 34	0.009 630	1.7713	131.7864	69.370	312.6239	163.8866	367.51
Pluto	2640.5	39.372 68	0.247 761	17.1712	110.2323	223.2097	243.0788	247.0643	366.75
	2840.5	39.441 89	0.249 070	17.1675	110.2404	223.4901	243.8453	247.7161	366.75

*Synodic period = (product of Ps of two planets) ÷ (difference of the Ps). Tabular values are relative to Earth.
†Values are actually for the Earth-Moon barycentre.

Asteroid	Diameter km	Mean Distance a AU	Eccentricity e	Inclination i °	Long. of Asc. Node Ω °	Long. of Perihelion $\tilde{\omega}$ °	Long. at Epoch L °	Sidereal Period P a	Synodic Period* S d
Elements are for epoch Julian Date 245 2800.5 (2003 Jun. 10).									
(1) Ceres	1003	2.765 620	0.079 389	10.5840	80.4802	154.5964	69.4558	4.5995	466.71
(2) Pallas	608	2.773 035	0.229 984	34.8499	173.1648	123.6240	24.3185	4.6180	466.19
(4) Vesta	538	2.361 298	0.088 576	7.1334	103.9376	254.1247	215.4715	3.6286	504.19
(10) Hygiea	450	3.135 543	0.119 419	3.8440	283.6530	237.4964	79.9874	5.5525	445.47
(31) Euphrosyne	370	3.148 001	0.226 815	26.3194	31.2615	93.3314	238.5305	5.5856	444.89
(704) Interamnia	350	3.067 204	0.146 997	17.3029	280.6208	16.0214	128.4468	5.3719	448.78
(511) Davida	323	3.170 684	0.184 668	15.9423	107.7630	86.8431	124.0791	5.6461	443.86
(65) Cybele	309	3.436 987	0.103 999	3.5474	155.8170	261.6112	339.9866	6.3721	433.23
(52) Europa	289	3.099 207	0.101 408	7.4690	129.0225	111.9633	20.6609	5.4562	447.20
(451) Patientia	276	3.059 837	0.077 452	15.2230	89.4158	70.6283	182.0530	5.3526	449.16
(15) Eunomia	272	2.644 028	0.185 403	11.7478	293.4905	30.6390	65.3494	4.2995	475.94
(16) Psyche	250	2.919 372	0.139 602	3.0954	150.3556	18.5673	243.0169	4.9883	456.82
(3) Juno	247	2.667 033	0.258 747	12.9719	170.1318	58.0667	222.5020	4.3557	474.08
(324) Bamberga	246	2.682 308	0.338 360	11.1072	328.0577	12.1835	242.1032	4.3932	472.88
(24) Themis	234	3.128 561	0.133 112	0.7600	35.9736	143.8622	187.4592	5.5339	445.80
(95) Arethusa	230	3.073 366	0.146 099	12.9740	243.3530	38.4170	126.8703	5.3881	448.48
(45) Eugenia	226	2.719 546	0.083 283	6.6121	147.9626	233.8047	80.7189	4.4850	470.05
(13) Egeria	224	2.576 467	0.084 652	16.5382	43.3069	124.5300	9.1387	4.1357	481.72
(19) Fortuna	215	2.441 875	0.159 078	1.5728	211.3859	33.5729	172.6594	3.8159	494.95
(107) Camilla	211	3.477 986	0.079 332	10.0465	173.1529	122.7033	287.3111	6.4865	431.81
(88) Thisbe	210	2.768 002	0.163 945	5.2179	276.7922	313.3479	200.5715	4.6054	466.55
(7) Iris	209	2.385 937	0.229 792	5.5238	259.8597	45.1056	74.0737	3.6856	501.24
(747) Winchester	205	2.992 666	0.344 683	18.1789	130.2108	45.8410	273.0556	5.1773	452.68
(41) Daphne	204	2.765 218	0.271 773	15.7662	178.1741	224.2442	193.3057	4.5985	466.74
(6) Hebe	201	2.425 192	0.201 242	14.7664	138.8463	17.7638	35.5313	3.7769	496.77
(241) Germania	200	3.052 225	0.096 408	5.5163	271.0610	346.6128	102.2338	5.3326	449.54
(29) Amphitrite	195	2.554 650	0.071 414	6.1020	356.5432	58.9972	24.1932	4.0833	483.70
(145) Adeona	195	2.674 096	0.143 267	12.6261	77.5027	122.3354	352.6487	4.3730	473.53
(194) Prokne	191	2.616 993	0.236 967	18.4970	159.5452	322.5916	327.5400	4.2337	478.19
(386) Siegena	191	2.893 564	0.172 948	20.2557	166.9523	27.3572	212.7253	4.9223	458.36

NATURAL SATELLITES OF THE PLANETS
BY PHILIP D. NICHOLSON

Of the 102 natural satellites listed in the table, all but four orbit the giant planets Jupiter (39), Saturn (30), Uranus (21), and Neptune (8). With a few exceptions, these moons may be divided into three groups, which presumably reflect their different origins. Closest to the planets are small ring moons, 20 km to 200 km in diameter and with strong evolutionary and dynamical connections to the planetary ring systems. Most of these objects were discovered during the *Voyager* flybys of 1979–1989, and all are very difficult to observe from Earth. These include the "shepherd" satellites Prometheus, Pandora, Cordelia, Ophelia, and Galatea; the "co-orbital" satellites Janus and Epimetheus; and Pan, which orbits within the Encke gap in Saturn's A ring. Metis and Adrastea are apparently the source of the tenuous Jovian ring.

Next come the larger "regular" satellites in near-circular orbits in or near the planets' equatorial planes, thought to have been formed in situ via accretion in circumplanetary disks at the dawn of the solar system. The dividing line between the first two groups is fuzzy, but the regular satellites may be considered to start beyond the Roche limit at ~2.5 planetary radii, that is, at Amalthea, Mimas, Portia, and Larissa. This group extends out to Callisto (J IV), Iapetus (S VIII), Oberon (U IV), and Proteus (N VIII) but probably does not include Triton (N I), which is now thought to have been captured. There are numerous orbital resonances among the regular satellites, including Io/Europa/Ganymede (1:2:4), Mimas/Tethys (1:2), Enceladus/Dione (1:2), and Titan/Hyperion (3:4); the origin of the orbital resonance is generally ascribed to orbital expansion driven by tidal interaction with Jupiter or Saturn. Temporary capture in similar resonances in the past may have been responsible for the anomalously large inclinations of Miranda and (perhaps) Naiad. Tidal energy dissipation within Io is responsible for this moon's spectacular volcanic activity, and similar heating at a lower level may still occur within Europa and Enceladus.

The third and outermost group—and the group whose numbers have increased so much in recent years—comprises the "irregular" satellites. These generally small bodies (2 km to 200 km in diameter, except for 340-km Nereid (N II)) move in quite eccentric orbits at large inclinations to the planets' orbital planes. Their orbits are not random; rather, they fall into several more-or-less tight clusters in semi-major axis and inclination: three or four at Jupiter (all but one retrograde) centred on Himalia, Ananke, Pasiphae, and Carme; three at Saturn (one retrograde) centred on 2000 S11, 2000 S3, and Phoebe; and probably two at Uranus (both retrograde) centred on Caliban and Sycorax. These clusters are believed to be due to collisional disruptions of a smaller number of original objects captured from heliocentric orbits. Not included in (presently recognized) clusters are 1975 JI, Sinope, 2000 S8, and Nereid. The orbits of the irregular satellites, along with that of the Earth's Moon, are subject to strong solar gravitational perturbations and thus maintain approximately fixed inclinations to their respective planet's orbital planes rather than to their equators.

TABLE OF NATURAL SATELLITES OF THE PLANETS

Name	Diameter km	Mass[A] Pt	Density t/m³	Visual Mag.[B]	Visual Albedo	Mean Distance from Planet 10³ km	Orbital Period d	Eccentricity	Orbit Incl.[C] °	Discovery
Satellite of Earth										
Moon*	3475.	73 490. (10)	3.34	−12.7	0.11	384.5	27.322	0.0549	5.16	—
Satellites of Mars										
I Phobos*	22.	0.010 7 (0.000 02)	1.87	11.4	0.07	9.38	0.319	0.015	1.1	A. Hall, 1877
II Deimos*	12.	0.002 2 (0.000 2)	2.3	12.5	0.07	23.46	1.262	0.0002	1.8v	A. Hall, 1877
Satellites of Jupiter										
XVI Metis	43.	—	—	17.5	0.06	128.	0.294	0.0012	0.02	S. Synnott, *Voyager 2*, 1979
XV Adrastea	16.	—	—	18.7	≈0.05	129.	0.297	0.0018	0.05	D. Jewitt et al., *Voyager 1*, 1979
V Amalthea*	167.	—	—	14.1	0.09	181.4	0.498	0.0031	0.39	E. Barnard, 1892
XIV Thebe**	99.	—	—	16.0	0.05	221.9	0.674	0.0177	1.07	S. Synnott, *Voyager 1*, 1979
I Io*[D]	3643.	89 330. (10)	3.53	5.0	0.62	421.8	1.769	0.0041	0.04	Galileo, 1610
II Europa*[D]	3122.	48 000. (10)	3.01	5.3	0.68	671.1	3.551	0.0101	0.47	Galileo, 1610
III Ganymede*[D]	5262.	148 200. (10)	1.94	4.6	0.44	1 070.4	7.155	0.0015	0.17	Galileo, 1610
IV Callisto*	4820.	107 600. (10)	1.83	5.6	0.19	1 882.7	16.689	0.0074	0.31	Galileo, 1610
1975 J1	4.[E]	—	—	21.0	—	7 507.	130.0	0.24	43.	C. Kowal, 1975[F]
XIII Leda	≈20.	—	—	19.5	—	11 165.	240.9	0.16	27.	C. Kowal, 1974
VI Himalia***	185.	—	—	14.6	0.03	11 461.	250.6	0.16	27.	C. Perrine, 1904
X Lysithea***	≈35.	—	—	18.3	—	11 717.	259.2	0.11	28.	S. Nicholson, 1938
VII Elara	85.	—	—	16.3	0.03	11 741.	259.6	0.22	26.	C. Perrine, 1905
2000 J11	3.[E]	—	—	22.4	—	12 555.	287.	0.25	28.	S. Sheppard et al., 2000
2001 J10	2.[E]	—	—	23.1	—	19 394	541.	0.14	146.	S. Sheppard et al., 2001
2000 J3	4.[E]	—	—	21.8	—	20 216.	585.	0.22	150.	S. Sheppard et al., 2000

Pronunciations of the names of the satellites are given on p. 180.

Visual magnitudes are at mean opposition distance.

*synchronous rotation; **probably synchronous; ***asynchronous; ****chaotic rotation; (no asterisk) rotation unknown.

[A]The numbers in parentheses are possible errors.

[B]Magnitudes for Jovian, Saturnian, and Uranian irregular satellites discovered in 1997–2001 are CCD-R magnitudes (675 nm); the solar V–R colour is 0.53.

[C]Inclinations of inner satellites (those closer than 100 planetary radii) are relative to the planet's *equator*. As customary, inclinations for outer satellites (those beyond Jupiter IV, Saturn VIII, Uranus IV, and Neptune I) are relative to the planet's *orbital plane*. Iapetus is an intermediate case. For our Moon, the inclination relative to Earth's orbital plane is 5°; relative to Earth's equator it varies between 18° and 29° in an 18.61-year cycle. A value >90° indicates retrograde motion.

[D]Laplace resonance. Longitudes satisfy: L(Io) − 3L(Europa) + 2L(Ganymede) ≈ 180°. Also, the mean motions are such that the three periods are nearly 1:2:4.

[E]Diameters assume an albedo of 0.06.

[F]Initially detected in 1975 and then lost; recovered in 2000 by S. Sheppard and D. Jewitt.

TABLE OF NATURAL SATELLITES OF THE PLANETS (continued)

Name	Diameter km	Mass[A] Pt	Density t/m³	Visual Mag.[B]	Visual Albedo	Mean Distance from Planet 10³ km	Orbital Period d	Eccentricity	Orbit Incl.[C] °	Discovery
Satellites of Jupiter (continued)										
2000 J7	5.[E]	—	—	21.2	—	20 964.	617.	0.22	149.	S. Sheppard et al., 2000
2001 J7	3.[E]	—	—	22.8	—	21 027	602.	0.23	149.	S. Sheppard et al., 2001
2000 J5	3.[E]	—	—	22.2	—	21 132.	624.	0.23	149.	S. Sheppard et al., 2000
2001 J9	2.[E]	—	—	23.1	—	21 168	604.	0.28	146.	S. Sheppard et al., 2001
2001 J3	4.[E]	—	—	22.1	—	21 252	613.	0.21	151.	S. Sheppard et al., 2001
XII Ananke***	≈30.	—	—	18.8	—	21 276.	610.5	0.24	149.	S. Nicholson, 1951
2001 J2	3.[E]	—	—	22.3	—	21 312	613.	0.23	149.	S. Sheppard et al., 2001
2001 J6	2[E]	—	—	23.2	—	23 029	686.	0.27	165.	S. Sheppard et al., 2001
2000 J6	3.[E]	—	—	22.5	—	23 078.	719.	0.26	165.	S. Sheppard et al., 2000
2001 J8	2.[E]	—	—	23.0	—	23 124	690.	0.27	165.	S. Sheppard et al., 2001
2000 J4	3.[E]	—	—	22.8	—	23 168.	723.	0.27	165.	S. Sheppard et al., 2000
2001 J4	3[E]	—	—	22.7	—	23 219	691.	0.28	150.	S. Sheppard et al., 2001
2000 J9	4.[E]	—	—	21.9	—	23 312.	730.	0.25	165.	S. Sheppard et al., 2000
2000 J10	3.[E]	—	—	22.5	—	23 387.	734.	0.16	166.	S. Sheppard et al., 2000
XI Carme	≈45.	—	—	17.6	—	23 404.	702.3	0.25	165.	S. Nicholson, 1938
2001 J11	3.[E]	—	—	22.7	—	23 547	708.	0.26	165.	S. Sheppard et al., 2001
VIII Pasiphae	≈60.	—	—	17.0	—	23 624.	708.0	0.41	151.	P. Melotte, 1908
2000 J2	4.[E]	—	—	21.8	—	23 745.	751.	0.24	165.	S. Sheppard et al., 2000
2001 J5	2[E]	—	—	23.0	—	23 808	715.	0.31	151.	S. Sheppard et al., 2001
2000 J8	4.[E]	—	—	21.7	—	23 911.	758.	0.43	153.	S. Sheppard et al., 2000
IX Sinope***	≈38.	—	—	18.1	—	23 939.	724.5	0.25	158.	S. Nicholson, 1914
1999 J1	7.[E]	—	—	20.7	—	24 100.	759.	0.28	147.	J. Scotti & T. Spahr, 1999
2001 J1	3.[E]	—	—	22.0	—	24 122	729.	0.32	152.	S. Sheppard et al., 2001
Satellites of Saturn										
XVIII Pan[G]	≈20.	—	—	19.4	≈0.5	133.6	0.575	≈0.	≈0.	M. Showalter, 1990
XV Atlas	≈30.	—	—	19.0	0.4	137.7	0.601	≈0.	≈0.	R. Terrile, *Voyager 1*, 1980
XVI Prometheus**[H]	100.	—	—	15.8	0.6	139.4	0.613	0.002	≈0.0	S. Collins, D. Carlson, *Voyager 1*, 1980
XVII Pandora**[H]	85.	—	—	16.4	0.5	141.7	0.628	0.004	≈0.0	S. Collins, D. Carlson, *Voyager 1*, 1980
X Janus*[I]	180.	1.9 (0.1)	0.66	14.4	0.6	151.5	0.695	0.007	0.2	A. Dollfus, 1966
XI Epimetheus*[I]	120.	0.5 (0.1)	0.61	15.6	0.5	151.5	0.695	0.021	0.3	J. Fountain, S. Larson, 1978
I Mimas*	397.	38. (1)	1.14	12.8	0.6	185.6	0.942	0.021	1.5	W. Herschel, 1789

[G]Orbits within the Encke gap. Discovered in *Voyager* images (1980–81).   [I]Co-orbital satellites.
[H]Prometheus and Pandora are shepherds of the F-ring.

TABLE OF NATURAL SATELLITES OF THE PLANETS (continued)

Name	Diameter km	Mass[A] Pt	Density t/m³	Visual Mag.[B]	Visual Albedo	Mean Distance from Planet 10³ km	Orbital Period d	Eccentricity	Orbit Incl.[C] °	Discovery
Satellites of Saturn (continued)										
II Enceladus*	499.	65. (2)	1.00	11.8	1.0	238.1	1.370	0.004	0.02	W. Herschel, 1789
III Tethys*	1060.	627. (5)	1.01	10.3	0.8	294.7	1.888	0.000	1.1	G. Cassini, 1684
XIII Telesto	25.	—	—	18.5	0.7	294.7	1.888[J]	≈0.	1.2	B. Smith et al., 1980
XIV Calypso**	19.	—	—	18.7	1.0	294.7	1.888[K]	≈0.	1.5	D. Pascu et al., 1980
IV Dione*	1120.	1097. (2)	1.50	10.4	0.6	377.4	2.737	0.002	0.02	G. Cassini, 1684
XII Helene	30.	—	—	18.4	0.6	377.4	2.737[L]	≈0.	0.2	P. Laques, J. Lecacheux, 1980
V Rhea*	1530.	2 308. (60)	1.24	9.7	0.6	527.1	4.517	0.001	0.4	G. Cassini, 1672
VI Titan**	5550.[M]	134 570. (20)	1.88	8.4	0.2	1 221.	15.945	0.029	0.3	C. Huygens, 1655
VII Hyperion****	283.	—	—	14.4	0.3	1 464.	21.276	0.104	0.4	W. Bond, G. Bond, W. Lassell, 1848
VIII Iapetus*	1436.	1 590. (150)	1.03	11.0v	0.08–0.4	3 561.	79.331	0.028	7.6	G. Cassini, 1671
2000 S5	14.[E]	—	—	21.9	—	11 365.	449.	0.33	46.	B. Gladman et al., 2000
2000 S6	10.[E]	—	—	22.5	—	11 440.	451.	0.32	47.	J. Kavelaars et al., 2000
IX Phoebe***	220.	—	—	16.5	0.08	12 944.	548.2	0.16	175.	W. Pickering, 1898
2000 S2	19.[E]	—	—	21.2	—	15 199.	687.	0.36	45.	B. Gladman et al., 2000
2000 S8	6.[E]	—	—	23.5	—	15 645.	729.	0.27	153.	J. Kavelaars et al., 2000
2000 S11	26.[E]	—	—	20.4	—	16 404.	783.	0.48	34.	M. Holman & T. Spahr, 2000
2000 S10	8.[E]	—	—	22.9	—	17 616.	872.	0.47	34.	J. Kavelaars et al., 2000
2000 S3	32.[E]	—	—	20.0	—	18 160.	893.	0.29	46.	B. Gladman et al., 2000
2000 S4	13.[E]	—	—	22.0	—	18 247.	926.	0.54	34.	J. Kavelaars et al., 2000
2000 S9	6.[E]	—	—	23.7	—	18 709.	951.	0.21	167.	B. Gladman et al., 2000
2000 S12	6.[E]	—	—	23.8	—	19 463.	1016.	0.11	176.	B. Gladman et al., 2000
2000 S7	6.[E]	—	—	23.8	—	20 371.	1067.	0.44	176.	B. Gladman et al., 2000
2000 S1	16.[E]	—	—	21.6	—	23 096.	1311.	0.34	173.	B. Gladman et al., 2000
Satellites of Uranus										
VI Cordelia[N]	25.[O]	—	—	24.2	—	49.8	0.335	≈0.	0.1	*Voyager 2*, 1986
VII Ophelia[N]	30.[O]	—	—	23.9	—	53.8	0.375	0.010	0.1	*Voyager 2*, 1986
VIII Bianca	45.[O]	—	—	23.1	—	59.2	0.435	0.001	0.2	*Voyager 2*, 1986

[K]Telesto librates about the trailing (#5) Lagrangian point of Tethys's orbit.
[K]Calypso librates about the leading (#4) Lagrangian point of Tethys's orbit.
[L]Helene librates about the leading (#4) Lagrangian point of Dione's orbit with a period of ≈ 790 d.
[M]Titan's cloud-top diameter. Solid-body diameter equals 5150 km.
[N]Cordelia and Ophelia are shepherds of the ε-ring.
[O]Diameter assuming the same albedo (0.07) as Puck.

TABLE OF NATURAL SATELLITES OF THE PLANETS (continued)

Name	Diameter km	Mass[A] Pt	Density t/m³	Visual Mag.[B]	Visual Albedo	Mean Distance from Planet 10³ km	Orbital Period d	Eccentricity	Orbit Incl.[C] °	Discovery
Satellites of Uranus (continued)										
IX Cressida	65.⁰	—	—	22.3	—	61.8	0.463	≈0.	≈0.	Voyager 2, 1986
X Desdemona	60.⁰	—	—	22.5	—	62.6	0.475	≈0.	0.1	Voyager 2, 1986
XI Juliet	85.⁰	—	—	21.7	—	64.4	0.492	0.001	0.1	Voyager 2, 1986
XII Portia	110.⁰	—	—	21.1	—	66.1	0.513	≈0.	0.1	Voyager 2, 1986
XIII Rosalind	60.⁰	—	—	22.5	—	70.0	0.558	≈0.	0.3	Voyager 2, 1986
XIV Belinda	68.⁰	—	—	22.1	—	75.3	0.624	≈0.	≈0.	Voyager 2, 1986
1986 U10	≈40.	—	—	23.6	—	76.4	0.638	≈0.	≈0.	E. Karkoschka, 1999[P]
XV Puck	155.	—	—	20.4	0.07	86.0	0.763	≈0.	0.3	Voyager 2, 1985
V Miranda*[Q]	472.	66. (8)	1.2	15.8	0.32	129.9	1.413	0.017	4.3	G. Kuiper, 1948
I Ariel*[Q]	1158.	1350. (120)	1.7	13.7	0.39	190.9	2.521	0.0012	0.04	W. Lassell, 1851
II Umbriel*[Q]	1169.	1170. (140)	1.4	14.5	0.21	266.0	4.144	0.0040	0.13	W. Lassell, 1851
III Titania*	1578.	3520. (90)	1.7	13.5	0.27	436.3	8.706	0.0012	0.11	W. Herschel, 1787
IV Oberon*	1523.	3010. (80)	1.6	13.7	0.23	583.4	13.463	0.0013	0.07	W. Herschel, 1787
XVI Caliban	60.⁰	—	—	22.4	—	7231.	579.	0.16	141.	B. Gladman et al. 1997
XX Stephano	20.⁰	—	—	24.1	—	8004.	677.	0.23	144.	B. Gladman et al., 1999
XVII Sycorax	120.⁰	—	—	20.8	—	12179.	1283.	0.52	159.	P. Nicholson et al. 1997
XVIII Prospero	30.⁰	—	—	23.2	—	16240.	1962.	0.44	152.	M. Holman et al., 1999
XIX Setebos	35.⁰	—	—	23.3	—	17501.	2209.	0.58	158.	J. Kavelaars et al. 1999
Satellites of Neptune										
III Naiad	60.	—	—	24.6	≈0.06	48.2	0.294	≈0.	4.7	Voyager 2, 1989
IV Thalassa	80.	—	—	23.9	≈0.06	50.1	0.311	≈0.	0.2	Voyager 2, 1989
V Despina	150.	—	—	22.5	0.06	52.5	0.335	≈0.	0.1	Voyager 2, 1989
VI Galatea	160.	—	—	22.4	≈0.06	62.0	0.429	≈0.	0.1	Voyager 2, 1989
VII Larissa**	190.	—	—	22.0	0.06	73.5	0.555	0.001	0.2	Voyager 2, 1989
VIII Proteus**	420.	—	—	20.3	0.06	117.6	1.122	≈0.	≈0.0	Voyager 2, 1989
I Triton*	2706.	21400. (50)	2.06	13.5	0.76	354.8	5.877	<0.0005	156.8	W. Lassell, 1846
II Nereid***	340.	—	—	19.7	0.16	5513.	360.14	0.76	7.2	G. Kuiper, 1949
Satellite of Pluto										
Charon*	1190.	1620 (90)	1.9	17.3	0.37	19.4	6.387	≈0.	≈0.	J. Christy, 1978

[P]In Voyager 2 (January 1986) images.
[Q]Near resonance(?). L(Miranda) – 3L(Ariel) + 2L(Umbriel) drifts slowly (period ≈ 12.5 years).

ORBITAL MOTION
BY ROY BISHOP

An understanding of orbital motion is central to an appreciation of the heavens. Whether you are observing a distant galaxy, the stars in a globular cluster, the waltz of Jupiter's Galilean satellites, the drift of the Moon during an occultation, or merely uttering an expletive as an artificial satellite passes through the field of your camera, an understanding of orbital motion adds a deep insight to all of these views.

Among early cosmologies were those of **Aristotle** (340 BC) and **Ptolemy** (140 AD), and the superior heliocentric one proposed by **Copernicus** (1543). These attempts at modelling the heavens used complex systems of circles upon circles, of epicycles, eccentrics, and deferents. John Milton, a contemporary of Galileo, wrote the following lines in his epic poem "Paradise Lost" (1674), possibly expressing his discontent with the Ptolemaic and Copernican systems of compounded circles:

> *To ask or search I blame thee not, for Heav'n*
> *Is as the Book of God before thee set,*
> *Wherein to read his wond'rous Works, and learn*
> *His Seasons, Hours, or Days, or Months, or Years:*
> *This to attain, whether Heav'n move or Earth,*
> *Imports not, if thou reck'n right; the rest*
> *From Man or Angel the great Architect*
> *Did wisely to conceal, and not divulge*
> *His secrets to be scann'd by them who ought*
> *Rather admire; or if they list to try*
> *Conjecture, he his Fabric of the Heav'ns*
> *Hath left to thir disputes, perhaps to move*
> *His laughter at thir quaint Opinions wide*
> *Hereafter, when they come to model Heav'n*
> *And calculate the Stars, how they will wield*
> *The mighty frame, how build, unbuild, contrive*
> *To save appearances, how gird the Sphere*
> *With Centric and Eccentric scribbl'd o'er,*
> *Cycle and Epicycle, Orb in Orb.*

Kepler (1609), using observations accumulated by Tycho, broke with the 2000-year preoccupation with circles when he discovered that the planets move in an elegantly simple way along elliptical paths. Although he had discovered *how* the planets move, Kepler was unable to explain quantitatively *why* they move in this way.

Galileo strongly supported the Copernican heliocentric universe (1632) and achieved brilliant insights concerning the motion of objects (1638); however, he ignored Kepler's ellipses and did not apply his mechanics to the sky.

Newton united the heavens and Earth by showing that the laws governing motions on Earth also apply to the heavens. In his *Principia* (1687), the greatest book in the physical sciences, Newton presented his three laws of motion and the first ever physical force law, his law of gravitation. He used these to explain the motions not only of bodies on Earth, but also of the planets, comets, stars, equinoxes, tides, etc. Newton was the first to realize that the Moon is falling toward Earth just as freely as does an apple, and that the elliptical orbit of the centre of mass of the Earth–Moon system is the path that results (as he described it) as these two bodies free-fall under the action of the Sun's gravitational force.

A common misconception concerning orbits is that the inward gravitational force is balanced by an outward "centrifugal force." Newton's view is simpler: there is only one force, the inward pull of gravity. There is *no physical agent* to cause an outward force, and if there *were* an outward supporting force, the two forces would cancel and, as Galileo realized, the body would then move along a straight line. If you choose a rotating reference frame and then ignore the rotation (mistake no. 1), you have to pretend there is a "centrifugal force" (mistake no. 2) in order to make sense of motions occurring within this frame. The two mistakes effectively cancel, but understanding is compromised.

Einstein's general theory of relativity (GTR) of 1915 superseded Newton's description of gravity. The arbiter of which is a good theory and which theory is wrong is nature. Newton's laws are accurate enough for most of NASA's calculations, but they do not work exactly. For example, if the computer programs used in the Global Positioning System (GPS) were based on Newton's gravitation, the system would be a multibillion-dollar boondoggle. Einstein's conception of gravitation is essential to its operation. In the case of strong gravitation and/or speeds approaching the speed of light, Newton's laws fail dramatically. The GTR may be wrong too, but so far it has passed all experimental tests.

According to Einstein's GTR, gravitation is not a mysterious force that one mass exerts upon a distant mass; gravitation is the geometry (non-Euclidean) of the 4-dimensional spacetime within which we and the stars exist. Golf balls (if air friction is ignored), satellites, planets and stars follow *geodesics*, the straightest possible, force-free paths through a spacetime whose geometry is shaped by mass-energy. The difficulty in intellectually grasping a non-Euclidean spacetime originates with us. Common sense is inadequate. This is not surprising, given that our common sense is based on the Euclidean, 3-dimensional geometry of straight lines, rectangles, and spheres we learned in the crib by age 2.

Gravitation is geometry. This is why no one has ever felt a force of gravity. Like the centrifugal force, it never did exist. A force of gravity was the glue Newton invented to make his naive Euclidean model of spacetime approximate the real universe. (Newton himself was well aware of the unsatisfactory nature of several of his assumptions, far more so than most people who came after him.) When you release a coin from your hand, you see the coin "fall" because the contact force of the ground on your feet (the *only* force you feel) accelerates you the other way. An orbiting astronaut experiences no such force, so he remains beside a released coin. Orbital motion could not be simpler—*no* forces are involved.

What would Milton have written had he been familiar with the conjectures of Newton and Einstein?

SOME ASTRONOMICAL AND PHYSICAL DATA
BY ROY BISHOP

Many of the numbers listed below are based on measurement. Exceptions include defined quantities (indicated by ≡), quantities calculated from defined quantities (e.g. m/ly, AU/pc), and numbers of mathematical origin such as π and conversion factors in angular measure. Of those based on measurement, some are known to only approximate precision and the equal sign is reduced to ≈. Many others are known to quite high precision (the uncertainties occur after the last digit given) and several are from "the 1998 CODATA recommended values of the fundamental physical constants" (see physics.nist.gov/constants). The units (*Système International* (SI) where possible), symbols and nomenclature are based on recommendations of the *International Astronomical Union* and the *International Union of Pure and Applied Physics*.

LENGTH

1 metre (m) = the distance travelled by light in a vacuum in $(299\,792\,458)^{-1}$ s

1 astronomical unit (AU) = $1.495\,978\,707 \times 10^{11}$ m = 499.004 784 light-s

1 light-year (ly) = $9.460\,536 \times 10^{15}$ m (based on avg. Gregorian year)
= 63 239.8 AU

1 parsec (pc) = $3.085\,678 \times 10^{16}$ m
= 206 264.8 AU = 3.261 631 ly

1 mile* ≡ 1.609 344 km

1 micron* ≡ 1 μm *Indicates deprecated unit;

1 Angstrom* ≡ 0.1 nm unit on right is preferred

TIME

1 second (s) ≡ 9 192 631 770 periods of the radiation involved in the transition between the two hyperfine levels of the ground state of the ^{133}Cs atom at mean sea level

Day: Mean sidereal (equinox to equinox) = 86 164.092 s
Mean rotation (fixed star to fixed star) = 86 164.100 s
Day (d) ≡ 86 400. s
Mean solar = 86 400.001 s

Month: Draconic (node to node) = 27.212 221 d
Tropical (equinox to equinox) = 27.321 582 d
Sidereal (fixed star to fixed star) = 27.321 662 d
Anomalistic (perigee to perigee) = 27.554 550 d
Synodic (new Moon to new Moon) = 29.530 589 d

Year: Eclipse (lunar node to lunar node) = 346.620 075 d
Tropical (equinox to equinox) (a) = 365.242 190 d
Average Gregorian ≡ 365.242 5 d
Average Julian ≡ 365.25 d
Sidereal (fixed star to fixed star) = 365.256 363 d
Anomalistic (perihelion to perihelion) = 365.259 635 d

EARTH

Mass = 5.974×10^{24} kg   Age ≈ 4.6 Ga   Central T ≈ 5000 to 6000 K

Radius: Equatorial, a = 6378.140 km   Polar, b = 6356.755 km
Mean = $(a^2 b)^{1/3}$ = 6371.004 km   Of metallic core = 3475 km

Solar parallax = 8.794 148″ (Earth equatorial radius ÷ 1 AU)

1° of latitude = 111.132 95 − 0.559 82 cos 2ϕ + 0.001 17 cos 4ϕ km (at latitude ϕ)

1° of longitude = 111.412 88 cos ϕ − 0.093 50 cos 3ϕ + 0.000 12 cos 5ϕ km

1 knot = 1 nautical mile ($\approx 1'$ of latitude) per hour $\equiv$ 1.852 km/h = 0.51444 m/s
Distance of sea horizon for eye h metres above sea level
  (allowing for refraction) $\approx 3.9h^{1/2}$ km $\approx 2.1h^{1/2}$ nautical miles
Standard atmospheric pressure (1 atm) $\equiv$ 101.325 kPa ($\approx$ 1 kg above 1 cm^2)
Values of atmospheric refraction for various elevations (assuming 1 atm, 10°C):
  90°: 0′; 44°: 1′; 26°: 2′; 18°: 3′; 11°: 5′; 6°: 8′; 4°: 12′; 2°: 18′; 0°: 34′
Speed of sound in standard atmosphere = 331 m/s $\approx$ 1 km/3 s $\approx 10^{-6} c$
Magnetic field at surface $\approx 5 \times 10^{-5}$ T (**B** field comes out of a N-seeking pole)
Magnetic poles: 76°N, 101°W; 66°S, 140°E
Standard acceleration of gravity $\equiv$ 9.806 65 m/s^2
Meteoritic flux $\approx 1 \times 10^{-15}$ kg/(m^{2}s) $\approx 10^4$ t/a over entire Earth
Obliquity of ecliptic = 23.4393° (2000.0)   Constant of aberration = 20.495 52″
Annual general precession = 50.29″ (2000.0); Precession period $\approx$ 25 800 a
Escape speed from Earth = 11.2 km/s   Mean orbital speed = 29.786 km/s
Escape speed at 1 AU from Sun = 42.1 km/s (= $\sqrt{2}$ × orbital speed)

SUN

Mass = 1.9891×10^{30} kg   Radius = 696 265 km   Eff. Temp. $\approx$ 5780 K
Output: Power = 3.85×10^{26} W, M_{bol} = 4.79
          Luminous intensity = 2.84×10^{27} cd, M_v = 4.82
At 1 AU outside Earth's atmosphere:
          Energy flux = 1.37 kW/m^2, m_{bol} = −26.82
          Illuminance = 1.27×10^5 lx, m_v = −26.75
Inclination of the solar equator on the ecliptic of date = 7.25°
Longitude of ascending node of the solar equator on the ecliptic of date = 76°
Period of rotation at equator = 25.38 d (sidereal), 27.275 d (mean synodic)
Solar wind speed near Earth $\approx$ 450 km/s (travel time, Sun to Earth $\approx$ 4 d)
Solar velocity = 19.4 km/s toward α = 18.07h, δ = +30° (solar apex)
Location in Milky Way Galaxy: $\approx$ 25 kly from centre, $\approx$ 50 ly N of galactic
  plane, on the inner edge of the Orion arm

MILKY WAY GALAXY

Mass $\approx 10^{12}$ solar masses   Diameter $\approx$ 300 kly (including the galactic halo)
Centre: α = 17h 45.7m, δ = −29°00′; N pole: α = 12h 51m, δ = 27°08′ (2000.0)
Rotation speed at Sun $\approx$ 230 km/s, period $\approx$ 200 Ma
Velocity relative to 3 K background radiation $\approx$ 600 km/s toward $\alpha \approx$ 10h, $\delta \approx$ −20°

CONSTANTS

Speed of light, $c \equiv$ 299 792 458 m/s (This, in effect, defines the metre.)
Planck's constant, h = 6.626 07 $\times 10^{-34}$ J·s = 4.135 667 $\times 10^{-15}$ eV·s
Gravitational constant, G = 6.674 $\times 10^{-11}$ N·m^2/kg^2
Elementary charge, e = 1.602 176 $\times 10^{-19}$ C
Constant in Coulomb's law $\equiv 10^{-7} c^2$ (SI units) (This defines the Coulomb.)
Avogadro constant, N_A = 6.022 142 $\times 10^{26}$ kmol^{-1}
Boltzmann constant, k = 1.380 65 $\times 10^{-23}$ J/K = 8.617 $\times 10^{-5}$ eV/K $\approx$ 1 eV/10^{4}K
Stefan-Boltzmann constant, σ = 5.6704 $\times 10^{-8}$ W/(m^{2}K^4)
Wien's Law: $\lambda_m T$ = 2.8978 $\times 10^{-3}$ m·K (per dλ)
Hubble constant, $H \approx$ 60 to 80 km/(s Mpc)
−273.15°C (degree Celsius) = 0 K (kelvin) (lowest thermodynamic temperature)
Volume of ideal gas at 0°C, 101.325 kPa = 22.4140 m^3/kmol
Water: fusion at 0°C: 0.333 MJ/kg   vaporization at 100°C: 2.26 MJ/kg
          specific heat & density (near 20°C): 4.18 kJ/(kg·C°) & 1.00 t/m^3

MASS AND ENERGY

Mass is a measure of sluggishness of response to a net force. (SI unit: kg)
Weight ($\neq$ mass) is the force required to support a body. (SI unit: N)
    (1 pound-force = 4.4482 N)

1 kilogram (kg) $\equiv$ mass of a platinum-iridium cylinder stored in Paris, France
1 atomic mass unit (u) $\equiv$ $1/12^{th}$ of the mass of an atom of ^{12}C
    $= 1.660\,539 \times 10^{-27}$ kg $= N_A^{-1} = 931.4940$ MeV
1 joule (J) $\equiv$ work done by a force of 1 N acting through a distance of 1 m
    $\approx$ the kinetic energy gained by this Handbook in falling freely 0.4 m
1 electron-volt (eV) $\equiv$ the kinetic energy gained by a particle carrying one unit
    of elementary electrical charge (e) in falling through an
    electrical potential difference of one volt (V)
    $= 1.602\,176 \times 10^{-19}$ J

Electron mass = $9.109\,38 \times 10^{-31}$ kg = 548.579 91 μu = 0.510 998 9 MeV
Proton mass = $1.672\,622 \times 10^{-27}$ kg = 1.007 276 467 u = 938.2720 MeV
Neutron mass = $1.674\,927 \times 10^{-27}$ kg = 1.008 664 92 u = 939.565 MeV

Some atomic masses:

^1H = 1.007 825 u	^5Li = 5.0125 u	^{16}O = 15.994 915 u
^2H = 2.014 102 u	^8Be = 8.005 305 u	^{56}Fe = 55.934 940 u
^4He = 4.002 603 u	^{12}C $\equiv$ 12.000 000 u	^{235}U = 235.043 928 u

Thermochemical calorie* (cal) = 4.184 J
1 erg*/s = 10^{-7} J/s = 10^{-7} W
1 BTU*/h = 0.2930 W   *Indicates deprecated unit;
1 horsepower* = 745.7 W   unit on right is preferred
1 eV per event = 23 060 cal/mol
$C + O_2 \rightarrow CO_2 + 4.1$ eV   4 $^1H \rightarrow ^4He + 26.73$ MeV

Highest cosmic ray energy (carried by protons) $\approx 10^{20}$ eV
Power output (average) of an adult human $\approx$ 100 W
1 kg of TNT or milkshake releases 4.20 MJ $\approx$ 1 kWh

Relation between rest mass (m), linear momentum (p), total energy (E), kinetic
    energy (KE), and $\gamma \equiv (1 - v^2/c^2)^{-0.5}$ where c is the speed of light and v is the
    speed of the object: $E = \gamma mc^2 = mc^2 + KE = [(mc^2)^2 + (pc)^2]^{0.5}$

MAGNITUDE RELATIONS

Log of light intensity ratio $\equiv$ 0.4 times magnitude difference
Distance Modulus (D) $\equiv$ apparent magnitude (m) $-$ absolute magnitude (M)
Log of distance in ly = $0.2D + 1.513\,435$ (neglecting absorption)
Magnitude of sum of magnitudes $m_i = -2.5 \log \Sigma_i 10^{-0.4 m_i}$
A light source of apparent visual magnitude m provides an illuminance
    E (lux) where: $E = 10^{-0.4(m + 13.99)}$
Moon's apparent visual magnitude at phase angle P degrees ($0° =$ full Moon)
    when at its average distance from Earth: $-12.7 + 0.026\,|P| + (4 \times 10^{-9})\,P^4$

DOPPLER RELATIONS FOR LIGHT

$\alpha \equiv$ angle between velocity of source and line from source to observer
$\beta \equiv v/c$
$\gamma \equiv (1 - \beta^2)^{-0.5}$
Frequency: $\nu = \nu_0 \gamma^{-1}(1 - \beta \cos \alpha)^{-1}$
$z \equiv (\lambda - \lambda_0)/\lambda_0 = \gamma(1 - \beta \cos \alpha) - 1$
For $\alpha = \pi$ radians: $z = (1 + \beta)^{0.5}(1 - \beta)^{-0.5} - 1$ ($\approx \beta$ if $\beta \ll 1$)
    $\beta = [(1 + z)^2 - 1][(1 + z)^2 + 1]^{-1}$

OPTICAL WAVELENGTH DATA

Bright-adapted (photopic) visible range $\approx 400 - 750$ nm
Dark-adapted (scotopic) visible range $\approx 400 - 620$ nm
Wavelength of peak sensitivity of human eye: ≈ 555 nm (photopic)
≈ 510 nm (scotopic)
Mechanical equivalent of light: 1 lm $\equiv 1/683$ W at 540 THz ($\lambda \approx 555$ nm)
i.e. 1.46 W/klm (A 60 W incandescent light bulb emits about 1 klm = 1000 lm.
Compared to an optimum light source that delivers all its energy as light
at 540 THz, a 60 W incandescent light bulb is $1.46/60 \approx 2.4\%$ efficient.)
Colours (representative wavelength, nm):
violet (420), blue (470), green (530), yellow (580), orange (610), red (660)

Some useful wavelengths (element, spectral designation or colour and/or
(Fraunhofer line)):

H Lyman α	121.6 nm	N_2^+ blue†	465.2	Hg yellow	579.1
Ca (K solar)	393.4	Hβ (F solar)*	486.1	Na (D$_2$ solar)	589.0
Ca (H solar)	396.8	O^{++} green*	495.9	Na (D$_1$ solar)	589.6
Hg violet	404.7	O^{++} green*	500.7	O red†	630.0
Hδ (h solar)	410.2	Hg green	546.1	He-Ne laser	632.8
Hγ (g solar)	434.0	O yel.-green†	557.7	O red†	636.4
Hg deep blue	435.8	Hg yellow	577.0	Hα (C solar)	656.3

*Strong contributor to the visual light of gaseous nebulae
†Strong auroral lines

ANGULAR RELATIONS

2π radians $= 360°$ $\pi = 3.141\,592\,653\,589\,793\,2... \approx (113 \div 355)^{-1}$
Number of square degrees on a sphere $= 41\,253$

For $360° = 24$ h, $15° = 1$ h, $15' = 1$ min, $15'' = 1$ s

Relations between sidereal time t, right ascension α, hour angle h, declination δ,
azimuth A (measured east of north), altitude a, and latitude ϕ:
$h = t - \alpha$
$\sin a = \sin \delta \sin \phi + \cos h \cos \delta \cos \phi$
$\cos \delta \sin h = -\cos a \sin A$
$\sin \delta = \sin a \sin \phi + \cos a \cos A \cos \phi$
Annual precession in $\alpha \approx 3.0750 + 1.3362 \sin \alpha \tan \delta$ seconds   (α must be
Annual precession in $\delta \approx 20.043'' \cos \alpha$ in degrees)

SOME SI SYMBOLS AND PREFIXES

m	metre	N	newton (kg·m/s^2)	f	femto	10^{-15}
kg	kilogram	J	joule (N·m)	p	pico	10^{-12}
s	second	W	watt (J/s)	n	nano	10^{-9}
min	minute	Pa	pascal (N/m^2)	μ	micro	10^{-6}
h	hour	t	tonne (10^3 kg)	m	milli	10^{-3}
d	day	Hz	hertz (s^{-1})	c	centi	10^{-2}
a	year	C	coulomb (A·s)	k	kilo	10^3
A	ampere	V	volt (J/C)	M	mega	10^6
rad	radian	T	tesla (J·A^{-1}m^{-2})	G	giga	10^9
sr	steradian	lm	lumen	T	tera	10^{12}
K	kelvin (temperature)	cd	candela (lm/sr)	P	peta	10^{15}
ha	hectare (10^4 m^2)	lx	lux (lm/m^2)	E	exa	10^{18}

VOYAGES IN OUR SOLAR SYSTEM
BY RANDY ATTWOOD

During the second half of the 20th century, humankind began its reconnaissance of the solar system. Although people have travelled only as far as the Moon, robotic space probes have been sent to all the planets but one–Pluto–plus a few asteroids and comets. Our understanding of the solar neighbourhood is increasing at a tremendous pace as a result of the improving sophistication of these spacecraft.

The following is a list of some of the important firsts in the short history of the exploration of our solar system. Note that all space missions are not recorded, not even all the space firsts. A short list of upcoming missions to watch for is also included.

Year	Name	Significance
1957	*Sputnik 1*	First artificial satellite of Earth (Oct. 4); USSR
1957	*Sputnik 2*	First living being in Earth orbit (a dog named Laika); USSR
1959	*Luna 1*	First to escape Earth's gravity; USSR
1959	*Luna 2*	First to impact on the Moon; USSR
1959	*Luna 3*	First to image the far side of the Moon; USSR
1961	*Vostok 1*	First human in Earth orbit (Yuri Gagarin, Apr. 12); USSR
1962	*Mariner 2*	First to fly by another planet, Venus; USA
1965	*Mariner 4*	First to fly by Mars and take pictures; USA
1966	*Luna 9*	First soft landing on the Moon; USSR
1966	*Venera 3*	First to impact on another planet, Venus; USSR
1966	*Luna 10*	First to orbit the Moon; USSR
1968	*Apollo 8*	First humans to escape Earth's gravity and orbit the Moon; USA (Frank Borman, James Lovell, William Anders) (Dec. 24)
1969	*Apollo 11*	First humans to land and walk on the Moon; USA (Neil Armstrong, Edwin Aldrin) (Jul. 20)
1970	*Venera 7*	First soft landing on another planet, Venus; USSR
1971	*Mariner 9*	First to orbit another planet, Mars; USA
1971	*Mariner 9*	First close views of outer satellites (Phobos, Deimos); USA
1972	*Apollo 17*	Last 2 of 12 men to walk on the Moon; USA
1973	*Pioneer 10*	First to fly by Jupiter, reach solar escape speed; USA
1974	*Mariner 10*	First to fly by and study Mercury; USA
1975	*Venera 9*	First to return surface pictures of Venus; USSR
1976	*Viking 1*	First to softly land on Mars, return pictures; USA
1979	*Voyager 1*	First closeup study of Jupiter and its moons; USA
1979	*Pioneer 11*	First to fly by Saturn; USA
1980	*Voyager 1*	First closeup study of Saturn and its moons; USA
1985	*ICE*	*International Cometary Explorer;* first to study a comet; USA
1986	*Voyager 2*	First closeup study of Uranus and its moons; USA
1986	*Giotto*	First images taken of a comet nucleus, Halley; ESA
1989	*Voyager 2*	First closeup study of Neptune and its moons; USA
1991	*Galileo*	First flyby, closeup photos of an asteroid, 951 Gaspra; USA
1994	*Galileo*	First satellite of an asteroid discovered, 243 Ida; USA
1995	*Ulysses*	First flyby above the Sun's south/north poles; ESA
1995	*Galileo*	First probe into Jupiter's atmosphere; USA
1998	*Deep Space 1*	First to use an autonomous navigation system; USA
2001	*NEAR Shoemaker*	First to orbit and make a "soft" landing on an asteroid, Eros; USA
2004	*Mars Rovers**	First long-range surface exploration of Mars; USA
2004	*Stardust*	First collection and return of cometary material, Wild 2; USA
2004	*Cassini*	First to orbit Saturn; USA
2004	*Huygens*	First to land on Titan; USA/ESA
2004	*Messenger**	Spacecraft to orbit and study Mercury; USA
2005	*Deep Impact**	First to impact on and study the interior of a comet, Temple 1; USA
2005	*Muses-C**	First asteroid sample return mission; Japan
2006	*Dawn**	Spacecraft to orbit asteroids Ceres and Vesta; USA
2015	*New Horizons**	First flyby of Pluto and its moon, Charon; USA

*Mission in planning stages but not yet launched

TABLE OF PRECESSION FOR ADVANCING 50 YEARS

Precession in right ascension for declination in row immediately below

RA for Dec − (h m)	RA for Dec + (h m)	Prec in Dec (′)	85° (m)	80° (m)	75° (m)	70° (m)	60° (m)	50° (m)	40° (m)	30° (m)	20° (m)	10° (m)	0° (m)	Prec in Dec (′)	RA for Dec + (h m)	RA for Dec − (h m)
12 00	0 00	16.7	2.56	2.56	2.56	2.56	2.56	2.56	2.56	2.56	2.56	2.56	2.56	−16.7	12 00	24 00
12 30	0 30	16.6	4.22	3.39	3.10	2.96	2.81	2.73	2.68	2.64	2.61	2.59	2.56	−16.6	11 30	23 30
13 00	1 00	16.1	5.85	4.20	3.64	3.35	3.06	2.90	2.80	2.73	2.67	2.61	2.56	−16.1	11 00	23 00
13 30	1 30	15.4	7.43	4.98	4.15	3.73	3.30	3.07	2.92	2.81	2.72	2.64	2.56	−15.4	10 30	22 30
14 00	2 00	14.5	8.92	5.72	4.64	4.09	3.53	3.22	3.03	2.88	2.76	2.66	2.56	−14.5	10 00	22 00
14 30	2 30	13.3	10.31	6.41	5.09	4.42	3.73	3.37	3.13	2.95	2.81	2.68	2.56	−13.3	9 30	21 30
15 00	3 00	11.8	11.56	7.03	5.50	4.72	3.92	3.50	3.22	3.02	2.85	2.70	2.56	−11.8	9 00	21 00
15 30	3 30	10.2	12.66	7.57	5.86	4.99	4.09	3.61	3.30	3.07	2.88	2.72	2.56	−10.2	8 30	20 30
16 00	4 00	8.4	13.58	8.03	6.16	5.21	4.23	3.71	3.37	3.12	2.91	2.73	2.56	−8.4	8 00	20 00
16 30	4 30	6.4	14.32	8.40	6.40	5.39	4.34	3.79	3.42	3.15	2.94	2.74	2.56	−6.4	7 30	19 30
17 00	5 00	4.3	14.85	8.66	6.57	5.52	4.42	3.84	3.46	3.18	2.95	2.75	2.56	−4.3	7 00	19 00
17 30	5 30	2.2	15.18	8.82	6.68	5.59	4.47	3.88	3.49	3.20	2.96	2.76	2.56	−2.2	6 30	18 30
18 00	6 00	0.0	15.29	8.88	6.72	5.62	4.49	3.89	3.50	3.20	2.97	2.76	2.56	0.0	6 00	18 00
0 00	12 00	−16.7	2.56	2.56	2.56	2.56	2.56	2.56	2.56	2.56	2.56	2.56	2.56	16.7	24 00	12 00
0 30	12 30	−16.6	0.90	1.74	2.02	2.16	2.31	2.39	2.44	2.48	2.51	2.54	2.56	16.6	23 30	11 30
1 00	13 00	−16.1	−0.73	0.93	1.49	1.77	2.06	2.22	2.32	2.39	2.46	2.51	2.56	16.1	23 00	11 00
1 30	13 30	−15.4	−2.31	0.14	0.97	1.39	1.82	2.05	2.20	2.31	2.41	2.49	2.56	15.4	22 30	10 30
2 00	14 00	−14.5	−3.80	−0.60	0.48	1.03	1.60	1.90	2.09	2.24	2.36	2.46	2.56	14.5	22 00	10 00
2 30	14 30	−13.3	−5.19	−1.28	0.03	0.70	1.39	1.75	1.99	2.17	2.31	2.44	2.56	13.3	21 30	9 30
3 00	15 00	−11.8	−6.44	−1.90	−0.38	0.40	1.20	1.62	1.90	2.11	2.27	2.42	2.56	11.8	21 00	9 00
3 30	15 30	−10.2	−7.54	−2.45	−0.74	0.13	1.03	1.51	1.82	2.05	2.24	2.41	2.56	10.2	20 30	8 30
4 00	16 00	−8.4	−8.46	−2.91	−1.04	−0.09	0.89	1.41	1.75	2.00	2.21	2.39	2.56	8.4	20 00	8 00
4 30	16 30	−6.4	−9.20	−3.27	−1.28	−0.27	0.78	1.33	1.70	1.97	2.19	2.38	2.56	6.4	19 30	7 30
5 00	17 00	−4.3	−9.73	−3.54	−1.45	−0.39	0.70	1.28	1.66	1.94	2.17	2.37	2.56	4.3	19 00	7 00
5 30	17 30	−2.2	−10.06	−3.70	−1.56	−0.47	0.65	1.25	1.63	1.92	2.16	2.37	2.56	2.2	18 30	6 30
6 00	18 00	0.0	−10.17	−3.75	−1.59	−0.50	0.63	1.23	1.63	1.92	2.16	2.36	2.56	0.0	18 00	6 00

If declination is positive, use inner RA scale; *if declination is negative, use outer RA scale and reverse the sign of the precession in declination.* To avoid interpolation in this table, which becomes increasingly inaccurate for large |Dec|, precession formulae may be used (see p. 32).

TIME

TIME AND TIME SCALES
BY ROY BISHOP

Time has been said to be nature's way of keeping everything from happening at once. In 1687, Isaac Newton (1642–1727) perceived time as being separate from and more fundamental than the spinning of changeable planets or the oily mechanisms of clocks: "Absolute, true, and mathematical time, of itself, and from its own nature flows equably without regard to anything external." This is the common sense or intuitive view most people have of time.

Albert Einstein (1879–1955) was the first to understand that time is but an abstraction that does not exist independently of clocks. In his special theory of relativity (1905), Einstein predicted that clocks moving relative to an observer run slower. This is called time dilation or the second-order Doppler effect (e.g. relative to a clock fixed beside a road, the wristwatch of a person driving past at a speed of 100 km/h loses 0.26 ps per minute). A decade later, in his theory of gravitation, the general theory of relativity, Einstein predicted that clocks lower or higher than the observer in a gravitational field run slower or faster, respectively, than the observer's clock. In the case of a lower clock, this is called the gravitational redshift (e.g. an alarm clock on the floor a metre below your bed loses 3.1 ps per 8-hour night relative to a watch on your wrist). These counterintuitive effects are not only real, but in recent years they have found their way into the consumer marketplace in the form of GPS (Global Positioning System) receivers. These handheld units receive signals from orbiting atomic clocks and rely on programs that allow for time dilation and gravitational redshift (see *Physics Today*, May 2002, p. 41). In astronomy, the general theory of relativity was mostly ignored until the last few decades of the 20th century when increasing precision of clocks and advances in theoretical astrophysics and cosmology demanded its use.

As to understanding time, Lord Kelvin (1824–1907) said that you know a physical quantity if you can measure it. Time can indeed be measured, with mind-boggling precision. For those who feel compelled to state "We still don't know what time actually is," perhaps the mystery resides merely in the meaning of this statement.

The essence of time is that isolated material changes occur in invariant ratios one with respect to another. That is, as Sir Hermann Bondi has put it: "Time is that which is manufactured by clocks." Thus, to deal with time, clocks must be devised and units and time scales established. Readers who wish to pursue this topic beyond the brief overview presented here should consult *The Measurement of Time*, by C. Audoin and B. Guinot, Cambridge University Press, 2001, and the *Explanatory Supplement to the Astronomical Almanac*, by P.K. Seidelmann (ed.), University Science Books, 1992.

Periodic Time Intervals and Clocks

There are three obvious, natural, periodic time intervals on Earth: the seasonal cycle (year), the cycle of lunar phases (month), and the day–night cycle (day). The cycle of the seasons is called the *tropical year* and contains 365.242 190 days. The cycle of lunar phases is known as the *synodic month* and equals 29.530 589 days. The average day–night (diurnal) cycle is the *mean solar day* and presently contains approximately 86 400.001 s. Other types of year, month, and day have been defined and are listed along with brief definitions and durations on p. 29.

The problem of accurately subdividing these natural intervals to make time locally available at any moment (i.e. timekeeping) was satisfactorily solved in 1657 by Christiaan Huygens, who invented the first practical pendulum clock. Through successive refinements the pendulum clock reigned supreme for nearly three centuries, until it was surpassed in precision by the quartz oscillator in the 1940s. Within another 20 years the quartz clock was, in turn, superseded by the cesium atomic clock, which, using the technique of *laser cooling* of atomic beams (see *Physics Today,* December 1997, p. 17, February 1998, p. 21, and March 2001, p. 37), today has a precision near 2 in 10^{15} (one second in 16 million years).

Earth's Rotation and Time Scales

Of the three obvious, natural, periodic time intervals on Earth (year, month, and day), the day dominates our lives and determines the various time scales we have created. The day is caused primarily by Earth's rotation on its axis. To count rotations, a reference or fiducial point is required. Four such points are of interest, and three of these are the basis of five time scales:

(1) Earth's rotation relative to the distant stars: Although the distant stars (or better, extragalactic sources) provide a reference frame to determine the "true" period of Earth's rotation (presently about 86 164.100 s), because of Earth's orbital motion and its rotational precession, this true period is not that of either the solar day or the RA/Dec coordinate grid used to specify astronomical positions. Hence no time scales are based on Earth's true rotational period.

(2) Earth's rotation relative to the equinox: The equator and poles of the RA/Dec celestial coordinate grid are aligned with Earth's mean equator and poles. ("Mean" denotes that small, periodic variations caused by the nutation of Earth's axis have been averaged out. Nutation involves the true pole moving relative to the mean pole with an amplitude of about 9″ and a variety of short periods up to 18.6 years.) Hence the RA/Dec grid slowly shifts relative to the distant stars as Earth's rotation axis precesses, a motion caused primarily by the torques exerted by the Moon and Sun on Earth's equatorial bulge. The gravitational influence of the other planets causes the plane of the ecliptic also to precess, although this *planetary precession* is far smaller than the *lunisolar precession* of the mean equator. The sum of these two precessions is called *general precession*. General precession causes the zero point of right ascension (the "Greenwich of the skies," the vernal equinox, or "first point of Aries") to drift westward along the ecliptic about 50″ per year. As a result, Earth's rotation period relative to the equinox (called the *mean sidereal day,* currently 86 164.092 s) is about 8.4 ms shorter than the time for one rotation. At any longitude on Earth, the RA of a star on the meridian (corrected for nutation) is the **Local Mean Sidereal Time** (**LMST**) at that instant. At the Greenwich meridian (0° longitude) this is called **Greenwich Mean Sidereal Time** (**GMST**). LMST may be used to set a telescope on an object of known right ascension. The hour angle of the object equals the sidereal time less the right ascension. LMST may be available from a sidereal clock, or it can be calculated as explained in the middle of p. 41. Because Earth makes one more rotation with respect to the other stars than it does with respect to the Sun during a year, sidereal time gains relative to time scales linked to the Sun (see below) by about 3 min 56 s per day, or 2 hours per month.

(3) Earth's rotation relative to the real Sun: A common misconception is that the Sun is highest in the sky and lies on the local north–south meridian at 12:00 noon. However, time based on the position of the Sun in the sky, known as local *apparent solar time* or *sundial time,* can differ by up to an hour or more from civil time (the time that we normally use). There are two reasons for this discrepancy. One reason is that the Sun's eastward annual apparent motion around the sky is far from uniform both because of Earth's elliptical orbit and because of the inclination of the celestial equator to the ecliptic. Thus apparent solar time does not have a uniform rate (see the next paragraph). The second reason for the difference between sundial time and civil time is addressed in the penultimate paragraph of this article.

(4) Earth's rotation relative to the mean Sun: If the Sun is replaced by a fictitious mean sun moving uniformly along the celestial equator, Earth's rotation relative to this mean sun defines *Local Mean (solar) Time* (**LMT**). Apparent solar time can differ by up to 16 min from LMT depending upon the time of year (see Sundial Correction on p. 100). Small, periodic shifts of Earth's crust relative to the axis of rotation (*polar motion*) affect astronomical time determinations through the resulting east–west shift in the meridian at latitudes away from the equator. LMT at the Greenwich meridian (0° longitude) when corrected for this polar motion is called *Universal Time* (**UT1**, or often simply **UT**). UT1 is determined using very long baseline interferometry, satellite laser-ranging data, lunar laser-ranging data, and GPS data (via the International GPS Service).

All of the above mean time scales (LMST, GMST, LMT, and UT1), being based upon Earth's rotation, are only as uniform as this rotation. By the mid-19th century, discrepancies between theory and the observed motion of the Moon indicated that, over the long term, Earth's rotation is slowing down. However, not until clocks became better timekeepers than the spinning Earth (c. 1940 when crystal-controlled clocks exceeded precisions of 1 in 10^{10}) was it realized how complex is the variable rotation of our planet. There are (i) long-, (ii) medium-, and (iii) short-term accelerations:

(i) Over many centuries there is a *secular* slowing caused by tidal friction of about 8 parts in 10^{13} per day (i.e. the day becomes one second longer about every 40 000 years).

(ii) Over a few decades there are *random* accelerations (positive and negative), apparently caused by core–mantle interactions and possibly by changes in ocean currents. These are about 10 times larger than the tidal deceleration and thus completely obscure the latter effect over time intervals of less than a century or so.

(iii) The largest accelerations in Earth's rotation rate are short-term ones: *periodic components* are associated mainly with lunar-induced tides (over two-week and monthly intervals) and seasonal meteorological factors (over semiannual and annual intervals); *nonperiodic* (chaotic) high-frequency variations are associated mainly with the global atmospheric wind and pressure distributions. These short-term accelerations are typically one or two orders of magnitude larger again than the random, decade fluctuations on which they are superimposed (see the article by John Wahr in the June 1986 issue of *Sky & Telescope,* p. 545).

Uniform Time Scales

(1) Based on orbital motion: Although Earth's axial rotation is not sufficiently predictable to serve as a precise clock, the orbital motions of our Moon, Earth, and the other planets are predictable to high accuracy. Through the dynamical equations describing these motions plus extended astronomical observations, a uniform time scale can be derived. Such a scale, known as *Ephemeris Time* (ET), was for several years (1952–1984) the basis of astronomical ephemerides. Early in the 20th century the UT1 and ET scales coincided, but since Earth's rotation rate has been generally slower than the ET rate, by 1970 UT1 was 40 s behind ET and was losing more than one second per year. During the next 15 years, Earth's rotation rate increased (part of the random decade fluctuations). During the 1990s, UT1 lost about 0.7 s per year relative to ET (actually TT, see two paragraphs ahead).

(2) **Based on atomic motion:** Atoms display a permanence and stability that planets, quartz crystals, and pendulums cannot. The idea of an atomic clock was proposed by the American physicist Isidor Rabi in 1945. In 1967, *the second became the basic unit of time* when it was given an atomic definition: 9 192 631 770 periods of the radiation involved in the transition between the two hyperfine levels of the ground state of the cesium 133 atom. This is known as the SI (for Système International) second (abbreviation s, *not* sec). The number 9 192 631 770 was chosen so that on the rotating geoid (i.e. for clocks fixed on Earth at mean sea level), the SI second is identical to the older ET second to within the precision of measurement.

The previous sentence implies that clocks on the geoid run at the same rate. What about Earth's rotation? Clocks nearer the equator move faster, so does time dilation not make them run slower relative to clocks at higher latitudes? Ignoring the Moon and Sun, if Earth did not rotate and had an isotropic density distribution, its geoid (mean sea-level surface) would be spherical, and clocks fixed on this geoid would, by symmetry, all run at the same rate (they would all be at rest and have similar positions in Earth's gravitational field). For a rotating Earth the equatorial bulge is such that clocks away from the poles are just enough higher in Earth's gravitational field that the resulting gravitational blueshift exactly cancels the time dilation associated with their rotational speed. This simple, elegant, and convenient result is a consequence of Einstein's principle of equivalence. In this instance, any two nearby clocks will have identical rates if they are located on the same surface perpendicular to the direction of the electromagnetic contact forces supporting them. Thus *all* clocks on the geoid run at the same rate. Whether or not the planet beneath is rotating is immaterial.

Because of several difficulties surrounding both the original concept of ET and its determination, and because atomic clocks had become readily available, in 1984 ET was abandoned in favour of *Terrestrial Dynamical Time* (TDT). The unit of TDT was the SI second on the rotating geoid, and its scale was chosen to agree with the 1984 ET scale. In 1991 TDT was renamed simply **Terrestrial Time (TT).** Because of uncertainties surrounding the realization of the geoid (the geoid would coincide with Earth's sea surface *if* the waters of the oceans were homogeneous and at rest), in 2000 TT was redefined in terms of TCG (see below). The unit of TT is very close to the SI second on the rotating geoid. TT is the time reference for apparent geocentric ephemerides, and it is realized via TAI (see below).

International Atomic Time (**TAI** = Temps Atomique International) is based on a weighted average of atomic clocks in many countries and presently is the most precise *achievable* time scale. Not even atomic clocks are perfect timekeepers, so TAI shifts unpredictably relative to the TT rate by a few microseconds over several years. TAI was arbitrarily set to agree with UT1 at the beginning of 1958, which led to the definition that TT be exactly 32.184 s ahead of TAI on 1977 January 1.0 TAI. This ensured continuity of TT with ET.

In 1991, when the general theory of relativity was explicitly adopted as the theoretical background for spacetime reference frames, two new time scales were introduced: *Geocentric Coordinate Time* (**TCG**) and *Barycentric Coordinate Time* (**TCB**) for nonrotating coordinate frames with origins located at the centres of mass of Earth and of the solar system, respectively. TCG is not influenced by Earth's gravitation, and TCB is not influenced by *any* gravitational fields of the solar system. These coordinate time scales provide a means to unambiguously date events. TCG is used for analyzing the motions of Earth-orbiting satellites, and TCB is used to study planet and space probe motions. Both TCG and TCB use the SI second.

The gravitational redshift causes TT to lose 22 ms per year relative to TCG (clocks on Earth are deep within Earth's gravitational well). In turn, TCG loses about 467 ms per year relative to TCB because of time dilation and gravitational redshift (the geocentric coordinate frame orbits with Earth deep within the Sun's gravitational well). Thus TCB gains nearly half a second per year relative to TT. The origins of TCG and TCB were chosen so that TCG, TCB, and TT had the same reading at Earth's centre of mass on 1977 January 1.0 (TAI), all three scales being set to be exactly 32.184 s ahead of TAI at that point in spacetime. TCB and TCG (and hence TT) are realized via TAI.

Another time scale, Barycentric Dynamical Time (TDB), was introduced in 1976 when it became necessary to acknowledge relativistic effects but before the general theory of relativity was accepted by astronomers. It is similar to TCB except its scale unit was adjusted to approximate TT. TDB is a needlessly complex time scale; however, because it has been used extensively (e.g. by the Jet Propulsion Laboratory for ephemerides used in planetary exploration), it was not totally abandoned when TCB was introduced in 1991.

(3) Based on pulsars: Millisecond radio pulsars (old, rapidly spinning neutron stars) display extraordinary stability in their rotation. Their stability, after allowing for spin-down, is almost as good as the best atomic clocks. However, uncertainties in predicting the spin-down rate of a pulsar and in Earth's motion relative to a pulsar, the elaborate equipment needed to observe a pulsar, and the complex data analysis required all make it unlikely that a pulsar will ever replace cesium clocks as the basis for a uniform time scale.

Uniform Time Scales with Steps (to track the mean Sun)

Closely related to UT1 (which follows Earth's variable rotation relative to the mean Sun) is *Coordinated Universal Time* **(UTC),** introduced in its present form in 1972. UTC, the basis of the world system of civil time, runs at the TAI rate and is offset an integral number of seconds from TAI so that it approximates UT1. When required (usually on June 30 or December 31), "leap seconds" are inserted into (or, if necessary, deleted from) UTC so that the difference UT1 − UTC = ΔUT1 does not exceed ±0.9 s. UTC now lags TAI, and as of 1999 January 1, 0h UT (when a leap second was last inserted) TAI − UTC = ΔAT = 32 s. Thus as this edition of the *Observer's Handbook* goes to press (summer 2002), TT − UTC = 32 s + 32.184 s = 64.184 s exactly (see the diagram on the next page). In 1998 and again in 2000 Earth's rotation sped up slightly; consequently, a leap second was not needed during the years 1999 through 2002. The next leap second will likely occur at the end of June 2003. UTC is readily available via radio time signals or GPS receivers. (Note: The term *Greenwich Mean Time* (GMT) over the years has had three different meanings: the same as UT1, UTC, and mean solar time at the Greenwich meridian with 0 hours corresponding to noon. To avoid confusion, the term *Greenwich Mean Time* should not be used.)

Anyone in North America can keep track of Earth's varying rotation by listening to the CHU or WWV radio time signals in which is coded the difference ΔUT1 = (UT1 − UTC) (see TIME SIGNALS on p. 41). It is interesting to record ΔUT1 about once a month and use these data to make a graphical display of (TT − UT1) as a function of time over several years. Note that at least until the end of June 2003, TT − UT1 = 64.184 − (UT1 − UTC).

(continued on next page)

This diagram displays the rate and scale relations between Earth-based time scales that run at or near the SI rate at sea level and which are not longitude dependent. At the rate Earth presently is rotating, the difference TAI – UTC will likely be increased by one second to 33 s at the end of June 2003.

Local Mean (solar) Time (LMT) would suffice for the inhabitants of an isolated village, but with the advent in the 19th century of rapid travel and communication (railways, steamships, and the telegraph), it became essential that clocks over a range of longitudes indicate the same time. To keep these clocks reasonably in phase with the day–night cycle and yet avoid the inconvenience to travellers of a local time that varies continuously with longitude, in 1884 Earth was divided into 24 **Standard Time** zones, adjacent zones generally differing by one hour and each ideally 15 degrees wide (see the time zone map on p. 43). All clocks within the same zone read the same time. The Canadian railway surveyor and construction engineer Sir Sandford Fleming (1827–1915) was instrumental in establishing this system of standard time zones. The zero zone is centred on the Greenwich meridian (longitude 0°), and, since 1972, standard time in that zone is UTC. Thus the world system of civil time is based on UTC and includes the "leap seconds," which keep UTC near UT1. Depending upon an observer's location within his or her standard time zone, standard time may differ by up to an hour or so from LMT (see the third paragraph on p. 107). This is the second reason why the Sun seldom, if ever, is on the observer's meridian at 12:00 noon, standard time.

Some countries observe **Daylight Saving Time** during the summer months. In Canada and the United States, clocks are generally* set one hour ahead of standard time at 2 a.m. local time on the first Sunday in April, and return to standard time at 2 a.m. local time on the last Sunday in October: "spring ahead, fall back."

---

*Saskatchewan, Arizona, Indiana, and Hawaii do *not* observe daylight saving time.

TIME SIGNALS

National time services distribute Coordinated Universal Time (UTC). UTC is coordinated through the Bureau International des Poids et Mesures (BIPM) in Sèvres, France so that most time services are synchronized to a tenth of a millisecond. Radio time signals available in North America include:

CHU Ottawa, Ontario, Canada 3.330, 7.335, 14.670 MHz
WWV Fort Collins, Colorado, USA 2.5, 5, 10, 15, 20 MHz

For CHU, each minute starts at the *beginning* of the tone following the voice announcement, the tone for the 29th second is omitted, and the tones for seconds 31 through 39 have a different sound from the others.

The difference $\Delta UT1 = UT1 - UTC$ to the nearest tenth of a second is coded in the signals. If UT1 is ahead of UTC, second markers beginning at the 1-second mark of each minute are doubled, the number of doubled markers indicating the number of tenths of a second UT1 is ahead of UTC. If UT1 is behind UTC, the doubled markers begin at the 9-second point.

Time signals are also available by telephone from the National Research Council in Ottawa. Within Canada, call (800) 363-5409; outside Canada, call (613) 745-1576.

MEAN SIDEREAL TIME, 2003

The following is the Greenwich Mean Sidereal Time (GMST) in hours on day 0 at 0h UT of each month ("day 0" is the last day of the previous month):

Jan. 6.6168	Apr. 12.5307	Jul. 18.5103	Oct. 0.5556
Feb. 8.6538	May 14.5020	Aug. 20.5473	Nov. 2.5926
Mar. 10.4937	Jun. 16.5390	Sep. 22.5843	Dec. 4.5639

(handwritten: →7.9731 for Penticton)

GMST (in hours) at hour t UT on day d of the month =
GMST at 0h UT on day $0 + 0.065710d + 1.002738t$
LMST (Local Mean Sidereal Time) = GMST − west longitude (or + east longitude)

LMST calculated by this method will be accurate to ±0.2 s provided t is stated to ±0.1 s or better and the observer's longitude is known to ±1″. (Note that t must be expressed in decimal hours UT. Also, to achieve ±0.1 s accuracy in t, the correction $\Delta UT1$ must be applied to UTC. See the TIME SIGNALS section above.)

JULIAN DATE (JD), 2003

The Julian Date (JD) is commonly used by astronomers to refer to the time of astronomical events, because it avoids some of the annoying complexities of the civil calendar. Julian Date 0.0 was the instant of Greenwich mean noon on January 1, 4713 BC (see "The Origin of the Julian Day System" by G. Moyer, *Sky & Telescope,* April 1981).

The Julian day **commences at noon** (12h) UT. To find the Julian Date at any time during 2003, determine the day of the month and time at the Greenwich meridian, convert this to a decimal day, and add it to one of the following numbers according to the month (these numbers are the Julian Dates for 0h UT on the 0th day of each month):

Jan. ...245 2639.5	Apr. ...245 2729.5	Jul. 245 2820.5	Oct. ...245 2912.5
Feb. ...245 2670.5	May ..245 2759.5	Aug. ..245 2851.5	Nov. ..245 2943.5
Mar. ..245 2698.5	Jun. ...245 2790.5	Sep. ..245 2882.5	Dec. ..245 2973.5

For example, 21:36 EDT on May 18 = 1:36 UT on May 19 = May 19.07 UT = 245 2759.5 + 19.07 = JD 245 2778.57.

The Julian Dates for 0h UT January 0 for the three previous years are 245 0000.5 plus: 1543 (2000), 1909 (2001), 2274 (2002).

STANDARD TIME ZONES

The map at the right shows the world system of standard time zones. It was prepared and provided by Her Majesty's Nautical Almanac Office. Over the open oceans, the time zones are uniformly spaced and are bounded by lines of longitude 15° apart. In populated regions, political and other considerations have considerably modified the ideal geometry.

As Earth rotates with sunlight shining from one side, at some line of longitude the day of the week must jump discontinuously ahead by one day (otherwise, Monday would be followed by Monday!). The line chosen for this jump is in the relatively unpopulated central part of the Pacific Ocean and approximates longitude 180°. It is called the International Date Line. A person travelling westward across this line has to advance the calendar date by one day, while an eastward-bound traveller moves back one day on the calendar.

The standard time zones are generally designated by letters of the alphabet. The zero time zone, centred on the longitude 0° meridian passing through the Airy Transit Circle at the Old Royal Observatory in Greenwich, England, is denoted Z. Standard time within this zone is Coordinated Universal Time (UTC). Zones A, B, C, ..., M (J excluded), run eastward at one-hour intervals to the International Date Line, while zones N, O, P, ..., Y run westward to the same boundary. Zones M and Y are only one-half hour wide. Also, as indicated on the map, there are several partial zones that are one-half hour different from the adjacent main zones.

In North America there are seven standard time zones. In terms of their name (and letter designation, hours behind the Greenwich zone, and the west longitude of the reference or standard meridian), these are:

(1) Newfoundland (P*, 3 h 30 min, 52.5°)
(2) Atlantic (Q, 4 h, 60°)
(3) Eastern (R, 5 h, 75°)
(4) Central (S, 6 h, 90°)
(5) Mountain (T, 7 h, 105°)
(6) Pacific (U, 8 h, 120°)
(7) Alaska (V, 9 h, 135°)

Note: Caution is advised when relying on the time-zone information given in this map. The zones are drawn based on the best information available as of July 2002 and are subject to change. Also, local jurisdictions, especially those near depicted zone boundaries, often adopt a a different time. For current official Canadian time zones visit **www.nrc.ca/inms/time/tze.html**. Current U.S. and world time zones can easily be found by doing an Internet search using the keywords "time zones."

WORLD MAP OF TIME ZONES

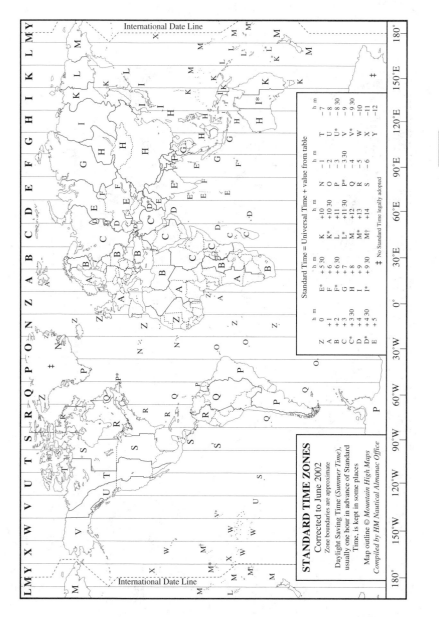

STANDARD TIME ZONES

Corrected to June 2002

Zone boundaries are approximate

Daylight Saving Time (*Summer Time*),
usually one hour in advance of Standard
Time, is kept in some places

Map outline © *Mountain High Maps*

Compiled by HM Nautical Almanac Office

Standard Time = Universal Time + value from table

	h m			h m
Z	0		E*	+5 30
A	+ 1		F	+ 6
B	+ 2		F*	+ 6 30
C	+ 3		G	+ 7
C*	+ 3 30		H	+ 8
D	+ 4		I	+ 9
D*	+ 4 30		I*	+ 9 30
E	+ 5			

	h m			h m
K	+10		N	− 1
K*	+10 30		O	− 2
L	+11		P*	− 3
L*	+11 30		P*	− 3 30
M	+12		Q	− 4
M*	+13		R	− 5
Mt	+14		S	− 6

	h m
T	− 7
U	− 8
U*	− 8 30
V	− 9
V*	− 9 30
W	−10
X	−11
Y	−12

‡ No Standard Time legally adopted

ASTRONOMICAL TWILIGHT AND SIDEREAL TIME
By Randall Brooks

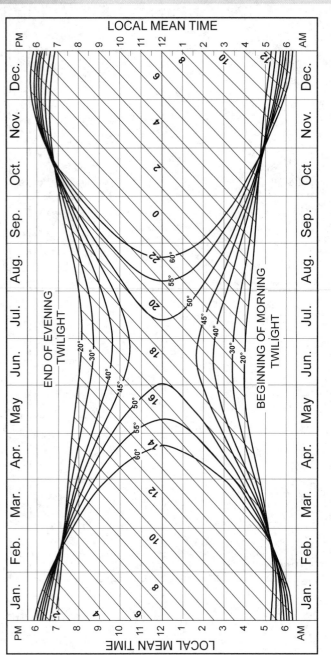

The diagram gives for any day of the year: (**1**) the local mean time (LMT) of the end and beginning of astronomical twilight at seven specified northern latitudes (curved lines); (**2**) the local mean sidereal time (LMST = right ascension at the observer's meridian) as a function of LMT (diagonal lines).

OPTICS AND OBSERVING

TELESCOPE PARAMETERS

Equations

Objective: f_o = focal length   *Eyepiece:* f_e = focal length
        D = diameter d_f = diameter of field stop
        FR = focal ratio θ_p = apparent angular field

Whole Instrument: M = angular magnification
                d_p = diameter of exit pupil
                θ_c = actual angular field

$$M = f_o/f_e = D/d_p \approx \theta_p/\theta_c \qquad \text{FR} = f_o/D \qquad d_f{}^* = f_o\theta_c \approx f_e\theta_p$$

$*(\theta_c$ and θ_p must be expressed in radians.)

Performance

D is assumed to be expressed in millimetres.

Light Grasp (LG) is the ratio of the light flux intercepted by a telescope's objective lens or mirror to that intercepted by a human eye having a 7-mm-diameter entrance pupil.

Limiting Visual Magnitude $m \approx 2.7 + 5 \log D$, assuming transparent, dark-sky conditions and magnification $M \geq 1D$. (See *Sky & Telescope, 45,* 401, 1973; *77,* 332, 1989; *78,* 522, 1989).

Smallest Resolvable Angle $\alpha \approx 116/D$ seconds of arc (Dawes's limit). However, atmospheric conditions seldom permit values less than 0.5″.

Useful Magnification Range $\approx 0.2D$ to $2D$. The lower limit $(0.2D)$ guarantees that, for most observers, all the light exiting a telescope can reach the retina. (The reciprocal of the coefficient to D is the diameter (in mm) of the telescope's exit pupil. Also, see the next section concerning exit pupils and magnification.) The upper limit $(2D)$ is determined by the wave nature of light and the optical limitations of the eye, although atmospheric turbulence usually limits the maximum magnification to 400× or less. For examination of double stars, detection of faint stars, and studying structure in bright nebulae, magnifications of up to $3D$ are sometimes useful.

Values for some common apertures are:

D (mm):	60	100	125	150	200	250	330	444
LG:	73	200	320	460	820	1300	2200	4000
m:	11.6	12.7	13.2	13.6	14.2	14.7	15.3	15.9
α:	1.93″	1.16″	0.93″	0.77″	0.58″	0.46″	0.35″	0.26″
$0.2D$:	12×	20×	25×	30×	40×	50×	66×	89×
$2D$:	120×	200×	250×	300×	400×	500×	660×	890×

TELESCOPE EXIT PUPILS
By Roy Bishop

The performance of a visual telescope is constrained by Earth's atmosphere, the wave aspect of light, the design of the telescope, imperfections in its optical system, and the properties of the human visual system. Telescope and eye meet at the *exit pupil* of the telescope, which is the image of the telescope's objective lens or mirror formed by its eyepiece. When a telescope is pointed at a bright area, such as the daytime sky, the exit pupil appears as a small disk of light hovering in the space just behind the eyepiece. (Insert a small piece of paper in this vicinity to demonstrate that this disk of light *really is* located behind the eyepiece.) Since the exit pupil is the narrowest point in the beam of light emerging from the telescope, it is here that the observer's eye must be located to make optimum use of the light passing through the telescope.

The diagram on p. 49 may be used to display the relation between the diameter of the exit pupil (d_p) of a telescope and the focal lengths (f_e) of various eyepieces. Both d_p and f_e are expressed in millimetres. The numbered scale around the upper right-hand corner of the diagram indicates the focal ratio (FR) of the objective lens or mirror of the telescope. (The FR equals the focal length of the objective divided by its diameter; see the previous page.) To prepare the diagram for a particular telescope, locate the FR of the telescope's objective on the FR scale, and draw a straight diagonal line from there to the origin (the lower left-hand corner). The diagram provides a visual display of the standard relation $d_p = f_e/\text{FR}$.

To determine, for example, the eyepiece focal length required to give an exit pupil of 3 mm on a certain telescope, locate $d_p = 3$ on the ordinate, run horizontally across to the diagonal line corresponding to the FR of that telescope, and from there drop vertically downward to the abscissa to find f_e. This procedure may, of course, be reversed: for a given f_e, find the corresponding d_p.

Magnification Ranges

The ranges H, M, L, and RFT blocked off along the ordinate of the diagram break the d_p scale into four sections, starting at 0.5 mm and increasing by factors of 2. Although this sectioning is somewhat arbitrary, it does correspond closely to what are usually considered to be the high (H), medium (M), low (L), and "richest-field telescope" (RFT) magnification ranges of any visual telescope—and the associated d_p ranges are easy to remember.

High Magnifications: In the case of the Moon, the planets, and all but the dimmest stars, the highest useful magnification is the point at which blurring due to diffraction (caused by the wave nature of light) becomes noticeable. This corresponds approximately to $d_p = 0.5$ mm, assuming good optics and negligible atmospheric turbulence (i.e. excellent "seeing"). Higher magnifications will not reveal any more detail in these images and will cause reductions in four desirable features: sharpness, brightness, field of view, and eye relief (the space between the eye and eyepiece). Also, as d_p is made progressively smaller, imperfections and debris in the interior of the eye (in the vitreous humour in front of the retina) become more noticeable and interfere with clear vision. However, for objects requiring the use of averted vision (e.g. faint stars, nebulae, and galaxies), the acuity of the eye is much reduced and very high magnifications ($d_p < 0.5$ mm) can sometimes be used to advantage (although only the brightest areas of nebulae and galaxies will still be visible at such magnifications).

Very Low Magnifications: Magnifications in the RFT range are useful because they yield wide fields of view, the brightest (highest luminance) images of extended objects, and for common telescope apertures, the most stars visible in one view (hence the term *richest field)*. The lowest magnification that still makes use of the full aperture of a telescope is determined by the point at which the diameter of the telescope's exit pupil matches the diameter of the *entrance pupil* of the observer's eye.

For the dark-adapted eye, the entrance-pupil diameter seldom equals the often-quoted figure of 7 mm, but depends, among other things, upon the age of the observer as indicated by the scale in the upper left portion of the diagram (see Kadlecová et al., *Nature, 182,* 1520, 1958; *Sky & Telescope,* May 1992, 502). Note that this scale indicates *average* values; the maximum diameter of the entrance pupil of the eye of any *one* individual may differ by up to a millimetre from these values. A horizontal line should be drawn across the diagram corresponding to the maximum diameter of one's own entrance pupil. This line will be an upper bound on d_p in the same sense that the line at $d_p = 0.5$ mm is a lower bound. Note that in daylight, the entrance pupil of the eye has a diameter in the range of 2 mm to 4 mm. Thus for daylight use of telescopes, the upper bound on d_p will be correspondingly reduced.

Ultra-Low Magnifications: If a d_p value larger than the entrance pupil of the eye is used, the iris of the observer's eye will cut off some of the light passing through the telescope to the retina; that is, the iris will have become the light-limiting aperture *(aperture stop)* of the system rather than the edge of the telescope's objective. In this case, the cornea of the eye together with the lenses of the telescope's eyepiece form an image of the observer's iris at the objective of the telescope; to the incoming starlight, a highly magnified image of the iris hovers as an annular skirt covering the outer region of the objective of the telescope! A telescope can be used at such "ultra-low" magnifications, but obviously a telescope of smaller aperture would perform as well. However, ultra-low magnifications on any telescope *do* have two advantages:

(1) A wider actual field of view, assuming the field stop of the eyepiece will permit this (an eyepiece requiring a 2-inch-diameter focuser is usually necessary).

(2) Ease of alignment of the entrance pupil of the eye with the exit pupil of the telescope, an aspect of viewing that is usually troublesome when these two pupils are nearly the same size. An oversize exit pupil provides "slop," making alignment less critical. This is particularly helpful when using binoculars during activities involving motion, such as boating or bird-watching. This is one advantage of using 7×50 (= $M \times D$) binoculars rather than 7×35 binoculars for daytime activities, although less than half of the light entering the larger binoculars can reach the observer's retinas.

Optimum Low Magnification: A value of d_p a millimetre or two *smaller* than the entrance pupil of the eye has several advantages:

(1) Viewing is more comfortable, since the observer can move a bit (move the head and/or scan the field) without cutting into the light beam and dimming the image. As mentioned above, ultra-low magnifications have the same advantage, but light is wasted.

(2) Light entering near the edge of the pupil of the dark-adapted eye is not as effective in stimulating the rod cells in the retina—the "scotopic Stiles-Crawford effect" (see VanLoo and Enoch, *Vision Research, 15,* 1005, 1975). Thus the smaller d_p will result in more effective use of the light.

(3) Aberrations in the cornea and lens of the eye are usually greatest in the peripheral regions and can distort star images. The smaller d_p will avoid the worst of these regions and produce sharper star images.

(4) With the higher magnification, structure in dim, extended objects, such as galaxies and bright and dark nebulae, will be more easily seen. (Our ability to see detail is greatly reduced in dim light, since the retina organizes its cells into larger units, thereby sacrificing resolution in order to improve signal-to-noise in the sparse patter of photons.)

(5) The background sky glow will be darker, producing views that some observers consider to be aesthetically more pleasing.

(The only disadvantage of having d_p a millimetre or two smaller than the entrance pupil of the eye is a somewhat reduced field of view, but this will be minimal if an eyepiece having a larger apparent angular field is available at this higher magnification.)

Using the Diagram

Once the diagonal line corresponding to a telescope's focal ratio has been drawn and the upper bound on d_p is established, the diagram at the right gives a concise and convenient display of the eyepiece/exit pupil/magnification range relations for a particular telescope and observer. One can see at a glance what range of eyepiece focal lengths is suitable.

Some examples:

(1) Consider the common 8-inch Schmidt-Cassegrain telescopes. These have $D = 200$ mm and (usually) FR = 10. The diagram indicates that eyepieces with focal lengths from 5 mm to 55 mm are usable for most observers. With a 32-mm eyepiece, the diagram gives $d_p = 3.2$ mm, in the L magnification range, and the magnification $M = D/d_p = 200/3.2 = 62\times$.

(2) If an observer wishes to use the full aperture of an FR = 4.5 telescope, a 40-mm eyepiece is ruled out. Similarly, a 70-year-old observer should probably not use even a 27-mm eyepiece on such a telescope and should not bother with 7 × 50 or 11 × 80 binoculars, unless ease of eye/exit pupil alignment is the main consideration.

(3) With ordinary eyepieces ($f_e \leq 55$ mm), a telescope with FR = 15 cannot be operated in the RFT range, unless a compressor lens is added to reduce its FR.

(4) There is no point in using extremely short focal length eyepieces and Barlow lenses on telescopes having large FRs. This is a common fault (among many others!) with camera/department store "junk telescopes."

(5) Exit-pupil diameters of about 1 mm and smaller cause "floaters" (mobile debris within the eye) to interfere with vision. This problem increases with age. To avoid the distraction of floaters, an observer might choose to keep exit-pupil diameters larger than 1.5 mm. For this lower limit the diagram indicates a minimum eyepiece focal length of, for example, 7 mm for a FR = 4.5 telescope and 24 mm for a FR = 16 telescope. With this restriction, to achieve a magnification of 250× for observing planets, a telescope would need an aperture of at least $D = M \times d_p = 250 \times 1.5 = 375$ mm. Hence, in addition to providing more light and greater resolution, a large-aperture telescope makes floaters less noticeable.

(6) Is a 20-mm eyepiece a "low power" eyepiece? As indicated by the diagram, the answer depends upon the focal ratio of the telescope. If FR = 4.5 the magnification M will be in the RFT range. If FR = 8, M will be low. If FR = 15, M will be medium. Similarly a 10-mm eyepiece will provide low, medium and high magnifications, respectively, for these three values of FR.

EXIT PUPILS DIAGRAM

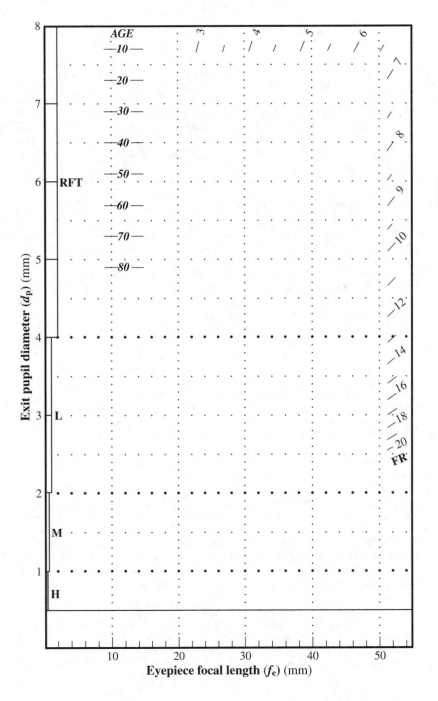

BINOCULARS
By Roy Bishop

Binoculars are indispensable for the experienced observer and the best choice for a beginner over a telescope. For the beginner unfamiliar with the large-scale features of the sky or who cannot yet identify a dozen constellations on any clear night, a telescope's narrow field of view and confusing image orientations will quickly cause more frustration than fun. The beginner is at a double disadvantage because he or she also does not know enough about astronomical telescopes to distinguish those that are worthy of the name from the common camera/department store "junk telescopes"— the $299 wonders with poor optics and impossibly wobbly mounts. How many such telescopes are gathering dust in closets, their young owners turned off astronomy and their parents a few hundred dollars poorer? Far better had the same investment been made in a good pair of binoculars. With their ease of use, wide field of view, and unreversed, upright images, binoculars are a great help in finding one's way around the sky, and provide many unique views of the heavens.

Binoculars magnifying 6 to 8 times are ideal for locating planets in the twilight, scanning the constellations, studying the larger dark nebulae and star fields of our galaxy, and viewing large comets. Binoculars magnifying 10 to 20 times provide the best views of objects spanning a few degrees, such as the Hyades, the Pleiades, the North American Nebula, and the Andromeda Galaxy; they also give the finest view of the slender crescent Moon, or of the full Moon with broken clouds blowing by.

Binoculars permit us to view the universe with both eyes, thereby providing more advantages: an improved sense of reality and depth (although parallax is negligible when viewing the heavens); more relaxed viewing; a complete view in the sense that the blind areas of one eye (associated with blood vessels and the region where the optic nerve attaches to the retina) are compensated by the field provided by the other eye; and dim objects appear brighter when viewed with two eyes.

Sizes: Binocular sizes are specified by numbers, for example, 7×50 and 8×30. The first number, including the "$\times$," is the angular magnification or "power"; the second number is the diameter of the front (objective) lenses in millimetres. That is, in the notation on p. 45: $M \times D$. Thus the exit pupil diameter is easily calculated from $D \div M$ (e.g. 7×35 binoculars have $35 \div 7 = 5$ mm exit pupils). Another important parameter is field of view. Binoculars have apparent angular field diameters of about $50°$ when equipped with standard eyepieces, to near $70°$ with wide-angle eyepieces. The actual field of view on the sky (typically $3°$ to $10°$) equals approximately the apparent field divided by the magnification. Thus the area of sky visible decreases rapidly with higher magnifications.

What is the best binocular size for astronomical use? There is no simple answer. Almost *any* pair of binoculars will show far more than can be seen with the unaided eyes; however, for astronomical use the objective lenses should be at least 30 mm in diameter. Also, small binoculars of high quality are more enjoyable to use than a large pair of low quality. For maximum light transmission and high-contrast images, binoculars with *multicoated* optics are preferable to those with merely *coated* optics (the former give greenish or deep red reflections from their surfaces, the latter bluish or violet).

Caveat emptor! Low-quality binoculars (and telescopes) are common. Images seen through low-quality binoculars are slightly fuzzy (usually not apparent to the inexperienced observer), one's eyes will be strained in trying to compensate for imperfectly aligned optics, and the focusing mechanism is usually flexible and crackling with an excess of grease used to mask poor workmanship. Avoid both zoom (variable magnification) binoculars and binoculars that do not have an adjustable focus—invariably these are of low quality. Considering that binoculars contain at least 14 pieces of glass with 36 optical surfaces, antireflection coatings on (hopefully) all air-to-glass surfaces, plus two focusing mechanisms and an interpupillary adjustment, it is not surprising that top-quality instruments are in the same price range as video cameras. Such prices buy crisp, high-contrast images, accurately aligned optics, precise, rugged, dust- and moisture-proof construction, and pleasurable service for a lifetime. Nevertheless, there is a big market for $99 binoculars and $299 telescopes, and manufacturers are happy to satisfy the demand. When it comes to optical equipment, quality usually matches price.

Stability: One aspect of binocular use not often appreciated is how much more can be seen if the binoculars are mounted on a stable support, such as a camera tripod. This eliminates the constant jiggling associated with hand-holding. Adapters for attaching binoculars to a tripod are available, although usually it is not difficult to make your own. A recent major advance in binocular design is "image-stabilization," an active optical system built into binoculars that compensates for the tremor associated with hand-holding. For example, the Canon company has introduced microprocessor-controlled binocular image stabilization, which gives near tripod-like stability with the convenience of hand-holding. Canon has produced 10×30, 12×36, 15×45, 15×50, and 18×50 models, the latter three being particularly impressive for astronomy (see *SkyNews,* July/August 1998, p. 12; and *Sky & Telescope,* July 2000, p. 59).

Rating Binoculars

A frequently cited figure for binocular performance is "Relative Brightness," which equals the square of the diameter (in millimetres) of the instrument's exit pupils. For example, for 7×50 binoculars this figure is $(50 \div 7)^2 = 51$. Although this is a measure of the surface brightness *(luminance)* of an extended object seen through the binoculars under nighttime conditions, it is a totally inadequate measure of binocular performance on the night sky. For instance, using this figure of merit, large 14×100 binoculars have practically the same rating as the unaided eyes (which, when young and in dim light, are effectively 1×7 binoculars)!

Since seeing depends upon light, and the amount of light passing through a pair of binoculars depends primarily upon the *area* of its objective lenses (diameter D), a D^2 dependence appears reasonable. However, although the amount of light going into the point images of stars increases as D^2, assuming constant magnification the increase in the luminance of the background sky as D increases leads to a somewhat slower improvement in the visibility of these stars. A similar muted improvement occurs for dim extended images, resulting in an approximately D^1 dependence, rather than D^2.

Also, for constant D the detail that can be seen in the night sky increases with the magnification M. The resulting lower luminance of the background sky allows fainter stars to be seen, and the visibility of structure in extended images improves as M increases because the image is larger and of fixed contrast relative to the sky background.

The simplest figure of merit for the performance of binoculars in low-light conditions that combines both variables is the mathematical product $M \times D$ (which looks the same as the binocular size specification!). In the case of two pairs of binoculars, one having twice the M and twice the D of the other, $M \times D$ indicates that "four times as much" should be visible in the larger instrument (e.g. 16×60 versus 8×30 binoculars). This is to be expected since in the larger instrument stars will be four times brighter and extended images will have four times the area from which the eyes can glean information, with luminances being the same in both instruments.

For many decades the venerable Carl Zeiss optical company has cited $\sqrt{(M \times D)}$ as a "Twilight Performance Factor" for binoculars, its value said to be proportional to the distance at which various binoculars will show the same detail. This is equivalent to $M \times D$ being proportional to *the amount of detail that can be seen at the same distance*. The latter situation is relevant for astronomy since, unlike a bird or other object on Earth, a star or a galaxy is always at essentially the *same distance* from the observer. $M \times D$ could be called the *visibility factor*.

Binocular Performance Diagram

The diagram at the right enables one to quickly compare binoculars in terms of their ability to reveal detail in the night sky. The vertical axis is magnification M; the horizontal axis is aperture D. The uniform grid of small dots is a guide to reading the diagram. The five straight lines indicate constant exit pupil diameters of 3, 4, 5, 6, and 7 mm, as indicated both by numbers and by circles of these diameters near the top ends of the lines. The five curved arcs indicate constant values of $M \times D$ (the visibility factor), increasing by successive powers of 2 toward the upper right (100, 200, 400, 800, and 1600). Each large dot represents a common size of binoculars. The arrows in the lower right corner indicate the directions on the diagram in which various quantities increase most rapidly.

Each straight line (constant exit pupil diameter) also corresponds to constant luminance of extended areas, such as the Orion Nebula or the background sky glow, with the luminance being proportional to the square of the exit pupil diameter (provided the entrance pupils of the observer's eyes are large enough to accommodate the exit pupils of the binoculars). However, exit pupils of 3 to 5 mm ensure (1) that all the light transmitted by the binoculars can enter the dark-adapted eyes no matter what the observer's age, (2) that alignment of exit pupils with dark-adapted eye pupils is relatively easy to achieve, (3) that the background sky glow will be subdued, and (4) that star images will be less distorted by aberrations in the observer's eyes (see the previous section).

Examples: Some examples apparent from the diagram: for viewing the night sky 10×50 binoculars will show about twice as much detail as 7×35s; 11×80 and 15×60 binoculars are equally capable, as are 8×30s and 6×42s (assuming one's eye pupils can accommodate the exit pupils of the instrument with the larger D); 10×50 binoculars are appreciably better than 7×50s for visibility (although, assuming equal apparent angular fields, 7×50s will show about twice as much sky area as will 10×50s). Canon's image-stabilized 15×45 binoculars are nearly equivalent to tripod-mounted 10×70s, with the *triple* advantage of smaller size, accommodating observers whose pupils will not open to 7 mm, and not requiring a tripod!

The visibility factor ($M \times D$) is applicable to the usual range of binocular sizes (exit pupils between about 3 mm and 7 mm), but should not be extrapolated indefinitely. For instance, as the magnification is increased on a telescope and the exit pupil approaches 1 mm or less, a point will be reached (dependent upon the darkness of the sky) where the background sky glow is imperceptible. A further increase in M will not cause a noticeable improvement in the visibility of stars, and the perceived contrast between an extended object and the sky will decrease. Also, the angular size of an extended object must be kept in mind. Once M is increased to the point at which the object fills the field of view of the instrument, the object may not be visible at all! For example, a large, dim comet coma may be visible in 15×60 binoculars ($M \times D = 900$) but be *invisible* in a 45×200 telescope ($M \times D = 9000$).

BINOCULAR PERFORMANCE DIAGRAM

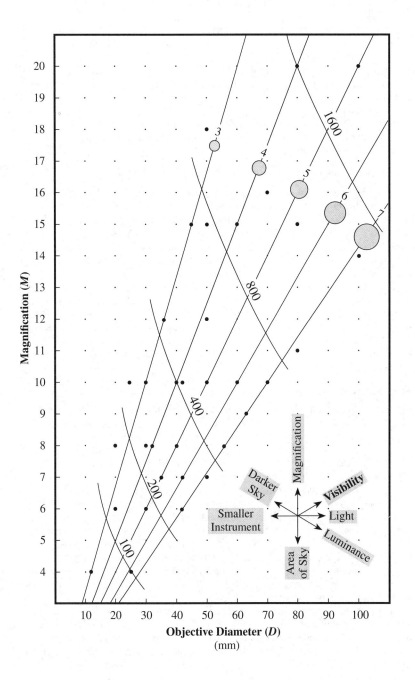

FILTERS
By Roy Bishop

Optical filters reflect and absorb some portion of the incident light. *Neutral-density filters* reflect and absorb light more or less uniformly across the visible spectrum. *Coloured (dye) filters* typically pass only one or two moderately broad portions of the spectrum. *Interference filters* are more selective and typically pass only one or two well-defined, narrow segments of the spectrum. All three types of filter are invaluable in astronomy.

In addition to categorization by physical type, filters may be categorized according to their intended use: for the Moon and planets (neutral-density and dye filters), for the Sun (neutral-density and interference filters), and for interstellar plasmas or emission nebulae (interference filters).

Lunar and Planetary Filters

As viewed in a telescope, the Moon and the planets Venus, Mars, and Jupiter are often uncomfortably bright. A neutral-density filter, which passes only 5% to 20% of the light, solves this problem while avoiding the loss in resolution that would accompany stopping down the aperture of the telescope to decrease the brightness to the same level. With a less-glaring image, light scattering in the observer's eye is reduced and fine details are easier to see. A neutral-density filter is typically about 26 mm in diameter and is attached to the forward-facing end of an eyepiece.

Dye filters can enhance the visibility of various planetary features. For instance, a red or yellow filter will absorb bluish light scattered by the Martian atmosphere and thereby improve the contrast of features on the surface of Mars. A green filter will increase the visibility of pale red and blue areas in the atmosphere of Jupiter (although the entire image will then appear green). Also, since they absorb an appreciable fraction of the light, dye filters or polarizing filters have the same advantage as a weak neutral-density filter when viewing bright objects.

Solar Filters

For observing the Sun a filter is essential and must be designed not only to reduce the brightness of the solar surface to a comfortable level but to block out the invisible but damaging infrared and ultraviolet radiation. Just because a filter makes the Sun dim enough to view comfortably is no guarantee that it is not transmitting damaging amounts of invisible radiation! This is no place to experiment with do-it-yourself filter designs—use only a proper solar filter from a reputable manufacturer. *Failure to use a proper filter when observing the Sun can cause immediate and irreversible damage to vision.*

A special warning: Heavy atmospheric haze near sunrise or sunset often dims the Sun so that it appears as a dull red disk, not uncomfortably bright to the eye. At such times resist the temptation to view the Sun with a telescope without using a solar filter. The atmosphere at such times is still relatively transparent in the invisible infrared portion of the spectrum, and the great light grasp of a telescope can result in thermal retinal damage! With the unaided eyes the retinal solar image, although just as bright, is much smaller and the eye can better dissipate the heat. Also, with unaided vision, one is less apt to fixate on the Sun for a prolonged period.

For white-light views of the Sun, a dark, broad-spectrum, neutral-density solar filter is needed. Aluminized Mylar and metal-coated glass are common designs, although they usually do not attenuate light uniformly across the visible spectrum (i.e. they are not perfect neutral-density filters). Aluminized Mylar gives a bluish colour to the solar image, while metal-coated glass filters usually give an orange colour.

The filter should be 50 mm or more in diameter and must be positioned to cover the *front* of the telescope. Ensure that the filter is *securely attached* so that a gust of wind or a bump cannot dislodge it. (Some small telescopes are sold with a "sun filter" designed to attach to the eyepiece, just before the observer's eye. Sunlight concentrated by the telescope can overheat and shatter a filter of this design. Such filters should be thrown in the garbage!)

For direct viewing of the Sun (not using binoculars or a telescope) shade #14 (no other shade) rectangular welder's glass may be used; this is available for a few dollars at welding supplies shops. These filters are not suitable for attaching to the front of binoculars or a telescope simply because their poor optical quality results in a fuzzy image.

Red, flame-like prominences at the Sun's limb and much structure in its chromosphere across the solar disk can be seen in hydrogen-alpha (Hα) light, a strong spectral line emitted by atomic hydrogen. This light is totally overwhelmed by the rest of the solar spectrum, so a neutral-density filter will not work. Advances in vacuum thin-film technology have made possible interference filters, filters that operate on the same principle as Fabry-Perot interferometers, involving the interference of multiply reflected beams of light. These filters can be constructed so they are transparent only to light having an extremely narrow range of wavelengths, typically 0.15 to 0.05 nm for solar viewing, although band-passes of up to 1 nm are used in solar prominence viewers that are designed to occult the solar disk. If this band-pass is centred on the Hα wavelength (656.3 nm), nearly all of the Sun's light will be blocked, leaving an image in Hα light.

Hα filters are expensive, particularly for band-passes near 0.05 nm that are needed for high-contrast images of the solar disk. Because Hα filters usually are mounted near the back end of a telescope, and because the wavelength of the centre of their narrow band-pass varies with the angle at which light rays enter the filter (a characteristic of interference filters), the focal ratio of the imaging telescope must be near f/20 for 0.15-nm band-pass filters and f/30 or higher for filters with narrower band-passes. Temperature control is usually required to keep the band-pass centred on the Hα wavelength, although some Hα filters are designed to be tilted in order to tune them to the Hα wavelength (the wavelength of peak transmittance is shifted toward shorter wavelengths when the filter is tilted away from 90° incidence).

Hα filters are usually mounted just ahead of the eyepiece (or film holder, if photography is planned). Also, Hα filters require a broadband "energy rejection prefilter," located at the front of the telescope. The prefilter has a band-pass of about 100 nm in the red part of the spectrum and blocks essentially all of the infrared, ultraviolet, and much of the visible part of the solar radiation from entering the telescope.

Nebula Filters

From the surface of Earth, the night sky is not completely dark. Even in the absence of light pollution (human-made and lunar), the air itself emits a feeble light called airglow. In higher latitudes, aurorae can also contribute to the glow of the atmosphere. Two other components of the light of the night sky are the zodiacal light and background starlight. The diffuse glow from all three sources reduces the contrast of celestial objects and, in the case of dim galaxies and nebulae, the object may be completely obscured by the brightness of the sky.

Filters transmit only a fraction of the incident light. Thus, employing them to see faint objects may seem counterproductive. However, there are objects in the heavens that emit light only at certain wavelengths. This behaviour is characteristic of plasmas—excited gases, matter composed of separate atoms that are energized either by ultraviolet radiation from nearby hot stars or by collisions such as occur in supernova explosion shock fronts. Such regions are called emission nebulae and include star-forming regions, planetary nebulae, and some supernova remnants. A filter that selectively blocks most of the background sky glow but is transparent to the wavelengths at which such objects emit most of their visible light will darken the sky background without appreciably dimming the object of interest. With narrow band-pass interference-type filters the effect can be dramatic, improving contrast and revealing details that otherwise are completely invisible. It is the next best thing to observing these objects from above Earth's atmosphere!

Dark-adapted (scotopic) human vision responds to light having wavelengths from approximately 400 to 620 nm. In bright light (photopic vision) the spectral range extends to somewhat longer wavelengths, about 750 nm. For both types of vision the response curve (sensitivity versus wavelength) is "bell-shaped," the wavelength of maximum sensitivity being in the middle of the visible range—near 510 nm for scotopic vision and 555 nm for photopic vision (see the figure "Nebular Filter Transmission" on the next page). The photopic sensation produced by 555-nm light is green; for scotopic vision colour is not produced, but at photopic levels 510-nm light appears blue-green.

Hydrogen is the predominant element in the universe. Atomic hydrogen, when excited by ultraviolet radiation from a nearby hot star, emits light in the visible spectrum at only four discrete wavelengths: 656, 486, 434, and 410 nm (designated as Hα, Hβ, Hγ, and Hδ, respectively, part of the "Balmer spectrum" of hydrogen). Scotopic vision is blind to 656-nm (Hα) light and relatively insensitive to the less intense 434- and 410-nm light. However, 486 nm (Hβ) lies near the 510-nm peak sensitivity of scotopic vision, and an Hβ ("H-beta") filter that has a narrow band-pass at this wavelength will greatly reduce the surrounding sky brightness and reveal Hβ-emitting nebulae.

The classic example is the Horsehead Nebula, a dark, silhouetted column of dust just southeast of the east end of Orion's belt. The surrounding hydrogen gas, excited probably by the nearby hot star ζ Orionis, fluoresces dimly with Hβ light. If the obscuring airglow is blocked by an Hβ filter, the dark Horsehead can distinctly be seen in a telescope having an aperture of 400 mm or greater. However, the number of objects that can be viewed advantageously with an Hβ filter is very limited, apparently because few nebulae emit strongly in Hβ light.

Two other strong nebular emission lines lie at 496 and 501 nm, nearly at the peak sensitivity of scotopic vision. Originally detected in 1864 by the British astronomer William Huggins, the origin of these lines was unknown at that time, and they were attributed to a hypothetical new element, "nebulium." In 1927, the American astrophysicist Ira Bowen identified the lines as due to doubly ionized oxygen (O^{++} or OIII), which glows brightly when very low-density nebular gas is strongly excited (high temperature). A filter that has a narrow band-pass spanning these two wavelengths gives striking views of highly excited nebulae. A good example is the Veil Nebula, a supernova remnant in eastern Cygnus. Through an OIII filter on a dark, transparent night, the direct view of the Veil in a large amateur telescope is more spectacular than any photograph or CCD image. Planetary nebulae (fluorescing, low-density shells of gas surrounding hot central stars) also show up well with an OIII filter; examples include the Helix Nebula, the Owl Nebula (M97), the Dumbbell Nebula (M27), and the Ring Nebula (M57).

Because of their narrow band-passes, Hβ and OIII filters are sometimes called *line filters,* although their band-passes are much wider than that of an Hα filter. Filters encompassing both the Hβ and OIII lines, such as the Lumicon Ultra High Contrast (UHC) filter, are termed *narrowband filters.* These filters also enhance views of many emission nebulae, although with the wider band-pass the sky background is brighter. With a large telescope under dark skies I find that the single most useful filter is the OIII line filter. With smaller apertures (less than about 200 mm), the narrowband Lumicon UHC filter (or equivalent filter from other manufacturers) may be preferable since it dims the stars less.

Some other nebulae that are greatly enhanced by OIII and narrowband filters include the Omega or Loon Nebula (M17), the Trifid Nebula (M20), the Lagoon Nebula (M8), the Rosette Nebula, the Eagle Nebula (M16), the North American Nebula, and the Eta Carina Nebula.

Nebular Filter Transmission

The dotted, dashed, and continuous curves show the transmission versus wavelength characteristic of four interference filters (in descending order in the legend): two line filters, a narrowband filter, and a broadband filter. The bell-shaped curves composed of small open and solid circles show the relative response of bright-adapted (photopic) vision and dark-adapted (scotopic) vision. In ascending sequence above the curves are spectral colours, nebula emission lines, and light pollution lines (M = mercury, S = high-pressure sodium, and LPS = low-pressure sodium). High-pressure sodium light sources emit an additional broad continuum spectrum that is not shown. The two unlabeled light pollution lines are strong airglow/auroral lines produced by atomic oxygen. (David Lane used a "Varian Model Cory 50 Conc. UV-Visible Spectrophotometer" owned by the Chemistry Department at Saint Mary's University to obtain the filter curves, and he also prepared the diagram.)

Stars emit light across the entire visible spectrum. Thus line filters and narrowband filters impair views of single stars, reflection nebulae, star clusters, and galaxies. Filters with wide band-passes extending from about 450 to 530 nm are called *broadband filters*. Examples are the Lumicon Deep Sky filter, the Orion SkyGlow filter, and the Meade Broadband filter. These decrease the airglow somewhat and block several of the brighter wavelengths emitted by sodium- and mercury-vapour streetlights, without dimming stars and galaxies too much. Thus they provide a modest improvement in the visibility of some objects from light-polluted sites. Because of their wide band-pass and high transmission at the Hα line, they are also useful for photography of emission nebulae. However, under dark skies an unfiltered view is preferable to that through a broadband filter.

LIMITING MAGNITUDES
By Douglas Pitcairn

Limiting Visual Magnitudes

One of the many difficulties with visual observing from the surface of our planet is the variability of the atmosphere. In any record of observations it is important to note the condition of the sky. Parameters such as brightness and contrast are greatly affected by the transparency of the sky and the presence of light pollution or aurorae.

One of the simplest ways to quantify local sky conditions is to note the magnitude of the faintest star visible with the unaided eye—the *limiting visual magnitude* (LVM). Although individuals differ in their ability to detect faint stars, these differences are generally small, and for any one observer such observations provide a consistent measure of sky quality.

The chart at the left shows a 9°-wide field in the vicinity of Polaris (the brightest star on the chart) and is useful for observers at latitude 20°N or higher. For orientation, the solid lines mark the beginning of the handle of the Little Dipper, as in the ALL-SKY MAPS on pp. 294–299. Several stars have their visual magnitudes indicated (with decimal points omitted). Using this field to determine your LVM has several advantages: it is always above the horizon in midnorthern latitudes; its altitude does not change with the time of night or year, so the variation of atmospheric extinction with altitude is not a consideration; there are no bright stars or planets in the field to dazzle the eye; the faint stars are quite well spaced and therefore easy to identify; and being a simple field, it can be memorized. Especially note the dashed spiral of descending magnitudes labelled "A" through "F."

Limiting Telescopic Magnitudes

Aperture, telescope design, eyepiece design, magnification, and the quality of optical surfaces are a few of the many variables that will determine the faintest stars visible through a given telescope and eyepiece. By determining an instrument's limiting magnitude—the *limiting telescopic magnitude* (LTM)—you can effectively assess the effect of these variables. The quality of the night sky will also affect the LTM. Therefore, changes in the LVM should be taken into account when determining the LTM. (The relationship between LTM and LVM is complex; readers may explore it using the excellent web-based calculator at **www.go.ednet.ns.ca/~larry/astro/maglimit.html**.) The LTM is a useful guide when attempting faint targets (Pluto in a 150-mm scope?), comparing the performance of different instruments ("Can my scope see as faint as yours?"), or determining whether a mirror or lens needs cleaning (many people clean their optics too often, assuming that dust degrades optical performance more than it actually does).

To help determine the LTM of your instrument, use the charts on the next page, which show an 8′-wide section of the northwest quadrant of M67 centred at RA 8h 50.1m and Dec +11°53′. This old open cluster lies 8° south-southeast of M44, Cancer's famous Beehive cluster. The accompanying table lists the visual magnitudes and the $B - V$ colour indices of the labelled stars. The diagram was constructed from

"Left-Right Correct" View

STAR	VISUAL	B-V
A	10.60	1.10
B	11.19	0.43
C	11.59	0.42
D	12.01	0.57
E	12.26	0.68
F	12.57	0.59
G	13.04	0.85
H	13.35	0.59
I	13.61	0.59
J	13.96	0.62
K	14.34	0.56
L	14.66	0.67
M	14.96	0.69
N	15.30	0.79
O	15.58	0.84
P	16.06	0.74
Q	16.31	0.99
R	16.62	0.81
S	17.05	1.26
T	17.38	1.17
U	17.64	1.31
V	18.04	1.27
W	18.38	0.76
X	18.69	1.17
Y	19.07	1.56
Z	19.29	0.61
a	19.42	1.34
b	20.10	0.00
c	20.35	0.83
d	20.61	1.55
e	21.03	0.32

"Mirror Reversed" View

The "left-right correct" chart is for telescopes with an even number of reflecting surfaces (e.g. Newtonian reflectors) and the "mirror-reversed" chart is for telescopes with an odd number of reflecting surfaces (e.g. a refractor with a diagonal).

a photograph taken by René Racine of the University of Montreal, who exposed a 103a-D plate at the f/3.67 focus of the Hale Reflector. The magnitudes are based on work by Racine and Ronald Gilliland of the Space Telescope Science Institute.

Correction for Atmospheric Extinction

Atmospheric extinction varies with altitude above the horizon. To normalize observations to the zenith (altitude 90°), the following values should be added to estimates of faintest visible magnitude obtained using the charts (format: altitude range/ **correction**):

$18° - 20°/$**0.5**; $20° - 24°/$**0.4**; $24° - 29°/$**0.3**; $29° - 36°/$**0.2**; $36° - 52°/$**0.1**; $52° - 90°/$**0.0**

These corrections are for near sea level and would be reduced at higher elevations. Also, excellent sky conditions are assumed; under less than ideal conditions the corrections are generally larger and can be quite uncertain, especially when the target area is closer to the horizon.

POLAR ALIGNMENT

The charts for the north celestial pole on the facing page can be used to align an equatorial mount in the northern hemisphere. To polar align a mount, that is, to point the polar axis of the mount at the north celestial pole, select a telescope/eyepiece combination for which you know, or have carefully measured, the size of the field of view. Depending on the accuracy required (see below), you can use the finderscope, guidescope, or main telescope. Point the chosen telescope in the same direction as the mount's polar axis. Simply adjusting the mount's declination until the setting circle reads 90° is not sufficient; instead, rotate the mount 180° in RA, and check whether the field rotates in the eyepiece without shifting. If not, make adjustments in declination until the amount of shift is minimal. To reduce the shift to an acceptable level, you may have to make further, one-time transverse adjustments, leaving the declination fixed. For example, on a German equatorial mount, shims can be inserted between a mounting ring and the mounting plate.

Next, using one of the charts, adjust the mount's altitude and azimuth so that the starfield seen in the eyepiece is centred at the pole. Circles corresponding to various field sizes are indicated on both charts; you can draw a circle corresponding to your own exact field size using a compass if you prefer.

Precise polar alignment is necessary for long-exposure photography; otherwise, the stars will be elongated as a result of "field rotation." With good guiding on a system that is free of mechanical flexure, the guidestar will remain stationary on the film or imaging CCD chip. However, because of polar misalignment, all other stars will trace tiny arcs about the guidestar. The length of a particular star's arc a depends upon the amount of polar misalignment p (in arcminutes), the length of the exposure t (in hours), the distance d (in millimetres) in the imaging plane between the star and the guidestar, the declination of the guidestar δ (in degrees), and the geometrical circumstances of the exposure. An approximate formula for a (in μm (microns)), assuming the worst possible geometry, is

$$a \approx ptd/(14\cos\delta).$$

For example, with $p = 5'$, $t = 1$ h, $d = 20$ mm, and $\delta = 20°$, we have $a \approx 7.6$ μm. You can use this formula to determine the value of p needed to keep a within a specified tolerance (such as 10 μm, a good target for high-resolution imaging), and then achieve the required polar-alignment accuracy using the above method. For example, to keep a under 5 μm with $t = 30$ min (0.5 h), $d = 20$ mm, and $\delta = 60°$, the required accuracy is $p \approx (5)(14)(\cos 60°)/(0.5)(20) = 3.5'$. If you need very high polar-alignment accuracy, you may want to shift the mount down by the amount of atmospheric refraction at the altitude of the pole (see p. 30 for some values of atmospheric refraction), so that the mount is aligned on the true pole instead of the refracted pole.

An alternative method for precise polar alignment is the *star drift method,* which involves alternately detecting the drift in declination of two stars near the celestial equator, one in the south and the other rising in the east, and making azimuth and altitude adjustments accordingly. If the first star drifts north, the mount's axis is pointing west of the true pole; if it drifts south, the axis is east of the pole. If the second star drifts north, the axis is pointing too high; if it drifts south, the axis is too low. The amount of misalignment p (in arcminutes) in terms of the amount of drift d (in arcseconds) and the length of time t the star is observed (in minutes) is given approximately by

$$p \approx 3.8d/t.$$

For example, if a star drifts 10″ in 5 min, the misalignment is $\approx 7.6'$; a rate of drift of 1″/min corresponds to a misalignment of $\approx 3.8'$.

CHARTS FOR THE NORTH CELESTIAL POLE

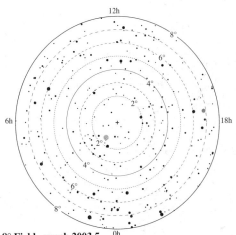

8° Field, epoch 2003.5
Magnitude limit = 10

The charts are precessed to epoch 2003.5. Polaris is drawn in light grey in both charts; the penultimate "handle" star in Ursa Minor, δ UMa, is drawn in dark grey in the 8° chart at an RA of approximately 17.5h. The north celestial pole is indicated with a crosshair in both charts. Circles corresponding to various diameters are drawn; a scale with tick marks placed at 1' intervals is provided on the 2° chart to facilitate the drawing of a circle of any other diameter using a compass.

See the accompanying text for instructions on using these charts for polar alignment.

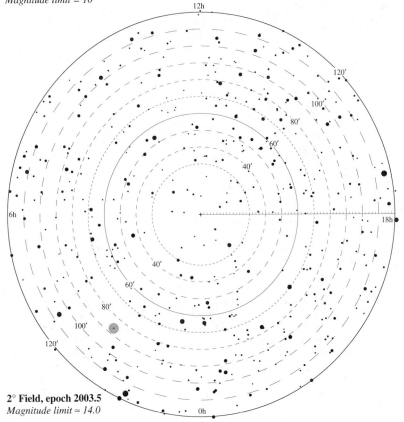

2° Field, epoch 2003.5
Magnitude limit ≈ 14.0

FREQUENCY OF NIGHTTIME CLOUD COVER
By Jay Anderson

APRIL–MAY MEAN NIGHTTIME CLOUD COVER IN PERCENT

The above maps are constructed from observations taken from 19 years of satellite observations beginning in 1981. Computer algorithms are used to determine
the amount of cloud within a one-degree longitude by one-degree latitude bin for
nighttime satellite passages using observations in several infrared wavelengths. The
observations suffer from small biases over snow and ice fields and lose some of their
reliability at high latitudes in spring. The chart at left is an average of April and May
observations; that on the right is for July and August.

In spring the clearest skies can be found in a band stretching from central Mexico
north-westward through Arizona and into southern California. In Canada best
observing prospects are found over southeast Alberta and southwest Saskatchewan,
but the cloud amounts are considerably larger than along the Mexico border. Cloud
cover is relatively uniform at Canadian latitudes, a result of the many storm systems
that travel along and near the border as warmer weather arrives.

High cloud frequencies are found along the Atlantic coast, the California shoreline
(mostly low cloud and fog), over the higher parts of the Rocky Mountain chain
(where cirrus cloudiness is endemic), and, to a lesser extent, over the Appalachians.

JULY–AUGUST MEAN NIGHTTIME CLOUD COVER IN PERCENT

Resolution of the cloud cover within the narrow valleys of the western mountains is not possible at the scale of the observations, although in April the heavy cloudiness of winter is mostly over.

In July and August the clear springtime skies of the southwestern deserts of the United States give way to an increased cloudiness as the "monsoon season" brings moisture and frequent thunderstorms into Arizona, New Mexico, and Colorado. California's interior retains its reputation as the sunniest location, but clearer skies return to the midwestern plains, extending northward into the Prairie provinces. Almost all regions are clearer than in the April–May chart, although the Appalachians and the Atlantic provinces continue to be among the cloudiest locations. As in the spring, the Cypress Hills area of Alberta and Saskatchewan experiences the most reliable nighttime skies in Canada.

The maps may be used for planning travel to star parties and sunnier climates and to special astronomical events. During April and May, cloud cover is changing rapidly across the centre of the continent, and the average cloudiness shown in the chart at the left is likely too optimistic for April and too pessimistic for May. These charts are more reliable than those used in previous years, particularly over Canada, where surface observations are sparse. In spite of the different data source used to construct these charts, the cloud patterns are not significantly different than those shown in past years using surface-based reports.

WEATHER RESOURCES ON THE INTERNET
By Allan Rahill

Visual astronomy is dependent on the weather, and astronomers rely on local forecasts. Despite public skepticism, weather forecasts are in fact quite accurate, provided they are from informed sources. Specialized services—usually involving a fee—are available for aviation, agriculture, forestry, and marine applications. Until recently there was no such service for astronomy, likely because there was no directly related economy. The Canada-France-Hawaii Observatory at Mauna Kea is now experimenting with local seeing and transparency forecasts to "queue schedule" observing activities. This marks a new era in which professional observatories are starting to make the best use of weather conditions and change planned observing activities accordingly.

Similar information is now freely available to amateur and professional astronomers worldwide via the Internet. With light pollution becoming more and more pervasive, amateur astronomers drive long distances to get to dark skies. They can avoid frustration by using the information and URLs below to plan their observing sessions.

Satellite Images

Many astronomers rely on satellite images to predict nighttime cloud cover. Real-time images are available from GOES satellites for eastern and western America; other satellites such as Meteosat give the same service for Europe and Africa. These satellites give three main types of images: visible, infrared (IR), and water vapour. Visible pictures are easy to interpret, but they are available only during the day; for nighttime tracking of clouds, IR images are available. Water vapour images don't track clouds; they indicate the total moisture in the air mass. Usually the darkest areas in those images have good correlation with the best sky transparency.

Particularly useful for short-term forecasting are IR satellite loops, which are available at many websites. IR images show the radiance emission from Earth and indicate the temperature of the ground and/or clouds. During cold seasons, the ground can be as cold if not colder than the air mass, and single IR satellite images are not very helpful in identifying low-level clouds such as stratocumulus. One way to separate clouds from the ground in these situations is to use a time-lapse loop and look for motion: the ground doesn't move but clouds do. Keep this trick in mind for northern latitudes from late fall to early spring.

There are many IR image enhancements available at various websites, and you should be aware that many of them don't display *any* low clouds, even with the trick mentioned above. One way to familiarize yourself with low cloud detection is to compare visible GOES images to IR enhancements in the early morning, when the ground is still cold. In some situations, you may be surprised by the amount of low cloud not displayed in the IR satellite images. By comparing IR and visible images, you can select a website that you feel gives accurate images and one that you are comfortable with. A website I recommend for IR satellite images, which gives you the ability to zoom into your region, choose different satellite image enhancements, and do animation easily is:

weather.unisys.com/satellite/sat_ir_hem.html

To make the best use of weather satellite images, you also should be aware of the behaviour of certain specific types of cloud. Low-level clouds such as stratus usually develop locally and generally move much slower than high clouds. These clouds appear during the night and usually get burned off by the Sun during the day. Coastal regions will usually see the low clouds moving inland in the evening and out to sea in the morning.

Also, cumulus, towering cumulus, and cumulonimbus clouds arise with day-time convective heating if the air mass is unstable. The depth or height of the cloud structure is related to the level of instability and can reach up to 20 000 m for severe thunderstorms. On satellite loops, these clouds appear as clear areas that are gradually filled with clouds during the day and that slowly vanish in the evening. In the summer, some of the most unstable cumulonimbus clouds will survive at night. Even though thunderstorms, associated with cumulonimbus clouds, can be far from your location, cirrus blowoff from these cells may reach you quite quickly, depending on the upper wind direction, and thus ruin your observing session. Satellite and radar loops are good ways to keep track of these thunderstorm lines.

Radar

Remote-controlled observatories, where the operator is not physically present, and star parties, where telescopes are often left set up and exposed, are becoming more popular. When the sky conditions are variable, there is one common worry: is there a fast-moving precipitation band approaching the observing site? The best way to track precipitation in the short term is with radar. The radar network is extensive across the United States; it also covers populated regions of Canada.

Radar images require careful interpretation. During the night, the temperature cools near the ground and creates a temperature inversion. On some nights with strong inversions, radar signals are refracted, or bent, toward the ground and scattered back to the radar, thus appearing as precipitation on the graphical displays. Similar situations occur in mountainous areas where higher terrain interrupts the radar signal. A radar loop will help you to distinguish theses areas: sometimes they are nearly motionless, and at other times they shift around in a chaotic jumble; precipitation moves in a smoother fashion, at times linearly. The best websites for access to radar loops for Canada and the United States, respectively, are:

www.weatheroffice.ec.gc.ca/radar/index_e.html (click on "composite image")
www.intellicast.com (click on "radar")

Weather Forecasts for Astronomy

Cloud Forecasts: Local media and television "experts" cannot always be relied upon when conditions are uncertain. Usually their forecasts cover a large area and the weather can be quite different within the region. Also, for most people, including many local weather forecasters, skies are considered clear despite thin, high cloudiness that may interfere with observing.

The best forecasts for clouds are via direct output from numerical models. Weather models are not perfect, but they are surprisingly good at capturing local effects and predicting cloud formation and dissipation. The biggest problem with numerical forecasting is convection (thunderstorms): it is like forecasting the next bubble in boiling water. Complex thunderstorm cells can be forecast much farther away than they actually appear, leading to poor cloud progression forecasts for regions hundreds of kilometres ahead.

Some weather channels and websites use animated forecasts to show cloud progression for the next day, but these animations generally have low resolution and are not very useful for astronomy. The only North American high-resolution cloud forecast I know of is produced at the Canadian Meteorological Centre (CMC), available at:

www.cmc.ec.gc.ca/cmc/htmls/clds_vis_e.html

Occasionally, especially in the fall when low clouds (stratocumulus) are omnipresent, a weather balloon can be launched into a cloud hole, and the resulting cloud forecast may be too optimistic for the surrounding regions. To avoid a bad forecast, always compare the cloud cover forecast with the latest satellite picture. In these situations, an old forecast may be a better choice; this is why the most recent old forecast, in addition to the current forecast, is available at this website.

Sky Transparency Forecasts: For deep-sky observing, sky transparency is critical because it largely determines how dark the sky will be. Aerosols—particles suspended in the atmosphere—and moisture reduce sky transparency and brighten the sky by diffusing the light in the sky. Aerosols include volcanic ash, pollen, sea salts, and smoke from forest fires. Spectacular examples of aerosol introduction into the atmosphere include Mount Saint Helens, which spread roughly 10^9 tonnes of ash into the atmosphere in 1980, and more recently in 2002 large forest fires over northern Quebec that spread smoke over all of northeastern North America. Specialized weather numerical models handle aerosol phenomena; websites that track aerosol envelopes with up to five-day forecasts across the world are:

toms.gsfc.nasa.gov/aerosols/today_aero.html
www.nrlmry.navy.mil/aerosol/#currentaerosolmodeling

Moisture is the only weather element affecting sky transparency that can be forecast with confidence. For many northern-latitude residents, moisture is the most important contributor to reduced sky transparency; despite clear skies, very often high-level ice crystals (extremely thin clouds) are present and can be seen only at sunset and sunrise. In addition, moisture from open waters, vegetation (evapo-transpiration), or moist soil can keep the low-level atmosphere humid.

Over the years, I have compared water-vapour satellite images to various observers' estimates of background sky brightness. The resulting sky transparency forecasts can be found at:

www.cmc.ec.gc.ca/cmc/htmls/transparence_e.html

There is a good correlation between the darkest areas in water-vapour images and the darkest observed sky conditions. There are some cases where the sky background is brighter than expected due to moisture trapped by a temperature inversion. Based on this observation and others, the forecasts above emphasize humidity near the surface and also near the tropopause (cirrus heights).

Seeing Forecasts: Seeing conditions determine the steadiness of images through a telescope and are relevant for planetary as well as deep-sky observing. When highest resolution is necessary for planetary imaging or visual observing, seeing should be at its best.

Favourable conditions occur when the atmosphere is turbulence-free all across the path of the light. The best weather pattern is weak wind circulation at all levels. These conditions take place more frequently over the southeastern United States than any other region of North America, with Atlantic Canada generally having the worst conditions among populated North American regions. Canadian and U.S. central prairies often experience blocking weather systems that give weak upper wind circulation and excellent seeing conditions.

Another pattern for excellent seeing takes place when moderate winds blow from the same direction at all levels, that is, when horizontal and vertical wind shear are weak at all levels. In other words, no jetstream (strong winds reaching 200–400 km/h at an altitude of 10–12 km) or sudden shifts or increase in wind speed with height are present.

At locations downwind from mountains when winds are moderate, it is best to be far away from the mountains, since "gravity waves"—vertical air-mass oscillations caused by the mountains—can downgrade seeing. In general, topography is quite important because rough terrain increases the wind shear in the low-level atmosphere, due to friction and gravity waves.

Temperature variation at the surface also plays a role in seeing conditions. Nights of excellent wind conditions as described above may nevertheless have marginal seeing. On such nights, temperatures quickly and steadily fall, and large telescopes have trouble cooling at the same rate as the surrounding air. This creates what is called "local seeing": thermal heat released from the optics (despite good ventilation) ruins the seeing despite the excellent weather pattern. The opposite is also true: the best planetary observations with a large telescope often take place just before thick clouds roll in or when looking through thin cirrostratus cloud. Under these conditions the temperature usually rises a few degrees before the clouds appear. Thin cirrostratus clouds usually keep the temperature steady, eliminating any negative local seeing effects. Thin clouds also play the role of a neutral-density filter, increasing fine detail and contrast on bright planets. Ground fog can also be associated with excellent seeing conditions (until the fog thickens) if you can keep your optics dry.

Predicting favourable seeing conditions requires a good ability to interpret weather charts, something that is difficult for most observers to do. The Canadian weather service now has an experimental seeing forecast available at their astro-weather website. The seeing forecast attempts to simulate wind shears, topography, and temperature effects and is available at:

www.cmc.ec.gc.ca/cmc/htmls/seeing_e.html

The Clear Sky Clock

The Canadian Meteorological Centre's numerical weather forecasts, given in the various URLs above, are unique because they are specifically designed for astronomers. However, they include 68 forecast images, covering all of North America, so it can be a chore to find the one you want. All the above weather forecasts for astronomy can be viewed at a glance for any particular observing site in North America with the Clear Sky Clock produced by Attilla Danko, available at:

www.cleardarksky.com/csk/

LIGHT POLLUTION
By David L. Crawford

A Lost Heritage: During this and the 20th century, most people have lost the spectacular view of the universe that our ancestors enjoyed on clear nights. The development of electrical lighting technology and the increase in urban population have caused a rapid increase in sky glow above towns and cities. Few members of the general public have ever seen a prime dark sky. For urban dwellers, star-studded nights are limited to simulations at planetaria. Comets Hyakutake and Hale-Bopp, the most spectacular comets of our time, were for many people merely dim fuzz-balls because of the glare of light pollution. Even in rural areas, poorly designed yard lights often obscure the splendour of the night sky. As Leslie Peltier, one of the most famous amateur astronomers of the twentieth century, stated eloquently in his autobiography *Starlight Nights:*

> *"The moon and the stars no longer come to the farm. The farmer has exchanged his birthright in them for the wattage of his all-night sun. His children will never know the blessed dark of night."*

The increased sky glow that adversely affects the environment is called *light pollution*, for it originates mainly from excess light that does nothing to increase useful nighttime illumination. It is light that sprays horizontally and upward into the sky from poorly designed lighting fixtures. It is light that glares into the eyes of motorists and homeowners, compromising visibility, safety, and security. It

A nighttime satellite view of central North America

is light that depresses property values by reducing the aesthetic quality of a neighbourhood. It is light that can seriously affect the circadian rhythm of all living things, including humans, as well as creating other hazards for many species (birds, sea turtles, etc.). In the United States and Canada over a billion dollars plus large amounts of energy are lost annually in generating this wasted light.

A Threat to Astronomy: Light pollution poses special perils to astronomy. Many observations, including most of those of cosmological interest, can be made only from prime observing sites, far removed from centres of population. Some older observatories, such as the David Dunlap in Ontario and Mount Wilson in California, are severely affected by light pollution from nearby urban centres. New observatories usually are located at remote sites, and amateur astronomers routinely drive large distances to escape the glare of towns and cities. The argument that all astronomy can be done from space is incorrect because it does not make sense to do in space, at much higher costs, what can be done from the ground. There are observations that can only be done from space, but more than three decades of space astronomy have greatly increased the need for ground-based observatories.

Solutions: There are solutions to the problem of light pollution; outdoor lighting ordinances have been instituted in a number of communities near large observatories, such as Tucson, Arizona, and San Diego, California. *The main solution is the use of full-cutoff lighting fixtures that direct all their light below the horizontal, such that the light source itself is not directly visible from the side—an almost universal fault with* *street and yard lights. Since this places the light where it is needed, less total light and thus less electrical energy is required.*

Inefficient street lighting

Additional major cost savings are realized by switching to light sources that are more efficient, that require less power to produce a given amount of light. The table below shows the efficiency of common types of outdoor lights; the comparative numbers indicate the approximate amount of electrical power (watts) required to produce the same amount of visible light (1000 lm). In addition to providing light at the lowest cost, low-pressure sodium (LPS) lights are nearly monochromatic, with the result that much of their glare can be filtered out by astronomers. Low-pressure sodium lights are especially good for street lighting, parking lot lighting, security lighting, and any application where colour rendering is not important.

Common Types of Outdoor Lights
(in increasing order of efficiency)

Type	Power (W/klm)
incandescent (ordinary bulbs)	60
mercury vapour (violet-white light)	24
metal halide (white)	17
high-pressure sodium (orange-gold)	12
low-pressure sodium (yellow)	8

A full-cutoff, efficient light fixture

Although full-cutoff, efficient light fixtures generally have a higher capital cost than polluting fixtures, this cost is quickly recovered through the much lower operating costs. Quite a few cities worldwide are realizing substantial savings each year through extensive use of LPS street lighting. For example, one can usually replace a 175-W mercury vapour lighting fixture with a full-cutoff, 35-W LPS fixture and get the same amount of useful light, with none of the glare and light trespass. The energy saving is remarkable, as is the better visibility.

Even less light pollution and more savings can be realized by using *no more light than is required.* In particular, too much light and/or poorly shielded lights can ruin adaptation to night lighting, blinding us just when we need to see. When we go from too bright to too dark or vice versa, "transient adaptation" is impaired and we have poor visibility for awhile. Do not exceed IESNA (Illuminating Engineering Society of North America) recommended lighting levels. Overkill never helps; it usually just adds glare and it always wastes energy. In addition, lights should be used only when necessary (timers are useful for controlling lights).

Increased lighting generally gives a perception of greater security, yet there is no statistically significant evidence that more lighting results in less crime. Criminals need light. "Security lights" provide this, may draw attention to a house or business that would otherwise not be noticed, and mask any additional light that criminals may need to do their work. Our cities and towns are far more brightly lit than ever, yet the crime rate soars. Security can best be provided by shielded, motion-activated lights that come on only when triggered by movement nearby. These serve to frighten criminals, alert others that there is a potential problem, and provide glare-free visibility (when properly installed so they are glare-free); they also use insignificant amounts of energy.

Lack of Awareness: The biggest problem in controlling light pollution is lack of awareness rather than resistance. After all, it costs money to light pollute! Unlike the case with many other forms of pollution, simple solutions are available; moreover, *everyone benefits* in applying these solutions. Most people are not yet conscious of the expense, the waste, and the harm associated with excess lighting. They put up with distant lights that shine directly into their eyes, not realizing that not only does this do *nothing* to illuminate the area near the light but that it also produces a veiling glare. The pollution usually involves not only the light itself but also other forms of environmental pollution associated with the production of the wasted light: the extraction, transportation, and burning of coal and oil. This general lack of awareness has been summarized nicely by Doug Pitcairn, an astronomy teacher in Nova Scotia:

> *"It surprises me how someone who would never think of leaving a plastic bottle on the ground at a picnic site will pay extra money each month to illuminate half the neighbourhood with unnecessary, distracting light."*

Education: Educating the public, government officials, lighting professionals, and astronomers is a major thrust of current programs. These efforts have helped. Most committees in the IESNA have been addressing these issues, and upcoming Recommended Practices and other documents are fully reflecting these concerns. As they are issued, one will expect to see them implemented, albeit on a slow time schedule. Astronomers and environmentalists should do all they can to help publicize these documents when they come out to help get them into existing practices in our communities.

The International Dark-Sky Association: The International Dark-Sky Association (IDA) is a tax-exempt, nonprofit, membership organization dedicated to overcoming this awareness problem. Its goal is to preserve dark skies while at the same time maximizing the quality and efficiency of nighttime outdoor lighting. The IDA needs your help. Memberships begin at $30 U.S. per year. To join this effort or to obtain further information on any aspects of the issue, write to the International Dark-Sky Association, 3225 N. First Avenue, Tucson AZ 85719, USA (phone: (520) 293-3198; fax: (520) 293-3192; email: ida@darksky.org; website: www.darksky.org). Plenty of useful information is on the website, including images, and content is added regularly. The IDA has many information sheets available to assist you in educating others—in several languages in addition to English and French—and can provide examples of lighting ordinances that have been enacted in many communities to enforce high-quality, effective nighttime lighting. For more information, see the July 1990 (p. 23) and September 1998 issues of *Sky & Telescope*.

Within Canada, the Royal Astronomical Society of Canada has an active Light Pollution Abatement Committee under the chairmanship of Robert Dick (his address: PO Box 79, Rideau Ferry ON K0G 1W0, email: rdick@ccs.carleton.ca); or you may contact the RASC directly (see p. 8). Also, some local centres of the RASC have taken action to address poor lighting practices in their areas.

Editor's Note: An indication that the IDA is making its message heard where it counts is the election of its executive director, David Crawford, as a Fellow of the Illuminating Engineering Society of North America in 1997. The IDA has members in 70 countries, and its total membership as of June 2002 was about 9000 (with 182 from Canada). Despite the almost 20% growth in membership over the previous July, this is still less than 10% of the community of amateur and professional astronomers. As Daniel Green of the Smithsonian Astrophysical Observatory has put it (see *Sky & Telescope,* May 1998, p. 10): "Where are all the astronomers?" Anyone who values the night sky should support this unique and deserving organization.

DEEP-SKY OBSERVING HINTS
BY ALAN DYER

In the 1960s and 1970s, few observers owned telescopes larger than 200-mm aperture. Today, 250-mm to 600-mm Dobsonian-mounted reflectors are commonplace. Using computerized telescopes, observers can now find thousands of objects at the push of a button. As a result, deep-sky observing has soared in popularity.

However, owners of less sophisticated, small-aperture instruments shouldn't think they are shut out of deep-sky viewing. In a dark sky an 80-mm to 100-mm telescope will show all the Messier objects and reveal hundreds of brighter NGC (New General Catalogue) objects. In fact, many large objects are best seen in fast (f/4 to f/6), small-aperture telescopes or in giant 70-mm and 80-mm binoculars. Contrary to popular belief, even slow f-ratio instruments (f/11 to f/16) are useful; their only disadvantage is the difficulty of achieving a low-power wide field. No matter what telescope you use, follow these techniques to get the most out of a night's deep-sky viewing:

- Always plan each night's observing: Prepare a list of a dozen or so objects for the night. Hunt them down on star charts or with computer programs first during the day to become familiar with their location.
- Seek out dark skies; a black sky improves contrast and makes up for lack of aperture.
- To preserve night vision, always use a dim red flashlight for reading charts.
- Avoid prolonged exposure to bright sunlight earlier in the day (such as a day at the beach); it will reduce your ability to dark adapt and make for tired eyes at night.
- Use averted vision; looking to one side of an object places it on a more sensitive part of the retina.
- Another technique for picking out faint objects is to jiggle the telescope (and the image) slightly.
- Don't be afraid to use high power; it often brings out small, faint objects such as planetary nebulae and galaxies and resolves detail in globulars, in small, rich open clusters, and in bright galaxies.
- Use a nebula filter on emission and planetary nebulae (see the section FILTERS on pp. 54–57); even in a dark sky, filters can dramatically enhance the view of these kinds of objects, often making obvious an otherwise elusive nebula.
- Be comfortable; sit down while at the eyepiece and be sure to dress warmly.
- Collimate and clean your optics; a poorly maintained telescope will produce distorted star images, reduce image contrast, and make it more difficult to see faint stars and other threshold objects.
- Don't expect to use analog setting circles; in a portable telescope "dial-type" circles will rarely be accurate.
- Digital setting circles and Go To telescopes can find objects precisely. While they are wonderful observing aids, they can overwhelm observers with thousands of targets, often supplying scant information about each one. When making a list for a night's viewing, books such as the three-volume *Burnham's Celestial Handbook* and the two-volume *Night Sky Observer's Guide* by Kepple and Sanner are still the best guides.
- Don't be in a rush to check off targets; take time to examine each object, and take notes or make drawings. Both will help train your eye to see subtle detail; you'll learn to see the most through your telescope.
- Consider keeping a logbook or journal of your nightly tours of the sky; including eyepiece impressions and drawings provides a record of your improving observing skills that is fun to look back upon in future years. See the section THE OBSERVING LOGBOOK (immediately following) for suggestions on organizing a journal.

THE OBSERVING LOGBOOK
BY PAUL MARKOV

There are many good reasons for maintaining an observing logbook: A logbook is useful for recalling the details of previous observations and comparing past observations with current ones; maintaining one will make your observing organized and methodical; and having to describe an object forces you to *look* for more details, thus sharpening your observing skills. Finally, if you are planning to apply for an observing certificate (e.g. the RASC's Explore the Universe, Messier, or Finest NGC Certificate; see p. 258), then a logbook with your observations may be required when submitting your application.

Logbooks can be chronological or sectional. In a chronological logbook all observations are listed sequentially by date, regardless of object type. In a sectional logbook observations are grouped by object type, such as open clusters and galaxies. With either format, you may want to keep a master index of objects for cross referencing to the correct page in your logbook.

What about the book itself? Typical choices are the simple three-ring binder with standard lined paper, spiral bound notebooks, and hardcover record/accounting books. In my opinion, the most practical is the three-ring binder because it allows you to insert auxiliary materials into your logbook with the help of a three-hole punch. With this choice, entering observations out of sequence is never an issue because you can easily rearrange the sheets. Also, should you wish to make a copy of your logbook for safe-keeping, it's much easier with loose sheets.

For recording observations, using a preprinted observing form offers these advantages: the fill-in-the-blank fields remind you to record the relevant data; many of these forms have a space for making a drawing of the observed object; and they give your book a neat and organized look. An example of an observing form can be found at **www.rasc.ca/handbook/obsform.pdf**; you may prefer to design your own observing form by using the fields suggested below. However, you can also use plain lined paper: you will never have to worry about running out of forms, and you will not need different forms for different types of objects.

There are two choices for recording your observations: using full sentences and using acronyms and abbreviations. Using full sentences is the preferred method if you enjoy re-reading your observations from past years, or if you want others to be able to easily read your logbook. But if your intent is to keep a data book for reference purposes only, then acronyms and abbreviations are the recommended choices.

It is useful to record the following information for each observing session: date; time of arrival and departure (if you have travelled somewhere to observe); location; names of other people at the observing site; sky transparency (i.e. clarity of the atmosphere, which is generally noted by faintest visible stellar magnitude; see pp. 56–57); seeing (i.e. the steadiness of the atmosphere: if stars and planets appear to shimmer, that indicates poor seeing; if they appear sharp and steady, that indicates good seeing), and environmental conditions (e.g. temperature, dew, wind, sources of light pollution, snow cover, and mosquitoes). You can also number each observing session sequentially for easy referencing within your logbook.

Be sure to standardize your time/date format. For recording time, choose either the military time or a.m./p.m. format. In addition, use alpha characters to specify the month rather than numbers. For example, use Aug. 5, 2002 instead of 8/5/2002; this will avoid ambiguity in reading the date.

For each object observed, record the following information as a minimum: date and time of observation, object name or designation, type of object, constellation, telescope and magnification used, type of filter (if any), and visual description. Making drawings is highly recommended and adds substantially to the appearance of your logbook. It is also important to record failed observations because these entries will remind you to try again in your next observing session.

If you are able to write neatly while observing, it is best to enter observations directly into your logbook. However, if this proves too difficult given the environmental circumstances, you can record your observations in a temporary notebook and transcribe them into your logbook the next day. A tape recorder can also be used if you are careful to ensure its mechanical integrity while in the field and if you are diligent enough to transcribe the recorded observations into your observing logbook regularly. Below are some suggestions on what to look for when observing deep-sky objects.

All Object Types: What is the shape of the object? What is its size (based on the field of view of your eyepiece)? Is averted vision required to see the object? Does averted vision allow you to see more detail? (If yes, describe the extra detail.) Is the object near (or in the same field of view as) other deep-sky objects or bright stars? What magnification gives the best view of the object? Does a filter improve the view? (See the section FILTERS on pp. 52–55.)

Open Cluster: Is there a greater concentration of stars in a specific part of the cluster? Is it fully resolved into its component stars, or are there any unresolved stars causing the cluster to appear nebulous? How many stars can you see (only if reasonable to count them)? Are there any bright stars within the cluster? Are there any coloured stars? (If so, describe their tints and locations within the cluster.) Does the cluster stand out from the background star field?

Globular Cluster: What is the degree of star concentration (high, medium, low)? How much can be resolved to component stars (none, outer edges, middle, to the core)?

Galaxy: Is it uniform in brightness, or does it have a brighter nucleus? Is it diffuse or stellar? Can any detail or mottling be seen in the arms? Are there any stars visible within the arms?

Emission or Reflection Nebula: Is the brightness even, or are there brighter/darker areas? Are the edges of the nebula well defined? Are there any stars within the nebula? Is there a hint of any colour?

Planetary Nebula: Is it stellar in appearance, or can a disk be seen? Are the edges well defined or diffuse? Are there any brighter/darker areas? Can a central star be seen? Is there a hint of any colour?

Dark Nebula: Is it easy or difficult to discern the dark nebula from the background sky? Are there any stars within the nebula?

Logbooks and Databases

If you enjoy using computers, an electronic database can be a helpful complement to an observing logbook. You can obtain commercially available deep-sky databases that allow you to enter your own observations for any object. These databases are also useful for creating observing lists and planning observing sessions. A highly recommended database, which also happens to be freeware, is the Saguaro Astronomy Club (SAC) database, available at **www.saguaroastro.org**. With minimal tweaking, the SAC database can be formatted to accept your own observations.

You can transcribe complete observations from your logbook into the database or simply enter four valuable pieces of information for each observed object: seen (Y/N), date, telescope used, and location. With these fields filled in, in a matter of seconds you can determine which and how many objects you have observed, and the date field for any object will direct you to the correct page in your observing logbook. You can also determine interesting facts such as from which observing location you observed the most objects or which telescope produced the most observations.

THE SKY MONTH BY MONTH

LEFT-HAND PAGES BY DAVID LANE

INTRODUCTION

In the descriptions on the next 24 pages (two pages for each month), the right ascension (RA), declination (Dec) (both for epoch J2000.0), distance from Earth's centre in astronomical units (Dist), visual magnitude (Mag), and equatorial angular diameter (Size) are tabulated for seven planets for 0h UT on the 1st, 11th, and 21st day of each month. The RA, Dec, distance, and diameter of the Sun are also given. Unless noted otherwise, the descriptive comments about the planets apply to the middle of the month. Any stated planet visibility times are in local standard time. "Northern observers" and "southern observers" are assumed to be at latitudes 45°N and 30°S, respectively. Descriptions are given first for northern observers and then for southern observers. Events of special interest are in **boldface.**

Sun—Data concerning the position, transit, orientation, rotation, and activity of the Sun plus times of sunrise and sunset appear on pp. 100–110. For detailed information on this year's solar eclipses, see ECLIPSES DURING 2003 on pp. 134–154.

Moon

The Moon's phases, perigee and apogee times, distances (distances from *Astronomical Tables of the Sun, Moon, and Planets,* by Jean Meeus, 2nd ed., Willmann-Bell, 1995), and conjunctions with the planets are given in the monthly tables. The phases new Moon, first quarter, full Moon, and last quarter correspond, respectively, to the Moon having a longitude that is 0°, 90°, 180°, and 270° east of that of the Sun. The age of the Moon is the time since the new phase; first quarter, full, and last quarter phases correspond approximately to 7.4, 14.8, and 22.1 days, respectively. For times of moonrise and moonset, see pp. 116–129.

The Sun's selenographic colongitude (SSC) indicates the position of the sunrise terminator as it moves across the face of the Moon and provides a method of ascertaining the angle of illumination of features on the Moon's surface. The SSC is the angle of the sunrise terminator measured toward the observer's east (i.e. westward on the Moon) starting from the lunar meridian that passes through the mean centre of the apparent disk. Its value increases by nearly 12.2° per day, or about 0.5° per hour, and is approximately 0°, 90°, 180°, and 270° at the first quarter, full, last quarter, and new phases, respectively. Values of the SSC are given on the following pages for the beginning of each month.

Selenographic longitude (λ) is measured toward the observer's west (i.e. eastward on the Moon) from the mean central lunar meridian. Thus sunrise will occur at a given point on the Moon when SSC = 360° – λ; values of 360° – λ for several lunar features are listed in the MAP OF MOON on pp. 114–115. The longitude of the sunset terminator differs by 180° from that of the sunrise terminator.

Libration is the apparent rocking motion of the Moon as it orbits Earth. As a consequence, over time, about 59% of the lunar surface can be viewed from Earth (see *Sky & Telescope,* July 1987, p. 60). Libration in longitude (up to ±8°) results from the nearly uniform axial rotation of the Moon combined with its varying orbital speed along its elliptical orbit, while libration in latitude (±7°) is caused by the tilt of the Moon's equator to its orbital plane. A smaller contribution (up to ±1°), called *diurnal libration,* is associated with the shifting of the observer due to Earth's rotation.

When the libration in longitude is positive, more of the Moon's east limb, the limb near Mare Crisium, is exposed to view (in reference to the lunar limbs, *east* and *west* are used in this lunar sense; see also the "E" and "W" labels on the MAP OF MOON). When the libration in latitude is positive, more of the Moon's north limb is exposed to view. The monthly dates of the greatest positive and negative values of the libration in longitude and latitude, favourable dates for viewing librated lunar limbs, and the dates of greatest northern and southern declination are given in the following pages.

The lunar graphics on the right-hand pages give the geocentric appearance of the Moon at 0h UT on the odd-numbered days of the month. They depict the Moon's phase (based on the SCC), size, and libration. A small dot of size proportional to the amount of libration appears near the limb that is librated. The graphics were prepared using images and data provided by Roger Fell, who generated the data using the Lunar Calculator computer program written by Alister Ling (see www.edmontonrasc.com/software/software.html#1).

The Moon's orbit is inclined 5°09' to the ecliptic. The gravitational influences of Earth and the Sun cause (1) the orbital plane to wobble and (2) the major axis of the orbit to precess. (1) The wobble shifts the line of nodes westward (retrograde) along the ecliptic with a period of 18.61 years. During 2003, the ascending node regresses from longitude 67.0° to 47.7°, moving from Taurus to Aries. Thus the ascending node is farther from the autumnal equinox (at longitude 180°), and the monthly range of the Moon's declination increases from its 1997 minimum of ±18° to ±27° by the end of 2003. (2) The precession shifts the perigee point eastward (direct) with a period of 8.85 years, although the positions of successive perigees fluctuate considerably from the mean motion. The Moon's mean equatorial plane, its mean orbital plane, and the plane of the ecliptic intersect along a common line of nodes, the equator being inclined at 1°32' to the ecliptic and at $1°32' + 5°09' = 6°41'$ to the orbit (i.e. the ascending node of the equator on the ecliptic coincides with the descending node of the orbit).

Planets—See CONTENTS or the INDEX for the location of more information on each of the planets.

Jupiter's Satellites—The configurations of Jupiter's Galilean satellites, provided by Larry Bogan, are given on the right side of the monthly pages. In these diagrams the vertical double line represents the equatorial diameter of the disk of Jupiter. Time is shown on the vertical scale, successive horizontal lines indicating 0h UT on the various days of the month. The relative east–west positions of the four satellites with respect to the disk of Jupiter are given by the four curves, where I = Io, II = Europa (dashed curve), III = Ganymede, and IV = Callisto. Note the "West–East" orientation given at the top of each diagram; these directions are those of the observer's sky, not Jupiter's limbs, and correspond to the view in an inverting telescope. For the various transits, occultations, and eclipses of Jupiter's Galilean satellites, see PHENOMENA OF THE GALILEAN SATELLITES on pp. 204–210. (Diagrams are also given for the five brightest satellites of Saturn. See CONFIGURATIONS OF SATURN'S BRIGHTEST SATELLITES on pp. 211–214.)

Minima of Algol—Predicted times of mideclipse are based on the formula heliocentric minimum = 244 1598.608 + 2.867315E and are expressed as geocentric times for comparison with observations (the first number is the Julian date for the minimum of 1972 October 8.108, and the second is the period of Algol in days; E is an integer).

Occultations Involving the Moon, Stars, Planets, and Asteroids—The footnotes give areas of visibility; see "Occultations" in the INDEX for more details.

THE SKY FOR 2003 JANUARY

		Mercury	Venus	Mars	Jupiter	Saturn	Uranus	Neptune	Sun
RA	1	20^{h}01^m	15^{h}29^m	15^{h}09^m	9^{h}18^m	5^{h}36^m	21^{h}55^m	20^{h}48^m	18^{h}44^m
	11	19^{h}34^m	16^{h}08^m	15^{h}35^m	9^{h}14^m	5^{h}33^m	21^{h}57^m	20^{h}49^m	19^{h}28^m
	21	18^{h}53^m	16^{h}52^m	16^{h}02^m	9^{h}10^m	5^{h}30^m	21^{h}59^m	20^{h}51^m	20^{h}11^m
Dec	1	−20°44′	−15°14′	−16°57′	+16°31′	+22°02′	−13°27′	−17°50′	−23°03′
	11	−18°52′	−17°23′	−18°40′	+16°51′	+22°02′	−13°17′	−17°44′	−21°54′
	21	−19°43′	−19°14′	−20°09′	+17°14′	+22°02′	−13°07′	−17°38′	−20°03′
Dist	1	0.85	0.60	2.05	4.48	8.08	20.68	30.94	0.983
	11	0.67	0.67	1.97	4.40	8.15	20.80	31.01	0.983
	21	0.75	0.75	1.88	4.35	8.23	20.89	31.05	0.984
Mag	1	0.1	−4.5	1.5	−2.5	−0.4	5.9	8.0	
	11	4.5	−4.4	1.5	−2.6	−0.3	5.9	8.0	
	21	0.9	−4.4	1.4	−2.6	−0.3	5.9	8.0	
Size	1	7.9″	27.9″	4.6″	44.0″	20.6″	3.4″	2.2″	32′32″
	11	10.0″	24.8″	4.8″	44.8″	20.4″	3.4″	2.2″	32′32″
	21	9.0″	22.3″	5.0″	45.4″	20.2″	3.4″	2.2″	32′30″

Moon—On Jan. 1.0 UT, the age of the Moon is 27.7 d. The Sun's selenographic colongitude is 242.89° and increases by 12.2° each day thereafter. The libration in longitude is maximum (east limb exposed) on Jan. 5 (+5°) and minimum (west limb exposed) on Jan. 17 (−5°). (See the paragraph concerning libration two pages earlier.) The libration in latitude is maximum (north limb exposed) on Jan. 7 (+7°) and minimum (south limb exposed) on Jan. 21 (−7°). Particularly favourable dates for viewing librated lunar limbs are Jan. 6 (8.3°) and Jan. 19 (8.0°). The Moon reaches its greatest northern declination on Jan. 17 (+26°) and its greatest southern declinations on Jan. 2 (−26°) and Jan. 30 (−26°).

Mercury is not easily observed by northern or southern observers until late in the month after it has both risen in the morning twilight and become brighter. Southern observers are favoured during this morning apparition of Mercury when, by month's end, it rises completely out of the twilight sky in the east-southeast. Northern observers can only observe Mercury during twilight in the southeast.

Venus is at greatest elongation west (47°) on Jan. 11. In this morning apparition, which favours southern observers, it rises about 4 h before the Sun for northern observers and stands about 15° high in the southeast at the beginning of morning twilight. Southern observers will find Venus about 20° high in the east at the beginning of morning twilight.

Mars begins the month in Libra, moves through Scorpius, and ends the month in Ophiuchus. Mars is at perihelion opposition with the Sun this year in August; therefore, this is a very good year to observe Mars (see pp. 185–190 for further details). In mid-January, it rises about 4 h before the Sun in the east-southeast and stands about 20° high in the south-southeast after the beginning of morning twilight. Mars rises near 1 a.m. in the east-southeast for southern observers and is about 35° high in the east at the beginning of morning twilight.

Jupiter, in Cancer, rises in the east-northeast during evening twilight for both northern and southern observers and is visible for the remainder of the night.

Saturn, in Taurus, was at opposition on 2002 Dec. 17. It stands about 40° high in the east at the end of evening twilight and sets during morning twilight. For southern observers, Saturn is about 35° high in the north-northeast at the end of evening twilight and sets near 3 a.m. The south side of its ring system faces Earth for the next 6 years (the rings were last edge-on in February 1996). During 2003, the tilt of the rings increases slightly from 26.7° in January to 27.0° in early April, closes to 24.8° in late October, and then increases slightly to 25.5° by late December.

Time (UT)			JANUARY EVENTS	Jupiter's Satellites	
d	h	m		West	East
Wed. 1	3	14	Algol at minimum		
			Mercury at ascending node		
Thu. 2	0	16	**Double shadow transit on Jupiter**		
	10		Mercury stationary		
	20	23	**New Moon**		
Fri. 3	18	44	**Double shadow transit on Jupiter**		
	23		Mercury 5° N of Moon		
Sat. 4	0		Quadrantid meteors peak		
	0	03	Algol at minimum		
	5		**Earth at perihelion** (147 103 Mm)		
	19		Neptune 5° N of Moon		
Mon. 6			Mercury at perihelion		
	1		Uranus 5° N of Moon		
	20	53	Algol at minimum		
Tue. 7	7	41	**Double shadow transit on Jupiter**		
Thu. 9	2	09	**Double shadow transit on Jupiter**		
	17	42	Algol at minimum		
Fri. 10	13	15	**First Quarter**		
	20	38	**Double shadow transit on Jupiter**		
Sat. 11	1		Moon at apogee (404 343 km)		
	3		**Venus greatest elongation W (47°)**		
	20		Mercury in inferior conjunction		
Sun. 12	14	31	Algol at minimum		
Tue. 14	9	48	**Double shadow transit on Jupiter**		
Wed. 15	11	20	Algol at minimum		
	20		Saturn 3° S of Moon		
	22		Venus 8° N of Antares		
Thu. 16			Mercury at greatest heliocentric lat. N		
	5	25	**Double shadow transit on Jupiter**		
Fri. 17	23	05	**Double shadow transit on Jupiter**		
	23	52	**Triple satellite transit on Jupiter**		
Sat. 18	8	10	Algol at minimum		
	10	48	**Full Moon**		
Sun. 19			Venus at greatest heliocentric lat. N		
	15		Jupiter 4° S of Moon		
Tue. 21			**Zodiacal Light** vis. in N lat. in W after evening twilight for next two weeks		
	4	59	Algol at minimum		
	12	24	**Double shadow transit on Jupiter**		
Wed. 22	23		Mercury stationary		
Thu. 23	22		Moon at perigee (369 898 km)		
Fri. 24	1	48	Algol at minimum		
Sat. 25	1	42	**Double shadow transit on Jupiter**		
	8	33	**Last Quarter**		
Sun. 26	22	37	Algol at minimum		
Mon. 27	15		**Mars 0.4° N of Moon, Occultation†**		
Tue. 28	15	01	**Double shadow transit on Jupiter**		
	19		Venus 4° N of Moon		
Wed. 29	19	27	Algol at minimum		
Thu. 30	10		Mercury 5° N of Moon		
Fri. 31	0		Neptune in conjunction with Sun		
	5		Mars 5° N of Antares		

†Samoa, central Pacific Ocean, southern South America

THE SKY FOR 2003 FEBRUARY

		Mercury	Venus	Mars	Jupiter	Saturn	Uranus	Neptune	Sun
RA	1	19^h11^m	17^h43^m	16^h32^m	9^h04^m	5^h28^m	22^h01^m	20^h52^m	20^h56^m
	11	19^h58^m	18^h31^m	16^h59^m	8^h59^m	5^h26^m	22^h03^m	20^h54^m	21^h37^m
	21	20^h56^m	19^h21^m	17^h27^m	8^h54^m	5^h26^m	22^h05^m	20^h55^m	22^h16^m
Dec	1	$-21°06'$	$-20°38'$	$-21°30'$	$+17°40'$	$+22°02'$	$-12°54'$	$-17°32'$	$-17°17'$
	11	$-20°58'$	$-21°05'$	$-22°27'$	$+18°03'$	$+22°03'$	$-12°42'$	$-17°26'$	$-14°14'$
	21	$-18°53'$	$-20°37'$	$-23°06'$	$+18°25'$	$+22°05'$	$-12°30'$	$-17°20'$	$-10°48'$
Dist	1	0.94	0.83	1.78	4.33	8.36	20.96	31.07	0.985
	11	1.10	0.91	1.69	4.34	8.49	21.00	31.05	0.987
	21	1.23	0.98	1.60	4.38	8.64	21.01	31.01	0.989
Mag	1	0.0	−4.3	1.3	−2.6	−0.2	5.9	8.0	
	11	−0.1	−4.2	1.2	−2.6	−0.1	5.9	8.0	
	21	−0.2	−4.2	1.1	−2.6	0.0	5.9	8.0	
Size	1	7.1″	20.0″	5.2″	45.6″	19.9″	3.3″	2.2″	32′28″
	11	6.1″	18.4″	5.5″	45.5″	19.6″	3.3″	2.2″	32′25″
	21	5.5″	17.0″	5.8″	45.0″	19.2″	3.3″	2.2″	32′20″

Moon—On Feb. 1.0 UT, the age of the Moon is 29.1 d. The Sun's selenographic colongitude is 259.85° and increases by 12.2° each day thereafter. The libration in longitude is maximum (east limb exposed) on Feb. 1 (+5°) and on Feb. 27 (+5°) and minimum (west limb exposed) on Feb. 13 (−6°). The libration in latitude is maximum (north limb exposed) on Feb. 3 (+7°) and minimum (south limb exposed) on Feb. 17 (−7°). A particularly favourable date for viewing a librated lunar limb is Feb. 17 (7.3°). The Moon reaches its greatest northern declination on Feb. 13 (+26°) and its greatest southern declination on Feb. 26 (−26°).

Mercury reaches greatest elongation west (25°) on Feb. 4. For southern observers, Mercury continues a favourable morning apparition and can be observed low in the east-southeast before sunrise for the entire month. Northern observers can find Mercury with difficulty very low in the southeast during morning twilight early in the month; it becomes lost in the glare of the Sun near midmonth.

Venus rises about 2.5 h before the Sun and is low in the southeast during morning twilight. For more favoured southern observers, Venus rises nearly 3.5 h before the Sun and stands nearly 25° high in the east at the beginning of morning twilight.

Mars moves from Ophiuchus to Sagittarius late in the month. It rises in the east by 3 a.m., but stands only about 15° high in the south-southeast at the beginning of morning twilight. For more favoured southern observers, Mars rises in the east-southeast soon after midnight and is about 45° high in the east at the beginning of morning twilight.

Jupiter, in Cancer, is at opposition on Feb. 2. It rises about 1.5 h before sunset for both northern and southern observers, transits before midnight, and sets during morning twilight.

Saturn, in Taurus, is stationary on Feb. 22 and returns to direct (eastward) motion. For northern observers, it is high in the south-southeast at the end of evening twilight and sets in the early morning in the west-northwest. For southern observers, Saturn stands about 40° high on the meridian in the north just after the end of evening twilight and sets near 1 a.m.

Time (UT)			FEBRUARY EVENTS	Jupiter's Satellites	
d	h	m		West	East

Sat.	1	4 19	**Double shadow transit on Jupiter**	1.0
		10 48	**New Moon**	
		16 16	Algol at minimum	2.0 — IV
Sun.	2	9	**Jupiter at opposition**	3.0
Mon.	3			I
Tue.	4	1	**Mercury greatest elongation W (25°)**	4.0 — III
		13 05	Algol at minimum	5.0
Wed.	5			6.0
Thu.	6			7.0
Fri.	7	9 55	Algol at minimum	II
		22	Moon at apogee (404 552 km)	8.0
Sat.	8			9.0
Sun.	9		Mercury at descending node	10.0
		11 11	**First Quarter**	
Mon.	10	6 44	Algol at minimum	11.0
Tue.	11			12.0
Wed.	12	3	Saturn 3° S of Moon	13.0
Thu.	13	3 33	Algol at minimum	14.0
Fri.	14			
Sat.	15	18	Jupiter 4° S of Moon	15.0
Sun.	16	0 22	Algol at minimum	16.0
		6	Vesta stationary	17.0
		23 51	**Full Moon**	
Mon.	17	22	Uranus in conjunction with Sun	18.0
Tue.	18	21 12	Algol at minimum	19.0
Wed.	19		Mercury at aphelion	20.0
			Zodiacal Light vis. in N lat. in W after evening twilight for next two weeks	21.0
		16	Moon at perigee (364 845 km)	22.0
Thu.	20			23.0
Fri.	21	0	Mercury 1.6° S of Neptune	24.0
		18 01	Algol at minimum	25.0
Sat.	22	10	Saturn stationary	
Sun.	23	16 46	**Last Quarter**	26.0
Mon.	24	14 50	Algol at minimum	27.0
Tue.	25	5	**Mars 1.9° N of Moon**	28.0
Wed.	26			29.0
Thu.	27	11	Venus 5° N of Moon	30.0
		11 40	Algol at minimum	
Fri.	28		Mars at descending node	31.0
		15	Neptune 5° N of Moon	

THE SKY FOR 2003 MARCH

		Mercury	Venus	Mars	Jupiter	Saturn	Uranus	Neptune	Sun
RA	1	21^h45^m	20^h00^m	17^h49^m	8^h50^m	5^h26^m	22^h07^m	20^h57^m	22^h46^m
	11	22^h50^m	20^h49^m	18^h17^m	8^h46^m	5^h27^m	22^h09^m	20^h58^m	23^h23^m
	21	23^h59^m	21^h37^m	18^h44^m	8^h44^m	5^h29^m	22^h11^m	20^h59^m	23^h59^m
Dec	1	$-15°40'$	$-19°34'$	$-23°26'$	$+18°39'$	$+22°07'$	$-12°21'$	$-17°15'$	$-7°50'$
	11	$-9°44'$	$-17°26'$	$-23°34'$	$+18°53'$	$+22°10'$	$-12°09'$	$-17°10'$	$-3°59'$
	21	$-1°46'$	$-14°29'$	$-23°26'$	$+19°02'$	$+22°13'$	$-11°58'$	$-17°05'$	$-0°02'$
Dist	1	1.30	1.04	1.53	4.44	8.77	20.99	30.95	0.991
	11	1.36	1.11	1.44	4.54	8.94	20.95	30.86	0.993
	21	1.35	1.17	1.35	4.65	9.10	20.88	30.75	0.996
Mag	1	-0.4	-4.1	1.0	-2.5	0.0	5.9	8.0	
	11	-0.9	-4.1	0.8	-2.5	0.0	5.9	8.0	
	21	-1.8	-4.0	0.7	-2.4	0.1	5.9	8.0	
Size	1	5.2″	16.1″	6.1″	44.4″	19.0″	3.3″	2.2″	32′17″
	11	5.0″	15.1″	6.5″	43.5″	18.6″	3.3″	2.2″	32′12″
	21	5.0″	14.2″	7.0″	42.4″	18.3″	3.4″	2.2″	32′07″

Moon—On Mar. 1.0 UT, the age of the Moon is 27.5 d. The Sun's selenographic colongitude is 240.44° and increases by 12.2° each day thereafter. The libration in longitude is maximum (east limb exposed) on Mar. 26 (+6°) and minimum (west limb exposed) on Mar. 13 (−7°). The libration in latitude is maximum (north limb exposed) on Mar. 2 (+7°) and on Mar. 29 (+7°) and minimum (south limb exposed) on Mar. 16 (−7°). The Moon reaches its greatest northern declination on Mar. 12 (+26°) and its greatest southern declination on Mar. 25 (−26°).

Mercury is not observable by northern observers until early April. For southern observers, it remains visible early in the month low in the east-southeast before sunrise. It brightens, but at the same time it slowly descends into the morning twilight, becoming lost in the glare of the Sun by about Mar. 10. Mercury is in superior conjunction with the Sun on Mar. 22.

Venus rises during morning twilight and is low in the east-southeast before becoming lost in the glare of the Sun. For more favoured southern observers, Venus rises about 3 h before the Sun and stands about 20° high in the east at the beginning of morning twilight.

Mars, in Sagittarius, rises in early morning in the southeast and climbs slowly to only about 15° high in the south-southeast after the beginning of morning twilight. For more favoured southern observers, Mars rises in the east-southeast near midnight and is nearly 60° high in the east at the beginning of morning twilight.

Jupiter, in Cancer, stands about 60° high in the southeast at the end of evening twilight and sets in the west-northwest at the beginning of morning twilight. Southern observers will find Jupiter about 20° high in the north-northeast at the end of evening twilight and setting in the west-northwest in early morning.

Saturn, in Taurus, stands about 60° high in the southwest at the end of evening twilight and sets by about 2 a.m. For less favoured southern observers, Saturn stands about 30° high in the northwest at the end of evening twilight and sets near 11 p.m.

Time (UT) d h m	MARCH EVENTS	Jupiter's Satellites West East
Sat. 1 15	Mercury 3° N of Moon	
Sun. 2 8 29	Algol at minimum	
Mon. 3 2 35	**New Moon**	
Tue. 4 13	Mercury 1.5° S of Uranus	
Wed. 5 5 18	Algol at minimum	
Thu. 6 23	Pallas in conjunction with Sun	
Fri. 7 17	Moon at apogee (404 382 km)	
Sat. 8 2 07	Algol at minimum	
15 48	Double satellite transit on Jupiter	
Sun. 9		
Mon. 10 22 57	Algol at minimum	
Tue. 11	Mercury at greatest heliocentric lat. S	
7 15	**First Quarter**	
12	Saturn 3° S of Moon	
Wed. 12 10	Juno stationary	
20	Venus 0.2° N of Neptune	
Thu. 13 19 46	Algol at minimum	
Fri. 14		
Sat. 15 0	Jupiter 4° S of Moon	
Sun. 16	Venus at descending node	
16 35	Algol at minimum	
Mon. 17		
Tue. 18 10 34	**Full Moon**	
Wed. 19 13 24	Algol at minimum	
19	Moon at perigee (359 816 km)	
Thu. 20		
Fri. 21 1 00	**Equinox**	
Sat. 22 0	Mercury in superior conjunction	
10 13	Algol at minimum	
Sun. 23 17	Pluto stationary	
Mon. 24		
Tue. 25 1 51	**Last Quarter**	
7 03	Algol at minimum	
18	Mars 3° N of Moon	
Wed. 26 23	**Vesta at opposition**	
Thu. 27 22	Neptune 5° N of Moon	
Fri. 28 3 52	Algol at minimum	
13	**Venus 0.05° N of Uranus**	
Sat. 29 8	Uranus 5° N of Moon	
10	Venus 5° N of Moon	
Sun. 30	Mercury at ascending node	
Mon. 31 0 41	Algol at minimum	

THE SKY FOR 2003 APRIL

		Mercury	Venus	Mars	Jupiter	Saturn	Uranus	Neptune	Sun
RA	1	1ʰ18ᵐ	22ʰ29ᵐ	19ʰ14ᵐ	8ʰ43ᵐ	5ʰ31ᵐ	22ʰ13ᵐ	21ʰ00ᵐ	0ʰ40ᵐ
	11	2ʰ23ᵐ	23ʰ14ᵐ	19ʰ41ᵐ	8ʰ43ᵐ	5ʰ35ᵐ	22ʰ15ᵐ	21ʰ01ᵐ	1ʰ16ᵐ
	21	3ʰ03ᵐ	23ʰ59ᵐ	20ʰ07ᵐ	8ʰ44ᵐ	5ʰ38ᵐ	22ʰ17ᵐ	21ʰ02ᵐ	1ʰ53ᵐ
Dec	1	+8°28′	−10°26′	−22°59′	+19°06′	+22°17′	−11°46′	−17°00′	+4°17′
	11	+16°26′	−6°15′	−22°18′	+19°05′	+22°21′	−11°37′	−16°57′	+8°04′
	21	+20°18′	−1°44′	−21°26′	+18°58′	+22°25′	−11°29′	−16°54′	+11°38′
Dist	1	1.24	1.24	1.25	4.80	9.28	20.78	30.60	0.999
	11	1.01	1.31	1.16	4.95	9.44	20.66	30.45	1.002
	21	0.77	1.37	1.07	5.10	9.58	20.53	30.28	1.005
Mag	1	−1.4	−4.0	0.5	−2.3	0.1	5.9	7.9	
	11	−0.6	−4.0	0.3	−2.3	0.1	5.9	7.9	
	21	0.9	−3.9	0.2	−2.2	0.1	5.9	7.9	
Size	1	5.4″	13.4″	7.5″	41.1″	17.9″	3.4″	2.2″	32′01″
	11	6.6″	12.8″	8.1″	39.9″	17.6″	3.4″	2.2″	31′56″
	21	8.8″	12.2″	8.7″	38.7″	17.4″	3.4″	2.2″	31′50″

Moon—On Apr. 1.0 UT, the age of the Moon is 28.9 d. The Sun's selenographic colongitude is 258.08° and increases by 12.2° each day thereafter. The libration in longitude is maximum (east limb exposed) on Apr. 23 (+7°) and minimum (west limb exposed) on Apr. 11 (−8°). The libration in latitude is maximum (north limb exposed) on Apr. 25 (+7°) and minimum (south limb exposed) on Apr. 13 (−7°). The Moon reaches its greatest northern declination on Apr. 9 (+26°) and its greatest southern declination on Apr. 21 (−26°). On Apr. 17 the Moon reaches its second closest perigee distance of the year (357 157 km). With a full Moon occurring only about one-half day earlier, extra large tides will occur (see the section TIDES AND THE EARTH–MOON SYSTEM on pp. 173–177).

Mercury emerges in the west-northwestern evening twilight early in the month, and at midmonth it sets nearly 2 h after the Sun and stands nearly 20° above the horizon at sunset. It reaches greatest elongation east (20°) on Apr. 16, which becomes the **best evening apparition of the year for northern observers.** In the second half of the month, Mercury fades rapidly as it descends into the evening twilight and is lost in the glare of the Sun late in the month. For less favoured southern observers, in the middle two weeks of the month Mercury rises just high enough in the west-northwestern evening twilight to be observed with difficulty.

Venus rises only about 1 h before the Sun for northern observers and is visible only with difficulty, due to the unfavourable tipping of the ecliptic, in the bright eastern dawn sky. For greatly favoured southern observers, Venus rises about 2.5 h before the Sun and stands about 15° high in the east at the beginning of morning twilight.

Mars moves from Sagittarius to Capricornus this month. It rises near 2 a.m. in the east-southeast and climbs slowly to only about 20° high in the southeast after morning twilight begins. For more favoured southern observers, Mars rises in the east-southeast before midnight and stands over 70° high in the east after morning twilight begins.

Jupiter, in Cancer, is stationary on Apr. 4 and returns to direct (eastward) motion. For northern observers, it stands over 60° high in the southwest at the end of evening twilight and sets in the west-northwest in early morning. Less favoured southern observers will find Jupiter about 40° high on the meridian at the end of evening twilight and setting shortly after midnight. Early in the month, Jupiter is about 1° southwest of M44.

Saturn, in Taurus, stands about 30° high in the west at the end of evening twilight and sets before midnight. For less favoured southern observers, Saturn is low in the northwest at the end of evening twilight and sets in midevening.

Time (UT) d h m	APRIL EVENTS	Jupiter's Satellites West East
Tue. 1 19 19	**New Moon**	
Wed. 2 21 30	Algol at minimum	
Thu. 3		
Fri. 4	Mercury at perihelion	
4	Moon at apogee (406 209 km)	
5	Jupiter stationary	
Sat. 5 18 19	Algol at minimum	
Sun. 6 2	**Daylight Saving Time begins**	
Mon. 7 22	Saturn 3° S of Moon	
Tue. 8 15 08	Algol at minimum	
Wed. 9 23 40	**First Quarter**	
Thu. 10		
Fri. 11 1 43	Double satellite transit on Jupiter	
8	Jupiter 4° S of Moon	
11 57	Algol at minimum	
Sat. 12		
Sun. 13		
Mon. 14	Mercury at greatest heliocentric lat. N	
8 46	Algol at minimum	
Tue. 15		
Wed. 16 15	**Mercury greatest elongation E (20°)**	
19 36	**Full Moon (Largest of 2003)**	
Thu. 17 5	Moon at perigee (357 157 km)	
	Large tides	
5 36	Algol at minimum	
Fri. 18		
Sat. 19	Venus at aphelion	
Sun. 20 2 25	Algol at minimum	
Mon. 21		
Tue. 22 17	Lyrid meteors peak	
23 14	Algol at minimum	
Wed. 23 7	Mars 3° N of Moon	
12 18	**Last Quarter**	
Thu. 24 4	Neptune 5° N of Moon	
Fri. 25 16	Uranus 5° N of Moon	
20 03	Algol at minimum	
Sat. 26 22	Mercury stationary	
Sun. 27		
Mon. 28 16 52	Algol at minimum	
17	Venus 3° N of Moon	
Tue. 29		
Wed. 30		

THE SKY FOR 2003 MAY

		Mercury	Venus	Mars	Jupiter	Saturn	Uranus	Neptune	Sun
RA	1	3^{h}07^m	0^{h}44^m	20^{h}32^m	8^{h}47^m	5^{h}43^m	22^{h}18^m	21^{h}02^m	2^{h}31^m
	11	2^{h}47^m	1^{h}29^m	20^{h}56^m	8^{h}51^m	5^{h}47^m	22^{h}19^m	21^{h}02^m	3^{h}10^m
	21	2^{h}39^m	2^{h}15^m	21^{h}19^m	8^{h}56^m	5^{h}52^m	22^{h}20^m	21^{h}02^m	3^{h}49^m
Dec	1	+19°24′	+2°55′	−20°23′	+18°47′	+22°28′	−11°22′	−16°52′	+14°52′
	11	+15°14′	+7°31′	−19°13′	+18°32′	+22°31′	−11°17′	−16°51′	+17°42′
	21	+12°13′	+11°52′	−17°58′	+18°12′	+22°34′	−11°14′	−16°52′	+20°03′
Dist	1	0.60	1.42	0.99	5.26	9.71	20.38	30.12	1.007
	11	0.56	1.47	0.91	5.42	9.82	20.22	29.95	1.010
	21	0.62	1.52	0.83	5.58	9.91	20.05	29.78	1.012
Mag	1	3.6	−3.9	−0.0	−2.1	0.1	5.9	7.9	
	11	4.7	−3.9	−0.2	−2.1	0.1	5.8	7.9	
	21	2.0	−3.9	−0.4	−2.0	0.1	5.8	7.9	
Size	1	11.2″	11.7″	9.4″	37.5″	17.1″	3.4″	2.2″	31′45″
	11	12.1″	11.3″	10.3″	36.4″	17.0″	3.5″	2.2″	31′41″
	21	10.8″	11.0″	11.2″	35.4″	16.8″	3.5″	2.2″	31′37″

Moon—On May 1.0 UT, the age of the Moon is 29.2 d. The Sun's selenographic colongitude is 264.02° and increases by 12.2° each day thereafter. The libration in longitude is maximum (east limb exposed) on May 21 (+7°) and minimum (west limb exposed) on May 9 (−8°). The libration in latitude is maximum (north limb exposed) on May 22 (+7°) and minimum (south limb exposed) on May 10 (−7°). The Moon reaches its greatest northern declination on May 6 (+26°) and its greatest southern declination on May 19 (−27°). There is a **total lunar eclipse** on May 16. Part or all of its umbral phases are visible in Europe, the western Middle East, Africa, the Americas, and Antarctica (see pp. 134–135 in ECLIPSES DURING 2003). There is an **annular solar eclipse** on May 31, whose wide path of annularity crosses central Greenland and northern Iceland. Partial phases are visible in parts of western Europe, the Middle East, Russia, Alaska, and parts of the Arctic regions of Canada (see pp. 135–136 in ECLIPSES DURING 2003).

Mercury is in inferior conjunction with the Sun on May 7, causing a rare **transit of the disk of Mercury across the disk of the Sun;** see 2003 TRANSIT OF MERCURY on pp. 199–203. Mercury is not easily observable by northern observers until late July. For southern observers, Mercury emerges in the east-northeast before sunrise in the second half of the month; however, it does not brighten sufficiently to be easily observed until the last few days of the month. **Mercury is in conjunction with Venus on May 28.**

Venus rises less than 1 h before the Sun for northern observers and is visible only with difficulty in the bright eastern dawn sky. For greatly favoured southern observers, Venus rises about 2 h before the Sun and stands about 10° high in the east-northeast just after the beginning of morning twilight. **Venus is in conjunction with Mercury on May 28.**

Mars, in Capricornus, rises near 1 a.m. in the east-southeast and climbs slowly to only about 20° high in the southeast after morning twilight begins. For more favoured southern observers, Mars rises in the east-southeast in late evening and stands nearly 80° high on the meridian after morning twilight begins.

Jupiter, in Cancer, stands about 30° high in the west after the end of evening twilight and sets in the west-northwest after midnight. For southern observers, Jupiter stands nearly 40° high in the north-northwest at the end of evening twilight and sets in the west-northwest in late evening.

Saturn moves from Taurus to Orion this month; its visibility has degraded considerably this month. It is very low in the west-northwest during evening twilight for both northern and southern observers and becomes lost in the twilight sky by the end of the month for northern observers and by early June for southern observers.

Time (UT)			MAY EVENTS	Jupiter's Satellites	
d	h	m		West	East

Thu.	1	8	Moon at apogee (**406 529 km**)	
		12 15	**New Moon**	
		13 41	Algol at minimum	
Fri.	2			
Sat.	3	11	Juno at opposition	
Sun.	4	10 30	Algol at minimum	
Mon.	5	9	Saturn 3° S of Moon	
		23	η-Aquarid meteors peak	
Tue.	6			
Wed.	7		Mercury at descending node	
		7	Mercury in inferior conjunction	
			Transit across Sun (pp. 199–203)	
		7 19	Algol at minimum	
Thu.	8	18	Jupiter 4° S of Moon	
Fri.	9	11 53	**First Quarter**	
Sat.	10	4 08	Algol at minimum	
Sun.	11			
Mon.	12		Venus at greatest heliocentric lat. S	
Tue.	13	0 56	Algol at minimum	
		14	Mars 2° S of Neptune	
Wed.	14			
Thu.	15	4	Vesta stationary	
		16	Moon at perigee (357 449 km)	
			Large tides	
		21 45	Algol at minimum	
Fri.	16	3	Neptune stationary	
		3 36	**Full Moon, total lunar eclipse** (p. 134)	
		23	Ceres in conjunction with Sun	
Sat.	17			
Sun.	18		Mercury at aphelion	
		18 34	Algol at minimum	
Mon.	19	14	Mercury stationary	
Tue.	20			
Wed.	21	12	Neptune 5° N of Moon	
		15 23	Algol at minimum	
		20	Mars 3° N of Moon	
Thu.	22			
Fri.	23	0	Uranus 5° N of Moon	
		0 31	**Last Quarter**	
Sat.	24	12 12	Algol at minimum	
Mon.	26			
Tue.	27	9 01	Algol at minimum	
Wed.	28	0	**Mercury 2° S of Venus**	
		13	Moon at apogee (406 168 km)	
Thu.	29	2	**Mercury 2° S of Moon**	
		4	**Venus 0.1° S of Moon, Occultation†**	
Fri.	30	5 50	Algol at minimum	
Sat.	31	4 20	**New Moon, annular eclipse** (p. 135)	

†Eastern E. Africa, Madagascar, India, Sri Lanka, Thailand, China, Taiwan, Japan

THE SKY FOR 2003 JUNE

		Mercury	Venus	Mars	Jupiter	Saturn	Uranus	Neptune	Sun
RA	1	2ʰ59ᵐ	3ʰ07ᵐ	21ʰ43ᵐ	9ʰ02ᵐ	5ʰ58ᵐ	22ʰ20ᵐ	21ʰ02ᵐ	4ʰ34ᵐ
	11	3ʰ42ᵐ	3ʰ56ᵐ	22ʰ02ᵐ	9ʰ08ᵐ	6ʰ04ᵐ	22ʰ20ᵐ	21ʰ02ᵐ	5ʰ15ᵐ
	21	4ʰ47ᵐ	4ʰ47ᵐ	22ʰ20ᵐ	9ʰ15ᵐ	6ʰ09ᵐ	22ʰ20ᵐ	21ʰ01ᵐ	5ʰ57ᵐ
Dec	1	+13°08′	+16°08′	−16°36′	+17°46′	+22°36′	−11°12′	−16°53′	+21°58′
	11	+16°47′	+19°21′	−15°26′	+17°18′	+22°37′	−11°12′	−16°55′	+23°02′
	21	+21°17′	+21°43′	−14°25′	+16°48′	+22°37′	−11°14′	−16°57′	+23°26′
Dist	1	0.78	1.57	0.75	5.74	9.98	19.87	29.61	1.014
	11	0.96	1.61	0.69	5.87	10.02	19.71	29.46	1.015
	21	1.16	1.64	0.62	6.00	10.05	19.55	29.34	1.016
Mag	1	0.8	−3.9	−0.7	−1.9	0.1	5.8	7.9	
	11	0.0	−3.9	−0.9	−1.9	0.0	5.8	7.9	
	21	−0.8	−3.9	−1.2	−1.9	0.0	5.8	7.9	
Size	1	8.6″	10.6″	12.4″	34.4″	16.7″	3.5″	2.3″	31′33″
	11	7.0″	10.4″	13.7″	33.6″	16.6″	3.6″	2.3″	31′30″
	21	5.8″	10.2″	15.1″	32.9″	16.6″	3.6″	2.3″	31′29″

Moon—On Jun. 1.0 UT, the age of the Moon is 0.8 d. The Sun's selenographic colongitude is 282.64° and increases by 12.2° each day thereafter. The libration in longitude is maximum (east limb exposed) on Jun. 19 (+7°) and minimum (west limb exposed) on Jun. 6 (−7°). The libration in latitude is maximum (north limb exposed) on Jun. 19 (+7°) and minimum (south limb exposed) on Jun. 6 (−7°). The Moon reaches its greatest northern declinations on Jun. 2 (+26°) and on Jun. 29 (+26°) and its greatest southern declination on Jun. 15 (−26°).

Mercury reaches greatest elongation west (24°) on Jun. 3; however, due to unfavourable geometry, it is not visible this month by northern observers. For southern observers, a favourable morning apparition continues. During the month, Mercury brightens by about two magnitudes as it slowly descends into the east-northeast morning twilight sky, becoming lost in the glare of the Sun late in the month. **Mercury is in conjunction with Venus on Jun. 21.**

Venus rises about 1 h before the Sun for northern observers and is visible only with difficulty in the bright east-northeastern dawn sky. For southern observers, Venus's visibility degrades considerably this month. At midmonth it rises during morning twilight and is still very low when it is lost in the glare of the Sun. **Venus is in conjunction with Mercury on Jun. 21.**

Mars moves from Capricornus to Aquarius early in the month. It rises before midnight in the east-southeast and climbs to about 25° high in the southeast after morning twilight begins. For more favoured southern observers, Mars rises in the east-southeast near 10 p.m. and stands about 70° high in the northwest at the beginning of morning twilight.

Jupiter, in Cancer, is visible low in the west during evening twilight and sets about 3 h after the Sun in the west-northwest. More favoured southern observers will find Jupiter about 25° high in the northwest at the end of evening twilight and setting about 4 h after the Sun in the west-northwest.

Saturn is in conjunction with the Sun on Jun. 24. It cannot be easily observed by northern observers this month; however, southern observers can glimpse Saturn very low in the west-northwest during evening twilight in the first few days of the month.

Pluto, in Ophiuchus, is at opposition on Jun. 9. See the finder chart for Pluto on p. 198.

Time (UT) d h m	JUNE EVENTS	Jupiter's Satellites West East
Sun. 1 10 49	**Double shadow transit on Jupiter**	
21	Saturn 4° S of Moon	
Mon. 2 2 38	Algol at minimum	
Tue. 3 6	**Mercury greatest elongation W (24°)**	
Wed. 4 23 27	Algol at minimum	
Thu. 5 6	Jupiter 4° S of Moon	
Fri. 6		
Sat. 7	Mercury at greatest heliocentric lat. S	
15	Uranus stationary	
20 16	Algol at minimum	
20 28	**First Quarter**	
Sun. 8 13 08	**Double shadow transit on Jupiter**	
Mon. 9 21	**Pluto at opposition**	
Tue. 10 17 05	Algol at minimum	
Wed. 11		
Thu. 12 23	Moon at perigee (360 425 km)	
Fri. 13 13 53	Algol at minimum	
Sat. 14 11 16	**Full Moon**	
Sun. 15 13 40	Double satellite transit on Jupiter	
Mon. 16 10 42	Algol at minimum	
Tue. 17 11 14	**Double shadow transit on Jupiter**	
21	Neptune 5° N of Moon	
Wed. 18 19	Venus 5° N of Aldebaran	
Thu. 19 6	**Mars 1.7° N of Moon**	
7 31	Algol at minimum	
8	Uranus 5° N of Moon	
12	Mercury 4° N of Aldebaran	
Fri. 20 23	Mars 3° S of Uranus	
Sat. 21 2	**Mercury 0.4° S of Venus**	
14 45	**Last Quarter**	
19 10	**Solstice**	
Sun. 22 4 20	Algol at minimum	
17 26	Double satellite transit on Jupiter	
Mon. 23		
Tue. 24 14	Saturn in conjunction with Sun	
Wed. 25 1 08	Algol at minimum	
2	Moon at apogee (405 232 km)	
Thu. 26	Mercury at ascending node	
Fri. 27 21 57	Algol at minimum	
Sat. 28		
Sun. 29 18 39	**New Moon**	
Mon. 30 18 46	Algol at minimum	

THE SKY FOR 2003 JULY

		Mercury	Venus	Mars	Jupiter	Saturn	Uranus	Neptune	Sun
RA	1	6^h15^m	5^h40^m	22^h35^m	9^h22^m	6^h15^m	22^h19^m	21^h00^m	6^h38^m
	11	7^h48^m	6^h33^m	22^h46^m	9^h30^m	6^h20^m	22^h18^m	20^h59^m	7^h19^m
	21	9^h09^m	7^h26^m	22^h53^m	9^h38^m	6^h26^m	22^h17^m	20^h58^m	8^h00^m
Dec	1	+24°09′	+23°06′	−13°37′	+16°14′	+22°36′	−11°17′	−17°01′	+23°09′
	11	+22°54′	+23°22′	−13°09′	+15°37′	+22°34′	−11°22′	−17°05′	+22°12′
	21	+18°06′	+22°30′	−13°05′	+14°58′	+22°32′	−11°29′	−17°09′	+20°36′
Dist	1	1.30	1.67	0.56	6.11	10.04	19.41	29.23	1.017
	11	1.32	1.69	0.51	6.20	10.02	19.28	29.15	1.017
	21	1.24	1.71	0.46	6.28	9.97	19.18	29.09	1.016
Mag	1	−1.8	−3.9	−1.4	−1.8	0.0	5.8	7.9	
	11	−1.5	−3.9	−1.7	−1.8	0.1	5.7	7.8	
	21	−0.6	−3.9	−2.0	−1.8	0.1	5.7	7.8	
Size	1	5.2″	10.0″	16.7″	32.3″	16.6″	3.6″	2.3″	31′28″
	11	5.1″	9.8″	18.4″	31.9″	16.6″	3.6″	2.3″	31′28″
	21	5.4″	9.7″	20.3″	31.5″	16.7″	3.7″	2.3″	31′29″

Moon—On Jul. 1.0 UT, the age of the Moon is 1.2 d. The Sun's selenographic colongitude is 289.28° and increases by 12.2° each day thereafter. The libration in longitude is maximum (east limb exposed) on Jul. 16 (+6°) and minimum (west limb exposed) on Jul. 2 (−6°) and Jul. 29 (−5°). The libration in latitude is maximum (north limb exposed) on Jul. 16 (+7°) and minimum (south limb exposed) on Jul. 3 (−7°) and Jul. 30 (−7°). The Moon reaches its greatest northern declination on Jul. 27 (+26°) and its greatest southern declination on Jul. 12 (−26°).

Mercury is in superior conjunction with the Sun on Jul. 5, following which the **best evening apparition of the year for southern observers** begins. It emerges in the west-northwestern evening twilight during the second half of the month. By month's end it sets nearly 2 h after the Sun and stands about 5° high at the end of evening twilight. Northern observers can only glimpse Mercury with difficulty very low in the west-northwest after sunset during the last week of the month. **Mercury is in conjunction with Jupiter on Jul. 26.**

Venus is visible only with great difficulty in the brightening east-northeastern dawn sky early in the month for both northern and southern observers. It is lost in the glare of the Sun by the third week of the month.

Mars, in Aquarius, is stationary on Jul. 30 and begins retrograde (westward) motion. It rises near the end of evening twilight in the east-southeast and is about 30° high on the meridian during morning twilight. For more favoured southern observers, Mars rises in the east-southeast in midevening and is visible for the remainder of the night.

Jupiter moves from Cancer to Leo on Jul. 30. It is visible very low in the west-north-west after sunset early in the month. Late in the month it becomes lost in the glare of the Sun. More favoured southern observers will find Jupiter nearly 10° high in the west-northwest at the end of evening twilight and setting about 2 h after the Sun, also in the west-northwest. **Jupiter is in conjunction with Mercury on Jul. 26.**

Saturn, in Gemini, slowly emerges in the east-northeast morning twilight in the second half of the month. By month's end it is still difficult to observe, more so by northern observers.

Time (UT) d h m	JULY EVENTS	Jupiter's Satellites West East
Tue. 1	Mercury at perihelion	1.0
Wed. 2 16	Juno stationary	2.0 III
21	Jupiter 4° S of Moon	IV
Thu. 3 15 34	Algol at minimum	3.0
Fri. 4 6	**Earth at aphelion** (152 100 Mm)	4.0 I
Sat. 5 10	Mercury in superior conjunction	5.0
Sun. 6 12 23	Algol at minimum	
Mon. 7	Venus at ascending node	6.0
2 32	**First Quarter**	7.0
Tue. 8 8	Venus 0.8° N of Saturn	8.0 II
Wed. 9 9 11	Algol at minimum	
Thu. 10 22	Moon at perigee (365 145 km)	9.0
Fri. 11	Mercury at greatest heliocentric lat. N	10.0
Sat. 12 6 00	Algol at minimum	11.0
Sun. 13 19 21	**Full Moon**	12.0
Mon. 14		13.0
Tue. 15 2 49	Algol at minimum	
5	Neptune 5° N of Moon	14.0
Wed. 16 16	Uranus 5° N of Moon	15.0
Thu. 17 8	**Mars 0.3° S of Moon, Occultation**†	16.0
23 37	Algol at minimum	
Fri. 18		17.0
Sat. 19		18.0
Sun. 20 20 26	Algol at minimum	19.0
Mon. 21 7 01	**Last Quarter**	20.0
Tue. 22 20	Moon at apogee (404 328 km)	
Wed. 23 17 15	Algol at minimum	21.0
Thu. 24		22.0
Fri. 25		23.0
Sat. 26	Saturn at perihelion	24.0
1	**Mercury 0.4° N of Jupiter**	25.0
14 03	Algol at minimum	
Sun. 27 0	Saturn 4° S of Moon	26.0
Mon. 28 6	S. δ-Aquarid meteors peak	27.0
Tue. 29 6 53	**New Moon**	28.0
10 52	Algol at minimum	
Wed. 30 11	Mercury 0.2° N of Regulus	29.0
13	Jupiter 4° S of Moon	30.0
22	Mars stationary	31.0
Thu. 31 1	Mercury 5° S of Moon	

†Central Pacific Ocean, Central America, northwest S. America, Caribbean, N. Atlantic Ocean

THE SKY FOR 2003 AUGUST

		Mercury	Venus	Mars	Jupiter	Saturn	Uranus	Neptune	Sun
RA	1	10^h17^m	8^h24^m	22^h56^m	9^h47^m	6^h32^m	22^h16^m	20^h57^m	8^h43^m
	11	11^h03^m	9^h14^m	22^h53^m	9^h56^m	6^h37^m	22^h15^m	20^h56^m	9^h21^m
	21	11^h33^m	10^h03^m	22^h45^m	10^h04^m	6^h41^m	22^h13^m	20^h55^m	9^h59^m
Dec	1	+11°09′	+20°16′	−13°29′	+14°12′	+22°29′	−11°37′	−17°14′	+18°11′
	11	+4°51′	+17°14′	−14°14′	+13°29′	+22°25′	−11°45′	−17°19′	+15°28′
	21	−0°14′	+13°23′	−15°10′	+12°44′	+22°21′	−11°53′	−17°23′	+12°20′
Dist	1	1.10	1.72	0.42	6.34	9.89	19.09	29.07	1.015
	11	0.96	1.73	0.39	6.37	9.79	19.04	29.07	1.014
	21	0.81	1.73	0.38	6.38	9.68	19.02	29.11	1.012
Mag	1	−0.1	−3.9	−2.3	−1.7	0.1	5.7	7.8	
	11	0.2	−3.9	−2.6	−1.7	0.2	5.7	7.8	
	21	0.6	−3.9	−2.8	−1.7	0.2	5.7	7.8	
Size	1	6.1″	9.7″	22.4″	31.1″	16.8″	3.7″	2.3″	31′31″
	11	7.0″	9.6″	23.9″	30.9″	17.0″	3.7″	2.3″	31′34″
	21	8.3″	9.6″	24.9″	30.8″	17.2″	3.7″	2.3″	31′37″

Moon—On Aug. 1.0 UT, the age of the Moon is 2.7 d. The Sun's selenographic colongitude is 308.19° and increases by 12.2° each day thereafter. The libration in longitude is maximum (east limb exposed) on Aug. 13 (+5°) and minimum (west limb exposed) on Aug. 25 (−5°). The libration in latitude is maximum (north limb exposed) on Aug. 12 (+7°) and minimum (south limb exposed) on Aug. 27 (−7°). A particularly favourable date for viewing a librated lunar limb is Aug. 11 (7.0°). The Moon reaches its greatest northern declination on Aug. 23 (+27°) and its greatest southern declination on Aug. 9 (−27°).

Mercury reaches greatest elongation east (27°) on Aug. 14 and continues its **best evening apparition of the year for southern observers.** It remains visible all month low in the west after sunset; however, it fades considerably in the second half of the month as it descends rapidly into the evening twilight, becoming lost in the glare of the Sun by month's end. Northern observers can only glimpse Mercury with difficulty very low in the west after sunset during the first week of the month.

Venus, in superior conjunction with the Sun on Aug. 18, is not observable this month.

Mars, in Aquarius, is at **opposition on Aug. 28.** It rises during evening twilight in the east-southeast, transits about 30° high near 1 a.m., and is low in the southwest when it becomes lost during morning twilight. For more favoured southern observers, Mars rises in the east-southeast during evening twilight, transits about 75° high near 1 a.m., and is in the west when it becomes lost in morning twilight.

Jupiter is in conjunction with the Sun on Aug. 22 and cannot be observed this month by northern observers. Southern observers can only glimpse Jupiter early in the month very low in the west-northwest after sunset.

Saturn, in Gemini, improves its visibility in the morning sky this month. By month's end, it stands about 30° above the eastern horizon at the beginning of morning twilight for northern observers and about 20° above the northeastern horizon for southern observers.

Uranus moves from Capricornus to Aquarius in January where it spends the rest of the year. It is at opposition on Aug. 24 and was in conjunction with the Sun on Feb. 17. Its southerly declination in 2003 makes it low in the sky for northern observers. See the finder chart for Uranus on p. 196.

Neptune, in Capricornus, is at opposition on Aug. 4 and was in conjunction with the Sun on Jan. 31. Its southerly declination in 2003 makes it low in the sky for northern observers. See the finder chart for Neptune on p. 197.

Time (UT) d h m	AUGUST EVENTS	Jupiter's Satellites West East
Fri. 1 7 40	Algol at minimum	
Sat. 2		
Sun. 3	Mercury at descending node	
Mon. 4	Transit of Earth as seen from Neptune	
	Mars at greatest heliocentric lat. S	
4 29	Algol at minimum	
14	**Neptune at opposition**	
Tue. 5 7 28	**First Quarter**	
Wed. 6 14	Moon at perigee (369 433 km)	
Thu. 7 1 17	Algol at minimum	
Fri. 8		
Sat. 9 22 06	Algol at minimum	
Sun. 10	Venus at perihelion	
Mon. 11	Neptune at descending node	
13	Neptune 5° N of Moon	
Tue. 12 4 48	**Full Moon**	
18 55	Algol at minimum	
Wed. 13 0	Uranus 5° N of Moon	
5	**Perseid meteors peak**	
17	**Mars 1.9° S of Moon**	
Thu. 14	Mercury at aphelion	
21	**Mercury greatest elongation E (27°)**	
Fri. 15 15 43	Algol at minimum	
Sat. 16		
Sun. 17		
Mon. 18 12 32	Algol at minimum	
18	Venus in superior conjunction	
Tue. 19 14	Moon at apogee (404 102 km)	
Wed. 20 0 48	**Last Quarter**	
Thu. 21 5	Venus 0.6° N of Jupiter	
9 20	Algol at minimum	
Fri. 22 10	Jupiter in conjunction with Sun	
Sat. 23 14	Saturn 4° S of Moon	
Sun. 24 6 09	Algol at minimum	
10	**Uranus at opposition**	
Tue. 26		
Wed. 27 2 58	Algol at minimum	
9 52	Mars closest approach (55 758 006 km)	
	nearest approach in ≈100 000 years	
17 26	**New Moon**	
Thu. 28 0	Mercury stationary	
18	**Mars at opposition**	
Fri. 29 1	Mercury 9° S of Moon	
23 46	Algol at minimum	
Sat. 30	Mars at perihelion	
6	Pluto stationary	
Sun. 31	Venus at greatest heliocentric lat. N	
19	Moon at perigee (367 926 km)	

THE SKY FOR 2003 SEPTEMBER

		Mercury	Venus	Mars	Jupiter	Saturn	Uranus	Neptune	Sun
RA	1	11^h37^m	10^h55^m	22^h34^m	10^h13^m	6^h46^m	22^h11^m	20^h54^m	10^h39^m
	11	11^h10^m	11^h41^m	22^h24^m	10^h21^m	6^h49^m	22^h10^m	20^h53^m	11^h15^m
	21	10^h54^m	12^h26^m	22^h17^m	10^h30^m	6^h52^m	22^h09^m	20^h52^m	11^h51^m
Dec	1	$-2°17'$	$+8°28'$	$-16°04'$	$+11°55'$	$+22°16'$	$-12°02'$	$-17°28'$	$+8°31'$
	11	$+1°29'$	$+3°35'$	$-16°29'$	$+11°09'$	$+22°13'$	$-12°11'$	$-17°32'$	$+4°49'$
	21	$+6°33'$	$-1°30'$	$-16°21'$	$+10°24'$	$+22°09'$	$-12°18'$	$-17°35'$	$+0°58'$
Dist	1	0.67	1.72	0.37	6.37	9.53	19.03	29.18	1.009
	11	0.64	1.71	0.39	6.35	9.39	19.07	29.27	1.007
	21	0.79	1.70	0.41	6.30	9.23	19.14	29.38	1.004
Mag	1	1.7	−3.9	−2.9	−1.7	0.2	5.7	7.8	
	11	4.9	−3.9	−2.7	−1.7	0.2	5.7	7.9	
	21	0.9	−3.9	−2.4	−1.7	0.1	5.7	7.9	
Size	1	10.0″	9.7″	25.0″	30.9″	17.5″	3.7″	2.3″	31′41″
	11	10.5″	9.7″	24.1″	31.0″	17.7″	3.7″	2.3″	31′46″
	21	8.5″	9.8″	22.6″	31.3″	18.0″	3.7″	2.3″	31′51″

Moon—On Sep. 1.0 UT, the age of the Moon is 4.3 d. The Sun's selenographic colongitude is 326.86° and increases by 12.2° each day thereafter. The libration in longitude is maximum (east limb exposed) on Sep. 9 (+5°) and minimum (west limb exposed) on Sep. 22 (−6°). The libration in latitude is maximum (north limb exposed) on Sep. 8 (+7°) and minimum (south limb exposed) on Sep. 23 (−7°). Particularly favourable dates for viewing librated lunar limbs are Sep. 9 (9.2°) and Sep. 22 (9.0°). The Moon reaches its greatest northern declination on Sep. 19 (+27°) and its greatest southern declination on Sep. 5 (−27°).

Mercury is in inferior conjunction with the Sun on Sep. 11. It slowly emerges in the eastern morning twilight during the second half of the month, reaching greatest elongation west (18°) on Sep. 27. It is only easily visible during the last week of the month when it both brightens and rises high enough in morning twilight to be observed. The geometry is poor for southern observers; as a result, it can only be glimpsed with difficulty very low in the east before sunrise during the last week of the month.

Venus cannot be observed by northern observers until mid-October; however, for southern observers it begins to slowly emerge in the western evening twilight sky in the second half of the month. This begins a favourable evening apparition of Venus for southern observers. By month's end it sets nearly 1 h after the Sun.

Mars, in Aquarius, is stationary on Sep. 29 and then returns to direct (eastward) motion. It rises in the east-southeast just before sunset and sets in the west-southwest before the beginning of morning twilight. For more favoured southern observers, Mars stands about 40° high in the east at the end of evening twilight and sets in the west-southwest during morning twilight.

Jupiter, in Leo, emerges in the dawn twilight during the month. By month's end, it stands about 10° above the eastern horizon at the beginning of morning twilight. Less favoured southern observers will find Jupiter slowly emerging in the east-northeastern dawn twilight in the second half of the month.

Saturn, in Gemini, rises before midnight and is high in the east before the beginning of morning twilight. For less-favoured southern observers, it rises near 2 a.m. and stands about 25° high in the northeast at the beginning of morning twilight.

Time (UT)			SEPTEMBER EVENTS	Jupiter's Satellites	
d	h	m		West	East
Mon. 1	20	35	Algol at minimum		
Tue. 2					
Wed. 3			Mercury at greatest heliocentric lat. S		
	12	34	**First Quarter**		
Thu. 4	17	23	Algol at minimum		
Fri. 5	21		Pallas stationary		
Sat. 6					
Sun. 7	14	12	Algol at minimum		
	19		Neptune 5° N of Moon		
Mon. 8					
Tue. 9	6		Uranus 5° N of Moon		
	13		**Mars 1.2° S of Moon, Occultation†**		
Wed. 10	11	01	Algol at minimum		
	16	36	**Full Moon** (the *Harvest Moon*)		
Thu. 11	2		Mercury in inferior conjunction		
Fri. 12					
Sat. 13	7	49	Algol at minimum		
Sun. 14					
Mon. 15					
Tue. 16	4	38	Algol at minimum		
	9		Moon at apogee (404 714 km)		
Wed. 17					
Thu. 18	19	03	**Last Quarter**		
Fri. 19	1	27	Algol at minimum		
	13		Mercury stationary		
Sat. 20	3		Saturn 5° S of Moon		
Sun. 21	22	15	Algol at minimum		
Mon. 22			Mercury at ascending node		
Tue. 23	10	47	**Equinox**		
Wed. 24			**Zodiacal Light** vis. in N lat. in E before morning twilight for next two weeks		
	4		Jupiter 4° S of Moon		
	17		Mercury 5° S of Moon		
	19	04	Algol at minimum		
Thu. 25					
Fri. 26	3	09	**New Moon**		
Sat. 27			Mercury at perihelion		
	0		**Mercury greatest elongation W (18°)**		
	15	53	Algol at minimum		
Sun. 28	6		Moon at perigee (362 835 km)		
Mon. 29	14		Mars stationary		
Tue. 30	12	41	Algol at minimum		

†Eastern Siberia, northern China

THE SKY FOR 2003 OCTOBER

		Mercury	Venus	Mars	Jupiter	Saturn	Uranus	Neptune	Sun
RA	1	11^{h}27^m	13^{h}12^m	22^{h}16^m	10^{h}37^m	6^{h}55^m	22^{h}07^m	20^{h}52^m	12^{h}27^m
	11	12^{h}28^m	13^{h}58^m	22^{h}19^m	10^{h}45^m	6^{h}56^m	22^{h}06^m	20^{h}51^m	13^{h}03^m
	21	13^{h}31^m	14^{h}46^m	22^{h}27^m	10^{h}52^m	6^{h}57^m	22^{h}06^m	20^{h}51^m	13^{h}41^m
Dec	1	+5°17′	−6°33′	−15°41′	+9°39′	+22°06′	−12°24′	−17°37′	−2°55′
	11	−0°59′	−11°23′	−14°33′	+8°56′	+22°04′	−12°30′	−17°39′	−6°46′
	21	−8°21′	−15°46′	−13°02′	+8°15′	+22°03′	−12°33′	−17°40′	−10°27′
Dist	1	1.06	1.67	0.45	6.23	9.07	19.23	29.52	1.001
	11	1.29	1.65	0.50	6.14	8.90	19.35	29.67	0.998
	21	1.40	1.62	0.56	6.03	8.74	19.49	29.83	0.996
Mag	1	−0.8	−3.9	−2.1	−1.7	0.1	5.7	7.9	
	11	−1.1	−3.9	−1.8	−1.8	0.1	5.8	7.9	
	21	−1.3	−3.9	−1.5	−1.8	0.0	5.8	7.9	
Size	1	6.3″	10.0″	20.7″	31.7″	18.3″	3.6″	2.3″	31′57″
	11	5.2″	10.1″	18.7″	32.2″	18.7″	3.6″	2.3″	32′02″
	21	4.8″	10.3″	16.8″	32.7″	19.0″	3.6″	2.2″	32′08″

Moon—On Oct. 1.0 UT, the age of the Moon is 4.9 d. The Sun's selenographic colongitude is 332.91° and increases by 12.2° each day thereafter. The libration in longitude is maximum (east limb exposed) on Oct. 5 (+6°) and minimum (west limb exposed) on Oct. 20 (−7°). The libration in latitude is maximum (north limb exposed) on Oct. 5 (+7°) and minimum (south limb exposed) on Oct. 20 (−7°). Particularly favourable dates for viewing librated lunar limbs are Oct. 6 (9.0°) and Oct. 20 (9.4°). The Moon reaches its greatest northern declination on Oct. 17 (+27°) and its greatest southern declinations on Oct. 2 (−27°) and Oct. 29 (−27°).

Mercury remains visible early in the month in the east before sunrise for northern observers. It brightens, but at the same time slowly descends into the morning twilight, becoming lost in the glare of the Sun by about Oct. 12. Mercury is in superior conjunction with the Sun on Oct. 25. Southern observers cannot easily observe Mercury this month.

Venus begins to slowly emerge in the west-southwestern evening twilight sky in the second half of the month; however, by month's end it still sets less than 1 h after the Sun. For more favoured southern observers, Venus is low in the west during evening twilight and at month's end sets about 1.5 h after the Sun.

Mars, in Aquarius, stands about 25° high in the south-southeast at the end of evening twilight and sets in the west-southwest near 2 a.m. For more favoured southern observers, Mars stands more than 65° high in the northeast at the end of evening twilight and sets in the west-southwest before the beginning of morning twilight.

Jupiter, in Leo, improves in visibility this month in the predawn sky. At midmonth Jupiter rises nearly 4 h before the Sun and stands about 20° above the eastern horizon at the beginning of morning twilight. Less favoured southern observers will find Jupiter only about 5° high in the east-northeast at the beginning of twilight.

Saturn, in Orion, is stationary on Oct. 26 and begins retrograde (westward) motion. It rises in the east-northeast in late evening for northern observers and near midnight for southern observers and is visible for the remainder of the night.

| Time (UT) | | | OCTOBER EVENTS | Jupiter's Satellites | |
| d | h | m | | West | East |

			OCTOBER EVENTS	
Wed.	1			
Thu.	2	19 09	**First Quarter**	
Fri.	3	9 30	Algol at minimum	
		22	Venus 3° N of Spica	
Sun.	5	0	Neptune 5° N of Moon	
Mon.	6	6 19	Algol at minimum	
		10	Uranus 5° N of Moon	
		15	**Mars 1.1° N of Moon, Occultation†**	
Tue.	7		Mercury at greatest heliocentric lat. N	
Wed.	8			
Thu.	9	3 08	Algol at minimum	
		9	Draconid meteors peak	
Fri.	10	7 27	**Full Moon** (the *Hunter's Moon*)	
Sat.	11	23 56	Algol at minimum	
Mon.	13	15	Pallas at opposition	
Tue.	14	2	Moon at apogee (405 692 km)	
		20 45	Algol at minimum	
Wed.	15	18 25	Double satellite transit on Jupiter	
Thu.	16			
Fri.	17	13	Saturn 5° S of Moon	
		17 34	Algol at minimum	
Sat.	18	12 31	**Last Quarter**	
Sun.	19			
Mon.	20	14 23	Algol at minimum	
Tue.	21	23	Jupiter 4° S of Moon	
Wed.	22	9	Orionid meteors peak	
		19 29	**Double shadow transit on Jupiter**	
Thu.	23	0	Neptune stationary	
		11 12	Algol at minimum	
Fri.	24		**Zodiacal Light** vis. in N lat. in E before morning twilight for next two weeks	
Sat.	25	10	Mercury in superior conjunction	
		12 50	**New Moon**	
Sun.	26		Venus at descending node	
		0	Saturn stationary	
		2	**Daylight Saving Time ends**	
		8 00	Algol at minimum	
		12	Moon at perigee (358 547 km) Large tides	
		20	**Venus 0.08° N of Moon, Occultation‡**	
Tue.	28			
Wed.	29	4 49	Algol at minimum	
		21 23	**Double shadow transit on Jupiter**	
		22 23	Double satellite transit on Jupiter	
Thu.	30		Mercury at descending node	
Fri.	31			

†Tasmania, New Zealand, most of Antarctica
‡Hawaiian Islands, central and most of southern S. America

THE SKY FOR 2003 NOVEMBER

		Mercury	Venus	Mars	Jupiter	Saturn	Uranus	Neptune	Sun
RA	1	14^{h}39^m	15^{h}41^m	22^{h}39^m	10^{h}59^m	6^{h}57^m	22^{h}05^m	20^{h}51^m	14^{h}23^m
	11	15^{h}42^m	16^{h}33^m	22^{h}54^m	11^{h}05^m	6^{h}56^m	22^{h}05^m	20^{h}52^m	15^{h}03^m
	21	16^{h}45^m	17^{h}27^m	23^{h}11^m	11^{h}10^m	6^{h}54^m	22^{h}05^m	20^{h}52^m	15^{h}44^m
Dec	1	−15°38′	−19°50′	−11°01′	+7°33′	+22°04′	−12°35′	−17°39′	−14°13′
	11	−20°52′	−22°36′	−8°57′	+6°59′	+22°05′	−12°35′	−17°38′	−17°14′
	21	−24°24′	−24°16′	−6°41′	+6°30′	+22°08′	−12°34′	−17°36′	−19°46′
Dist	1	1.44	1.58	0.63	5.90	8.57	19.66	30.02	0.993
	11	1.41	1.55	0.70	5.76	8.43	19.83	30.19	0.990
	21	1.33	1.50	0.77	5.61	8.30	20.00	30.36	0.988
Mag	1	−1.0	−3.9	−1.2	−1.8	−0.1	5.8	7.9	
	11	−0.6	−3.9	−0.9	−1.9	−0.1	5.8	7.9	
	21	−0.5	−3.9	−0.7	−2.0	−0.2	5.8	7.9	
Size	1	4.7″	10.5″	14.9″	33.4″	19.4″	3.6″	2.2″	32′13″
	11	4.8″	10.8″	13.5″	34.2″	19.7″	3.5″	2.2″	32′18″
	21	5.1″	11.1″	12.2″	35.1″	20.0″	3.5″	2.2″	32′23″

Moon—On Nov. 1.0 UT, the age of the Moon is 6.5 d. The Sun's selenographic colongitude is 350.66° and increases by 12.2° each day thereafter. The libration in longitude is maximum (east limb exposed) on Nov. 2 (+7°) and on Nov. 30 (+8°) and minimum (west limb exposed) on Nov. 17 (−8°). The libration in latitude is maximum (north limb exposed) on Nov. 2 (+7°) and on Nov. 29 (+7°) and minimum (south limb exposed) on Nov. 16 (−7°). Particularly favourable dates for viewing librated lunar limbs are Nov. 2 (9.2°), Nov. 17 (10.5°), and Nov. 30 (11.1°). The Moon reaches its greatest northern declination on Nov. 13 (+27°) and its greatest southern declination on Nov. 26 (−27°). There is a **total lunar eclipse** on Nov. 8–9 that favours observers in Europe, Western Africa, and eastern North and South America. Part or all of the umbral phases are visible from most major land masses on Earth (see pp. 136–137 in ECLIPSES DURING 2003), There is a **total solar eclipse** on Nov. 23–24 visible only from Antarctica and the neighbouring southern Indian Ocean. Partial phases are visible from most of Australia and southern New Zealand (see p. 137 in ECLIPSES DURING 2003). On Nov. 23 the Moon reaches its closest perigee distance of the year (356 811 km). With a new Moon occurring at nearly the same time, extra large tides will occur (see the section TIDES AND THE EARTH–MOON SYSTEM on pp. 173–177).

Mercury is not easily visible this month by northern observers; however, a favourable evening apparition for southern observers begins near midmonth when it both brightens and rises high enough in the west-southwest during morning twilight to be observed. By month's end it sets about 1.5 h after the Sun.

Venus continues to improve its visibility in the southwestern evening twilight this month. At month's end it sets more than 1.5 h after the Sun, but due to the unfavourable tipping of the ecliptic for northern observers, it remains embedded in twilight. For more favoured southern observers, at month's end Venus sets more than 2 h after the Sun and stands about 5° high in the west-southwest at the end of evening twilight.

Mars, in Aquarius, stands about 35° high in the south-southeast at the end of evening twilight and sets in the west-southwest near 1 a.m. For more favoured southern observers, Mars stands more than 65° high near the meridian soon after the end of evening twilight and sets in the west before 2 a.m.

Jupiter, in Leo, rises near 1 a.m. in the east and stands about 40° high in the southeast at the beginning of morning twilight. For southern observers, Jupiter rises by 2 a.m. and stands about 20° high in the east-northeast at the beginning of morning twilight.

Saturn, in Gemini, rises in the east-northeast in early evening for northern observers and in late evening for southern observers and is visible for the remainder of the night.

Time (UT)			NOVEMBER EVENTS	Jupiter's Satellites	
d	h	m		West	East

	d	h	m	Event	
Sat.	1	1	38	Algol at minimum	
		4	25	**First Quarter**	
		6		Neptune 5° N of Moon	
Sun.	2	15		Uranus 5° N of Moon	
Mon.	3	9		Mars 3° N of Moon	
		22	27	Algol at minimum	
Tue.	4	22		S. Taurid meteors peak	
Wed.	5				
Thu.	6	0	43	**Double shadow transit on Jupiter**	
		19	16	Algol at minimum	
Fri.	7				
Sat.	8	19		Uranus stationary	
Sun.	9	1	13	**Full Moon, total lunar eclipse** (p. 136)	
		16	05	Algol at minimum	
Mon.	10			Mercury at aphelion	
		7		Venus 4° N of Antares	
		12		Moon at apogee (406 301 km)	
Tue.	11				
Wed.	12	12	54	Algol at minimum	
Thu.	13			Pallas at opposition	
		19		Saturn 5° S of Moon	
		20		N. Taurid meteors peak	
Fri.	14				
Sat.	15	9	43	Algol at minimum	
Mon.	17	4	15	**Last Quarter**	
Tue.	18	3		Leonid meteors peak	
		6	32	Algol at minimum	
		12		Mercury 3° N of Antares	
		16		Jupiter 4° S of Moon	
Thu.	20				
Fri.	21	3	21	Algol at minimum	
Sat.	22				
Sun.	23	22	59	**New Moon, total solar eclipse** (p. 137)	
Sun.	23	23		Moon at perigee **(356 811 km)**	
		23		**Large tides**	
Mon.	24	0	10	Algol at minimum	
Tue.	25	3		**Mercury 0.3° N of Moon, Occultation†**	
		18		**Venus 2° N of Moon**	
Wed.	26	9		Ceres stationary	
		20	59	Algol at minimum	
Thu.	27				
Fri.	28	14		Neptune 5° N of Moon	
Sat.	29	17	48	Algol at minimum	
		22		Uranus 5° N of Moon	
Sun.	30			Mercury at greatest heliocentric lat. S	
				Venus at aphelion	
		17	16	**First Quarter**	

†S. Indian Ocean, most of Indonesia, Australia except N and NE, New Zealand, Easter Island

THE SKY FOR 2003 DECEMBER

		Mercury	Venus	Mars	Jupiter	Saturn	Uranus	Neptune	Sun
RA	1	17ʰ48ᵐ	18ʰ21ᵐ	23ʰ29ᵐ	11ʰ14ᵐ	6ʰ52ᵐ	22ʰ06ᵐ	20ʰ53ᵐ	16ʰ26ᵐ
	11	18ʰ41ᵐ	19ʰ16ᵐ	23ʰ49ᵐ	11ʰ17ᵐ	6ʰ49ᵐ	22ʰ07ᵐ	20ʰ54ᵐ	17ʰ10ᵐ
	21	18ʰ50ᵐ	20ʰ09ᵐ	0ʰ10ᵐ	11ʰ20ᵐ	6ʰ46ᵐ	22ʰ08ᵐ	20ʰ55ᵐ	17ʰ54ᵐ
Dec	1	−25°50′	−24°45′	−4°17′	+6°06′	+22°11′	−12°30′	−17°33′	−21°42′
	11	−24°59′	−23°58′	−1°46′	+5°47′	+22°15′	−12°25′	−17°29′	−22°56′
	21	−22°31′	−22°00′	+0°48′	+5°36′	+22°20′	−12°18′	−17°25′	−23°26′
Dist	1	1.18	1.46	0.85	5.46	8.20	20.17	30.52	0.986
	11	0.97	1.41	0.93	5.30	8.12	20.34	30.66	0.985
	21	0.74	1.36	1.01	5.14	8.07	20.50	30.79	0.984
Mag	1	−0.5	−3.9	−0.4	−2.0	−0.2	5.8	7.9	
	11	−0.4	−3.9	−0.2	−2.1	−0.3	5.9	8.0	
	21	1.5	−4.0	0.0	−2.2	−0.4	5.9	8.0	
Size	1	5.7″	11.4″	11.0″	36.1″	20.3″	3.5″	2.2″	32′26″
	11	6.9″	11.8″	10.1″	37.1″	20.5″	3.4″	2.2″	32′29″
	21	9.1″	12.2″	9.2″	38.3″	20.6″	3.4″	2.2″	32′31″

Moon—On Dec. 1.0 UT, the age of the Moon is 7.0 d. The Sun's selenographic colongitude is 355.76° and increases by 12.2° each day thereafter. The libration in longitude is maximum (east limb exposed) on Dec. 28 (+8°) and minimum (west limb exposed) on Dec. 15 (−7°). The libration in latitude is maximum (north limb exposed) on Dec. 26 (+7°) and minimum (south limb exposed) on Dec. 14 (−7°). Particularly favourable dates for viewing librated lunar limbs are Dec. 14 (9.5°) and Dec. 27 (10.5°). The Moon reaches its greatest northern declination on Dec. 10 (+27°) and its greatest southern declination on Dec. 23 (−27°).

Mercury reaches greatest elongation east (21°) on Dec. 9, continuing a favourable evening apparition for southern observers. It is visible low in the west-southwest after sunset until about Dec. 20 when it has both faded and descended into the evening twilight. Northern observers can only see Mercury during the first half of the month very low in the southwest after sunset.

Venus sets more than 2 h after the Sun and is visible low in the southwest during evening twilight. For more favoured southern observers, Venus sets more than 2 h after the Sun and stands more than 5° high in the west-southwest at the end of evening twilight.

Mars moves from Aquarius to Pisces early in the month. It stands more than 40° high near the meridian soon after the end of evening twilight and sets in the west soon after midnight. Southern observers will find Mars high in the northwest at the end of evening twilight and setting in the west near 1 a.m.

Jupiter, in Leo, rises before midnight in the east and stands about 50° high near the meridian at the beginning of morning twilight. For southern observers, Jupiter rises near midnight in the east and stands about 40° high in the northeast at the beginning of morning twilight.

Saturn, in Gemini, rises during evening twilight and is visible for the remainder of the night for both northern and southern observers. It is at opposition on Dec. 31.

Time (UT)			DECEMBER EVENTS	Jupiter's Satellites	
d	h	m		West	East
Mon. 1	16		Mars 4° N of Moon		
Tue. 2	13	35	Double satellite transit on Jupiter		
	14	37	Algol at minimum		
Wed. 3					
Thu. 4					
Fri. 5	11	26	Algol at minimum		
	19		Juno in conjunction with Sun		
Sat. 6					
Sun. 7	12		Moon at apogee (406 279 km)		
Mon. 8	8	15	Algol at minimum		
	19		Pallas stationary		
	20	37	**Full Moon**		
Tue. 9	6		**Mercury greatest elongation E (21°)**		
Wed. 10	22		Saturn 5° S of Moon		
Thu. 11	5	04	Algol at minimum		
Fri. 12	1		Ceres 1.1° N of Moon, Occultation†		
	5		Pluto in conjunction with Sun		
Sun. 14	1	53	Algol at minimum		
	4		**Geminid meteors peak**		
Tue. 16	4		Jupiter 4° S of Moon		
	17	42	**Last Quarter**		
	22	43	Algol at minimum		
Wed. 17	13		Mercury stationary		
Fri. 19			Mercury at ascending node		
	5	29	Double satellite transit on Jupiter		
	19	32	Algol at minimum		
Mon. 22			Venus at greatest heliocentric lat. S		
	7	04	**Solstice**		
	12		Moon at perigee (358 338 km)		
			Large tides		
	16	21	Algol at minimum		
Tue. 23	0		Ursid meteors peak		
	9	43	**New Moon**		
Wed. 24			Mercury at perihelion		
	10		Vesta in conjunction with Sun		
Thu. 25	13	10	Algol at minimum		
	16		Venus 3° N of Moon		
Fri. 26	1		Neptune 5° N of Moon		
Sat. 27	1		Mercury in inferior conjunction		
	8		Uranus 5° N of Moon		
Sun. 28	9	59	Algol at minimum		
Mon. 29			Mars at ascending node		
Tue. 30	7		Mars 4° N of Moon		
	7		Venus 1.9° S of Neptune		
	10	03	**First Quarter**		
Wed. 31	6	49	Algol at minimum		
	21		**Saturn at opposition**		

†South-eastern South Atlantic Ocean

THE SUN

EPHEMERIS FOR THE SUN

Sundial Correction

The **Greenwich Transit** time in the table at the right may be used to calculate the sundial correction at the observer's position. For example, to find the correction at Winnipeg on 2003 Aug. 16: At Greenwich the Sun transits at 12:04:55 on Aug. 13 and at 12:04:08 on Aug. 17. Thus, to the nearest minute, on Aug. 16 at both Greenwich and Winnipeg the Sun will transit at 12:04 local mean solar time (LMT), or 12:33 CST (Central Standard Time) since Winnipeg has a longitude correction of +29 min (see the 3rd paragraph on p. 107). Thus a 4-minute correction must be added to the reading of a simple sundial to obtain LMT, and an additional 29 minutes must be added to obtain CST.

A figure accurate to a second or two can be obtained by interpolating for longitude. The interpolated transit time at Greenwich for Aug. 16 is 12:04:20, the daily change in time being –11.8 s. Adjusting this for the longitude of Winnipeg: 12 h 4 min 20 s – (11.8 s × 6 h 29 min ÷ 24 h) = 12 h 4 min 17 s. Thus the sundial correction is 4 min 17 s. To find the standard time of the Sun's transit to the nearest second or two, the observer's longitude must be known to 10″ or better. For example, suppose an observer in Winnipeg is at longitude 97°13′50″W, or 6 h 28 min 55 s W of Greenwich. The time of transit will be 12:04:17 + 28 min 55 s = 12:33:12 CST (13:33:12 CDT).

Orientation of the Sun

The table at the right gives three angles that specify the orientation of the Sun.

P is the position angle of the axis of rotation, measured eastward in the observer's sky from the north point on the disk. Note that P varies between +26° (solar north pole tilted eastward) and –26° (tilted westward) during the year. This tilt is associated mainly with the inclination of the ecliptic in the observer's sky, with a smaller contribution from the Sun's 7.2° inclination to the ecliptic (the longitude of the ascending node of the solar equator on the ecliptic is 76°).

B_0 is the heliographic latitude of the centre of the disk, and is the result of the Sun's 7.2° inclination to the ecliptic. Note that positive values of B_0 correspond to the solar equator passing south of the centre of the disk, with the solar north pole being tipped toward the observer.

L_0 is the heliographic longitude of the centre of the disk measured from Carrington's solar prime meridian in the direction of rotation. L_0 decreases about 13° per day. The dates during the year when $L_0 = 0°$ are given in the table below. The rotation period of the Sun depends upon heliographic latitude. The synodic and sidereal periods of rotation at the solar equator are 27.275 days and 25.38 days, respectively.

Commencement (UT) of Numbered Synodic Solar Rotations

No*	Commences	No	Commences	No	Commences	No	Commences
1998	'02 Dec. 27.61	2002	Apr. 15.90	2006	Aug. 2.76	2010	Nov. 19.85
1999	'03 Jan. 23.95	2003	May 13.14	2007	Aug. 29.99	2011	Dec. 17.17
2000	Feb. 20.29	2004	Jun. 9.35	2008	Sep. 26.26	2012	'04 Jan. 13.50
2001	Mar. 19.61	2005	Jul. 6.55	2009	Oct. 23.55		

*Based on R.C. Carrington's Greenwich photoheliocentric series in which rotation number 1 commenced 1853 November 9.

EPHEMERIS FOR THE SUN, 2003

Date 0h UT	Greenwich Apparent RA (2003)	Dec	Transit UT	Orientation P	B0	L0	Date 0h UT	Greenwich Apparent RA (2003)	Dec	Transit UT	Orientation P	B0	L0
Jan. 1	18 44.1	−23 03	12:03:25	+2.3	−3.0	302.2	Jul. 4	6 50.6	+22 56	12:04:20	−1.5	+3.2	33.7
5	19 01.7	−22 41	12:05:16	+0.3	−3.4	249.5	8	7 07.1	+22 33	12:05:00	+0.3	+3.6	340.8
9	19 19.3	−22 11	12:07:00	−1.6	−3.9	196.8	12	7 23.4	+22 03	12:05:34	+2.1	+4.0	287.8
13	19 36.6	−21 35	12:08:35	−3.5	−4.3	144.1	16	7 39.6	+21 28	12:06:01	+3.9	+4.4	234.9
17	19 53.8	−20 52	12:10:00	−5.4	−4.7	91.5	20	7 55.7	+20 47	12:06:19	+5.6	+4.8	182.0
21	20 10.9	−20 02	12:11:13	−7.3	−5.1	38.8	24	8 11.7	+19 60	12:06:29	+7.3	+5.1	129.1
25	20 27.7	−19 07	12:12:15	−9.0	−5.5	346.1	28	8 27.5	+19 08	12:06:29	+9.0	+5.4	76.1
29	20 44.3	−18 06	12:13:04	−10.8	−5.8	293.5							
Feb. 2	21 00.7	−17 00	12:13:40	−12.4	−6.1	240.8	Aug. 1	8 43.1	+18 10	12:06:20	+10.6	+5.8	23.2
6	21 16.9	−15 49	12:14:04	−14.0	−6.3	188.1	5	8 58.6	+17 09	12:06:02	+12.2	+6.0	330.3
10	21 32.9	−14 33	12:14:14	−15.5	−6.6	135.5	9	9 13.9	+16 02	12:05:33	+13.7	+6.3	277.4
14	21 48.6	−13 14	12:14:12	−16.9	−6.8	82.8	13	9 29.1	+14 52	12:04:55	+15.2	+6.5	224.6
18	22 04.2	−11 51	12:13:57	−18.3	−6.9	30.1	17	9 44.1	+13 37	12:04:08	+16.5	+6.7	171.7
22	22 19.5	−10 26	12:13:32	−19.5	−7.1	337.4	21	9 58.9	+12 20	12:03:13	+17.8	+6.9	118.8
26	22 34.8	−8 57	12:12:57	−20.6	−7.2	284.8	25	10 13.7	+10 59	12:02:11	+19.0	+7.0	66.0
							29	10 28.3	+9 35	12:01:02	+20.2	+7.1	13.1
Mar. 2	22 49.8	−7 27	12:12:13	−21.7	−7.2	232.1	Sep. 2	10 42.9	+8 09	11:59:48	+21.2	+7.2	320.3
6	23 04.7	−5 55	12:11:22	−22.6	−7.3	179.4	6	10 57.3	+6 41	11:58:29	+22.2	+7.2	267.4
10	23 19.5	−4 21	12:10:23	−23.5	−7.2	126.7	10	11 11.7	+5 11	11:57:06	+23.0	+7.3	214.6
14	23 34.3	−2 47	12:09:19	−24.2	−7.2	74.0	14	11 26.1	+3 39	11:55:41	+23.8	+7.2	161.8
18	23 48.9	−1 12	12:08:11	−24.8	−7.1	21.2	18	11 40.4	+2 07	11:54:15	+24.5	+7.2	109.0
22	0 03.5	+0 23	12:07:00	−25.3	−7.0	328.5	22	11 54.8	+0 34	11:52:50	+25.1	+7.1	56.2
26	0 18.1	+1 57	12:05:47	−25.8	−6.9	275.8	26	12 09.2	−1 00	11:51:27	+25.5	+6.9	3.4
30	0 32.6	+3 31	12:04:35	−26.0	−6.7	223.0	30	12 23.6	−2 33	11:50:07	+25.9	+6.8	310.6
Apr. 3	0 47.2	+5 04	12:03:24	−26.2	−6.5	170.2	Oct. 4	12 38.1	−4 06	11:48:50	+26.1	+6.6	257.8
7	1 01.8	+6 35	12:02:15	−26.3	−6.2	117.5	8	12 52.7	−5 38	11:47:39	+26.3	+6.4	205.0
11	1 16.5	+8 05	12:01:09	−26.2	−5.9	64.7	12	13 07.3	−7 09	11:46:35	+26.3	+6.1	152.3
15	1 31.2	+9 32	12:00:08	−26.1	−5.6	11.9	16	13 22.1	−8 39	11:45:38	+26.2	+5.8	99.5
19	1 46.0	+10 57	11:59:12	−25.8	−5.3	319.0	20	13 37.1	−10 06	11:44:51	+26.0	+5.5	46.7
23	2 01.0	+12 19	11:58:23	−25.4	−5.0	266.2	24	13 52.3	−11 32	11:44:15	+25.6	+5.2	354.0
27	2 16.0	+13 38	11:57:41	−24.9	−4.6	213.4	28	14 07.6	−12 54	11:43:50	+25.2	+4.8	301.2
May 1	2 31.2	+14 53	11:57:08	−24.2	−4.2	160.5	Nov. 1	14 23.1	−14 13	11:43:36	+24.6	+4.4	248.5
5	2 46.6	+16 04	11:56:43	−23.5	−3.8	107.6	5	14 38.8	−15 29	11:43:35	+23.9	+4.0	195.8
9	3 02.1	+17 11	11:56:27	−22.6	−3.4	54.8	9	14 54.8	−16 40	11:43:47	+23.0	+3.6	143.0
13	3 17.7	+18 14	11:56:20	−21.6	−2.9	1.9	13	15 10.9	−17 47	11:44:13	+22.1	+3.1	90.3
17	3 33.5	+19 11	11:56:21	−20.5	−2.5	309.0	17	15 27.3	−18 49	11:44:53	+21.0	+2.7	37.5
21	3 49.4	+20 03	11:56:32	−19.4	−2.0	256.0	21	15 44.0	−19 46	11:45:46	+19.8	+2.2	344.8
25	4 05.5	+20 50	11:56:52	−18.1	−1.6	203.1	25	16 00.8	−20 37	11:46:52	+18.5	+1.7	292.1
29	4 21.7	+21 31	11:57:19	−16.7	−1.1	150.2	29	16 17.9	−21 22	11:48:10	+17.0	+1.2	239.4
Jun. 2	4 38.0	+22 06	11:57:54	−15.2	−0.6	97.3	Dec. 3	16 35.1	−22 00	11:49:39	+15.5	+0.7	186.7
6	4 54.5	+22 35	11:58:35	−13.7	−0.1	44.3	7	16 52.5	−22 32	11:51:17	+13.9	+0.2	133.9
10	5 11.0	+22 58	11:59:21	−12.1	+0.4	351.4	11	17 10.0	−22 57	11:53:04	+12.2	−0.3	81.2
14	5 27.6	+23 14	12:00:10	−10.4	+0.9	298.5	15	17 27.7	−23 14	11:54:56	+10.4	−0.9	28.5
18	5 44.2	+23 23	12:01:01	−8.7	+1.3	245.5	19	17 45.4	−23 24	11:56:53	+8.6	−1.4	335.8
22	6 00.8	+23 26	12:01:53	−6.9	+1.8	192.6	23	18 03.1	−23 26	11:58:53	+6.7	−1.9	283.1
26	6 17.5	+23 23	12:02:45	−5.2	+2.3	139.6	27	18 20.9	−23 21	12:00:52	+4.8	−2.4	230.5
30	6 34.1	+23 13	12:03:34	−3.4	+2.7	86.7	31	18 38.6	−23 09	12:02:49	+2.9	−2.8	177.8

SOLAR ACTIVITY
By Ken Tapping

The maximum of Solar Activity Cycle 23* is now definitely past, and the average level of activity is falling. However, 2001 brought a surprise or two. Activity had fallen to less than 150 solar flux units (sfu; see p. 106), when there was a sudden resurgence that took us higher than the maximum of the cycle, peaking at around 240 sfu and remaining above ≈210 sfu for more than a month. Although similar events have occurred in previous cycles, and a resurgence of activity during the decline after the maximum occurs in almost every cycle, none have occurred so soon after the maximum and stood out so starkly from the general rhythm of solar activity. If we ignore that surprising resurgence of activity, the maximum of Cycle 23 was the second lowest since 1946, when Canada started monitoring solar activity using the 10.7-cm solar flux. It's clear that we still have a lot to learn about causes of solar activity.

The figure shows solar activity as represented by the adjusted 10.7-cm solar microwave flux activity index (see p. 106) from 1947 to the present. The plotted values are averaged values of the index over each solar (≈27-day) rotation. The ≈11-year activity cycle is clearly evident, as is the dramatic resurgence of activity during 2001.

The term *solar activity* comprises all the Sun's variable aspects, such as the occurrence of sunspots and active regions, the variable emissions in soft X-rays, spectral lines such as CaII K and MgII K, emissions at radio wavelengths, and flares, a particularly dramatic form of solar activity. The Sun's brightness is also variable; measurements made using space-borne radiometers show that as the level of solar activity increases, the Sun becomes slightly brighter. All manifestations of solar activity are driven by an underlying engine: the varying spatial and temporal distribution of magnetic flux in the photosphere, chromosphere, and corona.

Deep below the photosphere the density is high enough for the solar material to drag the magnetic fields; differential rotation and convection give rise to electrical currents, which in turn produce magnetic fields. These fields form complex networks of twisted "magnetic flux ropes," containing enormous amounts of stored energy. The penetration of sections of these flux ropes through the photosphere and into the chromosphere and corona gives rise to the many observed forms of solar activity. Above the photosphere, however, the density is much lower, and the distribution and movement of the magnetic fields trap and confine the ionized gas of the solar atmosphere, supporting loops and filaments and forming the well-known and diverse photospheric, chromospheric, and coronal structures.

Most activity occurs in active regions: bipolar magnetic structures form when magnetic loops emerge through the photosphere into the overlying chromosphere and corona. The formation of a new region—an emerging flux region—is heralded by the

*The numbering system for solar activity cycles was started by Rudolph Wolf, who arbitrarily designated the activity maximum of 1750 as that of Cycle 1.

formation of small pores (≈1000 km across). These pores coalesce into a patch a few thousand kilometres across and eventually spread to form a patch of magnetic flux that may exceed 50 000 km in length. The average magnetic field strength in the patch is ≈0.01 T (100 gauss). The emergence of these magnetic fields modifies the spatial and density structure of the chromosphere, giving rise to enhanced emission in the calcium and magnesium II K spectral lines. These bright patches (called plage), which stand out prominently in filtergrams, are the most conspicuous aspect of active regions.

Concentrations of magnetic flux having strengths of the order of 0.1 T locally impede the transfer of energy from deeper within the Sun; therefore, the concentrations are ≈3000 K cooler than the surrounding (6000 K) photosphere. Although actually quite hot and shining quite brightly, in contrast with their hotter surroundings these flux concentrations appear as dark spots: sunspots. The first direct manifestation of solar activity to be observed, sunspots are present in most active regions. As a region grows, one or more large spots form at the leading end, and a scattering of smaller ones form at the trailing end.

Repeated episodes of magnetic flux emergence occur during the growth phase of the active region. The size the region reaches is directly related to how much magnetic flux it accumulates. As flux emergence slows and stops, so does the growth of the region. Fragmentation sets in, the spots disappear, and the remains are left as a large area of magnetic flux arranged in a network pattern, blending in slowly with the remains of other decayed active regions.

The redistribution of magnetic flux during the evolution of active regions leads to distortion and stressing of magnetic structures in the chromosphere and corona. Energy from below the photosphere is propagated into the chromospheric and coronal magnetic fields through twisting and motions of "footpoints," which are photospheric anchors of chromospheric or coronal magnetic loops. This is stored as magnetic energy in stressed loops and flux tubes. Evolution of the host active region requires that this energy be dissipated. This occurs noncatastrophically through slow reconnection and heating or explosively in mass ejections and flares.

The organization of the subphotospheric magnetic fields gives rise to a consistent pattern in the magnetic configuration of active regions. Each region is magnetically bipolar, with the bipoles arranged east–west on the disk. All bipoles lying in the same hemisphere are arranged with the same magnetic polarity leading (facing in the direction in which the region appears to move as it is carried across the disk by solar rotation—westward in the observer's sky). In the other hemisphere the leading and following magnetic polarities are reversed.

Exceptions do occur. Regions are sometimes formed that have a magnetic orientation perpendicular to or even the reverse of the norm for that hemisphere. Such regions usually try to move into the conventional orientation but are impeded by the magnetic linkages they have formed with their surroundings. These regions tend to produce flares as potential energy builds up in their magnetic structures and is subsequently released catastrophically.

The "conventional" magnetic configurations for active regions reverse on alternate activity cycles. For example, during Cycle 22, active regions in the northern solar hemisphere were oriented with their "negative" (i.e. south-seeking) magnetic polarity ends leading and "positive" (north-seeking) ends following, with the reverse situation in the southern hemisphere. In Cycle 23 this arrangement is reversed. A *magnetic* activity cycle, which is probably a more realistic description of the rhythms of solar activity, is equal to two of Wolf's activity cycles and takes about 22 years to complete.

Active regions are not isolated phenomena; they occur in complexes, comprising several active regions at various stages of development, together with the network elements remaining from decayed regions. This localization of activity gives rise to a rotational modulation of the 10.7-cm flux as active region clusters are carried across the disk and disappear around the west limb. To smooth out this modulation in long-term studies of solar activity, the data are averaged over solar rotations rather than by month. Active regions can persist for one or more solar rotations and the complexes for a dozen or so.

The large-scale organization of solar magnetic activity is also apparent in the spatial distribution of active regions during the solar cycle. The first activity of the new cycle is marked by the formation of active regions at high latitudes. As activity builds toward the maximum of the cycle, the number of active regions increases, and they tend to form at lower latitudes. As the activity wanes toward the next minimum, the number of regions decreases, but the average latitude continues to decrease until the last activity of the cycle is located near the equator. Then, as the new cycle starts, new active regions form at high latitudes.

The Solar Wind and Aurorae: The solar atmosphere is not stable; it is constantly flowing outward as a stream of particles and magnetic fields, the *solar wind.* The flow is strongest where the magnetic loops are very large and impose the least drag on the outwardly flowing particles. Because of their lower coronal densities, these regions produce a lower flux of X-rays and appear as dark patches in X-ray images, called coronal holes. The solar wind is not homogeneous or steady; its speed, density, and direction can change according to the positions of coronal holes and the nature of current solar activity.

The flow of the solar wind past Earth produces profound changes in Earth's magnetic field. The pressure of the solar wind pushes Earth's magnetic field out of its dipole shape into a long teardrop. The magnetic geometry in this tail makes it the site of many plasma instabilities. The flow of the solar wind over the interface between it and Earth's magnetic field (the magnetopause) excites many types of waves, which move along Earth's magnetic field lines and which can be detected on the ground at high magnetic latitudes. Increases in the density or velocity of the solar wind change the pressure equilibrium between the solar wind and the magnetosphere, producing fluctuations in the strength and direction of the magnetic field lines at ground level. If the fluctuations are strong enough, the events, called magnetic storms and substorms, can disrupt any human activity that involves connected metal networks covering large geographical areas, especially at high magnetic latitudes.

Complex interactions between the solar wind and Earth's magnetic field lead to an accumulation of trapped particles in the magnetosphere. During magnetic storms, instabilities and waves excited in the magnetosphere by the solar wind accelerate some of the trapped particles downward along Earth's magnetic field into increasingly dense atmosphere, where they collide with the atmospheric constituents, exciting them with sufficient energy to produce light. These displays are called *aurora borealis* and *aurora australis,* the northern and southern lights, respectively. Views from space show that aurorae fall in a rough circle (the auroral oval), centred around the magnetic pole, that is, in a definite band of magnetic latitudes. As activity increases, the auroral oval expands, covering lower and lower magnetic latitudes. It also becomes increasingly distorted. During the period of very high activity in March 1989, auroral displays were seen as far south as the Caribbean.

Aurorae occur in many forms and can be steady, moving, or rapidly pulsating, depending upon the nature of the particle streams causing them. Aurorae can appear green or red, although if they are faint, the eye cannot respond in colour and they appear grey. The greenish colour is due to spectral lines from oxygen (558 nm) and a range of lines from nitrogen covering the band 391 nm to 470 nm. Under highly disturbed conditions, red spectral line emissions at 630 nm and 636 nm and in a series of bands between

(text continued on p. 106)

AURORAL FORMS

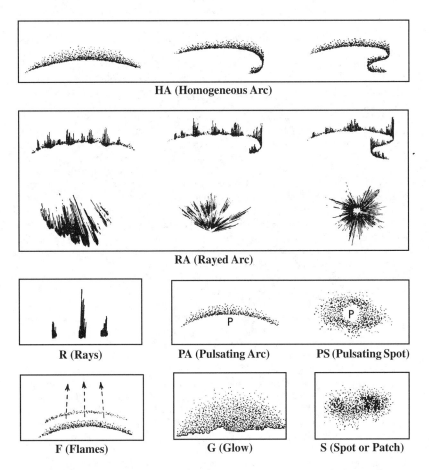

The above sketches illustrate standard auroral forms. This simplified classification was devised for visual observers during the International Geophysical Year over four decades ago (1957–58). Although there is great variety in auroral patterns, the sketches emphasize fundamental features and minimize variations that depend on the location of the observer. The light of the aurora is emitted by the upper fringes of Earth's atmosphere (heights of 100 to 400 km) as it is bombarded by electrons of the solar wind (solar wind protons contribute a smaller amount of energy). The modification of the trajectories of these particles by Earth's magnetic field restricts activity to high latitudes, producing the "aurora borealis" in the Northern Hemisphere and the "aurora australis" in the Southern Hemisphere. The wavelengths of four atmospheric molecular and atomic emission lines that can contribute strongly to auroral light are included in the list on p. 32. Whether aurorae appear coloured depends on their luminance—light that is too faint will not activate colour vision and appears white. When the luminance is sufficiently great, the relative contributions of blue, green, and red emission lines can result in a variety of auroral hues.

650 nm and 680 nm can also be seen. The green emissions are produced at a height of about 110 km; the red 630-nm and 636-nm emissions, due to atomic oxygen, originate at heights between 200 km and 400 km; the 650-nm to 680-nm emissions are produced at about 90 km.

The Impact and Measurement of Solar Activity: Solar activity has had profound effects upon Earth extending as far back in time as we have been able to look. The solar activity cycle is reflected in the growth rates of trees (determined from the study of tree rings) in recently living timber, wood from medieval buildings, and fossilized trees; it is also evident in the changes in the thickness of annual sedimentary deposits in lakes that dry up in summer.

There is extensive evidence of the dramatic effects solar activity has upon our activities. Magnetic storms due to solar activity induce currents in communications and power transmission systems having long distance wires, disrupting their operation for hours. The power blackouts in Quebec and Scandinavia produced by a large flare on 1989 March 10 are a particularly outstanding example. Railway signalling systems can also be affected. Increased X-ray emissions from flares cause enhanced ionization of Earth's atmosphere at D region heights (about 90 km), producing blackouts of short-wave communications.

Solar activity heats the upper atmosphere, causing it to expand further into space, increasing the drag experienced by artificial satellites in low orbits. It is ironic that the lifetime of the Solar Max satellite was dramatically shortened in this way. Above the atmosphere, satellites have no protection from high-energy particle fluxes produced by the Sun. Their electronic systems can be damaged, leading to catastrophic failures in some cases, as occurred with two Anik communications satellites in January 1994.

The oldest index of solar activity is the sunspot number. A number of techniques, many empirical, have been developed to combine observations from various observatories and observers to form the *International Sunspot Number.* This is a rather poor index; however, it has given us a database extending back to at least the 17th century.

Probably the best available index of solar activity, at least covering the last 50 years or so, is the *10.7-cm flux,* or $F_{10.7}$. This index is an objective measurement of the integrated emission at the 10.7-cm wavelength (a frequency of 2.8 GHz) from all sources present on the solar disk. It has been measured daily by the National Research Council of Canada for nearly 50 years and is now used worldwide as a primary index of solar activity. It is expressed in solar flux units (1 sfu = 10^{-22} W·m^{-2}Hz^{-1}). The 10.7-cm flux has the great advantage that it can be measured in any weather and requires no human involvement or "interpretation." When quiet, the Sun produces a 10.7-cm flux of 64 sfu, due to free-free thermal emission from the quiet solar corona. This index is expressed in two main forms: the *observed* and *adjusted* flux values.

The *observed* value is what is measured, and since this represents the impact of solar activity on Earth, it is useful in studying the consequences of solar activity here on Earth and our near-Earth space environment. The *adjusted* value is what we would observe at a constant distance from the Sun of one astronomical unit. This version of the index describes the activity of the Sun as a star, with the effect of the changing Earth–Sun distance taken out.

The 10.7-cm flux can be used as an objective proxy for other activity-related quantities. For example, the *adjusted* 10.7-cm flux can be used as a proxy for sunspot number through the relation *sunspot number* = $1.14 \times$ (*adjusted solar flux*) $- 73.21$, and the total *photospheric magnetic flux,* in units of 10^{22} Maxwells, equals (*adjusted flux*)/2 $- 10$.

We are a long way from understanding the nature and the extent of the effects solar activity has upon Earth. Some correlations, like that between miniskirt length and solar activity, are probably spurious; others might not be. As we exploit our environment more fully, we become increasingly sensitive to things that might affect it, even slightly.

TIMES OF SUNRISE AND SUNSET

The tables on the next three pages give the times of sunrise and sunset at four-day intervals for locations ranging from 20° to 62° north latitude. "Rise" and "set" correspond to the upper limb of the Sun appearing at the horizon for an observer at sea level. The times are local mean time (LMT) for the Greenwich meridian (i.e. UT at 0° longitude), although for North American observers the stated values may be read directly as LMT at the observer's position with an error less than 1 minute. The tables may be interpolated linearly for both nontabular latitudes and dates, and can be extrapolated beyond the 20° and 62° latitude limits a few degrees without significant loss of accuracy.

It is a common misconception that extreme values for sunrise and sunset times occur on the shortest and the longest days of the year. This is not the case and is due to the tilt of Earth's spin axis to the axis of its orbit and to Earth's varying speed along its elliptical orbit (as Kepler described in his second law). At midnorthern latitudes, the earliest sunset occurs early in December and the latest sunrise in early January whereas the shortest day (in the sense of hours of daylight) is December 21 or 22. For more information see *Sky & Telescope*, December 1988, p. 674 and July 1972, p. 20, and an article by Terence Hicks in *JRASC, 88*, p. 86, February 1994.

The standard time of an event at a particular location must take account of the observer's longitude relative to his or her standard meridian (see STANDARD TIME ZONES on pp. 42–43). The **table below** lists the latitude and the longitude correction (in minutes of time) for a number of cities in Canada and the United States. For example, to find the time of sunrise at Toronto on 2003 February 15: the latitude is 44°, and from the table the time of sunrise at 0° longitude is 7:00 UT (after interpolating for latitude). Thus, at Toronto, the time of sunrise will be approximately 7:00 LMT. Toronto is in the Eastern time zone (E) and is 18 minutes of time west of the standard meridian for this zone (75°W). Thus, sunrise in Toronto will occur at 7:18 EST (Eastern Standard Time). The longitude correction for any location may be found by converting the difference between the longitude of the place and that of its standard meridian to time (1° = 4 minutes of time), the correction being + if the place is west of its standard meridian, – if east.

Note: Due to a difference in height between the observer and the actual horizon, the observed time may differ by several minutes from the predicted time.

Canadian Cities				American Cities	
Brandon	50°+40C	Quebec	47°–15E	Atlanta	34°+37E
Calgary	51°+36M	Regina	50°+58C	Boston	42°–16E
Charlottetown	46°+12A	Resolute	75°+20C	Chicago	42°–10C
Corner Brook	49°+22N	Rimouski	48°–26E	Cincinnati	39°+38E
Edmonton	54°+34M	Saint John	45°+24A	Denver	40° 00M
Halifax	45°+14A	St. John's	48°+01N	Fairbanks	65°+50A
Hamilton	43°+20E	Sarnia	43°+29E	Flagstaff	35°+27M
Kelowna	50°–03P	Saskatoon	52°+67C	Kansas City	39°+18C
Kingston	44°+06E	Sudbury	47°+24E	Los Angeles	34°–07P
Kitchener	43°+22E	Thunder Bay	48°+57E	Miami	26°+21E
London	43°+25E	Toronto	44°+18E	Minneapolis	45°+13C
Moncton	46°+19A	Vancouver	49°+12P	New Orleans	30° 00C
Montreal	46°–06E	Victoria	48°+13P	New York	41°–04E
Niagara Falls	43°+16E	Whitehorse	61°+60P	San Francisco	38°+10P
Ottawa	45°+03E	Windsor, ON	42°+32E	Seattle	48°+09P
Pangnirtung	66°+23A	Winnipeg	50°+29C	Tucson	32°+24M
Prince George	54°+11P	Yellowknife	62°+38M	Washington	39°+08E

SUNRISE AND SUNSET, 2003 JANUARY–APRIL
UNIVERSAL TIME AT GREENWICH MERIDIAN

Latitude:	+20°		+30°		+35°		+40°		+45°		+50°		+54°		+58°		+62°	
Event:	RISE	SET	RISE	SET	RISE	SET	RISE	SET	RISE	SET	RISE	SET	RISE	SET	RISE	SET	RISE	SET
Jan. -2	6:34	17:30	6:55	17:09	7:07	16:57	7:21	16:43	7:38	16:26	7:58	16:06	8:19	15:45	8:46	15:18	9:25	14:40
2	6:35	17:33	6:56	17:12	7:08	17:00	7:22	16:46	7:38	16:30	7:59	16:09	8:19	15:49	8:45	15:23	9:22	14:46
6	6:36	17:35	6:57	17:15	7:09	17:03	7:22	16:50	7:38	16:34	7:58	16:14	8:17	15:54	8:43	15:29	9:19	14:53
10	6:37	17:38	6:57	17:18	7:09	17:07	7:21	16:53	7:37	16:38	7:56	16:19	8:15	16:00	8:40	15:36	9:14	15:02
14	6:38	17:40	6:57	17:21	7:08	17:10	7:21	16:58	7:35	16:43	7:54	16:25	8:12	16:06	8:35	15:43	9:07	15:11
18	6:38	17:43	6:56	17:25	7:07	17:14	7:19	17:02	7:33	16:48	7:51	16:31	8:08	16:13	8:30	15:51	9:00	15:22
22	6:38	17:45	6:55	17:28	7:05	17:18	7:17	17:07	7:30	16:53	7:47	16:37	8:03	16:21	8:24	16:00	8:51	15:33
26	6:37	17:48	6:54	17:32	7:03	17:22	7:14	17:11	7:27	16:59	7:42	16:43	7:57	16:28	8:17	16:09	8:42	15:44
30	6:36	17:50	6:52	17:35	7:01	17:26	7:11	17:16	7:23	17:04	7:37	16:50	7:51	16:36	8:09	16:18	8:32	15:55
Feb. 3	6:35	17:53	6:49	17:39	6:58	17:30	7:07	17:21	7:18	17:10	7:31	16:57	7:44	16:44	8:00	16:28	8:21	16:07
7	6:33	17:55	6:47	17:42	6:54	17:34	7:03	17:26	7:13	17:16	7:25	17:04	7:37	16:52	7:52	16:38	8:10	16:19
11	6:32	17:57	6:44	17:45	6:51	17:38	6:58	17:31	7:08	17:22	7:18	17:11	7:29	17:00	7:42	16:47	7:59	16:31
15	6:29	17:59	6:40	17:48	6:47	17:42	6:54	17:35	7:02	17:27	7:11	17:18	7:21	17:08	7:32	16:57	7:47	16:42
19	6:27	18:01	6:37	17:51	6:42	17:46	6:48	17:40	6:56	17:33	7:04	17:24	7:12	17:16	7:22	17:06	7:35	16:54
23	6:24	18:03	6:33	17:54	6:38	17:50	6:43	17:45	6:49	17:38	6:56	17:31	7:03	17:24	7:12	17:16	7:23	17:05
27	6:22	18:04	6:29	17:57	6:33	17:53	6:37	17:49	6:42	17:44	6:48	17:38	6:54	17:32	7:01	17:25	7:10	17:16
Mar. 3	6:19	18:06	6:24	18:00	6:28	17:57	6:31	17:53	6:35	17:49	6:40	17:45	6:45	17:40	6:51	17:35	6:58	17:28
7	6:16	18:07	6:20	18:03	6:22	18:00	6:25	17:58	6:28	17:55	6:32	17:51	6:35	17:48	6:40	17:44	6:45	17:39
11	6:12	18:08	6:15	18:05	6:17	18:04	6:19	18:02	6:21	18:00	6:23	17:58	6:26	17:56	6:29	17:53	6:32	17:50
15	6:09	18:09	6:11	18:08	6:11	18:07	6:12	18:06	6:14	18:05	6:15	18:04	6:16	18:03	6:17	18:02	6:19	18:00
19	6:05	18:11	6:06	18:10	6:06	18:10	6:06	18:10	6:06	18:10	6:06	18:11	6:06	18:11	6:06	18:11	6:06	18:11
23	6:02	18:12	6:01	18:13	6:00	18:14	6:00	18:15	5:59	18:16	5:57	18:17	5:56	18:18	5:55	18:20	5:53	18:22
27	5:58	18:13	5:56	18:15	5:55	18:17	5:53	18:19	5:51	18:21	5:49	18:23	5:46	18:26	5:44	18:29	5:40	18:33
31	5:55	18:14	5:51	18:18	5:49	18:20	5:47	18:23	5:44	18:26	5:40	18:30	5:37	18:33	5:32	18:38	5:27	18:43
Apr. 4	5:52	18:15	5:46	18:20	5:44	18:23	5:40	18:27	5:36	18:31	5:31	18:36	5:27	18:41	5:21	18:47	5:14	18:54
8	5:48	18:16	5:42	18:23	5:38	18:26	5:34	18:31	5:29	18:36	5:23	18:42	5:17	18:48	5:10	18:55	5:01	19:05
12	5:45	18:17	5:37	18:25	5:33	18:30	5:28	18:35	5:22	18:41	5:14	18:48	5:07	18:56	4:59	19:04	4:48	19:16
16	5:42	18:18	5:33	18:28	5:28	18:33	5:22	18:39	5:15	18:46	5:06	18:55	4:58	19:03	4:48	19:13	4:35	19:26
20	5:39	18:20	5:28	18:30	5:22	18:36	5:16	18:43	5:08	18:51	4:58	19:01	4:49	19:10	4:37	19:22	4:22	19:37
24	5:36	18:21	5:24	18:33	5:18	18:39	5:10	18:47	5:01	18:56	4:50	19:07	4:40	19:18	4:27	19:31	4:10	19:49
28	5:33	18:22	5:20	18:35	5:13	18:43	5:05	18:51	4:55	19:01	4:43	19:13	4:31	19:25	4:16	19:40	3:57	20:00

SUNRISE AND SUNSET, 2003 MAY–AUGUST
UNIVERSAL TIME AT GREENWICH MERIDIAN

Latitude / Event	+20° RISE	SET	+30° RISE	SET	+35° RISE	SET	+40° RISE	SET	+45° RISE	SET	+50° RISE	SET	+54° RISE	SET	+58° RISE	SET	+62° RISE	SET
May 2	5:31	18:24	5:17	18:38	5:09	18:46	5:00	18:55	4:49	19:06	4:36	19:19	4:23	19:33	4:06	19:49	3:45	20:11
6	5:28	18:25	5:13	18:40	5:05	18:49	4:55	18:59	4:43	19:11	4:29	19:26	4:15	19:40	3:57	19:58	3:33	20:22
10	5:26	18:27	5:10	18:43	5:01	18:52	4:50	19:03	4:38	19:16	4:22	19:32	4:07	19:47	3:48	20:07	3:22	20:33
14	5:25	18:28	5:08	18:45	4:58	18:55	4:46	19:07	4:33	19:21	4:16	19:37	4:00	19:54	3:39	20:15	3:11	20:44
18	5:23	18:30	5:05	18:48	4:55	18:59	4:43	19:11	4:28	19:25	4:11	19:43	3:53	20:01	3:31	20:24	3:00	20:55
22	5:22	18:32	5:03	18:50	4:52	19:02	4:39	19:14	4:24	19:29	4:06	19:48	3:47	20:07	3:23	20:31	2:50	21:05
26	5:21	18:33	5:01	18:53	4:50	19:04	4:37	19:18	4:21	19:34	4:02	19:53	3:42	20:13	3:16	20:39	2:40	21:15
30	5:20	18:35	5:00	18:55	4:48	19:07	4:34	19:21	4:18	19:37	3:58	19:58	3:37	20:18	3:10	20:46	2:32	21:25
Jun. 3	5:20	18:36	4:59	18:57	4:47	19:10	4:33	19:24	4:16	19:41	3:55	20:02	3:33	20:23	3:05	20:52	2:25	21:33
7	5:20	18:38	4:59	18:59	4:46	19:12	4:31	19:26	4:14	19:44	3:53	20:05	3:31	20:28	3:01	20:57	2:18	21:40
11	5:20	18:39	4:58	19:01	4:46	19:14	4:31	19:29	4:13	19:46	3:51	20:08	3:28	20:31	2:58	21:01	2:14	21:46
15	5:20	18:40	4:58	19:02	4:46	19:15	4:31	19:30	4:13	19:48	3:50	20:11	3:27	20:34	2:57	21:05	2:11	21:51
19	5:21	18:41	4:59	19:04	4:46	19:17	4:31	19:32	4:13	19:50	3:50	20:12	3:27	20:35	2:56	21:07	2:09	21:53
23	5:22	18:42	5:00	19:04	4:47	19:17	4:32	19:33	4:14	19:51	3:51	20:13	3:28	20:36	2:57	21:07	2:10	21:54
27	5:23	18:43	5:01	19:05	4:48	19:18	4:33	19:33	4:15	19:51	3:53	20:13	3:29	20:36	2:59	21:07	2:12	21:53
Jul. 1	5:24	18:43	5:02	19:05	4:49	19:18	4:35	19:33	4:17	19:50	3:55	20:13	3:32	20:35	3:02	21:05	2:16	21:50
5	5:25	18:44	5:04	19:05	4:51	19:18	4:37	19:32	4:19	19:49	3:58	20:11	3:35	20:33	3:06	21:03	2:22	21:46
9	5:27	18:43	5:06	19:04	4:53	19:17	4:39	19:31	4:22	19:48	4:01	20:09	3:39	20:30	3:11	20:59	2:29	21:40
13	5:28	18:43	5:08	19:03	4:56	19:15	4:42	19:29	4:25	19:46	4:05	20:06	3:44	20:27	3:17	20:54	2:37	21:33
17	5:30	18:42	5:10	19:02	4:58	19:14	4:45	19:27	4:29	19:43	4:09	20:02	3:49	20:22	3:23	20:48	2:46	21:24
21	5:31	18:41	5:12	19:00	5:01	19:11	4:48	19:24	4:33	19:39	4:14	19:58	3:55	20:17	3:30	20:41	2:56	21:15
25	5:33	18:40	5:15	18:58	5:04	19:09	4:52	19:21	4:37	19:35	4:19	19:53	4:01	20:11	3:38	20:34	3:06	21:05
29	5:34	18:39	5:17	18:56	5:07	19:06	4:55	19:17	4:41	19:31	4:24	19:48	4:08	20:04	3:46	20:26	3:17	20:54
Aug. 2	5:36	18:37	5:19	18:53	5:10	19:02	4:59	19:13	4:46	19:26	4:30	19:42	4:14	19:57	3:54	20:17	3:27	20:43
6	5:37	18:35	5:22	18:50	5:13	18:59	5:03	19:09	4:50	19:21	4:36	19:35	4:21	19:50	4:03	20:08	3:38	20:32
10	5:38	18:32	5:24	18:46	5:16	18:54	5:06	19:04	4:55	19:15	4:42	19:28	4:28	19:42	4:11	19:58	3:49	20:20
14	5:40	18:30	5:26	18:43	5:19	18:50	5:10	18:59	5:00	19:09	4:47	19:21	4:35	19:33	4:20	19:48	4:00	20:08
18	5:41	18:27	5:29	18:39	5:22	18:45	5:14	18:53	5:05	19:02	4:53	19:13	4:42	19:24	4:29	19:38	4:11	19:55
22	5:42	18:24	5:31	18:34	5:25	18:41	5:18	18:48	5:09	18:56	4:59	19:06	4:49	19:15	4:37	19:27	4:21	19:43
26	5:43	18:21	5:33	18:30	5:28	18:35	5:22	18:42	5:14	18:49	5:05	18:58	4:57	19:06	4:46	19:16	4:32	19:30
30	5:44	18:17	5:36	18:25	5:31	18:30	5:25	18:35	5:19	18:42	5:11	18:49	5:04	18:57	4:54	19:06	4:43	19:17

SUNRISE AND SUNSET, 2003 SEPTEMBER–DECEMBER
UNIVERSAL TIME AT GREENWICH MERIDIAN

Latitude: Event:	+20° RISE	+20° SET	+30° RISE	+30° SET	+35° RISE	+35° SET	+40° RISE	+40° SET	+45° RISE	+45° SET	+50° RISE	+50° SET	+54° RISE	+54° SET	+58° RISE	+58° SET	+62° RISE	+62° SET
Sep. 3	5:45	18:14	5:38	18:21	5:34	18:25	5:29	18:29	5:24	18:34	5:17	18:41	5:11	18:47	5:03	18:54	4:53	19:04
7	5:46	18:10	5:40	18:16	5:37	18:19	5:33	18:23	5:28	18:27	5:23	18:32	5:18	18:37	5:12	18:43	5:04	18:51
11	5:46	18:07	5:42	18:11	5:40	18:13	5:37	18:16	5:33	18:19	5:29	18:23	5:25	18:27	5:20	18:32	5:14	18:38
15	5:47	18:03	5:44	18:06	5:42	18:08	5:40	18:10	5:38	18:12	5:35	18:15	5:32	18:17	5:29	18:21	5:24	18:25
19	5:48	17:59	5:46	18:01	5:45	18:02	5:44	18:03	5:43	18:04	5:41	18:06	5:39	18:07	5:37	18:09	5:35	18:12
23	5:49	17:56	5:49	17:56	5:48	17:56	5:48	17:56	5:48	17:57	5:47	17:57	5:46	17:57	5:46	17:58	5:45	17:59
27	5:50	17:52	5:51	17:51	5:51	17:50	5:52	17:50	5:52	17:49	5:53	17:48	5:54	17:47	5:54	17:47	5:55	17:46
Oct. 1	5:51	17:49	5:53	17:46	5:54	17:45	5:56	17:43	5:57	17:41	5:59	17:39	6:01	17:38	6:03	17:35	6:06	17:33
5	5:52	17:45	5:55	17:41	5:57	17:39	6:00	17:37	6:02	17:34	6:05	17:31	6:08	17:28	6:12	17:24	6:16	17:20
9	5:53	17:42	5:58	17:36	6:01	17:34	6:04	17:30	6:07	17:27	6:12	17:22	6:16	17:18	6:21	17:13	6:27	17:07
13	5:54	17:38	6:00	17:32	6:04	17:28	6:08	17:24	6:12	17:20	6:18	17:14	6:23	17:09	6:29	17:02	6:37	16:54
17	5:55	17:35	6:03	17:28	6:07	17:23	6:12	17:18	6:18	17:13	6:24	17:06	6:31	16:59	6:38	16:51	6:48	16:41
21	5:57	17:32	6:06	17:23	6:11	17:18	6:16	17:13	6:23	17:06	6:31	16:58	6:38	16:50	6:48	16:41	6:59	16:29
25	5:58	17:30	6:08	17:20	6:14	17:14	6:21	17:07	6:28	16:59	6:37	16:50	6:46	16:41	6:57	16:31	7:10	16:17
29	6:00	17:27	6:11	17:16	6:18	17:09	6:25	17:02	6:34	16:53	6:44	16:43	6:54	16:33	7:06	16:21	7:22	16:05
Nov. 2	6:02	17:25	6:14	17:13	6:21	17:05	6:30	16:57	6:39	16:47	6:50	16:36	7:02	16:25	7:15	16:11	7:33	15:53
6	6:04	17:23	6:17	17:10	6:25	17:02	6:34	16:53	6:45	16:42	6:57	16:29	7:09	16:17	7:25	16:02	7:44	15:42
10	6:06	17:22	6:21	17:07	6:29	16:58	6:39	16:49	6:50	16:37	7:04	16:23	7:17	16:10	7:34	15:53	7:56	15:31
14	6:08	17:21	6:24	17:05	6:33	16:55	6:43	16:45	6:56	16:33	7:10	16:18	7:25	16:03	7:43	15:45	8:07	15:21
18	6:10	17:20	6:27	17:03	6:37	16:53	6:48	16:42	7:01	16:29	7:17	16:13	7:32	15:57	7:52	15:37	8:18	15:11
22	6:13	17:19	6:30	17:01	6:41	16:51	6:52	16:39	7:06	16:25	7:23	16:09	7:40	15:52	8:01	15:31	8:29	15:02
26	6:15	17:19	6:34	17:00	6:45	16:50	6:57	16:37	7:11	16:23	7:29	16:05	7:47	15:47	8:09	15:25	8:40	14:54
30	6:18	17:19	6:37	17:00	6:48	16:49	7:01	16:36	7:16	16:21	7:35	16:02	7:53	15:43	8:17	15:20	8:50	14:47
Dec. 4	6:20	17:20	6:40	17:00	6:52	16:48	7:05	16:35	7:21	16:19	7:40	16:00	7:59	15:40	8:24	15:16	8:59	14:41
8	6:23	17:21	6:43	17:00	6:55	16:48	7:09	16:35	7:25	16:18	7:45	15:59	8:05	15:38	8:31	15:13	9:07	14:36
12	6:25	17:22	6:46	17:01	6:58	16:49	7:12	16:35	7:29	16:18	7:49	15:58	8:09	15:38	8:36	15:11	9:14	14:33
16	6:27	17:23	6:49	17:02	7:01	16:50	7:15	16:36	7:32	16:19	7:52	15:58	8:13	15:38	8:40	15:10	9:19	14:32
20	6:30	17:25	6:51	17:04	7:03	16:51	7:17	16:37	7:34	16:20	7:55	16:00	8:16	15:39	8:44	15:11	9:23	14:32
24	6:32	17:27	6:53	17:06	7:05	16:54	7:19	16:39	7:36	16:22	7:57	16:02	8:18	15:41	8:46	15:13	9:25	14:34
28	6:33	17:29	6:55	17:08	7:07	16:56	7:21	16:42	7:38	16:25	7:58	16:05	8:19	15:44	8:46	15:17	9:25	14:38
32	6:35	17:32	6:56	17:11	7:08	16:59	7:22	16:45	7:38	16:28	7:59	16:08	8:19	15:48	8:46	15:21	9:23	14:44

TWILIGHT

There are three definitions for the beginning of morning and ending of evening twilight: (1) *Civil twilight*—centre of the Sun 6° below the horizon, brightest stars visible, artificial illumination required for most outdoor activities, marks the ending or beginning of night for aviation purposes; (2) *Nautical twilight*—centre of the Sun 12° below the horizon, horizon no longer visible; (3) *Astronomical twilight*—centre of the Sun 18° below the horizon, amount of sunlight scattered by the atmosphere is negligible.

The table below gives the beginning of morning and ending of evening astronomical twilight in UT at 0° longitude. For observers in North America the times may be handled in the same way as those of sunrise and sunset (see p. 107).

Latitude: M-E	+20° MORN	+20° EVE	+30° MORN	+30° EVE	+35° MORN	+35° EVE	+40° MORN	+40° EVE	+45° MORN	+45° EVE	+50° MORN	+50° EVE	+54° MORN	+54° EVE	+58° MORN	+58° EVE	+62° MORN	+62° EVE
Jan. 10	5:16	18:50	5:30	18:36	5:37	18:29	5:44	18:22	5:52	18:14	6:00	18:06	6:06	18:00	6:14	17:52	6:23	17:43
20	5:19	18:56	5:32	18:43	5:39	18:36	5:45	18:29	5:52	18:23	5:59	18:16	6:05	18:10	6:11	18:04	6:19	17:56
30	5:21	19:01	5:32	18:50	5:38	18:44	5:43	18:39	5:48	18:34	5:54	18:28	5:59	18:24	6:03	18:19	6:09	18:14
Feb. 9	5:20	19:06	5:29	18:57	5:34	18:53	5:38	18:49	5:41	18:46	5:45	18:42	5:48	18:40	5:50	18:37	5:53	18:35
19	5:18	19:11	5:24	19:05	5:27	19:02	5:29	19:00	5:31	18:58	5:32	18:57	5:33	18:57	5:33	18:57	5:32	18:58
Mar. 1	5:13	19:15	5:17	19:12	5:18	19:11	5:18	19:11	5:17	19:11	5:16	19:13	5:14	19:15	5:11	19:18	5:06	19:23
11	5:07	19:18	5:07	19:18	5:06	19:19	5:04	19:21	5:01	19:24	4:57	19:29	4:52	19:34	4:45	19:41	4:36	19:51
21	4:59	19:21	4:56	19:25	4:53	19:28	4:49	19:32	4:43	19:38	4:36	19:46	4:28	19:54	4:17	20:05	4:02	20:21
31	4:51	19:24	4:44	19:32	4:39	19:37	4:32	19:43	4:24	19:52	4:12	20:04	4:00	20:16	3:44	20:32	3:22	20:55
Apr. 10	4:41	19:28	4:31	19:39	4:23	19:46	4:14	19:55	4:02	20:07	3:47	20:23	3:30	20:40	3:08	21:03	2:36	21:37
20	4:32	19:31	4:17	19:46	4:08	19:56	3:56	20:08	3:40	20:24	3:20	20:45	2:58	21:07	2:27	21:40	1:34	22:36
30	4:23	19:36	4:04	19:54	3:52	20:07	3:37	20:22	3:18	20:41	2:52	21:08	2:22	21:39	1:34	22:29		
May 10	4:14	19:41	3:52	20:03	3:38	20:18	3:19	20:36	2:56	21:00	2:22	21:35	1:40	22:19				
20	4:07	19:46	3:41	20:12	3:24	20:29	3:03	20:51	2:34	21:21	1:50	22:05	0:37	23:26				
30	4:01	19:52	3:32	20:21	3:13	20:41	2:48	21:06	2:14	21:41	1:15	22:41						
Jun. 9	3:58	19:57	3:26	20:29	3:05	20:51	2:37	21:19	1:57	22:00	0:28	23:35						
19	3:57	20:00	3:23	20:36	3:00	20:58	2:30	21:29	1:44	22:15								
29	4:00	20:06	3:22	20:40	2:59	21:04	2:28	21:35	1:40	22:23								
Jul. 9	4:04	20:07	3:25	20:41	3:02	21:05	2:31	21:36	1:44	22:22	1:02	23:07						
19	4:09	20:04	3:31	20:41	3:08	21:01	2:39	21:30	1:56	22:13	1:41	22:29						
29	4:14	19:59	3:38	20:34	3:17	20:54	2:51	21:21	2:13	21:58	1:41	22:29						
Aug. 8	4:19	19:52	3:46	20:26	3:28	20:44	3:05	21:07	2:33	21:39	2:13	21:56	1:18	22:48				
18	4:24	19:44	3:55	20:16	3:39	20:31	3:19	20:54	2:52	21:17	2:41	21:25	2:05	22:00	0:53	23:05	0:18	23:22
28	4:28	19:34	4:03	20:04	3:50	20:17	3:33	20:34	3:11	20:55	3:05	20:56	2:39	21:21	1:59	22:00	1:57	21:54
Sep. 17	4:34	19:15	4:11	19:51	4:00	20:02	3:46	20:15	3:29	20:32	3:27	20:28	3:07	20:47	2:40	21:14	2:44	21:02
27	4:37	19:05	4:18	19:37	4:10	19:46	3:59	19:56	3:45	20:10	3:46	20:02	3:32	20:16	3:12	20:35	3:21	20:19
Oct. 7	4:39	18:56	4:25	19:24	4:19	19:30	4:10	19:38	4:00	19:48	4:04	19:37	3:54	19:47	3:40	20:01	3:52	19:42
17	4:42	18:49	4:31	19:10	4:27	19:15	4:21	19:20	4:14	19:27	4:21	19:14	4:14	19:21	4:05	19:30	4:20	19:09
27	4:45	18:43	4:37	18:58	4:35	19:00	4:32	19:03	4:27	19:07	4:37	18:53	4:33	18:57	4:27	19:02	4:45	18:41
Nov. 6	4:48	18:39	4:43	18:47	4:43	18:47	4:42	18:48	4:40	18:50	4:52	18:35	4:51	18:36	4:49	18:38	5:09	18:17
16	4:53	18:36	4:49	18:38	4:51	18:36	4:52	18:35	4:52	18:35	5:06	18:20	5:08	18:19	5:09	18:17	5:31	17:58
26	4:58	18:36	4:56	18:31	4:59	18:31	5:02	18:25	5:04	18:22	5:20	18:08	5:24	18:05	5:27	18:01	5:50	17:44
Dec. 6	5:03	18:38	5:03	18:26	5:07	18:25	5:12	18:17	5:16	18:13	5:33	18:01	5:38	17:55	5:44	17:50	6:06	17:36
16	5:09	18:42	5:10	18:25	5:16	18:18	5:21	18:13	5:27	18:07	5:44	17:57	5:51	17:51	5:58	17:44	6:17	17:34
26	5:14	18:47	5:17	18:25	5:23	18:21	5:30	18:11	5:37	18:06	5:53	17:58	6:00	17:51	6:08	17:43	6:22	17:39
Jan. 5	5:18	18:52	5:23	18:28	5:30	18:25	5:37	18:18	5:45	18:11	5:58	18:03	6:05	18:04	6:13	17:57	6:22	17:49

MIDNIGHT TWILIGHT AND MIDNIGHT SUN
BY ROY BISHOP

Astronomers generally desire dark skies, free of moonlight and man-made light pollution. As mentioned on the previous page, the beginning or end of *astronomical twilight* corresponds to the centre of the Sun being 18° below the horizon. At that point the amount of sunlight scattered by the upper layers of Earth's atmosphere is negligible; that is, it is less than the combined illuminance (about 2×10^{-3} lux) from starlight, airglow, and zodiacal light, the three main contributors to the light of the "dark" night sky.

For observers in countries at high latitudes (e.g. the United Kingdom, Norway, southern Argentina and Chile, and most of Canada), around the time of the summer solstice the Sun always lies less than 18° below the horizon, and the sky does not get dark at night. This "midnight twilight" phenomenon can be displayed in a graph as a function of latitude and time of year.

The **diagram** at the right indicates the brightness of the sky at local midnight at any time of the year for any latitude north of 45°N or south of 45°S. Below the lower curve the natural sky is dark. Between the two curves twilight prevails. Above the upper curve the Sun is in the sky. Place names in roman type (left-hand side) are in the Northern Hemisphere; place names in *italic* type (right-hand side) are in the *Southern Hemisphere*. On the horizontal axis use the roman-type months for the former, *italic*-type months for the latter. The diagram is simplified slightly in that the months are assumed to be of equal duration, and the seasonal pattern of months and summer solstices for Earth's two hemispheres are assumed to be identical except for a six-month phase shift.

The latitude of the Arctic and Antarctic Circles (90° subtract the obliquity of the ecliptic = 66°34′) is indicated by the dashed line. This line is *not* tangent to the Midnight Sun curve because at midnight on the summer solstice at either the Arctic or the Antarctic Circle the Sun is above the horizon. Atmospheric refraction raises the apparent Sun about 34′ above the true Sun. Also, rise/set is defined as the top limb of the Sun at a sea level horizon; thus the 16′ semidiameter of the Sun must also be taken into account. To see the top limb of the Sun on the horizon at local midnight on the summer solstice, an observer must be 34′ + 16′ = 50′ south of the Arctic Circle (or north of the Antarctic Circle), at latitude 65°44′.

By running a horizontal line across the chart at a selected latitude, the reader can determine the approximate dates when midnight twilight and, possibly, midnight sun begin and end for any locality at north or south latitudes above 48.6°, the lower limit for midnight twilight on the summer solstice. (Remarkably, when rounded to the nearest degree, the latter figure is the latitude of the longest east-west international border: the 2000-km-long 49th parallel between the United States and western Canada.)

Some examples: The diagram shows that at Grise Fiord (a hamlet on the stunning south coast of Ellesmere Island, and Canada's most northerly community) the sky is never dark from about March 10 until early October, and the midnight sun lasts from late April until mid-August. Note that Cape Horn at midnight is bathed in dim Antarctic twilight from early November until early February. Even at the latitude of Vancouver there is a period of almost a month each year when the sky never gets astronomically dark—although the natural night sky is obliterated *every* night near any town or city unless there is an electrical power failure! Finally, note that Earth's poles are astronomically dark for less than 3 months of the year.

MIDNIGHT TWILIGHT AND MIDNIGHT SUN DIAGRAM

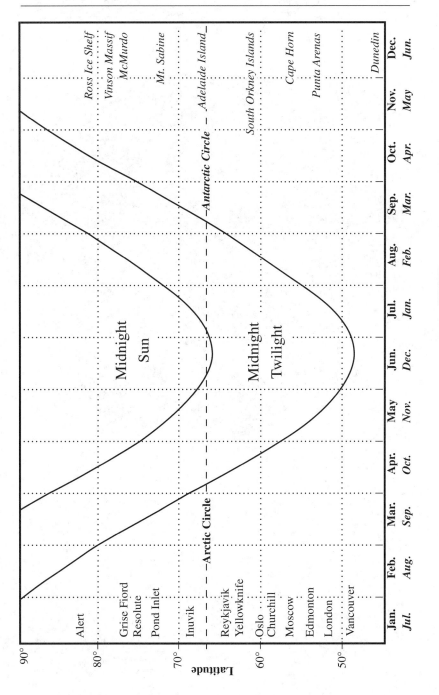

THE MOON

MAP OF MOON

By Roy Bishop

Maria	
LS	Lacus Somniorum (Lake of Dreams) (330°)
MC	Mare Crisium (Sea of Crises) (300°)
MFe	Mare Fecunditatis (Sea of Fertility) (310°)
MFr	Mare Frigoris (Sea of Cold) (0°)
MH	Mare Humorum (Sea of Moisture) (40°)
MI	Mare Imbrium (Sea of Rains) (20°)
MNe	Mare Nectaris (Sea of Nectar) (325°)
MNu	Mare Nubium (Sea of Clouds) (15°)
MS	Mare Serenitatis (Sea of Serenity) (340°)
MT	Mare Tranquillitatis (Sea of Tranquillity) (330°)
MV	Mare Vaporum (Sea of Vapors) (355°)
OP	Oceanus Procellarum (Ocean of Storms) (50°)
SA	Sinus Aestuum (Seething Bay) (8°)
SI	Sinus Iridum (Bay of Rainbows) (32°)
SM	Sinus Medii (Central Bay) (0°)
SR	Sinus Roris (Bay of Dew) (60°)

Lunar Probes

2 *Luna 2,* First to reach Moon (1959.9.13) (0°)
7 *Ranger 7,* First close pictures (1964.7.31) (21°)
9 *Luna 9,* First soft landing (1966.2.3) (64°)
11 *Apollo 11,* First men on Moon (1969.7.20) (337°)
12 *Apollo 12* (1969.11.19) (23°)
14 *Apollo 14* (1971.2.5) (17°)
15 *Apollo 15* (1971.7.30) (356°)
16 *Apollo 16* (1972.4.21) (344°)
17 *Apollo 17* (1972.12.11) (329°)

Angles in parentheses equal $360° - \lambda$, *where* λ *is the selenographic longitude of the centre of the feature.* $0°$ *marks the mean centre of the lunar disk and the angles increase toward the observer's east (i.e. westward on the Moon). These angles facilitate locating the feature on the accompanying map, and may be correlated with the Sun's selenographic colongitude (see THE SKY MONTH BY MONTH (pp. 74–99)) to determine the optimum times for viewing the feature.*

MAP OF MOON (continued)

Craters			Mountains
	43 Endymion (305°)	67 Mersenius (49°)	
	44 Eratosthenes (11°)	68 Newcomb (316°)	A Alpine Valley (356°)
21 Albategnius (356°)	45 Eudoxus (343°)	69 Petavius (298°)	B Alps Mts. (359°)
22 Alphonsus (3°)	46 Fracastorius (326°)	71 Piccolomini (327°)	E Altai Mts. (336°)
23 Arago (338°)	47 Furnerius (299°)	72 Plato (10°)	F Apennine Mts. (2°)
24 Archimedes (4°)	48 Gassendi (40°)	73 Plinius (336°)	G Carpathian Mts. (24°)
25 Aristarchus (47°)	49 Grimaldi (68°)	74 Posidonius (330°)	H Caucasus Mts. (352°)
26 Aristillus (358°)	51 Halley (354°)	75 Ptolemaeus (2°)	K Haemus Mts. (349°)
27 Aristoteles (342°)	52 Hercules (321°)	76 Reinhold (23°)	M Jura Mts. (34°)
28 Arzachel (2°)	53 Herschel (2°)	77 Ross (338°)	N Pyrenees Mts. (319°)
29 Atlas (315°)	54 Hevelius (66°)	78 Schickard (55°)	R Rheita Valley (312°)
31 Autolycus (358°)	55 Hipparchus (354°)	79 Schiller (40°)	S Riphaeus Mts. (27°)
32 Bessel (342°)	56 Julius Caesar (345°)	81 Snellius (304°)	V Spitzbergen (5°)
33 Bullialdus (22°)	57 Kepler (38°)	82 Stevinus (305°)	W Straight Range (20°)
34 Cassini (355°)	58 Langrenus (299°)	83 Taruntius (313°)	X Straight Wall (8°)
35 Catharina (336°)	59 Lansberg (27°)	84 Theophilus (333°)	Y Taurus Mts. (319°)
36 Clavius (15°)	61 Longomontanus (21°)	85 Timocharis (13°)	Z Teneriffe Mts. (13°)
37 Cleomedes (304°)	62 Macrobius (314°)	86 Tycho (11°)	
38 Cook (311°)	63 Maginus (6°)	87 Wilhelm (20°)	
39 Copernicus (20°)	64 Manilius (351°)		
41 Cyrillus (336°)	65 Maskelyne (330°)		
42 Delambre (342°)	66 Maurolycus (345°)		

UNIVERSAL TIME OF NEW MOON DATES

	2003			2004	
Jan. 2.8	May 1.5	Sep. 26.1	Jan. 21.9	May 19.2	Sep. 14.6
Feb. 1.4	May 31.2	Oct. 25.5	Feb. 20.4	Jun. 17.9	Oct. 14.1
Mar. 3.1	Jun. 29.8	Nov. 24.0	Mar. 20.9	Jul. 17.5	Nov. 12.6
Apr. 1.8	Jul. 29.3	Dec. 23.4	Apr. 19.6	Aug. 16.1	Dec. 12.1
	Aug. 27.7				

These dates will be useful for planning observing sessions, determining favourable dates for observing very thin lunar crescents, and setting Moon dials on clocks. The dates are indicated to lower precision in the calendar on the inside back cover.

TIMES OF MOONRISE AND MOONSET

The following 12 pages of tables give the times of moonrise and moonset for each day of the year for locations ranging from 20° to 62° north latitude. The tables may be interpolated linearly for nontabular latitudes and can be extrapolated beyond the 20° and 62° latitude limits a few degrees without significant loss of accuracy. "Rise" and "Set" correspond to the upper limb of the Moon appearing at the horizon for an observer at sea level. The times are local mean time (LMT) for the Greenwich meridian (i.e. UT at 0° longitude). Because of the relatively rapid eastward motion of the Moon, unlike the sunrise and sunset tables, for observers not near 0° longitude the times cannot be read directly as LMT; the table must be interpolated according to the observer's longitude. Also, to convert from the observer's LMT to standard time, the observer's longitude correction relative to his or her standard meridian must be applied. The chart at the right enables the sum of these two corrections to be determined easily in one step. However, the chart must first be set for your longitude.

To prepare the **Moonrise/Moonset Correction Diagram,** first mark your longitude on the *West or East Longitude* scale. Using a straight-edge, draw a diagonal line from this mark to the origin (the 0,0 point). Next, the *Correction in minutes* axis (which is subdivided at two-minute intervals) must be labelled. As a guide, the first three divisions have been tentatively labelled 0, ±2, ±4 (*use + if you are west of the prime meridian in Greenwich, England, – if east*); but, to these numbers must be added your longitude correction relative to your standard meridian (see the third paragraph on p. 107.) As an aid both for labelling and for reading the chart, the vertical lines at 10-minute intervals are wider. **Examples:** For Toronto, which is 4.5°W of its standard meridian of 75°, the longitude correction is +18 minutes, so an observer in Toronto would label the Correction axis divisions 18, 20, 22, 24,...; an observer in Boston (longitude correction –16) would label the axis –16, –14, –12,...; an observer in Hong Kong (east longitude, longitude correction +24) would label the axis: 24, 22, 20,...; an observer in Vienna (longitude correction –6) would label the axis: –6, –8, –10,....

The chart is now ready for use on any day from your position. Interpolating for nontabular latitudes, from the table obtain today's time for the event (moonrise, or moonset) and tomorrow's time if you are west of Greenwich, yesterday's time if east, enter the difference on the Tabular Delay axis, and run horizontally across to meet the diagonal line. The correction, to the nearest minute, can then be read directly below off the Correction axis. This correction is applied to the tabular "today's time" and results in the standard time of the event for your position. **Note:** Due to a difference in height between the observer and the actual horizon, the observed time may differ by several minutes from the predicted time.

MOONRISE/MOONSET CORRECTION DIAGRAM

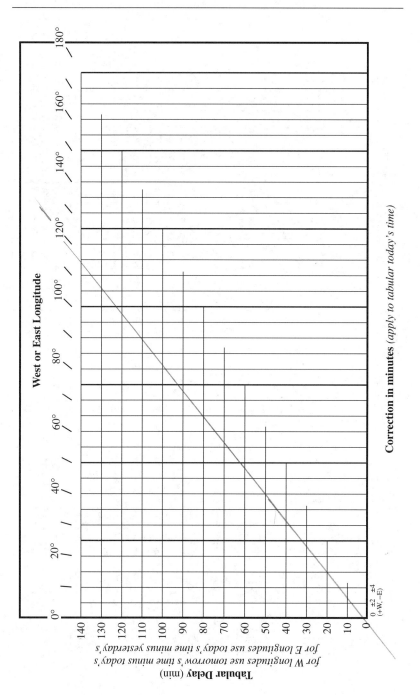

MOONRISE AND MOONSET, 2003 JANUARY
UNIVERSAL TIME AT GREENWICH MERIDIAN

Moon phases (left to right): ● (New)   ◐   ○ (Full)   ◑

Latitude/Event	+62° RISE	+62° SET	+58° RISE	+58° SET	+54° RISE	+54° SET	+50° RISE	+50° SET	+45° RISE	+45° SET	+40° RISE	+40° SET	+35° RISE	+35° SET	+30° RISE	+30° SET	+20° RISE	+20° SET
Jan. 1	8:33	12:47	7:42	13:39	7:09	14:13	6:44	14:38	6:20	15:03	6:01	15:23	5:45	15:39	5:32	15:53	5:08	16:18
2	10:03	13:24	9:01	14:27	8:23	15:04	7:56	15:32	7:30	15:58	7:09	16:19	6:52	16:36	6:37	16:51	6:12	17:17
3	10:54	14:38	9:57	15:35	9:21	16:11	8:54	16:37	8:29	17:02	8:08	17:22	7:51	17:39	7:37	17:53	7:12	18:17
4	11:15	16:15	10:31	16:58	10:01	17:27	9:38	17:50	9:16	18:11	8:57	18:29	8:42	18:44	8:29	18:56	8:06	19:18
5	11:24	17:55	10:52	18:25	10:29	18:47	10:11	19:05	9:52	19:22	9:37	19:36	9:24	19:48	9:13	19:58	8:54	20:16
6	11:28	19:30	11:06	19:51	10:49	20:06	10:35	20:18	10:21	20:31	10:10	20:41	10:00	20:50	9:51	20:58	9:36	21:11
7	11:29	21:00	11:15	21:12	11:04	21:22	10:55	21:29	10:45	21:37	10:37	21:44	10:30	21:49	10:24	21:54	10:14	22:02
8	11:30	22:25	11:22	22:30	11:16	22:34	11:11	22:38	11:06	22:41	11:01	22:44	10:58	22:46	10:54	22:48	10:48	22:52
9	11:30	23:48	11:28	23:47	11:27	23:45	11:26	23:44	11:25	23:43	11:24	23:43	11:23	23:42	11:22	23:41	11:21	23:40
10	11:30	—	11:34	—	11:37	—	11:40	—	11:43	—	11:46	—	11:48	—	11:50	—	11:53	—
11	11:30	1:10	11:40	1:02	11:48	0:56	11:55	0:51	12:02	0:46	12:08	0:41	12:13	0:37	12:18	0:34	12:26	0:28
12	11:31	2:34	11:48	2:19	12:01	2:07	12:12	1:58	12:23	1:48	12:32	1:40	12:41	1:33	12:48	1:27	13:00	1:17
13	11:33	4:01	11:58	3:38	12:17	3:20	12:32	3:06	12:47	2:52	13:00	2:40	13:11	2:31	13:21	2:22	13:37	2:07
14	11:38	5:32	12:13	4:59	12:38	4:35	12:57	4:16	13:17	3:57	13:33	3:42	13:46	3:30	13:58	3:19	14:19	3:00
15	11:49	7:05	12:35	6:19	13:07	5:49	13:30	5:26	13:54	5:03	14:12	4:45	14:28	4:30	14:42	4:17	15:05	3:54
16	12:14	8:31	13:12	7:34	13:48	6:58	14:14	6:32	14:40	6:07	15:00	5:47	15:17	5:30	15:32	5:15	15:57	4:51
17	13:09	9:33	14:08	8:34	14:44	7:58	15:11	7:31	15:36	7:05	15:57	6:44	16:14	6:27	16:29	6:13	16:53	5:47
18	14:36	10:06	15:24	9:17	15:56	8:44	16:20	8:20	16:43	7:56	17:02	7:36	17:17	7:20	17:31	7:06	17:54	6:42
19	16:18	10:20	16:53	9:44	17:18	9:18	17:37	8:58	17:56	8:38	18:12	8:21	18:25	8:07	18:36	7:55	18:55	7:34
20	18:04	10:26	18:27	10:02	18:44	9:43	18:58	9:27	19:12	9:12	19:24	8:59	19:33	8:48	19:42	8:39	19:57	8:22
21	19:48	10:30	20:01	10:14	20:12	10:01	20:20	9:51	20:29	9:41	20:36	9:32	20:42	9:24	20:48	9:18	20:57	9:06
22	21:29	10:31	21:34	10:23	21:38	10:17	21:42	10:11	21:45	10:06	21:48	10:01	21:50	9:57	21:52	9:53	21:56	9:47
23	23:10	10:32	23:07	10:31	23:04	10:30	23:03	10:30	23:01	10:29	22:59	10:28	22:58	10:28	22:56	10:27	22:54	10:27
24	—	10:33	—	10:39	—	10:44	—	10:48	—	10:52	—	10:55	—	10:59	—	11:01	23:53	11:06
25	0:51	10:34	0:39	10:47	0:31	10:58	0:24	11:07	0:16	11:16	0:10	11:24	0:05	11:30	0:01	11:36	—	11:46
26	2:34	10:36	2:14	10:58	1:58	11:15	1:46	11:29	1:33	11:44	1:23	11:55	1:14	12:05	1:06	12:14	0:53	12:30
27	4:21	10:40	3:49	11:14	3:26	11:38	3:08	11:57	2:50	12:16	2:36	12:32	2:23	12:45	2:13	12:57	1:54	13:17
28	6:08	10:51	5:22	11:38	4:51	12:09	4:28	12:33	4:06	12:57	3:48	13:15	3:32	13:31	3:19	13:45	2:57	14:08
29	7:45	11:16	6:45	12:16	6:09	12:53	5:42	13:20	5:16	13:46	4:56	14:07	4:39	14:24	4:24	14:39	3:59	15:04
30	8:50	12:14	7:49	13:15	7:11	13:53	6:44	14:20	6:18	14:46	5:57	15:06	5:40	15:24	5:25	15:38	4:59	16:03
31	9:20	13:43	8:30	14:33	7:57	15:05	7:33	15:29	7:08	15:53	6:49	16:11	6:33	16:27	6:19	16:40	5:55	17:03

MOONRISE AND MOONSET, 2003 FEBRUARY
UNIVERSAL TIME AT GREENWICH MERIDIAN

Latitude: Event:	+20° RISE	+20° SET	+30° RISE	+30° SET	+35° RISE	+35° SET	+40° RISE	+40° SET	+45° RISE	+45° SET	+50° RISE	+50° SET	+54° RISE	+54° SET	+58° RISE	+58° SET	+62° RISE	+62° SET
Feb. 1	6:45	18:02	7:06	17:43	7:18	17:31	7:32	17:18	7:49	17:03	8:09	16:43	8:29	16:24	8:56	15:59	9:32	15:23
2	7:30	18:59	7:46	18:43	7:56	18:35	8:07	18:25	8:20	18:13	8:36	17:58	8:52	17:44	9:12	17:26	9:37	17:01
3	8:09	19:52	8:22	19:42	8:29	19:36	8:37	19:29	8:46	19:21	8:58	19:11	9:09	19:01	9:22	18:50	9:39	18:34
4	8:45	20:43	8:53	20:37	8:57	20:34	9:02	20:30	9:08	20:26	9:15	20:21	9:22	20:16	9:30	20:10	9:40	20:02
5	9:19	21:32	9:22	21:31	9:24	21:31	9:26	21:30	9:28	21:30	9:31	21:29	9:33	21:28	9:36	21:28	9:40	21:27
6	9:51	22:20	9:50	22:24	9:49	22:27	9:48	22:29	9:46	22:32	9:45	22:36	9:44	22:40	9:42	22:44	9:40	22:50
7	10:23	23:09	10:17	23:17	10:14	23:22	10:10	23:28	10:05	23:35	10:00	23:43	9:54	23:51	9:48	—	9:40	—
8	10:57	23:58	10:46	—	10:40	—	10:33	—	10:25	—	10:15	—	10:06	—	9:55	0:00	9:40	0:13
9	11:32	—	11:17	0:11	11:09	0:19	10:59	0:28	10:47	0:38	10:34	0:50	10:20	1:03	10:03	1:18	9:41	1:38
10	12:11	0:49	11:52	1:06	11:41	1:17	11:29	1:28	11:14	1:42	10:56	1:59	10:38	2:16	10:15	2:38	9:45	3:07
11	12:55	1:42	12:33	2:03	12:20	2:16	12:05	2:30	11:47	2:47	11:25	3:08	11:03	3:30	10:34	3:58	9:52	4:38
12	13:44	2:37	13:19	3:01	13:05	3:15	12:48	3:31	12:28	3:51	12:03	4:15	11:37	4:41	11:03	5:15	10:09	6:08
13	14:38	3:33	14:12	3:58	13:58	4:13	13:40	4:31	13:20	4:51	12:53	5:17	12:26	5:44	11:49	6:22	10:48	7:23
14	15:37	4:29	15:12	4:54	14:58	5:08	14:42	5:25	14:22	5:45	13:57	6:10	13:31	6:36	12:57	7:12	12:02	8:07
15	16:38	5:22	16:17	5:45	16:05	5:58	15:50	6:13	15:33	6:31	15:12	6:53	14:50	7:16	14:22	7:45	13:41	8:27
16	17:41	6:12	17:24	6:31	17:14	6:42	17:03	6:54	16:50	7:09	16:33	7:27	16:17	7:44	15:57	8:06	15:29	8:36
17	18:44	6:59	18:32	7:13	18:25	7:21	18:18	7:30	18:09	7:40	17:58	7:53	17:47	8:05	17:34	8:20	17:17	8:40
18	19:45	7:42	19:39	7:51	19:36	7:56	19:32	8:01	19:28	8:07	19:22	8:15	19:17	8:22	19:11	8:31	19:03	8:42
19	20:46	8:24	20:46	8:26	20:46	8:28	20:46	8:30	20:46	8:32	20:46	8:34	20:46	8:36	20:47	8:39	20:47	8:42
20	21:46	9:04	21:52	9:01	21:56	8:59	22:00	8:57	22:04	8:55	22:10	8:52	22:15	8:50	22:22	8:47	22:31	8:43
21	22:47	9:45	22:59	9:36	23:06	9:31	23:13	9:26	23:23	9:19	23:34	9:11	23:45	9:04	23:59	8:55	—	8:45
22	23:49	10:28	—	10:14	—	10:06	—	9:57	—	9:46	—	9:33	—	9:20	—	9:05	0:16	8:48
23	—	11:14	0:06	10:55	0:16	10:44	0:27	10:32	0:41	10:17	0:58	9:59	1:14	9:41	1:35	9:18	2:04	8:55
24	0:51	12:04	1:13	11:42	1:25	11:28	1:40	11:13	1:57	10:55	2:19	10:32	2:41	10:09	3:10	9:39	3:53	9:14
25	1:53	12:59	2:18	12:34	2:32	12:19	2:49	12:02	3:09	11:41	3:35	11:15	4:01	10:49	4:37	10:12	5:35	9:59
26	2:53	13:56	3:19	13:31	3:34	13:16	3:52	12:58	4:13	12:37	4:39	12:10	5:07	11:43	5:46	11:04	6:51	11:20
27	3:50	14:55	4:14	14:31	4:29	14:17	4:46	14:00	5:06	13:41	5:31	13:16	5:57	12:50	6:33	12:15	7:28	12:58
28	4:40	15:53	5:03	15:32	5:16	15:20	5:30	15:06	5:48	14:49	6:10	14:28	6:32	14:07	7:01	13:39	7:43	

MOONRISE AND MOONSET, 2003 MARCH
UNIVERSAL TIME AT GREENWICH MERIDIAN

Latitude:	+20°		+30°		+35°		+40°		+45°		+50°		+54°		+58°		+62°	
Event:	RISE	SET	RISE	SET	RISE	SET	RISE	SET	RISE	SET	RISE	SET	RISE	SET	RISE	SET	RISE	SET
Mar. 1	5:26	16:50	5:44	16:33	5:55	16:23	6:07	16:12	6:22	15:58	6:39	15:42	6:57	15:26	7:19	15:05	7:49	14:37
2	6:06	17:44	6:21	17:31	6:29	17:24	6:38	17:16	6:49	17:07	7:02	16:55	7:15	16:44	7:31	16:30	7:51	16:11
3	6:43	18:35	6:53	18:28	6:58	18:23	7:05	18:19	7:12	18:13	7:20	18:06	7:29	17:59	7:39	17:51	7:52	17:41
4	7:18	19:25	7:22	19:22	7:25	19:21	7:28	19:19	7:32	19:17	7:36	19:15	7:40	19:13	7:45	19:10	7:51	19:06
5	7:50	20:13	7:50	20:16	7:50	20:17	7:50	20:19	7:50	20:20	7:51	20:23	7:51	20:25	7:51	20:27	7:51	20:30
6	8:22	21:02	8:18	21:09	8:15	21:13	8:12	21:18	8:09	21:23	8:05	21:30	8:01	21:36	7:56	21:44	7:50	21:54
7	8:55	21:51	8:46	22:02	8:41	22:09	8:35	22:17	8:28	22:26	8:20	22:37	8:12	22:48	8:02	23:01	7:50	23:19
8	9:30	22:41	9:16	22:57	9:08	23:06	8:59	23:17	8:49	23:30	8:37	23:45	8:24	—	8:10	—	7:50	—
9	10:07	23:33	9:49	23:53	9:39	—	9:27	—	9:13	—	8:57	—	8:40	0:01	8:20	0:20	7:52	0:46
10	10:48	—	10:26	—	10:14	0:04	10:00	0:18	9:43	0:34	9:22	0:54	9:01	1:14	8:34	1:40	7:56	2:17
11	11:33	0:26	11:09	0:49	10:55	1:03	10:39	1:19	10:20	1:38	9:55	2:01	9:31	2:26	8:57	2:58	8:07	3:48
12	12:24	1:21	11:59	1:46	11:44	2:01	11:26	2:18	11:05	2:39	10:39	3:05	10:12	3:32	9:34	4:09	8:33	5:11
13	13:20	2:16	12:55	2:41	12:40	2:56	12:22	3:14	12:02	3:34	11:36	4:01	11:09	4:28	10:31	5:06	9:29	6:08
14	14:19	3:09	13:56	3:33	13:43	3:47	13:27	4:03	13:08	4:23	12:45	4:47	12:20	5:12	11:48	5:45	10:59	6:35
15	15:21	4:00	15:02	4:21	14:50	4:33	14:37	4:47	14:22	5:03	14:03	5:24	13:43	5:44	13:19	6:10	12:44	6:46
16	16:23	4:48	16:09	5:04	16:01	5:14	15:51	5:25	15:40	5:37	15:26	5:53	15:12	6:08	14:55	6:26	14:33	6:51
17	17:26	5:32	17:17	5:44	17:12	5:50	17:06	5:57	17:00	6:06	16:52	6:16	16:44	6:26	16:34	6:38	16:21	6:53
18	18:28	6:15	18:26	6:21	18:24	6:24	18:22	6:27	18:20	6:31	18:18	6:36	18:15	6:41	18:13	6:46	18:09	6:53
19	19:31	6:57	19:34	6:56	19:36	6:56	19:38	6:56	19:41	6:55	19:44	6:55	19:48	6:55	19:52	6:54	19:57	6:54
20	20:33	7:39	20:43	7:32	20:49	7:28	20:55	7:24	21:03	7:20	21:12	7:14	21:21	7:08	21:32	7:02	21:46	6:54
21	21:37	8:22	21:53	8:10	22:02	8:03	22:12	7:55	22:24	7:46	22:39	7:35	22:54	7:24	23:13	7:11	23:38	6:54
22	22:42	9:09	23:03	8:51	23:15	8:41	23:28	8:29	23:45	8:16	—	7:59	—	7:43	—	7:23	—	6:56
23	23:47	9:59	—	9:37	—	9:24	—	9:10	—	8:52	0:05	8:31	0:26	8:09	0:53	7:41	1:32	7:01
24	—	10:53	0:11	10:28	0:25	10:14	0:41	9:57	1:01	9:37	1:26	9:11	1:51	8:45	2:26	8:09	3:22	7:13
25	0:49	11:51	1:14	11:25	1:30	11:10	1:47	10:52	2:09	10:30	2:36	10:03	3:04	9:35	3:43	8:56	4:51	7:48
26	1:47	12:50	2:12	12:25	2:27	12:10	2:44	11:53	3:05	11:33	3:32	11:07	3:59	10:40	4:37	10:02	5:38	9:01
27	2:39	13:48	3:02	13:26	3:16	13:13	3:32	12:58	3:50	12:40	4:14	12:17	4:37	11:54	5:09	11:23	5:56	10:38
28	3:25	14:45	3:45	14:26	3:57	14:16	4:10	14:03	4:26	13:49	4:45	13:31	5:04	13:13	5:29	12:49	6:02	12:17
29	4:07	15:39	4:23	15:25	4:32	15:17	4:42	15:08	4:54	14:57	5:09	14:44	5:23	14:31	5:41	14:14	6:04	13:53
30	4:44	16:30	4:55	16:21	5:02	16:16	5:09	16:10	5:17	16:03	5:28	15:55	5:37	15:46	5:49	15:36	6:05	15:23
31	5:19	17:20	5:25	17:16	5:29	17:14	5:33	17:11	5:38	17:08	5:43	17:04	5:49	17:00	5:56	16:55	6:04	16:49

MOONRISE AND MOONSET, 2003 APRIL
UNIVERSAL TIME AT GREENWICH MERIDIAN

Event:	+20° RISE	SET	+30° RISE	SET	+35° RISE	SET	+40° RISE	SET	+45° RISE	SET	+50° RISE	SET	+54° RISE	SET	+58° RISE	SET	+62° RISE	SET
Apr. 1	5:51	18:09	5:53	18:09	5:54	18:10	5:55	18:10	5:56	18:11	5:58	18:11	5:59	18:12	6:01	18:13	6:03	18:14
2	6:23	18:57	6:20	19:03	6:18	19:06	6:17	19:09	6:14	19:14	6:12	19:19	6:09	19:23	6:06	19:29	6:02	19:37
3	6:56	19:46	6:48	19:56	6:43	20:02	6:38	20:09	6:33	20:17	6:26	20:26	6:19	20:35	6:11	20:47	6:01	21:02
4	7:29	20:35	7:17	20:50	7:10	20:59	7:02	21:09	6:53	21:20	6:42	21:34	6:31	21:48	6:18	22:06	6:01	22:29
5	8:05	21:27	7:49	21:45	7:39	21:57	7:28	22:09	7:16	22:24	7:00	22:43	6:45	23:01	6:26	23:26	6:02	23:59
6	8:44	22:19	8:24	22:42	8:12	22:55	7:59	23:10	7:43	23:28	7:23	23:51	7:04	—	6:39	—	6:04	—
7	9:28	23:13	9:05	23:38	8:51	23:52	8:35	—	8:16	—	7:53	—	7:29	0:14	6:57	0:45	6:11	1:31
8	10:16	—	9:51	—	9:36	—	9:18	0:09	8:58	0:30	8:32	0:55	8:05	1:22	7:27	1:59	6:27	2:59
9	11:09	0:07	10:43	0:33	10:28	0:48	10:10	1:06	9:49	1:27	9:22	1:54	8:54	2:22	8:15	3:01	7:08	4:07
10	12:05	1:00	11:41	1:25	11:26	1:39	11:09	1:57	10:49	2:17	10:24	2:43	9:58	3:09	9:22	3:45	8:25	4:43
11	13:04	1:50	12:43	2:13	12:30	2:26	12:16	2:41	11:58	2:59	11:37	3:22	11:15	3:45	10:46	4:14	10:04	4:57
12	14:05	2:38	13:47	2:57	13:37	3:08	13:26	3:20	13:13	3:35	12:56	3:53	12:39	4:10	12:18	4:33	11:50	5:03
13	15:06	3:22	14:54	3:37	14:47	3:45	14:39	3:54	14:30	4:05	14:19	4:17	14:08	4:30	13:54	4:45	13:37	5:05
14	16:07	4:05	16:01	4:14	15:58	4:19	15:54	4:24	15:49	4:31	15:44	4:38	15:38	4:46	15:32	4:55	15:23	5:06
15	17:09	4:46	17:09	4:49	17:09	4:51	17:09	4:53	17:10	4:55	17:10	4:57	17:10	4:59	17:10	5:02	17:11	5:06
16	18:12	5:28	18:19	5:25	18:22	5:23	18:27	5:21	18:32	5:18	18:38	5:15	18:44	5:13	18:51	5:09	19:00	5:05
17	19:17	6:11	19:30	6:02	19:37	5:56	19:46	5:50	19:56	5:43	20:08	5:35	20:20	5:27	20:35	5:17	20:54	5:05
18	20:24	6:57	20:42	6:42	20:53	6:33	21:05	6:23	21:20	6:12	21:38	5:58	21:56	5:44	22:20	5:27	22:52	5:06
19	21:31	7:47	21:54	7:27	22:08	7:15	22:23	7:02	22:42	6:46	23:05	6:26	23:30	6:07	—	5:42	—	5:08
20	22:37	8:42	23:03	8:18	23:18	8:04	23:36	7:48	23:57	7:28	—	7:04	—	6:39	0:02	6:06	0:51	5:15
21	23:39	9:41	—	9:15	—	8:59	—	8:42	—	8:20	0:24	7:53	0:52	7:25	1:31	6:45	2:38	5:38
22	—	10:41	0:05	10:16	0:21	10:00	0:38	9:43	1:00	9:21	1:27	8:55	1:56	8:26	2:35	7:47	3:44	6:39
23	0:35	11:42	0:59	11:18	1:14	11:04	1:30	10:48	1:50	10:29	2:15	10:05	2:41	9:40	3:15	9:07	4:08	8:14
24	1:24	12:40	1:46	12:20	1:58	12:08	2:12	11:55	2:29	11:39	2:50	11:19	3:11	10:59	3:38	10:33	4:16	9:57
25	2:08	13:35	2:25	13:11	2:35	13:11	2:46	13:03	2:59	12:48	3:16	12:33	3:32	12:19	3:52	12:00	4:18	11:35
26	2:46	14:27	2:59	14:17	3:06	14:10	3:14	14:03	3:24	13:55	3:36	13:45	3:47	13:35	4:01	13:23	4:18	13:07
27	3:21	15:17	3:29	15:12	3:34	15:08	3:39	15:04	3:45	15:00	3:52	14:54	3:59	14:49	4:07	14:43	4:18	14:35
28	3:54	16:06	3:57	16:05	3:59	16:04	4:01	16:04	4:03	16:03	4:06	16:02	4:09	16:01	4:13	16:00	4:17	15:59
29	4:26	16:54	4:24	16:58	4:23	17:00	4:22	17:03	4:21	17:06	4:20	17:09	4:19	17:13	4:17	17:17	4:16	17:22
30	4:57	17:42	4:51	17:51	4:48	17:56	4:44	18:02	4:39	18:08	4:34	18:16	4:29	18:24	4:22	18:34	4:14	18:46

MOONRISE AND MOONSET, 2003 MAY
UNIVERSAL TIME AT GREENWICH MERIDIAN

| Latitude: | +20° | | +30° | | +35° | | +40° | | +45° | | +50° | | +54° | | +58° | | +62° | |
Event:	RISE	SET	RISE	SET	RISE	SET	RISE	SET	RISE	SET	RISE	SET	RISE	SET	RISE	SET	RISE	SET
May 1	5:30	18:31	5:20	18:45	5:13	18:53	5:06	19:01	4:58	19:12	4:49	19:24	4:39	19:37	4:28	19:52	4:14	20:13
2	6:05	19:22	5:50	19:40	5:42	19:50	5:32	20:02	5:20	20:16	5:06	20:33	4:52	20:50	4:35	21:12	4:13	21:42
3	6:44	20:15	6:24	20:36	6:13	20:49	6:01	21:03	5:46	21:20	5:27	21:42	5:09	22:04	4:46	22:33	4:15	23:15
4	7:26	21:08	7:03	21:32	6:50	21:47	6:35	22:03	6:17	22:23	5:54	22:48	5:32	23:14	5:02	23:49	4:19	—
5	8:12	22:02	7:47	22:28	7:32	22:43	7:15	23:01	6:55	23:22	6:30	23:49	6:03	—	5:27	—	4:30	0:46
6	9:03	22:55	8:37	23:20	8:22	23:35	8:04	23:53	7:42	—	7:15	—	6:47	0:17	6:08	0:56	5:00	2:03
7	9:57	23:45	9:32	—	9:17	—	9:00	—	8:39	0:14	8:13	0:40	7:46	1:08	7:08	1:46	6:05	2:49
8	10:54	—	10:31	0:09	10:18	0:23	10:02	0:39	9:44	0:58	9:21	1:22	8:57	1:47	8:25	2:19	7:37	3:08
9	11:53	0:32	11:34	0:53	11:22	1:05	11:10	1:19	10:54	1:35	10:36	1:55	10:11	2:15	9:52	2:40	9:19	3:15
10	12:51	1:17	12:37	1:33	12:29	1:42	12:19	1:53	12:08	2:06	11:55	2:21	11:41	2:36	11:24	2:54	11:02	3:18
11	13:50	1:58	13:42	2:10	13:37	2:16	13:31	2:23	13:24	2:32	13:16	2:42	13:08	2:52	12:58	3:04	12:45	3:19
12	14:50	2:39	14:47	2:44	14:45	2:48	14:43	2:51	14:41	2:56	14:39	3:01	14:36	3:05	14:33	3:11	14:29	3:18
13	15:51	3:19	15:54	3:19	15:56	3:19	15:58	3:18	16:01	3:18	16:04	3:18	16:06	3:18	16:10	3:18	16:15	3:18
14	16:54	4:00	17:03	3:54	17:09	3:50	17:15	3:46	17:22	3:42	17:31	3:36	17:40	3:31	17:51	3:25	18:05	3:17
15	18:00	4:44	18:15	4:32	18:24	4:25	18:35	4:17	18:47	4:08	19:02	3:57	19:17	3:46	19:35	3:33	20:01	3:17
16	19:08	5:32	19:29	5:14	19:41	5:04	19:55	4:52	20:12	4:39	20:33	4:22	20:54	4:06	21:22	3:45	22:02	3:18
17	20:17	6:25	20:41	6:03	20:56	5:50	21:13	5:35	21:33	5:17	21:59	4:55	22:25	4:32	23:02	4:03	—	3:22
18	21:23	7:24	21:49	6:58	22:05	6:43	22:23	6:26	22:45	6:05	23:12	5:39	23:41	5:12	—	4:34	0:01	3:34
19	22:24	8:26	22:49	8:00	23:05	7:44	23:22	7:26	23:43	7:04	—	6:37	—	6:08	0:22	5:27	1:34	4:15
20	23:18	9:29	23:41	9:04	23:54	8:49	—	8:32	—	8:12	0:09	7:46	0:36	7:20	1:14	6:43	2:15	5:42
21	—	10:30	—	10:09	—	9:56	0:09	9:41	0:28	9:24	0:50	9:02	1:13	8:40	1:43	8:11	2:27	7:29
22	0:05	11:28	0:24	11:11	0:35	11:01	0:47	10:49	1:02	10:36	1:20	10:19	1:38	10:02	2:00	9:41	2:31	9:12
23	0:46	12:22	1:00	12:10	1:08	12:03	1:18	11:54	1:29	11:45	1:42	11:33	1:55	11:22	2:11	11:07	2:32	10:48
24	1:22	13:14	1:32	13:06	1:37	13:02	1:44	12:57	1:51	12:51	2:00	12:44	2:08	12:37	2:18	12:29	2:31	12:18
25	1:56	14:03	2:01	14:00	2:03	13:59	2:07	13:57	2:10	13:55	2:15	13:53	2:19	13:50	2:24	13:47	2:30	13:44
26	2:28	14:51	2:28	14:53	2:28	14:54	2:28	14:56	2:28	14:58	2:28	15:00	2:28	15:02	2:29	15:04	2:29	15:07
27	3:00	15:39	2:55	15:46	2:52	15:50	2:49	15:55	2:46	16:00	2:42	16:07	2:38	16:13	2:33	16:21	2:27	16:31
28	3:32	16:28	3:23	16:39	3:17	16:46	3:11	16:54	3:05	17:03	2:56	17:14	2:48	17:25	2:39	17:39	2:26	17:56
29	4:06	17:18	3:52	17:34	3:45	17:44	3:36	17:54	3:25	18:07	3:13	18:23	3:00	18:39	2:45	18:58	2:26	19:25
30	4:43	18:10	4:25	18:30	4:15	18:42	4:03	18:56	3:49	19:12	3:32	19:32	3:16	19:53	2:55	20:19	2:27	20:57
31	5:24	19:03	5:03	19:27	4:50	19:41	4:36	19:57	4:18	20:16	3:57	20:40	3:36	21:05	3:09	21:38	2:30	22:30

MOONRISE AND MOONSET, 2003 JUNE
UNIVERSAL TIME AT GREENWICH MERIDIAN

Latitude: Event:	+62° RISE	SET	+58° RISE	SET	+54° RISE	SET	+50° RISE	SET	+45° RISE	SET	+40° RISE	SET	+35° RISE	SET	+30° RISE	SET	+20° RISE	SET
Jun. 1	2:38	23:54	3:31	22:49	4:05	22:11	4:30	21:43	4:55	21:17	5:14	20:56	5:31	20:38	5:45	20:23	6:09	19:58
2	3:01	—	4:06	23:45	4:45	23:06	5:13	22:38	5:39	22:11	6:00	21:50	6:18	21:32	6:33	21:17	6:59	20:51
3	3:54	0:51	5:00	—	5:39	23:49	6:07	23:23	6:33	22:58	6:54	22:38	7:12	22:21	7:27	22:07	7:53	21:42
4	5:19	1:17	6:12	0:23	6:46	—	7:11	23:58	7:36	23:37	7:55	23:20	8:11	23:05	8:25	22:52	8:49	22:30
5	6:59	1:26	7:37	0:47	8:03	0:19	8:24	—	8:44	—	9:00	23:55	9:14	23:43	9:26	23:33	9:46	23:15
6	8:40	1:30	9:06	1:02	9:25	0:42	9:40	0:25	9:56	0:09	10:08	—	10:19	—	10:28	—	10:44	23:57
7	10:21	1:31	10:37	1:13	10:49	0:59	10:59	0:47	11:09	0:36	11:17	0:26	11:25	0:17	11:31	0:10	11:42	—
8	12:01	1:31	12:08	1:21	12:14	1:13	12:18	1:06	12:23	0:59	12:27	0:53	12:31	0:48	12:34	0:44	12:39	0:36
9	13:41	1:30	13:41	1:27	13:40	1:25	13:39	1:23	13:39	1:21	13:38	1:20	13:38	1:18	13:38	1:17	13:37	1:15
10	15:25	1:29	15:16	1:34	15:09	1:37	15:03	1:40	14:57	1:43	14:51	1:46	14:47	1:48	14:43	1:50	14:37	1:53
11	17:15	1:29	16:56	1:41	16:41	1:51	16:29	1:59	16:17	2:07	16:07	2:14	15:59	2:20	15:52	2:25	15:39	2:34
12	19:11	1:29	18:40	1:50	18:16	2:07	17:58	2:21	17:40	2:34	17:26	2:46	17:14	2:56	17:03	3:04	16:45	3:19
13	21:12	1:31	20:23	2:05	19:51	2:29	19:27	2:48	19:03	3:08	18:45	3:24	18:29	3:37	18:16	3:49	17:53	4:09
14	23:03	1:38	21:55	2:28	21:16	3:01	20:48	3:26	20:21	3:50	20:00	4:10	19:42	4:26	19:27	4:40	19:01	5:04
15	—	2:01	23:03	3:09	22:23	3:49	21:54	4:17	21:27	4:44	21:05	5:06	20:47	5:24	20:32	5:39	20:06	6:05
16	0:11	3:07	23:43	4:15	23:09	4:54	22:44	5:23	22:19	5:50	22:00	6:11	21:43	6:29	21:29	6:44	21:05	7:10
17	0:34	4:50	—	5:41	23:39	6:14	23:19	6:38	22:59	7:02	22:43	7:21	22:29	7:37	22:17	7:50	21:56	8:13
18	0:41	6:39	0:05	7:14	—	7:38	23:45	7:57	23:30	8:16	23:17	8:32	23:07	8:45	22:57	8:56	22:41	9:15
19	0:43	8:22	0:19	8:44	0:00	9:01	—	9:15	23:54	9:29	23:46	9:40	23:38	9:50	23:32	9:58	23:20	10:12
20	0:43	9:56	0:27	10:10	0:15	10:21	0:05	10:29	—	10:38	—	10:45	—	10:51	—	10:57	23:55	11:06
21	0:42	11:25	0:34	11:31	0:27	11:36	0:21	11:40	0:15	11:44	0:10	11:47	0:06	11:50	0:02	11:53	—	11:57
22	0:41	12:50	0:39	12:49	0:37	12:49	0:35	12:48	0:34	12:48	0:32	12:47	0:31	12:47	0:30	12:46	0:28	12:46
23	0:40	14:14	0:44	14:06	0:47	14:00	0:49	13:55	0:52	13:50	0:54	13:46	0:56	13:43	0:57	13:40	1:00	13:34
24	0:39	15:38	0:49	15:24	0:57	15:12	1:03	15:03	1:10	14:53	1:16	14:45	1:21	14:39	1:25	14:33	1:33	14:23
25	0:38	17:06	0:55	16:43	1:08	16:25	1:19	16:11	1:30	15:57	1:39	15:46	1:47	15:36	1:54	15:27	2:06	15:12
26	0:38	18:37	1:03	18:03	1:22	17:39	1:37	17:20	1:52	17:02	2:05	16:47	2:16	16:34	2:26	16:23	2:42	16:04
27	0:40	20:10	1:15	19:23	1:40	18:52	2:00	18:29	2:20	18:06	2:36	17:48	2:49	17:33	3:01	17:19	3:22	16:57
28	0:47	21:39	1:34	20:38	2:06	20:01	2:30	19:34	2:53	19:09	3:12	18:48	3:28	18:31	3:42	18:16	4:06	17:51
29	1:03	22:48	2:05	21:40	2:42	21:01	3:09	20:33	3:36	20:06	3:56	19:45	4:14	19:27	4:29	19:12	4:54	18:46
30	1:46	23:22	2:53	22:24	3:32	21:48	4:00	21:22	4:27	20:56	4:48	20:35	5:06	20:18	5:21	20:04	5:47	19:38

MOONRISE AND MOONSET, 2003 JULY
UNIVERSAL TIME AT GREENWICH MERIDIAN

Latitude: Event:	+20° RISE	SET	+30° RISE	SET	+35° RISE	SET	+40° RISE	SET	+45° RISE	SET	+50° RISE	SET	+54° RISE	SET	+58° RISE	SET	+62° RISE	SET
Jul. 1	6:43	20:28	6:19	20:51	6:05	21:04	5:48	21:19	5:28	21:38	5:03	22:00	4:37	22:23	4:01	22:52	3:04	23:35
2	7:41	21:14	7:20	21:33	7:07	21:44	6:53	21:57	6:36	22:12	6:14	22:30	5:52	22:47	5:23	23:10	4:41	23:41
3	8:39	21:57	8:22	22:11	8:12	22:19	8:01	22:29	7:47	22:40	7:30	22:53	7:14	23:06	6:52	23:22	6:23	23:42
4	9:37	22:37	9:25	22:46	9:18	22:51	9:09	22:57	9:00	23:04	8:48	23:12	8:37	23:20	8:23	23:30	8:04	23:42
5	10:34	23:15	10:27	23:19	10:23	23:21	10:18	23:23	10:13	23:26	10:07	23:30	10:01	23:33	9:53	23:37	9:43	23:42
6	11:30	23:52	11:29	23:51	11:28	23:50	11:28	23:49	11:27	23:48	11:26	23:46	11:25	23:45	11:23	23:43	11:22	23:41
7	12:28	—	12:32	—	12:35	—	12:38	—	12:42	—	12:46	—	12:50	23:57	12:55	23:50	13:02	23:40
8	13:27	0:31	13:38	0:24	13:44	0:20	13:51	0:15	13:59	0:10	14:09	0:03	14:18	—	14:30	23:58	14:45	23:40
9	14:30	1:13	14:46	1:00	14:55	0:53	15:06	0:44	15:18	0:35	15:34	0:23	15:49	0:12	16:09	—	16:35	23:41
10	15:35	1:59	15:56	1:41	16:08	1:30	16:22	1:18	16:39	1:04	17:00	0:47	17:22	0:30	17:50	0:09	18:31	23:45
11	16:41	2:50	17:06	2:28	17:21	2:15	17:37	1:59	17:58	1:42	18:23	1:19	18:50	0:57	19:27	0:27	20:26	23:58
12	17:47	3:48	18:13	3:22	18:29	3:07	18:47	2:50	19:08	2:29	19:36	2:03	20:05	1:36	20:45	0:59	21:57	—
13	18:49	4:50	19:14	4:24	19:29	4:08	19:46	3:50	20:07	3:29	20:33	3:01	21:00	2:32	21:37	1:52	22:37	0:40
14	19:44	5:54	20:06	5:30	20:19	5:15	20:35	4:58	20:53	4:38	21:15	4:13	21:37	3:46	22:07	3:10	22:49	2:10
15	20:32	6:58	20:50	6:37	21:01	6:24	21:13	6:10	21:28	5:53	21:45	5:32	22:02	5:10	22:24	4:42	22:53	4:00
16	21:14	7:58	21:28	7:41	21:36	7:32	21:45	7:21	21:55	7:08	22:08	6:52	22:20	6:36	22:35	6:15	22:54	5:48
17	21:52	8:54	22:01	8:43	22:06	8:36	22:11	8:29	22:18	8:20	22:25	8:09	22:33	7:58	22:42	7:45	22:53	7:28
18	22:26	9:47	22:30	9:41	22:32	9:37	22:35	9:33	22:37	9:28	22:41	9:23	22:44	9:17	22:48	9:10	22:52	9:01
19	22:59	10:38	22:58	10:37	22:57	10:36	22:57	10:35	22:56	10:34	22:55	10:33	22:54	10:32	22:53	10:30	22:51	10:29
20	23:32	11:27	23:26	11:31	23:22	11:33	23:18	11:35	23:14	11:38	23:09	11:42	23:04	11:45	22:57	11:49	22:50	11:54
21	—	12:16	23:54	12:24	23:48	12:29	23:41	12:35	23:33	12:42	23:24	12:50	23:14	12:57	23:03	13:07	22:49	13:19
22	0:05	13:05	—	13:19	—	13:26	—	13:35	23:55	13:45	23:41	13:58	23:27	14:10	23:10	14:25	22:50	14:45
23	0:40	13:56	0:25	14:14	0:16	14:24	0:06	14:36	—	14:50	—	15:07	23:44	15:24	23:21	15:45	22:50	16:15
24	1:18	14:49	0:59	15:10	0:48	15:23	0:35	15:37	0:20	15:54	0:02	16:16	—	16:37	23:37	17:06	22:54	17:48
25	2:00	15:43	1:37	16:07	1:24	16:21	1:09	16:38	0:51	16:58	0:29	17:23	0:06	17:48	—	18:24	23:05	19:20
26	2:47	16:37	2:22	17:03	2:07	17:18	1:50	17:36	1:30	17:57	1:04	18:24	0:38	18:52	0:02	19:31	23:36	20:39
27	3:39	17:31	3:13	17:57	2:57	18:12	2:40	18:29	2:18	18:50	1:51	19:17	1:23	19:44	0:44	20:22	—	21:25
28	4:34	18:22	4:09	18:46	3:54	19:00	3:37	19:16	3:16	19:35	2:50	19:59	2:23	20:23	1:45	20:56	0:43	21:44
29	5:33	19:11	5:10	19:31	4:57	19:43	4:41	19:56	4:23	20:12	4:00	20:32	3:36	20:51	3:05	21:16	2:18	21:51
30	6:32	19:55	6:13	20:11	6:02	20:20	5:50	20:31	5:35	20:43	5:16	20:57	4:58	21:12	4:34	21:30	4:01	21:53
31	7:31	20:36	7:17	20:47	7:09	20:53	7:00	21:00	6:49	21:08	6:36	21:18	6:23	21:28	6:06	21:39	5:45	21:54

MOONRISE AND MOONSET, 2003 AUGUST
UNIVERSAL TIME AT GREENWICH MERIDIAN

Latitude: Event:	+62° RISE	+62° SET	+58° RISE	+58° SET	+54° RISE	+54° SET	+50° RISE	+50° SET	+45° RISE	+45° SET	+40° RISE	+40° SET	+35° RISE	+35° SET	+30° RISE	+30° SET	+20° RISE	+20° SET
Aug. 1	7:26	21:53	7:38	21:46	7:48	21:41	7:55	21:36	8:03	21:31	8:10	21:27	8:15	21:24	8:20	21:21	8:29	21:15
2	9:06	21:52	9:10	21:52	9:13	21:53	9:15	21:53	9:18	21:53	9:20	21:53	9:22	21:53	9:23	21:53	9:26	21:53
3	10:45	21:51	10:41	21:59	10:38	22:05	10:35	22:09	10:32	22:14	10:30	22:19	10:28	22:22	10:26	22:26	10:23	22:31
4	12:27	21:51	12:15	22:06	12:05	22:18	11:57	22:28	11:48	22:38	11:41	22:47	11:36	22:54	11:31	23:00	11:22	23:12
5	14:14	21:51	13:51	22:16	13:34	22:35	13:20	22:50	13:06	23:05	12:55	23:18	12:45	23:29	12:37	23:39	12:22	23:55
6	16:06	21:53	15:30	22:31	15:04	22:57	14:44	23:18	14:25	23:39	14:09	23:56	13:56	—	13:44	—	13:25	—
7	18:00	22:01	17:06	22:55	16:32	23:30	16:07	23:56	15:43	—	15:23	—	15:07	0:10	14:53	0:22	14:29	0:44
8	19:42	22:27	18:31	23:38	17:51	—	17:22	—	16:55	0:21	16:33	0:41	16:15	0:58	16:00	1:13	15:34	1:37
9	20:39	23:38	19:32	—	18:52	0:18	18:24	0:47	17:56	1:15	17:35	1:37	17:17	1:55	17:02	2:10	16:36	2:36
10	20:58	—	20:08	0:45	19:35	1:25	19:10	1:53	18:46	2:19	18:27	2:41	18:11	2:58	17:56	3:13	17:32	3:39
11	21:03	1:23	20:29	2:12	20:04	2:44	19:44	3:08	19:25	3:32	19:09	3:50	18:55	4:06	18:43	4:19	18:23	4:42
12	21:05	3:13	20:42	3:46	20:24	4:09	20:09	4:28	19:55	4:46	19:43	5:01	19:32	5:14	19:23	5:25	19:08	5:43
13	21:04	4:56	20:50	5:18	20:38	5:34	20:29	5:47	20:19	6:00	20:12	6:11	20:04	6:20	19:58	6:28	19:47	6:41
14	21:03	6:33	20:56	6:45	20:50	6:55	20:45	7:03	20:40	7:11	20:36	7:17	20:32	7:23	20:29	7:28	20:23	7:36
15	21:02	8:04	21:01	8:09	21:00	8:12	21:00	8:15	20:59	8:18	20:58	8:21	20:58	8:23	20:58	8:25	20:57	8:28
16	21:01	9:31	21:06	9:29	21:10	9:27	21:14	9:25	21:17	9:24	21:20	9:23	21:23	9:21	21:25	9:20	21:30	9:19
17	20:59	10:57	21:11	10:48	21:20	10:40	21:28	10:34	21:36	10:28	21:43	10:23	21:48	10:19	21:54	10:15	22:02	10:08
18	20:58	12:24	21:17	12:07	21:32	11:54	21:44	11:43	21:56	11:32	22:07	11:23	22:16	11:16	22:23	11:09	22:37	10:57
19	20:59	13:53	21:26	13:27	21:47	13:07	22:03	12:52	22:20	12:37	22:34	12:24	22:45	12:13	22:56	12:04	23:14	11:48
20	21:01	15:25	21:39	14:48	22:06	14:21	22:27	14:01	22:48	13:41	23:05	13:25	23:20	13:11	23:32	13:00	23:54	12:39
21	21:08	16:58	22:00	16:07	22:34	15:34	22:59	15:09	23:24	14:45	23:43	14:26	—	14:10	—	13:56	—	13:33
22	21:27	18:25	22:34	17:19	23:13	16:41	23:41	16:13	—	15:46	—	15:25	0:00	15:07	0:14	14:52	0:38	14:27
23	22:18	19:26	23:27	18:17	—	17:37	—	17:09	0:08	16:42	0:29	16:20	0:47	16:02	1:02	15:47	1:28	15:21
24	23:45	19:52	—	18:57	0:06	18:21	0:35	17:55	1:02	17:30	1:23	17:10	1:41	16:53	1:56	16:38	2:22	16:13
25	—	20:01	0:40	19:21	1:15	18:53	1:41	18:31	2:05	18:10	2:25	17:52	2:41	17:38	2:55	17:25	3:19	17:03
26	1:29	20:04	2:07	19:37	2:35	19:16	2:55	19:00	3:16	18:43	3:32	18:29	3:46	18:17	3:58	18:07	4:19	17:49
27	3:15	20:05	3:41	19:47	4:00	19:33	4:15	19:22	4:30	19:10	4:43	19:01	4:54	18:52	5:03	18:45	5:19	18:32
28	5:00	20:05	5:15	19:55	5:27	19:47	5:37	19:41	5:47	19:35	5:55	19:29	6:02	19:24	6:08	19:20	6:18	19:12
29	6:43	20:04	6:49	20:01	6:54	20:00	6:59	19:58	7:03	19:57	7:07	19:55	7:10	19:54	7:12	19:53	7:17	19:52
30	8:25	20:02	8:23	20:07	8:22	20:12	8:21	20:15	8:20	20:19	8:19	20:22	8:18	20:24	8:17	20:26	8:16	20:30
31	10:08	20:01	9:58	20:14	9:50	20:24	9:44	20:33	9:37	20:42	9:31	20:49	9:27	20:55	9:23	21:01	9:15	21:11

MOONRISE AND MOONSET, 2003 SEPTEMBER
UNIVERSAL TIME AT GREENWICH MERIDIAN

Sep.	+20° RISE	+20° SET	+30° RISE	+30° SET	+35° RISE	+35° SET	+40° RISE	+40° SET	+45° RISE	+45° SET	+50° RISE	+50° SET	+54° RISE	+54° SET	+58° RISE	+58° SET	+62° RISE	+62° SET
1	10:16	21:54	10:29	21:38	10:37	21:30	10:45	21:20	10:56	21:08	11:08	20:54	11:20	20:40	11:35	20:23	11:55	20:01
2	11:19	22:41	11:37	22:20	11:48	22:09	12:00	21:55	12:15	21:39	12:33	21:20	12:51	21:00	13:15	20:36	13:47	20:02
3	12:23	23:33	12:46	23:08	12:59	22:54	13:15	22:38	13:33	22:19	13:57	21:54	14:21	21:29	14:53	20:56	15:42	20:06
4	13:27	—	13:53	—	14:08	23:48	14:26	23:30	14:47	23:08	15:14	22:41	15:42	22:12	16:22	21:32	17:31	20:22
5	14:29	0:29	14:55	0:03	15:11	—	15:29	—	15:51	—	16:19	23:41	16:48	23:11	17:30	22:30	18:44	21:16
6	15:26	1:30	15:51	1:04	16:06	0:48	16:23	0:30	16:43	0:08	17:09	—	17:36	—	18:12	23:51	19:09	22:54
7	16:18	2:32	16:40	2:07	16:52	1:53	17:07	1:37	17:24	1:17	17:46	0:52	18:08	0:26	18:36	—	19:16	—
8	17:03	3:32	17:21	3:12	17:31	3:00	17:43	2:46	17:56	2:30	18:13	2:10	18:29	1:49	18:50	1:22	19:17	0:43
9	17:44	4:31	17:57	4:15	18:04	4:06	18:12	3:56	18:22	3:43	18:34	3:28	18:45	3:13	18:59	2:54	19:17	2:28
10	18:21	5:26	18:28	5:16	18:33	5:13	18:38	5:03	18:44	4:54	18:51	4:44	18:57	4:35	19:05	4:23	19:16	4:07
11	18:55	6:19	18:58	6:14	18:59	6:11	19:01	6:07	19:03	6:03	19:05	5:58	19:08	5:53	19:10	5:47	19:14	5:40
12	19:28	7:10	19:26	7:10	19:24	7:10	19:23	7:10	19:21	7:09	19:19	7:09	19:17	7:09	19:15	7:09	19:12	7:09
13	20:01	8:00	19:53	8:05	19:49	8:08	19:45	8:11	19:39	8:15	19:33	8:19	19:27	8:23	19:20	8:29	19:10	8:35
14	20:34	8:50	20:22	8:59	20:16	9:05	20:08	9:11	19:59	9:19	19:48	9:28	19:38	9:37	19:25	9:48	19:09	10:02
15	21:10	9:40	20:54	9:54	20:44	10:03	20:34	10:12	20:21	10:24	20:06	10:37	19:51	10:51	19:32	11:08	19:08	11:31
16	21:49	10:31	21:28	10:50	21:17	11:01	21:03	11:13	20:47	11:28	20:28	11:47	20:08	12:05	19:43	12:29	19:08	13:03
17	22:31	11:23	22:08	11:46	21:54	11:59	21:38	12:14	21:19	12:33	20:55	12:55	20:31	13:19	19:59	13:50	19:12	14:37
18	23:18	12:17	22:52	12:42	22:37	12:57	22:20	13:14	21:59	13:35	21:32	14:01	21:04	14:28	20:26	15:06	19:23	16:09
19	—	13:10	23:43	13:37	23:28	13:52	23:10	14:10	22:48	14:32	22:20	15:00	21:51	15:29	21:10	16:10	19:56	17:23
20	0:10	14:03	—	14:29	—	14:44	—	15:01	23:47	15:23	23:20	15:49	22:53	16:17	22:14	16:56	21:10	18:01
21	1:05	14:53	0:40	15:17	0:25	15:30	0:07	15:46	—	16:05	—	16:29	—	16:53	23:36	17:25	22:49	18:13
22	2:03	15:40	1:40	16:00	1:27	16:12	1:12	16:25	0:54	16:41	0:31	17:00	0:07	17:38	—	17:44	—	18:17
23	3:02	16:24	2:44	16:40	2:33	16:48	2:21	16:59	2:06	17:10	1:48	17:24	1:30	17:53	1:07	17:56	0:35	18:18
24	4:02	17:06	3:49	17:16	3:41	17:22	3:32	17:28	3:22	17:36	3:10	17:45	2:57	18:06	2:42	18:04	2:21	18:17
25	5:02	17:46	4:54	17:50	4:50	17:52	4:45	17:55	4:39	17:59	4:32	18:02	4:26	18:06	4:17	18:10	4:07	18:16
26	6:02	18:25	6:00	18:24	5:59	18:23	5:58	18:22	5:57	18:21	5:56	18:19	5:55	18:18	5:53	18:16	5:51	18:14
27	7:02	19:06	7:07	18:58	7:10	18:54	7:13	18:49	7:17	18:43	7:21	18:37	7:25	18:30	7:31	18:22	7:37	18:13
28	8:04	19:49	8:15	19:35	8:22	19:19	8:29	19:19	8:37	19:09	8:48	18:57	8:58	18:45	9:10	18:30	9:27	18:11
29	9:09	20:36	9:25	20:17	9:35	20:06	9:46	19:53	10:00	19:39	10:16	19:21	10:32	19:03	10:53	18:41	11:21	18:11
30	10:14	21:27	10:36	21:04	10:49	20:50	11:04	20:35	11:21	20:16	11:43	19:53	12:06	19:29	12:36	18:58	13:20	18:13

MOONRISE AND MOONSET, 2003 OCTOBER
UNIVERSAL TIME AT GREENWICH MERIDIAN

Latitude: Event:	+62° RISE	+62° SET	+58° RISE	+58° SET	+54° RISE	+54° SET	+50° RISE	+50° SET	+45° RISE	+45° SET	+40° RISE	+40° SET	+35° RISE	+35° SET	+30° RISE	+30° SET	+20° RISE	+20° SET
Oct. 1	15:18	18:22	14:12	19:28	13:33	20:07	13:05	20:36	12:39	21:03	12:18	21:24	12:00	21:42	11:45	21:58	11:20	22:24
2	16:48	18:59	15:28	20:20	14:45	21:02	14:15	21:32	13:47	22:01	13:25	22:23	13:06	22:41	12:50	22:57	12:24	23:24
3	17:22	20:30	16:17	21:35	15:38	22:13	15:10	22:41	14:43	23:07	14:22	23:28	14:04	23:45	13:49	—	13:23	—
4	17:30	22:20	16:44	23:04	16:13	23:34	15:50	23:57	15:27	—	15:08	—	14:52	—	14:39	0:00	14:16	0:25
5	17:31	—	17:00	—	16:37	—	16:19	—	16:00	0:19	15:45	0:37	15:33	0:52	15:21	1:04	15:02	1:26
6	17:31	0:06	17:10	0:36	16:54	0:58	16:40	1:15	16:27	1:32	16:16	1:45	16:07	1:57	15:58	2:07	15:44	2:25
7	17:29	1:46	17:16	2:05	17:06	2:19	16:58	2:31	16:49	2:43	16:42	2:52	16:36	3:01	16:30	3:08	16:21	3:20
8	17:27	3:19	17:21	3:30	17:17	3:38	17:13	3:44	17:09	3:51	17:05	3:57	17:02	4:02	17:00	4:06	16:55	4:13
9	17:25	4:49	17:25	4:52	17:26	4:54	17:26	4:56	17:27	4:58	17:27	4:59	17:27	5:01	17:28	5:02	17:28	5:04
10	17:23	6:16	17:30	6:11	17:35	6:08	17:40	6:06	17:44	6:03	17:48	6:00	17:52	5:58	17:55	5:57	18:00	5:54
11	17:21	7:42	17:34	7:31	17:45	7:22	17:54	7:15	18:03	7:07	18:11	7:01	18:17	6:56	18:23	6:51	18:34	6:43
12	17:19	9:11	17:41	8:51	17:57	8:36	18:10	8:24	18:24	8:12	18:35	8:03	18:45	7:53	18:54	7:46	19:08	7:33
13	17:19	10:42	17:49	10:12	18:12	9:51	18:30	9:34	18:48	9:17	19:03	9:03	19:16	8:52	19:27	8:41	19:46	8:24
14	17:20	12:16	18:03	11:34	18:32	11:05	18:55	10:43	19:17	10:22	19:36	10:04	19:51	9:50	20:04	9:37	20:27	9:16
15	17:26	13:51	18:24	12:52	19:01	12:16	19:28	11:50	19:54	11:25	20:14	11:05	20:31	10:48	20:46	10:34	21:12	10:09
16	17:45	15:16	19:00	14:02	19:41	13:21	20:11	12:51	20:38	12:24	21:00	12:02	21:19	11:44	21:34	11:28	22:01	11:02
17	18:42	16:08	19:55	14:54	20:36	14:13	21:05	13:41	21:32	13:17	21:54	12:55	22:12	12:37	22:27	12:21	22:54	11:54
18	20:14	16:25	21:09	15:29	21:44	14:53	22:10	14:27	22:35	14:01	22:55	13:41	23:11	13:24	23:25	13:09	23:49	12:44
19	21:56	16:30	22:35	15:50	23:02	15:22	23:23	15:00	23:44	14:39	—	14:21	—	14:07	—	13:54	—	13:32
20	23:41	16:31	—	16:04	—	15:43	—	15:26	—	15:10	0:00	14:56	0:14	14:44	0:26	14:34	0:47	14:16
21	—	16:31	0:07	16:13	0:26	15:59	0:41	15:48	0:57	15:36	1:09	15:26	1:20	15:18	1:29	15:10	1:45	14:58
22	1:25	16:29	1:40	16:20	1:52	16:12	2:02	16:06	2:12	15:59	2:20	15:54	2:27	15:49	2:33	15:45	2:43	15:37
23	3:09	16:27	3:15	16:25	3:20	16:24	3:24	16:22	3:28	16:21	3:32	16:20	3:35	16:19	3:38	16:18	3:42	16:17
24	4:54	16:25	4:52	16:31	4:50	16:36	4:49	16:39	4:47	16:43	4:46	16:47	4:45	16:50	4:44	16:52	4:43	16:57
25	6:43	16:23	6:32	16:37	6:23	16:49	6:16	16:58	6:08	17:07	6:02	17:15	5:57	17:22	5:52	17:28	5:45	17:39
26	8:38	16:22	8:16	16:46	7:59	17:05	7:46	17:20	7:32	17:35	7:21	17:48	7:12	17:59	7:03	18:08	6:49	18:25
27	10:40	16:22	10:03	17:00	9:37	17:28	9:17	17:49	8:57	18:10	8:41	18:27	8:28	18:42	8:16	18:54	7:57	19:16
28	12:46	16:26	11:48	17:25	11:12	18:01	10:46	18:28	10:21	18:54	10:01	19:15	9:44	19:32	9:30	19:47	9:05	20:13
29	14:38	16:47	13:17	18:08	12:34	18:51	12:04	19:21	11:36	19:50	11:14	20:12	10:55	20:31	10:39	20:47	10:13	21:14
30	15:32	18:04	14:17	19:18	13:36	19:59	13:07	20:28	12:39	20:56	12:16	21:18	11:58	21:36	11:42	21:51	11:16	22:17
31	15:44	19:55	14:51	20:46	14:17	21:20	13:52	21:44	13:27	22:08	13:07	22:27	12:51	22:43	12:37	22:57	12:12	23:20

MOONRISE AND MOONSET, 2003 NOVEMBER
UNIVERSAL TIME AT GREENWICH MERIDIAN

Latitude:	+20°		+30°		+35°		+40°		+45°		+50°		+54°		+58°		+62°	
Event:	RISE	SET	RISE	SET	RISE	SET	RISE	SET	RISE	SET	RISE	SET	RISE	SET	RISE	SET	RISE	SET
Nov. 1	13:01	—	13:22	—	13:34	23:50	13:48	23:37	14:04	23:22	14:24	23:03	14:44	22:44	15:10	22:20	15:45	21:46
2	13:44	0:20	14:01	0:01	14:10	—	14:20	—	14:33	—	14:48	—	15:02	—	15:21	23:50	15:45	23:28
3	14:23	1:16	14:34	1:02	14:40	0:54	14:47	0:45	14:56	0:34	15:06	0:20	15:16	0:07	15:28	—	15:43	—
4	14:57	2:10	15:04	2:01	15:07	1:55	15:11	1:49	15:16	1:43	15:21	1:34	15:26	1:26	15:33	1:16	15:41	1:03
5	15:30	3:00	15:31	2:57	15:32	2:54	15:33	2:52	15:34	2:49	15:35	2:46	15:36	2:42	15:37	2:38	15:39	2:33
6	16:02	3:50	15:58	3:51	15:56	3:52	15:54	3:53	15:51	3:54	15:48	3:55	15:45	3:56	15:41	3:58	15:36	3:59
7	16:35	4:39	16:26	4:45	16:21	4:49	16:16	4:53	16:09	4:58	16:02	5:04	15:54	5:09	15:45	5:16	15:34	5:25
8	17:09	5:28	16:55	5:40	16:48	5:46	16:39	5:54	16:29	6:02	16:17	6:13	16:05	6:23	15:51	6:36	15:32	6:52
9	17:45	6:19	17:27	6:35	17:17	6:44	17:05	6:55	16:52	7:07	16:35	7:22	16:19	7:38	15:58	7:57	15:31	8:22
10	18:25	7:10	18:03	7:31	17:50	7:42	17:36	7:56	17:19	8:12	16:58	8:32	16:37	8:52	16:10	9:19	15:31	9:56
11	19:08	8:03	18:43	8:27	18:29	8:41	18:12	8:57	17:53	9:16	17:28	9:40	17:02	10:05	16:28	10:39	15:34	11:32
12	19:56	8:57	19:29	9:22	19:14	9:38	18:56	9:55	18:34	10:17	18:07	10:44	17:38	11:13	16:58	11:52	15:47	13:03
13	20:47	9:49	20:20	10:16	20:05	10:31	19:47	10:50	19:25	11:12	18:57	11:40	18:27	12:09	17:45	12:51	16:28	14:09
14	21:41	10:39	21:16	11:05	21:01	11:20	20:44	11:38	20:23	11:59	19:57	12:26	19:30	12:53	18:52	13:32	17:49	14:35
15	22:37	11:27	22:15	11:50	22:02	12:04	21:47	12:20	21:29	12:38	21:06	13:02	20:43	13:25	20:13	13:57	19:28	14:43
16	23:33	12:11	23:15	12:31	23:05	12:42	22:52	12:55	22:38	13:11	22:21	13:29	22:03	13:48	21:41	14:12	21:10	14:44
17	—	12:52	—	13:07	—	13:16	—	13:26	23:50	13:38	23:38	13:51	23:26	14:05	23:10	14:22	22:51	14:44
18	0:29	13:31	0:16	13:41	0:09	13:47	0:00	13:53	—	14:01	—	14:10	—	14:19	—	14:29	—	14:42
19	1:26	14:09	1:19	14:14	1:14	14:16	1:09	14:19	1:03	14:22	0:56	14:26	0:50	14:30	0:41	14:35	0:31	14:40
20	2:24	14:47	2:22	14:46	2:21	14:45	2:20	14:44	2:19	14:44	2:17	14:42	2:16	14:41	2:14	14:40	2:11	14:38
21	3:23	15:27	3:27	15:20	3:30	15:16	3:33	15:11	3:36	15:06	3:40	14:59	3:44	14:53	3:49	14:46	3:56	14:36
22	4:25	16:11	4:36	15:58	4:42	15:50	4:49	15:41	4:58	15:31	5:08	15:19	5:18	15:07	5:30	14:53	5:46	14:34
23	5:31	16:59	5:48	16:40	5:58	16:29	6:09	16:17	6:22	16:02	6:39	15:44	6:55	15:26	7:16	15:04	7:44	14:33
24	6:41	17:54	7:03	17:31	7:16	17:17	7:31	17:01	7:49	16:42	8:11	16:18	8:34	15:54	9:05	15:22	9:51	14:35
25	7:51	18:55	8:17	18:29	8:32	18:13	8:50	17:55	9:11	17:33	9:38	17:05	10:07	16:36	10:47	15:55	11:58	14:44
26	8:59	20:00	9:26	19:33	9:42	19:18	10:01	18:59	10:23	18:37	10:52	18:08	11:22	17:38	12:05	16:55	13:29	15:32
27	10:01	21:06	10:27	20:42	10:42	20:27	10:59	20:10	11:20	19:50	11:47	19:24	12:14	18:57	12:52	18:20	13:53	17:20
28	10:55	22:10	11:17	21:49	11:31	21:37	11:46	21:23	12:03	21:06	12:25	20:45	12:47	20:24	13:16	19:56	13:58	19:16
29	11:42	23:09	12:00	22:53	12:10	22:44	12:22	22:34	12:36	22:21	12:52	22:06	13:09	21:50	13:30	21:31	13:58	21:05
30	12:23	—	12:35	—	12:43	23:48	12:51	23:41	13:01	23:32	13:13	23:22	13:24	23:13	13:38	23:00	13:56	22:45

MOONRISE AND MOONSET, 2003 DECEMBER
UNIVERSAL TIME AT GREENWICH MERIDIAN

Moon phase symbols along the top of the table: ○ ◑ ● ◐

Latitude:	+20°		+30°		+35°		+40°		+45°		+50°		+54°		+58°		+62°	
Event:	RISE	SET	RISE	SET	RISE	SET	RISE	SET	RISE	SET	RISE	SET	RISE	SET	RISE	SET	RISE	SET
Dec. 1	12:59	0:05	13:07	—	13:11	—	13:16	—	13:22	—	13:29	—	13:36	—	13:44	—	13:54	—
2	13:32	0:57	13:35	0:51	13:37	0:48	13:38	0:45	13:41	0:40	13:43	0:35	13:45	0:31	13:48	0:25	13:52	0:17
3	14:04	1:47	14:02	1:46	14:01	1:46	14:00	1:46	13:58	1:46	13:56	1:46	13:54	1:45	13:52	1:45	13:49	1:45
4	14:37	2:36	14:30	2:40	14:26	2:43	14:21	2:46	14:16	2:50	14:09	2:54	14:04	2:59	13:56	3:04	13:47	3:10
5	15:10	3:25	14:58	3:34	14:51	3:40	14:44	3:46	14:35	3:54	14:24	4:03	14:14	4:12	14:01	4:22	13:45	4:36
6	15:45	4:14	15:29	4:29	15:19	4:37	15:09	4:47	14:56	4:58	14:41	5:12	14:26	5:25	14:08	5:42	13:44	6:05
7	16:23	5:06	16:03	5:24	15:51	5:35	15:38	5:48	15:22	6:03	15:02	6:21	14:43	6:40	14:18	7:04	13:43	7:37
8	17:06	5:58	16:42	6:21	16:28	6:34	16:12	6:49	15:53	7:08	15:30	7:30	15:06	7:54	14:33	8:25	13:46	9:12
9	17:52	6:52	17:26	7:17	17:11	7:32	16:54	7:49	16:32	8:10	16:06	8:36	15:38	9:04	14:59	9:42	13:54	10:46
10	18:43	7:45	18:16	8:11	18:00	8:27	17:42	8:45	17:20	9:07	16:52	9:35	16:23	10:05	15:41	10:46	14:24	12:03
11	19:36	8:36	19:11	9:02	18:55	9:18	18:38	9:36	18:17	9:57	17:50	10:24	17:22	10:53	16:42	11:32	15:34	12:41
12	20:31	9:24	20:08	9:49	19:55	10:03	19:39	10:19	19:20	10:39	18:57	11:03	18:32	11:28	17:59	12:02	17:10	12:52
13	21:27	10:09	21:08	10:30	20:56	10:42	20:43	10:56	20:28	11:13	20:09	11:33	19:50	11:55	19:25	12:19	18:50	12:56
14	22:22	10:51	22:08	11:10	21:59	11:17	21:49	11:28	21:38	11:41	21:24	11:56	21:10	12:12	20:52	12:31	20:29	12:54
15	23:17	11:30	23:08	11:41	23:02	11:48	22:56	11:56	22:48	12:05	22:40	12:15	22:31	12:26	22:20	12:38	22:06	12:53
16	—	12:06	—	12:13	—	12:17	—	12:21	—	12:26	23:56	12:32	23:53	12:37	23:49	12:44	23:43	12:51
17	0:12	12:43	0:08	12:44	0:06	12:45	0:03	12:45	0:00	12:46	—	12:47	—	12:48	—	12:49	—	12:48
18	1:08	13:20	1:10	13:16	1:11	13:13	1:12	13:10	1:14	13:07	1:15	13:03	1:17	12:59	1:19	12:54	1:21	12:48
19	2:07	14:00	2:14	13:50	2:19	13:44	2:24	13:37	2:30	13:30	2:37	13:20	2:44	13:11	2:53	13:00	3:04	12:47
20	3:09	14:45	3:22	14:29	3:30	14:19	3:39	14:09	3:50	13:56	4:03	13:42	4:16	13:27	4:33	13:09	4:54	12:45
21	4:15	15:35	4:34	15:14	4:45	15:01	4:58	14:47	5:14	14:30	5:33	14:10	5:53	13:49	6:18	13:22	6:54	12:45
22	5:24	16:32	5:48	16:07	6:02	15:52	6:18	15:35	6:38	15:15	7:03	14:49	7:29	14:22	8:04	13:46	9:01	12:49
23	6:34	17:36	7:00	17:09	7:16	16:53	7:35	16:35	7:57	16:12	8:25	15:44	8:55	15:14	9:38	14:31	10:58	13:10
24	7:40	18:44	8:07	18:18	8:23	18:02	8:41	17:44	9:03	17:23	9:31	16:55	10:00	16:26	10:41	15:45	11:55	14:32
25	8:40	19:51	9:04	19:28	9:18	19:15	9:35	18:59	9:54	18:40	10:19	18:17	10:43	17:53	11:17	17:21	12:07	16:32
26	9:32	20:54	9:52	20:36	10:04	20:26	10:17	20:14	10:33	19:59	10:52	19:42	11:11	19:24	11:35	19:01	12:08	18:29
27	10:17	21:54	10:32	21:41	10:41	21:34	10:50	21:25	11:02	21:15	11:16	21:03	11:29	20:51	11:46	20:36	12:08	20:16
28	10:56	22:49	11:06	22:41	11:12	22:37	11:18	22:32	11:25	22:27	11:34	22:20	11:43	22:13	11:53	22:05	12:06	21:54
29	11:32	23:41	11:36	23:39	11:39	23:37	11:42	23:36	11:45	23:35	11:49	23:33	11:53	23:31	11:58	23:28	12:04	23:26
30	12:05	—	12:04	—	12:04	—	12:04	—	12:03	—	12:03	—	12:03	—	12:02	—	12:01	—
31	12:37	0:31	12:32	0:34	12:29	0:36	12:25	0:38	12:21	0:40	12:16	0:43	12:12	0:46	12:06	0:49	11:59	0:53

ECLIPSE PATTERNS
BY ROY BISHOP

Eclipse Seasons

The plane of the Moon's orbit is tilted about 5° to the plane of Earth's orbit, the ecliptic. Since 5° is considerably larger than the angular sizes of the Sun and Moon (≈0.5°), eclipses can occur only when the Sun is near (within about ±15° to ±18° for solar eclipses) one of the two points at which the Moon's orbit crosses the ecliptic (nodes). The *ascending* node is the one at which the Moon crosses to the *north* side of the ecliptic.

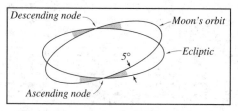

The Sun moves eastward along the ecliptic about 1° per day; thus the interval during which an eclipse can occur is at most about $(2 \times 18°) \div 1°/d = 36$ d, an *eclipse season*. Since the interval between new moons (29.5 days) is somewhat less, one or two solar eclipses will occur in each eclipse season. Six months later, when the Sun is near the other node, another eclipse season occurs. However, the plane of the Moon's orbit wobbles, making the nodes regress slowly westward along the ecliptic with a period of 18.61 years; thus the two eclipse seasons drift backward through the year, occurring about 19 days earlier each year. *The eclipse seasons of 2003 occur in May and November.*

In a calendar year,
- there can be as many as seven eclipses (solar and lunar combined, as last occurred in 1982) and as few as four (the usual number, as in 2003);
- there can be as many as five solar or lunar eclipses and as few as two;
- the number of total or annular solar eclipses can range from zero to two, the number of total lunar eclipses from zero to three.

In 2003, there are four eclipses: two lunar (both total) and two solar (one annular and one total).

The Saros

Eclipses of the Sun and Moon recur with various periodicities that are more or less approximate. These periodicities are interesting both as numerical curiosities and because they may be used to predict eclipses. The most famous periodicity, the *Saros*, has been known since ancient times. It is a consequence of a remarkable commensurability between three lunar average periods:

Synodic month (S) (new to new)	= 29.530 589 d, 223S	= 6585.3213 d
Draconic month (N) (node to node)	= 27.212 221 d, 242N	= 6585.3575 d
Anomalistic month (P) (perigee to perigee) = 27.554 550 d, 239P		= 6585.5375 d

Several aspects of this arithmetic are relevant to the pattern of eclipses (for brevity, the following comments are restricted primarily to the case of solar eclipses):

(1) An integer number of Ss (223) ensures a new Moon and hence the possibility of a second solar eclipse.

(2) $242N \approx 223S$ means that the new Moon will be at almost the same position relative to a node, ensuring that an eclipse *will* occur again and that it will occur on Earth's globe about the same distance north or south of the ecliptic plane as did the first eclipse.

(3) The Saros $(223S) = 6585.3213$ d $= 18$ years $+ only$ 10.3213 d or 11.3213 d (depending on the number of intervening leap years). Thus one Saros later Earth will be at almost the same point in its elliptical orbit and hence at nearly the same distance from the Sun. Moreover, the inclination of Earth toward the Sun (season) will be nearly the same; thus the same latitude region of Earth will be exposed to the eclipse.

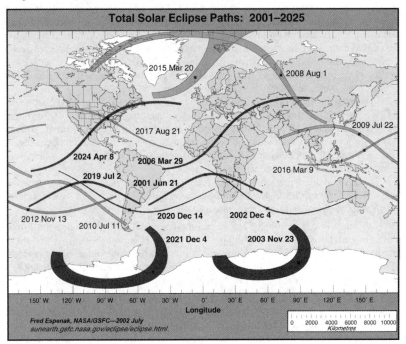

The figure shows the paths of all total solar eclipses, excluding hybrid annular/total eclipses, occurring during the years 2001–2025. There are 15 eclipses, one in each of the years 2001, 2002, 2003, 2006, 2008, 2009, 2010, 2012, 2015, 2016, 2017, 2019, 2020, 2021, and 2024. Because the 25-year period covered by the figure is somewhat longer than the 18-year Saros interval, the first four and last four eclipses, drawn with heavy shading and with labels in bold type, make up four Saros pairs, with Saros numbers 127, 142, 152, and 139, respectively. Note that the members of each pair are both total eclipses, are separated in time by one Saros, have similar path shapes, occur at similar latitudes, and that the later member is shifted 120° westward in longitude (see items (2) through (6) of the text explaining these features). The figure was produced by Fred Espenak and is presented here with his permission. For figures showing total solar eclipses, annular eclipses, and hybrid annular/total eclipses for the period 1801–2200 see sunearth.gsfc.nasa.gov/eclipse/SEatlas/SEatlas.html.

(4) $239P \approx 223S$ means that one Saros later the new Moon will be at almost the same point in its elliptical orbit and thus at the same distance from Earth. With the same lunar and solar distances, the type of eclipse (total or annular) will be the same. Since the eclipse will occur near the same geographic latitude (see (2) and (3)), the duration of totality or annularity, or the magnitude of partial eclipse if the eclipse is not central, will be almost the same as it was one Saros earlier.

(5) $242N - 223S = 0.0361$ d $= 0.87$ h. This, together with the 0.55°/h eastward speed of the Moon in its orbit, means that after one Saros, the Moon will be about 0.5° west of its former position relative to its node. Thus a Saros series does not last forever; there will be about $36°/0.5° \approx 72$ eclipses in a Saros series (the number ranges from 69 to 86). Furthermore, any one Saros series will last for about $72 \times 18 \approx 1300$ years (the range is 1226 to 1532 years).

A Saros series begins with about 10 partial eclipses of increasing magnitude in the north or south polar region, depending upon whether the eclipses are occurring near the ascending or descending lunar node, respectively. These are followed by about 50 central eclipses (either total or annular), which over many centuries progressively shift southward or northward across Earth (about 300-km shift in latitude with each successive eclipse). The series ends with 10 or so partial eclipses of decreasing magnitude in the opposite polar region.

Currently, for solar eclipses 39 Saros series are running simultaneously, numbers 117 through 155 (for lunar eclipses, 41 Saros series are running, numbers 109 through 149). That is, in any 18-year 11-day interval, one eclipse from each of these 39 (and 41) series takes place, after which the whole pattern repeats. Those series occurring at the lunar ascending node are given odd numbers; those at the descending node, even numbers (vice versa for lunar eclipses).

The eclipse sequence of the year 2003 is similar to that of the four-eclipse year 1985, except that the May annular solar eclipse was partial in 1985 (both in north polar regions, and odd Saros number 147).

(6) The Saros $= 223S = 6585.3213$ d, and the fractional 0.3213 d $\approx$ one-third of a day. Thus each successive solar eclipse in a Saros series will be shifted one-third of the way westward (120° in longitude) around Earth. After three Saros periods (3×6585.3213 d $\approx 19\,756$ d, or approximately 54 years and 1 month), a cycle known as the *Exeligmos*, the eclipse will be back at approximately the same geographic longitude, although shifted about 1000 km in latitude. Two examples follow.

(a) Two total lunar eclipses will be visible from much of North America in 2003, on the nights of May 15/16 (Saros 121) and November 8/9 (Saros 126). One Saros earlier, nearly identical eclipses occurred on 1985 May 4 (Saros 121) and 1985 October 28 (Saros 126), except they were visible about 120° further east, from Europe and Asia, not from North America.

(b) The total solar eclipse of 2024 April 8 (no. 30 of Saros 139), which sweeps northeastward across eastern North America, will be geographically similar to that of 1970 March 7 (no. 27 of Saros 139), which followed the eastern seaboard of North America one Exeligmos earlier.

The Metonic Cycle

The sequence of lunar phases and the year repeat their relative pattern at 19-year intervals, a cycle known to astronomers in ancient Babylon and which was discovered independently around 430 BC by a Greek astronomer, Meton. We have

$235S = 235 \times 29.530\,589 = 6939.6884$ d;
19 years $= 6939$ d or 6940 d (depending on leap years).

Also, $255N$ is also very close to 19 years:

$255N = 255 \times 27.212\,221 = 6939.1164$ d.

Thus solar and lunar eclipses also repeat on a 19-year "Metonic" cycle. Since $255N$ is less than $235S$, the Moon does not reach the same phase (new or full for an eclipse) until it has moved eastward relative to the node by

$(235S - 255N) \times 24h \times 0.55°/h = 7.5°.$

Thus a Metonic eclipse series will have only

eclipse season width on the ecliptic $(36°) \div 7.5° \approx 4$ or 5 eclipses;

and the geographic latitude of successive solar eclipses in a series will change substantially (north or south, depending upon whether the Moon is at its ascending node or descending node, respectively).

What about the Moon's position in its orbit relative to its perigee? Using the anomalistic month P (the Moon returns to perigee on average every 27.554 550 d),

$235S \div P = 251.85$, which is *not* near an integer.

Thus in a Metonic series the Moon's distance is not the same from one eclipse to another. Hence the type of solar eclipse (total or annular) will vary within the series.

With only about four eclipses in a series, a mix of eclipse types, and scattered geographic occurrence, a Metonic eclipse series is not as elegant or useful as a Saros series. The main feature of a Metonic eclipse series is that, like lunar phases, the successive eclipses occur on (almost) the *same day* of the year.

Examples of the Metonic cycle for a lunar phase, lunar eclipses, and two recent Western Hemisphere total solar eclipses are given below. The numbers in parentheses are Saros numbers.

Full Moon	Lunar Eclipses	Solar Eclipses
1946 Sep. 10	1965 May 15 (no eclipse)	1960 Feb. 26 (no eclipse)
1965 Sep. 10	1984 May 15 Penum. (111)	**1979** Feb. 26 Total (120)
1984 Sep. 10	**2003** May 16 Total (121)	**1998** Feb. 26 Total (130)
2003 Sep. 10	2022 May 16 Total (131)	2017 Feb. 26 Annular (140)
2022 Sep. 10	2041 May 16 Partial (141)	2036 Feb. 27 Partial (150)
2041 Sep. 10	2060 May 16 (no eclipse)	2055 Feb. 27 (no eclipse)

ECLIPSES DURING 2003

BY FRED ESPENAK

Two central solar and two total lunar eclipses occur in 2003 as follows:

2003 May 16:	Total lunar eclipse
2003 May 31:	Annular solar eclipse
2003 Nov. 9:	Total lunar eclipse
2003 Nov. 23:	Total solar eclipse

Predictions for the eclipses are summarized in Figures 1 through 6. World maps show the regions of visibility for each eclipse. The lunar eclipse diagrams also include the path of the Moon through Earth's shadows. Contact times for each principal phase are tabulated along with the magnitudes and geocentric coordinates of the Sun and Moon at greatest eclipse.

Total Lunar Eclipse of May 16

The first eclipse of the year, a total lunar eclipse, is well-placed for Western Hemisphere observers. The eclipse occurs just half a day after perigee so the Moon will appear quite large (33.4 arc-min). During this event, the Moon is low on the ecliptic in Libra, approximately 15° west of the first-magnitude star alpha Scorpii (Antares).

The Moon's path moves through the northern part of Earth's umbral shadow. Although the eclipse is not central, the total phase still lasts 1 h 37 min. The eclipse begins at 01:05 UT with first penumbral contact. An hour later, the partial eclipse commences with first umbral contact at 02:03 UT. The total umbral eclipse begins at 03:14 UT and ends at 04:07 UT. The partial phase ends at 05:17 UT, and the Moon leaves the penumbral shadow at 06:15 UT. The Moon's path through Earth's shadows as well as a map illustrating worldwide visibility of the event are shown in Figure 1 (p. 149).

At the instant of greatest eclipse (03:40 UT), the Moon will lie in the zenith for observers in southern Brazil near its western border with Bolivia and Paraguay. At this time, the umbral magnitude[1] peaks at 1.134 as the Moon's southern limb passes 8.6 arc-min north of the shadow's axis. In contrast, the Moon's northern limb will lie 4.5 arc-min from the northern edge of the umbra and 25.3 arc-min from the shadow centre. Thus the northern sections of the Moon will appear much brighter than the southern part, which will lie deeper in the shadow. Since the Moon traverses a large range of umbral depths during totality, its appearance will likely change dramatically with time. However, it's impossible to predict the exact brightness distribution in the umbra so observers are encouraged to estimate the Danjon value at different times during totality (see Danjon Scale of Lunar Eclipse Brightness below). Note that it may also be necessary to assign different Danjon values to different portions of the Moon (i.e. north vs. south).

During totality, the spring constellations will be well-placed for viewing. Spica (m_V = +0.98) lies 32° west of the eclipsed Moon, while Arcturus (m_V = −0.05) is 43° to the northwest. Jupiter will appear low in the west in Cancer.

The eclipse will be widely visible from the Americas, Europe, and Africa. The eastern half of North America will witness the entire event, while the partial phases will already be in progress at moonrise as seen by observers in the western portions of the continent. Similarly, the Moon sets in Europe during various stages of the eclipse.

---

[1] Umbral magnitude of a lunar eclipse is defined as the fraction of the Moon's diameter covered by the umbral shadow. The magnitude is <1.0 for partial eclipses and >1.0 for total eclipses.

Observers in Ontario, Quebec, the Maritime Provinces, and the eastern United States will see all phases of the eclipse. Farther to the west, the eclipse begins before moonrise, but totality will still be visible except from Yukon and Alaska.

Table 1 (p. 144) lists predicted umbral immersion and emersion times for 20 well-defined lunar craters. The timing of craters is useful in determining the atmospheric enlargement of Earth's shadow (see Crater Timings During Lunar Eclipses below).

Annular Solar Eclipse of May 31

The first solar eclipse of 2003, which takes place in the Northern Hemisphere, is a very unusual annular eclipse (Figure 2, p. 150). The axis of the Moon's shadow passes to the far north where it barely grazes Earth's surface. In fact, the northern edge of the antumbra[2] actually misses our planet so that one path limit is defined by the day/night terminator rather than by the shadow's upper edge. As a result, the track of annularity has a peculiar D shape, which is nearly 1200 km wide. Since the eclipse occurs just three weeks before the northern summer solstice, Earth's northern axis is pointed sunward by 22.8°. As seen from the Sun, the antumbral shadow actually passes between the North Pole and the terminator. As a consequence of this extraordinary geometry, the path of annularity runs from east to west instead of vice versa. As a member of Saros[3] 147, this is the first central eclipse of the series (sunearth.gsfc.nasa.gov/eclipse/SEsaros/SEsaros147.html).

The event transpires near the Moon's ascending node in central Taurus 5° north of Aldebaran. Since apogee occurs three days earlier (May 28 at 13 UT), the Moon's apparent diameter (29.6 arc-min) is still too small to completely cover the Sun (31.6 arc-min), resulting in an annular eclipse.

The Moon's antumbral shadow first touches down on Earth at 03:45 UT in northern Scotland, about 100 km north of Glasgow (Figure 3, p. 151). The antumbra quickly extends northward as it travels on a northwestern trajectory. In Scotland, the Northwest Highlands, Loch Ness, the Isle of Lewis (Outer Hebrides), the Orkney Islands, and the Shetland Islands all lie in the annular track; here, maximum eclipse occurs at or shortly after sunrise. Several minutes later, the shadow's edge reaches the Faeroe Islands (03:51 UT), where annularity lasts 3 min 8 s with the Sun 4° above the northeastern horizon.

By 03:59 UT, the leading edge of the antumbra arrives along the southeastern coast of Iceland. Travelling with a ground speed of over 0.5 km/s, the shadow sweeps across the entire North Atlantic nation in 8 min. The shadow is so broad that the duration of the 3.5-min annular phase varies by less than 5 s across all of Iceland.

After traversing the Denmark Strait, the highly elliptical antumbra bisects Greenland, where over a third of the enormous island lies within the track. Crossing the ill-named land mass, the path width rapidly shrinks as the grazing antumbra begins its return to space. Just before reaching Baffin Island, the shadow leaves Earth in the Davis Strait (04:31 UT). From start to finish, the antumbra sweeps over its entire path in a little under 47 min.

The central line of the eclipse forms a short C-shaped curve that begins south

[2] The antumbra begins at the vertex of the umbral shadow and extends out into space away from the Sun. During a solar eclipse, an observer within the antumbra will see an annular eclipse.

[3] A Saros cycle is a period of 223 lunations or synodic months (6585.3216 days or 18.03 years). Eclipses separated by one Saros share nearly identical characteristics. This occurs because 223 synodic months is almost equal to 242 draconic months (6585.3572 days) and 239 anomalistic months (6585.5375 days). Since the periods are not perfect, the eclipses in a Saros series slowly evolve. Each Saros series lasts about 12 centuries.

of Iceland and crosses the country near Reykjavik. Greatest eclipse[4] occurs at 04:08:18 UT about 200 km northwest of the Scandinavian island nation. At that point, the duration of the annular phase lasts 3 min 37 s with the Sun 2.9° above the northeastern horizon. The central line ends near Greenland after running its complete course in 12 min.

Coordinates of the annular path and central line circumstances are presented in Table 2 (p. 144). Partial phases of the eclipse are visible from much of Europe (except Spain and Portugal) and the Middle East, where the event occurs at sunrise, as well as from central and northern Asia (excluding most of China, South East Asia, and Japan). In the Western Hemisphere, the partial eclipse is visible from northern Canada and Alaska during the afternoon of May 30. Local circumstances for a number of cities are listed in Table 3 (pp. 145–147). All times are given in Universal Time. The Sun's altitude and azimuth, the eclipse magnitude,[5] and obscuration[6] are all given at the instant of maximum eclipse.

A detailed report on this eclipse is available from NASA's Technical Publication series (see NASA Solar Eclipse Bulletins below). Additional information is also available at the 2003 annular solar eclipse website:

sunearth.gsfc.nasa.gov/eclipse/ASE2003/ASE2003.html

Total Lunar Eclipse of November 9

The second lunar eclipse of the year occurs six lunations after the first. It takes place at the ascending node of Luna's orbit in Aries. This time, the Moon is 1.4 days shy of apogee and appears 12% smaller (= 29.4 arc-min) than it was during May's eclipse. The Moon's trajectory takes it well to the south of the umbral shadow's central axis, resulting in a total eclipse that lasts just 25 min. At midtotality, the Moon's southern limb is a scant 0.6 arc-min from the umbra's edge. Even the northern limb is 23.4 arc-min from the centre of the shadow. Assuming that the transparency of Earth's atmosphere remains relatively unchanged, the November eclipse will be dramatically brighter than the May event because of the shallow umbral depth. Since different parts of the Moon will pass through radically different portions of Earth's umbral shadow, a large variation in shadow brightness can be expected. The totally eclipsed Moon will appear to have a bright rim along its southern edge. Observers are encouraged to estimate the Danjon value at midtotality (see Danjon Scale of Lunar Eclipse Brightness below).

The near grazing geometry of this event suggests that it is a transition eclipse in its Saros series. Indeed, it is the very last total eclipse of Saros 126 (sunearth.gsfc.nasa.gov/eclipse/LEsaros/LEsaros126.html). This series produced 13 total lunar eclipses during the past 234 years. The next 19 eclipses in the family will all be partial eclipses of decreasing duration and magnitude.

The penumbral phase of November's eclipse begins at 22:15 UT (on Nov. 8), but most observers will not be able to visually detect the shadow until about 23:00 UT. The partial eclipse commences with first umbral contact at 23:33 UT. Totality begins

---

[4] The instant of greatest eclipse occurs when the distance between the Moon's shadow axis and Earth's geocentre reaches a minimum. Although greatest eclipse differs slightly from the instants of greatest magnitude and greatest duration (for total eclipses), the differences are quite small.

[5] Eclipse magnitude is defined as the fraction of the Sun's *diameter* occulted by the Moon.

[6] Eclipse obscuration is defined as the fraction of the Sun's *surface area* occulted by the Moon.

at 01:06 UT and lasts until 01:31 UT. The partial and penumbral phases end at 03:05 UT and 04:22 UT, respectively.

At the instant of midtotality (01:19 UT), the Moon will stand at the zenith for observers near the Cape Verde Islands in the Atlantic. At that time, the umbral eclipse magnitude will be 1.022. The entire eclipse will be visible from Europe and most of Africa as well as the eastern Americas. Various stages of the eclipse are in progress at moonset for observers throughout Asia. In the Western Hemisphere, the ingressing partial phases will already be in progress at moonrise for observers in western Canada and the United States. The Moon's path through Earth's shadows as well as a map illustrating worldwide visibility of the event are shown in Figure 4 (p. 152). Note that no eclipse is visible from easternmost Asia, Japan, Indonesia, and Australia.

Table 4 (p. 147) lists predicted umbral immersion and emersion times for 20 well-defined lunar craters. The timing of craters is useful in determining the atmospheric enlargement of Earth's shadow (see Crater Timings During Lunar Eclipses below).

Total Solar Eclipse of November 23

The final event of 2003 is a total solar eclipse visible from the Southern Hemisphere (Figure 5, p. 153). The path of the Moon's umbral shadow begins at 22:19 UT in the southern Indian Ocean, about 1100 km southeast of Kerguelen Island (Figure 6, p. 154). Curving south, the 500-km-wide umbral path reaches the coast of Antarctica at 22:35 UT. The Shackleton Ice Shelf and Russia's Mirnyy research station lie in the path, where the central line duration is 1 min 55 s and the Sun stands 13° above the frozen landscape. Quickly moving inland, the elongated shadow sweeps over the desolate interior of the continent, encountering no permanently staffed research stations for the next half hour.

Greatest eclipse occurs in Wilkes Land at 22:49:17 UT. At this point, the duration of totality reaches its maximum of 1 min 55 s at solar altitude of 15°. The duration and altitude slowly drop as the umbra's path curves from southwest to northwest. Just like May's annular eclipse, the November event features a lunar shadow moving in the "wrong" direction. Once again, the explanation lies in the deep southern track of the umbra coupled with the close proximity of the eclipse with the winter solstice. As viewed from the Sun's direction, the shadow passes around the "back" side of the pole between Earth's axis of rotation and the terminator.

The umbra reaches the Antarctic coast in Queen Maud Land and several more research stations (Asuka, Novolazarevskaya, Maitri) before the path ends and the shadow leaves Earth's surface (23:19 UT) one hour after it began.

The rest of Antarctica, New Zealand, most of Australia, and southern Argentina and Chile will see a partial eclipse. Coordinates for the path of totality and central line circumstances are presented in Table 5 (p. 148). Local circumstances for a selection of cities throughout the path are given in Table 6 (p. 148). All times are given in Universal Time. The Sun's altitude and azimuth and the eclipse magnitude and obscuration are all given at the instant of maximum eclipse.

A detailed report on this eclipse is available from NASA's Technical Publication series (see NASA Solar Eclipse Bulletins below). Additional information is also available at the 2003 total solar eclipse website:

sunearth.gsfc.nasa.gov/eclipse/TSE2003/TSE2003.html

Solar Eclipse Figures

For each solar eclipse, an orthographic projection map of Earth shows the path of penumbral (partial) and umbral (total or annular) eclipse. North is to the top in all cases and the daylight terminator is plotted for the instant of greatest eclipse. An asterisk (*) indicates the subsolar point[7] on Earth.

The limits of the Moon's penumbral shadow delineate the region of visibility of the partial solar eclipse. This irregular or saddle-shaped region often covers more than half of the daylight hemisphere of Earth and consists of several distinct zones or limits. At the northern and/or southern boundaries lie the limits of the penumbra's path. Partial eclipses have only one of these limits, as do central eclipses when the Moon's shadow axis falls no closer than about 0.45 radii from Earth's centre. Great loops at the western and eastern extremes of the penumbra's path identify the areas where the eclipse begins/ends at sunrise and sunset, respectively. If the penumbra has both a northern and southern limit, the rising and setting curves form two separate, closed loops. Otherwise, the curves are connected in a distorted figure 8. Bisecting the "eclipse begins/ends at sunrise and sunset" loops is the curve of maximum eclipse at sunrise (western loop) and sunset (eastern loop). The points P1 and P4 mark the coordinates where the penumbral shadow first contacts (partial eclipse begins) and last contacts (partial eclipse ends) Earth's surface.

A curve of maximum eclipse is the locus of all points where the eclipse is at a maximum at a given time. Curves of maximum eclipse are plotted at each half hour Universal Time. They generally run between the penumbral limits in the north/south direction or from the "maximum eclipse at sunrise and sunset" curves to one of the limits. If the eclipse is central (i.e. total or annular), the curves of maximum eclipse run through the outlines of the umbral shadow, which are plotted at 10-min intervals. The curves of constant eclipse magnitude delineate the locus of all points where the magnitude at maximum eclipse is constant. These curves run exclusively between the curves of maximum eclipse at sunrise and sunset. Furthermore, they are parallel to the northern/southern penumbral limits and the umbral paths of central eclipses. In fact, the northern and southern limits of the penumbra can be thought of as curves of constant magnitude 0.0. The adjacent curves are for magnitudes 0.2, 0.4, 0.6, and 0.8 (i.e. 20%, 40%, 60%, and 80%). For total eclipses, the northern and southern limits of the umbra are curves of constant magnitude of 1.0. Umbral path limits for annular eclipses are curves of maximum eclipse magnitude.

Greatest eclipse is defined as the instant when the axis of the Moon's shadow passes closest to Earth's centre. Although greatest eclipse differs slightly from the instants of greatest magnitude and greatest duration (for total eclipses), the differences are usually negligible. The point on Earth's surface intersected by the axis at greatest eclipse is marked by an asterisk. For partial eclipses, the shadow axis misses Earth entirely, so the point of greatest eclipse lies on the day/night terminator and the Sun appears in the horizon.

Data pertinent to the eclipse appear with each map. At the top are listed the instant of conjunction of the Sun and Moon in right ascension and the instant of greatest eclipse, expressed in Universal Times and Julian Dates. The eclipse magnitude is defined as the fraction of the Sun's diameter obscured by the Moon at greatest eclipse. For central eclipses (total or annular), the magnitude is replaced by the geocentric ratio of diameters of the Moon and the Sun. Gamma is the minimum distance of the Moon's shadow axis from Earth's centre in Earth radii at greatest eclipse. The Saros series of the eclipse is listed, followed by the member position. The first member number identifies the sequence position of the eclipse in the Saros, while the second is the total number of eclipses in the series.

---

[7] The subsolar point is the geographic location where the Sun appears directly overhead (zenith).

In the upper left and right corners are the geocentric coordinates of the Sun and the Moon, respectively, at the instant of greatest eclipse. They are:

RA   Right ascension
Dec   Declination
S.D.   Apparent semi-diameter
H.P.   Horizontal parallax

To the lower left are exterior contact times of the Moon's penumbral shadow with Earth, which are defined as follows:

P1   Instant of first exterior tangency of penumbra with Earth's limb.
       (partial eclipse begins)
P4   Instant of last exterior tangency of penumbra with Earth's limb.
       (partial eclipse ends)

For central eclipses, the lower right corner lists exterior/interior contact times of the Moon's umbral shadow with Earth's limb, which are defined as follows:

U1   Instant of first exterior tangency of umbra with Earth's limb.
       (umbral [total/annular] eclipse begins)
U2   Instant of first interior tangency of umbra with Earth's limb.
U3   Instant of last interior tangency of umbra with Earth's limb.
U4   Instant of last exterior tangency of umbra with Earth's limb.
       (umbral [total/annular] eclipse ends)

At bottom centre are the geographic coordinates of the position of greatest eclipse along with the local circumstances at that location (i.e. Sun altitude, Sun azimuth, path width, and duration of totality/annularity). At bottom left is a list of parameters used in the eclipse predictions, while bottom right gives the Moon's geocentric libration (optical + physical) at greatest eclipse.

Lunar Eclipse Figures

Each lunar eclipse has two diagrams associated with it along with data pertinent to the eclipse. The top figure shows the path of the Moon through Earth's penumbral and umbral shadows. Above this figure are listed the instant of conjunction in right ascension of the Moon with Earth's shadow axis and the instant of greatest eclipse, expressed as both Universal Times and Julian Dates. The penumbral and umbral magnitudes are defined as the fraction of the Moon's diameter immersed in the two shadows at greatest eclipse. The radii of the penumbral and umbral shadows, P. Radius and U. Radius, respectively, are also listed. Gamma is the minimum distance in Earth radii of the Moon's centre from Earth's shadow axis at greatest eclipse, and Axis is the same parameter expressed in degrees. The Saros series of the eclipse is listed, followed by a pair of numbers. The first number identifies the sequence position of the eclipse in the Saros; the second is the total number of eclipses in the series.

In the upper left and right corners are the geocentric coordinates of the Sun and the Moon, respectively, at the instant of greatest eclipse. They are:

RA   Right ascension
Dec.   Declination
S.D.   Apparent semi-diameter
H.P.   Horizontal parallax

To the lower left are the semi, or half, durations of the penumbral, umbral (partial), and total eclipses. Below them are the Sun/Moon ephemerides used in the predictions, followed by the extrapolated value of ΔT (the difference between Terrestrial Time and

Universal Time). To the lower right are the contact times of the Moon with Earth's penumbral and umbral shadows, defined as follows:

P1   Instant of first exterior tangency of Moon with penumbra.
        (penumbral eclipse begins)

U1   Instant of first exterior tangency of Moon with umbra.
        (partial umbral eclipse begins)

U2   Instant of first interior tangency of Moon with umbra.
        (total umbral eclipse begins)

U3   Instant of last interior tangency of Moon with umbra.
        (total umbral eclipse ends)

U4   Instant of last exterior tangency of Moon with umbra.
        (partial umbral eclipse ends)

P4   Instant of last exterior tangency of Moon with penumbra.
        (penumbral eclipse ends)

The bottom figure is a cylindrical equidistant projection map of Earth that shows the regions of visibility for each stage of the eclipse. In particular, the moonrise/moonset terminator is plotted for each contact and is labelled accordingly. The point where the Moon is in the zenith at greatest eclipse is indicated by an asterisk. The region that is completely unshaded will observe the entire eclipse, while the darkly shaded area will witness none of the event. The remaining lightly shaded areas will experience moonrise or moonset while the eclipse is in progress. The shaded zones east of the asterisk will witness moonset before the eclipse ends, and the shaded zones west will witness moonrise after the eclipse has begun.

Danjon Scale of Lunar Eclipse Brightness

The Moon's appearance during a total lunar eclipse can vary enormously from one eclipse to the next. Obviously, the geometry of the Moon's path through the umbra plays an important role. Not as apparent is the effect of Earth's atmosphere on total eclipses. Although the physical mass of Earth blocks off all direct sunlight from the umbra, the planet's atmosphere refracts some of the Sun's rays into the shadow. Earth's atmosphere contains varying amounts of water (clouds, mist, precipitation) and solid particles (meteoric dust, organic debris, volcanic ash). This material significantly filters and attenuates the sunlight before it is refracted into the umbra. For instance, eclipses following large or frequent volcanic eruptions, which dump huge quantities of ash into the atmosphere, are often very dark and red for several years. Extensive cloud cover along Earth's limb also tends to darken the eclipse by blocking sunlight.

The French astronomer André-Louis Danjon proposed a useful five-point scale for evaluating the visual appearance and brightness of the Moon during total lunar eclipses. L values for various luminosities are defined as follows:

L=0   Very dark eclipse.
        Moon almost invisible, especially at midtotality.

L=1   Dark eclipse, grey or brownish in coloration.
        Details distinguishable only with difficulty.

L=2   Deep-red or rust-coloured eclipse.
        Very dark central shadow, while outer umbra is relatively bright.

L=3   Brick-red eclipse.
        Umbral shadow usually has a bright or yellow rim.

L=4   Very bright copper-red or orange eclipse.
        Umbral shadow has a bluish, very bright rim.

The assignment of an *L* value to lunar eclipses is best done with the naked eye, binoculars, or a small telescope near the time of midtotality. It's also useful to examine the Moon's appearance just after the beginning and before the end of totality. The Moon is then near the edge of the shadow; this provides an opportunity to assign an *L* value to the outer umbra. In making any evaluations, the instrumentation and the time should both be recorded. Also note any variations in colour and brightness in different parts of the umbra, as well as the apparent sharpness of the shadow's edge. Pay attention to the visibility of lunar features within the umbra. Notes and sketches made during the eclipse are often invaluable in recalling important details, events, and impressions.

Crater Timings During Lunar Eclipses

In 1702, Pierre de La Hire made a curious observation about Earth's umbra. In order to accurately predict the duration of a lunar eclipse, he found it necessary to increase the radius of the shadow one arc-minute larger than warranted by geometric considerations. Although the effect is clearly related to Earth's atmosphere, it is not completely understood, since the shadow enlargement seems to vary from one eclipse to the next. The enlargement can be measured through careful timings of lunar craters as they enter and exit the umbra.

Such observations are best made using a low-power telescope and a clock or watch synchronized with radio time signals. Timings should be made to a precision of 0.1 min. Record the instant when the most abrupt gradient at the umbra's edge crosses the apparent centre of the crater. In the case of large craters like Tycho and Copernicus, record the times when the shadow touches the two opposite edges of the crater. The average of these times is equal to the instant of crater bisection.

As a planning guide, Tables 1 and 2 list 20 well-defined craters with predicted umbral immersion and emersion times during the two lunar eclipses of 2003. The predictions assume a 2% enlargement of the umbra and include corrections for the effects of Earth's oblateness. Naturally, you should be thoroughly familiar with these features before an eclipse in order to prevent confusion and misidentification. The four umbral contacts with the Moon's limb can also be used in determining the shadow's enlargement. However, these events are less distinct and difficult to time accurately. Observers are encouraged to make crater timings and to send their results to *Sky & Telescope* (Sky Publishing Corporation, 49 Bay State Road, Cambridge MA 02138-1200, USA) for analysis.

Eclipse Altitudes and Azimuths

The altitude *a* and azimuth *A* of the Sun and Moon during an eclipse depend on the time and the observer's geographic coordinates. They are calculated as follows:

$$h = 15 (GST + UT - \alpha) + \lambda$$
$$a = \arcsin [\sin \delta \sin \phi + \cos \delta \cos h \cos \phi]$$
$$A = \arctan [-(\cos \delta \sin h)/(\sin \delta \cos \phi - \cos \delta \cos h \sin \phi)]$$

where

h = hour angle of Sun or Moon
a = altitude
A = azimuth
GST = Greenwich Sidereal Time at 0:00 UT
UT = Universal Time
α = right ascension of Sun or Moon
δ = declination of Sun or Moon

$$\lambda \;\; = \text{observer's longitude (east +, west --)}$$
$$\phi \;\; = \text{observer's latitude (north +, south --)}$$

During the eclipses of 2003, the values for GST and the geocentric right ascension and declination of the Sun or the Moon (at greatest eclipse) are as follows:

Eclipse	Date	GST	α	δ
Total lunar	2003 May 16	15.563	15.512	−18.592
Annular solar	2003 May 31	16.550	4.509	21.849
Total lunar	2003 Nov. 9	3.188	2.927	16.330
Total solar	2003 Nov. 23	4.166	15.940	−20.406

Eclipses During 2004

Next year, there will be two partial solar and two total lunar eclipses:

2004 May 4	Total lunar eclipse
2004 Apr. 19	Partial solar eclipse
2004 Oct. 14	Partial solar eclipse
2004 Oct. 28	Total lunar eclipse

A full report on eclipses during 2004 will be published next year in the *Observer's Handbook 2004*.

NASA Solar Eclipse Bulletins

Special bulletins containing detailed predictions and meteorological data for future solar eclipses of interest are prepared by F. Espenak and J. Anderson and are published through NASA's Publication series. The bulletins are provided as a public service to both the professional and lay communities, including educators and the media. A list of currently available bulletins and an order form can be found at:

sunearth.gsfc.nasa.gov/eclipse/SEpubs/RPrequest.html

Single copies of the eclipse bulletins are available at no cost by sending a 9 × 12-in. self-addressed envelope stamped with postage for 11 oz. (310 g). Please print the eclipse year on the lower left corner of the envelope. Use stamps only; cash and cheques cannot be accepted. Requests from outside the United States and Canada should include 10 international postal coupons. Mail requests to: Fred Espenak, NASA/Goddard Space Flight Center, Code 693, Greenbelt MD 20771, USA.

The NASA eclipse bulletins are also available over the Internet, including out-of-print bulletins. Using a Web browser, they can be read or downloaded via the World Wide Web from the GSFC/SDAC (Solar Data Analysis Center) eclipse page:

umbra.nascom.nasa.gov/eclipse/index.html

The original Microsoft Word text files and PICT figures (Macintosh format) are also available via anonymous ftp. They are stored as BinHex-encoded, StuffIt-compressed Mac folders with the .hqx suffixes. For PCs, the text is available in a zip-compressed format in files with the .zip suffix. There are three subdirectories: figures (GIF format), maps (JPEG format), and tables.

Eclipse Websites

A special solar and lunar eclipse website is available via the Internet at:

sunearth.gsfc.nasa.gov/eclipse/eclipse.html

The site features predictions and maps for all solar and lunar eclipses well into the 21st century. Special emphasis is placed on eclipses occurring during the next two years with detailed path maps, tables, graphs, and meteorological data. Additional catalogues list every solar and lunar eclipse over a 5000-year period.

Detailed information on solar and lunar eclipse photography and tips on eclipse observing and eye safety may be found at:

www.MrEclipse.com

Acknowledgments

All eclipse predictions were generated on a Power Macintosh 8500/150 using algorithms developed from the *Explanatory Supplement* (1974) with additional algorithms from Meeus, Grosjean, and Vanderleen (1966). The solar and lunar ephemerides were generated from Newcomb and the *Improved Lunar Ephemeris*. For lunar eclipses, the diameter of the umbral shadow was enlarged by 2% to compensate for Earth's atmosphere; corrections for the effects of oblateness have been included. Text and table composition was done on a Macintosh using Microsoft Word. Additional figure annotation was performed with Claris MacDraw Pro.

All calculations, diagrams, tables, and opinions presented in this paper are those of the author, and he assumes full responsibility for their accuracy.

This publication is available electronically via the Internet along with additional information and updates at:

sunearth.gsfc.nasa.gov/eclipse/OH/OH2003.html

References

Eckert, W.J., Jones, R., and Clark, H.K., *Improved Lunar Ephemeris 1952–1959,* Naval Observatory, Washington, DC, 1954.

Espenak, F., *Fifty Year Canon of Solar Eclipses: 1986–2035,* Sky Publishing Corp., Cambridge, MA, 1988.

Espenak, F., *Fifty Year Canon of Lunar Eclipses: 1986–2035,* Sky Publishing Corp., Cambridge, MA, 1989.

Espenak, F. & Anderson, J., *Central Solar Eclipses of 2003,* NASA, Washington, DC, 2002.

Explanatory Supplement to the Astronomical Ephemeris and the American Ephemeris and Nautical Almanac, Her Majesty's Nautical Almanac Office, London, 1974.

Littmann, M., Willcox, K., & Espenak, F., *Totality—Eclipses of the Sun,* Oxford University Press, New York, 1999.

Meeus, J., Grosjean, C.C., & Vanderleen, W., *Canon of Solar Eclipses,* Pergamon Press, New York, 1966.

Meeus, J. & Mucke, H., *Canon of Lunar Eclipses: –2002 to +2526,* Astronomisches Buro, Wien, 1979.

Newcomb, S., "Tables of the Motion of the Earth on its Axis Around the Sun," *Astron. Papers Amer. Eph., Vol. 6, Part I,* 1895.

TABLE 1—CRATER IMMERSION AND EMERSION TIMES FOR THE TOTAL LUNAR ECLIPSE OF 2003 MAY 16

UT of Immersion	Crater Name	UT of Emersion	Crater Name
2:09	Grimaldi	4:17	Aristarchus
2:10	Billy	4:19	Grimaldi
2:15	Campanus	4:24	Plato
2:19	Tycho	4:25	Kepler
2:22	Kepler	4:27	Billy
2:28	Aristarchus	4:29	Pytheas
2:29	Copernicus	4:31	Timocharis
2:34	Pytheas	4:33	Copernicus
2:41	Timocharis	4:34	Aristoteles
2:42	Dionysius	4:37	Eudoxus
2:44	Manilius	4:39	Campanus
2:47	Menelaus	4:46	Manilius
2:49	Goclenius	4:48	Tycho
2:50	Plinius	4:49	Menelaus
2:54	Langrenus	4:53	Plinius
2:55	Taruntius	4:54	Dionysius
2:56	Plato	5:02	Proclus
2:58	Proclus	5:06	Taruntius
2:59	Eudoxus	5:09	Goclenius
3:02	Aristoteles	5:13	Langrenus

Predictions include 2% enlargement of the umbral shadow due to Earth's atmosphere.

TABLE 2—PATH OF THE ANTUMBRAL SHADOW ANNULAR SOLAR ECLIPSE OF 2003 MAY 31

Universal Time	Northern Limit Lat.	Long.	Southern Limit Lat.	Long.	Centre Line Lat.	Long.	Alt °	Central Durat.
Limits	56°47′ N	4°36′ W	56°47′ N	4°36′ W	62°25′ N	21°15′ W	0	—
03:46	57°11′ N	5°32′ W	59°17′ N	1°00′ W	—	—	—	—
03:48	57°53′ N	7°18′ W	61°24′ N	0°46′ E	—	—	—	—
03:50	58°34′ N	9°07′ W	63°01′ N	1°28′ E	—	—	—	—
03:52	59°15′ N	10°59′ W	64°26′ N	1°39′ E	—	—	—	—
03:54	59°55′ N	12°54′ W	65°42′ N	1°27′ E	—	—	—	—
03:56	60°34′ N	14°53′ W	66°52′ N	0°57′ E	—	—	—	—
03:58	61°11′ N	16°54′ W	67°58′ N	0°08′ E	—	—	—	—
04:00	61°48′ N	19°00′ W	69°00′ N	0°57′ W	—	—	—	—
04:02	62°23′ N	21°09′ W	69°58′ N	2°20′ W	—	—	—	—
04:04	62°57′ N	23°22′ W	70°53′ N	4°02′ W	64°41′ N	20°30′ W	2	3m36s
04:06	63°30′ N	25°39′ W	71°44′ N	6°03′ W	65°45′ N	21°58′ W	3	3m37s
04:08	64°02′ N	28°00′ W	72°30′ N	8°26′ W	66°28′ N	24°08′ W	3	3m37s
04:10	64°32′ N	30°25′ W	73°13′ N	11°11′ W	66°54′ N	26°52′ W	3	3m37s
04:12	65°00′ N	32°55′ W	73°50′ N	14°20′ W	66°58′ N	30°11′ W	2	3m36s
04:14	65°27′ N	35°28′ W	74°22′ N	17°54′ W	66°03′ N	34°43′ W	1	3m36s
04:16	65°52′ N	38°06′ W	74°46′ N	21°53′ W	—	—	—	—
04:18	66°15′ N	40°48′ W	75°02′ N	26°16′ W	—	—	—	—
04:20	66°36′ N	43°34′ W	75°09′ N	31°01′ W	—	—	—	—
04:22	66°56′ N	46°24′ W	75°04′ N	36°02′ W	—	—	—	—
04:24	67°13′ N	49°17′ W	74°45′ N	41°13′ W	—	—	—	—
04:26	67°28′ N	52°14′ W	74°08′ N	46°27′ W	—	—	—	—
04:28	67°41′ N	55°14′ W	73°06′ N	51°37′ W	—	—	—	—
04:30	67°51′ N	58°17′ W	71°18′ N	56°38′ W	—	—	—	—
Limits	67°57′ N	60°20′ W	67°57′ N	60°20′ W	65°29′ N	35°41′ W	0	—

TABLE 3—LOCAL CIRCUMSTANCES FOR SOLAR ECLIPSE OF 2003 MAY 31

Geographic Location	Eclipse Begins h:m	Maximum Eclipse h:m	Eclipse Ends h:m	Sun Alt °	Sun Az °	Ecl. Mag.	Ecl. Obs.
AUSTRIA							
Vienna	— r	3:20	4:19	2	59	0.827	0.761
BELARUS							
Minsk	2:26	3:24	4:26	12	68	0.816	0.749
BELGIUM							
Antwerpen (Antwerp)	— r	3:38 r	4:29	0	53	0.840	0.776
Brussels	— r	3:40 r	4:28	0	53	0.801	0.730
BULGARIA							
Sofia	— r	3:08	4:06	2	61	0.744	0.662
CANADA							
Whitehorse, YT	4:27	5:22	— s	3	311	0.610	0.506
Yellowknife, NT	4:13	5:00 s	— s	0	325	0.691	0.599
CZECH REPUBLIC							
Praha (Prague)	— r	3:24	4:23	3	58	0.849	0.787
DENMARK							
Københavns (Copenhagen)	— r	3:34	4:33	6	59	0.888	0.834
EGYPT							
Cairo	— r	2:57 r	3:39	0	64	0.494	0.377
ENGLAND							
Birmingham	— r	3:56 r	4:34	0	52	0.639	0.539
Leeds	— r	3:48 r	4:36	0	50	0.805	0.735
Liverpool	— r	3:56 r	4:36	0	51	0.682	0.588
London	— r	3:55 r	4:32	0	53	0.625	0.522
Manchester	— r	3:53 r	4:36	0	51	0.729	0.644
Newcastle upon Tyne	— r	3:41 r	4:38	0	49	0.922	0.868
FINLAND							
Helsinki	2:36	3:36	4:39	14	70	0.858	0.799
FRANCE							
Lille	— r	3:46 r	4:29	0	54	0.715	0.627
Lyon	— r	3:59 r	4:20	0	57	0.358	0.238
Marseille	— r	4:05 r	4:16	0	59	0.184	0.090
Paris	— r	3:57 r	4:26	0	55	0.500	0.383
GERMANY							
Berlin	— r	3:28	4:27	4	58	0.869	0.811
Düsseldorf	— r	3:30	4:28	1	53	0.882	0.826
Frankfurt	— r	3:28	4:25	0	54	0.869	0.810
Hamburg	— r	3:32	4:30	3	56	0.886	0.831
Cologne	— r	3:30	4:27	0	54	0.880	0.823
München (Munich)	— r	3:23	4:21	0	56	0.844	0.782
Stuttgart	— r	3:30 r	4:23	0	55	0.836	0.772
GREECE							
Athens	— r	3:08 r	3:57	0	62	0.667	0.571
HUNGARY							
Budapest	— r	3:18	4:16	3	60	0.810	0.741

TABLE 3—LOCAL CIRCUMSTANCES FOR SOLAR ECLIPSE OF 2003 MAY 31 (continued)

Geographic Location	Eclipse Begins h:m	Maximum Eclipse h:m	Eclipse Ends h:m	Sun Alt °	Sun Az °	Ecl. Mag.	Ecl. Obs.	
ICELAND Reykjavík	— r	4:04	5:01	2	36	0.968	0.880	ANNULAR
INDIA Delhi	2:07	2:33	3:01	33	81	0.065	0.020	
IRAN Tehran	1:53	2:46	3:43	15	74	0.464	0.345	
IRAQ Baghdad	— r	2:44	3:39	9	70	0.489	0.372	
ISRAEL Tel Aviv-Yafo	— r	2:47	3:41	2	65	0.540	0.427	
ITALY Rome	— r	3:41 r	4:10	0	60	0.463	0.344	
JORDAN 'Ammān	— r	2:46	3:40	2	65	0.531	0.417	
LEBANON Beirut	— r	2:49	3:44	3	66	0.562	0.452	
NETHERLANDS Amsterdam	— r	3:33	4:30	1	53	0.895	0.840	
NORWAY Oslo	2:43	3:41	4:41	8	59	0.910	0.858	
POLAND Warsaw	2:27	3:24	4:25	7	63	0.837	0.773	
ROMANIA Bucureşti (Bucharest)	— r	3:09	4:08	5	64	0.748	0.667	
RUSSIA Gorki	2:24	3:25	4:32	21	82	0.738	0.656	
Moscow	2:24	3:25	4:30	18	77	0.773	0.698	
Novosibirsk	2:32	3:36	4:44	44	119	0.414	0.295	
St. Petersburg	2:34	3:34	4:39	16	74	0.833	0.770	
Volgograd	2:11	3:10	4:14	18	77	0.675	0.581	
SAUDI ARABIA Riyadh	— r	2:31	3:17	5	68	0.327	0.209	
SCOTLAND Glasgow	— r	3:47 r	4:40	0	48	0.906	0.853	
SLOVAKIA Bratislava	— r	3:20	4:18	3	59	0.823	0.757	
SLOVENIA Ljubljana	— r	3:19 r	4:16	0	57	0.815	0.747	
SWEDEN Stockholm	2:38	3:37	4:39	11	64	0.883	0.828	

All times are Universal Time.
'r' indicates eclipse in progress at sunrise. 's' indicates eclipse in progress at sunset.

TABLE 3—LOCAL CIRCUMSTANCES FOR SOLAR ECLIPSE OF 2003 MAY 31 (continued)

Geographic Location	Eclipse Begins h:m	Maximum Eclipse h:m	Eclipse Ends h:m	Sun Alt °	Sun Az °	Ecl. Mag.	Ecl. Obs.
SWITZERLAND							
Bern	— r	3:44 r	4:21	0	57	0.606	0.501
SYRIA							
Damascus	— r	2:48	3:43	3	66	0.552	0.440
TURKEY							
Istanbul	— r	3:03	4:01	4	64	0.696	0.605
UKRAINE							
Kiev	2:19	3:17	4:19	11	69	0.777	0.702
Odessa	2:14	3:10	4:11	9	67	0.742	0.660
UNITED STATES							
Anchorage, AK	4:31	5:28	6:21	9	300	0.530	0.417
Juneau, AK	4:31	5:25	— s	2	313	0.586	0.479

All times are Universal Time.
'r' indicates eclipse in progress at sunrise. 's' indicates eclipse in progress at sunset.

TABLE 4—CRATER IMMERSION AND EMERSION TIMES FOR THE TOTAL LUNAR ECLIPSE OF 2003 NOVEMBER 9

UT of Immersion	Crater Name	UT of Emersion	Crater Name
23:40	Aristarchus	1:51	Grimaldi
23:46	Grimaldi	1:54	Billy
23:48	Kepler	1:58	Campanus
23:50	Plato	1:59	Tycho
23:51	Pytheas	2:08	Kepler
23:53	Timocharis	2:10	Aristarchus
23:55	Copernicus	2:18	Copernicus
23:56	Billy	2:21	Pytheas
23:59	Aristoteles	2:26	Timocharis
0:01	Eudoxus	2:33	Plato
0:07	Manilius	2:36	Manilius
0:10	Menelaus	2:38	Dionysius
0:14	Plinius	2:40	Menelaus
0:15	Campanus	2:42	Eudoxus
0:17	Dionysius	2:43	Aristoteles
0:24	Proclus	2:44	Plinius
0:28	Taruntius	2:47	Goclenius
0:34	Tycho	2:53	Taruntius
0:35	Goclenius	2:54	Langrenus
0:39	Langrenus	2:55	Proclus

Predictions include 2% enlargement of the umbral shadow due to Earth's atmosphere.

TABLE 5—PATH OF THE UMBRAL SHADOW TOTAL SOLAR ECLIPSE OF 2003 NOVEMBER 23

Universal Time	Northern Limit Lat.	Long.	Southern Limit Lat.	Long.	Centre Line Lat.	Long.	Alt °	Width km	Central Durat.
Limits	50°56′ S	84°28′ E	54°10′ S	79°01′ E	52°27′ S	82°00′ E	0	497	1m34s
22:24	57°29′ S	94°56′ E	—	—	55°33′ S	87°37′ E	5	534	1m41s
22:26	59°06′ S	96°23′ E	—	—	57°43′ S	90°14′ E	7	544	1m45s
22:28	60°34′ S	97°27′ E	57°25′ S	84°16′ E	59°28′ S	91°46′ E	9	545	1m47s
22:30	61°57′ S	98°14′ E	59°27′ S	86°14′ E	61°00′ S	92°47′ E	10	543	1m49s
22:32	63°16′ S	98°47′ E	61°08′ S	87°18′ E	62°26′ S	93°26′ E	11	539	1m51s
22:34	64°32′ S	99°08′ E	62°38′ S	87°51′ E	63°47′ S	93°48′ E	12	533	1m53s
22:36	65°46′ S	99°18′ E	64°01′ S	88°02′ E	65°04′ S	93°55′ E	13	528	1m54s
22:38	66°58′ S	99°18′ E	65°20′ S	87°54′ E	66°19′ S	93°49′ E	13	522	1m55s
22:40	68°09′ S	99°06′ E	66°34′ S	87°29′ E	67°31′ S	93°28′ E	14	516	1m56s
22:42	69°18′ S	98°43′ E	67°45′ S	86°46′ E	68°41′ S	92°54′ E	14	511	1m56s
22:44	70°26′ S	98°06′ E	68°54′ S	85°45′ E	69°49′ S	92°04′ E	15	506	1m57s
22:46	71°33′ S	97°16′ E	69°59′ S	84°24′ E	70°55′ S	90°57′ E	15	502	1m57s
22:48	72°39′ S	96°08′ E	71°02′ S	82°42′ E	72°00′ S	89°30′ E	15	498	1m57s
22:50	73°43′ S	94°41′ E	72°01′ S	80°35′ E	73°02′ S	87°41′ E	15	494	1m57s
22:52	74°46′ S	92°50′ E	72°57′ S	78°00′ E	74°02′ S	85°26′ E	15	491	1m57s
22:54	75°47′ S	90°30′ E	73°48′ S	74°54′ E	74°59′ S	82°40′ E	15	489	1m57s
22:56	76°46′ S	87°36′ E	74°33′ S	71°12′ E	75°52′ S	79°17′ E	14	487	1m56s
22:58	77°41′ S	83°59′ E	75°11′ S	66°52′ E	76°39′ S	75°13′ E	14	486	1m56s
23:00	78°32′ S	79°30′ E	75°40′ S	61°50′ E	77°20′ S	70°20′ E	14	485	1m55s
23:02	79°16′ S	74°01′ E	75°57′ S	56°08′ E	77°53′ S	64°36′ E	13	485	1m54s
23:04	79°52′ S	67°23′ E	75°59′ S	49°50′ E	78°13′ S	58°01′ E	12	486	1m53s
23:06	80°15′ S	59°36′ E	75°41′ S	43°05′ E	78°19′ S	50°41′ E	11	487	1m51s
23:08	80°22′ S	50°52′ E	74°56′ S	36°06′ E	78°05′ S	42°53′ E	10	489	1m50s
23:10	80°09′ S	41°37′ E	73°26′ S	29°05′ E	77°27′ S	34°59′ E	9	493	1m48s
23:12	79°32′ S	32°28′ E	—	—	76°17′ S	27°23′ E	7	497	1m45s
23:14	78°25′ S	24°02′ E	—	—	74°14′ S	20°23′ E	5	502	1m41s
Limits	69°35′ S	8°46′ E	69°06′ S	21°36′ E	69°27′ S	14°49′ E	0	504	1m34s

TABLE 6—LOCAL CIRCUMSTANCES FOR SOLAR ECLIPSE OF 2003 NOVEMBER 23

Geographic Location	Eclipse Begins h:m	Maximum Eclipse h:m	Eclipse Ends h:m	Sun Alt °	Sun Az °	Ecl. Mag.	Ecl. Obs.
AUSTRALIA							
Adelaide	20:55	21:41	22:30	25	98	0.438	0.328
Blacktown	21:02	21:42	22:25	36	92	0.260	0.154
Brisbane	21:04	21:32	22:01	35	97	0.109	0.043
Canberra	21:01	21:44	22:30	35	92	0.311	0.201
Melbourne	21:01	21:47	22:37	32	92	0.408	0.296
Newcastle	21:02	21:41	22:22	36	92	0.232	0.131
Perth	— r	21:40	22:28	6	110	0.612	0.525
Southport	21:05	21:33	22:02	35	96	0.113	0.045
Sydney	21:02	21:42	22:25	36	92	0.257	0.152
Wollongong	21:02	21:43	22:27	36	92	0.271	0.165
NEW ZEALAND							
Christchurch	21:43	22:19	22:55	56	56	0.135	0.059
Wellington	21:53	22:17	22:42	59	57	0.057	0.016

All times are Universal Time.
'r' indicates eclipse in progress at sunrise.

FIGURE 1—TOTAL LUNAR ECLIPSE OF 2003 MAY 16

Geocentric Conjunction = 03:25:00.2 UT   J.D. = 2452775.642364
Greatest Eclipse = 03:40:10.2 UT   J.D. = 2452775.652896

Penumbral Magnitude = 2.09960   P. Radius = 1.3118°   Gamma = 0.41230
Umbral Magnitude = 1.13353   U. Radius = 0.7739°   Axis = 0.42120°

Saros Series = 121   Member = 55 of 84

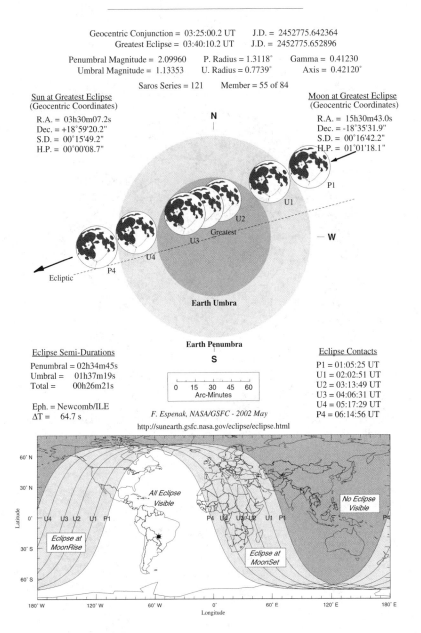

Sun at Greatest Eclipse
(Geocentric Coordinates)

R.A. = 03h30m07.2s
Dec. = +18°59'20.2"
S.D. = 00°15'49.2"
H.P. = 00°00'08.7"

Moon at Greatest Eclipse
(Geocentric Coordinates)

R.A. = 15h30m43.0s
Dec. = -18°35'31.9"
S.D. = 00°16'42.2"
H.P. = 01°01'18.1"

Eclipse Semi-Durations

Penumbral = 02h34m45s
Umbral =   01h37m19s
Total =   00h26m21s

Eph. = Newcomb/ILE
ΔT =   64.7 s

F. Espenak, NASA/GSFC - 2002 May
http://sunearth.gsfc.nasa.gov/eclipse/eclipse.html

Eclipse Contacts

P1 = 01:05:25 UT
U1 = 02:02:51 UT
U2 = 03:13:49 UT
U3 = 04:06:31 UT
U4 = 05:17:29 UT
P4 = 06:14:56 UT

FIGURE 2—ANNULAR SOLAR ECLIPSE OF 2003 MAY 31

Geocentric Conjunction = 04:38:15.6 UT   J.D. = 2452790.693236
Greatest Eclipse = 04:08:17.6 UT   J.D. = 2452790.672426

Eclipse Magnitude = 0.93842   Gamma = 0.99598

Saros Series = 147   Member = 22 of 80

Sun at Greatest Eclipse
(Geocentric Coordinates)
R.A. = 04h30m33.5s
Dec. = +21°50'57.1"
S.D. = 00°15'46.5"
H.P. = 00°00'08.7"

Moon at Greatest Eclipse
(Geocentric Coordinates)
R.A. = 04h29m35.5s
Dec. = +22°43'13.2"
S.D. = 00°14'48.1"
H.P. = 00°54'19.3"

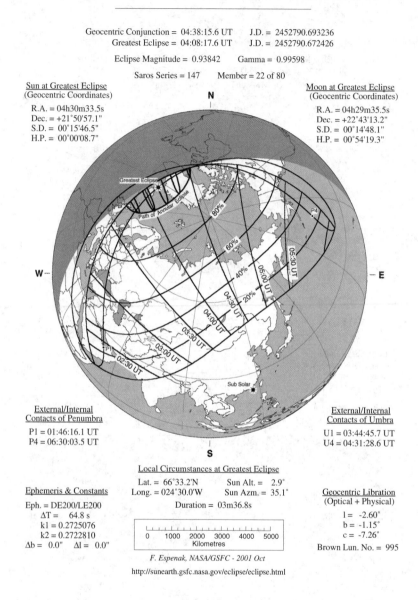

External/Internal
Contacts of Penumbra
P1 = 01:46:16.1 UT
P4 = 06:30:03.5 UT

External/Internal
Contacts of Umbra
U1 = 03:44:45.7 UT
U4 = 04:31:28.6 UT

Local Circumstances at Greatest Eclipse
Lat. = 66°33.2'N   Sun Alt. =   2.9°
Long. = 024°30.0'W   Sun Azm. = 35.1°
Duration = 03m36.8s

Ephemeris & Constants
Eph. = DE200/LE200
ΔT =   64.8 s
k1 = 0.2725076
k2 = 0.2722810
Δb = 0.0"   Δl = 0.0"

Geocentric Libration
(Optical + Physical)
l = -2.60°
b = -1.15°
c = -7.26°
Brown Lun. No. = 995

| 0 | 1000 | 2000 | 3000 | 4000 | 5000 |
Kilometres

F. Espenak, NASA/GSFC - 2001 Oct

http://sunearth.gsfc.nasa.gov/eclipse/eclipse.html

FIGURE 3—ANNULAR SOLAR ECLIPSE OF 2003 MAY 31

FIGURE 4—TOTAL LUNAR ECLIPSE OF 2003 NOVEMBER 9

Geocentric Conjunction = 00:57:15.2 UT   J.D. = 2452952.539759
Greatest Eclipse = 01:18:32.5 UT   J.D. = 2452952.554542

Penumbral Magnitude = 2.14017   P. Radius = 1.1945°   Gamma = -0.43195
Umbral Magnitude = 1.02219   U. Radius = 0.6455°   Axis = 0.38914°

Saros Series = 126   Member = 45 of 72

Sun at Greatest Eclipse
(Geocentric Coordinates)

R.A. = 14h54m59.8s
Dec. = -16°41'23.3"
S.D. = 00°16'08.7"
H.P. = 00°00'08.9"

Moon at Greatest Eclipse
(Geocentric Coordinates)

R.A. = 02h55m37.0s
Dec. = +16°19'48.5"
S.D. = 00°14'43.8"
H.P. = 00°54'03.6"

Eclipse Semi-Durations

Penumbral = 03h03m24s
Umbral =   01h46m02s
Total =   00h12m16s

Eph. = Newcomb/ILE
ΔT =   64.8 s

Eclipse Contacts

P1 = 22:15:09 UT
U1 = 23:32:30 UT
U2 = 01:06:16 UT
U3 = 01:30:48 UT
U4 = 03:04:34 UT
P4 = 04:21:57 UT

F. Espenak, NASA/GSFC - 2002 May
http://sunearth.gsfc.nasa.gov/eclipse/eclipse.html

FIGURE 5—TOTAL SOLAR ECLIPSE OF 2003 NOVEMBER 23

Geocentric Conjunction = 23:20:14.6 UT   J.D. = 2452967.472391
Greatest Eclipse = 22:49:16.7 UT   J.D. = 2452967.450887

Eclipse Magnitude = 1.03788   Gamma = -0.96381

Saros Series = 152   Member = 12 of 70

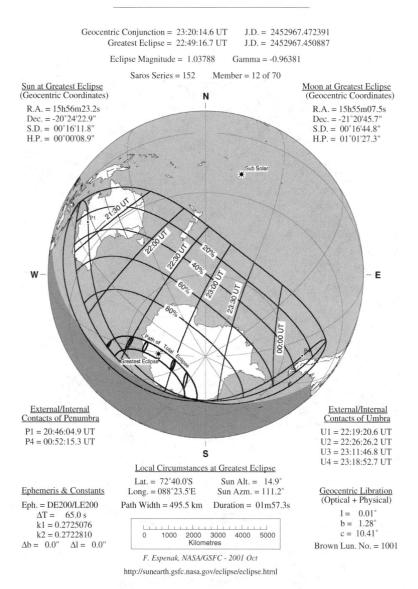

Sun at Greatest Eclipse
(Geocentric Coordinates)

R.A. = 15h56m23.2s
Dec. = -20°24'22.9"
S.D. = 00°16'11.8"
H.P. = 00°00'08.9"

Moon at Greatest Eclipse
(Geocentric Coordinates)

R.A. = 15h55m07.5s
Dec. = -21°20'45.7"
S.D. = 00°16'44.8"
H.P. = 01°01'27.3"

External/Internal
Contacts of Penumbra

P1 = 20:46:04.9 UT
P4 = 00:52:15.3 UT

External/Internal
Contacts of Umbra

U1 = 22:19:20.6 UT
U2 = 22:26:26.2 UT
U3 = 23:11:46.8 UT
U4 = 23:18:52.7 UT

Local Circumstances at Greatest Eclipse

Lat. = 72°40.0'S   Sun Alt. = 14.9°
Long. = 088°23.5'E   Sun Azm. = 111.2°
Path Width = 495.5 km   Duration = 01m57.3s

Ephemeris & Constants

Eph. = DE200/LE200
ΔT =   65.0 s
k1 = 0.2725076
k2 = 0.2722810
Δb = 0.0"   Δl = 0.0"

Geocentric Libration
(Optical + Physical)

l =   0.01°
b =   1.28°
c = 10.41°

Brown Lun. No. = 1001

0	1000	2000	3000	4000	5000

Kilometres

F. Espenak, NASA/GSFC - 2001 Oct

http://sunearth.gsfc.nasa.gov/eclipse/eclipse.html

FIGURE 6—TOTAL SOLAR ECLIPSE OF 2003 NOVEMBER 23

WEATHER FOR THE 2003 SOLAR ECLIPSES
BY JAY ANDERSON

2003 MAY 31 ANNULAR ECLIPSE

The first of the two polar eclipses of 2003 occurs in the middle of the night in an area of the globe noted for its cloudiness and precipitation—an inauspicious omen for the year. Weather prospects are not particularly favourable: the best possible prospects are found on the Greenland icecap. From a meteorological perspective, there is little to differentiate Greenland, Iceland, and Scotland.

The area between Iceland and Greenland is home to the Icelandic low, a persistent feature of the North Atlantic that controls the weather between Greenland and Europe. When the low is active, cloud systems spawned by the contrast between Arctic and maritime air masses are expelled toward Scotland, bringing the wet weather that defines the Hebridean character. In Iceland the semipermanent low is always a nuisance as far as astronomy is concerned.

Location	Clear	Percent Frequency of			Probability of Seeing Eclipse
		Scattered	Broken	Overcast	
Greenland					
Egedesminde (Aasiaat)*	4.8	24.4	32.5	38.2	0.30
Godthaab (Nuuk)	6.2	19.1	21.8	52.9	0.25
Holsteinsborg (Sisimiut)	13.5	21.1	20.7	44.8	0.33
Jakobshavn (Ilulissat)*	11.4	20.0	42.9	25.8	0.37
Sonder Stromfjord (Kangerlussuaq)	7.8	29.6	42.2	20.4	0.40
Iceland					
Akureyri*	3.0	18.4	29.3	49.3	0.24
Raufarhofn*	6.8	15.1	22.3	55.9	0.23
Blonduos*	1.1	17	11.6	70.2	0.16
Stykkisholmur*	4.1	15.6	31.1	49.1	0.24
Hjardarnes*	0.5	23.2	24.7	51.6	0.23
Reykjavík*	0.9	26.9	35.2	36.9	0.29
Keflavik*	2.4	20.7	32.3	44.7	0.26
Eyrarbakki*	1.1	26.3	28.3	44.3	0.27
Vestmannaeyjar*	2.8	25.2	23.2	48.8	0.26
United Kingdom					
Lerwick, Shetland Is.*	0.6	21.2	39.1	39.1	0.26
Kirkwall, Orkney Is.*	1.9	25.0	41.2	31.8	0.31
Wick*	2.4	22.4	47.6	27.6	0.31
Stornoway*	2.3	32.0	36.5	29.2	0.34
Aberdeen	1.8	25.9	40.5	31.8	0.31
Invergordon Harbour*	6.7	21.2	32.0	40.1	0.30
Inverness*	1.7	17.8	56.1	24.4	0.30
Kinloss RAF*	1.6	24.1	52.4	21.8	0.33
Lossiemouth RAF*	2.5	25.3	51.0	21.1	0.34
Edinburgh	2.6	27.2	46.0	24.3	0.34
Glasgow	3.3	27.8	44.0	24.9	0.35

*In central eclipse zone

Greenland

Settlement in Greenland is confined to the coastal regions, mostly on the west side facing the Canadian Arctic islands. This area has a high frequency of cloud, but the weather is highly variable because of the rugged terrain and the distant icecap. Cold but dry foehn (chinook) winds from the icecap often bring sunny weather to one patch of coast while nearby areas remain under the cloud as they flow to the sea. Passing low-pressure systems, heading northward toward Baffin Bay, also contribute to the topsy-turvy weather.

In spite of the gloomy outlook, Greenland's west coast is the best of the sites for viewing this eclipse, with 5% to 11% chance of clear skies at the eclipse hour and a nominal probability of seeing the event that ranges from 30% to 37%. Even better is the icecap in the interior of the island: cold and dry and seemingly blessed with a considerably higher frequency of clear skies. The actual advantage is difficult to determine because there are only a limited number of measurements. Russian satellite observations from the 1970s suggest a clear sky or scattered cloud frequency of 60% to 68% and an overcast condition on only 18% of May days. These data seem to be verified by the records of some of the icecap expeditions of past years. Temperatures on the icecap may range into the –20s (°C), and the wind is persistent.

Iceland

The frequency of clear skies in Iceland on a May night is less than 5% at nearly all locations on the island except Raufarhofn on the northeast coast. Overcast skies are generally observed about 50% of the hours at eclipse time. Reykjavík, with a low frequency of overcast skies (37%), offers marginally better prospects than other sites on the island. Because this eclipse is very low in the sky—only 2° or 3° above the horizon—the effect of even a little cloud is magnified by the long view through the atmosphere. An optimistic assessment would suggest that the chances of seeing the eclipse are around 25% generally, with Reykjavík sporting a slightly higher value.

Scotland

From a cloud perspective, Scotland is similar to Iceland, with a very low frequency of clear skies. Scattered cloud is found more often, however, with the result that the chances in the British Isles rise to 30% or 35%, especially at the more southerly sites such as Invergordon and Lossiemouth. Stornoway on the Hebrides also has similar cloud prospects but at the cost of a more limited ability to travel to find a break in the clouds.

Strategy

Movement is limited in Greenland, but alternative eclipse sites can be selected in Iceland and Scotland if weather forecasts prove promising. The area covered by the eclipse is relatively small and reachable within a few hours of travel. In Iceland the best roads follow the coast, mandating a roundabout trip to the opposite side of the island if weather conditions dictate. Scotland's highways provide a convenient route to any part of the shadow zone. Computer models and forecasts should allow the selection of the most promising site a day in advance. Last-minute adjustments can be made with the help of satellite imagery.

2003 NOVEMBER 23 TOTAL ECLIPSE

The second eclipse of the year has weather prospects nearly as dismal as the first. The Antarctic coast is one of the world's most active weather regimes, with an endless series of low-pressure disturbances pushing against the land, each accompanied by a generous retinue of cloud. Downslope winds flowing off of the Antarctic icecap push the cloud away from the land and bring clear skies, but the effect is highly variable in the rugged landscape. Some sites on the coast offer a mean cloud cover of three- or four-tenths, but most exceed seven-tenths. Chances of seeing the eclipse at Mirnyy are about 37%. Inland, on the icecap, chances increase to 50% or 60% but there are no observing sites. The challenge inland is coping with cold temperatures in the –20s and 30s (°C) and windchill values that average 10°C to 15°C colder.

VIEWING A SOLAR ECLIPSE—A WARNING

Solar eclipses are among the most widely publicized and observed celestial events. It is essential to be aware of the visual danger associated with a solar eclipse. The safety rule is simple but not widely appreciated: **Never look at the surface of the Sun, either directly with the unaided eyes or through binoculars or a telescope.** To do so one risks permanent partial blindness, and this can occur almost instantly in the case of telescopic viewing. Viewing our Sun is just as dangerous on any clear day, but at the time of an eclipse people have a reason to want to look at it—and often resort to dangerous methods.

A direct view of the Sun is safe only if a suitable filter is used in a proper manner. In the case of binoculars or a telescope, the filter must be one that attaches *securely* to the *front* end of the instrument, never one that attaches to the eyepiece end (the heat developed near the eyepiece can shatter such a filter).

Filters specifically designed for solar viewing include aluminized Mylar and glass filters plated with a slightly transparent, metallic film. Such filters may be purchased at telescope supply stores. Shade #14 (no other shade) rectangular welder's glass may be used; however, since these filters are of low optical quality, they are useful only for views not involving binoculars or a telescope. All of these are commercial items and cannot be replaced with ordinary household items. For example, layers of photographic colour film, coloured glass, stacked sunglasses, crossed polarizers, smoked glass, or photographic neutral-density filters must never be used. Although one may devise a combination that dims the *visible* sunlight to a comfortable level, the makeshift filter may be quite transparent in the infrared part of the solar spectrum, and this invisible radiation will damage the retina of the observer's eye. For the same reason, one must never rely on clouds or heavy atmospheric haze to dim the solar image when using a telescope. Two layers of fully exposed and developed, silver-based, black and white photographic film provides adequate protection, but many modern films, including all colour films, are based on dyes that do not provide protection in the infrared. Thus it is best to avoid using filters made of photographic film.

One of the simplest, safest, and least known ways to observe the partial phases of a solar eclipse is *pinhole mirror projection*. Take a small pocket mirror and, with masking tape, cover all but a small section of the mirror's surface. The shape and size of the small opening are not critical, but a square about 6 mm on a side works well. Prop the mirror up on a sunny windowsill and orient the mirror so the reflected sunlight shines on the ceiling or a wall of the room—but not directly into anyone's eyes! The spot of light on the viewing surface will be a *pinhole image* of the solar disk. The mirror has a great advantage over the usual "pinhole-in-a-box arrangement" in that the image can be aimed across a substantial distance to a convenient viewing screen. The greater the projection distance, the larger, but dimmer, the Sun's image. The size of the mirror aperture should be adjusted for the best compromise between image brightness and image sharpness. With this simple device the progress of a solar eclipse can be viewed in complete safety by a group of children in a darkened room.

A sharper and brighter image of the solar disk may be projected onto a white viewing screen placed 30 or 40 cm behind the eyepiece of binoculars or a small telescope (the telescope aperture should be stopped down to about 50 mm in order to limit the intensity of sunlight passing through the instrument, and the viewing screen should be shielded from direct sunlight). However, one must *not* look through the instrument when aiming it, and, especially if children are present, a physical barrier should be used to prevent anyone from attempting to look into the eyepiece. If the telescope has a finderscope, it should be either covered or removed.

OCCULTATIONS BY THE MOON
By David W. Dunham

The Moon often passes between Earth and a star, an event called an *occultation*. During an occultation, a star suddenly disappears as the east limb of the Moon crosses the line between the star and the observer. The star reappears from behind the west limb some time later. Because the Moon moves through an angle about equal to its own diameter every hour, the longest time for an occultation is about an hour. The time is shorter if the occultation is not central. Solar eclipses are actually occultations: the star being occulted by the Moon is the Sun.

Since observing occultations is rather easy, amateur astronomers should try this activity. The slow, majestic drift of the Moon in its orbit is an interesting part of such observations, and the disappearance or reappearance of a star at the Moon's limb is a remarkable sight, particularly when it occurs as a *graze* near the Moon's northern or southern limb. During a graze, a star may disappear and reappear several times in succession as mountains and valleys in the Moon's polar regions drift by it. On rarer occasions the Moon occults a planet. (See THE SKY FOR JULY (p. 89) for an occultation of Mars, the only planet occulted this year in North America; Venus is occulted in Hawaii in October.)

Lunar occultation and graze observations refine our knowledge of the shape of the lunar profile and the fundamental star coordinate system. These observations complement those made by other techniques, such as Clementine laser ranging and photographs. Improved knowledge of the lunar profile is useful in determinations of the Sun's diameter from solar eclipse records. Occultation observations are also useful for detecting double stars and measuring their separations. Binaries with separations as small as 0.02″ have been discovered visually during grazes. Doubles with separations in this range are useful for filling the gap between doubles that can be directly resolved and those whose duplicity has been discovered spectroscopically.

Observations

The **International Lunar Occultation Centre (ILOC)** analyzes lunar occultation observations and is the world clearinghouse for such observations. Anyone interested in pursuing a systematic program of lunar occultation observations should write to the ILOC, Geodesy and Geophysics Division, Hydrographic Department, Tsukiji 5-3-1, Chuo-ku, Tokyo 104-0045, Japan for their booklet *Guide to Lunar Occultation Observations*. ILOC's web address is www1.kaiho.mlit.go.jp/KOHO/iloc/obsrep/.

Observers in North America should also contact the **International Occultation Timing Association (IOTA),** 5403 Bluebird Trail, Stillwater OK 74074, USA; email: business@occultations.org. IOTA provides predictions and coordination services for occultation observers. Detailed predictions for any grazing occultation are available ($1.50 U.S. each; free by email); instructions explaining the use of predictions are also available ($5 U.S.). Annual membership in IOTA is $30 U.S. in North America, $35 U.S. overseas. Less expensive online rates are available. Membership includes free graze predictions, descriptive materials, and a subscription to *Occultation Newsletter* (available separately for $20 U.S. in North America, $25 overseas). IOTA's administrative web address is www.occultations.org, and its site for predictions, updates, observations, and other technical information is www.lunar-occultations.com/iota.

For observers in the southwestern Pacific (New Zealand, Australia, Papua New Guinea, and nearby areas), the Royal Astronomical Society of New Zealand (RASNZ) provides occultation data (total lunar, lunar grazing, planetary, and Jupiter's satellites), plus comprehensive instructions for new observers. See the RASNZ website: occsec.wellington.net.nz/sitemap.htm.

The main information required in a lunar occultation observation is the time of the event and the observer's location. Supplementary data include the seeing conditions, telescope size, timing method, estimate of the observer's reaction time and the accuracy of the timing, and whether or not the reaction time correction has been applied. The timing should be accurate to 0.5 s or better (a shortwave radio time signal and tape recorder provide a simple, permanent time record, but a video record provides higher accuracy). The observer's longitude, latitude, and altitude should be reported to the nearest tenth of a second of arc and 10 m, respectively, and should be accurate to at least 0.5″ or 16 m. These can be determined from either GPS measurements (10 min of position averaging and an unobstructed view of the sky above 15° altitude are needed) or a suitable topographical map. For Canada, the maps are available from the Canada Map Office, Natural Resources Canada, 130 Bentley Ave., Nepean ON K2E 6T9. In the United States (except Alaska), write to U.S. Geological Survey, Map Sales, Box 25286, Denver CO 80225, asking for an index to topographical maps in your state, or call (800) USA-MAPS. For Alaska, write to U.S. Geological Survey, Map Sales, 101-12th Ave. #12, Fairbanks AK 99701. Parts of USGS maps can be viewed and printed at www.topozone.com.

Observers are encouraged to develop a video capability for recording occultations in order to obtain reliable and accurate timings. Inexpensive yet sensitive video cameras are now available. Visual timings must be accurate to ±0.2 s to be good enough for further improvement of the lunar profile and other parameters, except for grazes, where ±0.5 s is adequate. For asteroidal occultations, especially the shorter duration events of 10 s or less, video or photoelectric observations are much preferred.

Pages 164–172 give tables of occultation predictions and a table and maps of northern or southern limits for grazing occultations.

1. TOTAL OCCULTATION PREDICTIONS

PREDICTIONS BY THE INTERNATIONAL LUNAR OCCULTATION CENTRE, JAPAN

The total occultation predictions, as given in the tables on pp. 164–166, are for the 18 standard stations identified on the map below; the longitudes and latitudes of these stations are given in the table headings.

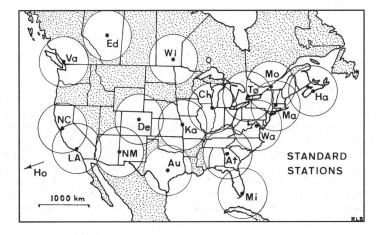

The predictions are limited to stars of magnitude 5.0 and brighter. The first five columns give for each occultation the date, the Zodiacal Catalogue (ZC) number of the star, its magnitude, the phenomenon (DD or DB = disappearance at dark limb or bright limb, respectively; RD or RB = reappearance at dark limb or bright limb, respectively), and the elongation of the Moon from the Sun in degrees. Under each station are given the Universal Time of the event, factors A and B (see below), and the position angle P (from the north point, eastward around the Moon's limb to the point of occurrence of the phenomenon). In several places, predictions have been replaced by the cryptic notations GBG (after moonset), GSM (before moonrise), NB2 (Sun's altitude greater than $-6°$), NSG (after sunrise), and NBM (before sunset). If A and B give an unrealistic representation, as in the case of near grazes, they are omitted.

The terms A and B are for determining corrections to the times of the events for stations within 500 km of the standard stations. If Lo* and La* represent the longitude and latitude of the standard station, and Lo and La those of the observer, then for the observer,

UT of event =
UT of event at the standard station + A(Lo − Lo*) + B(La − La*) ,

where Lo, etc., are expressed in degrees, and A and B are in minutes of time per degree. Longitude measured *west* of Greenwich is assumed to be *positive* (which is opposite to the IAU convention and that used by IOTA's *Occult* software). Due regard must be paid to the algebraic signs of the terms. To convert UT to the standard time of the observer, see the section STANDARD TIME ZONES on pp. 42–43.

As an example, consider the occultation of ZC 1030 (ε Gem or Mebsuta) on 2003 January 17 as seen from Regina. For Regina, Lo = 104.61° and La = 50.45°. The nearest standard station is Winnipeg, for which Lo* = 97.20° and La* = 49.90°. Therefore, the UT of the disappearance at the dark limb (DD) is 0:51.5 − 0.7 × (104.61° − 97.20°) min + 0.9 × (50.45° − 49.90°) min = 0:46.8. The elongation of the Moon is 162°, which corresponds to the waxing gibbous phase (between first quarter and full Moon). The position angle of disappearance is approximately 114°.

The number of events observable from any location increases *rapidly* as predictions are extended to fainter stars. Observers who wish to pursue such work can obtain software or more extensive lists from Walter Robinson, 515 W. Kump, Bonner Springs KS 66012–1439, USA, by providing accurate geographical coordinates and a long, self-addressed envelope (with postage); or, better, write to webmaster@lunar-occultations.com.

2. GRAZE PREDICTIONS AND DATA ON OCCULTED STARS
By Eberhard Riedel and David W. Dunham

(A) GRAZE PREDICTIONS

The table on pp. 167–168 lists lunar grazing occultation predictions for much of North America for 2003. The events are limited to stars of magnitude 7.0 or brighter (paths for stars down to magnitude 7.5 are shown when the Moon is 40% or less sunlit) that will graze the limb of the Moon when it is at a favourable elongation from the Sun and at least as high above a land horizon in degrees as the star's magnitude (e.g. a third-magnitude star is included only if its altitude is at least 3°). The star's USNO reference number is the ZC number, unless the number is prefixed with an X. In the latter case, the star is not in the ZC and its number is from the XZ catalogue, a more extensive catalogue of zodiacal stars prepared originally at the U.S. Naval Observatory but now updated at the Japanese National Observatory.

The maps on pp. 169–172 show the predicted graze tracks. The maps are "false" projections, since the latitude and longitude scales are both linear. This makes it much easier for measuring coordinates or plotting locations with known coordinates than is possible with any other type of projection. The longitude scale is compressed by a factor of cos 50°. The maps are not detailed enough for locating oneself in the 2- or 3-km-wide zone where multiple disappearances of the star may occur. To obtain detailed predictions of any graze for plotting on larger-scale maps of your region, write to (or email) IOTA (see p. 158).

Each track is keyed to the sequential number in the table. The computer-drawn number appears at the east and west ends of the track and is aligned parallel to it. Some overlapping numbers have been omitted for legibility; in these cases, check the other end of the track for the number. Conditions are represented by three different types of lines:

    solid line = dark limb, night
    dashed line = bright limb, night
    dotted line = dark or bright limb, day

Thicker lines are drawn for first-magnitude stars and planets. Many tracks begin and/ or end with the letter A, B, or S: A denotes that the Moon is at a low altitude, B that the bright limb interferes, and S that sunlight or twilight interferes. The tick marks along the tracks indicate multiples of 10 min of every hour. For example, if the time for the west end of the track is 3:16.2, the tick marks proceeding eastward correspond to 3:20, 3:30, etc. Time always increases from west to east along the path. *The time ticks, track numbers, and the A, B, and S letters are on the side of the limit with an occultation,* that is north of southern limits and south of northern limits. The locations for the North American standard stations for lunar total occultation predictions are indicated by asterisks on the graze maps (see the map on p. 159). For grazes of planets, a *partial occultation* of the object will occur at the northern or southern limit. The line plotted is the centre of the partial occultation zone, typically several kilometres wide.

(B) NAMES OF OCCULTED STARS

The stars that are occulted by the Moon are stars that lie along the zodiac; hence they are known by their number in the ZC compiled by James Robertson and published in the *Astronomical Papers Prepared for the Use of the American Ephemeris and Nautical Almanac,* vol. 10, pt. 2 (U.S. Government Printing Office, Washington, 1940). Robertson's ZC has been out of print for several years. In 1986, Isao Sato, a member of the Lunar Occultation Observers Group in Japan, republished the ZC. This new edition is based on the epoch J2000 and includes much new data, particularly on double stars. Since stars are not usually recognized by their ZC numbers, the equivalent Bayer designations or Flamsteed numbers of the stars occulted during the year are given in the table on the next page. The ZC and XZ catalogues are available through IOTA's website.

ZC	Name	ZC	Name	ZC	Name
76	14 Cet	1088	47 Gem	1951	81 Vir
83	15 Cet	1094	49 Gem	1962	82 Vir
212	95 Psc	1099	52 Gem	2182	26 Lib
219	μ Psc	1117	57 Gem	2192	28 Lib
354	ξ Ari	1169	76 Gem	2290	δ Sco (Dschubba)
422	σ Ari	1170	κ Gem	2347	o Sco
601	39 Tau	1206	ω Cnc	2359	ρ Oph
631	51 Tau	1211	4 Cnc	2411	25 Sco
633	53 Tau	1251	λ Cnc	2443	26 Oph
634	56 Tau	1270	28 Cnc	2500	θ Oph
660	υ Tau	1363	ξ Cnc	2558	V3894 Sgr
664	72 Tau	1365	79 Cnc	2601	7 Sgr
743	98 Tau	1484	η Leo	2721	φ Sgr
767	103 Tau	1544	46 Leo	2750	σ Sgr (Nunki)
822	118 Tau	1702	ν Vir	2784	τ Sgr
839	121 Tau	1821	γ Vir (Porrima)	2910	ω Sgr
852	125 Tau	1866	44 Vir	2914	60 Sgr
882	132 Tau	1869	46 Vir	3130	33 Cap
900	139 Tau	1875	48 Vir	3158	37 Cap
932	TU Gem	1891	θ Vir (Apami-Ati)	3160	38 Cap
1030	ε Gem (Mebsuta)	1937	72 Vir	3343	τ¹ Aqr
1055	37 Gem	1941	74 Vir	3349	τ² Aqr
1061	39 Gem	1947	77 Vir	3428	ψ³ Aqr
1062	40 Gem				

(C) OCCULTED STARS KNOWN TO BE DOUBLE

In the table at the right are data on double stars for which graze predictions are given. This information is from DSFILE, a comprehensive file of zodiacal double star data compiled by Don Stockbauer, Henk Bulder, Mitsuru Sôma, and David Dunham; most of the data for the ZC stars are in the Sato ZC catalogue. The successive columns give the USNO reference number of the star, the number of the graze track, the double star code (d), the magnitudes of the brighter (A) and dimmer (B) components, the separation in seconds of arc, and the position angle of B from A measured eastward from north. If the star is triple, the third component's magnitude is given under C, and its separation and position angle from A are given in the last columns. The last three stars are not in the ZC, so their XZ numbers are given.

The parameters are given for the epoch of the occultation, computed from orbital elements when available or from extrapolations from a long series of observations. If there is little change in the available observations, the last-observed separation and P.A. are used. Components fainter than magnitude 11.5 are not listed, and some very close doubles whose parameters are not known, generally with separations less than 0.2″, are also not listed. The latter include spectroscopic binaries (code J, U, or sometimes V) and visual occultation doubles (most codes K and X, and many Vs).

The codes have the following meanings:

A, C, or G .... visual double
B or V .... close double, usually discovered by occultation
D .... primary of wide pair; secondary has separate catalogue entry
E .... secondary star of wide pair
F .... prediction is for the following component of a visual double
H .... triple, with close occultation pair and third visual component; prediction uses a mean position

I..................... data for B component computed from orbital elements, but the B component is itself a close double, with data for the C component referred to B rather than A

K .... possible double from elements

Q .... = O, but A component may be close double (if triple, C-component data are computed from orbital elements)

R .... triple; close pair = O and C component also has orbit relative to centre of close pair

W .... = A or C, but A component is a spectroscopic binary

X .... probable double from occultation

Y .... triple, K or X (B component) and A or C (C component)

Z.................... triple, O (B component) and V (C component)

Some close pairs have rapid orbital motion so the current position angle is unknown.

USNO	Graze #	d	A	B	Sep. "	P.A. °	C	Sep. "	P.A. °
83	231	A	6.9	10.8	30.5	307			
212	111	O	7.6	7.9	0.1	135			
631	41	O	5.9	7.9	0.1	263			
651	19	X	6.7	6.7	0.2	55			
688	21, 78, 113	M	6.8	10.0	1.9	283			
743	185	W	6.2	6.4	0.0	246	9.9	94.6	289
767	43, 130	M	5.6	8.7	0.4	207	8.6	35.3	197
822	80, 147	D	5.9	6.7	4.8	206			
852	69, 148, 186, 206	L	5.2	8.5	0.3	313			
1105	166, 209	V	7.0	7.7	0.2	231			
1170	73	A	3.7	8.2	7.4	241			
1211	169, 236, 237	C	6.2	11.0	45.5	23			
1363	213	M	5.7	6.2	0.3	62			
1365	214	C	6.9	6.9	0.1	107			
1484	27, 85, 216	C	4.1	4.6	0.1	93			
1821	55	O	3.5	3.5	1.3	252			
1821	222	O	3.5	3.5	1.2	247			
1866	119	Y	6.7	6.7	0.1	90	11.1	20.9	55
1869	118	M	6.2	8.9	0.8	174	13.1	4.2	136
1875	29, 120	M	7.2	7.6	0.6	196			
1891	245	T	4.5	6.8	0.5	338	9.4	7.1	343
1937	10	A	6.1	11.4	29.8	16			
1951	136	M	7.8	8.0	2.7	40	11.0	14.1	328
2065	137	C	6.6	10.0	39.7	42			
2147	248	V	7.2	9.0	0.3	163			
2181	151	C	7.1	8.1	47.4	140			
2236	123	M	7.6	7.6	1.8	224			
2290	152, 249	L	3.0	4.6	0.2				
2357	140	M	7.0	8.7	0.4	318			
2359	139	E	5.0	5.7	3.1	337			
2424	173	A	6.9	11.0	3.1	356			
2524	58, 142	M	6.2	8.6	0.3	191			
2601	225	Y	6.9	9.4	0.2	212	13.0	8.9	26
2750	36	Y	2.9	2.9	0.1	90	9.5	9.0	244
2848	105	A	5.6	8.6	7.8	142			
3052	94, 178, 252	M	6.5	8.7	1.7	200			
3343	1, 180	A	5.8	9.0	20.1	123	10.0	63.4	34
3413	17, 108	A	6.4	10.9	3.5	256			
3428	143	A	5.2	11.2	1.7	144			
X06274	68	H	8.5	8.5	0.1	80	10.6	4.7	62
X09881	46	V	7.7	8.4	0.3	69			
X15556	114	O	7.5	9.6	1.9	236			

TABLE OF TOTAL LUNAR OCCULTATION PREDICTIONS

DATE	ZC	MAG	PH	ELG°	HALIFAX 63.6°W, 44.6°N TIME (UT)	A m	B m	P°	MONTREAL 73.6°W, 45.5°N TIME (UT)	A m	B m	P°	TORONTO 79.4°W, 43.7°N TIME (UT)	A m	B m	P°
Apr. 21	2650	4.7	RD	243	NB2				NB2				9:31.8	-1.7	-1.1	326
May 20	2910	4.8	RD	237	NB2				8:25.3	-1.7	0.6	244	8:13.6	-1.8	0.9	243
Jul. 17	3349	4.2	RD	225	NB2				7:59.8	-2.1	0.1	267	7:46.7	-2.3	0.3	273
Aug. 3	1821	2.9	DD	60	0:22.9	-0.7	-1.7	107	0:13.5	-0.9	-1.7	113	0:11.0	-1.0	-1.7	120
3	1821	2.9	RB	61	1:22.4	-0.2	-1.9	312	1:17.2	-0.5	-1.9	309	1:17.5	-0.6	-1.8	304
7	2359	4.8	DD	114	GBG				GBG				3:59.6	-0.7	0.0	43
21	709	4.3	RD	284	—				7:34.8	0.4	3.1	198	7:31.7	0.4	2.8	204
Sep. 1	2118	2.9	RB	66	16:28.0	-0.3	0.1	311	GSM				GSM			
2	2290	2.5	DD	83	22:57.4	—	—	171	22:48.5	—	—	184				
2	2290	2.5	RB	83	23:32.8	—	—	226	23:11.2	—	—	218				
5	2784	3.4	DD	122	23:15.6	-1.5	-0.4	138	NBM				NBM			
17	660	4.4	RD	255	NB2				9:30.1	-1.9	0.7	255	9:17.4	-1.9	1.0	256
Oct. 4	2910	4.8	DD	106	0:45.8	-1.3	-0.1	60	0:32.2	-1.4	0.4	48	0:22.3	-1.6	0.7	46
4	2914	5.0	DD	106	2:23.7	-1.1	-1.1	86	2:11.3	-1.2	-0.6	71	2:04.6	-1.4	-0.3	66
16	852	5.0	RD	243	1:34.8	—	—	330	—				—			
27	2347	4.8	DD	34	GBG				22:11.6	-1.2	-1.9	137	NBM			
Nov. 12	852	5.0	RD	217	NB2				10:22.2	-1.9	1.2	219	10:04.2	—	—	199
17	1484	3.6	RD	273	NB2				10:55.0	-1.7	-0.8	294	10:45.1	-1.9	0.0	281
20	1821	2.9	DB	312	11:40.0	-1.0	-1.0	142	11:31.2	-0.6	-1.2	155	11:31.4	-0.2	-2.0	171
20	1821	2.9	RD	312	12:50.7	-1.6	-0.6	294	12:33.7	-1.8	0.3	279	12:21.3	-2.1	1.3	262
26	2784	3.4	DD	41	20:56.5	-1.2	-0.4	65	NBM				NBM			
Dec. 21	2290	2.5	DB	333	11:02.3	-0.1	-0.4	150	GSM				GSM			
21	2290	2.5	RD	333	11:55.9	-1.5	1.2	262	11:41.8	-1.6	2.1	245	GSM			

DATE	ZC	MAG	PH	ELG°	WINNIPEG 97.2°W, 49.9°N TIME (UT)	A m	B m	P°	EDMONTON 113.4°W, 53.6°N TIME (UT)	A m	B m	P°	VANCOUVER 123.1°W, 49.2°N TIME (UT)	A m	B m	P°
Jan. 14	628	4.8	DD	133	GBG				10:55.8	0.1	-1.3	82	11:03.6	0.1	-1.7	101
17	1030	3.2	DD	162	0:51.5	-0.7	0.9	114	0:50.2	-0.1	1.5	89	NSG			
22	1702	4.2	RD	232									11:01.5	—	—	9
Feb. 13	1030	3.2	DD	136	GBG				12:20.5	0.4	-1.2	92	12:30.3	0.4	-1.4	106
14	1170	3.7	DD	148	GBG				13:14.9	0.2	-0.9	57	13:20.7	0.2	-1.0	72
Mar. 21	2118	2.9	DB	225	GBG				GBG				15:10.8	-0.8	-1.9	135
25	2721	3.3	RD	276	NB2				NB2				12:49.2	-1.0	0.4	308
Apr. 21	2650	4.7	RD	243	9:07.1	-0.8	0.0	323	GSM				GSM			
May 4	709	4.3	DD	29	GBG				4:58.2	-0.1	-0.2	35	4:59.6	0.0	-0.7	57
10	1484	3.6	DD	99	—								4:33.4	-2.0	-0.2	75
20	2910	4.8	RD	237	7:53.3	-1.3	1.4	245	GSM				GSM			
20	2914	5.0	RD	238	9:33.4	-1.5	0.7	249	GSM				GSM			
Jul. 9	2118	2.9	DD	119	6:09.9	-0.7	-1.4	88	5:49.7	-1.1	-1.2	88	5:41.7	-1.5	-0.9	97
9	2118	2.9	RB	119	GBG				6:49.6	-0.8	-1.7	319	6:48.5	-1.0	-1.6	314
17	3349	4.2	RD	225	7:08.0	—	—	313					GSM			
Aug. 2	1821	2.9	DD	60	23:42.3	-1.0	-1.4	134	23:22.7	-0.8	-1.2	149	23:24.8	-0.1	-2.3	177
3	1821	2.9	RB	60	0:51.8	-1.1	-1.5	296	0:27.4	-1.4	-0.7	281	0:11.0	-2.3	0.6	256
21	709	4.3	RD	284	7:48.6	0.1	1.9	238	7:57.5	0.2	1.6	256	7:53.7	0.4	1.4	259
Sep. 1	2053	4.6	DD	59	GBG				GBG				3:42.5	-0.8	-1.6	109
17	656	4.4	RD	254	7:49.4	0.2	3.1	199	7:58.0	-0.1	2.2	228	7:48.3	0.0	2.0	233
17	660	4.4	RD	254	8:45.3	-2.2	-0.3	302								
Oct. 4	2914	5.0	DD	106	1:41.7	-1.3	0.5	41	1:23.3	-1.4	1.2	32	NSG			
7	3349	4.2	DD	145	7:31.3	-1.8	-3.2	117	7:01.6	-1.3	-0.6	78	6:49.3	-1.6	0.0	73
Nov. 12	852	5.0	RD	216	9:45.4	-1.7	1.8	224	9:25.6	-1.4	1.3	243	9:04.6	-1.3	2.1	235
17	1484	3.6	RD	273	10:18.5	-1.2	0.5	289	10:04.5	-0.8	0.6	299	9:54.5	-0.6	1.0	287
20	1821	2.9	DB	311	11:17.2	-0.2	-1.4	168	11:11.3	-0.1	-0.8	161	GSM			
20	1821	2.9	RD	312	12:02.0	-1.3	2.1	258	11:54.9	-0.6	2.2	258	GSM			
Dec. 28	3349	4.2	DD	63	—				3:46.8	—	—	140	—			
28	3349	4.2	RD	64	—				3:56.7	—	—	158	—			

See pp. 159–160 for an explanation of this table.

TABLE OF TOTAL LUNAR OCCULTATION PREDICTIONS (continued)

DATE	ZC	MAG	PH	ELG °	MASSACHUSETTS 72.5°W, 42.5°N TIME (UT)	A m	B m	P °	WASHINGTON, D.C. 77.0°W, 38.9°N TIME (UT)	A m	B m	P °	CHICAGO 87.7°W, 41.9°N TIME (UT)	A m	B m	P °
Apr. 21	2650	4.7	RD	243	NB2				9:41.7	-2.0	-1.2	317	9:20.3	-1.5	-0.6	318
May 12	1702	4.2	DD	123	—				1:27.0	—	—	52	NSG			
20	2910	4.8	RD	237	8:25.2	-1.8	0.7	240	8:13.3	-2.0	1.1	236	7:56.7	-1.8	1.4	239
20	2914	5.0	RD	238	NB2				NB2				9:44.1	-1.8	0.7	238
Jul. 17	3349	4.2	RD	225	8:01.5	-2.1	0.3	260	7:50.3	-2.3	0.5	261	7:26.6	-2.3	0.5	283
Aug. 3	1821	2.9	DD	60	0:19.6	-0.9	-1.7	115	0:21.8	-0.9	-1.8	124	0:05.4	-1.1	-1.8	132
3	1821	2.9	RB	61	1:23.4	-0.4	-1.9	307	1:27.6	-0.6	-1.8	300	1:14.4	-0.9	-1.7	296
7	2359	4.8	RD	115	4:04.1	-0.5	-0.4	53	4:02.4	-0.8	-0.3	57	3:51.6	-1.2	0.3	43
21	709	4.3	RD	284	7:23.7	—	—	186	7:14.7	—	—	184	7:29.9	0.3	2.4	214
Sep. 17	660	4.4	RD	255	9:29.3	-1.9	1.2	244	9:15.4	-1.9	1.7	238	8:59.7	-1.9	1.1	262
Oct. 4	2910	4.8	DD	106	0:32.7	-1.6	0.4	54	0:23.1	-1.8	0.6	55	0:06.3	-1.8	1.2	45
4	2914	5.0	DD	106	2:14.5	-1.3	-0.7	77	2:10.0	-1.6	-0.5	78	1:52.4	-1.6	0.2	60
27	2347	4.8	DD	34	22:19.0	-1.3	-2.1	143	NBM				NBM			
Nov. 12	852	5.0	RD	217	10:18.0	—	—	203	—				—			
17	1484	3.6	RD	273	10:59.0	-1.9	-0.6	286	10:49.4	-2.5	0.5	268	10:27.6	-2.0	1.1	266
20	1821	2.9	DB	312	11:36.1	-0.5	-1.7	163	11:44.8	—	—	190	11:42.3	—	—	207
20	1821	2.9	DB	312	12:34.8	-2.1	0.4	272	12:18.7	—	—	246	11:52.4	—	—	224
Dec. 21	2290	2.5	DB	333	11:06.8	—	—	178	—				—			
21	2290	2.5	RD	333	11:36.3	—	—	235	—							

DATE	ZC	MAG	PH	ELG °	MIAMI 80.3°W, 25.8°N TIME (UT)	A m	B m	P °	ATLANTA 84.3°W, 33.8°N TIME (UT)	A m	B m	P °	AUSTIN 97.8°W, 30.2°N TIME (UT)	A m	B m	P °
Jan. 22	1702	4.2	RD	233	—				—				12:05.1	0.5	-4.0	5
25	2033	4.3	RD	269	6:20.5	—	—	3	—				GSM			
27	2307	4.1	RD	296	8:31.8	0.3	-1.3	335	GSM				GSM			
27	2310	4.6	RD	296	9:02.8	-0.4	-0.4	308	8:58.0	0.1	-0.7	328	GSM			
Mar. 12	900	4.9	DD	99	1:51.7	-3.2	3.6	35	—				1:30.3	—	—	2
20	1941	4.8	RD	204	3:24.2	-0.5	-1.1	325	3:11.1	0.1	-2.2	353	3:14.7	-0.1	-0.7	323
Apr. 21	2650	4.7	RD	244	9:46.2	-2.6	-0.6	288	9:31.6	-2.1	-0.7	304	9:06.1	-1.8	0.2	285
May 10	1484	3.6	DD	99	5:52.5	—	—	49	—				5:30.7	-1.4	-0.5	74
12	1702	4.2	DD	123	1:09.1	-2.2	-0.9	114	0:57.0	-2.3	0.2	97	NSG			
14	1941	4.8	DD	150	0:29.7	-2.5	2.3	70	—				NSG			
19	2721	3.3	RD	222	4:14.0	-0.6	0.3	289	GSM				GSM			
20	2910	4.8	RD	237	7:39.3	—	—	202	7:50.5	-2.2	1.9	225	7:03.7	—	—	189
20	2914	5.0	RD	238	9:31.9	—	—	191	9:42.9	-1.9	1.3	221	9:07.5	-2.4	2.3	217
Jul. 9	2118	2.9	DD	119	GBG				GBG				6:38.3	-0.9	-1.6	118
17	3349	4.2	RD	225	7:30.4	-2.3	1.4	241	7:29.6	-2.4	0.8	263	6:56.3	-1.9	0.9	272
17	MARS	-1.9	DB	225	8:14.8	—	—	346	—				—			
17	MARS	-1.9	RD	225	8:52.1	—	—	297	—				—			
26	900	4.9	DD	326	8:56.8	—	—	3	—				—			
26	900	4.9	RD	326	9:13.8	—	—	328	—				—			
Aug. 3	1821	2.9	DD	60	0:45.6	-0.7	-2.4	151	0:24.5	-1.0	-2.1	140	0:22.1	-0.5	-2.9	170
3	1821	2.9	RB	61	1:44.8	-0.8	-1.1	274	1:30.8	-0.9	-1.5	287	1:16.9	-2.0	-0.8	264
7	2359	4.8	RD	115	4:05.3	-1.4	-0.7	85	3:56.1	-1.4	-0.3	64	3:31.8	-2.3	0.0	72
21	709	4.3	RD	284	—				7:04.8	—	—	184	7:08.1	0.9	2.5	201
22	852	5.0	RD	296	10:15.0	-2.4	-0.1	288	—				—			
Sep. 5	2650	4.7	DD	112	GBG				GBG				6:10.5	—	—	8
17	660	4.4	RD	254	8:34.6	-0.6	3.9	200	8:52.7	-1.6	2.1	234	8:25.9	-1.3	1.7	248
Oct. 4	2910	4.8	DD	105	0:07.4	-2.6	0.5	77	0:04.0	-2.2	1.0	60	NBM			
4	2914	5.0	DD	106	2:12.0	-2.7	-1.1	103	1:58.3	-2.0	-0.2	78	1:27.3	-2.4	0.6	71
Nov. 17	1484	3.6	RD	273	—				10:14.1	—	—	224	—			
19	1702	4.2	RD	297	8:30.2	-0.5	-1.5	332					GSM			

TABLE OF TOTAL LUNAR OCCULTATION PREDICTIONS (continued)

DATE	ZC	MAG	PH	ELG °	KANSAS CITY 94.5°W, 39.0°N				DENVER 105.0°W, 39.8°N				NEW MEX., ARIZ. 109.0°W, 34.0°N			
					TIME (UT)	A m	B m	P °	TIME (UT)	A m	B m	P °	TIME (UT)	A m	B m	P °
Jan. 17	1030	3.2	DD	162	—				0:40.5	-1.0	-0.1	132	NSG			
17	1030	3.2	RD	163	—				R:O.B.				1:00.9	—	—	191
22	1702	4.2	RD	232	—				R:O.B.				11:51.4	-0.5	-2.8	346
24	1941	4.8	RD	259	—				—				13:17.4	0.4	-3.8	7
Apr. 21	2650	4.7	DD	243	9:11.4	-1.5	-0.2	306	8:57.9	-1.2	0.3	296	8:50.0	-1.4	0.7	279
May 10	1484	3.6	DD	99	—				5:14.4	-2.2	-0.1	61	5:10.4	-1.7	-1.0	87
20	2910	4.8	RD	237	7:39.8	-1.8	1.9	230	7:23.3	-1.7	2.5	219	—			
20	2914	5.0	RD	238	9:28.6	-2.0	1.1	236	9:09.2	-1.9	1.5	236	8:50.5	-2.2	2.3	221
Jul. 9	2118	2.9	DD	119	6:27.5	-0.7	-1.5	102	6:16.9	-1.1	-1.4	100	6:20.4	-1.3	-1.5	110
9	2118	2.9	RB	119	GBG				GBG				7:28.5	-0.8	-1.6	293
17	3349	4.2	RD	225	7:09.7	-2.1	0.6	287	6:50.8	-1.5	0.5	298	6:41.6	-1.2	0.8	286
Aug. 2	1821	2.9	DD	60	24:03.7	-1.0	-2.0	146	23:53.0	-0.6	-2.3	164	24:09.5	—	—	191
3	1821	2.9	RB	60	1:11.6	-1.3	-1.5	285	0:53.9	-1.9	-1.0	271	0:46.0	—	—	247
7	2359	4.8	DD	114	3:40.2	-1.8	0.4	50	3:17.5	-2.5	0.7	54	3:04.1	-2.7	0.4	72
21	709	4.3	RD	284	7:26.0	0.4	2.2	217	7:32.0	0.4	1.8	231	GSM			
Sep. 17	656	4.4	RD	254	—				7:19.5	—	—	186	7:01.2	—	—	172
17	660	4.4	RD	254	8:44.0	-1.7	1.2	265	8:26.5	-1.8	0.7	287	8:15.5	-1.4	0.9	279
Oct. 4	2914	5.0	DD	106	1:39.7	-1.8	0.6	58	1:20.5	-1.9	1.1	50	NSG			
Nov. 17	1484	3.6	RD	273	10:08.7	-1.9	2.7	247	9:54.4	-1.2	2.6	247	—			

DATE	ZC	MAG	PH	ELG °	LOS ANGELES 118.3°W, 34.1°N				N. CALIFORNIA 122.0°W, 38.0°N				HONOLULU 157.9°W, 21.3°N			
					TIME (UT)	A m	B m	P °	TIME (UT)	A m	B m	P °	TIME (UT)	A m	B m	P °
Jan. 14	628	4.8	DD	133	GBG				11:27.5	0.9	-3.1	139	—			
20	1484	3.6	RD	209	—				—				16:13.7	—	—	3
22	1702	4.2	RD	232	11:42.7	-1.2	-2.0	326	11:30.7	-1.1	-1.9	330	—			
24	1941	4.8	RD	259	13:14.2	-0.8	-2.2	342	13:03.2	-0.6	-2.1	345	—			
28	2500	3.4	RD	313	NB2				NB2				15:30.1	-2.0	2.3	239
Feb. 11	709	4.8	DD	110	—				—				6:58.4	-2.8	1.0	66
Mar. 10	656	4.4	DD	79	—				—				8:27.5	-1.2	0.8	53
16	1484	3.6	DD	152	—				—				10:27.5	-2.2	-1.0	104
21	2118	2.9	DB	225	GBG				15:34.9	-0.9	-2.4	153	—			
22	2241	5.0	DD	236	—				—				11:00.6	-1.2	0.2	283
25	2721	3.3	RD	276	12:52.5	-1.9	0.2	286	12:47.1	-1.6	0.3	291	—			
Apr. 19	2359	4.8	RD	220	GBG				GBG				15:41.6	-1.8	0.8	236
21	2650	4.7	RD	243	8:38.4	-1.2	1.1	266	GSM				—			
May 10	1484	3.6	DD	99	4:54.8	-1.7	-1.3	105	4:43.4	-1.8	-1.2	103	—			
15	2118	2.9	DD	171	GBG				GBG				12:40.8	-1.3	-3.2	166
15	2118	2.9	RB	172	GBG				GBG				13:25.2	-1.4	0.5	242
20	2914	5.0	RD	237	8:30.4	—	—	208	8:34.8	-1.8	2.8	216	—			
23	3349	4.2	RD	276	NB2				NB2				13:07.2	—	—	332
Jul. 9	2118	2.9	DD	118	6:06.7	-1.6	-1.4	113	5:55.5	-1.7	-1.2	109	—			
9	2118	2.9	RB	119	7:19.4	-1.1	-1.6	295	7:08.7	-1.2	-1.7	301	—			
17	3349	4.2	RD	224	6:32.9	-0.7	0.8	286	6:33.6	-0.5	0.7	294	GSM			
24	656	4.4	RD	307	NB2				NB2				15:33.0	-0.9	1.8	239
Aug. 9	2721	3.3	DD	144	GBG				GBG				10:01.1	-1.1	2.0	32
Sep. 1	2053	4.6	DD	59	4:12.3	-0.7	-1.9	130	4:02.3	-0.8	-1.8	122	NSG			
17	656	4.4	RD	254	7:12.6	0.7	2.7	198	7:24.3	0.4	2.3	213	GSM			
17	660	4.4	RD	254	8:02.2	-1.5	0.1	300	—				—			
23	1484	3.6	RD	327	NB2				NB2				14:55.9	—	—	212
28	2118	2.9	DD	39	—				—				23:16.2	-3.6	1.7	72
29	2118	2.9	RB	39	—				—				0:00.7	0.4	-3.6	2
Oct. 3	2784	3.4	DD	96	—				6:04.6	—	—	143	4:57.2	-3.2	-2.0	132
7	3349	4.2	DD	145	—				6:56.3	-3.0	-1.1	102	5:15.0	-1.8	1.2	76
26	VEN	-3.9	RB	17	—				—				18:32.0	0.2	-1.0	324
31	2910	4.8	DD	79	—				GBG				7:48.8	—	—	139
Nov. 10	599	4.5	RD	197	—				—				13:57.7	-2.3	0.6	246
12	852	5.0	RD	216	—				8:23.4	—	—	182	7:38.7	0.8	2.7	206
17	1484	3.6	RD	273	9:22.8	—	—	215	9:37.0	-0.3	2.5	245	—			
Dec. 17	1821	2.9	DB	285	—				—				22:25.2	-0.7	-0.3	76

See pp. 159–160 for an explanation of this table.

TABLE OF GRAZING LUNAR OCCULTATION PREDICTIONS

The table below and on the next page lists lunar grazing occultation predictions for much of North America for 2003. The eight maps following the table show the graze tracks (see the descriptive text on pp. 160–161).

For each graze is given:

No. .... a chronological sequential number used on the maps
Date .... the date
USNO d ... the star's USNO (U.S. Naval Observatory) reference number (see the bottom of p. 160) and its duplicity code (in the **"d"** column—see section (C) on pp. 162–163 concerning double stars)
m .... its visual magnitude
%sl .... the percent of the Moon sunlit (+ for waxing, – for waning)
L .... whether the track is a northern (N) or southern (S) limit
W.U.T. ..... the Universal Time at the west end of the track
Lo., La. .... the longitude and latitude of the west end of the track

No.	Date	USNO d	m	%sl	L	W.U.T.	Lo.	La.	No.	Date	USNO d	m	%sl	L	W.U.T.	Lo.	La.
1	Jan. 7	3343 A	5.7	19+	S	3:33.6	–130	45	54	14	1239	6.6	80+	S	11:38.5	–111	55
2	8	3458	6.2	26+	S	1:18.1	–90	20	55	19	1821 O	3.6	99–	S	6:59.2	–59	55
3	8	3480	7.2	28+	S	5:00.8	–130	44	56	20	1962	5.0	95–	S	9:17.0	–92	55
4	9	25	7.4	35+	S	2:06.8	–80	20	57	22	2217	5.5	80–	S	7:29.0	–100	55
5	9	44	7.4	37+	S	5:58.1	–130	38	58	24	2524 M	6.0	59–	S	6:59.1	–71	47
6	12	354 K	5.5	63+	S	0:25.7	–118	50	59	27	3012	6.9	26–	S	10:22.0	–99	28
7	16	882 V	5.0	94+	S	1:43.2	–123	26	60	27	X54084	7.4	26–	S	11:21.9	–113	28
8	17	1030	3.1	98+	S	0:42.6	–121	26	61	27	X28741	7.2	26–	S	11:22.7	–113	29
9	22	1709	6.5	80–	S	14:00.1	–100	55	62	Apr. 4	355	7.4	4+	S	2:17.9	–116	35
10	24	1937 A	6.1	60–	S	11:56.1	–130	40	63	5	X04181	7.5	9+	S	2:26.7	–96	55
11	26	2182	6.2	38–	S	11:43.5	–72	55	64	5	466	7.3	9+	S	2:57.4	–125	37
12	26	2192	6.2	37–	S	13:58.7	–130	49	65	6	595 K	6.8	15+	S	3:14.7	–126	50
13	28	2459	7.2	18–	S	10:19.7	–62	52	66	6	X06070 X	6.9	21+	S	23:53.3	–78	39
14	28	2469	6.5	18–	S	12:22.5	–72	55	67	7	716	6.3	22+	N	1:01.1	–92	34
15	28	2483	7.1	17–	S	13:39.7	–114	50	68	7	X06274 H	7.4	23+	N	4:41.6	–96	55
16	28	2500 J	3.3	16–	N	15:47.7	–130	45	69	8	852 L	5.2	31+	N	1:25.9	–106	22
17	Feb. 4	3413 A	6.1	7+	S	2:49.4	–130	25	70	8	867	6.8	31+	N	3:14.4	–106	55
18	5	3529 K	6.5	13+	S	2:11.7	–130	45	71	8	877	6.5	32+	N	5:05.5	–130	51
19	10	651 X	6.0	63+	S	21:27.8	–64	52	72	8	X07656 V	7.3	33+	N	6:03.2	–130	44
20	10	665 U	5.7	64+	S	23:31.4	–86	20	73	10	1170 A	3.6	53+	S	7:52.6	–87	55
21	11	688 M	6.8	65+	N	4:50.7	–93	25	74	11	1270 V	6.0	61+	N	1:12.7	–102	24
22	12	X07145	6.8	76+	S	7:17.5	–130	51	75	13	1544	5.4	83+	N	8:03.8	–101	55
23	12	839	5.4	76+	S	7:47.9	–72	55	76	26	3374	6.1	22–	S	11:27.3	–118	27
24	12	835	7.0	75+	N	6:55.3	–95	55	77	May 4	X05829	7.5	5+	N	0:44.3	–85	35
25	13	1099	5.8	89+	S	23:33.2	–95	52	78	4	688 M	6.8	5+	N	1:49.1	–84	55
26	14	1117 K	5.0	90+	S	2:59.6	–130	35	79	4	X05956	7.5	6+	N	4:05.5	–130	40
27	16	1484 C	3.5	100–	N	22:27.7	–73	41	80	5	822 D	5.8	11+	N	3:07.1	–114	50
28	20	1864	6.7	86–	S	3:28.2	–84	52	81	7	1117 K	5.0	27+	S	5:23.1	–85	55
29	20	1875 M	6.7	86–	S	6:10.5	–97	55	82	8	X12313	7.3	34+	N	0:48.5	–88	32
30	21	1996	6.7	77–	S	5:18.2	–94	45	83	8	X12558	7.2	37+	N	5:26.6	–130	40
31	21	1997	6.8	77–	S	5:37.2	–91	55	84	8	1251	5.9	37+	N	6:07.6	–130	43
32	23	2282	5.8	53–	S	10:21.7	–130	36	85	10	1484 C	3.5	57+	N	4:55.3	–118	55
33	24	2443 K	5.7	41–	S	12:58.7	–111	55	86	11	1598 K	6.5	68+	N	4:18.9	–128	51
34	25	2579	7.4	31–	S	11:36.0	–76	55	87	12	1702	4.0	77+	N	1:13.8	–89	47
35	25	X24526	7.5	30–	S	14:35.7	–130	46	88	14	1941	4.7	93+	N	0:39.4	–88	32
36	26	2750 Y	2.0	22–	N	10:00.5	–92	31	89	14	1962	5.0	95+	S	7:40.3	–92	36
37	Mar. 5	X01461	7.2	7+	S	22:26.1	–65	45	90	16	2217	5.5	0E	S	3:43.7	–115	48
38	8	394	7.5	21+	S	3:01.0	–130	23	91	19	2721 X	3.2	87–	N	3:58.8	–74	41
39	9	517	6.1	31+	S	7:00.4	–126	55	92	20	2910 K	4.7	78–	S	6:54.2	–107	35
40	10	633 V	5.5	39+	S	5:07.9	–130	53	93	20	2914 V	4.8	77–	S	8:08.0	–125	34
41	10	631 O	5.6	39+	N	4:45.7	–130	54	94	21	3052 M	6.4	68–	S	6:24.2	–86	35
42	10	634	5.3	39+	S	5:41.0	–130	45	95	24	3458	6.2	37–	N	9:39.6	–106	24
43	11	767 M	5.5	48+	N	3:45.8	–125	44	96	25	25	7.4	27–	N	10:17.6	–114	28
44	12	900	4.8	57+	N	1:43.2	–95	30	97	28	355	7.4	6–	N	11:34.2	–111	22
45	12	902	6.6	57+	N	2:31.1	–85	41	98	Jun. 2	932	7.3	4+	N	3:37.4	–118	42
46	12	X09881 V	6.8	66+	S	23:10.9	–75	51	99	3	1061	6.2	7+	N	0:23.8	–67	46
47	12	1046	7.0	66+	S	23:35.4	–81	33	100	3	1094	7.0	9+	N	6:15.0	–130	54
48	13	1049	6.8	66+	S	0:02.4	–87	38	101	5	1334	7.0	22+	N	3:49.5	–90	55
49	13	1055	5.7	67+	S	2:21.8	–79	55	102	6	1435	6.5	30+	N	1:02.5	–83	38
50	13	1061	6.2	67+	N	3:44.6	–104	41	103	6	1436	6.8	31+	N	1:41.1	–89	42
51	13	1062 K	6.4	68+	N	4:05.3	–102	51	104	7	1569	6.9	43+	N	5:54.0	–106	55
52	13	1068	7.0	68+	S	5:02.8	–130	49	105	16	2848 A	5.6	95–	S	6:56.9	–130	34
53	13	1099	5.8	71+	S	11:08.3	–129	55	106	18	3158	5.7	81–	N	11:53.3	–103	20

TABLE OF GRAZING LUNAR OCCULTATION PREDICTIONS (continued)

No.	Date	USNO d	m	%sl	L	W.U.T.	Lo.	La.	No.	Date	USNO d	m	%sl	L	W.U.T.	Lo.	La.
107	Jun. 18	3160	6.7	81-	N	10:49.0	-123	20	182	Oct. 14	601 X	5.9	87-	N	5:04.0	-87	20
108	20	3413 A	6.1	62-	N	10:36.8	-107	20	183	14	621 V	6.1	86-	N	9:17.2	-130	36
109	22	95 K	7.0	42-	N	11:10.7	-113	20	184	15	740	6.3	80-	N	5:01.9	-120	23
110	23	202	6.9	34-	N	7:39.2	-91	24	185	15	743 W	5.8	80-	N	6:27.0	-90	20
111	23	212 O	7.2	33-	N	10:24.4	-130	23	186	16	852 L	5.2	72-	N	1:26.6	-70	42
112	25	X03834	7.5	17-	N	9:47.3	-113	47	187	17	1042	6.7	62-	N	8:16.6	-109	20
113	27	688 M	6.8	5-	N	11:50.0	-119	26	188	18	1169	5.3	52-	N	8:36.0	-130	44
114	Jul. 4	X15556 O	7.3	18+	N	0:35.8	-80	28	189	19	1283	7.0	42-	N	7:08.0	-91	20
115	4	1535	6.8	19+	N	3:13.3	-76	55	190	19	1290	6.9	42-	N	8:28.5	-122	30
116	4	1544	5.4	20+	N	4:51.7	-130	48	191	20	X14421	7.3	32-	N	8:08.2	-102	30
117	7	1864	6.7	50+	N	2:38.4	-104	39	192	20	1408 K	7.3	32-	N	8:29.7	-114	45
118	7	1869 M	6.2	50+	N	3:52.0	-93	55	193	20	1416	7.0	31-	N	10:03.4	-128	23
119	7	1866 Y	5.8	50+	S	4:23.6	-81	41	194	21	1535	6.8	21-	S	11:24.1	-89	50
120	7	1875 M	6.7	51+	N	5:24.6	-130	43	195	21	1544	5.4	21-	S	12:29.2	-130	42
121	8	1997	6.8	63+	N	5:45.7	-130	27	196	22	1647	6.7	13-	N	11:10.7	-119	44
122	10	2230 X	6.7	81+	N	1:20.9	-80	45	197	22	1659	6.7	12-	N	13:18.4	-130	44
123	10	2236 M	6.9	82+	N	1:32.1	-96	27	198	23	1758	6.9	6-	N	11:46.0	-109	38
124	13	2721 X	3.2	99+	N	0:21.9	-71	44	199	27	2347	4.5	8+	N	22:48.8	-83	29
125	17	Mars	-1.7	86-	N	8:03.4	-89	20	200	27	X22292	7.0	8+	N	22:49.0	-82	37
126	17	3349	4.0	86-	N	6:34.0	-119	50	201	28	X22362	7.5	9+	N	1:30.8	-125	45
127	19	X00375	6.9	70-	N	6:03.4	-100	49	202	Nov. 2	X29964	7.0	60+	N	5:12.6	-86	20
128	19	49	6.1	69-	N	7:29.9	-111	20	203	7	219	4.8	96+	S	2:02.2	-84	20
129	21	283	6.6	50-	N	8:57.1	-125	20	204	9	434	6.9	9E	N	1:04.4	-81	20
130	25	767 M	5.5	15-	N	11:06.3	-130	41	205	10	660 V	4.3	97-	N	21:43.8	-58	44
131	26	900	4.8	8-	N	9:03.9	-88	23	206	12	852 L	5.2	91-	N	8:53.3	-104	43
132	26	902	6.6	8-	N	9:41.1	-103	37	207	13	994 X	6.6	85-	N	5:44.7	-130	27
133	27	1061	6.2	4-	N	11:30.3	-118	39	208	14	1089	6.7	79-	N	1:08.2	-75	48
134	Aug. 1	1612	7.3	10+	N	3:32.2	-117	45	209	14	1105 V	6.5	78-	N	3:05.8	-86	23
135	4	1947	7.0	35+	N	0:54.8	-70	55	210	14	1108 V	7.0	78-	N	4:12.3	-82	20
136	4	1951 M	7.1	36+	N	2:51.7	-117	30	211	15	1251	5.9	68-	N	8:10.4	-110	49
137	5	2065 C	6.5	46+	N	0:34.5	-80	38	212	15	1270 V	6.0	67-	N	12:19.3	-130	52
138	6	2217	5.5	61+	N	6:35.6	-130	32	213	16	1363 M	5.2	59-	N	5:39.4	-97	22
139	7	2359 E	5.7	70+	N	3:22.3	-111	54	214	16	1365 C	6.0	59-	N	6:06.1	-102	21
140	7	2357 M	6.8	70+	N	3:35.5	-98	55	215	16	1373	6.5	59-	S	8:29.5	-84	29
141	8	2514	6.4	80+	N	2:46.6	-118	30	216	17	1484 C	3.5	48-	N	9:05.6	-130	31
142	8	2524 M	6.0	81+	N	5:16.8	-130	44	217	18	1586	7.5	38-	N	7:26.2	-97	42
143	14	3428 A	5.0	95-	N	7:55.0	-83	20	218	18	1598 K	6.5	37-	N	10:08.1	-130	47
144	17	219	4.8	76-	N	3:58.2	-90	21	219	19	1702	4.0	27-	N	8:03.4	-93	32
145	21	X05956	7.5	38-	N	5:39.3	-84	36	220	19	1709	6.5	27-	S	10:28.7	-125	51
146	21	716	6.3	38-	N	8:42.1	-124	26	221	20	X18646	7.2	17-	N	9:53.7	-100	36
147	22	822 D	5.8	29-	N	5:04.0	-74	45	222	20	1821 O	3.6	17-	S	11:26.9	-125	49
148	22	852 L	5.2	28-	N	9:21.0	-102	20	223	20	1825	5.9	17-	S	12:14.5	-130	42
149	Sep. 1	X20068	7.5	22+	N	0:33.6	-90	21	224	21	1947	7.0	9-	N	10:33.7	-99	29
150	2	2173	6.9	34+	N	3:05.3	-130	21	225	25	2601 Y	6.8	5+	S	22:45.5	-82	26
151	2	2181 C	6.8	34+	N	4:15.9	-130	33	226	26	2621	7.5	6+	N	1:02.2	-109	20
152	2	2290 L	2.3	43+	S	22:37.4	-88	55	227	26	X24693	7.2	6+	S	1:15.9	-104	20
153	5	2650	4.7	68+	N	6:03.5	-118	20	228	28	2965	7.2	22+	S	1:43.1	-78	20
154	5	2643	6.7	68+	S	5:05.0	-122	28	229	28	X29427	7.5	30+	S	22:09.5	-84	47
155	5	2784 V	3.3	76+	S	23:08.8	-85	43	230	Dec. 3	76	5.9	72+	S	3:03.5	-94	20
156	6	2796	6.8	76+	N	0:28.8	-88	39	231	3	83 A	6.6	73+	S	3:32.8	-130	27
157	8	3130	5.4	94+	N	9:47.0	-130	39	232	4	219	4.8	83+	S	10:14.6	-130	53
158	15	413	6.7	81-	N	7:21.1	-81	20	233	6	422	5.5	94+	S	4:18.2	-130	43
159	15	434	6.9	80-	N	13:17.8	-130	44	234	11	1088	5.8	95-	N	6:50.5	-130	30
160	17	X05675	7.0	64-	N	6:31.4	-87	20	235	12	1206	5.9	90-	N	4:36.4	-128	27
161	17	660 V	4.3	64-	N	7:38.7	-130	32	236	12	1211 C	6.3	90-	N	5:27.8	-130	43
162	17	664 K	5.5	64-	N	8:01.4	-130	23	237	12	1211 C	6.3	90-	S	5:40.4	-82	30
163	20	1088	5.8	35-	N	10:11.1	-96	20	238	13	1334	7.0	83-	N	7:00.7	-111	55
164	20	1089	6.7	35-	N	10:08.6	-130	38	239	14	1435	6.5	75-	N	4:47.8	-112	49
165	20	X10660 X	7.4	34-	N	10:24.9	-130	27	240	14	1436	6.8	75-	N	5:33.9	-126	54
166	20	1105 V	6.5	34-	N	12:43.6	-130	38	241	15	1544	5.4	66-	S	3:47.8	-77	36
167	20	X10805	7.3	34-	N	13:12.6	-130	49	242	15	1578 K	6.8	62-	S	15:16.9	-124	55
168	21	1206	5.9	26-	N	7:10.5	-77	20	243	16	1669	6.7	54-	S	8:25.9	-128	43
169	21	1211 C	6.3	26-	N	7:44.5	-97	35	244	17	1758	6.9	44-	N	6:16.8	-81	35
170	21	X12313	7.3	25-	N	11:06.2	-130	39	245	18	1891 T	4.1	35-	N	10:58.7	-62	55
171	24	1586	7.5	4-	N	11:57.5	-109	34	246	20	2132	7.3	13-	S	9:09.1	-78	21
172	Oct. 1	2411	6.7	29+	S	0:15.7	-79	38	247	20	2136	6.6	13-	S	10:15.8	-84	41
173	1	2424 A	6.9	30+	S	2:32.4	-111	20	248	20	2147 V	6.9	12-	S	12:07.4	-117	30
174	1	2427	7.2	31+	S	3:09.7	-124	32	249	21	2290 L	2.3	6-	N	11:17.8	-81	45
175	1	2558	6.3	40+	N	23:17.1	-81	24	250	21	X21949	7.3	5-	S	11:57.0	-89	39
176	3	2784 X	3.3	55+	S	6:14.4	-130	31	251	25	X27602	7.5	4+	S	0:34.7	-112	37
177	4	2914 V	4.8	63+	S	2:51.8	-75	20	252	26	3052 M	6.4	9+	S	0:22.0	-112	40
178	4	3052 M	6.4	73+	S	23:53.4	-79	21	253	28	3349	4.0	27+	S	3:42.8	-130	46
179	6	3227	6.3	84+	S	9:15.1	-117	20	254	28	3458	6.2	34+	S	22:18.7	-86	45
180	7	3343 A	5.7	90+	S	5:23.0	-130	35	255	29	X31717	7.4	36+	S	3:21.5	-82	20
181	7	3349	4.0	91+	S	6:55.9	-130	25	256	30	X00347	7.0	46+	S	1:09.1	-110	20

GRAZING OCCULTATION MAPS

JANUARY 1 – FEBRUARY 20

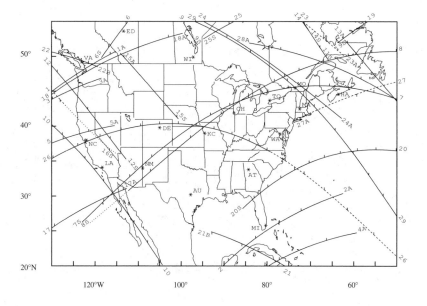

FEBRUARY 21 – MARCH 31

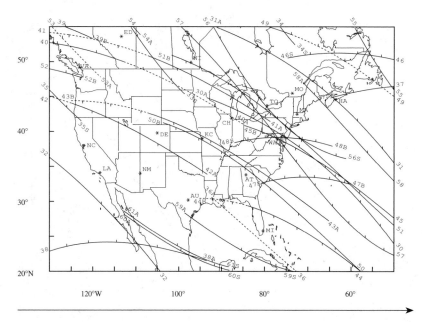

GRAZING OCCULTATION MAPS (continued)

APRIL 1 – MAY 20

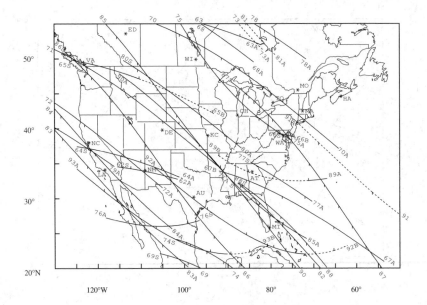

MAY 21 – JULY 20

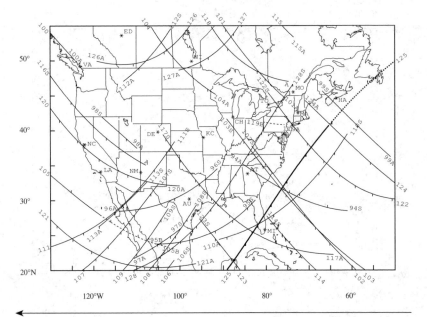

GRAZING OCCULTATION MAPS (continued)

JULY 21 – SEPTEMBER 19

SEPTEMBER 20 – OCTOBER 20

GRAZING OCCULTATION MAPS (continued)

OCTOBER 21 – NOVEMBER 20

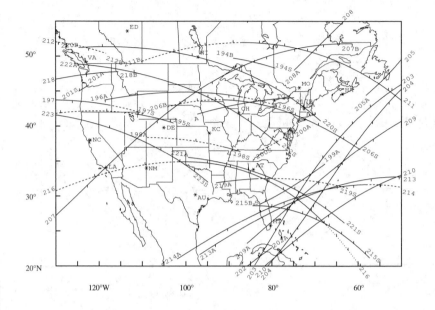

NOVEMBER 21 – DECEMBER 31

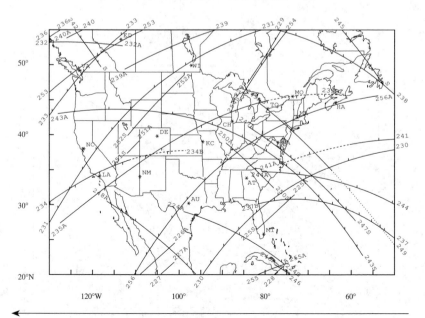

TIDES AND THE EARTH–MOON SYSTEM
BY ROY BISHOP

The tidal aspect of gravitation produces some of the most interesting phenomena in the universe, from the structure of interacting galaxies, such as M51, to the volcanoes of Io, the fragmentation of Comet Shoemaker-Levy 9 by Jupiter in 1992, the synchronous rotation of our Moon, and the pulse of the seas on our planet. Perhaps because they occur at our feet, the tides of the oceans are often overlooked when considering the heavens; yet the pulse of the tides is the heartbeat of a greater universe beyond Earth.

Newtonian Tides

Tides were known to the ancients, but an understanding of their origin came only three centuries ago with the publication of Newton's *Principia* (1687). In the Newtonian context, tides originate in the fact that the force of gravity decreases with distance from a massive body. The Moon exerts a force on Earth, and Earth responds by accelerating toward the Moon; however, the waters on the hemisphere facing the Moon, being closer to the Moon, accelerate more and fall ahead of Earth. Similarly, Earth itself accelerates more than the waters on the other hemisphere and falls ahead of these waters. Thus two tidal bulges are produced, one on the side of Earth facing the Moon and one on the side facing away from the Moon.

Note that the waters directly under the Moon and the waters farthest from the Moon do not rise up because of the slightly larger and smaller, respectively, lunar gravity at these two locations; all that results from the Moon's action on the waters at these two points is a slight decrease in the pressure on the floor of the sea. The two tidal bulges form because the variation in the Moon's gravity causes the *surrounding* waters on each hemisphere to flow horizontally across Earth's surface into these regions:

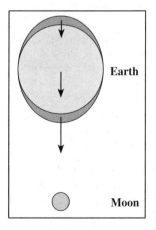

In order of decreasing length, the arrows indicate the force per unit mass (acceleration) produced by the Moon's gravity on the near side, centre, and far side of Earth. It is the resulting horizontal flow of the water across Earth's surface toward the two points nearest and farthest from the Moon that produces the two tidal bulges (indicated by heavy shading).

As Earth rotates on its axis, the orientation of these two bulges in relation to the Moon remains fixed; hence the rise and fall of the oceans on Earth. If Earth had no rigidity, the entire planet would flex freely in the same fashion, and there would be virtually no water tides. The very existence of the tides indicates that on a time scale of several hours our planet displays considerable rigidity.

Because of the Moon's orbital motion, it transits on average 50.47 min later each day. Thus on successive days, high tides recur about 50 min later; or for the many regions experiencing two high tides daily, these tides recur at intervals of 12 h 25 min.

The Sun exerts a gravitational force 180 times stronger than that exerted by the Moon on Earth; however, because the Moon is so much closer, the *variation* in the Moon's force across Earth's diameter is about 2.2 times larger than the variation in the Sun's force. As described above, it is this variation that produces tides; thus the pair of bulges raised by the Moon is considerably larger than the pair raised by the Sun. As the Moon goes through its monthly cycle of phases, these two pairs of tidal bulges get in and out of step, combining in step to produce *spring tides* (no connection with the season) when the Moon is new or full (syzygy) and out of step to produce *neap tides* when the Moon is at first or last quarter (quadrature).

Another factor having a substantial influence on tidal ranges is the elliptical shape of the Moon's orbit. Although the Moon is only 9% to 12% closer at perigee than at apogee, because the *variation* in its gravitational force varies inversely as the cube of its distance (the force itself varies inversely as the square of the distance), the Moon's tidal influence is 30% to 48% greater at perigee than at apogee. Because the Sun tidally influences the shape of the Moon's orbit, exceptionally close perigees coincide with full or new Moon, and the resulting extreme tides are known as *perigean spring tides*. If the lunar orbit were fixed in orientation, such tides would recur at half-year intervals; however, the major axis of the lunar orbit rotates in the direct sense with a period of 8.85 years, making the average interval between perigean spring tides about 24 days longer than half a year (206 days).

Influences on the Tides

There are many astronomical factors influencing the tides. These can be sorted according to the periods they produce. The periods of the more important factors are:

(1) semidiurnal, 12 h 00 min (two solar-induced tidal bulges, as described above);

(2) semidiurnal, 12 h 25 min (two lunar-induced tidal bulges, as described above);

(3) diurnal, 24 h 50 min (the changing declinations of the Moon and Sun shift the pairs of tidal bulges out of Earth's equatorial plane, resulting in a tidal component with a one-day period; this is the dominant tide in some areas, such as parts of the southern coast of Canada's Gulf of St. Lawrence);

(4) semimonthly, 13.66 days (variation in the Moon's declination);

(5) semimonthly, 14.77 days (spring–neap cycle, described above);

(6) monthly, 27.55 days (perigee–apogee cycle, described above);

(7) semiannual, 182.6 days (variation in the Sun's declination);

(8) semiannual, 206 days (perigean spring tide cycle, described above);

(9) annual, 365.26 days (perihelion–aphelion variation in the Sun's tidal influence);

(10) 8.85 years (rotation period of the Moon's perigee); and

(11) 18.61 years (rotation period of the nodes of the Moon's orbit).

In addition to astronomical factors, the tides on Earth are strongly influenced by the sizes, boundaries, and depths of ocean basins and inlets and by Earth's rotation, winds, and barometric pressure fluctuations. Using Newton's gravitation and laws of motion, the French physicist Pierre-Simon Laplace (1749–1827) developed the dynamical theory of the tides on the rotating Earth (*Mécanique Céleste*, 1799), but because of the complexity of the tides the full application of his theory was not possible until the advent of the digital computer in the last third of the 20th century.

Tides typically have ranges (vertical high to low) of a metre or two, but there are regions in the oceans where the various influences conspire to produce virtually no tides at all and others where the tides are greatly amplified. Among the latter regions are the Sea of Okhotsk, the Gulf of Alaska, the northern coast of Australia, the English channel, and in Canada: Ungava Bay in northern Quebec and the Bay of Fundy between New Brunswick and Nova Scotia. The tidal ranges in these regions are of the order of 10 m.

Fundy Tides

The highest ocean tides on Earth occur in Minas Basin, the eastern extremity of the Bay of Fundy in eastern Canada, where the mean vertical range is 12 m and can reach 16 m (52 ft.) when the various factors affecting the tides are in phase (although the highest tides occur typically a day or two after the astronomical influences reach their peak).

The primary cause of the immense tides of Fundy is a resonance of the Bay of Fundy/Gulf of Maine system. The system is effectively bounded at its outer end by the edge of the continental shelf with its approximately 40:1 increase in depth. The system has a natural period of approximately 13 hours, a Q-value* of about 5, and is driven near resonance, not directly by the Moon, but by the dominant semidiurnal tides of the Atlantic Ocean. Like a father pushing his daughter on a swing, the gentle Atlantic tidal pulse pushes the waters of the Bay of Fundy/Gulf of Maine basin at nearly the optimum frequency to cause a large oscillation. The seventh Astronomer Royal, G.B. Airy (1801–1892), first developed the theory of the behaviour of tides in restricted arms of the ocean such as the Fundy system.

Because the lunar tidal period (12.4 hours) is nearer to the system's resonant period than is the solar tidal period (12.0 hours), Fundy tides respond more to the perigee–apogee influence than they do to the spring–neap influence. Although the variation in the Moon's distance is not obvious when viewing the Moon directly, near the head of the Bay of Fundy the 3-m to 6-m *increase* in the vertical tidal range makes it obvious when the Moon is near perigee, clear skies or cloudy!

The most dramatic view of the vertical range of Fundy tides is at the Minas Basin Pulp & Power Company wharf in the town of Hantsport, Nova Scotia. Remarkably, this site is practically unknown; it is not advertised, and no special provisions have been made to accommodate spectators.

Perhaps the most awesome display of the tides on our planet occurs at Cape Split, Nova Scotia, on the southern side of the entrance to Minas Basin. (Cape Split may be reached by a pleasant two-hour walk along a popular hiking trail from the village of Scots Bay.) Here, at the time of the midpoint of an incoming tide, for a considerable distance the forest on the towering cliffs is filled with a hollow roar produced by the turbulence of the waters surging over the submarine ridges below. The currents exceed 8 knots (4 m/s), and the flow in the deep, 5-km-wide channel on the north side of Cape Split equals the combined flow of all the streams and rivers of Earth ($\approx$4 km^3/h). Three hours later the spectacle pauses and then begins flowing in the opposite direction.

The highest of the high tides on the Bay of Fundy occur on rare occasions when a perigean spring tide coincides with a low barometric-pressure storm system sweeping northward up the Gulf of Maine and accompanied by hurricane-force southerly winds. The close Moon, the in-phase solar tide, the reduced air pressure above the

---

*The Q-value, or quality-value, of an oscillator indicates its efficiency. A large Q means low energy loss per cycle and a well-defined resonant frequency.

water, and the wind drag pushing more water into the Bay of Fundy all contribute to an especially high tide. An additional favourable influence is if all this occurs near an equinox, for then the axis of the tidal bulges of the spring tide is at a right angle to Earth's rotation axis, optimizing the tidal range (if the axes were parallel there would be no tidal cycle). This right-angle-axes enhancement of the tides is strengthened in those years when the declination range of the Moon (±18° to ±29°) is near a minimum, a situation that recurs with the 18.61-year period of the retrograde motion of the nodes of its orbit. (The declination range was at its ±18° minimum in 1959, 1978, and 1997 and will be again in 2015. See p. 75 for the shift in the longitude of the ascending node of the Moon's orbit during 2003.) Furthermore, since perihelion occurs in January, the highest tides of all will tend to occur just prior to the March equinox or after the September equinox. The infamous Bay of Fundy "Saxby gale" of 1869 October 5 was a time when all seven of these factors coincided (perigee, spring tide, low pressure, south wind, equinox, minimum declination range, perihelion enhancement). Since weather is unpredictable, so, too, is the next major tidal flood in the Bay of Fundy.

Tidal Friction

Tidal friction, which occurs primarily in shallow seas around the margins of the oceans, transforms Earth's rotational kinetic energy into heat at a rate of about 3.5 TW. This is comparable to humankind's total rate of energy use. Approximately 1% of this energy transformation occurs in the Bay of Fundy, and, since 1984, a tiny portion of this (20 MW peak) is being turned into commercial electric power at the Annapolis Basin tidal power plant in Nova Scotia. The only other large-scale tidal power installation is in France on the Rance estuary (240 MW peak).

Tidal friction also transfers angular momentum from Earth to the Moon, lengthening the day and increasing the size of the orbit of the Moon. The day is lengthening by about 1 second every 40 000 years—imperceptible on a human time scale but of profound significance to Earth's rotation over a few billion years. (For example, 900 million years ago, when Earth was already 80% of its present age, there were about 480 18-hour days in a year.) The Moon is receding about 3.8 cm per year, with the result that within 600 million years total solar eclipses will cease. Presently we are well into the transitional phase: annular eclipses already outnumber total solar eclipses. New moons occur, on average, almost one day earlier each successive month; however, because of the increasing size of the lunar orbit, in about 300 million years the lunar (synodic) month will have lengthened to equal the average calendar month (although the average month will then contain only about twenty-eight 26-hour days).

If the Sun does not first incinerate our planet, there will come a day that is as long as the lunar month (each then equal to about 40 present days), and a more distant Moon will stand stationary in the sky, as does Earth now in the lunar sky. But this situation will not endure, for solar tides will still be present and will reduce the angular momentum of the Earth–Moon system, causing the Moon to approach Earth once more.

General Relativity and Tides

Einstein's theory of gravitation, general relativity, superseded Newton's theory nearly a century ago, yet descriptions of the tides almost invariably ignore Einstein (as has this article to this point). The reasons for using the older, wrong theory are: (1) Newton's theory describes the gentle tides on Earth to high accuracy; (2) the mathematics involved is much simpler than that of general relativity; (3) the Newtonian description of the tides is compatible with cultivated common sense. Because of this last reason, Newton's concepts regarding motion and gravitation form the essential foundation for anyone attempting to understand the tides. One must climb up on Newton's towering shoulders before it is possible to focus clearly on Einstein.

As mentioned in the article *Orbital Motion* (see p. 28), Newton's Euclidean universe with its force of gravity never did exist. Although Newton's ideas are more than adequate for describing the tides on Earth, for some purposes, such as the Global Positioning System (GPS), Newton's concepts of space, time, and gravitation are inadequate. We inhabit an Einsteinian universe, a universe in which gravitation is a manifestation of the structure of spacetime, the four-dimensional stage of our existence in which space and time are interwoven. The geometry of spacetime is curved by the mass–energy of matter, and the curvature tells matter how to move.

The Moon's mass alters the structure of spacetime at its location, and this distortion propagates outward, becoming more dilute with the volume encompassed according to the inverse cube of the distance. At Earth, the distortion results in the waters of the oceans following slightly different paths through spacetime than does the rigid planet beneath, producing the characteristic egglike shape of the tidal effect. The tidal heartbeat is that of the very fabric of spacetime. The tides at our feet carry a profound message.

References

For more information, see the superb introduction *The Tides* by E.P. Clancy, Anchor Books, Doubleday and Co., 1969 (now, unfortunately, out of print). For a detailed account of the evolution of our understanding of the tides see *Tides, A Scientific History,* by D.E. Cartwright, Cambridge University Press, 1999. (Note, however, that neither Clancy nor Cartwright mention general relativity.) For a popular account of general relativity, see *A Journey into Gravity and Spacetime,* by J.A. Wheeler, Scientific American Library, 1990. An article dealing specifically with the tides of Fundy and tidal power installations has been written by Christopher Garrett (*Endeavour 8,* #2, 58–64, 1984). The major astronomical factors influencing the tides (the phases, perigees, and apogees of the Moon) are tabulated in THE SKY MONTH BY MONTH section (pp. 76–99) of this Handbook. These may be perused to determine days favourable for large tides. Detailed predictions for tides in Canadian waters, produced by the Department of Fisheries and Oceans Canada, are published in *Canadian Tide and Current Tables,* the six volumes of which are individually available from Canadian Government bookstores and other authorized chart dealers; see www.lau.chs-shc.dfo-mpo.gc.ca/marees/produits/accueil.htm for a list of dealers and also for predictions for particular locations.

PLANETS AND SATELLITES

GENERAL INTRODUCTION

PLANETARY HELIOCENTRIC LONGITUDES, 2003

The heliocentric longitude of a planet is the angle between the vernal equinox and the planet, as seen from the Sun. It is measured in the ecliptic plane, in the direction of the orbital motion of the planet (counterclockwise as viewed from the north side of the ecliptic plane). Knowing these heliocentric longitudes and the distances of the planets from the Sun (see p. 21), one can construct a diagram or model showing the relative orientations of the Sun and planets on any date.

UT	Me °	V °	E °	Ma °	J °	S °	U °	N °	P °
Jan. 1.0	44	137	100	202	131	86	328	310	258
Feb. 1.0	203	187	132	216	133	87	329	311	258
Mar. 1.0	284	232	160	230	135	88	329	311	258
Apr. 1.0	56	282	191	246	138	89	329	311	258
May 1.0	207	329	220	262	140	91	330	311	258
Jun. 1.0	296	18	250	280	142	92	330	311	259
Jul. 1.0	75	66	279	298	145	93	330	312	259
Aug. 1.0	220	117	308	317	147	94	331	312	259
Sep. 1.0	309	167	338	337	150	95	331	312	259
Oct. 1.0	101	215	7	356	152	96	331	312	259
Nov. 1.0	231	265	38	15	154	97	332	312	259
Dec. 1.0	320	312	68	33	157	99	332	313	260
Jan. 1.0	125	1	100	51	159	100	332	313	260

MAGNITUDES OF NAKED-EYE PLANETS IN 2003

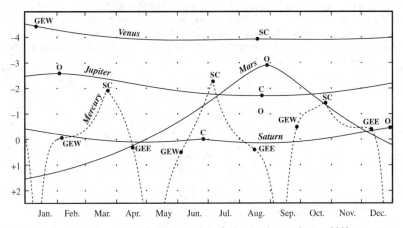

The visual magnitudes of the five, classical (naked-eye) planets during 2003 are given. Oppositions (O), conjunctions (C), inferior and superior conjunctions (IC, SC), and greatest elongations east and west (GEE, GEW) are indicated. See the diagram explaining these terms at the right.

PRONUNCIATION OF PLANET NAMES

Mercury	mûr′kū-rē
Venus	vē′nŭs
Earth	ûrth
Mars	màrz
Jupiter	jōo′pĭ-tēr
Saturn	sàt′ûrn
Uranus	yoor′à-nŭs
Neptune	nĕp′tyoͦon
Pluto	ploͦo′tō

à àsk;   ē wē; ĕ mĕt; ē makēr;   ĭ bĭt;
ō gō; oo book; oͦo mooͦn;   ū ūnite; ŭ ŭp; û ûrn

SOLAR SYSTEM GEOMETRY

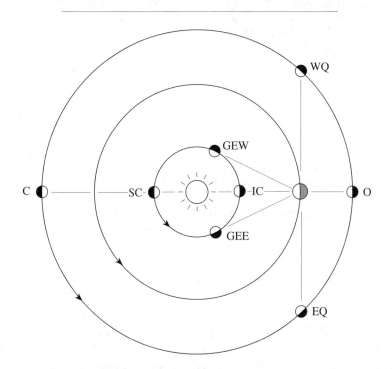

The diagram is a simplified view of our solar system, from the north side. Earth is shown (middle orbit) together with an inferior planet (i.e. Mercury or Venus) and a superior planet (e.g. Mars). Four special geometrical configurations of the inferior planet relative to Earth are shown; in counterclockwise chronological sequence they are inferior conjunction (IC), greatest elongation west (GEW), superior conjunction (SC), and greatest elongation east (GEE). Four special configurations of the superior planet relative to Earth are also shown; in clockwise chronological sequence they are opposition (O), eastern quadrature (EQ), conjunction (C), and western quadrature (WQ).

TELESCOPIC APPEARANCE OF THE PLANETS

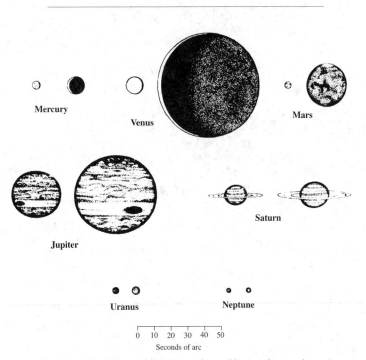

Mercury

Venus

Mars

Jupiter

Saturn

Uranus

Neptune

```
0   10  20  30  40  50
      Seconds of arc
```

The apparent maximum and minimum observable size of seven planets is illustrated along with characteristic telescopic appearance.

PRONUNCIATION OF SATELLITE NAMES

Adrastea	à-drăs'tē-à	Galatea	gàl'à-tē'à	Pasiphae	pà-sĭf'à-ē'
Amalthea	ăm''l-thē'à	Ganymede	găn'ĕ-mēd'	Phobos	fō'bŏs
Ananke	a'năn-kē	Helene	hà-lēn'	Phoebe	fē'bē
Ariel	âr'ē-ĕl	Himalia	hĭm'à-lĭ-à	Portia	pôr'shà
Atlas	ăt'lăs	Hyperion	hī-pēr'ĭ-ŏn	Prometheus	prŏ-mē'thē-ŭs
Belinda	bà-lĭn'dà	Iapetus	ī-ăp'ĕ-tŭs	Prospero	prŏs'pĕr-ō
Bianca	bē-āng'kà	Io	ī'ō	Proteus	prō'tē-ŭs
Caliban	kăl'ĭ-băn	Janus	jā'nŭs	Puck	pŭk
Callisto	kà-lĭs'tō	Juliet	joo'lē-ĕt	Rhea	rē'à
Calypso	kà-lĭp'sō	Larissa	là-rĭs'à	Rosalind	rŏz'à-lĭnd
Carme	kàr'mē	Leda	lē'dà	Setebos	sĕt'ē-bōs
Charon	kâr'ĕn	Lysithea	lĭs'ĭ-thē'à	Sinope	sĭ-nō'pē
Cordelia	kôr-dēl'yà	Metis	mē'tĭs	Stephano	stĕf'à-nō
Cressida	krĕs'ĭ-dà	Mimas	mī'măs	Sycorax	sĭk'ō-răks
Deimos	dī'mŏs	Miranda	mĭ-răn'dà	Telesto	tà-lĕs'tō
Desdemona	dĕz'dà-mō'nà	Moon	moon	Tethys	tē'thĭs
Despina	dĭs-pīn'à	Naiad	nī'àd	Thalassa	thà-làs'à
Dione	dī-ō'nē	Nereid	nēr'ē-ĭd	Thebe	thē'be
Elara	ē'làr-à	Oberon	ō'bà-rŏn	Titan	tī't'n
Enceladus	ĕn-sĕl'à-dŭs	Ophelia	ō-fēl'yà	Titania	tī'tā'nē-à
Epimetheus	ĕp'à-mē'thē-ŭs	Pan	păn	Triton	trī't'n
Europa	yoo-rō'pà	Pandora	păn-dôr'à	Umbriel	ŭm'brē-ĕl'

ā dāte; ă tăp; â câre; à àsk; ē wē; ĕ mĕt; ī īce; ĭ bĭt; ō gō; ŏ hŏt; ô ôrb; oo book; oo moon; ŭ ŭp

RIGHT ASCENSIONS OF THE SUN AND PLANETS IN 2003

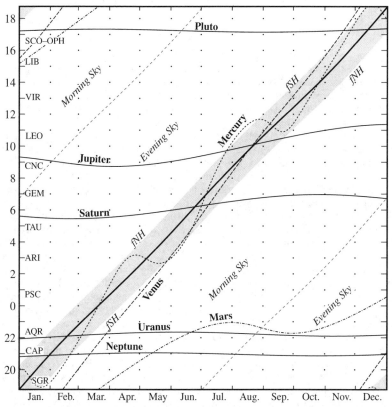

This diagram shows the variation during the year in the right ascension (vertical axis) of the Sun and the planets. The slightly curved, heavy diagonal line represents the Sun; the shaded regions approximately indicate parts of the night sky affected by twilight. The two thin, dashed diagonal lines at the upper left and bottom right represent the boundary between the evening sky and the morning sky.

The diagram may be used as a quick reference to determine in what part of the sky a planet may be found (including in which constellation—note the names along the vertical axis), when a superior planet is in conjunction with the Sun or at opposition (opposition is approximately where its curve intersects the dashed diagonal lines, and note that, due to retrograde motion, this point is also where the planet's curve has its maximum negative slope), when Mercury and Venus have their various greatest elongations and conjunctions, and when there are conjunctions of planets. For example, the Dec. 31 opposition of Saturn can be read from the extreme right of the diagram, and note the almost simultaneous conjunction of Jupiter, Venus, and the Sun around Aug. 20.

For observers in midlatitudes, at certain times of the year the ecliptic stands steeply to the horizon in the western evening sky or the eastern morning sky, making apparitions of planets in these parts of the sky favourable from the Northern Hemisphere ("fNH" on the diagram) or favourable from the Southern Hemisphere ("fSH").

For more information on all these events, see THE SKY MONTH BY MONTH *(pp. 74–99) and* THE PLANETS FOR 2003 *(immediately following).*

THE PLANETS FOR 2003
By Terence Dickinson

INTRODUCTION

Planetary observing is perhaps the most widely accessible and diversified category of amateur astronomical pursuits. Planets can be seen on almost any clear night of the year. Indeed, in heavily light-polluted cities they are sometimes the *only* celestial objects visible. With dark skies ever more remote from population centres, planetary observing is returning—partly by default—to take its place as an important part of the amateur astronomer's repertoire.

But a factor more important than sky conditions is needed to explain the expanding interest in planetary observing. There is a widespread recognition among amateur astronomers that high-quality optics are essential for good views of the planets; the increased commercial availability of such instruments—especially previously unavailable systems such as apochromatic refractors and Maksutov-Newtonians—means that planetary observing is more accessible than ever.

Planetary observing divides into three distinct categories, each with its opportunities and limitations. *Unaided-eye* observing consists of detecting, identifying, and monitoring the night-to-night and week-to-week motion and visibility of the five brighter planets. *Binoculars* add Uranus and Neptune along with the Galilean satellites of Jupiter. Binoculars are ideal for tracking planetary motion against the backdrop of stars, many of which are too faint for naked-eye detection. But it is only through *telescopic* observing that the planets reveal their uniqueness, and this section concentrates on that aspect. For a listing of unaided-eye highlights such as conjunctions, see THE SKY MONTH BY MONTH section on pp. 74–99.

Urban and suburban locales unsuited for many aspects of astronomy can be perfectly acceptable for telescopic planetary observing. Atmospheric turbulence—seeing—is often no worse, and sometimes better, in urban areas. However, observers should avoid using telescopes on pavement, balconies, or immediately beside a house or substantial building due to the heat radiated to the surrounding atmosphere from these structures. Also, avoid looking over these objects if possible. A typical grassed backyard is fine in most instances. For optimum performance all telescopes (except small refractors) require from 10 min to an hour to cool to outside temperature when taken outdoors. Hazy but otherwise cloudless nights are usually just as good as, and sometimes better than, clear skies for steady telescopic images of planets.

More than any other class of telescopic observing, planetary observing is most affected by seeing. Many nights are rendered useless for planet watching by ever-present ripples and undulations in Earth's atmosphere. Planets within 15° of the horizon are virtually always afflicted (as many observers of Mars noted in the summer of 2001 from Canadian latitudes). Minimum altitude for expectations of reasonable seeing is 25°. A further problem with low-altitude planetary targets is dispersion associated with atmospheric refraction. Refraction causes celestial objects to appear displaced to higher altitudes. Since the effect is wavelength-dependent (being less for longer wavelengths), for planets at low altitudes this produces a red fringe on the lower side of the planet and a green (or blue) fringe on the upper; the effect also introduces chromatic smearing to the whole image.

Regardless of the type of telescope used for planetary observing, optical quality is far more critical than aperture. In no other type of observing are the effects of less-than-perfect optics more apparent. Other factors that can significantly degrade a telescope's planetary performance include a large *central obstruction* in the optical system (all Schmidt-Cassegrains, Maksutov-Cassegrains, and Newtonians with secondary mirror diameters exceeding 20% of their apertures), *secondary mirror supports* (most Newtonians), *chromatic aberration* (most achromatic refractors over 90 mm), *internal air currents* (all types, refractors least), optical component *cool-down time* (mostly aperture-dependent, telescopes over 200 mm can take hours), *improperly light-baffled optics,* and *dirty optics.*

In the remarks below, when a planetary phenomenon is stated as being visible in a certain minimum aperture, good seeing and a moderate level of observer experience are assumed. When a specific minimum aperture is cited, an unobstructed optical system (i.e. a refractor) is assumed. Somewhat larger apertures are often required if centrally obstructed systems are used or the observer is inexperienced.

Editor's Note: The tables and figures that appear in this section were prepared by the editor or other contributors; the editor assumes full responsibility for their accuracy.

MERCURY

Of the five planets visible to the unaided eye, Mercury is by far the most difficult to observe and is seldom conveniently located for either unaided eye or telescopic observation. The problem for observers is Mercury's tight orbit, which constrains the planet to a small zone on either side of the Sun as viewed from Earth. When Mercury is east of the Sun we may see it as an evening "star" low in the west just after sunset. When it is west of the Sun we might view Mercury as a morning "star" in the east before sunrise. But due to the celestial geometry of the tilt of Earth's axis and Mercury's orbit, we get much better views of Mercury at certain times of the year.

MERCURY—MOST FAVOURABLE EVENING VIEW IN 2003 FROM NORTHERN LATITUDES

Date 0h UT		Mag.	Angular Diameter "	Percent Illuminated	Elongation from Sun °	Apparent RA (2003) h m	Dec ° '
Apr.	1	+1.4	5.4	91	10	1 18	+8 29
	6	−1.1	5.9	80	15	1 53	+12 51
	11	−0.6	6.6	59	18	2 23	+16 27
	16	0.1	7.6	41	20	2 47	+18 58
	21	+0.9	8.8	25	19	3 03	+20 18
	26	+2.0	10.0	13	15	3 09	+20 26
May	1	+3.6	11.2	4	10	3 07	+19 25

From midlatitudes, the best time to see the planet in the *evening* sky is within a month or two of the spring equinox and in the *morning* sky within a month or two of the autumn equinox (this applies to both northern and southern latitudes, although the respective seasons are six months out of phase). Binoculars are of great assistance in searching for the planet about 40 min to an hour after sunset or before sunrise during the periods when it is visible. The planet's brightness, which varies by more than two magnitudes, is a more important factor influencing its visibility than its angular distance from the Sun during any particular elongation. Mercury's true colour is almost pure white, but absorption from Earth's atmosphere within 15° of the horizon, where Mercury is most easily seen, usually imparts a yellow or ochre hue to the planet.

Telescopic observers will find the rapidly changing phases of Mercury of interest. The planet appears to zip from gibbous to crescent phase in about three weeks during each of its evening elongations. The phases are accessible to users of 75-mm or larger telescopes; the 30% phase can be detected at 50×. Large apertures (over 200 mm) rarely offer an advantage due to the crippling effects of poor seeing at lower altitudes, especially following sunset when the planet is most frequently observed. Experienced planetary observers often report their most satisfying telescopic observations of Mercury in the morning sky. Near favourable western elongations, the planet may be easily located at least an hour before sunrise, then followed to higher altitudes into the daytime sky. Seeing often remains steady more than an hour after sunrise by which time the planet may be 30° above the horizon. Under such conditions the phase is sharply defined, and the small disk takes on a unique appearance, paler than Venus, with a vaguely textured surface. Surface details, although suspected in moments of fine seeing, are always elusive. Contrasts between the planet's surface features are lower than on the lunar surface, although in other respects the two bodies are similar.

VENUS

Venus is the only world in the solar system that closely resembles Earth in size and mass. It also comes nearer to Earth than any other planet, at times approaching as close as 0.27 AU. Despite the fundamental similarity, surface conditions on Earth and Venus differ greatly. The clouds and haze that cloak the planet are highly reflective, making Venus the brightest natural celestial object in the nighttime sky apart from our Moon. Whenever it is visible, it is readily recognized. Because its orbit is within that of Earth's, Venus is never separated from the Sun by an angle greater than 47°. However, this is more than sufficient for the dazzling object to dominate the morning or evening sky.

Like Mercury, Venus exhibits phases, although they are much more easily detected in small telescopes because of Venus's greater size. When it is far from us near the other side of its orbit, we see the planet nearly fully illuminated, but because of its distance it appears small—about 10″ in diameter. As Venus moves closer to Earth, the phase decreases (we see less of the illuminated portion of the planet), but the diameter increases until it is a thin slice nearly a minute of arc in diameter. It takes Venus several months to move from one of these extremes to the other, compared to just a few weeks for Mercury.

As 2003 opens, Venus is near greatest elongation west (Jan. 11) and dominates the morning sky. It remains visible through the first half of the year, with ecliptic geometry leading to particularly favourable circumstances for southern observers. After superior conjunction on Aug. 18, it emerges in the evening dusk in late September, with southern observers once again favoured. Circumstances improve for all observers as Venus heads toward greatest elongation east on 2004 Mar. 29.

For telescopic observers, the following information will be useful: on Jan. 1, Venus is 44% illuminated and 28″ in apparent diameter; Mar. 1, 71%, 16″; Jun. 1, 93%, 11″; Oct. 1, 98%, 10″; Dec. 1, 90%, 11″.

When Venus is about a 20% crescent, even rigidly held, good-quality binoculars can be used to distinguish that the planet is not spherical or a point source. The new image-stabilized binoculars beautifully display the crescent Venus. A 60-mm refractor should be capable of revealing the shape of all but the gibbous and full phases. Experienced observers prefer to observe Venus during the daytime, and indeed the planet is bright enough to be seen with the unaided eye if one knows where to look.

Because of Venus's high surface brightness (about 40 times greater than Jupiter's), Venus can accommodate the highest magnifications a telescope can deliver. The author has used magnifications over 4× per millimetre of aperture on occasion and regularly employs 1.5× to 3× per millimetre on the planet, particularly in bright twilight when the sky is moderately dark but Venus is still high enough to avoid low-altitude seeing degradation. Venus's cloud-shrouded surface appears to most observers to be feature-less no matter what type of telescope is used or what the planet's phase. Broad streaks and splotches in the clouds, revealed in blue-filtered and ultraviolet images of Venus, may be vaguely detected telescopically using a violet filter (#38A or #47), although sketches of these features seldom match among different observers.

MARS

This is a very special year for Mars, or, to be more precise, for the inhabitants of Earth who enjoy watching Mars! In late August, the red planet makes its closest approach to Earth in recorded history. The extended coverage provided here is intended to encourage everyone, especially newcomers to observational astronomy, to follow the progress of Mars through the closest approach period in August and September, and to emphasize that *this is by far the best opportunity during the next 15 years to see detail on the planet's surface using modest-aperture telescopes.*

Even without any astronomical equipment, Mars is often considered the most interesting planet to observe with the unaided eye. It moves rapidly among the stars— its motion can often be detected after an interval of less than a week—and it varies in brightness over a far greater range than any other planet. Mars can be distinguished by its pale orange-red colour, a hue that originates with rust-coloured dust that covers much of the planet. As 2003 opens, Mars is a morning-sky object about 5° from Venus on the Scorpius/Libra border. During the next six months it moves eastward through Scorpius, Sagittarius, Capricornus, and into Aquarius as it brightens from magnitude +2 to –1, and its ochre glow dominates the eastern sky after midnight. Mars remains in Aquarius for the next five months (July through November) where it becomes the dominant starlike object in the night sky in late summer and autumn. On July 1, Mars is magnitude –1.5 and brightens rapidly at the approximate rate of one-tenth of a magnitude every four days until it reaches magnitude –2.9 in late August, which is the maximum possible brightness for Mars. Opposition is on August 28, when Mars is visible throughout the night. Around opposition, Mars will draw attention to itself because of its distinctive rusty hue, which will be enhanced (to human eyes) by the exceptional brilliance.

This opposition of Mars is as good as it gets for telescopic observers—in theory anyway. The last opposition, in June 2001, turned into a disappointment for many because just days after the planet's closest approach to Earth, a dust storm broke out in the Hellas basin which quickly spread to envelope 80% of the Martian globe. By early July, the familiar dark areas of our neighbour world were completely obscured, and they remained that way for months. It was the biggest dust storm seen on Mars in three decades. What are the chances of this happening again? Statistically, a major dust storm is unlikely to strike two successive oppositions. However, so little is known about the atmospheric dynamics behind the storms that predicting storm activity is impossible at present.

What makes this year's opposition exceptional is the fact that Mars is nearest Earth just three days before Martian perihelion (see the diagram OPPOSITIONS OF MARS 1997–2010 on p. 188). Closest approach occurs August 27 at 9:52 UT when the distance between the two worlds is 0.372 719 25 AU, or 55 758 006 km, which is *the nearest to Earth that Mars has been for approximately 100 000 years*. Mars will not be closer to Earth until 2287 August 28, when the planet will be 70 000 km nearer. To give this year's event full perspective, though, keep in mind that the closest approach of Mars to Earth during the opposition of 1924 was only 1900 km greater, hardly a significant difference.

For the past 150 years, both amateur and research astronomers have awaited perihelion oppositions for the best views of Mars because the desert planet is always 22″ to 25″ in apparent diameter compared to 14″ at aphelion oppositions. This almost two-to-one difference in apparent diameter actually translates into a more than three-to-one variation when calculated as apparent surface area—a more practical comparison for visual observers—which is why planetary observers so anticipate the minimum approaches. Perihelion oppositions occur at intervals of 15 to 17 years; the most recent was in 1988 (23.8″ apparent diameter), and the next after this year's will be in 2018 (24.3″). This August, Mars will be 25.1″ in diameter, the maximum possible.

At the last opposition, in 2001, Mars reached 20.8″ and (before the dust storm) substantial detail on the planet was distinguished with typical backyard telescopes such as a 200-mm Newtonian. Many observers, though, were disappointed in the event apart from the dust storm. In fact, 2001 was not a favourable opposition for midnorthern latitude observers because Mars was stationed 25° south of the celestial equator. That placed the planet just 20° above the southern horizon for observers at 45° north latitude, not high enough to avoid the image-degrading effects of poor seeing so close to the horizon. This year's event will be different in two respects: improved sky position for northern observers and a larger apparent diameter. So northern-latitude observers are urged not to judge what will be seen this year based on the 2001 experience.

Mars will be greater than 20″ apparent diameter for 11 weeks, from July 19 to October 4, an unprecedented extended prime observing window—unequalled since 1924 and unrivalled since 1988. Further, throughout this same period Mars will be within 2° of 15° south of the celestial equator, placing the planet 30° above the south horizon for the observer at 45° north latitude. This is high enough to ensure some nights of decent seeing for almost everyone. Observers using 100-mm or larger telescopes (barring a big dust storm on Mars) should be able to record enough detail to identify many of the prominent features shown on the accompanying map. In moments of good seeing, observers using 200-mm or larger telescopes of good optical quality will see an overwhelming amount of fine detail.

Most of Mars is a peach-coloured desert with darker greyish zones (also deserts) of varying size and prominence. The clarity of the surface features depends to a large extent on the transparency of the Martian atmosphere. In addition to local dust storms, ice clouds and haze can lower contrast across sectors of the disk. But when the Martian air is clear, and the seeing conditions on Earth permit, the subtle colour and fine detail of the planet's surface are exquisite and compelling in a telescope. Throughout the prime observing window, the Martian southern regions are tilted toward Earth. The regions from the equator to −40° Martian latitude are most prominently displayed. Meridiani Sinus and Sabaeus Sinus are the most distinctive darker features in this zone. The large dark marking known as Syrtis Major, although tilted southward on the Martian disk at this apparition, will still be easy to see.

By coincidence, the Martian northern hemisphere winter solstice occurs on September 29, just one month after the date of closest approach. That means the south polar cap (the only visible cap during this close approach window) will start out small and end up large as the carbon dioxide atmosphere in the frigid polar zone freezes to the ground as the temperature drops. Even though the planet will diminish in apparent size into 2004, the cap should remain visible in telescopes as it continues to enlarge.

(text continued on p. 190)

MARS—EPHEMERIS FOR PHYSICAL OBSERVATIONS, 2003

Date 0h UT	Dist. AU	Mag.	Equat. Diam. "	Percent Illum.	Position Angle °	Incl. °	L(1) °	Δ °/d
Jan. 16	1.925	+1.4	4.9	93	37	+10	299.3	9.68
Feb. 17	1.638	+1.1	5.7	91	31	+1	349.7	9.67
Mar. 21	1.346	+0.7	7.0	88	21	−7	40.2	9.68
Apr. 22	1.066	+0.2	8.8	87	9	−15	90.6	9.67
May 24	0.812	−0.5	11.5	87	358	−20	141.1	9.64
Jun. 1	0.754	−0.7	12.4	87	355	−20	64.0	9.61
9	0.699	−0.9	13.4	87	352	−21	347.1	9.58
17	0.646	−1.1	14.5	88	350	−21	270.5	9.52
25	0.597	−1.3	15.7	89	348	−21	194.3	9.46
Jul. 3	0.550	−1.5	17.0	90	346	−21	118.6	9.39
11	0.508	−1.8	18.4	92	345	−21	43.5	9.30
19	0.470	−2.0	19.9	93	344	−21	329.1	9.19
27	0.437	−2.2	21.5	95	344	−20	255.6	9.09
Aug. 4	0.409	−2.4	22.9	97	344	−20	182.9	8.98
12	0.389	−2.6	24.1	98	344	−20	111.1	8.89
20	0.377	−2.8	24.8	99	345	−19	40.0	8.84
28	0.373	−2.9	25.1	100	346	−19	329.3	8.84
Sep. 5	0.378	−2.8	24.8	99	348	−19	258.6	8.89
13	0.392	−2.6	23.9	99	349	−19	187.5	8.98
21	0.414	−2.4	22.6	97	349	−19	115.8	9.06
29	0.444	−2.1	21.1	95	350	−20	43.3	9.19
Oct.. 7	0.480	−1.9	19.5	94	349	−21	329.8	9.29
15	0.522	−1.7	17.9	92	349	−22	255.5	9.38
23	0.569	−1.4	16.5	91	347	−23	180.5	9.48
31	0.620	−1.2	15.1	90	346	−23	104.7	9.55
Nov. 8	0.674	−1.0	13.9	89	344	−24	28.3	9.61
16	0.732	−0.8	12.8	88	342	−25	311.4	9.66
24	0.793	−0.6	11.8	87	340	−26	234.1	9.75
Dec. 26	1.058	+0.1	8.9	87	330	−26	282.2	

The above table gives information useful for observers of Mars during 2003. Data are given at 8-day intervals while Mars is greater than 12″ in equatorial diameter (Jun. 1 to Nov. 24), otherwise the intervals are approximately one-month. The columns give (1) the date; (2) the distance of Mars from Earth in astronomical units; (3) the visual magnitude of Mars; (4) its apparent equatorial angular diameter; (5) the percent of its disk illuminated; (6) the position angle of its rotation axis, measured counterclockwise from north (clockwise in telescopes having an odd number of reflections); (7) the inclination of its rotation axis to the plane of the sky, positive if its north pole is tipped toward Earth; and two quantities, (8) L(1) and (9) Δ, which can be used to calculate the planetographic longitude L of the central meridian of the observed geometric disk of Mars at any moment. L increases westward on Mars (eastward on the celestial sphere).

For a given date and time (UT) of observation, L is equal to L(1) for the nearest preceding date in the table, less Δ multiplied by the number of complete days elapsed since that date. To the result, add 14.6° multiplied by the time in hours elapsed since 0h UT. If the result is less than 0°, add 360°; if the result is 360° or larger, subtract 360°. The answer is accurate to better than 1°, provided the time of observation is accurate to ±2 minutes. This value of L can then be used to orient the map on p. 189 to the view of Mars seen in a telescope.

OPPOSITIONS OF MARS, 1997–2010

Diagram by Roy Bishop

The above diagram represents the orbits of Earth and Mars as viewed from the north eclip-tic pole. Straight lines link simultaneous positions of the two planets for seven successive oppositions of Mars, beginning with that of the year 1997. The separation of the two planets (in astronomical units) at the various oppositions is indicated beside each of the connecting lines. The months inside of Earth's orbit indicate the position of Earth during the year (both planets orbit counterclockwise). For each orbit, two tick marks labelled A and P indicate the aphelion point and the perihelion point, respectively. The direction of the vernal equinox is shown (toward the late September position of Earth). Around the orbit of Mars is indicated its declination (ranges between +27° and –28°) and the constellation in which Mars resides when at opposition.

Four views of Mars are shown—at its two equinoxes and two solstices. These views show the portion of Mars illuminated by the Sun, the location and approximate size of its north polar cap, and the apparent size of Mars (labelled in arc-seconds) for oppositions occurring at these points in its orbit. The seasons of the Martian northern hemisphere are indicated around the outer margin of the diagram, and are very nearly one season ahead of those on Earth at the same orbital position. (For the southern hemisphere of Mars, the season and the configuration of the south polar cap are the same as those of the diametri-cally opposite view.) Note that the maximum angular diameter Mars can attain (25″) occurs near its perihelion, at a late-August opposition.

As an example of the information that can be read from this diagram: the 2003 opposi-tion of Mars occurs in late August with Mars 0.37 AU from Earth. Mars will be close to its maximum angular diameter, over 24″, and located near declination –15°, close to the Capricornus-Aquarius border. It will be late autumn in the northern hemisphere on Mars, with a large but hidden north polar cap and a small, observable south polar cap.

MAP OF MARS

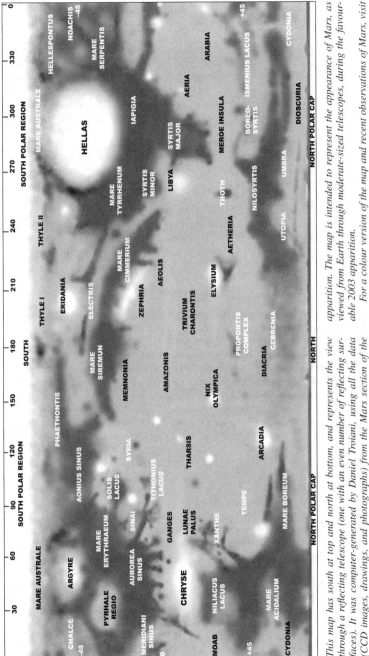

This map has south at top and north at bottom, and represents the view through a reflecting telescope (one with an even number of reflecting surfaces). It was computer-generated by Daniel Troiani, using all the data (CCD images, drawings, and photographs) from the Mars section of the Association of Lunar and Planetary Observers (ALPO) during the 2001 apparition. The map is intended to represent the appearance of Mars, as viewed from Earth through moderate-sized telescopes, during the favourable 2003 apparition.

For a colour version of the map and recent observations of Mars, visit the Mars section of the ALPO website, www.lpl.arizona.edu/alpo.

Coloured eyepiece filters can improve the visibility of darker Martian surface features and reduce glare in larger-aperture telescopes. Deep yellow, orange, or red filters enhance the contrast of the dark areas. Smaller telescopes benefit most from a #21 or #23A filter; for larger instruments try #23A or #25. These filters also slightly improve the seeing by eliminating shorter (mostly blue) wavelengths of light, which are more susceptible to atmospheric turbulence.

For the first time in decades, a new planetary filter has entered the field. Developed by Sirius Optics, the planetary-contrast filter (PC-1) employs the interference technology of nebula filters to heighten contrast on the planets using any type of telescope. Observers' opinions vary, but many report improvements in detail visible on Mars and Jupiter. The PC-1 filter seems to function best on achromatic refractors, particularly 100-mm aperture and over, by significantly cutting the false colour introduced by chromatic aberration. This alone improves planetary contrast. Observers should also be aware that this filter introduces a yellow-green cast to the planet, although it is not as blatant as the hues imparted by the colour filters mentioned above.

Planetary filters are most effective when used *after* the observer is fully familiar with the planet's appearance without a filter. This is the only way to properly gauge the filters' effectiveness (if any). But in the case of Mars, there is also an aesthetic issue. Much of the history and lore of Mars connects to the planet's colour in the sky, as well as the hues visible telescopically on its surface. The ideas of Schaparelli and Lowell from the late 19th century stem at least partly from the beautiful mix of coral, greenish-grey, yellow, and white that greets the observer's gaze across the interplanetary gulf that separates Earth from Mars.

JUPITER

Jupiter, the solar system's largest planet, is a colossal ball of hydrogen and helium without any solid surface comparable to land masses on Earth. Jupiter likely has a small rocky core encased in a thick mantle of metallic hydrogen which is enveloped by a massive atmospheric cloak topped by a quilt of multicoloured clouds. These clouds are the visible surface of Jupiter—a realm of constant change characterized by alternating dark belts and brighter zones. The zones are ammonia ice-crystal clouds, the belts mainly ammonium hydrosulphide clouds. Frequently the belts intrude on the zones with dark rifts or loops called festoons.

The equatorial region of Jupiter's clouds rotates 5 min faster than the rest of the planet: 9 h 50 min compared to 9 h 55 min. This means constant interaction as one region slips by the other at about 400 km/h. It also means that there are basically two rotational systems from the viewpoint of week-to-week telescopic observation (see Jupiter—Table of Daily Central Meridians, 2003 on p. 193 for daily longitudes of Jupiter's regions System I and System II). Jupiter's rapid rotation also makes the great globe markedly bulged at the equator.

Two dark belts, the North Equatorial Belt and the South Equatorial Belt, are obvious in the smallest telescopes. Larger instruments reveal several more narrow dark belts along with the famous Great Red Spot, a salmon-coloured oval vortex observed for centuries on the south edge of the South Equatorial Belt. Historically, the Red Spot has varied from being blatantly obvious to nearly invisible. For example, in 1997 it was detectable with a 100-mm aperture but could hardly be described as prominent because it closely matched its surroundings in hue and contrast. In 2003 observers should find the Red Spot near longitude 80° in System II (see Jupiter—Daily Central Meridians and Time of Transit of Great Red Spot on p. 192 for instructions on determining when the Great Red Spot crosses Jupiter's central meridian).

The smallest of telescopes will reveal Jupiter's four large satellites, each of which is equal to or larger than Earth's satellite. They provide a never-ending fascination for amateur astronomers. (For the configurations of the Galilean satellites see the right side of the pages in the THE SKY MONTH BY MONTH section on pp. 77–99.) Sometimes the satellites are paired on either side of the belted planet; frequently one is missing—either behind Jupiter, in the planet's shadow, or in front of Jupiter. In the latter case the satellite usually blends in against Jupiter's bright clouds and is difficult to see (more on this below). Even more interesting are the occasions when one of the satellites casts its shadow on the disk of the planet (see PHENOMENA OF THE GALILEAN SATELLITES on pp. 204–210). The tiny black shadow can be particularly evident if it is cast on one of the bright zones of Jupiter. This phenomenon sometimes is evident in a 60-mm refractor under good seeing conditions. On rarer occasions, *two* shadows are cast on the face of Jupiter. These "double shadow transits" appear in bold type in the tables on pp. 205–210 and are included in the right-hand pages of THE SKY MONTH BY MONTH section on pp. 77–99.

The satellite umbral shadows vary significantly in size from one to another. Mean opposition angular diameters are Io 0.9″, Europa 0.6″, Ganymede 1.1″, and Callisto 0.5″. The enormous contrast between the dark shadows and the bright Jovian clouds makes these tiny features visible even though they are smaller than the nominal resolution limit of a small telescope. Furthermore, the satellites' penumbral shadows are quite large, especially Callisto's, which adds a few tenths of an arc-second to their effective visual diameters. The satellites themselves have the following mean opposition apparent diameters: Io 1.2″, Europa 1.0″, Ganymede 1.7″, and Callisto 1.6″. A 150-mm telescope reveals the size differences as well as colour variations among the satellites.

When the Galilean satellites transit the disk of Jupiter, they are seldom visible in telescopes under 100 mm and are best seen near the planet's limb when entering or leaving the disk. Tracking a satellite transit completely across Jupiter is a challenging observation. Each satellite has a characteristic appearance when superimposed on the Jovian cloudscape. Europa is bright white, similar to the brightest Jovian clouds. When traversing a white cloud zone in the central sector of Jupiter, Europa is usually invisible. However, it stands out well when near the limb or against a dark belt. Callisto, the darkest satellite, is best seen in the reverse circumstances. When seen against a pale zone this greyish satellite can be mistaken for a satellite shadow, but it is often lost against a dark belt. Ganymede is intermediate in surface brightness, but because of its great size, it is the easiest of the four to track completely across Jupiter's face. Io, innermost of the Galilean satellites, is also the most frequently seen in transit. It is close to Europa in brightness but is generally easier to follow over typical cloud features, probably due to its slightly greater diameter. Near opposition, a transiting satellite often appears adjacent to its own shadow. These events are especially worth a look. Jupiter's other satellites are photographic objects for large instruments.

As 2003 opens, Jupiter is nearing its Feb. 2 opposition in Cancer, in the southeastern evening sky after dusk. For southern observers it is in the northeast. In late July Jupiter moves into Leo, where it remains for the rest of the year. At the same time it becomes lost in the solar glare—conjunction with the Sun occurs on Aug. 22. In late September Jupiter peeks above the eastern horizon in dawn twilight,

Jupiter—2003		
Date UT	Mag.	Equat. Diam. ″
Jan. 1.0	−2.5	44.0
Feb. 1.0	−2.6	45.6
Mar. 1.0	−2.5	44.4
Apr. 1.0	−2.3	41.1
May 1.0	−2.1	37.5
Jun. 1.0	−1.9	34.4
Jul. 1.0	−1.8	32.3
Aug. 1.0	−1.7	31.1
Sep. 1.0	−1.7	30.9
Oct. 1.0	−1.7	31.7
Nov. 1.0	−1.8	33.4
Dec. 1.0	−2.0	36.1
Jan. 1.0	−2.2	39.6

with the celestial geometry favouring northern observers. In October it is a prominent early-morning luminary, and it becomes progressively higher in the morning sky as the year closes.

JUPITER—DAILY CENTRAL MERIDIANS AND TIME OF TRANSIT OF GREAT RED SPOT

The table at the right can be used to calculate the longitude of the central meridian of the observed disk of Jupiter during the months January–June and October–December (when Jupiter is well placed for observation). System I is the most rapidly rotating region between the middle of the North Equatorial Belt and the middle of the South Equatorial Belt. System II applies to the rest of the planet. The rotation rate of System I is 36.577±0.008 °/h and that of System II is 36.259±0.008 °/h. These figures, together with the closest tabular value, can be used to determine the longitude of a system's central meridian for any given date and time (UT) of observation. **Example:** At 22:30 PST Jan. 3 = 6:30 UT Jan. 4 the longitude of the central meridian of System II is

$$254.8 + (36.259 \times 6.5) = 490.5°;$$

putting this angle in the range 0°–360° by subtracting 360° leaves a longitude of 130.5°, accurate to about 0.1°.

The table may also be used to determine when the Great Red Spot (GRS) (near longitude 80° in System II) will cross the central meridian of the disk of Jupiter. **Example:** Suppose an observer in Ontario, Canada (time zone: Eastern Standard, –5 h) is viewing Jupiter on the evening of Dec. 15. At 0h UT Dec. 16 (19h EST December 15) the table gives approximately 13° for the longitude of the central meridian in System II. A further rotation of

$$80° - 13° = 67°$$

will bring the GRS to the central meridian, which will require

$$67° \div 36.259°/h = 1.85 \text{ h} = 1 \text{ h } 51 \text{ min.}$$

Thus the GRS will transit at

$$1:51 \text{ UT Dec. } 16 = 20:51 \text{ EST Dec. } 15.$$

Note that the GRS slowly drifts in longitude, so the 80° figure is only a guide. By timing a transit of the GRS and using the table, you can update its longitude.

SATURN

Saturn is the telescopic showpiece of the night sky. The chilling beauty of the small pale orb floating in a field of velvet is something no photographs or descriptions can adequately duplicate. Any telescope magnifying more than 30× will show the rings. The view is exquisite in 100- to 200-mm instruments. The rings consist of billions of particles—largely water ice—that range in size from microscopic specks to flying mountains kilometres across. The reason "rings" is plural is that gaps and brightness differences define hundreds of distinct rings. However, from Earth only the three most prominent components—known simply as rings A, B, and C—can be distinguished visually. (See the diagram Saturn—Main Ring Features Visible from Earth on p. 195.)

(text continued on p. 194)

JUPITER—TABLE OF DAILY CENTRAL MERIDIANS, 2003

Date 0h UT	System I	II	Date 0h UT	System I	II	Date 0h UT	System I	II	Date 0h UT	System I	II	Date 0h UT	System I	II
JANUARY			25	317.4	155.4	21	360.1	138.6	15	33.9	112.8	6	63.2	123.3
0	107.8	13.2	26	115.3	305.8	22	157.9	288.7	16	191.6	262.8	7	221.0	273.5
1	265.9	163.6	27	273.3	96.1	23	315.6	78.8	17	349.3	52.8	8	18.8	63.7
2	63.9	314.0	28	71.3	246.4	24	113.4	229.0	18	146.9	202.9	9	176.6	213.9
3	221.9	104.4	**MARCH**			25	271.2	19.1	19	304.6	352.9	10	334.5	4.1
4	20.0	254.8	1	229.2	36.8	26	68.9	169.2	20	102.2	142.9	11	132.3	154.2
5	178.0	45.2	2	27.2	187.1	27	226.7	319.3	21	259.9	293.0	12	290.1	304.4
6	336.1	195.6	3	185.1	337.4	28	24.4	109.5	22	57.6	83.0	13	87.9	94.6
7	134.1	346.0	4	343.1	127.7	29	182.2	259.6	23	215.2	233.0	14	245.8	244.8
8	292.1	136.5	5	141.0	278.1	30	339.9	49.7	24	12.9	23.1	15	43.6	35.1
9	90.2	286.9	6	299.0	68.4	**MAY**			25	170.5	173.1	16	201.5	185.3
10	248.2	77.3	7	96.9	218.7	1	137.6	199.8	26	328.2	323.1	17	359.3	335.5
11	46.3	227.7	8	254.8	9.0	2	295.4	349.9	27	125.9	113.1	18	157.1	125.7
12	204.3	18.1	9	52.8	159.3	3	93.1	140.0	28	283.5	263.2	19	315.0	275.9
13	2.4	168.5	10	210.7	309.6	4	250.9	290.1	29	81.2	53.2	20	112.8	66.1
14	160.4	318.9	11	8.6	99.9	5	48.6	80.2	30	238.8	203.2	21	270.7	216.3
15	318.4	109.3	12	166.5	250.2	6	206.3	230.3	*JULY TO*			22	68.5	6.6
16	116.5	259.8	13	324.5	40.5	7	4.0	20.4	*SEPTEMBER*			23	226.4	156.8
17	274.5	50.2	14	122.4	190.7	8	161.8	170.5	*SUPPRESSED*			24	24.2	307.0
18	72.6	200.6	15	280.3	341.0	9	319.5	320.6				25	182.1	97.2
19	230.6	351.0	16	78.2	131.3	10	117.2	110.7	**OCTOBER**			26	340.0	247.5
20	28.7	141.4	17	236.1	281.6	11	274.9	260.8	1	143.3	118.1	27	137.8	37.7
21	186.7	291.8	18	34.0	71.8	12	72.6	50.9	2	301.1	268.2	28	295.7	187.9
22	344.8	82.2	19	191.9	222.1	13	230.3	200.9	3	98.8	58.3	29	93.6	338.2
23	142.8	232.7	20	349.7	12.3	14	28.1	351.0	4	256.5	208.5	30	251.5	128.4
24	300.8	23.1	21	147.6	162.6	15	185.8	141.1	5	54.3	358.6	**DECEMBER**		
25	98.9	173.5	22	305.5	312.8	16	343.5	291.2	6	212.0	148.7	1	49.3	278.7
26	256.9	323.9	23	103.4	103.1	17	141.2	81.3	7	9.8	298.8	2	207.2	68.9
27	55.0	114.3	24	261.3	253.3	18	298.9	231.3	8	167.5	88.9	3	5.1	219.2
28	213.0	264.7	25	59.1	43.6	19	96.6	21.4	9	325.3	239.0	4	163.0	9.4
29	11.1	55.1	26	217.0	193.8	20	254.3	171.5	10	123.0	29.2	5	320.9	159.7
30	169.1	205.5	27	14.8	344.0	21	52.0	321.5	11	280.8	179.3	6	118.8	310.0
31	327.1	355.9	28	172.7	134.3	22	209.7	111.6	12	78.5	329.4	7	276.7	100.2
FEBRUARY			29	330.6	284.5	23	7.4	261.7	13	236.3	119.6	8	74.6	250.5
1	125.2	146.4	30	128.4	74.7	24	165.0	51.7	14	34.1	269.7	9	232.5	40.8
2	283.2	296.8	31	286.2	224.9	25	322.7	201.8	15	191.8	59.8	10	30.4	191.0
3	81.2	87.2	**APRIL**			26	120.4	351.8	16	349.6	210.0	11	188.3	341.3
4	239.3	237.6	1	84.1	15.1	27	278.1	141.9	17	147.4	360.1	12	346.2	131.6
5	37.3	28.0	2	241.9	165.3	28	75.8	292.0	18	305.1	150.2	13	144.1	281.9
6	195.3	178.4	3	39.7	315.5	29	233.5	82.0	19	102.9	300.4	14	302.0	72.1
7	353.3	328.7	4	197.6	105.7	30	31.2	232.1	20	260.7	90.5	15	99.9	222.4
8	151.4	119.1	5	355.4	255.9	31	188.8	22.1	21	58.5	240.7	16	257.8	12.7
9	309.4	269.5	6	153.2	46.1	**JUNE**			22	216.2	30.8	17	55.8	163.0
10	107.4	59.9	7	311.0	196.3	1	346.5	172.2	23	14.0	181.0	18	213.7	313.3
11	265.4	210.3	8	108.9	346.5	2	144.2	322.2	24	171.8	331.1	19	11.6	103.6
12	63.4	0.7	9	266.7	136.7	3	301.9	112.3	25	329.6	121.3	20	169.5	253.9
13	221.4	151.1	10	64.5	286.8	4	99.6	262.3	26	127.4	271.4	21	327.5	44.2
14	19.5	301.5	11	222.3	77.0	5	257.2	52.4	27	285.2	61.6	22	125.4	194.5
15	177.5	91.8	12	20.1	227.2	6	54.9	202.4	28	83.0	211.7	23	283.4	344.8
16	335.5	242.2	13	177.9	17.4	7	212.6	352.4	29	240.8	1.9	24	81.3	135.1
17	133.5	32.6	14	335.7	167.5	8	10.2	142.5	30	38.5	152.1	25	239.2	285.5
18	291.5	182.9	15	133.4	317.7	9	167.9	292.5	31	196.3	302.2	26	37.2	75.8
19	89.5	333.3	16	291.2	107.8	10	325.6	82.6	**NOVEMBER**			27	195.1	226.1
20	247.4	123.7	17	89.0	258.0	11	123.3	232.6	1	354.1	92.4	28	353.1	16.4
21	45.4	274.0	18	246.8	48.1	12	280.9	22.6	2	152.0	242.6	29	151.1	166.7
22	203.4	64.4	19	44.6	198.3	13	78.6	172.7	3	309.8	32.8	30	309.0	317.1
23	1.4	214.7	20	202.3	348.4	14	236.3	322.7	4	107.6	182.9	31	107.0	107.4
24	159.4	5.1							5	265.4	333.1	32	264.9	257.7

Cassini's division, a gap between rings A and B discovered in 1675, is visible in small telescopes when the ring system is well inclined to our view. Cassini's division is a region less densely populated with ring particles than adjacent rings. Ring B, the brightest, overpowers ring C to such an extent that ring C, also known as the *crepe ring,* is seen only with difficulty in small telescopes. A Saturn phenomenon easily seen with backyard telescopes is the shadow of the planet on the rings. From one to four months before or after opposition the shadow falling on the rings is very apparent, often giving the scene a powerful three-dimensional aura.

In addition to the rings, Saturn has a family of at least 30 satellites. Titan, the largest, is easily seen in any telescope as an 8th-magnitude object orbiting Saturn in about 16 days. At east and west elongation Titan appears about five ring diameters from the planet. Telescopes over 60 mm in aperture should reveal 10th-magnitude Rhea at less than two ring diameters from Saturn. The satellite Iapetus has the peculiar property of being five times brighter at western elongation (magnitude 10.1) than at eastern elongation (11.9). One side of the satellite has the reflectivity of snow while the other resembles dark rock. When brightest, Iapetus is located about 12 ring diameters west of the parent planet. Of the remaining satellites, Tethys and Dione may be glimpsed in a 150-mm telescope, but the others require larger apertures. (See CONFIGURATIONS OF SATURN'S BRIGHTEST SATELLITES on pp. 211–214.)

The disk of Saturn appears about one-sixth the area of Jupiter through the same telescope with the same magnification. In telescopes less than 75-mm aperture, probably no features will ever be seen on the cloud deck of the planet other than the shadow cast by the rings. As the size of the telescope is increased, the pale equatorial region, a dusky equatorial band, and the darker polar regions become evident. Saturn has a belt system like Jupiter's, but it is much less active and the contrast is reduced. Seldom in telescopes less than 100-mm aperture do more than one or two belts come into view. Saturn is at perihelion on Jul. 26, and its angular diameter in 2003 exceeds that of any opposition in more than a quarter of a century (although it is less than 0.01″ greater than that in 2002).

Saturn begins the year in the evening sky in Taurus, having been at opposition on 2002 Dec. 17. It moves eastward and enters Orion in May before becoming lost in the solar glare by early June. It is in conjunction with the Sun on Jun. 24 and is not well placed for telescopic observing until August in the morning sky, by which time it has moved into Gemini. Saturn is at opposition on Dec. 31 when it is 8.05 AU, or 67 light-min, from Earth, 20.6″ in diameter, and the rings are 46.6″ across.

After having been edge-on to Earth in 1995 and 1996, Saturn's rings are now open to their maximum possible extent with their south side facing Earth. During January, the ring tilt is 26.7° as seen from Earth. By April, the rings will have opened to 27.0°. The tilt remains above 24.8° for the rest of the year. This makes 2003 an excellent year for examining the divisions and structural subtleties of the rings.

Saturn—2003			
Date UT	Mag.	Equat. Diam. ″	Ring Incl. °
Jan. 1.0	−0.4	20.6	−26.7
Feb. 1.0	−0.2	19.9	−26.8
Mar. 1.0	0.0	19.0	−26.9
Apr. 1.0	0.1	17.9	−27.0
May 1.0	0.1	17.1	−27.0
Jun. 1.0	0.1	16.7	−26.8
Jul. 1.0	0.0	16.6	−26.4
Aug. 1.0	0.1	16.8	−25.9
Sep. 1.0	0.1	17.5	−25.3
Oct. 1.0	0.1	18.3	−24.9
Nov. 1.0	−0.1	19.4	−24.8
Dec. 1.0	−0.2	20.3	−25.1
Jan. 1.0	−0.5	20.6	−25.5

(text continued on p. 196)

SATURN—MAIN RING FEATURES VISIBLE FROM EARTH

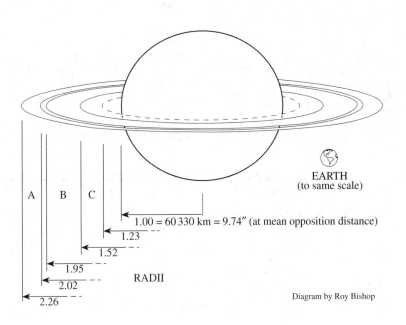

EARTH
(to same scale)

$1.00 = 60\,330$ km $= 9.74''$ (at mean opposition distance)

A   B   C

1.23
1.52
1.95
2.02
2.26

RADII

Diagram by Roy Bishop

SATURN'S RING SYSTEM—MAIN STRUCTURAL REGIONS

Ring	Radius**	Discoverer
D	1.11 – 1.23	*Voyager 1* (1980)
C*	1.23 – 1.52	W.C. & G.P. Bond, W.R. Dawes (1850)
B*	1.52 – 1.95 }	{ Galileo (1610), C. Huygens (1659),
A*	2.02 – 2.26 }	{ G.D. Cassini (1675)
F	2.33	*Pioneer 11* (1979)
G	2.8	*Voyager 1* (1980)
E	3. – 8.	W.A. Feibelman (1966)

*Visible from Earth. Also, the E ring can be detected when Saturn's ring system appears edge-on.
**In units of Saturn's equatorial radius (60 330 km).

URANUS

At magnitude 5.7, Uranus can be seen with the unaided eye under a clear, dark sky. However, it is much more easily located with binoculars. A 75-mm telescope will reveal its small, greenish, featureless disk.

Unlike the three other giant planets, the axis of Uranus is tipped almost parallel to the plane of the solar system. This means that we view Uranus nearly pole-on at certain points in its 84-year orbit. The southern (and counterclockwise turning) hemisphere of Uranus is now angled slightly toward Earth. Its south pole appeared nearest to (and slightly south of) the centre of its disk in 1985. Uranus has at least 21 satellites, all smaller than Earth's Moon, none of which can be detected in small or moderate-sized telescopes.

Uranus is at opposition in Aquarius on Aug. 24, when it is 19.02 AU, or 2.6 light-h, from Earth. It is then magnitude 5.7 and 3.7″ in apparent diameter. Use the chart below to locate this distant planet.

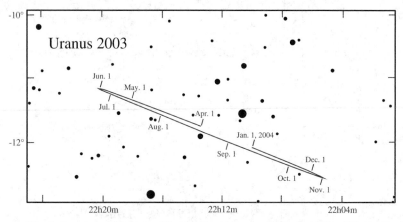

The finder chart above, provided by David Lane, shows the path of Uranus in Aquarius during the nine-month period 2003 April–December. Coordinates are for epoch 2000.0, and the magnitude limit is 9.0. Tick marks are drawn along the path at the beginning of each month. The two 5th-magnitude stars in the lower half of the chart are in south-central Aquarius south of the ecliptic, lying unmarked above the "I" of "AQUARIUS" in the SEPTEMBER ALL-SKY MAP on p. 298.

Along the five-month retrograde portion of its track, from Jun. 8 to Nov. 9 and centred at the Aug. 24 opposition, Uranus ranges between 5.7 and 5.8 in magnitude. It is brighter than the several 7th-magnitude stars drawn in the chart.

NEPTUNE

Neptune is an 8th-magnitude binocular object—an easy target in 7 × 50 or larger glasses—but seeing the planet as a disk rather than a point of light is a different matter. Magnifications over 200× are usually necessary, and even then Neptune is just a tiny bluish dot with no hard edge due to limb darkening. Neptune's large satellite, Triton, can be seen by an experienced observer using a 300-mm telescope. Triton varies between 8″ and 17″ from Neptune.

In 2003 Neptune is in Capricornus and may be easily identified using the chart below. At opposition on Aug. 4, Neptune is magnitude 7.8, 29.07 AU, or 4.04 light-h, from Earth, and 2.3″ in diameter.

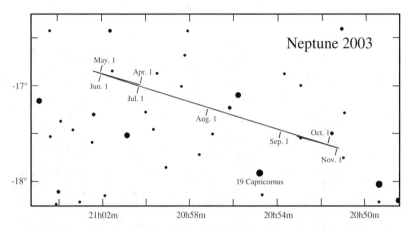

The finder chart above, provided by David Lane, shows the path of Neptune in Capricornus during the eight-month period 2003 April–November. Coordinates are in epoch 2000.0, and the magnitude limit is 9.0. Tick marks are drawn along the path at the beginning of each month. The 4rd-magnitude star θ Cap is just to the left of the chart, and 6th-magnitude 19 Capricornus is labelled. In the SEP-TEMBER ALL-SKY MAP *on p. 298, θ lies just underneath the ecliptic, below and to the left of the single letter "F."*

Along the five-month retrograde portion of its track, from May. 16 to Oct. 23 and centred at the Aug. 4 opposition, Neptune ranges between 7.8 and 7.9 in magnitude.

PLUTO

Besides being the solar system's smallest planet, Pluto is different from the other eight in almost every respect. Its unique characteristics include its orbit, which is so elliptical that the planet was closer to the Sun than was Neptune from 1980 through 1999.

Opposition is on Jun. 9, when the planet will be at magnitude 13.8 and 29.65 AU, or 4.11 light-h, from Earth. It can be identified using the chart at the right and a 200-mm or larger telescope. Pluto was near perihelion throughout the 1980s and 1990s and as bright as it ever gets. At that time, a few observers (with good optics, transparent skies, steady seeing, and high magnifications) succeeded in sighting Pluto with telescopes as small as 100-mm refractors.

FINDER CHART FOR PLUTO, 2003
BY IAN CAMERON

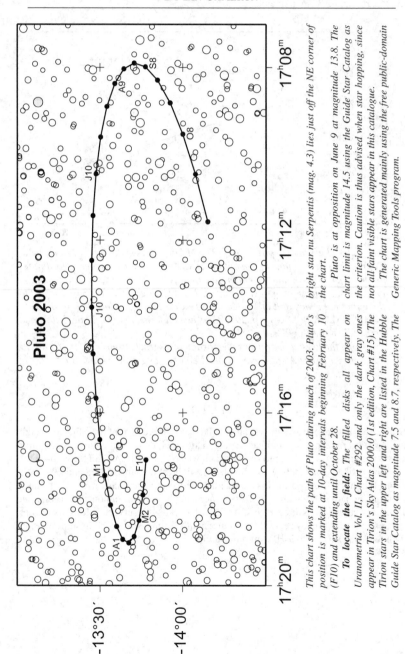

This chart shows the path of Pluto during much of 2003. Pluto's position is marked at 10-day intervals beginning February 10 (F10) and extending until October 28.

To locate the field: The filled disks all appear on Uranometria Vol. II, Chart #292 and only the dark gray ones appear in Tirion's Sky Atlas 2000.0 (1st edition, Chart #15). The Tirion stars in the upper left and right are listed in the Hubble Guide Star Catalog as magnitude 7.5 and 8.7, respectively. The bright star nu Serpentis (mag. 4.3) lies just off the NE corner of the chart.

Pluto is at opposition on June 9 at magnitude 13.8. The chart limit is magnitude 14.5 using the Guide Star Catalog as the criterion. Caution is thus advised when star hopping, since not all faint visible stars appear in this catalogue.

The chart is generated mainly using the free public-domain Generic Mapping Tools program.

2003 TRANSIT OF MERCURY
BY FRED ESPENAK

A transit, or passage of a planet across the face of the Sun, is a relatively rare occurrence. As seen from Earth, only transits of Mercury and Venus are possible. On average, there are 13 transits of Mercury each century. In comparison, transits of Venus occur in pairs separated by approximately 8 years with more than a century separating each pair.

On Wednesday, 2003 May 7, Mercury will transit the Sun; the last transit of Mercury was in November 1999. The entire event will be widely visible from Europe, Africa, and Asia, as shown in the map in Figure 1 (p. 200). Observers in Japan, Australia, and New Zealand will witness the beginning of the transit, but the Sun will set before the event ends. In contrast, observers in western Africa, eastern North America, and eastern South America will see the end of the event, since the transit will already be in progress at sunrise from those regions.

The principal events occurring during a transit are conveniently characterized by contacts, analogous to the contacts of an annular solar eclipse. The transit begins with contact I, which is the instant the planet's disk is externally tangent with the Sun. Shortly after contact I, the planet can be seen as a small notch in the solar limb. The entire disk of the planet is first seen at contact II, when the planet is internally tangent with the Sun. During the next several hours, the silhouetted planet slowly traverses the brilliant solar disk. At contact III, the planet reaches the opposite limb and once again is internally tangent with the Sun. Finally, the transit ends at contact IV, when the planet's limb is externally tangent to the Sun. Contacts I and II define the phase called *ingress*, while contacts III and IV are known as *egress*.

TABLE 1—GEOCENTRIC PHASES OF THE 2003 TRANSIT OF MERCURY

Event	Universal Time	Position Angle*
Contact I	05:12:56	15°
Contact II	05:17:24	14°
Greatest transit	07:52:23	333°
Contact III	10:27:19	292°
Contact IV	10:31:46	291°

*Position angle is defined as the direction of Mercury with respect to the centre of the Sun's disk as measured counterclockwise from the celestial north point on the Sun.

Table 1 lists the contact times and the time of greatest transit, which is the instant Mercury passes closest to the Sun's centre (i.e. minimum separation). During the 2003 transit, Mercury's minimum separation from the Sun is 708 arc-s. Figure 1 shows the path of Mercury across the Sun's disk, and the scale gives the Universal Time of Mercury's position at any instant during the transit. The celestial coordinates of the Sun and Mercury are provided at greatest transit as well as the times of the major contacts. The world map at the bottom of Figure 1 shows regions of visibility of the event.

Note that these times are for an observer at Earth's centre. The actual contact times for any given observer may differ by up to several minutes. This is due to effects of parallax, since Mercury's 12 arc-s diameter disk may be shifted up to nearly 16 arc-s from its geocentric coordinates, depending on the observer's exact position on Earth. Table 2 lists predicted contact times and corresponding altitudes of the Sun for major cities around the world with an emphasis on Canada and the United States.

Since Mercury is only 1/194 of the Sun's apparent diameter, a telescope with a

(text continued on p. 202)

FIGURE 1—TRANSIT OF MERCURY OF 2003 MAY 7

Greatest Transit = 07:52:23.3 UT   J.D. = 2452766.828047

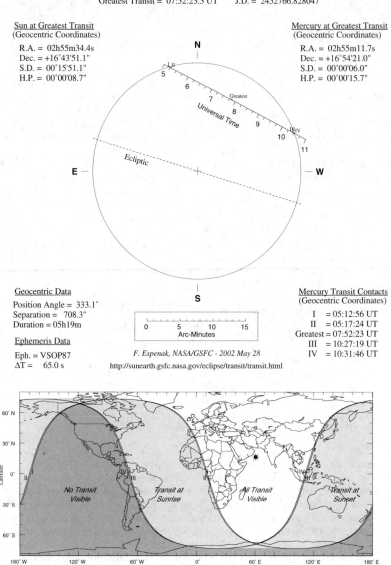

Sun at Greatest Transit
(Geocentric Coordinates)

R.A. = 02h55m34.4s
Dec. = +16°43'51.1"
S.D. = 00°15'51.1"
H.P. = 00°00'08.7"

Mercury at Greatest Transit
(Geocentric Coordinates)

R.A. = 02h55m11.7s
Dec. = +16°54'21.0"
S.D. = 00°00'06.0"
H.P. = 00°00'15.7"

Geocentric Data

Position Angle = 333.1°
Separation = 708.3"
Duration = 05h19m

Ephemeris Data

Eph. = VSOP87
ΔT = 65.0 s

Mercury Transit Contacts
(Geocentric Coordinates)

I = 05:12:56 UT
II = 05:17:24 UT
Greatest = 07:52:23 UT
III = 10:27:19 UT
IV = 10:31:46 UT

F. Espenak, NASA/GSFC - 2002 May 28
http://sunearth.gsfc.nasa.gov/eclipse/transit/transit.html

TABLE 2—LOCAL CIRCUMSTANCES FOR TRANSIT OF MERCURY OF 2003 MAY 7

———————————— Transit Contacts ————————————

Location	External Sun Ingress h m s	Alt °	Internal Sun Ingress h m s	Alt °	Greatest Sun Transit h m s	Alt °	Internal Sun Egress h m s	Alt °	External Sun Egress h m s	Alt °
CANADA										
Halifax, NS	—	–	—	–	—	–	10:29:39	15	10:34:03	16
Hamilton, ON	—	–	—	–	—	–	10:29:42	3	10:34:07	4
Montreal, QC	—	–	—	–	—	–	10:29:40	8	10:34:05	9
North York, ON	—	–	—	–	—	–	10:29:42	4	10:34:07	5
Ottawa, ON	—	–	—	–	—	–	10:29:40	7	10:34:05	8
Quebec, QC	—	–	—	–	—	–	10:29:38	10	10:34:03	11
Saint John's, NF	—	–	—	–	—	–	10:29:30	23	10:33:55	23
Toronto, ON	—	–	—	–	—	–	10:29:42	4	10:34:07	5
UNITED STATES										
Baltimore, MD	—	–	—	–	—	–	10:29:46	4	10:34:11	5
Boston, MA	—	–	—	–	—	–	10:29:43	9	10:34:08	10
Cleveland, OH	—	–	—	–	—	–	10:29:43	1	10:34:09	2
Columbus, OH	—	–	—	–	—	–			10:34:10	1
Detroit, MI	—	–	—	–	—	–	10:29:42	1	10:34:07	2
Hartford, CT	—	–	—	–	—	–	10:29:44	8	10:34:09	9
New York, NY	—	–	—	–	—	–	10:29:45	7	10:34:10	7
Norfolk, VA	—	–	—	–	—	–	10:29:48	4	10:34:13	5
Philadelphia, PA	—	–	—	–	—	–	10:29:46	6	10:34:11	6
Pittsburgh, PA	—	–	—	–	—	–	10:29:45	2	10:34:10	3
Providence, RI	—	–	—	–	—	–	10:29:44	9	10:34:09	10
Raleigh, NC	—	–	—	–	—	–	10:29:49	2	10:34:14	3
Richmond, VA	—	–	—	–	—	–	10:29:48	3	10:34:13	4
Washington, DC	—	–	—	–	—	–	10:29:47	4	10:34:12	5
WORLD LOCATIONS										
Sydney, Australia	5:14:13	20	5:18:43	19	—	–	—	–	—	–
Dacca, Bangladesh	5:12:45	78	5:17:11	79	7:51:15	62	10:25:30	27	10:29:58	26
Sao Paulo, Brazil	—	–	—	–	—	–	10:28:55	12	10:33:22	13
Beijing, China	5:11:48	63	5:16:15	63	7:50:59	37	10:26:02	8	10:30:30	7
Shanghai, China	5:12:05	66	5:16:31	66	7:50:57	34	10:25:45	1	10:30:14	1
Cairo, Egypt	5:12:31	26	5:16:57	26	7:52:15	60	10:27:11	74	10:31:36	74
London, England	5:11:25	6	5:15:50	7	7:52:21	31	10:28:25	51	10:32:50	51
Paris, France	5:11:32	7	5:15:57	8	7:52:22	33	10:28:21	54	10:32:45	54
Berlin, Germany	5:11:30	14	5:15:55	15	7:52:11	38	10:28:05	54	10:32:29	54
Athens, Greece	5:12:08	20	5:16:34	21	7:52:16	51	10:27:35	69	10:32:00	69
Victoria, Hong Kong	5:12:32	76	5:16:59	75	7:51:01	40	10:25:24	5	10:29:53	4
Bombay, India	5:13:04	63	5:17:31	64	7:51:34	79	10:25:39	42	10:30:06	41
Calcutta, India	5:12:49	77	5:17:15	78	7:51:17	64	10:25:29	28	10:29:57	27
Jakarta, Indonesia	5:13:50	66	5:18:18	66	7:51:21	40	10:24:45	4	10:29:15	3
Tehran, Iran	5:12:21	42	5:16:47	43	7:51:49	69	10:26:40	58	10:31:06	57
Jerusalem, Israel	5:12:28	29	5:16:54	30	07:52:09	62	10:27:05	71	10:31:30	70
Rome, Italy	5:11:53	12	5:16:18	13	7:52:23	42	10:28:00	64	10:32:25	64
Tokyo, Japan	5:11:40	51	5:16:06	50	7:50:56	19	—	–	—	–
Seoul, South Korea	5:11:46	59	5:16:13	58	7:50:57	29				
Moscow, Russia	5:11:30	28	5:15:56	29	7:51:51	47	10:27:32	49	10:31:57	49
Madrid, Spain	—	–	5:16:12	1	7:52:37	30	10:28:30	58	10:32:54	58
Bangkok, Thailand	5:13:04	87	5:17:32	87	7:51:12	52	10:25:09	16	10:29:37	14
Istanbul, Turkey	5:12:02	24	5:16:28	25	7:52:09	53	10:27:28	65	10:31:53	65
Caracas, Venezuela	—	–	—	–	—	–	10:29:51	4	10:34:17	5

All times are in Universal Time; delta T = 65.0 s.

magnification of 50× to 100× is recommended to observe this event. Naturally, the telescope must be suitably equipped with adequate filtration to ensure safe solar viewing. The visual and photographic requirements for observing a transit are identical to those for solar viewing. Amateurs can make a scientific contribution by timing the four contacts. Observing techniques and equipment are similar to those used for lunar occultations. Since poor seeing often increases the uncertainty in contact timings, an estimate of the possible error associated with each timing should be included. Transit timings and geographic coordinates of the observing site (measured from a topographic map or GPS receiver) should be sent to A.L.P.O. Mercury/Venus Transit Section, PO Box 16131, San Francisco CA 94116, USA.

Actually, white light observations of contacts I and IV are not technically possible, since Mercury is only visible *after* contact I and *before* contact IV. However, if hydrogen-alpha filtration is available, the planet may be visible against either prominences or the chromosphere before and after contacts I and IV, respectively. Definitions of contacts II and III also require clarification. They're often mistaken for the instant when the planet appears internally tangent to the Sun. However, just before contact II, the so-called "black drop effect" is seen. At that time, the transiting planet seems to be attached to the Sun's limb by a thin column or thread. The true instant of contact II is when the thread breaks and the planet is completely surrounded by sunlight. Contact III occurs in exactly the reverse order. Atmospheric seeing often makes it difficult to measure contact timings with a precision better than several seconds.

Additional Comments

All transits of Mercury fall within several days of May 8 and November 10. Since Mercury's orbit is inclined 7° to Earth's, it intersects the ecliptic at two points, or nodes, which cross the Sun each year on those dates. If Mercury passes through inferior conjunction at that time, a transit will occur. During November transits, Mercury is near perihelion and exhibits a disk only 10 arc-s in diameter. By comparison, the planet is near aphelion during May transits and appears 12 arc-s across. However, the probability of a May transit is smaller by a factor of almost 2. Mercury's slower orbital motion at aphelion makes it less likely to cross the node during the critical period. November transits recur at intervals of 7, 13, or 33 years, while May transits recur only over the latter two intervals. Table 3 lists all transits of Mercury from 2001 through 2100.

TABLE 3—TRANSITS OF MERCURY: 2001–2100

Date	Universal Time	Separation
2003 May 7	07:52	708″
2006 Nov. 8	21:41	423″
2016 May 9	14:57	319″
2019 Nov. 11	15:20	76″
2032 Nov. 13	08:54	572″
2039 Nov. 7	08:46	822″
2049 May 7	14:24	512″
2052 Nov. 9	02:30	319″
2062 May 10	21:37	521″
2065 Nov. 11	20:07	181″
2078 Nov. 14	13:42	674″
2085 Nov. 7	13:36	718″
2095 May 8	21:08	310″
2098 Nov. 10	07:18	215″

Edmund Halley was the first to realize that transits could be used to measure the distance from Earth to the Sun, thereby establishing the absolute scale of the solar system from Kepler's third law. Unfortunately, his method is somewhat impractical, since contact timings of the required accuracy are difficult to make. Nevertheless, expeditions during 1761 and 1769 to observe the transits of Venus gave astronomers their first good value for the astronomical unit.

Because Venus's orbit is considerably larger than Mercury's, transits of Venus are much rarer. Indeed, only six such events have occurred since the invention of the telescope (1631, 1639, 1761, 1769, 1874, and 1882). Venus's orbital nodes pass across the Sun during early December and early June; therefore, transits of Venus are only possible at these times. Transits of Venus show a clear pattern of recurrence at intervals of 8, 121.5, 8, and 105.5 years. Table 4 lists all transits of Venus from 1901 through 2200 (note that all transits during this 300-year period in fact fall in the 122 years between 2004 and 2125).

TABLE 4—TRANSITS OF VENUS: 1901–2200

Date	Universal Time	Separation
2004 Jun. 8	**08:19**	**627″**
2012 Jun. 6	01:28	553″
2117 Dec. 11	02:48	724″
2125 Dec. 8	16:01	733″

The 2004 transit of Venus will be the first one since 1882. The final stages of the transit will be visible from eastern Canada and the United States. Since Venus will subtend 58 arc-s, it should be visible to the naked eye using suitable filtration. The first transit of Venus in nearly 122 years is most eagerly anticipated. Full details will be published next year in the *Observer's Handbook 2004*. Visit the following website for additional information: sunearth.gsfc.nasa.gov/eclipse/transit/transit.html.

Acknowledgments

The 2003 transit predictions were generated on an Apple iMac computer using algorithms developed from Meeus (1989) and the *Explanatory Supplement* (1974). Ephemerides for the Sun and Mercury were generated from VSOP87. The next transit of Mercury occurs on 2006 November 8–9 and is visible from the Americas, eastern Asia, Australia, and New Zealand.

The author wishes to thank Goddard's *Living With a Star* program for support of this work. All calculations, diagrams, tables, and opinions presented in this paper are those of the author, and he assumes full responsibility for their accuracy.

This publication is available electronically via the Internet along with additional information and updates at: sunearth.gsfc.nasa.gov/eclipse/OH/transit03.html.

References

Explanatory Supplement to the Astronomical Ephemeris and the American Ephemeris and Nautical Almanac, Her Majesty's Nautical Almanac Office, London, 1974.

Maor, E., *June 8, 2004—Venus in Transit*, Princeton University Press, Princeton, 2000.

Meeus, J., "Transits of Mercury, 1920 to 2080," *J.B.A.A., 67,* 30, 1956.

Meeus, J., "Transits of Venus, 3000 BC to AD 3000," *J.B.A.A., 68,* 98, 1958.

Meeus, J., *Transits*, Willmann-Bell, Inc., Richmond, 1989.

Newcomb, S., "Tables of the Motion of the Earth on its Axis Around the Sun," *Astron. Papers Amer. Eph., Vol. 6, Part I,* 1895.

Newcomb, S., "Transits of Mercury, 1677–1881," *Astron. Papers Amer. Eph., Vol. 6, Part IV,* 1898.

PHENOMENA OF THE GALILEAN SATELLITES

The tables on the next six pages give the various transits, occultations, and eclipses of the four great satellites of Jupiter during January–June and October–December. Jupiter is not well-placed for observing during the other three months since it is in conjunction with the Sun on Aug. 22. Double shadow transits and triple satellite transits are indicated in **bold.**

Since the satellite phenomena are not instantaneous but take up to several minutes, the predicted times are for the middle of each event. The predictions were generated by the Institut de Mécanique Céleste et de Calcul des Ephémérides in Paris.

Satellites are denoted using the standard designations: I = Io; II = Europa; III = Ganymede; IV = Callisto. Events are denoted using the following abbreviations:

Ec = eclipse; Oc = occultation; Tr = transit of satellite; Sh = transit of shadow; I = ingress; E = egress; D = disappearance; R = reappearance

The general motion of the satellites and the successive phenomena are shown in the diagram at right, which is a view of Jupiter and the orbit of one of its satellites looking down from the north side. Satellites move from east to west across the face of the planet and from west to east behind it (here "east" and "west" are used in the sense of the observer's sky, not in the Jovian sense). Before opposition, shadows fall to the west and after opposition, to the east (as in the diagram).

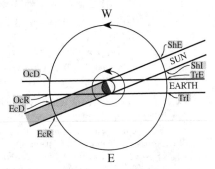

The sequence of phenomena for the outer satellite shown in the diagram, counterclockwise beginning at the lower right, is transit ingress (TrI), transit egress (TrE), shadow ingress (ShI), shadow egress (ShE), occultation disappearance (OcD), occultation reappearance (OcR), eclipse disappearance (EcD), and eclipse reappearance (EcR). The actual sequence will depend on the actual Sun–Jupiter–Earth angle and the size of the satellite's orbit.

Approximately three-quarters of the phenomena listed will not be visible from any one location because they occur when Jupiter is near or below the horizon or when daylight interferes. In practice, an observer usually knows when Jupiter will be conveniently placed in the night sky; if not, he or she can check THE SKY MONTH BY MONTH section (pp. 74–99) for this information. The table can then be scanned to see if there are any events during the intended observing period. For example, an observer near Victoria, B.C., on the evening of Jan. 6 would know that Jupiter is well-placed in the late-night sky. If planning to observe from 10 p.m. to 1:00 a.m. PST (8 h behind UT), he or she could scan the table for events in the interval Jan. 7, 6:00 to 9:00 UT and find that there are four events, beginning at 11:11 p.m. PST, involving double shadow and satellite transits of Io and Europa. The configuration of the four Galilean satellites during that evening is given in the diagram on the right-hand side of p. 77 in the THE SKY MONTH BY MONTH section.

Callisto is the only Galilean satellite that is not eclipsed during each of its revolutions. This year, however, all 22 revolutions of this outlying satellite result in eclipses. Callisto is part of a rare triple satellite transit on Jan. 17, a double shadow transit on Jun. 17, and a double satellite transit with Ganymede on Dec. 19. A total of 1809 events appear in the following tables, an average of one event every 3 h 39 min.

SATELLITES OF JUPITER, UT OF 2003 GEOCENTRIC PHENOMENA

JANUARY

```
0   4:35  II  ShI
    5:48  I   ShI
    6:08  II  TrI
    6:33  I   TrI
    7:29  II  ShE
    8:05  I   ShE
    8:50  I   TrE
    9:02  II  TrE
   23:06  IV  ShI

1   3:00  I   EcD
    3:51  IV  ShE
    6:02  IV  TrI
    6:04  I   OcR
   10:48  IV  TrE
   21:30  III ShI
   23:18  II  EcD

2   0:16  I   ShI
    0:24  III TrI
    0:59  I   TrI
    1:05  III ShE
    2:33  I   ShE
    3:16  I   TrE
    3:37  II  OcR
    4:01  III TrE
   21:28  I   EcD

3   0:30  I   OcR
   17:53  II  ShI
   18:44  I   ShI
   19:17  II  TrI
   19:25  I   TrI
   20:47  II  ShE
   21:01  I   ShE
   21:42  I   TrE
   22:12  II  TrE

4  15:57  I   EcD
   18:57  I   OcR

5  11:30  III EcD
   12:35  II  EcD
   13:13  I   ShI
   13:51  I   TrI
   15:30  I   ShE
   16:08  I   TrE
   16:45  II  OcR
   17:49  III OcR

6  10:25  I   EcD
   13:23  I   OcR

7   7:11  II  ShI
    7:41  I   ShI
    8:18  I   TrI
    8:27  II  TrI
    9:58  I   ShE
   10:06  II  ShE
   10:34  I   TrE
   11:21  II  TrE

8   4:54  I   EcD
    7:49  I   OcR
```

```
9   1:27  III ShI
    1:52  II  EcD
    2:09  I   ShI
    2:44  I   TrI
    3:46  III TrI
    4:26  I   ShE
    5:01  I   TrE
    5:03  III ShE
    5:53  II  OcR
    6:44  IV  EcD
    7:23  III TrE
   11:36  IV  EcR
   12:13  IV  OcD
   17:04  IV  OcR
   23:22  I   EcD

10  2:15  I   OcR
   20:29  II  ShI
   20:38  I   ShI
   21:10  I   TrI
   21:35  II  TrI
   22:55  I   ShE
   23:24  II  ShE
   23:27  I   TrE

11  0:30  II  TrE
   17:51  I   EcD
   20:41  I   OcR

12 15:06  I   ShI
   15:08  II  EcD
   15:29  III EcD
   15:36  I   TrI
   17:23  I   ShE
   17:53  I   TrE
   19:00  II  OcR
   21:10  III OcR

13 12:19  I   EcD
   15:07  I   OcR

14  9:34  I   ShI
    9:48  II  ShI
   10:02  I   TrI
   10:44  II  TrI
   11:52  I   ShE
   12:19  I   TrE
   12:42  II  ShE
   13:38  II  TrE

15  6:48  I   EcD
    9:34  I   OcR

16  4:03  I   ShI
    4:25  II  EcD
    4:28  I   TrI
    5:25  III ShI
    6:20  I   ShE
    6:45  I   TrE
    7:05  III TrI
    8:07  II  OcR
    9:01  III ShE
   10:42  III TrE

17  1:17  I   EcD
    4:00  I   OcR
   17:04  IV  TrI
   20:38  IV  TrI
   21:52  IV  ShE
   22:31  I   ShI
   22:54  I   TrI
   23:05  II  ShI
   23:52  II  TrI
```

```
18  0:48  I   ShE
    1:11  I   TrE
    1:24  IV  TrE
    2:00  II  ShE
    2:46  II  TrE
   19:45  I   EcD
   22:26  I   OcR

19 17:00  I   ShI
   17:19  I   TrI
   17:42  II  EcD
   19:17  I   ShE
   19:28  III EcD
   19:37  I   TrE
   21:14  II  OcR

20  0:28  III OcR
   14:14  I   EcD
   16:52  I   OcR

21 11:28  I   ShI
   11:45  I   TrI
   12:24  II  ShI
   13:00  II  TrI
   13:45  I   ShE
   14:02  I   TrE
   15:19  II  ShE
   15:54  II  TrE

22  8:42  I   EcD
   11:18  I   OcR

23  5:56  I   ShI
    6:11  I   TrI
    6:59  II  EcD
    8:14  I   ShE
    8:28  I   TrE
    9:23  III ShI
   10:21  II  OcR
   10:22  III TrI
   12:59  III ShE
   13:59  III TrE

24  3:11  I   EcD
    5:44  I   OcR

25  0:25  I   ShI
    0:37  I   TrI
    1:42  II  ShI
    2:07  II  TrI
    2:42  I   ShE
    2:54  I   TrE
    4:37  II  ShE
    5:02  II  TrE
   21:40  I   EcD

26  0:10  I   OcR
    0:45  IV  EcD
    7:20  IV  OcR
   18:53  I   ShI
   19:03  I   TrI
   20:16  II  EcD
   21:10  I   ShE
   21:20  I   TrE
   23:27  II  OcR
   23:27  III EcD

27  3:44  III OcR
   16:08  I   EcD
   18:36  I   OcR
```

```
28 13:22  I   ShI
   13:29  I   TrI
   15:01  II  ShI
   15:15  II  TrI
   15:39  I   ShE
   15:46  I   TrE
   17:56  II  ShE
   18:10  II  TrE

29 10:37  I   EcD
   13:02  I   OcR

30  7:50  I   ShI
    7:55  I   TrI
    9:32  II  EcD
   10:07  I   ShE
   10:12  I   TrE
   12:34  II  OcR
   13:21  III ShI
   13:38  III TrI
   16:59  III ShE
   17:15  III TrE

31  5:05  I   EcD
    7:27  I   OcR
```

FEBRUARY

```
1   2:19  I   ShI
    2:20  I   TrI
    4:19  II  ShI
    4:22  II  TrI
    4:36  I   ShE
    4:38  I   TrE
    7:14  II  ShE
    7:17  II  TrE
   23:34  I   EcD

2   1:53  I   OcR
   20:46  I   TrI
   20:47  I   ShI
   22:48  II  OcD
   23:03  I   TrE
   23:04  I   ShE

3   1:42  II  EcR
    3:20  III OcD
    7:04  III EcR
   10:48  IV  TrI
   11:04  IV  ShI
   15:34  IV  TrE
   15:52  IV  ShE
   18:01  I   OcD
   20:21  I   EcR

4  15:12  I   TrI
   15:15  I   ShI
   17:29  I   TrE
   17:30  II  TrI
   17:33  I   ShE
   17:38  II  ShI
   20:25  II  TrE
   20:33  II  ShE

5  12:27  I   OcD
   14:50  I   EcR
```

```
6   9:38  I   TrI
    9:44  I   ShI
   11:54  II  OcD
   11:55  I   TrE
   12:01  I   ShE
   14:59  I   EcR
   16:53  III TrI
   17:20  III ShI
   20:30  III TrE
   20:57  III ShE

7   6:53  I   OcD
    9:18  I   EcR

8   4:04  I   TrI
    4:12  I   ShI
    6:21  I   TrE
    6:30  I   ShE
    6:37  II  TrI
    6:56  II  ShI
    9:32  II  TrE
    9:50  II  ShE

9   1:19  I   OcD
    3:47  I   EcR
   22:30  I   TrI
   22:41  I   ShI

10  0:47  I   TrE
    0:58  I   ShE
    1:01  II  OcD
    4:16  II  EcR
    6:36  III OcD
   11:03  III EcR
   19:45  I   OcD
   22:16  I   EcR

11 16:34  IV  OcD
   16:56  I   TrI
   17:10  I   ShI
   19:13  I   TrE
   19:27  I   ShE
   19:46  II  TrI
   20:15  II  ShI
   22:40  II  TrE
   23:09  II  ShE
   23:40  IV  EcR

12 14:11  I   OcD
   16:44  I   EcR

13 11:22  I   TrI
   11:38  I   ShI
   13:39  I   TrE
   13:55  I   ShE
   14:08  II  OcD
   17:33  II  EcR
   20:10  III TrI
   21:19  III ShI
   23:47  III TrE

14  0:57  III ShE
    8:37  I   OcD
   11:13  I   EcR

15  5:48  I   TrI
    6:07  I   ShI
    8:05  I   TrE
    8:24  I   ShE
    8:53  II  TrI
    9:33  II  ShI
   11:48  II  TrE
   12:27  II  ShE
```

SATELLITES OF JUPITER, UT OF 2003 GEOCENTRIC PHENOMENA (ct'd)

FEBRUARY (ct'd)

Date	Time	Sat	Phen
16	3:03	I	OcD
	5:42	I	EcR
17	0:14	I	TrI
	0:35	I	ShI
	2:31	I	TrE
	2:52	I	ShE
	3:15	II	OcD
	6:50	II	EcR
	9:53	III	OcD
	15:02	III	EcR
	21:29	I	OcD
18	0:11	I	EcR
	18:40	I	TrI
	19:04	I	ShI
	20:57	I	TrE
	21:21	I	ShE
	22:02	II	TrI
	22:52	II	ShI
19	0:56	II	TrE
	1:46	II	ShE
	15:56	I	OcD
	18:39	I	EcR
20	1:00	IV	TrI
	5:03	IV	ShI
	5:46	IV	TrE
	9:52	IV	ShE
	13:06	I	TrI
	13:32	I	ShI
	15:23	I	TrE
	15:49	I	ShE
	16:22	II	OcD
	20:07	II	EcR
	23:28	III	TrI
21	1:18	III	ShI
	3:04	III	TrE
	4:55	III	ShE
	10:22	I	OcD
	13:08	I	EcR
22	7:32	I	TrI
	8:01	I	ShI
	9:49	I	TrE
	10:18	I	ShE
	11:10	II	TrI
	12:10	II	ShI
	14:04	II	TrE
	15:04	II	ShE
23	4:48	I	OcD
	7:37	I	EcR
24	1:58	I	TrI
	2:29	I	ShI
	4:15	I	TrE
	4:47	I	ShE
	5:30	II	EcR
	9:25	II	EcR
	13:13	III	OcD
	19:02	III	EcR
	23:14	I	OcD
25	2:05	I	EcR
	20:25	I	TrI
	20:58	I	ShI
	22:42	I	TrE
	23:15	I	ShE

Date	Time	Sat	Phen
26	0:19	II	TrI
	1:28	II	ShI
	3:13	II	TrE
	4:23	II	ShE
	17:41	I	OcD
	20:34	I	EcR
27	14:51	I	TrI
	15:27	I	ShI
	17:08	I	TrE
	17:44	I	ShE
	18:38	II	OcD
	22:42	II	EcR
28	2:48	III	TrI
	5:16	III	ShI
	6:25	III	TrE
	6:55	IV	OcD
	8:54	III	ShE
	11:46	IV	OcR
	12:07	I	OcD
	12:49	IV	EcD
	15:03	I	EcR
	17:43	IV	EcR

MARCH

Date	Time	Sat	Phen
1	9:17	I	TrI
	9:55	I	ShI
	11:34	I	TrE
	12:12	I	ShE
	13:28	II	TrI
	14:47	II	ShI
	16:22	II	TrE
	17:41	II	ShE
2	6:34	I	OcD
	9:32	I	EcR
3	3:44	I	TrI
	4:24	I	ShI
	6:01	I	TrE
	6:41	I	ShE
	7:46	II	OcD
	11:59	II	EcR
	16:35	III	OcD
	23:02	III	EcR
4	1:00	I	OcD
	4:00	I	EcR
	22:10	I	TrI
	22:52	I	ShI
5	0:27	I	TrE
	1:10	I	ShE
	2:38	II	TrI
	4:06	II	ShI
	5:32	II	TrE
	7:00	II	ShE
	19:27	I	OcD
	22:29	I	EcR
6	16:37	I	TrI
	17:21	I	ShI
	18:54	I	TrE
	19:38	I	ShE
	20:55	II	OcD

Date	Time	Sat	Phen
7	1:17	II	EcR
	6:12	III	TrI
	9:15	III	ShI
	9:48	III	TrE
	12:52	III	ShE
	13:53	I	OcD
	16:58	I	EcR
8	11:03	I	TrI
	11:50	I	ShI
	13:20	I	TrE
	14:07	I	ShE
	15:44	IV	TrI
	15:48	II	TrI
	17:24	II	ShI
	18:42	II	TrE
	20:18	II	ShE
	20:29	IV	TrE
	23:05	IV	ShI
9	3:52	IV	ShE
	8:20	I	OcD
	11:27	I	EcR
10	5:30	I	TrI
	6:18	I	ShI
	7:47	I	TrE
	8:35	I	ShE
	10:04	II	OcD
	14:34	II	EcR
	20:01	III	OcD
11	2:47	I	OcD
	3:02	III	EcR
	5:55	I	EcR
	23:57	I	TrI
12	0:47	I	ShI
	2:14	I	TrE
	3:04	I	ShE
	4:59	II	TrI
	6:43	II	ShI
	7:53	II	TrE
	9:36	II	ShE
	21:14	I	OcD
13	0:24	I	EcR
	18:24	I	TrI
	19:16	I	ShI
	20:41	I	TrE
	21:33	I	ShE
	23:14	II	OcD
14	3:52	II	EcR
	9:40	III	TrI
	13:14	III	ShI
	13:16	III	TrE
	15:41	I	OcD
	16:51	III	ShE
	18:53	I	EcR
15	12:51	I	TrI
	13:44	I	ShI
	15:07	I	TrE
	16:01	I	ShE
	18:10	II	TrI
	20:01	II	ShI
	21:04	II	TrE
	22:54	II	ShE
16	10:08	I	OcD
	13:22	I	EcR
	21:58	IV	OcD

Date	Time	Sat	Phen
17	2:50	IV	OcR
	6:52	IV	EcD
	7:18	I	TrI
	8:13	I	ShI
	9:34	I	TrE
	10:30	I	ShE
	11:46	IV	EcR
	12:25	II	OcD
	17:09	II	EcR
	23:31	III	OcD
18	3:10	III	OcR
	3:22	III	EcD
	4:35	I	OcD
	7:01	III	EcR
	7:50	I	EcR
19	1:45	I	TrI
	2:42	I	ShI
	4:01	I	TrE
	4:58	I	ShE
	7:22	II	TrI
	9:20	II	ShI
	10:16	II	TrE
	12:13	II	ShE
	23:02	I	OcD
20	2:19	I	EcR
	20:12	I	TrI
	21:10	I	ShI
	22:28	I	TrE
	23:27	I	ShE
21	1:36	II	OcD
	6:27	II	EcR
	13:13	III	TrI
	16:49	III	TrE
	17:14	III	ShI
	17:29	I	OcD
	20:48	I	EcR
	20:51	III	ShE
22	14:39	I	TrI
	15:39	I	ShI
	16:56	I	TrE
	17:56	I	ShE
	20:34	II	TrI
	22:38	II	ShI
	23:28	II	TrE
23	1:31	II	ShE
	11:57	I	OcD
	15:17	I	EcR
24	9:06	I	TrI
	10:08	I	ShI
	11:23	I	TrE
	12:24	I	ShE
	14:48	II	OcD
	19:45	II	EcR
25	3:06	III	OcD
	6:24	I	OcD
	6:44	III	OcR
	7:16	IV	TrI
	7:21	III	EcD
	9:45	I	EcR
	11:00	III	EcR
	12:02	IV	TrE
	17:06	IV	ShI
	21:53	IV	ShE

Date	Time	Sat	Phen
26	3:34	I	TrI
	4:36	I	ShI
	5:50	I	TrE
	6:53	I	ShE
	9:48	II	TrI
	11:56	II	ShI
	12:41	II	TrE
	14:50	II	ShE
27	0:52	I	OcD
	4:14	I	EcR
	22:01	I	TrI
	23:05	I	ShI
28	0:18	I	TrE
	1:22	I	ShE
	4:00	II	OcD
	9:03	II	EcR
	16:50	III	TrI
	19:19	I	OcD
	20:26	III	TrE
	21:14	III	ShI
	22:43	I	EcR
29	0:50	III	ShE
	16:29	I	TrI
	17:34	I	ShI
	18:45	I	TrE
	19:51	I	ShE
	23:01	II	TrI
30	1:15	II	ShI
	1:54	II	TrE
	4:08	II	ShE
	13:47	I	OcD
	17:12	I	EcR
31	10:56	I	TrI
	12:02	I	ShI
	13:13	I	TrE
	14:19	I	ShE
	17:13	II	OcD
	22:20	II	EcR

APRIL

Date	Time	Sat	Phen
1	6:45	III	OcD
	8:14	I	OcD
	10:23	III	OcR
	11:20	III	EcD
	11:41	I	EcR
	15:00	III	EcR
2	5:24	I	TrI
	6:31	I	ShI
	7:40	I	TrE
	8:48	I	ShE
	12:15	II	TrI
	13:58	IV	OcD
	14:33	II	ShI
	15:08	II	TrE
	17:26	II	ShE
	18:50	IV	OcR
3	0:56	IV	EcD
	2:42	IV	OcD
	5:49	IV	EcR
	6:09	I	EcR
	23:52	I	TrI

SATELLITES OF JUPITER, UT OF 2003 GEOCENTRIC PHENOMENA (ct'd)

APRIL (ct'd)

4	1:00	I	ShI
	2:08	I	TrE
	3:17	I	ShE
	6:26	II	OcD
	11:38	II	EcR
	20:32	III	TrI
	21:10	I	OcD
5	0:08	III	TrE
	0:38	I	EcR
	1:13	III	ShI
	4:50	III	ShE
	18:19	I	TrI
	19:29	I	ShI
	20:36	I	TrE
	21:45	I	ShE
6	1:29	II	TrI
	3:52	II	ShI
	4:22	II	TrE
	6:44	II	ShE
	15:38	I	OcD
	19:07	I	EcR
7	12:47	I	TrI
	13:57	I	ShI
	15:04	I	TrE
	16:14	I	ShE
	19:40	II	OcD
8	0:56	II	EcR
	10:06	I	OcD
	10:28	III	OcD
	13:36	I	EcR
	14:07	III	OcR
	15:20	III	EcD
	18:59	III	EcR
9	7:15	I	TrI
	8:26	I	ShI
	9:32	I	TrE
	10:43	I	ShE
	14:45	II	TrI
	17:10	II	ShI
	17:37	II	TrE
	20:03	II	ShE
10	4:34	I	OcD
	8:05	I	EcR
	23:45	IV	TrI
11	1:43	I	TrI
	2:55	I	ShI
	4:00	I	TrE
	4:31	IV	TrE
	5:11	I	ShE
	8:55	II	OcD
	11:07	IV	ShI
	14:14	II	EcR
	15:53	IV	ShE
	23:02	I	OcD
12	0:19	III	TrI
	2:33	I	EcR
	3:54	III	TrE
	5:13	III	ShI
	8:49	III	ShE
	20:11	I	TrI
	21:24	I	ShI
	22:28	I	TrE
	23:40	I	ShE
13	4:00	II	TrI
	6:28	II	ShI
	6:53	II	TrE
	9:21	II	ShE
	17:30	I	OcD
	21:02	I	EcR
14	14:39	I	TrI
	15:52	I	ShI
	16:56	I	TrE
	18:09	I	ShE
	22:10	II	OcD
15	3:32	II	EcR
	11:58	I	OcD
	14:18	III	OcD
	15:31	I	EcR
	17:56	III	OcR
	19:20	III	EcD
	23:00	III	EcR
16	9:08	I	TrI
	10:21	I	ShI
	11:24	I	TrE
	12:38	I	ShE
	17:17	II	TrI
	19:47	II	ShI
	20:09	II	TrE
	22:39	II	ShE
17	6:27	I	OcD
	10:00	I	EcR
18	3:36	I	TrI
	4:50	I	ShI
	5:52	I	TrE
	7:06	I	ShE
	11:26	II	OcD
	16:50	II	EcR
19	0:55	I	OcD
	4:09	III	TrI
	4:28	I	EcR
	6:56	IV	OcD
	7:44	III	TrE
	9:12	III	ShI
	11:48	IV	OcR
	12:48	III	ShE
	18:59	IV	EcD
	22:04	I	TrI
	23:19	I	ShI
	23:52	IV	EcR
20	0:21	I	TrE
	1:35	I	ShE
	6:33	II	TrI
	9:05	II	ShI
	9:26	II	TrE
	11:57	II	ShE
	19:23	I	OcD
	22:57	I	EcR
21	16:33	I	TrI
	17:47	I	ShI
	18:49	I	TrE
	20:04	I	ShE
22	0:42	II	OcD
	6:08	II	EcR
	13:52	I	OcD
	17:26	I	EcR
	18:11	III	OcD
	21:49	III	OcR
	23:20	III	EcD
23	3:00	III	EcR
	11:01	I	TrI
	12:16	I	ShI
	13:18	I	TrE
	14:33	I	ShE
	19:51	II	TrI
	22:23	II	ShI
	22:43	II	TrE
24	1:15	II	ShE
	8:20	I	OcD
	11:55	I	EcR
25	5:30	I	TrI
	6:45	I	ShI
	7:46	I	TrE
	9:02	I	ShE
	13:59	II	OcD
	19:26	II	EcR
26	2:49	I	OcD
	6:24	I	EcR
	8:04	III	TrI
	11:39	III	TrE
	13:11	III	ShI
	16:48	III	ShE
	23:58	I	TrI
27	1:14	I	ShI
	2:15	I	TrE
	3:30	I	ShE
	9:08	II	TrI
	11:41	II	ShI
	12:00	II	TrE
	14:33	II	ShE
	17:12	IV	TrI
	21:18	I	OcD
	21:58	IV	TrE
28	0:52	I	EcR
	5:10	IV	ShI
	9:54	IV	ShE
	18:27	I	TrI
	19:42	I	ShI
	20:43	I	TrE
	21:59	I	ShE
29	3:17	II	OcD
	8:44	II	EcR
	15:46	I	OcD
	19:21	I	EcR
	22:09	III	OcD
30	1:47	III	OcR
	3:20	III	EcD
	7:00	III	EcR
	12:56	I	TrI
	14:11	I	ShI
	15:12	I	TrE
	16:28	I	ShE
	22:26	II	TrI

MAY

1	1:00	II	ShI
	1:19	II	TrE
	3:51	II	ShE
	10:15	I	OcD
	13:50	I	EcR
2	7:24	I	TrI
	8:40	I	ShI
	9:41	I	TrE
	10:57	I	ShE
	16:35	II	OcD
	22:03	II	EcR
3	4:44	I	OcD
	8:19	I	EcR
	12:03	III	TrI
	15:38	III	TrE
	17:10	III	ShI
	20:47	III	ShE
4	1:53	I	TrI
	3:09	I	ShI
	4:10	I	TrE
	5:25	I	ShE
	11:45	II	TrI
	14:18	II	ShI
	14:37	II	TrE
	17:09	II	ShE
	23:13	I	OcD
5	2:47	I	EcR
	20:22	I	TrI
	21:38	I	ShI
	22:39	I	TrE
	23:54	I	ShE
6	0:49	IV	OcD
	5:43	IV	OcR
	5:53	II	OcD
	11:21	II	EcR
	13:03	IV	EcD
	17:42	I	OcD
	17:55	IV	OcR
	21:16	I	EcR
7	2:10	III	OcD
	5:48	III	OcR
	7:19	III	EcD
	10:59	III	EcR
	14:51	I	TrI
	16:06	I	ShI
	17:08	I	TrE
	18:23	I	ShE
8	1:04	II	TrI
	3:36	II	ShI
	3:56	II	TrE
	6:28	II	ShE
	12:11	I	OcD
	15:45	I	EcR
9	9:20	I	TrI
	10:35	I	ShI
	11:37	I	TrE
	12:52	I	ShE
	19:12	II	OcD
10	0:39	II	EcR
	6:40	I	OcD
	10:14	I	EcR
	16:06	III	TrI
	19:42	III	TrE
	21:11	III	ShI
11	0:47	III	ShE
	3:49	I	TrI
	5:04	I	ShI
	6:06	I	TrE
	7:21	I	ShE
	14:23	II	TrI
	16:54	II	ShI
	17:15	II	TrE
	19:45	II	ShE
12	1:09	I	OcD
	4:42	I	EcR
	22:18	I	TrI
	23:33	I	ShI
13	0:35	I	TrE
	1:49	I	ShE
	8:32	II	OcD
	13:57	II	EcR
	19:38	I	OcD
	23:11	I	EcR
14	6:14	III	OcD
	9:53	III	OcR
	11:18	III	EcD
	11:29	IV	TrI
	14:58	III	EcR
	16:16	IV	TrE
	16:47	I	TrI
	18:01	I	ShI
	19:04	I	TrE
	20:18	I	ShE
	23:11	IV	ShI
15	3:43	II	TrI
	3:55	IV	ShE
	6:12	II	ShI
	6:35	II	TrE
	9:03	II	ShE
	14:08	I	OcD
	17:40	I	EcR
16	11:17	I	TrI
	12:30	I	ShI
	13:33	I	TrE
	14:47	I	ShE
	21:52	II	OcD
17	3:16	II	EcR
	8:37	I	OcD
	12:09	I	EcR
	20:13	III	TrI
	23:49	III	TrE
18	1:10	III	ShI
	4:47	III	ShE
	5:46	I	TrI
	6:59	I	ShI
	8:03	I	TrE
	9:16	I	ShE
	17:03	II	TrI
	19:30	II	ShI
	19:55	II	TrE
	22:21	II	ShE
19	3:06	I	OcD
	6:37	I	EcR
20	0:15	I	TrI
	1:28	I	ShI
	2:32	I	TrE
	3:45	I	ShE
	11:12	II	OcD
	16:34	II	EcR
	21:36	I	OcD

SATELLITES OF JUPITER, UT OF 2003 GEOCENTRIC PHENOMENA (ct'd)

MAY (ct'd)

21	1:06	I	EcR
	10:22	III	OcD
	14:01	III	OcR
	15:18	III	EcD
	18:45	I	TrI
	18:58	III	EcR
	19:57	I	ShI
	21:02	I	TrE
	22:14	I	ShE
22	6:24	II	TrI
	8:48	II	ShI
	9:15	II	TrE
	11:39	II	ShE
	16:05	I	OcD
	19:32	IV	OcD
	19:35	I	EcR
23	0:26	IV	OcR
	7:08	IV	EcD
	11:58	IV	EcR
	13:14	I	TrI
	14:25	I	ShI
	15:31	I	TrE
	16:42	I	ShE
24	0:33	II	OcD
	5:52	II	EcR
	10:34	I	OcD
	14:04	I	EcR
25	0:23	III	TrI
	3:59	III	TrE
	5:10	III	ShI
	7:43	I	TrI
	8:47	III	ShE
	8:54	I	ShI
	10:00	I	TrE
	11:11	I	ShE
	19:44	II	TrI
	22:06	II	ShI
	22:36	II	TrE
26	0:57	II	ShE
	5:04	I	OcD
	8:32	I	EcR
27	2:13	I	TrI
	3:23	I	ShI
	4:30	I	TrE
	5:40	I	ShE
	13:54	II	OcD
	19:11	II	EcR
	23:33	I	OcD
28	3:01	I	EcR
	14:33	III	OcD
	18:12	III	OcR
	19:17	III	EcD
	20:43	I	TrI
	21:52	I	ShI
	22:57	III	EcR
	23:00	I	TrE
29	0:09	I	ShE
	9:05	II	TrI
	11:24	II	ShI
	11:57	II	TrE
	14:15	II	ShE
	18:03	I	OcD
	21:30	I	EcR

30	15:12	I	TrI
	16:21	I	ShI
	17:29	I	TrE
	18:38	I	ShE
31	3:16	II	OcD
	6:28	IV	TrI
	8:29	II	EcR
	11:15	IV	TrE
	12:32	I	OcD
	15:58	I	EcR
	17:13	IV	ShI
	21:55	IV	ShE

JUNE

1	4:35	III	TrI
	8:11	III	TrE
	9:09	III	ShI
	9:42	I	TrI
	10:49	**I**	**ShI**
	11:59	I	TrE
	12:46	III	ShE
	13:06	I	ShE
	22:27	II	TrI
2	0:41	II	ShI
	1:18	II	TrE
	3:33	II	ShE
	7:02	I	OcD
	10:27	I	EcR
3	4:11	I	TrI
	5:18	I	ShI
	6:28	I	TrE
	7:35	I	ShE
	16:38	II	OcD
	21:48	II	EcR
4	1:32	I	OcD
	4:56	I	EcR
	18:48	III	OcD
	22:27	III	OcR
	22:41	I	TrI
	23:17	III	EcD
	23:47	I	ShI
5	0:58	I	TrE
	2:04	I	ShE
	2:57	III	EcR
	11:48	II	TrI
	13:59	II	ShI
	14:40	II	TrE
	16:50	II	ShE
	20:01	I	OcD
	23:25	I	EcR
6	17:11	I	TrI
	18:16	I	ShI
	19:28	I	TrE
	20:33	I	ShE
7	6:00	II	OcD
	11:06	II	EcR
	14:31	I	OcD
	17:53	I	EcR

8	8:49	III	TrI
	11:41	I	TrI
	12:26	III	TrE
	12:44	I	ShI
	13:08	**III**	**ShI**
	13:58	I	TrE
	14:52	IV	OcD
	15:02	I	ShE
	16:46	III	ShE
	19:47	IV	OcR
9	1:10	II	TrI
	1:11	IV	EcD
	3:17	II	ShI
	4:02	II	TrE
	6:00	IV	EcR
	6:08	II	ShE
	9:01	I	OcD
	12:22	I	EcR
10	6:10	I	TrI
	7:13	I	ShI
	8:28	I	TrE
	9:30	I	ShE
	19:23	II	OcD
11	0:25	II	EcR
	3:31	I	OcD
	6:51	I	EcR
	23:04	III	OcD
12	0:40	I	TrI
	1:42	I	ShI
	2:44	III	OcR
	2:58	I	TrE
	3:17	III	EcD
	3:59	I	ShE
	6:56	III	EcR
	14:32	II	TrI
	16:34	II	ShI
	17:24	II	TrE
	19:26	II	ShE
	22:00	I	OcD
13	1:19	I	EcR
	19:10	I	TrI
	20:11	I	ShI
	21:27	I	TrE
	22:28	I	ShE
14	8:45	II	OcD
	13:43	II	EcR
	16:30	I	OcD
	19:48	I	EcR
15	13:06	III	TrI
	13:40	I	TrI
	14:40	I	ShI
	15:57	I	TrE
	16:44	III	TrE
	16:57	I	ShE
	17:08	III	ShI
	20:45	III	ShE
16	3:54	II	TrI
	5:52	II	ShI
	6:46	II	TrE
	8:43	II	ShE
	11:00	I	OcD
	14:17	I	EcR

17	2:01	IV	TrI
	6:50	IV	TrE
	8:10	I	TrI
	9:08	I	ShI
	10:27	I	TrE
	11:14	**IV**	**ShI**
	11:26	I	ShE
	15:56	IV	ShE
	22:09	II	OcD
18	3:02	II	EcR
	5:30	I	OcD
	8:45	I	EcR
19	2:40	I	TrI
	3:23	III	OcD
	3:37	I	ShI
	4:57	I	TrE
	5:55	I	ShE
	7:03	III	OcR
	7:16	III	EcD
	10:56	III	EcR
	17:17	II	TrI
	19:10	II	ShI
	20:09	II	TrE
	22:01	II	ShE
20	0:00	I	OcD
	3:14	I	EcR
	21:10	I	TrI
	22:06	I	ShI
	23:27	I	TrE
21	0:23	I	ShE
	11:32	II	OcD
	16:20	II	EcR
	18:30	I	OcD
	21:43	I	EcR
22	15:40	I	TrI
	16:35	I	ShI
	17:26	III	TrI
	17:57	I	TrE
	18:52	I	ShE
	21:03	III	TrE
	21:07	III	ShI
23	0:44	III	ShE
	6:39	II	TrI
	8:27	II	ShI
	9:31	II	TrE
	11:18	II	ShE
	13:00	I	OcD
	16:11	I	EcR
24	10:10	I	TrI
	11:03	I	ShI
	12:28	I	TrE
	13:21	I	ShE
25	0:56	II	OcD
	5:39	II	EcR
	7:30	I	OcD
	10:40	I	EcR
	10:44	IV	OcD
	15:38	IV	OcR
	19:14	IV	EcD

26	0:01	IV	EcR
	4:40	I	TrI
	5:32	I	ShI
	6:58	I	TrE
	7:43	III	OcD
	7:50	I	ShE
	14:55	III	EcR
	20:02	II	TrI
	21:45	II	ShI
	22:54	II	TrE
27	0:36	II	ShE
	2:00	I	OcD
	5:08	I	EcR
	23:10	I	TrI
28	0:01	I	ShI
	1:28	I	TrE
	2:19	I	ShE
	14:20	II	OcD
	18:57	II	EcR
	20:30	I	OcD
	23:37	I	EcR
29	17:40	I	TrI
	18:30	I	ShI
	19:58	I	TrE
	20:47	I	ShE
	21:47	III	TrI
30	1:07	III	ShI
	1:26	III	TrE
	4:45	III	ShE
	9:25	II	TrI
	11:02	II	ShI
	12:17	II	TrE
	13:53	II	ShE
	15:00	I	OcD
	18:06	I	EcR

JUL. TO SEP.
SUPPRESSED

OCTOBER

1	0:29	II	TrE
	4:52	III	ShI
	7:26	III	TrI
	8:27	III	ShE
	11:01	III	TrE
	13:47	I	ShI
	14:26	I	TrI
	16:05	I	ShE
	16:43	I	TrE
2	10:57	I	EcD
	13:54	I	OcR
	15:20	II	EcD
	19:35	II	OcR
3	8:16	I	ShI
	8:56	I	TrI
	10:33	I	ShE
	11:13	I	TrE

SATELLITES OF JUPITER, UT OF 2003 GEOCENTRIC PHENOMENA (ct'd)

OCTOBER (ct'd)

4	5:26	I	EcD
	7:27	IV	EcD
	8:24	I	OcR
	9:41	II	ShI
	11:02	II	TrI
	11:54	IV	EcR
	12:32	II	ShE
	13:52	II	TrE
	14:03	IV	OcD
	18:27	IV	OcR
	18:55	III	EcD
5	1:19	III	OcR
	2:44	I	ShI
	3:26	I	TrI
	5:02	I	ShE
	5:43	I	TrE
	23:54	I	EcD
6	2:53	I	OcR
	4:38	II	EcD
	8:59	II	OcR
	21:13	I	ShI
	21:56	I	TrI
	23:30	I	ShE
7	0:13	I	TrE
	18:22	I	EcD
	21:23	I	OcR
	22:58	II	ShI
8	0:24	II	TrI
	1:48	II	ShE
	3:15	II	TrE
	8:51	III	ShI
	11:50	III	TrI
	12:26	III	ShE
	15:24	III	TrE
	15:41	I	ShI
	16:26	I	TrI
	17:59	I	ShE
	18:43	I	TrE
9	12:51	I	EcD
	15:53	I	OcR
	17:56	II	EcD
	22:23	II	OcR
10	10:10	I	ShI
	10:56	I	TrI
	12:27	I	ShE
	13:13	I	TrE
11	7:19	I	EcD
	10:23	I	OcR
	12:15	II	ShI
	13:47	II	TrI
	15:05	II	ShE
	16:38	II	TrE
	22:52	III	EcD
12	4:38	I	ShI
	5:26	I	TrI
	5:40	III	OcR
	6:56	I	ShE
	7:43	I	TrE
	17:14	IV	ShI
	21:34	IV	ShE

13	0:45	IV	TrI
	1:47	I	EcD
	4:53	I	OcR
	4:58	IV	TrE
	7:14	II	EcD
	11:46	II	OcR
	23:07	I	ShI
	23:55	I	TrI
14	1:24	I	ShE
	2:13	I	TrE
	20:15	I	EcD
	23:22	I	OcR
15	1:32	II	ShI
	3:10	II	TrI
	4:22	II	ShE
	6:00	II	TrE
	12:49	III	ShI
	16:12	III	TrI
	16:23	III	ShE
	17:35	I	ShI
	18:25	I	TrI
	19:44	III	TrE
	19:52	I	ShE
	20:42	I	TrE
16	14:44	I	EcD
	17:52	I	OcR
	20:32	II	EcD
17	1:10	II	OcR
	12:04	I	ShI
	12:55	I	TrI
	14:21	I	ShE
	15:12	I	TrE
18	9:12	I	EcD
	12:22	I	OcR
	14:49	II	ShI
	16:32	II	TrI
	17:39	II	ShE
	19:22	II	TrE
19	2:50	III	EcD
	6:32	I	ShI
	7:25	I	TrI
	8:49	I	ShE
	9:42	I	TrE
	9:59	III	OcR
20	3:40	I	EcD
	6:51	I	OcR
	9:50	II	EcD
	14:32	II	OcR
21	1:01	I	ShI
	1:27	IV	EcD
	1:55	I	TrI
	3:18	I	ShE
	4:11	I	TrE
	5:51	IV	EcR
	10:16	IV	OcD
	14:28	IV	OcR
	22:09	I	EcD

22	1:21	I	OcR
	4:05	II	ShI
	5:54	II	TrI
	6:56	II	ShE
	8:44	II	TrE
	16:48	III	ShI
	19:29	**I**	**ShI**
	20:21	III	ShE
	20:24	I	TrI
	20:32	III	TrI
	21:46	I	ShE
	22:41	I	TrE
23	0:03	III	TrE
	16:37	I	EcD
	19:50	I	OcR
	23:08	II	EcD
24	3:55	II	OcR
	13:58	I	ShI
	14:54	I	TrI
	16:14	I	ShE
	17:11	I	TrE
25	11:05	I	EcD
	14:20	I	OcR
	17:22	II	ShI
	19:16	II	TrI
	20:13	II	ShE
	22:06	II	TrE
26	6:48	III	EcD
	8:26	I	ShI
	9:23	I	TrI
	10:23	III	EcR
	10:43	I	ShE
	10:44	III	OcD
	11:40	I	TrE
	14:17	III	OcR
27	5:34	I	EcD
	8:49	I	OcR
	12:25	II	EcD
	17:17	II	OcR
28	2:54	I	ShI
	3:53	I	TrI
	5:11	I	ShE
	6:10	I	TrE
29	0:02	I	EcD
	3:19	I	OcR
	6:39	II	ShI
	8:38	II	TrI
	9:29	II	ShE
	11:12	IV	ShI
	11:27	II	TrE
	15:28	IV	ShE
	20:40	IV	TrI
	20:45	III	ShI
	21:23	**I**	**ShI**
	22:23	I	TrI
	23:40	I	ShE
30	0:18	III	ShE
	0:39	I	TrE
	0:40	IV	TrI
	0:49	III	TrI
	4:19	III	TrE
	18:30	I	EcD
	21:48	I	OcR

31	1:43	II	EcD
	6:40	II	OcR
	15:51	I	ShI
	16:52	I	TrI
	18:08	I	ShE
	19:08	I	TrE

NOVEMBER

1	12:59	I	EcD
	16:18	I	OcR
	19:56	II	ShI
	21:59	II	TrI
	22:46	II	ShE
2	0:49	II	TrE
	10:20	I	ShI
	10:46	III	EcD
	11:22	I	TrI
	12:36	I	ShE
	13:38	I	TrE
	14:21	III	EcR
	15:02	III	OcD
	18:33	III	OcR
3	7:27	I	EcD
	10:47	I	OcR
	15:00	II	EcD
	20:01	II	OcR
4	4:48	I	ShI
	5:51	I	TrI
	7:05	I	ShE
	8:07	I	TrE
5	1:55	I	EcD
	5:16	I	OcR
	9:13	II	ShI
	11:20	II	TrI
	12:03	II	ShE
	14:10	II	TrE
	23:16	I	ShI
6	0:20	I	TrI
	0:43	**III**	**ShI**
	1:33	I	ShE
	2:36	I	TrE
	4:15	III	ShE
	5:04	III	TrI
	8:33	III	TrE
	19:27	IV	EcD
	20:23	I	EcD
	23:46	I	OcR
	23:46	IV	EcR
7	4:18	II	EcD
	6:04	IV	OcD
	9:23	II	OcR
	10:00	IV	OcR
	17:45	I	ShI
	18:50	I	TrI
	20:01	I	ShE
	21:06	I	TrE
8	14:52	I	EcD
	18:15	I	OcR
	22:30	II	ShI

9	0:41	II	TrI
	1:20	II	ShE
	3:30	II	TrE
	12:13	I	ShI
	13:19	I	TrI
	14:30	I	ShE
	14:44	III	EcD
	15:35	I	TrE
	18:18	III	EcR
	19:16	III	OcD
	22:46	III	OcR
10	9:20	I	EcD
	12:44	I	OcR
	17:36	II	EcD
	22:43	II	OcR
11	6:42	I	ShI
	7:48	I	TrI
	8:58	I	ShE
	10:04	I	TrE
12	3:48	I	EcD
	7:13	I	OcR
	11:47	II	ShI
	14:01	II	TrI
	14:37	II	ShE
	16:51	II	TrE
13	1:10	I	ShI
	2:17	I	TrI
	3:26	I	ShE
	4:33	I	TrE
	4:41	III	ShI
	8:13	III	ShE
	9:17	III	TrI
	12:44	III	TrE
	22:17	I	EcD
14	1:42	I	OcR
	6:53	II	EcD
	12:04	II	OcR
	19:38	I	ShI
	20:46	I	TrI
	21:55	I	ShE
	23:02	I	TrE
15	5:11	IV	ShI
	9:21	IV	ShE
	16:06	IV	TrI
	16:45	I	EcD
	19:50	IV	TrE
	20:11	I	OcR
16	1:04	II	ShI
	3:22	II	TrI
	3:54	II	ShE
	6:11	II	TrE
	14:07	I	ShI
	15:16	I	TrI
	16:23	I	ShE
	17:31	I	TrE
	18:42	III	EcD
	22:16	III	EcR
	23:27	III	OcD
17	2:56	III	OcR
	11:13	I	EcD
	14:40	I	OcR
	20:11	II	EcD

SATELLITES OF JUPITER, UT OF 2003 GEOCENTRIC PHENOMENA (ct'd)

NOVEMBER (ct'd)

```
18  1:24  II  OcR
    8:35   I  ShI
    9:45   I  TrI
   10:51   I  ShE
   12:00   I  TrE
19  5:41   I  EcD
    9:09   I  OcR
   14:21  II  ShI
   16:42  II  TrI
   17:11  II  ShE
   19:31  II  TrE
20  3:03   I  ShI
    4:14   I  TrI
    5:20   I  ShE
    6:29   I  TrE
    8:38 III  ShI
   12:10 III  ShE
   13:26 III  TrI
   16:52 III  TrE
21  0:10   I  EcD
    3:38   I  OcR
    9:28  II  EcD
   14:44  II  OcR
   21:32   I  ShI
   22:42   I  TrI
   23:48   I  ShE
22  0:58   I  TrE
   18:38   I  EcD
   22:07   I  OcR
23  3:38  II  ShI
    6:01  II  TrI
    6:28  II  ShE
    8:50  II  TrE
   13:27  IV  EcD
   16:00   I  ShI
   17:11   I  TrI
   17:41  IV  EcR
   18:16   I  ShE
   19:27   I  TrE
   22:39 III  EcD
24  1:17  IV  OcD
    2:13 III  EcR
    3:35 III  OcD
    4:56  IV  OcR
    7:02 III  OcR
   13:06   I  EcD
   16:36   I  OcR
   22:45  II  EcD
25  4:03  II  OcR
   10:28   I  ShI
   11:40   I  TrI
   12:45   I  ShE
   13:55   I  TrE
26  7:34   I  EcD
   11:04   I  OcR
   16:55  II  ShI
   19:20  II  TrI
   19:45  II  ShE
   22:09  II  TrE
```

```
27  4:57   I  ShI
    6:09   I  TrI
    7:13   I  ShE
    8:24   I  TrE
   12:37 III  ShI
   16:08 III  ShE
   17:33 III  TrI
   20:58 III  TrE
28  2:03   I  EcD
    5:33   I  OcR
   12:03  II  EcD
   17:21  II  OcR
   23:25   I  ShI
29  0:38   I  TrI
    1:41   I  ShE
    2:53   I  TrE
   20:31   I  EcD
30  0:02   I  OcR
    6:12  II  ShI
    8:39  II  TrI
    9:02  II  ShE
   11:27  II  TrE
   17:53   I  ShI
   19:06   I  TrI
   20:09   I  ShE
   21:21   I  TrE
```

DECEMBER

```
 1  2:36 III  EcD
    6:10 III  EcR
    7:39 III  OcD
   11:05 III  OcR
   14:59   I  EcD
   18:30   I  OcR
   23:08  IV  ShI
 2  1:20  II  EcD
    3:13  IV  ShE
    6:39  II  OcR
   10:54  IV  TrI
   12:22   I  ShI
   13:35   I  TrI
   14:21  IV  TrE
   14:38   I  ShE
   15:50   I  TrE
 3  9:28   I  EcD
   12:59   I  OcR
   19:29  II  ShI
   21:57  II  TrI
   22:19  II  ShE
 4  0:46  II  TrE
    6:50   I  ShI
    8:03   I  TrI
    9:06   I  ShE
   10:18   I  TrE
   16:35 III  ShI
   20:05 III  ShE
   21:36 III  TrI
 5  0:59 III  TrE
    3:56   I  EcD
    7:27   I  OcR
   14:37  II  EcD
   19:57  II  OcR
```

```
 6  1:18   I  ShI
    2:32   I  TrI
    3:34   I  ShE
    4:47   I  TrE
   22:24   I  EcD
 7  1:56   I  OcR
    8:46  II  ShI
   11:15  II  TrI
   11:36  II  ShE
   14:03  II  TrE
   19:47   I  ShI
   21:00   I  TrI
   22:02   I  ShE
   23:15   I  TrE
 8  6:34 III  EcD
   10:07 III  EcR
   11:40 III  OcD
   15:04 III  OcR
   16:52   I  EcD
   20:24   I  OcR
 9  3:54  II  EcD
    9:14  II  OcR
   14:15   I  ShI
   15:28   I  TrI
   16:31   I  ShE
   17:43   I  TrE
10  7:28  IV  EcD
   11:21   I  EcD
   11:36  IV  EcR
   14:52   I  OcR
   19:45  IV  OcD
   22:04  II  ShI
   23:07  IV  OcR
11  0:33  II  TrI
    0:54  II  ShE
    3:21  II  TrE
    8:43   I  ShI
    9:57   I  TrI
   10:59   I  ShE
   12:12   I  TrE
   20:32 III  ShI
12  0:02 III  ShE
    1:35 III  TrI
    4:56 III  TrE
    5:49   I  EcD
    9:21   I  OcR
   17:12  II  EcD
   22:31  II  OcR
13  3:12   I  ShI
    4:25   I  TrI
    5:27   I  ShE
    6:40   I  TrE
14  0:17   I  EcD
    3:49   I  OcR
   11:21  II  ShI
   13:49  II  TrI
   14:11  II  ShE
   16:38  II  TrE
   21:40   I  ShI
   22:53   I  TrI
   23:56   I  ShE
```

```
15  1:08   I  TrE
   10:31 III  EcD
   14:04 III  EcR
   15:37 III  OcD
   18:46   I  EcD
   19:00 III  OcR
   22:17   I  OcR
16  6:28  II  EcD
   11:47  II  OcR
   16:08   I  ShI
   17:21   I  TrI
   18:24   I  ShE
   19:36   I  TrE
17 13:14   I  EcD
   16:45   I  OcR
18  0:38  II  ShI
    3:06  II  TrI
    3:28  II  ShE
    5:54  II  TrE
   10:36   I  ShI
   11:49   I  TrI
   12:52   I  ShE
   14:04   I  TrE
   17:06  IV  ShI
   21:05  IV  ShE
19  0:30 III  ShI
    3:59 III  ShE
    4:54  IV  TrI
    5:29 III  TrI
    7:42   I  EcD
    8:04  IV  TrE
    8:49 III  TrE
   11:13   I  OcR
   19:46  II  EcD
20  1:03  II  OcR
    5:05   I  ShI
    6:17   I  TrI
    7:20   I  ShE
    8:32   I  TrE
21  2:11   I  EcD
    5:41   I  OcR
   13:55  II  ShI
   16:22  II  TrI
   16:45  II  ShE
   19:10  II  TrE
   23:33   I  ShI
22  0:45   I  TrI
    1:49   I  ShE
    2:59   I  TrE
   14:30 III  EcD
   18:02 III  EcR
   19:30 III  OcD
   20:39   I  EcD
   22:52 III  OcR
23  0:09   I  OcR
    9:03  II  EcD
   14:17  II  OcR
   18:01   I  ShI
   19:13   I  TrI
   20:17   I  ShE
   21:27   I  TrE
24 15:07   I  EcD
   18:37   I  OcR
```

```
25  3:12  II  ShI
    5:37  II  TrI
    6:03  II  ShE
    8:25  II  TrE
   12:29   I  ShI
   13:40   I  TrI
   14:45   I  ShE
   15:55   I  TrE
26  4:27 III  ShI
    7:56 III  ShE
    9:18 III  TrI
    9:36   I  EcD
   12:37 III  TrE
   13:04   I  OcR
   22:20  II  EcD
27  1:27  IV  EcD
    3:32  II  OcR
    5:30  IV  EcR
    6:58   I  ShI
    8:08   I  TrI
    9:13   I  ShE
   10:23   I  TrE
   13:19  IV  OcD
   16:23  IV  OcR
28  4:04   I  EcD
    7:32   I  OcR
   16:30  II  ShI
   18:52  II  TrI
   19:20  II  ShE
   21:40  II  TrE
29  1:26   I  ShI
    2:36   I  TrI
    3:42   I  ShE
    4:50   I  TrE
   18:28 III  EcD
   21:59 III  EcR
   22:32   I  EcD
   23:18 III  OcD
30  2:00   I  OcR
    2:39 III  OcR
   11:36  II  EcD
   16:46  II  OcR
   19:54   I  ShI
   21:03   I  TrI
   22:10   I  ShE
   23:18   I  TrE
31 17:00   I  EcD
   20:27   I  OcR
32  5:47  II  ShI
    8:07  II  TrI
    8:38  II  ShE
   10:55  II  TrE
   14:22   I  ShI
   15:31   I  TrI
   16:38   I  ShE
   17:45   I  TrE
```

CONFIGURATIONS OF SATURN'S BRIGHTEST SATELLITES
BY LARRY D. BOGAN

The diagrams on the next three pages give the relative locations of the five brightest satellites of Saturn for January through April and August through December 2003. The names and magnitudes of these satellites, in order of increasing distance from Saturn, are Enceladus 11.8, Tethys 10.3, Dione 10.4, Rhea 9.7, and Titan 8.4.

The curves in the diagrams show the elongations of the satellites from Saturn for day 0.0 UT to day 32.0 UT for each month. The dashed curves represent Enceladus and Dione, the first and third out from Saturn. The narrow, central, vertical band represents the disk of Saturn, and the wider band the outer edge of Saturn's "A" ring.

At the top of each monthly diagram is a scale drawing of Saturn, its rings, and the orbits of four of the five brightest satellites as seen through an inverting telescope (in the Northern Hemisphere). South is up. Because of the small size of the scale drawing, no orbit is shown for the innermost satellite, Enceladus. Due to its faintness and proximity to the bright rings, Enceladus is best seen when near a maximum elongation, but even then good seeing, good optics, and an aperture of at least 250 mm are required.

During 2003, we see Saturn and its satellites from south of the ring plane. The tilt for 2003 only varies between 25.3° and 27.0° during the year. The direction of motion of the satellites is clockwise as viewed with a telescope having an even number (0, 2, 4,...) of reflections in its optics.

A particular configuration of the satellites may be determined by drawing a horizontal line across the monthly curves at the time (UT) of interest. The intersection of this line with the curves gives the relative elongations of the satellites. Project these elongations onto the drawing of the orbits at the top of the diagram. The east side of the "A" ring vertical band has been extended up to the drawing to facilitate transfer of each elongation. A millimetre scale, pair of dividers, or a strip of paper on which to mark enables one to do this quickly and accurately.

The direction of the orbital motion of a satellite determines on which side of its orbit (north or south) a satellite is located. A satellite *moving right* (east) will be *above* (south of) Saturn in the scale drawing, and a satellite *moving left* (west) will be *below* (north of) Saturn in the drawing. The March diagram shows an example configuration for March 2 at 9:00 p.m. EST (March 3 at 2h UT).

Greatest Elongations and Conjunctions for Iapetus

Iapetus has a magnitude comparable to the five plotted satellites, but varies from magnitude 10.1 (western elongation) to 11.9 (eastern elongation). Its orbit is about 2.9 times the size of Titan's and is tilted 15° to Saturn's ring plane; its period is 79 days. Iapetus is easiest to find near conjunctions when it is just north or south of Saturn. The table below lists times (UT) of greatest elongations and conjunctions during 2003.

Eastern Elong.		Inferior Conj.		Western Elong.		Superior Conj.	
Jan. 6	14.6h	Jan. 27	1.1h	Feb. 15	6.4h	Mar. 6	5.7h
Mar. 26	17.7h	Apr. 16	19.6h	May 6	13.1h	May 26	0.8h
Jun. 16	1.4h	Jul. 7	7.4h	Jul. 27	0.0h	Aug. 15	13.9h
Sep. 5	14.0h	Sep. 26	9.9h	Oct. 15	15.3h	Nov. 3	19.4h
Nov. 24	5.7h	Dec. 14	11.1h	—		—	

Note: Two freeware computer programs that display the configurations of Saturn's satellites are *SATSAT2* and *Meridian*. *SATSAT2*, by Dan Bruton, is a DOS program and is available at www.physics.sfasu.edu/astro/dansoftware.html. *Meridian*, by Claude Duplessis, is a Windows program and is available at page.infinit.net/merid/index.html.

CONFIGURATIONS OF SATURN'S SATELLITES
2003 JANUARY–MARCH

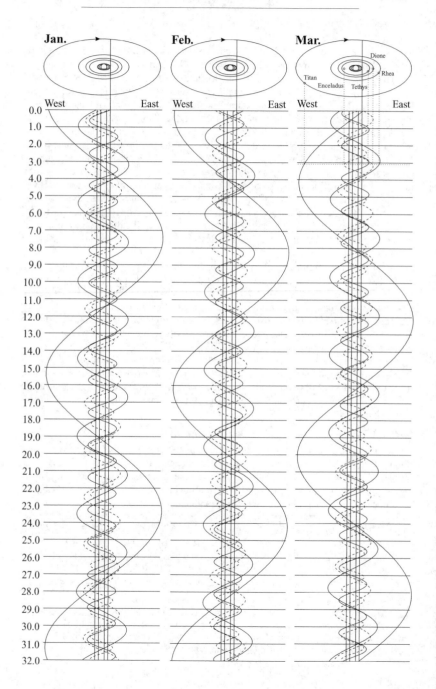

CONFIGURATIONS OF SATURN'S SATELLITES
2003 APRIL, AUGUST, SEPTEMBER

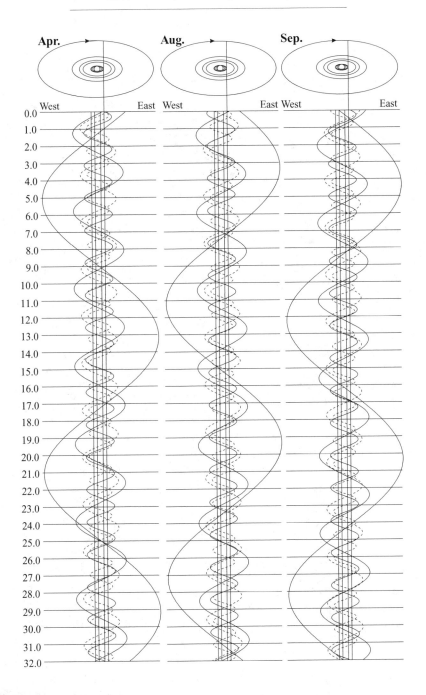

CONFIGURATIONS OF SATURN'S SATELLITES
2003 OCTOBER–DECEMBER

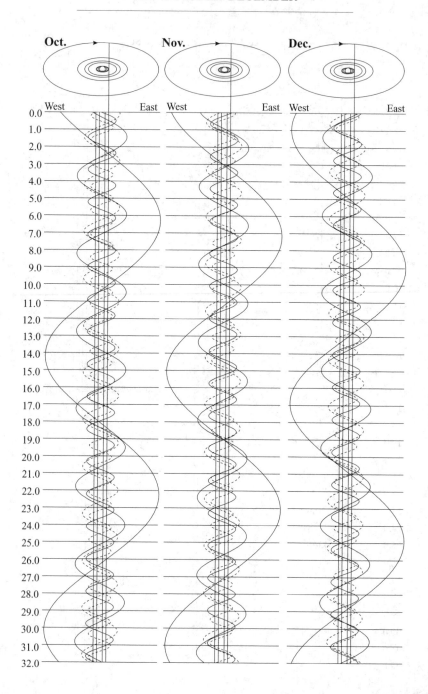

ASTEROIDS

THE BRIGHTEST ASTEROIDS

On the next two pages are ephemerides for asteroids (identified by number and name) that will be brighter than or equal to visual magnitude 10.0 and more than 90° from the Sun during 2002. The positions are based on TT, although the equivalent but older designation "ET" appears on the tables. TT differs by about one minute from UT (see TIME AND TIME SCALES on pp. 35–40). "Mag" is visual magnitude. These data were derived from current osculating elements.

Using the ephemerides provided and an appropriate star atlas, charts displaying the motion of each asteroid can be produced. For example, the chart below, provided by David Lane, shows the path of Vesta as it moves through its retrograde loop in Virgo from January to July.

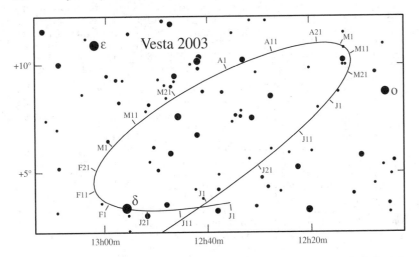

The coordinates in the chart are for epoch 2000.0, and the chart magnitude limit is 8.0; Vesta remains brighter than this limit during the depicted period. Tick marks along Vesta's path indicate its position on the 1st, 11th, and 21st day of each month, beginning with Jan. 1 (J1) and proceeding clockwise through Jul. 1 (also J1). The brightest star in the chart is magnitude-2.8 ε Vir. Note the proximity of Vesta to magnitude-3.4 δ Vir: Vesta is just 1.2′ south of this bright star at 21h UT on Jan. 25. In the MAY ALL-SKY MAP on p. 296, δ Vir and ε Vir appear just to right of the label "VIRGO."

Vesta brightens to visual magnitude 5.9 when at opposition on Mar. 26, and will then be bright enough to be seen with the naked eye. With a diameter of 538 km and opposition distance of 1.28 AU, Vesta will have an angular diameter of 0.58″ and may be resolvable with large telescopes under steady skies.

Ceres was the first asteroid discovered, on the first day of the 19th century, hence its designation (1) Ceres. (2) Pallas, (3) Juno, and (4) Vesta were discovered in the following few years. For most of the century Vesta was thought to be larger than Ceres because of its brightness; however Ceres is in fact the largest asteroid, almost twice the diameter of third-place Vesta.

For a listing of the orbital elements of selected asteroids see p. 21.

EPHEMERIDES FOR THE BRIGHTEST ASTEROIDS IN 2003
By Brian Marsden

(1) Ceres

Date 0h ET	RA (2000) h m	Dec ° '	Mag.
Oct. 18	7 32.3	+23 32	8.5
28	7 40.9	+23 49	8.3
Nov. 7	7 47.3	+24 13	8.2
17	7 51.3	+24 47	8.0
27	7 52.6	+25 33	7.8
Dec. 7	7 50.9	+26 29	7.5
17	7 46.2	+27 33	7.3
27	7 38.7	+28 41	7.1

(2) Pallas

Date 0h ET	RA (2000) h m	Dec ° '	Mag.
Jul. 20	1 47.3	+1 44	9.7
30	1 55.3	+0 42	9.5
Aug. 9	2 01.7	−0 40	9.4
19	2 06.6	−2 25	9.2
29	2 09.4	−4 32	9.0
Sep. 8	2 10.1	−7 01	8.8
18	2 08.4	−9 46	8.6
28	2 04.4	−12 42	8.4
Oct. 8	1 58.4	−15 35	8.3
18	1 51.0	−18 15	8.2
28	1 43.0	−20 28	8.3
Nov. 7	1 35.4	−22 08	8.4
17	1 29.1	−23 11	8.6
27	1 25.0	−23 38	8.7
Dec. 7	1 23.2	−23 33	8.8
17	1 24.0	−23 02	9.0
27	1 27.4	−22 11	9.1

(4) Vesta

Date 0h ET	RA (2000) h m	Dec ° '	Mag.
Jan. 1	12 34.6	+3 43	7.6
11	12 44.4	+3 23	7.4
21	12 52.4	+3 19	7.2
31	12 58.2	+3 33	7.0
Feb. 10	13 01.4	+4 05	6.8
20	13 01.7	+4 56	6.6
Mar. 2	12 59.1	+6 02	6.3
12	12 53.6	+7 18	6.1
22	12 45.8	+8 36	5.9
Apr. 1	12 36.8	+9 45	5.9
11	12 27.8	+10 35	6.0
21	12 20.1	+11 01	6.2
May 1	12 14.6	+11 00	6.4
11	12 11.9	+10 34	6.6
21	12 12.1	+9 45	6.8
31	12 15.1	+8 39	6.9
Jun. 10	12 20.7	+7 18	7.1
20	12 28.4	+5 45	7.2

(6) Hebe

Date 0h ET	RA (2000) h m	Dec ° '	Mag.
Oct. 28	7 46.2	+7 29	9.8
Nov. 7	7 53.4	+6 56	9.7
17	7 57.9	+6 32	9.5
27	7 59.3	+6 23	9.4
Dec. 7	7 57.4	+6 33	9.2
17	7 52.4	+7 03	9.0
27	7 44.5	+7 56	8.8

(8) Flora

Date 0h ET	RA (2000) h m	Dec ° '	Mag.
May 21	18 23.4	−18 41	10.0
31	18 16.8	−18 53	9.7
Jun. 10	18 07.6	−19 10	9.5
20	17 56.7	−19 32	9.2
30	17 45.3	−19 56	9.4
Jul. 10	17 35.0	−20 21	9.6
20	17 26.8	−20 48	9.8
30	17 21.6	−21 16	10.0

(9) Metis

Date 0h ET	RA (2000) h m	Dec ° '	Mag.
May 11	16 05.4	−19 07	9.9
21	15 55.2	−18 56	9.6
31	15 44.8	−18 45	9.9

(12) Victoria

Date 0h ET	RA (2000) h m	Dec ° '	Mag.
May 1	17 34.7	−21 14	10.0
11	17 34.2	−20 06	9.7
21	17 30.2	−18 48	9.4
31	17 23.2	−17 24	9.0
Jun. 10	17 14.3	−16 00	8.8
20	17 05.1	−14 41	8.9
30	16 57.1	−13 37	9.1
Jul. 10	16 51.9	−12 50	9.4
20	16 50.2	−12 25	9.6
30	16 52.2	−12 17	9.8
Aug. 9	16 57.9	−12 25	10.0

(14) Irene

Date 0h ET	RA (2000) h m	Dec ° '	Mag.
Dec. 7	5 19.2	+20 59	9.7
17	5 08.3	+21 21	9.7
27	4 57.8	+21 43	10.0

(15) Eunomia

Date 0h ET	RA (2000) h m	Dec ° '	Mag.
Dec. 7	9 59.5	+8 33	10.0
17	10 01.4	+7 32	9.9
27	10 00.5	+6 43	9.7

(20) Massalia

Date 0h ET	RA (2000) h m	Dec ° '	Mag.
Jan. 1	4 46.9	+21 17	9.0
11	4 41.8	+21 09	9.3
21	4 40.4	+21 08	9.5
31	4 42.8	+21 15	9.8
Feb. 10	4 48.7	+21 29	10.0

(29) Amphitrite

Date 0h ET	RA (2000) h m	Dec ° '	Mag.
Sep. 28	4 40.1	+28 37	10.0
Oct. 8	4 43.8	+29 23	9.9
18	4 44.4	+30 04	9.7
28	4 41.5	+30 39	9.4
Nov. 7	4 35.1	+31 04	9.2
17	4 25.9	+31 15	9.0
27	4 14.9	+31 10	8.8
Dec. 7	4 03.9	+30 49	8.9
17	3 54.3	+30 17	9.1
27	3 47.4	+29 39	9.4

(40) Harmonia

Date 0h ET	RA (2000) h m	Dec ° '	Mag.
May 1	14 52.1	−10 20	9.8
11	14 41.9	−9 48	9.9

(511) Davida

Date 0h ET	RA (2000) h m	Dec ° '	Mag.
Jan. 1	6 47.9	+19 48	9.5
11	6 38.9	+21 06	9.7
21	6 30.9	+22 21	10.0

PLANETARY APPULSES AND OCCULTATIONS
By David W. Dunham and James Stamm

As planets, satellites, asteroids, and comets move across the sky, they occasionally pass near an observer's line of sight to a distant star. Such close passes are called *appulses*. More rarely, the moving object's trajectory will carry it directly between the observer and the star, thereby producing an *occultation*. Astronomers have learned much about various solar system bodies by carefully monitoring the changing apparent brightness of stars during the immersion and emersion phases of occultations. If the occulting body does not have an atmosphere, the occultation is virtually instantaneous; if there is an atmosphere, it causes the star's disappearance and reappearance to occur gradually. If a planet has rings or other debris in its environs, the extent and degree of transparency of this material can be precisely mapped. The rings of Uranus, the ring arcs of Neptune, and the atmosphere of Pluto were all discovered by occultation observations. In addition, if an occultation is observed at several appropriately distributed sites, it is often possible to determine the size and shape of the occulting body more accurately than by other Earth-based techniques.

Amateur astronomers can sometimes make important contributions to occultation observing campaigns. This is particularly true for asteroid occultations, for which the event path across Earth is often very narrow and uncertain in location (due to uncertainties in both the star's position and the ephemeris of the asteroid). By recording the times of the star's disappearance and reappearance as seen from several sites (i.e. by noting the edges of the asteroid's shadow as it sweeps across Earth), the asteroid's profile can be directly determined. Often timings of adequate accuracy can be made by visual observers using modest telescopes.

When observing an occultation, it is important that an observer know his or her location to within a fraction of a kilometre. Geographic longitude and latitude as well as the altitude of an observing site can be determined from a high-quality topographic map or from some map websites. If observations are to be of maximum value, the times of immersion and emersion must be determined as accurately as possible—certainly to better than 0.5 s, and better than 0.2 s for the shortest events (those less than about 10 s in duration). **Photoelectric equipment** with high-speed digital recording systems is well suited for this work. Attaching a low-light-level **video camera** to a telescope is another good method for accurately timing these events. **Visual observers** equipped with tape recorders and shortwave time-signal receivers can also make useful contributions. Even simple measurements of the duration of an occultation made with an ordinary stopwatch can be of value. **CCD observers** should be aware that most of these systems are incapable of timing accuracies better than about 2 s; hence visual observation may be better. A trick that some CCD observers have used is to turn off the telescope clock drive shortly before the predicted time and let the images trail. The occultation will appear as a break in the trail that can be measured to a few tenths of a second if the moment the drive is turned off is accurately timed.

Occultation observations are coordinated in North America by the International Occultation Timing Association (IOTA). IOTA member or not, IOTA wants to inform you and others in your area able to locate stars to 11th magnitude of last-minute prediction updates. Please email the longitude and latitude (or location from the nearest town) of convenient observing sites, telescope size(s), and an indication of whether you are mobile to dunham@erols.com. Within a few days of each event, improved predictions may be obtained from recorded telephone messages at (301) 474-4945 (Greenbelt, MD) or from the asteroidal occultation section of IOTA's website: www.lunar-occultations.com/iota. Individuals interested in joining IOTA should refer to p. 158 in the section OCCULTATIONS BY THE MOON in this Handbook for membership information.

More information is in the *Solar System Photometry Handbook* (Willmann-Bell, Inc., 1983), *Sky & Telescope* (usually the February issue), and occasional papers in the *Astronomical Journal, Icarus,* and other scientific journals.

Observations of asteroidal and planetary occultations, *including* negative observations, should be sent to Jan Manek, Stefanik Observatory, Petrin 205, 118 46 Praha (Prague) 1, Czech Republic (email: jmanek@mbox.vol.cz) for publication by IOTA. When reporting timings, describe your geographic longitude, latitude, and altitude (to the nearest second of arc and 30 m, respectively), telescope size, timing method, the start and end time of observation, an estimate of the observer's reaction time (if applicable) and the accuracy of the timing, and whether the reaction time correction has been applied.

The following two-page table of predictions of asteroidal and planetary occultations visible from North America for 2003 is based on predictions by Edwin Goffin in Belgium.

The successive columns in the table list: (1) the date and time of the event; (2) the name of the occulting body; (3) the apparent magnitude of the asteroid or planet; (4) the catalogue number of the occulted star; (5) the apparent visual magnitude of the star; (6) the right ascension and (7) declination of the star; (8) the expected magnitude change from the combined brightness; (9) the predicted maximum duration of the occultation in seconds; and (10) the approximate region from which the occultation is predicted to be visible. Due to uncertainties in the catalogue positions of the stars and the ephemerides of the asteroids from which these predictions are derived, the exact region of visibility of an occultation cannot be derived until CCD observations link the star and asteroid to the new HIPPARCOS reference frame, usually about a week prior to the event.

For North American observers, finder charts and further details on these and other occultations can be found in the *2003 Planetary Occultation Supplement to Occultation Newsletter* available from IOTA. (See p. 158 in this Handbook for information on IOTA and on the Royal Astronomical Society of New Zealand. The latter organization provides information on occultations visible from the southwestern Pacific region.)

Notes regarding some of the events in the table:

(1) Jan. 21: Venus's 22″ disk will be 55% sunlit, with the star's reappearance visible on the dark side. The star is double, with 9.1- and 9.8-mag. components separated by 0.6″; the secondary will reappear, then the primary about 16 s later.

(2) Mar. 21: The star's 10.8-mag. companion, 73″ away in PA 270°, will be occulted about 10.7 h later in the Eastern Hemisphere.

(3) Mar. 29: Chiron is the largest Centaur object, actually a large comet.

(4) Jun. 8: The asteroid's full name is Klytaemnestra. The star's 14.5-mag. companion, 2.6″ away in PA 160°, will be occulted about 0.6 min earlier along a path about five path widths north of that for the primary, but the companion's occultation will be very difficult, since the asteroid will be one magnitude brighter.

(5) Jul. 7: The star's 9.3-mag. companion 18″ away in PA 16° will not be occulted.

(6) Sep. 13: The star's 10.7-mag. companion, 11″ away in PA 61°, will be occulted in central Argentina 23 s later.

(7) Sep. 25: The star is HIP 39424 = SAO 79896, with spectral type K0 and diameter 2 mas, requiring 0.2 s to cover for a central event.

IOTA SELECTED LIST OF NORTH AMERICAN OCCULTATIONS BY SOLAR SYSTEM OBJECTS FOR THE YEAR 2003

Date	UT	Occulting Body	(Mag.)	Star	RA (2000) h m s	Dec ° ' "	ΔMag.	Dur. s	Nominal Path
Jan. 1	3:11	233 Asterope	12.1	TYC 0726-00419	5 38 56.52	+14 28 20.2	1.9	10	Cuba to southern Mexico
2	4:36	44 Nysa	10.1	SAO 93324	3 10 58.45	+12 36 53.0	0.9	34	Western Mexico to Hudson Bay
11	3:46	441 Bathilde	12.5	SAO 117679	9 25 22.50	+4 17 8.2	4.8	9	Nova Scotia to southern California
15	4:12	95 Arethusa	12.0	TYC 0191-00774	7 39 58.71	+5 46 47.0	1.5	11	Northern Florida to central Baja California
21	11:08	Venus	−4.4	SAO 160149	16 53 54.55	−19 18 51.0	0.0	495	E North America and Central America
22	2:26	95 Arethusa	12.1	TYC 0190-01917	7 33 58.62	+5 48 53.6	1.0	12	Washington, DC to central California
24	22:19	511 Davida	10.1	TYC 1879-01831	6 28 13.63	+22 48 34.9	0.6	35	Newfoundland to southern Quebec
29	1:56	203 Pompeja	13.2	TYC 1885-01254	6 9 11.42	+27 37 29.2	1.7	19	Labrador to southern California
Feb. 8	6:37	275 Sapientia	11.8	TAC +17° 3131	8 57 26.06	+17 18 2.9	1.5	11	Virginia to southern Alaska
21	7:39	404 Arsinoë	12.0	TYC 1984-01884	11 42 12.09	+26 46 7.7	1.3	11	Western Mexico to southern California
Mar. 1	11:08	36 Atalante	13.3	TYC 4944-00158	12 25 34.42	−3 0 15.1	3.1	8	New England to northern California
5	3:26	602 Marianna	13.6	TYC 2430-01038	6 32 17.67	+34 29 53.3	3.0	14	Alabama to western Ontario
17	3:09	117 Lomia	12.7	TYC 1416-00054	9 40 40.82	+20 37 39.2	2.5	15	Newfoundland to N Baja California Norte
21	7:22	Jupiter	−2.4	SAO 98075	8 43 56.13	+19 2 3.2	0.0	23K	All of North and Central America
29	11:38	2060 Chiron	17.2	TYC 6296-00177	19 12 43.89	−15 44 47.1	6.2	14	Southern California to Minnesota
Apr. 8	7:56	173 Ino	12.8	TYC 0329-00371	14 43 27.04	+25 7 23.9	1.7	11	North Carolina to northern Alaska
24	1:02	51 Nemausa	12.3	TYC 1330-00949	6 44 31.83	+15 50 8.5	1.1	5	Southern Ontario to Nova Scotia
24	3:24	403 Cyane	12.8	SAO 157804	13 14 3.69	−17 25 36.5	3.2	5	Louisiana to Idaho
28	4:13	1051 Merope	16.1	SAO 117258	8 54 54.71	+3 54 42.9	6.6	5	Central California to New Brunswick
30	3:38	211 Isolda	13.1	TYC 0256-01454	10 35 24.86	+3 36 45.6	3.4	55	Guatemala to West Indies
30	7:34	92 Undina	11.4	TAC −02° 8673	14 46 48.33	−2 59 10.1	0.7	10	South Carolina to Oregon
May 4	11:16	503 Evelyn	13.8	TYC 6230-01594	16 54 40.05	−22 2 34.5	4.6	8	Kansas to southern California
8	11:21	777 Gutemberga	15.8	SAO 164164	21 8 15.47	−12 52 50.8	7.7	5	Western Mexico to southern Texas
16	2:31	74 Galatea	14.7	SAO 98128	8 47 39.44	+14 47 25.0	5.2	6	New Mexico to southern Florida
Jun. 8	7:20	179 Klytaemnestra	13.4	SAO 157983	13 31 40.71	−15 16 40.3	4.6	15	Central California to Alberta
18	8:21	85 Io	11.2	TYC 0530-01006	21 4 12.90	+2 26 29.6	0.7	32	Southern Mexico to western Hudson Bay
26	4:40	976 Benjamina	13.6	SAO 181454	18 25 15.49	+17 31 7.1	4.1	7	North Carolina to Oregon
Jul. 7	2:06	469 Argentina	13.6	SAO 182362	14 14 30.84	−29 14 21.2	5.0	18	Southern Mexico to Newfoundland
13	2:48	747 Winchester	13.7	TAC −02° 9343	16 24 34.15	−2 40 33.7	2.4	15	Newfoundland to western Mexico
24	6:24	336 Lacadiera	12.3	TYC 6264-00511	18 14 5.24	−15 7 44.8	1.1	15	New York to central California
29	6:54	654 Zelinda	12.6	TYC 6285-03426	18 48 47.40	−17 8 51.3	1.4	11	Virginia to Oregon

IOTA SELECTED LIST OF NORTH AMERICAN OCCULTATIONS BY SOLAR SYSTEM OBJECTS FOR THE YEAR 2003 (continued)

Date	UT	Occulting Body	(Mag.)	Star	(Mag.)	RA (2000) h m s	Dec ° ′ ″	ΔMag.	Dur. s	Nominal Path
Aug. 20	6:49	105 Artemis	11.6	TYC 1128-01774	10.4	21 41 26.31	+12 14 53.9	1.5	11	N Quebec to central Baja California
25	11:25	136 Austria	12.6	SAO 109060	9.6	0 11 55.83	+6 34 41.5	3.1	8	New York to S Baja California Sur
Sep. 3	4:38	505 Cava	14.3	TYC 6850-00368	10.0	18 7 43.55	−27 12 2.1	4.3	20	Washington to West Virginia
7	0:55	63 Ausonia	10.2	PPM 709674	10.4	23 28 11.61	−1 21 46.2	0.7	11	Newfoundland to southern Ontario
13	8:37	521 Brixia	12.9	SAO 95084	8.0	5 59 24.51	+17 48 52.8	4.9	4	Honduras to West Indies
22	0:12	21 Lutetia	12.3	SAO 159469	9.1	15 44 12.89	−19 47 14.2	3.3	3	Southern Ontario to New England
23	1:20	84 Klio	11.2	TYC 5222-00381	10.3	21 52 0.88	−6 49 14.3	1.3	25	Eastern Virginia to Wisconsin
25	5:24	94 Aurora	13.4	χ Geminorum	5.1	8 3 31.07	+27 47 39.6	8.3	7	Quebec, Labrador, SE Greenland
Oct. 9	2:59	1354 Botha	15.4	SAO 109453	9.0	0 46 46.29	+2 21 24.4	6.4	4	N Florida to southern Baja California Sur
10	13:41	756 Liliana	15.3	SAO 93448	6.9	3 28 36.35	11 23 25.6	8.4	6	NW Australia, Papua New Guinea, Yukon
17	2:43	1177 Gonnessia	14.2	TYC 1739-00870	10.7	0 50 35.23	+23 34 31.8	3.6	7	Nunavut to central California
24	2:21	978 Aidamina	14.0	SAO 126952	8.3	21 38 24.63	+8 35 4.6	5.7	6	Washington to western Central America
Nov. 3	9:31	130 Elektra	11.0	TYC 5883-00961	11.1	4 11 4.46	−15 24 26.7	0.7	20	Southern Florida to Yucatan
4	7:38	1191 Alfaterna	15.5	TYC 0114-01937	9.8	5 35 23.45	+0 14 21.3	5.7	6	Newfoundland to western Mexico
5	7:06	72 Feronia	14.1	SAO 117986	8.4	9 54 53.30	+7 10 18.4	5.8	4	Indiana to Virginia
15	8:48	Saturn	0.5	SAO 78867	8.6	6 55 20.97	+22 6 7.9	0.0	13K	All of North and Central America
16	10:04	200 Dynamene	13.8	TYC 0268-00843	10.9	11 5 27.92	+5 44 56.3	2.9	5	Southern California to Georgia
16	13:22	185 Eunike	11.6	TYC 5343-00009	9.7	5 17 2.30	−13 9 39.3	2.0	17	Utah to Hawaii
25	13:13	Saturn	0.5	SAO 78832	8.3	6 53 21.64	+22 8 59.4	0.0	9K	Western North America
Dec. 2	2:50	102 Miriam	12.6	TYC 1303-01486	11.4	5 51 31.38	+16 54 56.0	1.5	8	Newfoundland to southern California
18	0:19	104 Klymene	11.8	TYC 1872-00207	11.4	6 1 53.76	+26 38 26.8	1.0	12	Newfoundland to Texas
24	9:03	34 Circe	11.9	TYC 0759-00636	11.8	6 49 36.31	+13 57 7.8	0.8	11	Central Florida to N Baja California Norte
31	6:56	208 Lacrimosa	13.4	SAO 98314	9.0	9 3 4.89	+19 10 15.8	4.4	6	Northern Florida to southern California

METEORS, COMETS, AND DUST

METEORS

BY ROBERT L. HAWKES

The term *meteor* applies to the streak of light (and related phenomena such as ionization) produced when an interplanetary particle (a *meteoroid*) enters Earth's upper atmosphere and ablates (evaporates). Heights of ablation typically range from 65 to 135 km above Earth's surface (higher-speed meteors ablate at greater heights). Evaporated meteoroid atoms undergo high-speed collisions with atmospheric constituents, and it is the decay of these excited states that produces the meteor luminosity. Most meteoroids are very small; a bright visual meteor is typically produced by a grain smaller than a pea. Very bright meteors are termed *fireballs* (see FIREBALLS, p. 225). If a solid object reaches the ground, it is termed a *meteorite*.

The meteoroid complex can be conveniently divided into two parts: a *stream* component, made up of particles in highly correlated orbits, and a more or less random *sporadic* component. About 5 to 10 sporadic meteors per hour are visible (by a single observer with dark-adapted eyes) from a dark-sky location on any given night. When Earth's orbit intersects a meteor stream, an enhancement of the meteor rate—a meteor *shower*—is observed. Perspective causes the parallel paths of shower meteors to appear to radiate from a point when plotted on a star map. The constellation in which this point of divergence, or *radiant,* seems to lie is used in naming the shower. When two or more showers have radiants in the same constellation, a nearby bright star is used in the designation (e.g. the η-Aquarids). The radiant of the Quadrantid shower, named after the obsolete constellation Quadrans Muralis, is in Boötes.

The sporadic meteor component is derived from the stream component by dispersion due to collisions with smaller meteoroids, radiative effects, and differential gravitational perturbations on particles ejected from the parent comet with different relative velocities. The division between shower and sporadic meteors is not precise, and there continues to be debate regarding the validity of some minor meteor showers. A detailed list of showers, including some minor ones, is available in the meteor shower calendar published by the International Meteor Organization (IMO) (see **www.imo.net**).

The activity of a meteor shower is usually specified by the *zenithal hourly rate* (ZHR). The ZHR is the number of meteors a single perfect observer would see per hour from a shower with a radiant directly overhead in a dark-sky location under exceptional conditions and with complete dark adaptation, where +6.5 magnitude stars are visible. Even from dark-sky locations an observer will observe fainter meteors effectively over a much smaller field of view. Thus the ZHR figures are *not* expected visual meteor rates, which will always be significantly less than the ZHR (as a general rule of thumb, a typical single observer might see hourly rates of one-third the ZHR). They do, however, provide a widely accepted standardized method to report meteor rates.

In a number of cases orbital similarity permits a link between a meteor shower and a parent object. For example, the η-Aquarids and Orionids are derived from P/Comet Halley, the Leonids from P/Comet Tempel-Tuttle, the Perseids from P/Comet Swift-Tuttle, and the Taurid complex from P/Comet Encke.

Dedicated amateur meteor astronomers contribute the most visual observations. It is critical to choose a dark-sky location free from obstructions and to allow at least 20 min for dark adaptation. In general, one should not observe near the horizon (at least 40° elevation) and should look roughly 40° away from the radiant of the shower. Carefully estimate your limiting magnitude to the nearest tenth of a magnitude (see the LIMITING

MAGNITUDES section on pp. 58–59), and record it, the UT of the observing session, and observing direction (centre of field of view). The simplest observation method involves making an instantaneous decision regarding whether each meteor belongs to a shower (from the radiant and apparent speed). The shower association, brightness, and time for each meteor can be recorded orally on a tape recorder for uninterrupted observing periods. Visual observations of this type (after application of correction factors) are valuable for determining rate profiles and population indices of showers. Extensive information on observing meteors by visual and other methods is available from the IMO, the North American Meteor Network (www.namnmeteors.org), and the American Meteor Society (www.amsmeteors.org). These organizations also collect and analyze visual observations from amateurs.

Telescopic observations of meteors (usually employing binoculars) allow the plotting of trails with more precision and emphasize those showers rich in faint meteors. Photographic observations can be made with normal or wide-angle lenses, typically using exposures of 5 to 30 min. A rotating shutter permits determination of apparent angular velocity. Increasingly, amateurs are using video equipment for meteor observations. A standard home camcorder is limited to about magnitude +2 and will lead to very low rates, but image intensifiers coupled to video cameras make powerful meteor-observing systems. One can simply use the macro lens of the camcorder to form an image of the output phosphor of the image intensifier. This method (when used with a fast objective lens of focal length 50 mm) extends the sensitivity to magnitude +9, with sporadic meteor rates of typically 15/hour over a field of view of approximately 25°. Intermediate sensitivity can be achieved using specialized unintensified, low-light-level monochrome CCD cameras. Software exists that can automatically detect meteors from video records and log shower associations (MetRec, see www.imo.net; and MeteorScan, contact Peter.S.Gural@saic.com). Any of these techniques can be extended to simultaneous observations from two stations, and triangulation will yield the precise trajectory and orbital information. Baselines of 20 to 150 km are appropriate, with intersection heights at about 90 km.

Addition of a diffraction grating in front of the objective lens can be used to make meteor spectra with photographic or video observation techniques. Typically gratings with 200 to 800 lines per millimetre are used for this work. The dominant spectral lines are due to atomic emission lines from meteoric constituents (as well as oxygen and nitrogen from the atmosphere). The following elements have been identified in meteor spectra: Al, Ca, Co, Cr, Fe, H, Li, Mg, Mn, N, Na, Ni, O, Si, Sr, and Ti. A few molecules have also been identified, including AlO, CaO, CN, FeO, MgO, and N_2. In high-velocity meteors the forbidden oxygen line at 557.7 nm is a prominent feature, typically persisting for one second after the passage of the meteor.

Recently, brief optical flashes due to impacts on the darkened limb of the Moon have been obtained during major meteor showers. Typically these flashes last for less than 1/15 s. To view such flashes, one couples a video-rate (30 frames per second) CCD camera to a telescope typically in the 200- to 300-mm size. Two coincident systems are needed to confirm potential events. The physical mechanism of light production during these impacts is not well understood.

Serendipitous recording of meteor trails at high spatial resolution on photographic or CCD images through telescopes can be of great value in helping to better define the mode of fragmentation and ablation of meteors (which continues to be only poorly understood). If you obtain such images, please contact the author at rhawkes@mta.ca.

In addition to the above web resources, other resources are the *Handbook for Visual Meteor Observers,* available from the International Meteor Organization, and Neil Bone's book *Meteors* (Sky Publishing, 1993), which provides an excellent introduction to visual, telescopic, and photographic observation. And for those looking for information at a more advanced level, see the recent publication *Meteors in the Earth's Atmosphere,* E. Murad and I.P. Williams, eds., Cambridge University Press, 2002.

TABLE OF METEOR SHOWERS, 2003

The more prominent nighttime showers visible from the Northern Hemisphere are included in the following table, with the most visually impressive ones given in **bold** type. Explanations of the entries are given following the table.

Shower	Max (UT)			λ (2000)	D (d)	ZHR	R	Moon (%)	r	RA h m	Dec (°)	v (km/s)
Quadrantid	Jan.	4	0h	283.16	0.8	90	✓	2	2.1	15 30	+50	41
Lyrid	Apr.	22	17h	32.1	6	15	✓	59	2.9	18 08	+34	48
η–Aquarid	May	5	23h	45.0	8	40	>03	17	2.7	22 27	–01	65
S δ–Aquarid	Jul.	29	6h	125.7	12	20	>23	0	3.2	22 38	–16	41
Perseid	Aug.	13	5h	140.0	5	100	✓	99	2.4	3 06	+58	60
Draconid	Oct.	9	4h	195.4	1	10	✓	99	2.6	17 28	+54	20
Orionid	Oct.	22	9h	208.5	8	25	>23	13	2.8	6 22	+16	66
S Taurid	Nov.	4	22h	222	30	10	✓	85	2.3	3 28	+13	28
N Taurid	Nov.	13	20h	231	30	15	✓	81	2.3	3 55	+22	29
Leonid	Nov.	18	3h	235.3	2	15	>00	41	2.5	10 18	+22	71
Geminid	Dec.	14	4h	262.1	3	95	✓	72	2.6	7 30	+33	35
Ursid	Dec.	23	0h	270.7	2	20	✓	0	3.0	14 28	+75	34

The column labelled **Max** lists the date and hour (Universal Time) of the 2003 intersection of Earth with the densest region of the stream. These maxima are based on the solar longitude values (λ) for each shower given in the third column (epoch 2000). Many streams have a complex rate profile; for example, the η-Aquarid and Orionid showers have earlier peaks for faint meteors than for bright meteors. Most showers show activity over a number of days, and the next column, *D,* gives the number of days on each side of the maximum that show significant meteor activity from that shower. Some showers (e.g. the Quadrantids) are highly concentrated with strong displays lasting only a few hours, while others are spread over weeks (e.g. the Taurid complex). Concentrated showers are more likely to be of recent formation. There are no records of the Quadrantid shower before the 19th century, while several showers have been observed for hundreds or thousands of years (e.g. the Perseids). Some showers (such as the recent Leonid displays) have meteoroids concentrated in a small region of the orbit and hence have much higher peak rates in certain years.

The column labelled **ZHR** gives the predicted zenithal hourly rate.

The higher the radiant is in the sky, the more direct the projection of the stream cross section on the sky area above the observer and the higher the apparent activity. The *R* column indicates when the radiant is above the horizon for an observer at 43°N latitude; for example, >23 means that the shower can be observed after 11 p.m. local time. A ✓ means that the radiant is above the horizon throughout night hours. The number of meteors observed varies strongly with limiting magnitude; therefore, effective meteor observations must be made in the absence of significant moonlight. In the **Moon** column the percentage of illumination of the Moon at the date of shower maximum is given. The rise and set times of the Moon must also be taken into account, however.

The relative number of bright and faint meteors is given by the *population index, r,* which is defined as the ratio of the cumulative number of meteors brighter than magnitude $M + 1$ to the cumulative number brighter than magnitude M. The number of meteors observed is a strong function of limiting sensitivity. For example, for a limiting magnitude of +3.5, a shower with a ZHR of 60 and a population index $r = 2.8$ would have the number of observable meteors per hour reduced to less than three meteors per hour.

The next two columns give the right ascension (**RA**) and declination (**Dec**) of the shower radiant. A typical shower is active over several days, and the apparent radiant moves somewhat during this period. The tables published by the IMO (www.imo.net) give the daily motion of the radiant, which must be taken into account if one is observing meteor showers on dates significantly removed from the maximum of the shower. Meteors can only be observed when the radiant is above the local horizon (or nearly so). Finally, the geocentric speed *v* of the meteors in each shower is given in kilometres per second.

RADIO DETECTION OF METEORS
BY PHILIP GEBHARDT

The term *meteor* applies not only to the streak of light produced by a meteoroid, but also to the column of ionized atoms and molecules along the path behind the meteoroid. These meteor trails are capable of scattering radio signals from terrestrial stations. Unlike visual observation, radio detection of sporadic meteors or shower meteors can be undertaken in daylight and during inclement weather. Similarly, a night sky illuminated by the full Moon has no adverse effect on radio detection. Radio detection rates tend to be higher than visual observation rates because particles down to 10^{-5} kg can be detected visually, while particles down to 10^{-10} kg can be detected by radio. Assuming a density of 1 t/m^3, these mass limits correspond to diameters of about 3 mm and 0.06 mm, respectively.

Two types of meteor trails exist, *underdense* and *overdense;* they are determined by the density of free electrons. Reradiated signals from underdense trails (fewer than 2×10^{14} electrons per metre) rise above the receiver noise almost instantaneously and then decay exponentially. The duration of many meteor bursts is about a second or less. Reflected signals from overdense trails may have higher amplitude and longer duration, but destructive interference due to reflection from different parts of the trail can produce fluctuations in the signal. Note that other means of signal propagation may be heard on the FM band, but only meteor signals have their characteristic fast rise-time and short duration.

Data for selected meteor showers appear in the table on the previous page. These data are for visual observations and should be considered as guidelines only for radio purposes. The sporadic meteor rate (visual and radio) peaks about 6 a.m. local time (i.e. on the advancing side of Earth in its orbit) and is minimum near 6 p.m. The rate will vary from a few per hour for off-peak times for sporadic meteors to several hundred per hour during a very active shower. Frequencies between 20 and 150 MHz are typically used for meteor detection. Both amplitude and duration of meteor bursts are frequency-dependent—they decrease with increasing frequency. At the lower frequencies, however, galactic as well as human-made noise (particularly in urban areas) become limiting factors. Also, as the wavelength becomes comparable to the width of the meteor trail, the echo strength decreases.

The commercial FM broadcast band (88 to 108 MHz) provides the best introductory opportunity for meteor detection. The abundance of over-the-horizon stations transmitting 24 hours a day ensures that a meteor burst can be heard from a suitably positioned meteor regardless of the time of day.

The technique involves listening on a frequency not used by a local FM station. A receiver with a digital frequency readout is therefore an asset. Frequencies throughout North America are assigned at 200-kHz intervals between 88.1 and 107.9 MHz. In the absence of a clear frequency, it is possible to use a frequency occupied by a station with a very weak signal although weak meteor bursts will be masked. Alternatively, a TV set (channels 2 through 6) can be used, provided the set is connected to an antenna rather than through cable TV. For either the FM band or the TV channels, an outdoor antenna is preferable. It is also possible to listen using the FM radio in your car.

Further information can be found on the following websites:

www.odxa.on.ca/meteor.html
www.imo.net/calendar/cal03.html
www.spaceweather.com/glossary/nasameteorradar.html
www.ionosonde.iap-kborn.de/sky_main.htm

Also see *Sky & Telescope, 94,* no. 6 (December 1997), p. 108.

FIREBALLS
By Jeremy Tatum and Damien Lemay

Exceptionally bright meteors that are spectacular enough to attract the attention of the public and light up the countryside over a wide area are generally referred to as fireballs. With camera networks and satellite-based detections now providing statistical information on the entry of fireballs into Earth's atmosphere, the main reasons to collect fireball reports are to assist with meteorite recovery and to provide orbital information for recovered meteorites. Rapid recovery of meteorites is vital for the study of short-lived radioactive isotopes produced by cosmic ray bombardment of the meteorite while in interplanetary space. Small but potentially recoverable meteorites can be produced by fireballs that are no brighter than magnitude −6. A very slow fireball with no indication of terminal breakup is a good candidate for meteorite survival. The presence of delayed sound indicates penetration into the lower atmosphere and probable meteorite fall. The value of a meteorite is significantly greater when we know something of its atmospheric trajectory and orbit. Visual data can, under favourable circumstances, be used to obtain an approximate atmospheric trajectory. The Meteorites and Impacts Advisory Committee, MIAC (Comité consultatif sur les météorites et les impacts, CCMI), of the Canadian Space Agency maintains a website with images and information on fireballs, meteorites, and impact craters at miac.uqac.uquebec.ca/. For information on recent Canadian fireball or meteorite events, check the MIAC/CCMI bulletin board at:

miac.uqac.uquebec.ca/MIAC/wwwboard/wwwboard.html

Also, for a summary of actual observations received by MIAC, see:

hyperion.cc.uregina.ca/~astro/MIAC

The preferred method for submitting fireball reports is to complete an electronic fireball-reporting form at one of the following locations:

Canada (only): miac.uqac.uquebec.ca/MIAC/fireball.htm
United States (AMS): www.amsmeteors.org
Global (IMO): www.imo.net/fireball/report.html
North American Meteor Network (NAMN):
   visual: www.namnmeteors.org/fireball_form.html
   photographic: www.namnmeteors.org/photo_form.html

Reports should include the following information:

(1) The name, telephone number, and address of the observer(s).
(2) The time of occurrence (and uncertainty in this time).
(3) The location of the observer at the time the fireball was seen (preferably in precise longitude and latitude).
(4) The beginning and ending points of the fireball, in terms of either right ascension and declination or azimuth and elevation. If possible, indicate the uncertainty in these angles. Indicate whether the true beginning was observed and whether the ending point was blocked by horizon objects.
(5) A direct apparent magnitude estimate if possible; if not, note whether the fireball was brighter than, approximately equal to, or fainter than the full Moon.
(6) The duration of the fireball and the persistent train (if any).
(7) A qualitative description of the event (colour, flares, fragmentation, and sound). Report the absence as well as the presence of features such as sound and fragmentation. In the case of sound, report the delay between the fireball appearance and the sound.
(8) The existence of any video or photographic records.

Within Canada, you may instead email your report to fireball@mta.ca (MIAC/CCMI); outside Canada use fidac@imo.net.

METEORITE IDENTIFICATION
By Richard K. Herd

Meteorites are rocks that have fallen to Earth from space. Some have lain on Earth for many thousands of years; others are recent arrivals. Those observed to traverse Earth's atmosphere, and recovered based on those observations, are called meteorite *falls*. Those with no record of arrival are meteorite *finds* when recognized. Meteorites are named for where they are found. Over 25 000 meteorites are known worldwide: 18 000 are from Antarctica and a few thousand from deserts in Africa and Asia. The best and most up-to-date reference on meteorites is *The Cambridge Encyclopedia of Meteorites* by O. Richard Norton, Cambridge University Press, 2002.

Often there is confusion over when and where meteorites have fallen or have been preserved, and also over what they are and look like. All are significantly different than Earth rocks. Samples sent to experts for identification, even by other scientists, are usually "meteorwrongs"—terrestrial rocks or minerals, human-made slag, metals, alloys, or concrete—that rarely resemble meteorites. Over 60 identified meteorites are known in Canada. There have been three falls since 1994: Tagish Lake, B.C., 2000 January 18; Kitchener, Ontario, 1998 July 12; and St-Robert, Quebec, 1994 June 14.

Meteorites probably begin as streams of fragments *(meteoroids)* that are debris from collisions between larger objects. The calculated orbits of several falls intersect the Asteroid Belt; their ultimate origin in space and time may be elsewhere. About 20 meteorites have come from the Moon. The petrological and isotopic evidence is compelling that a similar number are from Mars, blasted off the surface by impacts. Based on the meteorites' reflectance spectra or density, links have been suggested between other types or groups of meteorites and specific asteroids or asteroid types or comets, but the provenance of most is uncertain. Yet they are an unparalleled source of information about our solar system, from its primitive beginnings to the present. Some preserve extrasolar mineral grains and primordial compounds made in other stars, yielding information about the origin of the universe. In the absence of extensive space exploration, and to prepare for it, they are scientifically invaluable.

Popular ideas about when and where meteorites fall are connected with the observation of *meteors,* the brief streaks of light produced when high-speed, interplanetary particles enter Earth's upper atmosphere. Sporadic meteors and *meteor showers* do not result in meteorites; their fragile cometary debris fragments are reduced to dust high in the atmosphere. Earth collects over 100 tonnes of cosmic dust debris per day. In contrast, stronger, larger space rocks can survive a fiery passage through the atmosphere and result in meteorites. These first appear as bright *fireballs,* are slowed to terminal speeds by atmospheric friction, and cease to show a bright trail long before they reach Earth's surface. Fireballs, which may seem very close, are usually quite high in the atmosphere, 50 km or further from the observer. Even if an extraterrestrial object does reach the surface, it is likely to plunge into the 70% that is water or be lost among forests, jungles, or mountainous regions. In only uncommonly recorded cases have meteorites struck or landed within a few metres of humans (see "Possible Hazards of Meteorite Falls" by C.E. Spratt, *JRASC, 85,* p. 263, October 1991). Rare meteoroids of masses exceeding 100 tonnes are not slowed appreciably by Earth's atmosphere and produce impact craters. The larger impacts may have dramatically altered the history of life on our planet, but they do not result in meteorites—the kinetic energy is sufficiently high to vaporize the impacting body completely and to deform and melt the target area in a fraction of a second. Crater diameters are typically 10 times the diameter of the impacting body. Glassy *tektites* found scattered over several continents may be evidence of such impacts, but they do not have meteorite compositions or characteristics. Information about meteorites, tektites, and impacts is now widely available on the Internet.

Meteorites are divided into three groups that vary widely both in appearance and properties: *stones* or *stony meteorites (aerolites), stony-irons (siderolites),* and *irons* or *iron meteorites (siderites).* All usually contain metallic nickel-iron compounds (with traces of other metals) and are mildly to strongly magnetic. Those that have lain on Earth's surface for long periods may be rusted almost beyond recognition. Some require laboratory tests to confirm their identity. Specimens generally have a quite soft, dull black to brown fusion crust; more prevalent on stones and stony-irons, it may have partially flaked off. Meteorites never contain bubble-like cavities, nor are they ever almost perfectly spherical and smooth. During atmospheric entry, only their surface is affected. Surfaces of irons and stony-irons are dimpled rather than bulbous. They rust easily so there may be no bright metal showing. Stony meteorites do not show protuberances; weathered varieties are rusty, even on broken surfaces. Fresh stony meteorites may have a whitish rock interior, with bright metal specks. Their crusts are black or smoky grey, varying from quite glassy to dull; telltale lines and bubbled patches orient their flight through the air. More metallic samples may also be oriented.

Stones are the most abundant; they resemble some terrestrial rocks but are denser. Most (called *chondrites*) consist of spheres of silicate minerals (called *chondrules)* visible on broken, cut, or polished surfaces and scattered grains of metal. Chondrites are the oldest, most primitive, least altered meteorites. Rare stony meteorites without chondrules are called *achondrites;* these are thought to be melt products from chondrites, samples of younger volcanic planetary surfaces. In August 1996, NASA scientists announced the discovery of fossil and chemical evidence of bacterial life in an ancient achondrite from Mars, but other scientists disagree. This controversy has resulted in renewed interest in missions to Mars and in finding water and life on Mars and elsewhere, even in extreme conditions on Earth. Irons and stony-irons are dense, with up to equal amounts of silicates and iron, and are often irregular in shape. They are thought to be core/mantle material of planets formed by melting chondrites.

Rare *carbonaceous chondrites* are grey to black, some resembling charcoal with silicate inclusions. The dark colour is from iron oxides and sulphides. They contain a few percent carbon in very fine-grained carbonates, carbides, graphite, diamonds, and primitive organic molecules, detectable mainly by isotopic analyses. They may have had biologically significant roles in providing seeds for the origin of life. They probably come from comet nucleii or similar ice-rich asteroids. Their organic molecules originate in interstellar space as coatings on dust. The study of interplanetary or interstellar dust particles has become important in deciphering the origins of meteorites and, therefore, of our solar system and everything in it. We are all composed of recycled stardust.

The Geological Survey of Canada (GSC) maintains the National Meteorite Collection of about 2000 specimens, identifies meteorites, and supports research on them. It also offers to pay the owner a minimum of $500 for the first specimen of any new Canadian meteorite. Should you find a suspected meteorite, you may forward it to **Geological Survey of Canada, Natural Resources Canada, 601 Booth St., Ottawa ON K1A 0E8, Attention: Meteorite Identification** (telephone: (613) 992-4042; fax: (613) 943-1286; email: herd@nrcan.gc.ca). The specimen will be examined and reported on free of charge. If it is too large for mailing, a description of its appearance (or a photograph) and its exact location should be sent. The GSC also makes available a free brochure on meteorites, with pictures of meteorites and comparative nonmeteorites. Write to the GSC's Publication Office at the above address. Meteorites of Canadian origin are subject to the provisions of the Cultural Property Export and Import Act and may not be exported from Canada without a permit.

METEORITE IMPACT CRATERS OF NORTH AMERICA
By Richard A.F. Grieve

The first recognition of meteorite impact craters on Earth, and the basis of their scientific investigation, was in North America. Daniel Barringer, an American engineer and entrepreneur, first argued in 1905 that an approximately 1-km-diameter hole in the Arizona desert was the result of the impact of a large iron meteorite. Barringer had hoped to exploit the several million tonnes of iron meteorite that he believed lay buried beneath the crater floor. Unfortunately, virtually all of the impacting body had been destroyed as a consequence of the extreme pressures and temperatures generated by the impact. Barringer's ideas were controversial, and it was not until 1960, when Ed Chao and Gene Shoemaker discovered coesite, the high-pressure form of the mineral quartz, that what is now known as Barringer or Meteor Crater (#3 in the accompanying table and map) was unequivocally proven to be of impact origin. It was 30 years after Barringer's proposal for an impact origin for Meteor Crater that American scientists John Boon and Claude Albritton Jr. suggested that several other puzzling, generally circular features in the American midwest were, in fact, further evidence of meteorite impact on Earth. These structures—Decatureville, Flynn Creek, Jeptha Knob, Kentland, Serpent Mound, Sierra Madera, Upheaval Dome, Wells Creek—had been postulated earlier as being due to explosive volcanism. The lack of a crater rim and meteorite fragments at any of these sites led to the realization that these were no longer prerequisite evidence for defining an ancient meteorite impact crater.

As in the United States, crater investigations in Canada stemmed from an interest in their economic potential. Discovery of the New Quebec Crater in the 1940s on military air photographs prompted Fred Chubb, a prospector, to seek support for a visit to this remote, circular landmark. He hoped to confirm that it was a large kimberlite "pipe," similar to the diamond-bearing ones of South Africa. Vic Meen of the Royal Ontario Museum led two expeditions to the site in 1950 and 1951 and concluded, based on its morphology and lack of volcanic evidence, that meteorite impact was the most likely cause of the crater. On the strength of Meen's discovery, Carlyle Beals, the Dominion Astronomer for Canada, instituted a crater research program at the Dominion Observatory, which included a systematic search of aerial photographs and led to confirmation of the Holleford crater. As the Observatory program became known, others reported unusual, circular topographic features in Canada (e.g. Brent, Clearwater).

Research programs at government laboratories and universities in Canada, the United States, Germany, Austria, South Africa, and Russia, in particular, have confirmed over 160 impact sites on Earth. Only about 10% retain meteorite fragments. In craters larger than approximately 1 km in diameter, the extreme shock pressures and temperatures vaporize and melt the impacting body. The bulk of these impact sites are identified by characteristic deformation features in the target rocks, features uniquely produced in nature only by hypervelocity impact and known as shock metamorphic features.

Approximately five meteorite craters are added to the world list each year. In 2002, three new structures were identified in North America, all in the United States: Cloud Creek, Wyoming; Rock Elm, Wisconsin; and Wetumpka, Alabama. Many of the recent additions have been identified through the discovery of shock features, which in turn led to recognition of a degraded and sometimes partially buried circular structure. In a few cases, such as Beaverhead, where shatter cones are simply found within an intensely disturbed oval zone, no circular morphologic feature is yet apparent. In the following table, therefore, values for crater diameter may represent a defined outer margin, whether an upraised rim or a peripheral fault, or the diameter may be a reconstruction from geologic and geophysical data with no obvious, morphological counterpart.

For crater images and more information, visit unb.ca/passc/ImpactDatabase.

TABLE OF METEORITE IMPACT CRATERS OF NORTH AMERICA

#	Name, Location	Lat. (N)	Long. (W)	Diam. km	Age* Ma	Surface Expression	Visible Geologic Features
1	Ames, Oklahoma, USA	36° 15'	98° 12'	16.	470. (30)	buried 3 km	none
2	Avak, Alaska, USA	71 15	156 38	12.	100. (5)	buried 30 m	none
3	Barringer (Meteor) Crater, Arizona, USA	35 02	111 01	1.2	0.049 (0.003)	rimmed polygonal crater	fragments of meteorite, highly shocked sandstone
4	Beaverhead, Montana, USA	44 36	113 00	60.	≈600.	oval area of crushed sandstone, and shatter cones	shatter cones
5	Brent, Ontario	46 05	78 29	3.8	450. (30)	sediment-filled shallow depression	fracturing
6	Calvin, Michigan, USA	41 50	85 57	8.5	450. (10)	buried 400 m	none
7	Carswell, Saskatchewan	58 27	109 30	39.	115. (10)	discontinuous circular ridge	shatter cones, breccia, impact melt
8	Charlevoix, Quebec	47 32	70 18	54.	357. (15)	semicircular trough, central peak	breccia, shatter cones, impact melt
9	Chesapeake Bay, Virginia, USA	37 17	76 01	85	35.5 (0.6)	buried 400–500 m, ring structure	none
10	Chicxulub, Mexico	21 20	89 30	180.	64.98 (0.05)	buried 1 km, ring of sink holes	none (related to the K/T mass extinction event)
11	Clearwater East, Quebec	56 05	74 07	26.	290. (20)	circular lake	sedimentary float
12	Clearwater West, Quebec	56 13	74 30	36.	290. (20)	island ring in circular lake	impact melt, breccias
13	Cloud Creek, Wyoming, USA	43 07	106 45	7.	190. (30)	buried 1.1 km	none
14	Couture, Quebec	60 08	75 20	8.	430. (25)	circular lake	breccia float
15	Crooked Creek, Missouri, USA	37 50	91 23	7.	320. (80)	oval area of disturbed rocks, shallow marginal depression	breccia, shatter cones
16	Decaturville, Missouri, USA	37 54	92 43	6.	<300.	slight oval depression	breccia, shatter cones
17	Deep Bay, Saskatchewan	56 24	102 59	13.	100. (50)	circular bay	sedimentary float
18	Des Plaines, Illinois, USA	42 03	87 52	8.	<280.	buried, 15–100 m	none
19	Eagle Butte, Alberta	49 42	110 30	10.	<65.	minor structural disturbance	shatter cones
20	Elbow, Saskatchewan	50 59	106 43	8.	395. (25)	buried, small mound	none
21	Flynn Creek, Tennessee, USA	36 17	85 40	3.8	360. (20)	sediment-filled shallow depression with small central peak	breccia, shatter cones
22	Glasford, Illinois, USA	40 36	89 47	4.	<430.	buried 350 m	none
23	Glover Bluff, Wisconsin, USA	43 58	89 32	8.	<500.	disturbed dolomite exposed	shatter cones
24	Gow, Saskatchewan	56 27	104 29	5.	<250.	lake and central island	breccia, impact melt
25	Haughton, NWT	75 22	89 41	24.	23.4 (1.0)	shallow circular depression	shatter cones, breccia
26	Haviland, Kansas, USA	37 35	99 10	0.015	<0.001	excavated depression	fragments of meteorite
27	Holleford, Ontario	44 28	76 38	2.4	550. (100)	sediment-filled shallow depression	sedimentary fill
28	Ile Rouleau, Quebec	50 41	73 53	4.	<300.	island is central peak of submerged structure	shatter cones, breccia dykes
29	Kentland, Indiana, USA	40 45	87 24	13.	<97.	central peak exposed in quarries, rest buried	breccia, shatter cones, disturbed rocks

* Numbers in parentheses are possible errors.

TABLE OF METEORITE IMPACT CRATERS OF NORTH AMERICA (ct'd)

#	Name, Location	Lat. (N)	Long. (W)	Diam. km	Age* Ma	Surface Expression	Visible Geologic Features
30	La Moinerie, Quebec	57 26	66 37	8.	400. (50)	lake-filled, depression	breccia float
31	Manicouagan, Quebec	51 23	68 42	100.	214. (1)	circumferential lake, central peak	impact melt, breccia
32	Manson, Iowa, USA	42 35	94 33	35.	73.8 (0.3)	none, central elevation buried 30 m	none
33	Maple Creek, Saskatchewan	49 48	109 06	6.	<75.	buried, small mound	disturbed rocks
34	Marquez, Texas, USA	31 17	96 18	12.7	58. (2)	circular area of disturbed rock	shatter cones
35	Middlesboro, Kentucky, USA	36 37	83 44	6.	<300.	circular depression	disturbed rocks
36	Mistastin, Labrador	55 53	63 18	28.	38. (4)	elliptical lake and central island	breccia, impact melt
37	Montagnais, Nova Scotia	42 53	64 13	45.	50.5 (0.8)	none, under water (115 m) and sediment	none
38	New Quebec, Quebec	61 17	73 40	3.4	1.4 (0.1)	rimmed, circular lake	raised rim, impact melt
39	Newporte, North Dakota, USA	48 58	101 58	3.	<500.	none, buried 3 km	none
40	Nicholson, NWT	62 40	102 41	12.5	<400.	irregular lake with islands	breccia
41	Odessa, Texas, USA	31 45	102 29	0.17	<0.05	sediment-filled depression with very slight rim, 4 others buried & smaller	fragments of meteorite
42	Pilot, NWT	60 17	111 01	6.	445. (2)	circular lake	fracturing, breccia float
43	Presqu'ile, Quebec	49 43	74 48	24.	<500.	none, heavily eroded	shatter cones
44	Red Wing, North Dakota, USA	47 36	103 33	9.	200. (25)	none, buried 1.5 km	none
45	Rock Elm, Wisconsin, USA	44 43	92 14	6.	<505.	circular rim depression, central dome	shatter cones, breccia
46	St. Martin, Manitoba	51 47	98 32	40.	220. (32)	none, partially buried	impact melt
47	Serpent Mound, Ohio, USA	39 02	83 24	8.	<320.	circular area of disturbed rock, slight central peak	breccia, shatter cones
48	Sierra Madera, Texas, USA	30 36	102 55	13.	<100.	central hills, annular depression, outer ring of hills	breccia, shatter cones
49	Slate Islands, Ontario	48 40	87 00	30.	≈450.	islands are central peak of submerged structure	shatter cones, breccia dykes
50	Steen River, Alberta	59 30	117 38	25.	95. (7)	none, buried 200 m	none
51	Sudbury, Ontario	46 36	81 11	250.	1850. (3)	deformed elliptical basin	breccia, impact melt, shatter cones, breccia dykes
52	Upheaval Dome, Utah, USA	38 26	109 54	10.	<65.	circular area of disturbed rock	breccia dykes
53	Viewfield, Saskatchewan	49 35	103 34	25.	190. (20)	buried 1 km	breccia dykes
54	Wanapitei, Ontario	46 45	80 45	7.5	37. (2)	lake-filled, depression	breccia float
55	Wells Creek, Tennessee, USA	36 23	87 40	12.	200. (100)	basin with central hill, inner and outer annular valleys, ridges	breccia, shatter cones
56	West Hawk Lake, Manitoba	49 46	95 11	2.4	100. (50)	circular lake	none
57	Wetumpka, Alabama, USA	32 31	86 10	6.5	81. (1.5)	arcuate outer ridge, central depression	breccia

* Numbers in parentheses are possible errors.

MAP OF NORTH AMERICAN METEORITE IMPACT STRUCTURES

Of the 160 plus impact structures identified on Earth, 57 are in North America (29 in Canada, 27 in the United States, and 1 in Mexico). These are identified on the above map; the numbers correspond to the listing in the table on the preceding two pages. Although the oceans cover 70% of Earth, only two impact structures have been identified on the seafloor (#37 and Mjølnir, in the Barents Sea). Also, with the exception of structure #51, all of those shown occurred within approximately the last 10% of Earth's history. Evidence of many earlier craters has been erased by geologic processes. It is possible, however, to calculate a terrestrial cratering rate by focusing only on geologically stable areas of Earth (known as cratons), with low erosion and sedimentation rate. One such area is the North American craton. These rate calculations indicate that Earth has received at least 10 000 impacts sufficient to result in craters greater than 20 km in diameter over the last 3.5 billion years. Very early in Earth history, the cratering rate was even higher, perhaps as high as 100 times the current rate. Doubtless some of these impacts have had profound influence upon the evolution of life on this planet. For example, Chicxulub (#10), the very large structure in Mexico, is linked to a major extinction event 65 million years ago. Some impact craters are the source of considerable economic resources: in North America, hydrocarbons are extracted from #1, 2, 6, 34, 39, 44, 48, 50, 53; #7 produces uranium; and #51 is the site of a world-class nickel and copper mining camp.

COMETS IN 2003

By Brian G. Marsden

Listed below are the periodic comets expected at perihelion in 2003. The orbital elements are given with sufficient precision to allow an ephemeris computation good to about one arcminute (1′). The angular elements are referred to the ecliptic and mean equinox J2000.0.

Comet	Perihelion Date T TT	Dist. q AU	Eccen. e	Rev. Per. P a	Arg. Peri. ω °	Asc. Node Ω °	Incl. i °
116P	Jan. 21.59	2.1698	0.3755	6.5	173.41	21.08	3.62
79P	Feb. 15.32	1.2300	0.5941	5.3	253.07	307.97	2.89
P/1992 Q1	18.84	1.5904	0.6716	10.7	48.01	343.64	18.06
65P	May 11.86	2.4459	0.3187	6.8	196.38	68.42	10.38
127P	Jun. 12.46	2.1591	0.3696	6.3	6.50	14.01	14.40
36P	July 6.65	3.0883	0.2590	8.5	202.21	182.40	9.93
118P	16.83	2.0111	0.4222	6.5	302.09	152.04	8.48
100P	Aug. 18.03	1.9797	0.4191	6.3	181.53	37.89	25.66
66P	28.23	1.2743	0.7877	14.7	257.25	22.21	18.70
94P	29.23	2.2311	0.3648	6.6	92.94	70.94	6.18
81P	Sep. 25.94	1.5904	0.5388	6.4	41.75	136.14	3.24
53P	Oct. 9.43	2.4154	0.5520	12.5	134.10	149.00	6.61
123P	Dec. 9.12	2.1287	0.4485	7.6	102.92	46.62	15.35
2P	29.88	0.3385	0.8473	3.3	186.50	334.59	11.77

For an explanation of these elements see p. 20; the elements are for an epoch within 20 days of perihelion.

The returns of 2P/Encke, 65P/Gunn, and 116P/Wild are favorable, and those of 53P/Van Biesbroeck, 79P/du Toit-Hartley, and 123P/West-Hartley are fair. The returns of 36P/Whipple, 66P/du Toit, 81P/Wild, 94P/Russell, and 100P/Hartley are poor, and those of 118P/Shoemaker-Levy, 127P/Holt-Olmstead, and P/1992 Q1 (Brewington) are very poor.

For ephemerides for these and other comets, visit:

cfa-www.harvard.edu/iau/ephemerides/comets

OBSERVING COMETS
BY DAVID H. LEVY

Comets are interesting and fun to observe because each has its own unique, changing appearance. Observationally, comets are very much like deep-sky objects. Even in large telescopes an observer can confuse a comet with a galaxy or a diffuse planetary nebula. Comets near a telescope's limit are virtually impossible to spot without an accurate position extracted from a detailed atlas like *Uranometria* or *Millennium*. It is difficult to define a telescope's limiting magnitude for comets because the more diffuse a comet, the more difficult it is to find. Typically, under a dark sky a 150-mm telescope will catch a 9th magnitude comet, a 200-mm telescope will see 10th, and a 400-mm should have no trouble with a 13th magnitude comet.

If you are sure you have discovered a comet, follow the procedure given in this Handbook (see REPORTING OF ASTRONOMICAL DISCOVERIES on p. 9). For more information on comet observing and hunting, read *Observing Comets, Asteroids, Meteors, and the Zodiacal Light,* by Stephen J. Edberg and David H. Levy (Cambridge University Press, 1994).

Magnitude Estimates

The brightness of the coma can be estimated using a variety of methods, the most common of which is the "In-Out" method:

(**1**) Study the coma until you become familiar with its "average" brightness, an easy process if the coma is of uniform brightness but rather difficult if there is a strong central condensation.

(**2**) Using a variable star chart or some source in which star magnitudes are listed, find a comparison star at approximately the same altitude as the comet.

(**3**) Defocus the star to the size of the in-focus coma.

(**4**) Compare the star's out-of-focus brightness with that of the coma.

Repeat the last three steps with a second star, or more if needed, until an interpolation can be made.

Physical Characteristics

A comet magnitude estimate becomes more useful if an estimate of the coma diameter is made at the same time. An observer seeing a 3′ (3 minutes of arc) coma, for example, will estimate much brighter than another observer who sees only a 1′ coma at the same time. The simplest way of estimating coma size is to draw the coma with the embedded and surrounding field stars and then compare the drawing to an atlas, using its scale to determine the size.

A nightly measurement of a comet's degree of condensation is a good way of studying its changing behaviour. A comet undergoing an outburst of dust from its nucleus might begin its display by showing almost overnight the development of an increased condensation. Use an integer scale from 0 to 9, where 0 means a diffuse coma with absolutely uniform brightness, 3 means a diffuse coma with gradually increasing brightness toward the centre, 6 involves a definite central condensation, and 9 refers to an almost stellar image.

Because of the changing Earth–Sun–comet geometry and the changing activity in a comet, the length and position angle of a tail should be measured. A rough way to measure the length of a tail is to sketch it and compare with a detailed atlas, as with the coma. Observers can also measure the position angle using an atlas and a protractor.

Visual Comet Hunting

The key ingredient to a successful comet search is perseverance. Although there are stories of people finding comets very quickly (Mark Whitaker discovered Comet Whitaker-Thomas 1968 V after three nights of comet hunting), these are the exception. Don Machholz searched for some 1700 hours for each of his first two comets, and I spent more than 917 hours before my first discovery. In contrast, neither Alan Hale nor Tom Bopp were comet hunting when they independently discovered what later became the Great Comet of 1997.

It is important to know the sky well before beginning a comet search program, but it is more important to know the difference between the fuzzy appearances of comets compared to galaxies, nebulae, and clusters. Observing all the objects in Messier's Catalogue (see pp. 275–278) provides an excellent education in what these distant objects look like, and observing as many known comets as possible is good preparation for recognizing an interloper. Generally, comets lack the bilateral symmetry of spiral galaxies and the mottled appearance of globular clusters. More important, they usually have unsharp edges, fading off into space so that it is often difficult to tell where the comet ends and the sky begins.

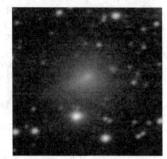

David Levy's 2nd comet, **C/1987 A1,** *was discovered within an hour of his completing the draft for his Cambridge book* Observing Variable Stars. *Photograph by Jim Scotti with the Spacewatch 0.9-m reflector.*

Although most comet hunters still use traditional star atlases to check their suspects, some are moving into a new mode of comet hunting. These hunters have attached encoders to their telescopes that allow an instant reading of the suspect's position in right ascension and declination. If the telescope has been properly set up, this approach allows faster checking of suspicious objects. However, a sense of the nature of the fuzzy object in the field of view is still important since thousands of nonstellar objects dot the sky.

Comets may appear at any time, but they are usually found within 90° of the Sun. Good areas to search are in the evening western sky during the week after full Moon and in the morning eastern sky before dawn around new Moon. Although comet hunters differ in their approaches to searching, one way is to use an altazimuth mount and make horizontal sweeps. In the western sky, begin near the end of twilight at the horizon, sweep across, then return to the point of origin, move upward about half a field of view and sweep again, etc. In the morning reverse the process.

Photographic and Electronic Comet Hunting

It is now possible to discover comets photographically and by using CCDs. With film and a wide-angle camera like a Schmidt camera, take photographs of selected areas of sky, then repeat these exposures after at least 45 minutes. Using a stereomicroscope or a blink microscope, it is then possible to spot moving objects. Through a stereomicroscope, the comet will appear to "float" above or "sink" below the stellar background, an elegant way to discover comets. If a blink microscope is used, the comet will appear to jump back and forth.

Using a CCD, take at least three images of each field, then examine either visually or by a moving-object detection program. Visual inspection is like blinking, so moving objects appear to move steadily through the three pictures, then jump back and begin moving again.

Finally, it is possible to discover comets over the Internet. Since images from the SOHO spacecraft are made available soon after they are taken, amateur astronomers can scan these images for Sun-grazing comets. RASC member Michael Boschat won the 2001 Ken Chilton Prize for his discoveries of several SOHO comets in this way.

Designation of Comets

At the International Astronomical Union's 22nd General Assembly in The Hague in 1994, Commission 20 of the IAU approved a resolution that changes the way comets are designated. Under the old system, a comet was designated according to its order of discovery or recovery in a given year (e.g. 1982i, Comet Halley, was the ninth comet to appear in 1982). After cometary information was complete for a given year, each comet also received a Roman numeral designation based on the order of perihelion passage (e.g. Halley at its last return was also known as 1986 III).

Under the new system, which went into effect in January 1995 but which is retroactive to every comet for which a reasonable orbit is available, a comet is assigned only one designation which is similar to, although not identical to, the provisional designation system for asteroids. With this system the year is divided into periods called *half-months* beginning with A (the first half of January) and concluding with Y (the last half of December), omitting the letter I. In addition, there is a letter indicating the comet's status: C for a long period comet, P for a "periodic comet" (defined as having a period of less than 200 years), X for a comet for which a reasonable orbit cannot be computed, and D for a disappeared comet. Once the orbit of a periodic comet is well known, that comet receives a permanent number according to the order in which the comet's periodicity was recognized. Thus Comet Hale-Bopp, as the first comet to be found in the O part of 1995, is labelled C/1995 O1. Comet Shoemaker-Levy 9 was 1993e; its new designation as the second comet to be found in the F part of 1993 is D/1993 F2. The new designation for Comet Halley is 1P/Halley.

When a comet becomes well known, the vast majority of scientists, press, and public ignore the official designation, preferring instead to use more easily remembered names. Our experience with comets Hale-Bopp and C/1996 B2 (Hyakutake) showed clearly that people were more comfortable with proper names. However, with 2 comets named Hyakutake, more than 200 named SOHO, and more than 50 named LINEAR, we need to become familiar with the official designation in order to separate one comet from the others.

A handful of comets are named not for their discoverers but for their orbit computors. The most famous of these is P/Halley, which has been well observed since at least 240 BC. It was finally identified as a comet appearing every 76 years or so by Edmond Halley in 1705. Two others are 2P/Encke and 27P/Crommelin.

In the event that the cometary nature of an object is established after it was originally given an asteroidal designation, the original designation remains. When Gene and Carolyn Shoemaker and I discovered Asteroid 1990 UL3 using the Palomar 18-inch telescope, for example, its orbit appeared to be more cometary than asteroidal. A few weeks after discovery, Steve Larson and I took a series of images through the Kuiper 61-inch telescope that clearly showed a tail, and the identification was changed to periodic comet Shoemaker-Levy 2. The mixed designation C/1990 UL3 applies.

Editor's Note: David Levy is the discoverer of 21 comets: 8 by visual searches (comets Levy-Rudenko 1984t, Levy 1987a, Levy 1987y, Levy 1988e, Okazaki-Levy-Rudenko 1989r, Levy 1990c, P/Levy 1991q, and Takamizawa-Levy 1994f) and 13 comets discovered photographically at Palomar under the combined name Shoemaker-Levy. One of these, Shoemaker-Levy 9 (D/1993 F2), collided with Jupiter in July 1994. Brief descriptions of the first 12 to be discovered are given in *JRASC, 85,* 384, 1991. In 1990, David Levy and H.E. Holt discovered the first Martian Trojan asteroid: 1990MB.

INTERPLANETARY DUST
BY ROY BISHOP

Outside of the astronomical community it is not generally realized that the inner solar system contains a vast cloud of dust. The particles in this cloud are concentrated near the plane of the ecliptic and toward the Sun, their spatial particle density in the ecliptic falling off somewhat more rapidly than the reciprocal of their distance from the Sun. Measurements from spacecraft indicate that the cloud extends well beyond the orbit of Mars but is negligible in the vicinity of Jupiter's orbit and beyond.

The particles composing the cloud have a continuum of sizes, from pebble-sized clumps down to specks with diameters comparable to the wavelength of visible light and smaller. The smaller particles are the more numerous, although the mass distribution appears to peak near 10^{-8} kg, corresponding to a particle diameter of a few tenths of a millimetre. The total mass of the cloud is small, amounting to perhaps 10^{-14} of the mass of the solar system. It is as if the satellites of Mars had been pulverized and spread throughout the inner solar system.

Like the planetary system, the interplanetary dust cloud is not static. Its particles generally move in orbits about the Sun. In addition, the particles undergo continual fragmentation due to collisions, sputtering associated with bombardment by the solar wind, electrostatic bursting, and sublimation. This progression toward smaller and smaller sizes is of crucial significance for the cloud, since particles with diameters appreciably less than a tenth of a millimetre have a sufficiently large surface-to-volume ratio that the radiation pressure of sunlight has a significant effect upon their motion—aberration of sunlight results in a small backward force which slows the dust particles (the Poynting–Robertson Effect), and they slowly spiral inward toward the Sun. During a total solar eclipse in 1983, instruments carried by a balloon detected a ring-like concentration of dust only a couple of solar diameters from the Sun. Its inner edge apparently marks the point at which solar heat vaporizes the infalling particles. The resulting tiny gas molecules, like the smallest particles of dust, are blown out of the solar system by the dominant radiation pressure and interactions with the solar wind.

Because of the above-mentioned influences on the sizes and motions of the dust particles, the estimated mean life of a cloud particle is about 10^4 years. Since this is much less than the age of the solar system, it is obvious that the cloud must be in a dynamic equilibrium—that is, it must be gaining new material as it loses the old. Part of the tail of a bright comet is the result of significant quantities of dust ejected from its nucleus, and it is generally assumed that comets provide a sizeable fraction of the supply of new dust to the cloud. Since comet nuclei are believed to consist of the undifferentiated matter that the solar system formed out of, much of the dust of the interplanetary cloud is most likely composed of this same low-density, fragile, primitive material. IRAS (Infrared Astronomical Satellite) data indicate that collisions of asteroids are also a significant source of dust, but it is not yet known whether comets or asteroids provide the greater input of dust to the cloud.

To an observer on Earth, the most noticeable aspect of the dust cloud is meteors—larger particles of the cloud that encounter Earth at high speeds and vaporize in the upper atmosphere. In addition, sunlight scattered by the dust cloud appears as a faint (fortunately!) glow in the vicinity of the ecliptic. This glow is brightest toward the Sun, is due primarily to particles with diameters between a few micrometres and a millimetre, and is referred to as the *zodiacal light*. A slight brightening in the sky opposite the Sun, called the *Gegenschein* (German for "counterglow"), is due to a phase effect (analogous to full moon) and also, possibly, to a concentration of dust at the L3 Lagrangian Point of the Earth–Sun system. As astronomical objects, the zodiacal light and the Gegenschein are unusual in that they can be seen only with the unaided eye. Because of their large angular sizes and indistinct borders, both are invisible in binoculars or a telescope.

The Zodiacal Light

Poetic references to the zodiacal light go back several centuries (e.g. see *The Observatory, 108,* 181, 1988). The 19th-century poet Edward FitzGerald is noted for his translation of the famous poem "Rubaiyat" by the Persian Omar Khayyam. In one of the stanzas, Khayyam's reference to the morning was altered by FitzGerald into haunting references to the zodiacal light: "Dreaming when Dawn's Left Hand was in the Sky" (in midnorthern latitudes, the zodiacal light and the first glow of the early autumn dawn combine to produce a large, glowing, ghostly figure having an upraised left arm); and "Before the phantom of False morning died" (the zodiacal light soon vanishes in the glow of the true dawn).

When conditions are favourable, the zodiacal light is indeed a mysterious and beautiful sight. Because the zodiacal light is brightest nearest the Sun, it is best seen after the end of evening twilight and before the beginning of morning twilight (for times of twilight, see the index) and when the ecliptic is at a steep angle relative to the horizon. In the tropics the ecliptic is always at a steep angle to the horizon, and the short duration of twilight is an added advantage. In midnorthern latitudes the optimum geometry occurs in the evening western sky in February and March, and in the morning eastern sky in September and October. The zodiacal light appears as a huge, softly radiant pyramid of white light with its base near the horizon and its axis centred on the zodiac. In its brightest parts it exceeds the luminance of the central Milky Way.

Despite its brightness, most people have not seen the zodiacal light. As mentioned above, certain times of night and year are more favourable than others. In addition, moonlight, haze, or light pollution rule out any chance of seeing this phenomenon. Even with a dark, transparent sky the inexperienced observer may confuse the zodiacal light with twilight and thus ignore it, or may not notice it because he or she is expecting a much smaller object.

The Gegenschein

The zodiacal light extends all around the zodiac with a shallow minimum in brightness some 120° to 150° from the Sun; nevertheless, this "zodiacal band" or "light bridge" is exceedingly faint and is visible only from high-altitude sites having very dark, transparent skies. However, the slight brightening in the vicinity of the antisolar point can be seen from most dark observing sites, provided the air is transparent.

The Gegenschein is very faint. Haze, moonlight, bright nearby stars, planets, or light pollution will hide it completely. Most observers, including experienced ones, have not seen it. The Gegenschein is sufficiently faint that, except from high-altitude sites with very dark skies, a person will not notice it without making a special effort to *look* for it. It is a ghostly apparition best seen near midnight, and in midnorthern latitudes, in the autumn or winter when the antisolar point is nearest the zenith. To avoid interference from bright stars or the Milky Way, the periods late September to early November and late January to early February are best. At these times, the Gegenschein is in Pisces and Cancer, respectively. It appears as a faint yet distinct, somewhat elliptical glow perhaps 10° in diameter. The luminance of the Gegenschein is about 10^{-4} cd/m^2, some 10 orders of magnitude dimmer than the brightest light the human eye can tolerate.

Don't determine the antisolar point before you look—imagination is too powerful. Find the antisolar point by locating the Gegenschein, and *then* check your star charts!

STARS

CONSTELLATIONS—NAMES AND ABBREVIATIONS

Nominative & Pronunciation	Genitive & Pronunciation	Abbr.	Meaning
Andromeda, ăn-drŏm′ē-dà	Andromedae, ăn-drŏm′ē-dē′	And	Daughter of Cassiopeia
Antlia, ănt′lĭ-à	Antliae, ănt′lē-ē′	Ant	The Air Pump
Apus, ā′pŭs	Apodis, ăp′à-dĭs	Aps	Bird of Paradise
Aquarius, à-kwâr′ē-ŭs	Aquarii, à-kwâr′ē-ī′	Aqr	The Water-bearer
Aquila, à-kwĭl′à	Aquilae, à-kwĭl′ē	Aql	The Eagle
Ara, ā′rà	Arae, ā′rē	Ara	The Altar
Aries, âr′ēz	Arietis, à-rī′ē-tĭs	Ari	The Ram
Auriga, ô-rī′gà	Aurigae, ô-rī′jē	Aur	The Charioteer
Bootes, bō-ō′tēz	Bootis, bō-ō′tĭs	Boo	The Herdsman
Caelum, sē′lŭm	Caeli, sē′lī	Cae	The Chisel
Camelopardalis kà-mĕl′ō-pàr′dà-lĭs	Camelopardalis kà-mĕl′ō-pàr′dà-lĭs	Cam	The Giraffe
Cancer, kăn′sēr	Cancri, kăn′krē	Cnc	The Crab
Canes Venatici kā′nēz vē-năt′ī-sī	Canum Venaticorum kā′nŭm vē-năt′ī-kôr′ŭm	CVn	The Hunting Dogs
Canis Major, kā′nĭs mā′jēr	Canis Majoris, kā′nĭs mā-jôr′ĭs	CMa	The Big Dog
Canis Minor, kā′nĭs mī′nēr	Canis Minoris, kā′nĭs mī-ñôr′ĭs	CMi	The Little Dog
Capricornus, kăp′rĭ-kôr-nŭs	Capricorni, kăp′rĭ-kôr-nī	Cap	The Goat
Carina, kà-rī′-nà	Carinae, kà-rī′-nē	Car	The Keel
Cassiopeia, kăs′ī-ō-pē′yà	Cassiopeiae, kăs′ī-ō-pē′yē	Cas	The Queen
Centaurus, sĕn-tôr′ŭs	Centauri, sĕn-tôr′ī	Cen	The Centaur
Cepheus, sē′fē-ŭs	Cephei, sē′fē-ī′	Cep	The King
Cetus, sē′tŭs	Ceti, sē′tī	Cet	The Whale
Chamaeleon, kà-mē′lē-ŭn	Chamaeleontis, kà-mē′lē-ŏn′tĭs	Cha	The Chameleon
Circinus, sûr′sĭ-nŭs	Circini, sûr′sĭ-nī	Cir	The Compasses
Columba, kō-lŭm′bà	Columbae, kō-lŭm′bē	Col	The Dove
Coma Berenices kō′mà bĕr′ē-nī′sēz	Comae Berenices kō′mē bĕr′ē-nī′sēz	Com	Berenice's Hair
Corona Australis kō-rō′nà ôs-trā′lĭs	Coronae Australis kō-rō′nē ôs-trā′lĭs	CrA	The Southern Crown
Corona Borealis kō-rō′nà bôr′ē-ăl′ĭs	Coronae Borealis kō-rō′nē bôr′ē-ăl′ĭs	CrB	The Northern Crown
Corvus, kôr′vŭs	Corvi, kôr′vī	Crv	The Crow
Crater, krā′tēr	Crateris, krā-tēr′ĭs	Crt	The Cup
Crux, krŭks	Crucis, krōō′sĭs	Cru	The Cross
Cygnus, sĭg′nŭs	Cygni, sĭg′nī	Cyg	The Swan
Delphinus, dĕl-fī′nŭs	Delphini, dĕl-fī′nī	Del	The Dolphin
Dorado, dō-rà′dō	Doradus, dō-rà′dŭs	Dor	The Swordfish
Draco, drā′kō	Draconis, drā′kō′nĭs	Dra	The Dragon
Equuleus, ē-kwōō′lē-ŭs	Equulei, ē-kwōō′lē-ī′	Equ	The Little Horse
Eridanus, ē-rĭd′à-nŭs	Eridani, ē-rĭd′à-nī′	Eri	The River
Fornax, fôr′năks	Fornacis, fôr-năs′ĭs	For	The Furnace
Gemini, jĕm′ī-nī	Geminorum, jĕm′ī-nôr′ŭm	Gem	The Twins
Grus, grŭs	Gruis, grōō′ĭs	Gru	The Crane (bird)
Hercules, hûr′kū-lēz	Herculis, hûr′kū-lĭs	Her	The Son of Zeus
Horologium, hŏr′ō-lō′jĭ-ŭm	Horologii, hŏr′ō-lō′jĭ-ī	Hor	The Clock
Hydra, hī′drà	Hydrae, hī′drē	Hya	The Water Snake (♀)
Hydrus, hī′drŭs	Hydri, hī′drī	Hyi	The Water Snake (♂)
Indus, ĭn′dŭs	Indi, ĭn′dī	Ind	The Indian
Lacerta, là-sûr′tà	Lacertae, là-sûr′tē	Lac	The Lizard

CONSTELLATIONS—NAMES AND PRONUNCIATIONS (continued)

Nominative & Pronunciation	Genitive & Pronunciation	Abbr.	Meaning
Leo, lē'ō	Leonis, lē'ō'nĭs	Leo	The Lion
Leo Minor, lē'ō mī'nĕr	Leonis Minoris	LMi	The Little Lion
	lē'ō'nĭs mī-nôr'ĭs		
Lepus, lē'pŭs	Leporis, lĕp'ôr-ĭs	Lep	The Hare
Libra, lē'brà	Librae, lē'brē	Lib	The Balance
Lupus, lōo'pŭs	Lupi, lōo'pī	Lup	The Wolf
Lynx, lĭnks	Lyncis, lĭn'sĭs	Lyn	The Lynx
Lyra, lī'rà	Lyrae, lī'rē	Lyr	The Lyre
Mensa, mĕn'sà	Mensae, mĕn'sē	Men	The Table
Microscopium	Microscopii	Mic	The Microscope
mī'krō-skō'pē-ŭm	mī'krō-skō'pē-ī'		
Monoceros, mō-nŏs'ēr-ŏs	Monocerotis, mō-nŏs'ēr-ō'tĭs	Mon	The Unicorn
Musca, mŭs'kà	Muscae, mŭs'ē	Mus	The Fly
Norma, nôr'mà	Normae, nôr'mē	Nor	The Square
Octans, ŏk'tănz	Octantis, ŏk'tăn'tĭs	Oct	The Octant
Ophiuchus, ō'fē-ū'kŭs	Ophiuchi, ō'fē-ū'kī	Oph	The Serpent-bearer
Orion, ō-rī'ŏn	Orionis, ôr'ē-ō'nĭs	Ori	The Hunter
Pavo, pā'vō	Pavonis, pà-vō'nĭs	Pav	The Peacock
Pegasus, pĕg'à-sŭs	Pegasi, pĕg'à-sī	Peg	The Winged Horse
Perseus, pûr'sē-ŭs	Persei, pûr'sē-ī'	Per	Rescuer of
			Andromeda
Phoenix, fē'nĭks	Phoenicis, fē-nī'cĭs	Phe	The Phoenix
Pictor, pĭk'tēr	Pictoris, pĭk-tor'ĭs	Pic	The Painter
Pisces, pī'sēz	Piscium, pĭsh'ē-ŭm	Psc	The Fishes
Piscis Austrinus,	Piscis Austrini,	PsA	The Southern Fish
pī'sĭs ôs-trī'nŭs	pī'sĭs ôs-trī'nī		
Puppis, pŭp'ĭs	Puppis, pŭp'ĭs	Pup	The Stern
Pyxis, pĭk'sĭs	Pyxidis, pĭk'sĭ-dĭs	Pyx	The Compass
Reticulum, rē-tĭk'-ū-lŭm	Reticuli, rē-tĭk'-ū-lī	Ret	The Reticle
Sagitta, sà-jĭt'à	Sagittae, sà-jĭt'ē	Sge	The Arrow
Sagittarius, săj'ĭ-târ'ē-ŭs	Sagittarii, săj'ĭ-târ'ē-ī'	Sgr	The Archer
Scorpius, skôr'pē-ŭs	Scorpii, skôr'pē-ī	Sco	The Scorpion
Sculptor, skŭlp'tēr	Sculptoris, skŭlp'tôr'ĭs	Scl	The Sculptor
Scutum, skū'tŭm	Scuti, skōo'tī	Sct	The Shield
Serpens, sûr'pĕnz	Serpentis, sûr-pĕn'tĭs	Ser	The Serpent
Sextans, sĕks'tănz	Sextantis, sĕks-tăn'tĭs	Sex	The Sextant
Taurus, tôr'ŭs	Tauri, tôr'ī	Tau	The Bull
Telescopium tĕl'à-skō'pē-ŭm	Telescopii, tĕl'à-skō'pē-ī	Tel	The Telescope
Triangulum, trī-ăng'gū-lŭm	Trianguli, trī-ăng'gū-lī'	Tri	The Triangle
Triangulum Australe	Trianguli Australis	TrA	The Southern
trī-ăng'gū-lŭm ôs-trā'lē	trī-ăng'gū-lī' ôs-trā'lĭs		Triangle
Tucana, tōo-kăn'à	Tucanae, tōo-kăn'ē	Tuc	The Toucan
Ursa Major, ûr'sà mā'jĕr	Ursae Majoris, ûr'sē mà-jôr'ĭs	UMa	The Great Bear
Ursa Minor, ûr'sà mī'nĕr	Ursae Minoris, ûr'sē mī-nôr'ĭs	UMi	The Little Bear
Vela, vē'là	Velorum, vē-lôr'ŭm	Vel	The Sails
Virgo, vûr'gō	Virginis, vûr'jĭn-ĭs	Vir	The Maiden
Volans, vō'lănz	Volantis, vō-lăn'tĭs	Vol	The Flying Fish
Vulpecula, vŭl-pĕk'ū-là	Vulpeculae, vŭl-pĕk'ū-lē'	Vul	The Fox

ă dāte; ă tăp; â câre; à àsk;   ē wē; ĕ mĕt; ē makēr;   ī īce; ĭ bĭt;   ō gō; ŏ hŏt; ô ôrb; ōo mōon; ū ūnite; ŭ ŭp; û ûrn

In terms of area (based on the official IAU boundaries), of the 88 constellations the 3 largest are Hydra (1303 square degrees), Virgo (1294), and Ursa Major (1280); the 3 smallest: Sagitta (80), Equuleus (72), and Crux (68). A complete list of the areas of the constellations appears in the 1972 edition of *The Handbook of the British Astronomical Association,* and was reproduced in the June 1976 issue of *Sky & Telescope* (p. 408).

FINDING LIST OF SOME NAMED STARS

Name & Pronunciation	Con.	RA	Name & Pronunciation	Con.	RA
Acamar, ā′kà-màr	θ Eri	2	Gienah, jē′nà	γ Crv	12
Achernar, ā′kĕr-nàr	α Eri	1	Hadar, hăd′ar	β Cen	14
Acrux, ā′krŭks	α Cru	12	Hamal, hăm′al	α Ari	2
Adara, à-dā′rà	ε CMa	6	Kaus Australis,	ε Sgr	18
Al Na′ir, ăl-nâr′	α Gru	22	kôs ôs-trā′lĭs		
Albireo, ăl-bĭr′ē-ō	β Cyg	19	Kochab, kō′kăb	β UMi	14
Alcor, ăl-kôr′	80 UMa	13	Markab, màr′kăb	α Peg	23
Alcyone, ăl-sī′ō-nē	η Tau	3	Megrez, me′grĕz	δ UMa	12
Aldebaran,	α Tau	4	Menkar, mĕn′kàr	α Cet	3
ăl-dĕb′à-ràn			Menkent, mĕn′kĕnt	τ Cen	14
Alderamin,	α Cep	21	Merak, mē′răk	β UMa	11
ăl-dĕr′à-mĭn			Merope, mĕr′ō-pē	23 Tau	3
Algeiba, ăl-jē′bà	γ Leo	10	Miaplacidus,	β Car	9
Algenib, ăl-jē′nĭb	γ Peg	0	mī′à-plăs′ĭ-dŭs		
Algol, ăl′gŏl	β Per	3	Mintaka, mĭn-tà′kà	δ Ori	5
Alioth, ăl′ĭ-ŏth	ε UMa	12	Mira, mī′rà	o Cet	2
Alkaid, ăl-kād′	η UMa	13	Mirach, mī′răk	β And	1
Almach, ăl′măk	γ And	2	Mirfak, mir′făk	α Per	3
Alnilam, ăl-nī′lăm	ε Ori	5	Mizar, mi′zàr	ζ UMa	13
Alphard, ăl′fàrd	α Hya	9	Nunki, nŭn′kē	σ Sgr	18
Alphecca, ăl-fĕk′à	α CrB	15	Peacock, pē′kŏk	α Pav	20
Alpheratz, ăl-fē′răts	α And	0	Phecda, fĕk′dà	γ UMa	11
Altair, ăl-târ′	α Aqi	19	Polaris, pō-lâr′ĭs	α UMi	2
Ankaa, ăn′kà	α Phe	0	Pollux, pŏl′ŭks	β Gem	7
Antares, ăn-tā′rēs	α Sco	16	Procyon, prō′sĭ-ŏn	α CMi	7
Arcturus, ark-tū′rŭs	α Boo	14	Pulcherrima,	ε Boo	14
Atria, ā′trĭ-a	α TrA	16	pŭl-kĕr′ĭ-mà		
Avior, ă-vĭ-ôr′	ε Car	8	Rasalgethi,	α Her	17
Bellatrix, bĕ-lā′trĭks	γ Ori	5	ràs′ăl-jē′thē		
Betelgeuse, bĕt′ĕl-jūz	α Ori	5	Rasalhague, ràs′ăl-hāg	α Oph	17
Canopus, kà-nō′pŭs	α Car	6	Regulus, rĕg′ū-lŭs	α Leo	10
Capella, kàp-pĕl′à	α Aur	5	Rigel, rī′gĕl	β Ori	5
Caph, kăf	β Cas	0	Rigil Kentaurus,	α Cen	14
Castor, kàs′tĕr	α Gem	7	rī′jĭl kĕn-tô′rŭs		
Cor Caroli, kôr kăr′ŏ-lī	α CVn	12	Sabik, sā′bĭk	η Oph	17
Deneb, dĕn′ĕb	α Cyg	20	Scheat, shē′ăt	β Peg	23
Denebola, dĕn-nĕb′ō-la	β Leo	11	Schedar, shĕd′àr	α Cas	0
Diphda, dĭf′dà	β Cet	0	Shaula, shô′là	λ Sco	17
Dubhe, dŭb′ē	α UMa	11	Sirius, sĭr′ĭ-ŭs	α CMa	6
Elnath, ĕl′năth	β Tau	5	Spica, spī′kà	α Vir	13
Eltanin, ĕl-tā′nĭn	γ Dra	17	Suhail, sŭ-hāl′	λ Vel	9
Enif, ĕn′ĭf	ε Peg	21	Thuban, thoo′ban	α Dra	14
Fomalhaut, fō′măl-ôt	α PsA	22	Vega, ve′gà	α Lyr	18
Gacrux, gà′krŭks	γ Cru	12	Zubenelgenubi,	α Lib	14
Gemma, jĕm′à	α CrB	15	zoo-bĕn′ĕl-jē-nū′bē		

Key to pronunciation on previous page.

THE BRIGHTEST STARS

By Robert F. Garrison and Toomas Karmo

We list the 314 stars brighter than or equal to apparent magnitude 3.55. Data for visual doubles are for the brighter component (A); the last column describes the companion(s). Where the double is too close to be resolved conveniently, data are for combined light (AB).

Apparent Visual Magnitude (**V**): Apparent magnitudes are from HIPPARCOS; the photoelectric system is that of H.L. Johnson and W.W. Morgan, *Ap. J. 117* (1953). The (yellow) *V* filter corresponds roughly to the response of the eye. The probable error of a *V* value is at most 0.03.

Colour Index (**B − V**): Since *B* on this system is the brightness of a star through a blue filter, the difference *B − V,* here taken from HIPPARCOS, measures apparent colour (as possibly reddened by interstellar dust; although, in general, *B − V* and spectral type are well correlated). The probable error of a *B − V* value is at most 0.02.

Spectral Classification (**MK Type**): The "temperature type" (O, B, A, F, G, K, M) is given first, followed by a finer subtype (0–9) and a "luminosity class" (Roman numerals I–V, with "a" or "b" added occasionally to indicate slightly brighter or fainter stars within the class). O stars are hottest, M stars coolest; Ia stars are the most luminous supergiants, III stars are giants, and V stars are dwarfs. (V stars form the largest class in the cosmos, comprising the main sequence.) Other MK symbols include "e" for hydrogen emission; "f" for broad, nonhydrogen emission in hot stars; "m" for strong metallic absorption; "n" or "nn" for unusually broad absorption (a signature of rotation); "p" for peculiarities; "s" for a mixture of broad and sharp lines; and ":" for a minor uncertainty. The types are the best available from Garrison's unpublished spectrograms and the literature.

Parallax (**π**): Parallaxes, in milliarcseconds (mas), are from HIPPARCOS.

Absolute Visual Magnitude (**M_V**) and *Distance in Light-Years* (**D**): Absolute magnitudes and distances are determined from parallaxes, except where a colon follows the absolute magnitude; in these cases, both quantities are determined from a calibration of the spectral classification. Corrections are made for interstellar absorption, by comparing, under an unpublished intrinsic-colour calibration from Garrison, spectral classification with *B − V.*

Proper Motion (**μ**) and *Position Angle* (**PA**): Proper motion and PA are derived from D. Hoffleit and C. Jaschek, *The Bright Star Catalogue,* Yale, 1982. Proper motion is the absolute value of the vector resultant from *The Bright Star Catalogue* (BSC) individual-coordinate proper motions. PA is the direction of the proper motion, as an angle measured from north through east.

Radial Velocity (**RV**): Radial velocities are from BSC. "SB" indicates a spectroscopic binary, an unresolved system whose duplicity is revealed by periodic Doppler oscillations in its spectrum and for which an orbit is generally known. If the lines of both stars are detectable, "SB2" is used; "+" and "−"indicate, respectively, motion away from and toward the observer. "V" indicates a variable velocity in a star not observable as a spectroscopic binary. (In most "V" cases the orbit is unknown.)

Remarks: Remarks include data on variability and spectra, particulars on any companions, and traditional names. Our sources for traditional names include BSC and M.E. Bakich, *The Cambridge Guide to the Constellations,* Cambridge University Press, 1995. Navigation-star names are **bold**.

TABLE OF BRIGHTEST STARS

Star Name	RA (2003.5) h m	Dec ° '	V	B–V	MK Type	π mas	Mv	D ly	μ "/yr	PA °	RV km/s	Remarks
Sun	—	—	−26.75	0.63	G2 V	—	4.8	8 lm	—	—	varies	Sun
α And	00 08.6	+29 07	2.07	−0.04	B9p IV: (HgMn)	34	−0.5	97	0.209	139	−12 SB	Alpheratz
β Cas	00 09.4	+59 10	2.28	0.38	F2 III	60	1.2	54	0.555	109	+11 SB	Caph
γ Peg	00 13.4	+15 12	2.83	−0.19	B2 IV	10	−2.4	333	0.008	176	+4 SB	Algenib; var: 2.25–2.31, 0.10 d
α Hyi	00 25.9	−77 14	2.82	0.62	G1 IV	134	3.4	24	2.255	82	23	
α Phe	00 26.5	−42 17	2.40	1.08	K0 IIIb	42	−0.3	77	0.442	152	+75 SB	Ankaa; var: 2.80–2.87, 0.15 d
δ And A	00 39.5	+30 53	3.27	1.27	K3 III	32	0.9	101	0.161	122	−7 SB	
α Cas	00 40.7	+56 33	2.24	1.17	K0 IIIa	14	−2.5	228	0.058	117	−4 V?	Schedar
β Cet	00 43.8	−17 58	2.04	1.02	K0 III	34	−1.0	96	0.234	81	13	Diphda
η Cas A	00 49.3	+57 50	3.46	0.59	G0 V	168	4.6	19	1.218	115	+9 SB	Achird; B: 7.51, K4 Ve, 12"
γ Cas	00 56.9	+60 44	2.15	−0.05	B0 IVnpe (shell)	5	−5.0	613	0.026	90	−7 SB	Cih; var: 1.6–3.0; B: 8.8..2"
β Phe AB	01 06.2	−46 42	3.32	0.89	G8 III	16	0.3:	147	0.030	279	−1	AB similar in light, spectrum, 1"
η Cet	01 08.8	−10 10	3.46	1.16	K1.5 III CN1	28	−0.1	118	0.250	121	12	
β And	01 09.9	+35 38	2.07	1.58	M0 IIIa	16	−1.9	199	0.210	121	+3 V	Mirach
δ Cas	01 26.0	+60 15	2.66	0.16	A5 IV	33	0.2	99	0.303	99	+7 SB	Ruchbah; ecl.? 2.68–2.76, 759 d
γ Phe	01 28.5	−43 18	3.41	1.54	K7 IIIa	14	−1.6	234	0.204	184	+26 SB	var: 3.39–3.49
α Eri	01 37.8	−57 13	0.45	−0.16	B3 Vnp (shell)	23	−2.9	144	0.108	105	+16 V	Achernar
τ Cet	01 44.2	−15 55	3.49	0.73	G8 V	274	5.7	12	1.921	296	−16	
α Tri	01 53.3	+29 36	3.42	0.49	F6 IV	51	1.8	64	0.230	177	−13 SB	Mothallah
ε Cas	01 54.6	+63 41	3.35	−0.15	B3 IV:p (shell)	7	−2.5	442	0.036	114	−8 V	Segin
β Ari	01 54.8	+20 50	2.64	0.17	A4 V	55	1.3	60	0.145	138	−2 SB	Sheratan
α Hyi	01 58.9	−61 33	2.86	0.29	F0 III–IVn	46	1.1	71	0.271	83	+1 V	
γ And A	02 04.1	+42 21	2.10	1.87	K3 IIb	9	−3.0	355	0.066	136	−12 SB	Almach; B: 5.4, B9 V, 10"; C: 6.2, A0 V; BC: 1"
α Ari	02 07.4	+23 29	2.01	1.15	K2 IIIab	49	0.5	66	0.238	127	−14 SB	Hamal
β Tri	02 09.8	+35 00	3.01	0.14	A5 IV	26	0.1	124	0.153	104	+10 SB2	
ο Cet A	02 19.5	−2 58	6.47	0.97	M5–10 IIIe	8	3.0	418	0.232	183	+64 V	Mira; LPV, 2–10; B: VZ Cet, 9.5v, Bpe, 1"
α UMi A	02 35.8	+89 17	1.97	0.64	F5–8 Ib	8	−4.1	431	0.046	95	−17 SB	Polaris; low amp. Cep., 4 d; B: 8.2, F3 V, 18"
γ Cet AB	02 43.5	+3 15	3.56	0.11	A2 Va	40	1.3	82	0.203	224	−5 V	Kaffaljidhmah; A: 3.57; B: 6.23.3"
θ Eri A	02 58.4	−40 17	3.28	0.17	A5 IV	20	−0.3	161	0.065	294	+12 SB2	Acamar; B: 4.35, A1 Va, 8"
α Cet	03 02.5	+4 06	2.54	1.63	M2 III	15	−1.7	220	0.075	189	−26	Menkar
γ Per	03 05.1	+53 31	2.91	0.72	G8 III + A2 V	13	−0.8:	196	0.002	180	+3 SB	composite spectrum
ρ Per	03 05.4	+38 51	3.32	1.53	M4 II	10	−1.3	325	0.165	128	28	semiregular var.: 3.3–4.0
β Per	03 08.4	+40 58	2.09	0.00	B8 V + F:	35	−0.5	93	0.004	124	+4 SB	Algol; ecl.: 2.12–3.4.2.87 d; composite
α Per	03 24.6	+49 52	1.79	0.48	F5 Ib	6	−4.9	592	0.033	131	−2 V	Mirfak; in open cluster
δ Per	03 43.2	+47 48	3.01	−0.13	B5 IIIn	6	−3.1	528	0.042	139	+4 SB	
δ Eri	03 43.4	−9 45	3.52	0.92	K0 IV	111	3.4	29	0.752	352	−6	Rana

(handwritten marginal note at left: "Codec Polaris = 43' =", with arrow pointing to the α UMi A row)

TABLE OF BRIGHTEST STARS (continued)

Star Name	RA (2003.5) h m	Dec ° '	V	B−V	MK Type	π mas	Mv	D ly	μ "/yr	PA °	RV km/s	Remarks
γ Hyi	3 47.2	−74 14	3.26	1.59	M2 III	15	−1.0	214	0.128	24	16	
η Tau	3 47.7	+24 07	2.85	−0.09	B7 IIIn	9	−1.6:	212	0.048	157	+10 V?	Alcyone; in Pleiades
ζ Per A	3 54.4	+31 54	2.84	0.27	B1 Ib	3	−6.0	982	0.011	146	+20 SB	B: 9.16, B8 V, 13″
ε Per A	3 58.1	+40 01	2.90	−0.20	B0.5 IV	6	−3.4	538	0.029	145	+1 SB2	B: 7.39, B9.5 V, 9″
γ Eri	3 58.2	−13 30	2.97	1.59	M1 IIIb	15	−1.6	221	0.124	153	62	Zaurak; calcium, chromium weak
λ Tau A	4 00.9	+12 30	3.41	−0.10	G8 II–III	9	−2.3	370	0.011	218	+18 SB2	ecl.: 3.3–3.8, 3.95 d; B: A4 IV
α Ret A	4 14.5	−62 28	3.33	0.92	B3 V	20	−0.5	163	0.068	43	+36 SB?	
ε Tau	4 28.8	+19 11	3.53	1.01	K0 III	21	0.1	155	0.114	108	39	Ain; in Hyades
θ² Tau	4 28.9	+15 53	3.40	0.18	A7 III	22	0.2	149	0.105	103	+40 SB	in Hyades
α Dor AB	4 34.1	−55 02	3.62	−0.08	A0p V: (Si)	19	0.2	176	0.051	89	26	A: 3.8; B: 4.3, B9 IV, 0.2″
α Tau A	4 36.1	+16 31	0.87	1.54	K5 III	50	−0.8	65	0.200	161	+54 SB	Aldebaran; var.: 0.75–0.95
π³ Ori	4 50.0	+06 58	3.19	0.48	F6 V	125	3.7	26	0.463	88	+24 SB2	Tabit
ι Aur	4 57.2	+33 10	2.69	1.49	K3 II	6	−3.6	512	0.018	167	18	Hasseleh; var.?
ε Aur A	5 02.2	+43 50	3.03	0.54	A9 Iae + B	2	−8.0:	7824	0.004	166	−3 SB	Almaaz; ecl.: 2.94–3.83, 9892 d
ε Lep	5 05.6	−22 22	3.19	1.46	K4 III	14	−2.0	227	0.073	166	1	
η Aur	5 06.8	+41 14	3.18	−0.15	B3 V	15	−1.2	219	0.073	157	+7 V?	Hoedus II
β Eri	5 08.0	−05 05	2.78	0.16	A3 IVn	37	0.4	89	0.128	231	−9	Cursa
μ Lep	5 13.1	−16 12	3.29	−0.11	B9p IV: (HgMn)	18	−0.4	184	0.043	129	28	
β Ori A	5 14.7	−08 12	0.18	−0.03	B8 Ia	4	−6.6	773	0.004	236	+21 SB	**Rigel**; var.: 2.97–3.36, 2 d
α Aur AB	5 16.9	+46 00	0.08	0.80	G6:III + G2:III	77	−0.8	42	0.430	169	+30 SB	**Capella**; B: 7.6, B5 V, 9″; C: 7.6; BC: 0.1″
η Ori AB	5 24.7	−02 24	3.35	−0.24	B0.5 V + B	4	−3.9	901	0.003	288	+20 SB2	composite: A: 0.6; B: 1.1, 0.04″
γ Ori	5 25.3	+06 21	1.64	−0.22	B2 III	13	−2.8	243	0.018	221	+18 SB?	Bellatrix
β Tau	5 26.5	+28 37	1.65	−0.13	B7 III	25	−1.3	131	0.178	172	+9 V	El Nath; ecl.: 3.14–3.35,8 d: A: 3.6; B: 5.0, 1.6″
β Lep A	5 28.4	−20 45	2.81	0.81	G5 II	20	−0.7	159	0.090	185	−14	Nihal
δ Ori A	5 32.2	−00 18	2.25	−0.18	O9.5 II	4	−5.4	916	0.002	252	+16 SB	Mintaka; B: 7.4, 2.6″
α Lep	5 32.9	−17 49	2.58	0.21	F0 Ib	3	−5.5	1283	0.006	279	24	Arneb
β Dor	5 33.7	−62 29	3.76	0.64	F7–G2 Ib	3	−4.2	1038	0.007	8	+7 V	Cepheid: 3.43–4.06, 9.8 d
λ Ori A	5 35.3	+09 56	3.39	−0.16	O8 III	3	−4.6	1055	0.006	191	34	Meissa; B: 5.61, B0 V, 4″
ι Ori A	5 35.6	−05 54	2.75	−0.21	O9 III	2	−5.6	1325	0.005	284	+22 SB2	Hatsya; B: 7.3, B7 IIIp(He wk), 11″
ε Ori	5 36.4	−01 12	1.69	−0.18	B0 Ia	2	−6.6	1342	0.004	236	+26 SB	Alnilam
ζ Tau	5 37.9	+21 09	2.97	−0.15	B2 IIIpe (shell)	8	−2.8	417	0.023	177	+20 SB	var.: 2.90–3.03; B: 5.0, 0.007″
α Col A	5 39.8	−34 04	2.65	−0.12	B7 IV	12	−1.9	268	0.026	178	+35 V?	Phakt
ζ Ori A	5 40.9	−01 56	1.74	−0.20	O9.5 Ib	4	−5.5	817	0.002	207	+18 SB	Alnitak; B: 4.2, B0 III, 2.4″
ζ Lep	5 47.1	−14 49	3.55	0.10	A2 Vann	46	1.7	70	0.023	263	+20 SB?	
κ Ori	5 47.9	−09 40	2.07	−0.17	B0.5 Ia	5	−5.0:	815	0.006	211	+21 V?	Saiph
β Col	5 51.1	−35 46	3.12	1.15	K1.5 III	38	0.2	86	0.405	7	+89 V	Wasn

TABLE OF BRIGHTEST STARS (continued)

Star Name	RA (2003.5) h m	Dec ° '	V	B–V	MK Type	π mas	Mv	D ly	μ "/yr	PA °	RV km/s	Remarks	
α Ori	5 55.4	+7 24	0.45	1.50	M2 Iab	8	−5.0:	522	0.028	68	+21 SB	var: 0.4–1.3	**Betelgeuse**
β Aur	5 59.8	+44 57	1.90	0.08	A1 IV	40	−0.2	82	0.055	269	−18 SB2	ecl.: 1.93–2.02, 4 d (mags. equal)	Menkalinan
θ Aur AB	6 00.0	+37 13	2.65	−0.08	A0p II: (Si)	19	−1.0	173	0.097	149	+30 SB	B: 7.2, G2 V, 4"	
η Gem	6 15.1	+22 30	3.31	1.60	M3 III	9	−1.8	349	0.068	259	+19 SB	var: 3.3–3.9; B: 8.8, 1.6"	Propus
ζ CMa	6 20.4	−30 04	3.02	−0.16	B2.5 V	10	−2.2	336	0.006	59	+32 SB		Furud
β CMa	6 22.9	−17 57	1.98	−0.24	B1 II–III	7	−4.0	499	0.014	253	+34 SB	var: 1.93–2.00, 0.25 d	Mirzam
μ Gem	6 23.2	+22 31	2.87	1.62	M3 IIIab	14	−1.5	232	0.125	154	55		Tejat Posterior
α Car	6 24.0	−52 42	−0.62	0.16	A9 Ib	10	−5.4	313	0.034	50	21	var: 2.76–3.02	**Canopus**
ν Pup	6 37.9	−43 12	3.17	−0.10	B8 IIIn	8	−2.4	423	0.010	234	21		
γ Gem	6 37.9	+16 24	1.93	0.00	A1 IVs	31	−0.6	105	0.061	136	+28 SB		Alhena
ε Gem	6 44.1	+25 08	3.06	1.38	G8 Ib	4	−5.0	903	0.016	195	−13 SB		Mebsuta
α CMa A	6 45.3	−16 43	−1.44	0.01	A0mA1 Va	379	1.5	9	1.324	204	−8 SB	B: 8.5, WDA, 50 y, 10" (1980)	**Sirius**
ξ Gem	6 45.5	+12 54	3.35	0.44	F5 IV	57	2.2	57	0.224	211	+25 V?		Alzirr
α Pic	6 48.2	−61 57	3.24	0.23	A6 Vn	33	0.7	99	0.275	345	21		
τ Pup	6 50.0	−50 37	2.94	1.21	K1 III	18	−1.9	183	0.079	157	+36 SB		
ε CMa A	6 58.8	−28 59	1.50	−0.21	B2 II	8	−4.1	431	0.002	27	27		**Adhara**
σ CMa	7 01.9	−27 56	3.49	1.73	K7 Ib	3	−4.7	1216	0.008	284	22	var: 3.43–3.49	
o² CMa	7 03.2	−23 50	3.02	−0.08	B3 Ia	1	−6.6	2567	0.007	262	+48 SB		
δ CMa	7 08.5	−26 24	1.83	0.67	F8 Ia	2	−7.2	1791	0.008	291	+34 SB		Wezen
L₂ Pup	7 13.6	−44 39	4.42	1.33	M5 IIIe	16	1.5	198	0.346	18	+53 V?	long-period var: 2.6–6.2	HR2748
π Pup	7 17.3	−37 06	2.86	1.62	K3 Ib	3	−5.1	1094	0.012	284	16		
δ Gem AB	7 20.3	+21 59	3.50	0.37	F0 IV	55	2.2	59	0.029	241	+4 SB	B: 8.2, K3 V, 0.2"	Wasat
η CMa	7 24.2	−29 19	2.45	−0.08	B5 Ia	1	−7.5	3196	0.008	284	+41 V		Aludra
β CMi	7 27.3	+8 17	2.89	−0.10	B8 V	19	−0.8	170	0.065	233	+22 SB		Gomeisa
σ Pup A	7 29.3	−43 19	3.25	1.51	K5 III	18	−1.6	184	0.195	342	+88 SB	B: 8.6, G5: V, 22"	
α Gem A	7 34.8	+31 53	1.58	0.03	A1mA2 Va	63	0.6	52	0.199	239	+6 SB	AB: 3" separation	Castor
α Gem B	7 34.8	+31 53	1.93	0.03	A2mA5 V:	63	1.0	52	0.199	239	−1 SB	BA: 3" separation	Castor
α CMi A	7 39.5	+5 13	0.41	0.43	F5 IV–V	286	2.8	11	1.248	214	−3 SB	B: 10.3, 4"	**Procyon**
β Gem	7 45.5	+28 01	1.16	0.99	K0 IIIb	97	1.1	34	0.629	265	+3 V		**Pollux**
ξ Pup	7 49.4	−24 52	3.34	1.22	G6 Ia	2	−7.5:	3260	0.033	240	+3 SB		Asmidiske
χ Car	7 56.9	−53 00	3.46	−0.18	B3 IVp (note)	8	−2.0	387	0.042	306	+19 V	Si II strong	
ζ Pup	8 03.7	−40 01	2.21	−0.27	O5 Iafn	2	−6.1	1399	0.033	290	−24 V?		Naos
ρ Pup	8 07.7	−24 19	2.83	0.46	F2mF5 II: (var)	52	1.4	63	0.100	299	+46 SB	delta Del spec.; var: 2.68–2.78, 0.14 d	
γ² Vel	8 09.6	−47 21	1.75	−0.15	WC8 + O9 I:	4	−5.8	840	0.007	304	+35 SB2	var: 1.6–1.8, 154 s	
β Cnc	8 16.7	+9 10	3.59	1.48	K4 III	11	−1.2	290	0.068	220	22		Tarf
ε Car	8 22.6	−59 31	2.17	1.20	K3:III + B2:V	5	−4.8	632	0.030	301	2	ecl.? 3.1–3.4p, 785 d	Avior

TABLE OF BRIGHTEST STARS (continued)

Star Name	RA (2003.5) h m	Dec ° '	V	B–V	MK Type	π mas	Mv	D ly	μ "/yr	PA °	RV km/s	Remarks
o UMa A	8 30.6	+60 42	3.35	0.86	G5 III	18	−0.3	184	0.171	230	20	var: 3.3–3.8, 358 d
δ Vel AB	8 44.8	−54 43	1.99	0.04	A1 Va	41	0.0	80	0.082	164	+2 V?	B: 5.0, 2"
ε Hya ABC	8 47.0	+6 24	3.38	0.69	G5:III + A:	24	0.0	135	0.198	254	+36 SB	composite A: 3.8; B: 4.7, 0.2"; C: 7.8,3"
ζ Hya	8 55.6	+5 56	3.11	0.98	G9 II-III	22	−0.2	151	0.101	277	23	
ι UMa A	8 59.4	+48 02	3.12	0.22	A7 IVn	68	−2.2	48	0.501	242	+9 SB	BC: 10.8, M1 V, 4" Talitha
λ Vel	9 08.1	−43 27	2.23	1.67	K4 Ib-IIa	6	−4.8	573	0.026	299	18	var: 2.14–2.22
a Car	9 11.1	−58 59	3.43	0.07	B2 IV-V	8	−2.2	418	0.028	283	+23 SB2	ecl: 3.2–3.6, 6.7 d HR3659
β Car	9 13.2	−69 44	1.67	0.07	A1 III	29	−1.1	111	0.183	304	−5 V?	Miaplacidus
ι Car	9 17.2	−59 17	2.21	0.19	A7 Ib	5	−4.4	694	0.019	285	13	var: 2.2–2.5 Tureis
α Lyn	9 21.3	+34 23	3.14	1.55	K7 IIIab	15	−1.3	222	0.223	273	38	
κ Vel	9 22.2	−55 02	2.47	−0.14	B2 IV-V	6	−3.9	539	0.012	315	+22 SB	
α Hya	9 27.8	−8 40	1.99	1.44	K3 II-III	18	−2.1	177	0.034	327	−4 V?	Alphard
N Vel	9 31.3	−57 03	3.16	1.54	K5 III	14	−1.3	238	0.034	268	−14	HR3803
θ UMa	9 33.1	+51 41	3.17	0.48	F6 IV	74	2.6	44	1.094	240	+15 SB	
o Leo AB	9 41.3	+9 53	3.52	0.52	F5 II + A5?	24	0.1	135	0.149	254	+27 SB	A: occ. bin. (mags. equal) Subra
l Car	9 45.3	−62 31	3.69	1.01	F9-G5 Ib	2	−5.8	1509	0.016	281	+4 V	Cepheid var: 3.39–4.12, 35.5 d HR3884
ε Leo	9 46.0	+23 45	2.97	0.81	G1 II	13	−1.6	251	0.048	252	+4 V?	Ras Elased Australis
υ Car AB	9 47.2	−65 05	3.10	0.29	A6 II	2	−2.5:	326	0.012	305	14	B: 6.26, B7 III, 5"
φ Vel	9 57.0	−54 35	3.52	−0.07	B5 Ib	2	−5.5	1929	0.013	293	14	
η Leo	10 07.5	+16 45	3.48	−0.03	A0 Ib	2	−5.6	2131	0.006	189	+3 V	B: 4.5, 0.1"
α Leo A	10 08.6	+11 57	1.36	−0.09	B7 Vn	42	−0.6	77	0.248	271	+6 SB	**Regulus**
ω Car	10 13.8	−70 03	3.29	−0.07	B8 IIIn	9	−2.1	370	0.032	275	+7 V	
ζ Leo	10 16.9	+23 24	3.43	0.31	F0 IIIa	13	−1.1	260	0.023	124	−16 SB	Adhafera
q Car	10 17.2	−61 21	3.39	1.54	K3 IIa	13	−4.2	736	0.027	276	8	var: 3.36–3.42 HR4050
λ UMa	10 17.3	+42 54	3.45	0.03	A1 IV	24	0.4	134	0.170	255	+18 V	Tania Borealis
γ Leo A	10 20.2	+19 49	2.61	1.13	K1 IIIb Fe-0.5	26	−0.7	126	0.342	116	−37 SB	AB: 5" separation Algieba
γ Leo B	10 20.2	+19 49	3.16	1.42	G7 III Fe-1	26	−1.9	126	0.358	119	−36 V	BA: 5" separation Algieba
μ UMa	10 22.5	+41 29	3.06	1.60	M0 IIIp	13	−1.5	249	0.088	290	−21 SB	var: 3.27–3.37 Tania Australis
ρ Car	10 32.2	−61 42	3.30	−0.09	B4 Vne	7	−2.0:	326	0.021	287	26	Ca II emission HR4140
θ Car	10 43.1	−64 25	2.74	−0.22	B0.5 Vp	7	−3.1	439	0.022	291	+24 SB	nitrogen enhanced
ν Vel AB	10 46.9	−49 26	2.90	1.07	G5 III + F8:V	28	−0.9	116	0.085	125	+6 SB	B: 6.4, 2"
ν Hya	10 49.8	−16 13	3.11	1.20	K2 III	24	−0.3	138	0.215	24	−1	
β UMa	11 02.0	+56 22	2.34	0.03	A0mA1 IV-V	41	0.4	79	0.087	70	−12 SB	Merak
α UMa AB	11 03.9	+61 44	1.81	1.06	K0 IIIa	26	−1.3	124	0.138	239	−9 SB	A: 1.86, B: 4.8, A8 V, <1" Dubhe
ψ UMa	11 09.9	+44 29	3.00	1.14	K1 III	22	−0.5	147	0.075	245	−4	
δ Leo	11 14.3	+20 30	2.56	0.13	A4 IV	57	1.3	58	0.197	133	−20 V	Zosma

TABLE OF BRIGHTEST STARS (continued)

Star Name	RA (2003.5) h m	Dec ° '	V	B–V	MK Type	π mas	Mv	D ly	μ "/yr	PA °	RV km/s	Remarks	Name
θ Leo	11 14.4	+15 25	3.33	0.00	A2 IV (K var.)	18	-0.2	178	0.104	216	+8 V		Chort
ν UMa	11 18.7	+33 05	3.49	1.40	K3 III Ba0.3	8	-3.2	421	0.036	309	-9 SB	B: 9.5, 7"	Alula Borealis
ξ Hya	11 33.2	-31 53	3.54	0.95	G7 III	25	0.0	129	0.211	259	-5 V		
λ Cen	11 35.9	-63 02	3.11	-0.04	B9.5 IIn	8	-2.5	410	0.039	258	-1 V		
β Leo	11 49.2	+14 33	2.14	0.09	A3 Va	90	1.9	36	0.511	257	0 V		Denebola
γ UMa	11 54.0	+53 41	2.41	0.04	A0 Van	39	0.2	84	0.094	86	-13 SB		Phad
δ Cen	12 08.5	-50 45	2.58	-0.13	B2 IVne	8	-3.1	395	0.034	249	+11 V	var: 2.51–2.65	
ε Crv	12 10.3	-22 38	3.02	1.33	K2 III	11	-2.3	303	0.073	278	5		Minkar
δ Cru	12 15.3	-58 46	2.79	-0.19	B2 IV	9	-2.6	364	0.039	255	+22 V?	var: 2.25–2.31p, 3.7 h	
δ UMa	12 15.6	+57 01	3.32	0.08	A2 Van	40	1.4	81	0.102	88	-13 V		Megrez
γ Crv	12 16.0	-17 34	2.58	-0.11	B8 III	20	-0.9	165	0.163	276	-4 SB	sp. var.?	Gienah Ghurab
α Cru A	12 26.8	-63 07	1.25	-0.20	B0.5 IV	10	-4.0	321	0.031	248	-11 SB	AB: 5"	Acrux
α Cru B	12 26.8	-63 07	1.64	-0.18	B1 Vn	10	-3.6	321	0.030	236	-1	BA: 5"	Acrux
δ Crv A	12 30.0	-16 32	2.94	-0.01	B9.5 IVn	37	-2.0	88	0.255	236	+9 V	B: 8.26, K2 V, 24"	Algorab
γ Cru	12 31.4	-57 08	1.59	1.60	M3.5 III	37	-0.7	88	0.269	174	21	var: 1.6–1.9	Gacrux
β Crv	12 34.6	-23 25	2.65	0.89	G5 II	23	-0.5	140	0.059	179	-8	var: 2.17–2.24p, 2 h	Kraz
α Mus	12 37.4	-69 09	2.69	-0.18	B2 IV–V	11	-2.3	306	0.043	248	+13 V		
γ Cen A	12 41.7	-48 59	2.95	-0.02	A1 IV	25	-0.1	130	0.190	268	-6 SB	AB: 5"	
γ Cen B	12 41.7	-48 59	2.85	-0.02	A0 IV	25	-0.1	130	0.190	268	-6 SB	BA: 5"	
γ Vir AB	12 41.7	-1 28	2.74	0.37	F1 V + F0mF2 V	85	2.2	39	0.567	271	-20 SB	var: 3.48, B: 3.50, 4"	Porrima
β Mus AB	12 46.5	-68 08	3.51	-0.18	B2 V + B2.5 V	10	-2.2:	424	0.041	233	+42 V	A: 3.58, B: 4.10, 1"	
β Cru	12 47.9	-59 42	1.25	-0.24	B0.5 III	9	-4.0	352	0.042	246	+16 SB	var: 1.23–1.31, 0.7 d?	Becrux
ε UMa	12 54.2	+55 56	1.76	-0.02	A0p IV: (CrEu)	40	-0.2	81	0.109	95	-9 SB?	var: 1.76–1.79, 5.1 d	Alioth
δ Vir	12 55.8	+3 23	3.39	1.57	M3 III	16	-0.5	202	0.474	263	-18 V?		Auva
α² CVn A	12 56.2	+38 18	2.85	-0.06	A0p (SiEu)	30	0.4	110	0.242	282	-3 V	B: 5.6, F0 V, 20"	Cor Caroli
ε Vir	13 02.4	+10 56	2.85	0.93	G9 IIIab	32	0.4	102	0.274	274	-14		Vindemiatrix
γ Hya	13 19.1	-23 11	2.99	0.92	G8 IIIa	25	-0.6	132	0.081	127	-5 V?		
ι Cen	13 20.8	-36 44	2.75	0.07	A2 Va	56	1.4	59	0.351	255	0		
ζ UMa A	13 24.1	+54 54	2.23	0.06	A1 Va	42	0.3	78	0.122	102	-6 SB2	B: 3.94, A1mA7 IV–V, 14"	Mizar
α Vir	13 25.4	-11 11	0.98	-0.24	B1 V	12	-3.6	262	0.054	232	+1 SB2	var: 0.97–1.04; mult. 3.1, 4.5, 7.5	Spica
ζ Vir	13 34.9	-0 37	3.38	0.11	A2 IV	45	1.6	73	0.287	277	-13		Heze
ε Cen	13 40.1	-53 29	2.29	-0.17	B1 III	9	-3.3	376	0.028	232	3		
η UMa	13 47.7	+49 18	1.85	-0.19	B3 V	32	-1.8	101	0.127	264	-11 SB?		Alkaid
ν Cen	13 49.7	-41 42	3.41	-0.23	B2 IV	7	-2.4	475	0.035	227	+9 SB		
μ Cen	13 49.8	-42 29	3.47	-0.17	B2 IV–V pne	6	-2.8	527	0.034	220	+9 SB	variable shell: 2.92–3.43	
η Boo	13 54.9	+18 23	2.68	0.58	G0 IV	88	2.4	37	0.370	190	0 SB		Mufrid

TABLE OF BRIGHTEST STARS (continued)

Star Name	RA (2003.5) h m	Dec ° ′	V	B–V	MK Type	π mas	Mv	D ly	μ ″/yr	PA °	RV km/s	Remarks	
ζ Cen	13 55.8	−47 18	2.55	−0.18	B2.5 IV	8	−2.9	384	0.072	232	+7 SB2	var: 0.61–0.68; B: 3.9, 1″	
β Cen AB	14 04.1	−60 23	0.58	−0.23	B1 III	6	−5.5	526	0.030	221	+6 SB		**Hadar**
θ Hya	14 06.6	−26 42	3.25	1.09	K2 IIIb	32	0.2	101	0.049	163	27		Menkent
π Cen	14 06.9	−36 23	2.06	1.01	K0 IIIb	54	0.1	61	0.738	225	1		
α Boo	14 15.8	+19 10	−0.05	1.24	K1.5 III Fe−0.5	89	−0.6	37	2.281	209	−5 V?	high space velocity	Arcturus
ι Lup	14 19.6	−46 04	3.55	−0.18	B2.5 IVn	9	−1.7	352	0.014	266	22		
γ Boo	14 32.2	+38 18	3.04	0.19	A7 IV+	38	1.0	85	0.189	322	−37 V		Seginus
η Cen	14 35.7	−42 10	2.33	−0.16	B1.5 IV pne	11	−2.8	308	0.049	226	0 SB	variable shell	
α Cen B	14 39.8	−60 51	1.24	0.90	K1 V	742	6.2	4	3.678	281	−21 V?	BA: 21″; C: Proxima, 12.4, M5e, 2°	
α Cen A	14 39.9	−60 51	0.14	0.71	G2 V	742	4.2	4	3.678	281	−25 SB	AB: 21″	**Rigil Kentaurus**
α Lup	14 42.2	−47 24	2.30	−0.15	B1.5 III	6	−4.1	548	0.026	220	+5 SB	var: 2.28–2.31, 0.26 d	
α Cir	14 42.8	−64 59	3.18	0.26	A7p (Sr)	61	1.9	53	0.302	218	+7 SB?	B: 8.6, K5 V, 16″	
ε Boo AB	14 45.1	+27 04	2.65	1.34	K0 II–III+A0 V	16	−2.6	210	0.054	289	−12 SB	A: 2.70; B: 5.12, 3″	Izar
β UMi	14 50.7	+74 08	2.07	1.97	K4 III	26	−1.1	126	0.036	286	+17 V		Kochab
α Lib A	14 50.9	−16 01	2.75	0.15	A3 III–IV	42	0.7	77	0.130	237	−23 SB		Zubenelgenubi
β Lup	14 58.8	−43 09	2.68	−0.18	B2 IV	6	−3.5	523	0.057	221	0 SB		
κ Cen	14 59.4	−42 07	3.34	−0.21	B2 V	6	−2.8	539	0.033	215	+8 SB		
β Boo	15 02.1	+40 23	3.49	0.96	G8 IIIa (note)	15	−0.7	219	0.056	235	−20	Ba 0.4, Fe −0.5	Nekkar
σ Lib	15 04.3	−25 18	3.25	1.67	M2.5 III	11	−1.9	292	0.087	237	−4	var: 3.20–3.36	Brachium
ζ Lup	15 12.5	−52 07	3.41	0.92	G8 III	28	0.1	116	0.128	237	−10		
δ Boo	15 15.6	+33 18	3.46	0.96	G8 III Fe−1	28	0.6	117	0.143	144	−12 SB		
β Lib	15 17.2	−9 24	2.61	−0.07	B8 IIIn	20	−1.0	160	0.101	275	−35 SB		Zubeneschemali
γ TrA	15 19.2	−68 42	2.87	0.01	A1 IIIn	18	−0.8	183	0.067	243	−3 V		
γ UMi	15 20.7	+71 49	3.01	0.06	A3 III	7	−0.1	147	0.031	308	−4 V		Pherkad
δ Lup	15 21.6	−40 40	3.22	−0.23	B1.5 IVn	6	−2.8	510	0.036	207	0 V?		
ε Lup AB	15 22.9	−44 42	3.56	−0.19	B2 IV–V	6	−2.5	504	0.024	232	+8 SB2	A: 3.5; B: 5.0, <1″	
ι Dra	15 25.0	+58 57	3.29	1.17	K2 III	32	0.8	102	0.020	311	−11		Ed Asich
α CrB	15 34.8	+26 42	2.22	0.03	A0 IV (composite)	44	0.3	75	0.151	127	+2 SB	ecl.: 2.21–2.32, 17.4 d	Alphecca
γ Lup AB	15 35.4	−41 11	3.40	−0.22	B2 Vn	6	−2.8	567	0.035	207	+2 V	A: 3.5; B: 3.6, <1″; similar spectra	
α Ser	15 44.4	+6 25	2.63	1.17	K2 IIIb CN1	45	0.9	73	0.143	72	+3 V?	var.?	Unuk al Hai
μ Ser	15 49.8	−3 26	3.54	−0.04	A0 III	21	0.3	156	0.094	253	−9 SB		
β TrA	15 55.5	−63 26	2.83	0.32	F0 IV	81	2.3	40	0.438	205	0		
π Sco A	15 59.1	−26 07	2.89	−0.18	B1 V + B2 V	7	−3.0	459	0.028	198	−3 SB2	A: occ. bin.: 3.4 + 4.5, 0.0003″ sep.	
T CrB	15 59.6	+25 55	10.08	1.34	gM3: + Bep	0	−9.3	...	0.013	327	−29 SB	recurrent nova 1866, 1946;	
η Lup A	16 00.4	−38 24	3.42	−0.21	B2.5 IVn	7	−2.5	493	0.040	213	+8 V	A: 3.47, B: 7.70, 15″	
δ Sco AB	16 00.5	−22 38	2.29	−0.12	B0.3 IV	8	−4.4:	522	0.027	202	−7 SB	AB: sep. < 1″; C: 4.9, B2 IV–V, 8″	Dschubba

TABLE OF BRIGHTEST STARS (continued)

Star Name	RA (2003.5) h m	Dec ° '	V	B–V	MK Type	π mas	Mv	D ly	μ "/yr	PA °	RV km/s	Remarks
β Sco AB	16 05.6	−19 49	2.56	−0.07	B0.5 V	6	−4.2	530	0.022	196	−1 SB	A: 2.78; B: 5.04, 1"; C: 4.93, 14" Graffias
δ Oph	16 14.5	−3 42	2.73	1.58	M1 III	19	−0.8	170	0.153	198	−20 V	Yed Prior
ε Oph	16 18.5	−4 42	3.23	0.97	G9.5 IIIb	30	0.8	107	0.089	64	−10 V	Yed Posterior
σ Sco A	16 21.4	−25 36	2.91	0.13	B1 III	4	−4.8:	522	0.025	201	+3 SB	var.: 2.94–3.06, 0.25 d; B: 8.3, B9 V, 20"
η Dra A	16 24.0	+61 30	2.73	0.91	G8 IIIab	37	0.7	88	0.064	338	−14 SB?	B: 8.7, 6"
α Sco A	16 29.6	−26 26	1.06	1.87	M1.5 Iab	5	−5.8	604	0.024	197	−3 SB	B: 5.37, B2.5 V, 3" Antares
β Her	16 30.4	+21 29	2.78	0.95	G7 IIIa	22	−0.5	148	0.100	260	−26 SB	Kornephoros
τ Sco	16 36.1	−28 13	2.82	−0.21	B0 V	8	−3.1	430	0.026	198	+2 V	
ζ Oph	16 37.4	−10 34	2.54	0.04	O9.5 Vn	7	−4.3	458	0.026	28	−15 V	
ζ Her AB	16 41.4	+31 36	2.81	0.65	G1 IV	93	2.5	35	0.614	310	−70 SB	A: 2.90; B: 5.53, G7 V, 1.1"
η Her	16 43.0	+38 55	3.48	0.92	G7.5 IIIb Fe-1	29	0.1	112	0.089	158	+8 V?	
α TrA	16 49.0	−69 02	1.91	1.45	K2 IIb–IIIa	8	−5.0	415	0.044	141	−3	Atria
ε Sco	16 50.4	−34 18	2.29	1.14	K2 III	50	0.1	65	0.661	247	−3	
μ¹ Sco	16 52.1	−38 03	3.00	−0.20	B1.5 IVn	4	−4.1	821	0.031	202	−25 SB2	ecl.: 2.80–3.08, 1.4 d
κ Oph	16 57.8	+9 22	3.19	1.16	K2 III	38	1.1	86	0.293	268	−56	
ζ Dra	16 58.9	+65 43	3.12	−0.12	B6 III	6	−4.5	574	0.033	200	−6	Aldhibah
η Oph AB	17 08.8	−15 44	2.43	0.06	A2.5 Va	39	0.8	84	0.102	310	−17 V	A: 3.0; B: 3.5, A3 V, 1" Sabik
η Sco	17 10.6	−43 15	3.30	0.44	F2p (Cr)	46	1.4	72	0.286	22	−1 SB	
α Her AB	17 12.4	+14 23	2.78	1.16	M5 Ib–II	9	−3.5:	1369	0.035	175	−27	var.: 3.0–4.0; B: 5.4, 5" Rasalgethi
π Her	17 14.8	+36 48	3.16	1.44	K3 IIab	9	−2.2	367	0.029	348	−33 V	
δ Her	17 15.2	+24 50	3.12	0.08	A1 Vann	42	1.2	78	0.159	276	−26	B: 8.8, 9" Sarin
θ Oph	17 22.2	−25 00	3.27	−0.19	B2 IV	6	−3.1	563	0.021	188	−40 SB	occ. bin.: 3.4, 5.4; var: 3.25–3.29, 0.14 d
β Ara	17 25.6	−55 32	2.84	1.48	K3 Ib–IIa	5	−4.1	603	0.024	188	−2 SB	
γ Ara A	17 25.7	−56 23	3.31	−0.15	B1 Ib	3	−5.7:	652	0.011	182	0	broad lines for Ib; B: 10.0, 18"
β Dra A	17 30.5	+52 18	2.79	0.95	G2 Ib–IIa	9	−2.9	361	0.026	170	−3 V	B: 11.5, 4" Rastaban
υ Sco	17 31.0	−37 18	2.70	−0.18	B2 IV	6	−3.5	518	0.032	301	−20 V	
α Ara	17 32.1	−49 53	2.84	−0.14	B2 Vne	13	−1.8	242	0.075	182	8 SB	
λ Sco	17 33.8	−37 06	1.62	−0.23	B1.5 IV	5	−3.6:	359	0.029	199	0 SB	var.: 1.59–1.65, 0.21 d Shaula
α Oph	17 35.1	+12 33	2.08	0.16	A5 Vnn	70	1.3	47	0.255	178	−3 SB2	Rasalhague
θ Sco	17 37.6	−43 00	1.97	0.41	F1 III	12	−3.0	272	0.016	157	+13 SB?	Sargas
ξ Ser	17 37.8	−15 24	3.54	0.26	F0 IIIb	31	0.9	105	0.076	90	−43 SB	
κ Sco	17 42.7	−39 02	2.39	−0.17	B1.5 III	7	−3.6	464	0.030	216	−14 SB	var: 2.39–2.42, 0.2 d
β Oph	17 43.6	+4 34	2.76	1.17	K2 III	40	0.7	82	0.164	194	−12 V	Cebalrai
μ Her A	17 46.6	+27 43	3.42	0.75	G5 IV	119	3.6	27	0.808	345	−16 V	
ι¹ Sco	17 47.8	−40 08	2.99	0.51	F2 Ia	2	−8.0:	3619	0.006	202	−28 SB	BC: 9.78, 33"

TABLE OF BRIGHTEST STARS (continued)

Star Name	RA (2003.5) h m	Dec ° '	V	B–V	MK Type	π mas	Mv	D ly	μ "/yr	PA °	RV km/s	Remarks	Name
G Sco	17 50.1	–37 03	3.19	1.19	K2 III	26	–0.6	127	0.064	58	25		HR6630
γ Dra	17 56.7	+51 29	2.24	1.52	K5 III	22	–1.1	148	0.025	213	–28		Eltanin
ν Oph	17 59.2	–9 46	3.32	0.99	G9.5 IIIa	21	0.0	153	0.118	184	13		Nash
γ² Sgr	18 06.0	–30 25	2.98	0.98	K0 III	34	0.1	96	0.192	196	+22 SB		
η Sgr A	18 17.9	–36 46	3.10	1.50	M3.5 IIIab	22	–0.1	149	0.210	218	+1 V?	var: 3.08–3.12; B: 8.33, G8: IV:, 4"	
δ Sgr	18 21.2	–29 50	2.72	1.38	K2.5 IIIa	11	–3.3	306	0.050	127	–20		Kaus Meridionalis
η Ser	18 21.5	–2 54	3.23	0.94	K0 III–IV	53	1.4	62	0.890	218	+9 V?		
ε Sgr	18 24.4	–34 23	1.79	–0.03	A0 III:n (shell?)	23	–1.4	145	0.129	194	–15		Kaus Australis
α Tel	18 27.2	–45 58	3.49	–0.18	B3 IV	13	–1.0	249	0.048	198	0 V?		
λ Sgr	18 28.2	–25 25	2.82	1.03	K1 IIIb	42	0.4	77	0.190	193	–43		Kaus Borealis
α Lyr	18 37.1	+38 47	0.03	0.00	A0 Va	129	0.6	25	0.348	35	–14 V		**Vega**
φ Sgr	18 45.9	–26 59	3.17	–0.11	B8 III	14	–1.0	231	0.052	89	+22 SB	similar companion, 0.1"	
β Lyr	18 50.2	+33 22	3.52	0.00	B7 Vpe (shell)	4	–4.1	881	0.002	180	–19 SB	ecl.: 3.34–4.34, 12.9 d	Sheliak
σ Sgr	18 55.5	–26 18	2.05	–0.13	B3 IV	15	–2.4	224	0.056	166	–11 V		Nunki
ξ² Sgr	18 57.9	–21 06	3.52	1.15	K1 III	3	0.1	913	0.035	111	–20		
γ Lyr	18 59.1	+32 42	3.25	–0.05	B9 II	5	–3.3	634	0.007	288	–21 V		Sulaphat
ζ Sgr AB	19 02.8	–29 52	3.27	0.06	A2 IV–V + A4:V:	37	1.1	89	0.014	266	+22 SB	A: 3.2; B: 3.5, <1"	Ascella
ζ Aql A	19 05.6	+13 52	2.99	0.01	A0 Vann	39	0.9	83	0.095	184	–25 SB		
λ Aql	19 06.4	–4 53	3.43	–0.10	B9 Vnp (kB7HeA0)	26	0.6	125	0.090	193	–12 V		
τ Sgr	19 07.2	–27 40	3.32	1.17	K1.5 IIIb	27	–0.4	120	0.035	192	+45 SB		
π Sgr ABC	19 10.0	–21 01	2.88	0.38	F2 II–III	7	–3.1	440	0.035	180	–10	A: 3.7; B: 3.8; C: 6.0, <1"	Albaldah
δ Dra	19 12.6	+67 40	3.07	0.99	G9 III	33	0.6	100	0.130	44	25		Nodus Secundus
δ Aql	19 25.7	+3 07	3.36	0.32	F2 IV	65	2.6	50	0.267	72	–30 SB		Deneb Okab
β Cyg A	19 30.9	+27 58	3.36	1.09	K3 Ib + B9.5 V	8	–2.3	385	0.002	153	–24 V	B: 6.4, F1 V, 2"	Albireo
δ Cyg AB	19 45.1	+45 08	2.86	0.00	B9.5 III	19	–0.7	171	0.069	45	–20 SB	B: 5.11, 35"; C: Δm = 1.5, 0.4"	
γ Aql	19 46.4	+10 37	2.72	1.51	K3 II	7	–2.6:	326	0.016	83	–2 V		Tarazed
α Aql	19 51.0	+8 53	0.76	0.22	A7 Vnn	194	2.1	17	0.662	54	–26		**Altair**
η Aql	19 52.7	+1 01	3.87	0.63	F6–G1 Ib	3	–4.3	1173	0.009	131	–15 SB	Cepheid var: 3.53–4.33, 7.2 d	
γ Sge	19 58.9	+19 30	3.51	1.57	M0 III	12	–0.9	274	0.070	69	–33		
θ Aql	20 11.5	–0 49	3.24	–0.07	B9.5 III	11	–1.4	287	0.037	79	–27 SB2		
β Cap A	20 21.2	–14 46	3.05	0.79	K0: II: + A5: V:n	9	–1.4	344	0.039	86	–19 SB	A: mult.: 4.0 + 4.3 + 4.8 + 6.7, <1"	Dabih
γ Cyg	20 22.4	+40 16	2.23	0.67	F8 Ib	2	–4.1:	522	0.001	27	–8		Sadr
α Pav	20 25.9	–56 43	1.94	–0.12	B2.5 V	18	–2.1	183	0.087	169	+2 SB		Peacock
α Ind	20 37.8	–47 17	3.11	1.00	K0 III CN–1	32	–0.1	101	0.090	39	–1		
α Cyg	20 41.6	+45 18	1.25	0.09	A2 Ia	1	–7.5:	1467	0.005	11	–5 V		**Deneb**
β Pav	20 45.3	–66 11	3.42	0.16	A6 IV	23	0.6	141	0.041	295	10		

TABLE OF BRIGHTEST STARS (continued)

Star Name	RA (2003.5) h m	Dec ° '	V	B–V	MK Type	π mas	Mv	D ly	μ "/yr	PA °	RV km/s	Remarks
η Cep	20 45.4	+61 51	3.41	0.91	K0 IV	70	2.7	47	0.827	6	−87	
ε Cyg	20 46.4	+33 59	2.48	1.02	K0 III	45	0.7	72	0.484	47	−11 SB	Gienah
ζ Cyg	21 13.1	+30 14	3.21	0.99	G8 IIIa Ba 0.6	22	0.2	151	0.052	181	+17 SB	
α Cep	21 18.7	+62 36	2.45	0.26	A7 Van	67	1.4	49	0.159	71	−10 V	Alderamin
β Cep	21 28.7	+70 35	3.23	−0.20	B1 III	5	−4.0:	815	0.016	38	−8 SB	Alfirk var: 3.16–3.27, 0.2 d; B: 7.8, 13″
β Aqr	21 31.7	−5 33	2.91	0.83	G0 Ib	5	−3.5	612	0.020	105	7	Sadalsuud
ε Peg	21 44.4	+9 53	2.38	1.52	K2 Ib	5	−5.2	672	0.030	81	+5 V	Enif var: 0.7–3.5 (flare in 1972)
δ Cap	21 47.2	−16 07	2.85	0.18	A3mF2 IV:	85	2.2	39	0.394	138	−6 SB	var: 2.83–3.05, 1 d; occ. bin.: 3.2 + 5.2
γ Gru	21 54.1	−37 21	3.00	−0.08	B8 IV–Vs	16	−1.1	203	0.104	99	−2 V?	
α Aqr	22 06.0	−0 18	2.95	0.97	G2 Ib	4	−4.3	756	0.016	104	+8 V?	Sadalmelik
α Gru	22 08.5	−46 57	1.73	−0.07	B7 Vn	32	−0.9	101	0.198	139	12	Alnair
θ Peg	22 10.4	+6 13	3.52	0.09	A2mA1 IV–V	34	1.0	97	0.277	83	−6 SB2	Baham
ζ Cep	22 11.0	+58 13	3.39	1.56	K1.5 Ib	4	−4.2	726	0.015	58	−18 SB	
α Tuc	22 18.7	−60 15	2.87	1.39	K3 III	16	−2.2	199	0.071	237	+42 SB	
δ Cep A	22 29.3	+58 26	4.07	0.78	F5–G2 Ib	3	−4.4	950	0.012	67	−16 SB	prototype Cep. var: 3.55–4.41, 5.4 d
ζ Peg	22 41.6	+10 51	3.41	−0.09	B8.5 III	16	−0.7	208	0.080	96	+7 V?	Homam
β Gru	22 42.9	−46 52	2.07	1.60	M5 III	19	−1.4	170	0.138	92	2	var: 2.0–2.3
η Peg	22 43.2	+30 14	2.93	0.85	G8 II + F0 V	3	−1.2	1113	0.025	148	+4 SB	Matar
ε Gru	22 48.8	−51 18	3.49	0.08	A2 Va	25	0.4	130	0.126	120	0 V	
ι Cep	22 49.8	+66 13	3.51	1.05	K0 III	28	0.6	115	0.137	209	−12	
μ Peg	22 50.2	+24 37	3.51	0.93	G8 III	28	0.8	117	0.152	104	14	Sadalbari
δ Aqr	22 54.8	−15 48	3.27	0.07	A3p (weak 4481)	20	−0.1	159	0.047	242	+18 V	Skat
α PsA	22 57.8	−29 36	1.17	0.15	A3 Va	130	1.6	25	0.373	116		**Fomalhaut**
β Peg	23 03.9	+28 06	2.44	1.66	M2 II–III	16	−1.7	199	0.236	53	+9 V	Scheat var: 2.31–2.74
α Peg	23 04.9	+15 13	2.49	0.00	A0 III–IV	23	−0.9	140	0.073	121	−4 SB	Markab
γ Cep	23 39.5	+77 39	3.21	1.03	K1 III–IV	72	2.1	45	0.168	337	−42	Alrai

THE NEAREST STARS
By Alan H. Batten

The *annual parallax* of a star is the difference between its direction as seen from Earth and the Sun. Astronomers began to look for stellar parallax as soon as they began to take seriously the idea that the Sun, and not Earth, is the centre of the planetary system. The great distances of the other stars ensured, however, that determination of parallax would be beyond the powers of early telescopes. James Bradley (1693–1762) came close to succeeding and correctly deduced that even the largest parallaxes must be less than 2″, but about another century was to elapse before success was achieved. Then, between 1838 and 1840, Bessel, Struve, and Henderson all published trustworthy parallaxes for three different stars. Two of those star systems, α Centauri (Henderson) and 61 Cygni (Bessel), are indeed so close to us that they appear in this table. Struve measured the parallax of Vega, which, although a relatively close neighbour of the Sun, lies some distance beyond the limit adopted here. Progress in measuring other parallaxes remained rather slow until it became possible, toward the end of the 19th century, to apply photography to the problem.

A table like the one presented here looks rather static, but if we think on a long enough time scale, the stars within the sphere of approximately 17 ly radius, centred on the Sun, are changing all the time—moving in and out of the sphere. Proxima Centauri has not always been our nearest neighbour nor will it always be, even though it is at present coming closer to us. Calculations by R.A.J. Matthews some time ago indicated that 32 000 years ago L726-8 was closer to us and that in another 33 000 years Ross 248 will be closer. More recent calculations by García-Sanchez and others, based on HIPPARCOS measurements, extend the picture over some tens of millions of years. Seven million years ago, Algol would have featured in this table; it also would have been appreciably brighter in the sky than Sirius now is. In 1.4 million years, Gliese 710 (now over 60 ly away from us) will be only 1.3 ly away and a moderately bright naked-eye star. All such calculations are approximate, of course, because there are still uncertainties in our knowledge of the distances and motions of the stars.

The table emphasizes the relative rarity of massive hot stars. Ignoring the white dwarfs, which are not massive, only Sirius, Procyon, and Altair are hotter and more massive than the Sun, and only α Centauri equals the Sun in these respects. Most of the objects in the table are very faint, cool stars. On the other hand, there is only one example of a "brown dwarf": LP944-20 (at 16.22 ly in the table). These objects are not massive enough to shine by the light of thermonuclear reactions, and they derive their energy from their gravitational contraction. They are necessarily difficult to detect, and there may be others still to be found within the region covered by this table, including some of the suspected unseen companions to some of the stars. The recently resolved component G208-44B is described as "in the transition region between stars and brown dwarfs." Another known brown dwarf, Gliese 229B, lies just beyond the limit of this table.

The HIPPARCOS-based Table

Some years ago the table was revised to include results from HIPPARCOS, the satellite launched to obtain high-precision parallaxes and proper motions for a large number of stars down to an approximate limiting magnitude $V = 12.5$. The results largely confirm earlier ground-based work, at least for nearby stars. Parallaxes are now more precisely known, so the order of stars in the list has been changed—but mostly not by very much, and not at all until ε Eridani. According to HIPPARCOS, however, the next star in this list, CD–36°15693, is a whole light-year nearer than we thought; the last star in the old table, AC+79°3888, now lies beyond the arbitrary adopted limit of 17 ly. HIPPARCOS has added four new stars to the table and recent ground-based observations a fifth (L372-58 or LHS 1565). Two stars, HIP 82725 and 85605, which were added on the strength of the initial HIPPARCOS list, have been deleted because a new analysis throws considerable doubt on the originally measured parallaxes of about 203 mas. We still rely on ground-based observations for stars fainter than $V = 12.5$ and for BD+20°2465, close in the sky to the much brighter (but much more distant) γ Leonis. Most data for stars not observed by HIPPARCOS are from the *Yale Catalogue of Trigonometrical Parallaxes*. A few parallaxes have been determined with the Hubble Space Telescope with even greater precision than those determined by HIPPARCOS. For the time being, however, I think it better to keep as many parallaxes as possible on a uniform system.

We can either incorporate the HIPPARCOS data in weighted means with the ground-based data or assume that the new values are definitive. Although the latter is somewhat unfair to the earlier work, I have adopted it to make immediately clear what HIPPARCOS has achieved. There are few significant differences between the results of the two treatments. The satellite's results have been published in 16 volumes, also available on CD-ROM. Table 3.6.1 of Volume 1 lists the 150 stars closest to the Sun measured by HIPPARCOS and contains all the information presented here, except the radial velocities. I have taken all the stars from that table, out to and including Altair, and interspersed stars from the Yale Catalogue that have parallaxes within the same limit, and L372-58. Our new table contains 37 single stars, 11 pairs (including common-proper-motion pairs), and 4 triples (α Centauri A and B, with Proxima, L789-6, a pair whose brighter component is a spectroscopic binary, G208-45 with G208-44 A and B, which have recently been resolved, and o^2 Eridani A, B and C), 71 objects in all, not counting the planetary companions mentioned below.

HIPPARCOS parallaxes are quoted in milliarcseconds (mas, 0″.001) rather than the arcseconds formerly used. I have adopted the new units since the elimination of the zero and decimal point before the significant figures makes room for more information, as described below. I have given HIPPARCOS parallaxes to the nearest tenth of a milliarcsecond. They are not that precise, even though the HIPPARCOS catalogue quotes them to five significant figures. The best determined values have uncertainties of several tenths of a milliarcsecond; most are uncertain by one or two milliarcseconds—better than ground-based observations, but not outstandingly so. A few are considerably less certain than good ground-based determinations. Most Yale Catalogue parallaxes are given to the nearest tenth of a milliarcsecond, but I have rounded them off. Readers, therefore, may tell at once, by the appearance of a figure after the decimal point, whether a given parallax was determined from HIPPARCOS. The order in which stars appear, however, is decided by that fourth significant figure, even if it is suppressed. That is why the star LP731-58 appears, at first sight, to be out of order in the table.

Recently we have learned more about LP944-20, the least luminous object known near the Sun and, as mentioned above, a brown dwarf. The spectral type of such a cool object is necessarily uncertain and M9V is the earliest this can be. There are no good photometric measurements of the visual magnitude of the star, but from measurements in the red and infrared its absolute bolometric magnitude is found to be 14.32. Again, the bolometric correction for so cool an object is uncertain, but I have tried to give an approximate estimate of the likely absolute visual magnitude (17.*). The star BD+20°2465 is very close in the sky to a 10.2 magnitude star with almost the same proper motion and a parallax of 183 mas. The two may well form a common-proper-motion pair, but the fainter one at a distance of 17.8 ly falls outside the scope of the present table. The faint star DENIS 1048-39, thought on discovery to lie within the limits of the table, has now been found to have a trigonometrical parallax that places it just beyond the distance of Altair. There are a few other known objects that may eventually prove to be near enough to the Sun to qualify for this table, but I will not include them until trigonometric parallaxes have been determined.

Many years ago we used to indicate in this table stars believed to have unseen companions. The existence of these companions was inferred from astrometric observations, mainly those made by Peter van de Kamp and his colleagues. The most famous example was Barnard's star, which van de Kamp believed to have one, or even two, planetary companions. Later, doubts arose about the interpretation of many of these observations and the companions were no longer indicated. Radial-velocity measurements can now be made with sufficient precision to detect the effect of planets at least as large as Jupiter. Two stars in this table, BD+36°2147 (also known as Lalande 21185 and one of the stars that van de Kamp listed) and BD−15°6290 (Gleise 876), do have planetary companions. In addition, 61 Cygni B and ε Eridani may have such companions. On the other hand, there is still no firm evidence for companions of Barnard's star, and the object near Proxima Centauri that was thought to have been photographed has not been confirmed by either astrometric or spectroscopic observation. A thorough study of both components of α Centauri has failed to reveal any planetary companions of either and has set rather strict limits on the nature of any such companions that could have escaped detection.

Subject to these comments, the table is arranged as previously. Successive columns give the name or designation of the star, the right ascension **(RA)** and declination **(Dec)** for the equinox 2000, the parallax **(π)** in milliarcseconds, the distance **(D)** in light-years (if you prefer the scientific unit of parsecs, just take the reciprocal of the parallax; one parsec is approximately 3.26 ly). Subsequent columns give the spectral type **(Sp.,** on the MK system whenever possible), the total proper motion **(μ)** in milliarcseconds/year, the position angle of the proper motion **(θ)** measured in degrees from north through east, the total space motion **(W)** in kilometres per second for those stars with known radial velocities, and the apparent and absolute visual magnitudes (**V** and **M_V**, respectively). Distances of HIPPARCOS stars are given to 0.01 ly and of the others to 0.1 ly. Again, I stress that we rarely know distances that precisely. Except for stars new to the list, I have usually retained the spectral types previously used. The K and M stars were classified by R.F. Wing some years ago. Recent reclassification resulted in few significant changes. Many M-type stars are flare stars, variable in both magnitude and spectral type. The space motion is given the same sign as the radial velocity (+ for recession). This is a little misleading for the two components of BD+59°1915, whose radial velocities are small, and which are travelling together, despite the difference in sign of their space motions. Only the radial velocity of o² Eridani C is given, but B and C are a known orbital pair. Several of the radial velocities are based on only one or two observations and are the least reliable data in the table. The velocities of the centres of mass of the binaries α Centauri, Sirius, Procyon, and 70 Ophiuchi are, however, reasonably well known. I have taken magnitudes from HIPPARCOS whenever possible, except for 70 Ophiuchi, for which the HIPPARCOS value appears to refer to the total light of the system. Magnitudes quoted to only one decimal are not photoelectrically determined.

HIPPARCOS has determined parallaxes and proper motions separately for each component of some binary systems. The components of α Centauri have the same parallax, but those of 61 Cygni are different; the components of Procyon are between them in distance, and BD+59°1915B turns out to be closer than its brighter companion. The two components of the common-proper-motion pair CD−25°10553, included in earlier versions of this table, have been removed because further analysis makes it doubtful that they are as close as previously thought. I have suppressed parallax and proper-motion entries for those components of binaries for which separate determinations were *not* made, sometimes condensing the entry to a single line. Only the B components of two BD stars are in the table: they form optical pairs with their respective brighter and more distant components.

Unfortunately, there is no uniform nomenclature for these predominantly faint stars; for some, names exist in several different systems. Preferred designations are as follows: proper names and Bayer Greek letters, Bonn or Cordoba *Durchmusterungen* numbers, and a miscellany of designations for fainter stars; usually I chose the one I thought most familiar.

With so much new data, some errors are likely to have made their way into the table. Either the editor or I will be pleased to have them pointed out. The preparation of this table was greatly assisted by access to the HIPPARCOS and SIMBAD catalogues provided by the Canadian Astronomy Data Centre.

Editor's Note: For more information, see "Our Changing Views of the Solar Neighbourhood," A.H. Batten, *JRASC, 92,* 1998, 231–237.

TABLE OF NEAREST STARS

Name	RA (2000) Dec h m ° ′		π mas	D ly	Sp.	μ mas/y	θ °	W km/s	V	M_V
Sun					G2V				−26.72	4.85
Proxima	14 30	−62 41	772.3	4.22	M5.5Ve	3 853	281	−29	11.01	15.45
α Cen A	14 40	−60 50	742.1	4.40	G2V	3 709	277	−32	−0.01	4.34
B					K1V	3 724	285	−32	1.35	5.70
Barnard's	17 58	+4 41	549.0	5.94	M5V	10 358	356	−139	9.54	13.24
Wolf 359	10 56	+7 01	419	7.79	M6.5Ve	4 702	235	+55	13.46	16.57
BD+36°2147	11 03	+35 58	392.4	8.31	M2+V	4 802	187	−104	7.49	10.46
Sirius A	6 45	−16 43	379.2	8.60	A1Vm	1 339	204	−18	−1.44	1.45
B					DA2				8.44	11.33
L726-8 A	1 39	−17 57	373	8.7	M5.5Ve	3 360	80	+52	12.56	15.42
B					M5.5Ve			+53	12.96	15.82
Ross 154	18 50	−23 50	336.5	9.69	M3.6Ve	6 660	107	−10	10.37	13.00
Ross 248	23 42	+44 09	316	10.3	M5.5Ve	1 588	176	−84	12.27	14.77
ε Eri	3 33	−9 27	310.8	10.50	K2V	977	271	+22	3.72	6.18
CD−36°15693	23 06	−35 51	303.9	10.73	M2V	6 896	79	+108	7.35	9.76
Ross 128	11 48	+0 48	299.6	10.89	M4+V	1 361	154	−26	11.12	13.50
L789-6 ABC	22 39	−15 17	290	11.2	M5+Ve	3 256	47	−80	12.32	14.63
61 Cyg A	21 07	+38 45	287.1	11.36	K5V	5 281	52	−108	5.20	7.49
Procyon A	7 39	+5 13	285.9	11.41	F5IV–V	1 259	215	−21	0.40	2.68
B					DF				10.7	13.0
61 Cyg B	21 07	+38 45	285.4	11.43	K7V	5 172	53	−107	6.05	8.33
BD+59°1915 B	18 43	+59 38	284.5	11.47	M4V	2 312	323	+39	9.70	11.97
A				280.3	11.64	M3.5V	2 238	324	−38	8.94	11.18
BD+43°44 A	0 18	+44 01	280.3	11.64	M2V	2 918	82	+51	8.09	10.33
B					M4V			+54	11.10	13.34
G51-15	8 30	+26 48	276	11.8	M6.5Ve	1 270	242		14.81	17.01
ε Ind	22 03	−56 47	275.8	11.83	K4Ve	4 704	123	−90	4.69	6.89
τ Cet	1 44	−15 56	274.2	11.90	G8V	1 922	296	−37	3.49	5.68
L372-58	3 36	−44 30	273	11.9	M4.5V	831	119		13.03	15.21
L725-32	1 12	−17 00	269.1	12.12	M5.5Ve	1 372	62	+37	12.10	14.25
BD+5°1668	7 27	+5 14	263.3	12.39	M4V	3 738	171	+72	9.84	11.94
Kapteyn's	5 12	−45 01	255.3	12.78	M1VIp	8 671	131	+294	8.86	10.89
CD−39°14192	21 17	−38 52	253.4	12.87	M0Ve	3 455	251	+69	6.69	8.71
Krüger 60 A	22 28	+57 42	249.5	13.07	M3.5V	990	242	−30	9.59	11.58
B					M4Ve			−37	11.3	13.3

TABLE OF NEAREST STARS (continued)

Name	RA (2000) h m	Dec ° '	D mas	D ly	Sp.	W mas/y	W °	W km/s	V	M_V
Ross 614 A	6 29	−2 49	242.9	13.43	M4.0Ve	930	132	+30	11.1	13.0
B					M5.5V				14.4	16.3
BD−12°4523	16 30	−12 40	234.5	13.91	M4V	1 189	185	−27	10.10	11.95
CD−37°15492	0 05	−37 21	229.3	14.23	M2V	6 100	113	+128	8.56	10.36
Wolf 424 A	12 33	+09 03	228	14.3	M5+Ve	1 811	277	−38	13.10	14.89
B									13.4	15.2
BD−13°637 B	3 22	−13 16	227.5	14.34		320	201		12.16	13.94
van Maanen's	0 49	+5 23	227.0	14.37	DG	2 978	156	+82	12.37	14.15
L1159-16	2 00	+13 01	224	14.6	M4.5Ve	2 096	148		12.26	14.01
L143-23	10 45	−61 10	222	14.7	M4	1 657	348		13.87	15.60
BD+68°946	17 36	+68 20	220.9	14.77	M3.5V	1 310	194	−36	9.15	10.87
LP731-58	10 48	−11 21	221	14.8	M6.5V	1 645	158		15.60	17.32
CD−46°11540	17 29	−46 53	220.4	14.80	M3V	1 050	147		9.38	11.10
G208-45	19 54	+44 24	220	14.8	M6Ve	616	139		14.01	15.72
44 A					M6Ve	681	142		13.47	15.18
44 B									16.76	18.47
BD−15°6346 B	23 07	−14 52	216.5	15.07		140	53		12.24	13.92
L145-141	11 46	−64 50	216.4	15.07	DC:	2 688	97		11.50	13.18
G158-27	0 07	−7 34	213	15.3	M5−5.5V	2 028	204		13.74	15.38
BD−15°6290	22 53	−14 16	212.7	15.34	M5V	1 174	125	+28	10.16	11.80
BD+44°2051 A	11 05	+43 32	206.9	15.77	M1V	4 511	282	+122	8.82	10.40
B					M5de				14.40	15.93
BD+50°1725	10 11	+49 27	205.2	15.90	K7V	1 452	250	−42	6.60	8.16
BD+20°2465	10 20	+19 52	205	15.9	M3.5Ve	491	264	+16	9.43	10.99
CD−49°13515	21 34	−49 00	202.5	16.11	M2V	819	183	+22	8.66	10.19
LP944-20	3 40	−35 26	201	16.22	≥M9V	439	176	+14		17.*
CD−44°11909	17 37	−44 18	198.3	16.43	M4V	1 176	217	−66	10.94	12.43
o² Eri A	4 15	−7 39	198.2	16.46	K1V	4 088	213	−106	4.43	5.92
B					DA	4 070	212	−100	9.52	11.01
C					M4.5Ve			(−45)	11.17	12.66
BD+43°4305 A	22 47	+44 20	198.1	16.47	M4−Ve	841	237	−20	10.29	11.77
70 Oph A	18 05	+2 30	196.6	16.59	K0V	971	173	−24	4.20	5.67
B					K4V				5.99	7.46
Altair	19 51	+8 52	194.4	16.78	A7V	661	54	−31	0.76	2.20

DOUBLE AND MULTIPLE STARS
By Brian D. Mason

Approximately 85% of stars are found in double or multiple systems. While the first detection of these double systems dates back to the early 17th century, it was not until systematic work with large-aperture telescopes was done (notably by William Herschel) that the physical rather than the optical nature of these systems was ascertained. The larger the aperture of the telescope, the closer the stars that can be separated under good conditions. The resolving power in arcseconds can be estimated as $120/D$, where D is the diameter of the telescope objective in millimetres. Astronomers using long-baseline optical interferometry have measured double-star separations less than a milliarcsecond (0.001").

The double stars in the table (two pages ahead) were selected to cover a wide variety of interests. While wide or slowly moving pairs are good for evaluating optical performance or estimating seeing, with the preponderance of inexpensive, large-aperture telescopes and the availability of interferometry for the amateur (in *Sky & Telescope* see the articles by A. Maurer, p. 91, March 1997, and H.A. McAlister, p. 34, November 1996), closer systems have been added to the list. Of the 40 listed systems, 9 have separations less than one arcsecond and 7 more between one and two arcseconds. A pair of binaries with white dwarf secondaries (α CMa and α CMi) is included to demonstrate the detection difficulty imposed by a large magnitude difference. Nine of the systems are found south of the equator. Since many of the stars selected exhibit significant motion, the predicted position angles and separations are given for both 2003.0 and 2004.0. P.A. (Position Angle) is the angular direction of the fainter star (B) from the brighter (A), measured counterclockwise from north (*clockwise* in an optical system having an *odd* number of reflections). Note that data for 2003.0 have been changed for some systems due to improvements in orbit calculations or more recent measurements. For systems with no orbit determination the most recently measured position is tabulated. Also included are notes on selected systems.

Other double stars appear in THE NEAREST STARS (pp. 251–255) and THE BRIGHTEST STARS (pp. 241–250) sections in this Handbook. For more information about observing double stars, see the following articles in *Sky & Telescope:* A. Adler (Jan. 2001, 131); S. Haas (May 2000, 112); L. Argüelles (Feb. 2000, 111); R. Tanguay (Feb. 1999, 116); J. Mullaney (Mar. 1993, 112); J. Ashbrook (Nov. 1980, 379); J. Meeus (Jan. and Feb. 1971, 21, 88); and C.E. Worley (Aug., Sep., and Nov. 1961, 73, 140, 261).

Notes on some double and multiple stars in the table:

γ And: The AB system is striking in colour, the brighter star golden and the secondary blue. The B component is itself a triple system consisting of a close (2.7-day period) spectroscopic binary and the wider BC pair also listed in the table. (In the NOVEMBER ALL-SKY MAP on p. 299, γ And is the bright star immediately west of the word "Algol.")

α CMa: The companion to Sirius is a difficult target, usually observable only during periods of exceptional seeing when you can use the highest magnification and move the primary off the field of view. The white dwarf secondary, predicted by Bessel and first observed by Alvan Clark, remains a challenging target for visual observers.

α CMi: Like Sirius, Procyon has a white dwarf companion. It was first detected in 1840 by the variation in the proper motion of the star but not resolved until 1896 by Shaeberle with the 36-in. refractor of Lick Observatory.

ζ Cnc: A gorgeous and easily seen triple system, the wide C component (not in the table) is quite bright and is well separated (6″). While its period is very uncertain, preliminary orbital analysis yields a period of about 1150 years. A new, close component to C has been found by infrared adaptive optics and lunar occultation; it has been confirmed with reprocessing of the HIPPARCOS data. An astrometric solution by Wulff Heintz yields a period of 17 years for the new close companion to C. For an excellent history of this system, see Roger Griffin's article in the February 2000 *Observatory*.

10 UMa: This pair of stars, one slightly hotter than the Sun and the other slightly cooler, is at a distance of 57 light-years. In spite of their name, these stars now fall within the constellation boundary of Lynx. They're very fast movers!

ξ UMa: Many "firsts" are associated with this system. It was one of the first discovered systems (Herschel), one of the first systems whose motion led to the discovery of the physical (rather than optical) nature of double stars (Struve), and was the first star to have an orbit calculated for it (Savary). Always relatively wide and with an obvious position angle change of 6° per year, this is a system that will never fail to please, observing season to observing season. For more information on this system, see Roger Griffin's article in the October 1998 *Observatory*. (In the MAY ALL-SKY MAP on p. 296, ξ UMa is the star nearest to the letter "S" in the word "BERENICES.")

24 Com: A well-separated pair with a significant magnitude and colour difference.

ζ UMa: This is the well-known bright multiple star Mizar (the intermediate separation pair is listed in the table). The wider pairing with Alcor is at a separation of 708″. Mizar is also the first known spectroscopic binary and was first resolved by Francis Pease using the 20-ft. beam interferometer mounted on the front end of the 100-in. at Mt. Wilson (see **www.mtwilson.edu/Tour/100inch/20ftl**). It has subsequently been resolved using the Navy Prototype Optical Interferometer (NPOI). See **www.nofs.navy.mil/projects/npoi/science/mizarmov.gif** for a movie of the orbital motion showing recent resolutions of the NPOI. For a list of nearby doubles, see the article by Sissy Haas listed above.

α Cen: Our closest neighbour is a quick-moving double star. The brighter component is a near twin of the Sun, while the B component is cooler. The C component, Proxima, which is slightly closer to the Sun, is an extremely faint red dwarf, 2.2° away.

λ Oph: Also known as Marfic or Marfik, the elbow of Ophiuchus, this is a nice, easily separated double showing slow but clear motion.

α Her: A slowly moving, easy-to-separate system, this binary has a significant colour difference between the two companions, A being reddish and B (itself a close double) appearing green. The period is very uncertain. See also the *Variable Star of the Year* in the 1998 *Observer's Handbook*. (In the JULY ALL-SKY MAP on p. 297, α Her is the star in the stick pattern of HERCULES closest to OPHIUCHUS.)

70 Oph: This is a very wide but short period system due to its close proximity to the Sun. Previous indications of an additional astrometric companion seem to have been laid to rest by high-resolution spectroscopy. A significant colour difference is noted for this system.

β Cyg: Also known as Albireo. If a neophyte doubts the colour of stars, this jewel of the summer sky should change that view. Appearing as brilliant yellow and a deep blue, this wide double has shown no apparent motion. The A component also has a close companion, discovered by speckle interferometry, at a separation of about 0.4″. (In the JULY ALL-SKY MAP on p. 297, β Cyg lies at the south end of the stick pattern for CYGNUS.)

δ Cyg: The bright blue colours of this binary make it an attractive system, but the large difference in magnitude makes it quite a challenge. It is slow moving, and the orbital period quoted here must be classified as preliminary.

π Aql: Called *Seat* by the Dutch scholar Grotius, this slow-moving object is a good test system to rate resolving power and seeing.

TABLE OF DOUBLE AND MULTIPLE STARS

Star	RA (2000) h m	Dec ° '	Magnitudes comb. A B	2003.0 P.A. °	Sep. "	2004.0 P.A. °	Sep. "	Period years
85 Peg	0 02.2	+27 05	5.7 5.8 8.8	214	0.8	223	0.8	26
γ Ari	1 53.5	+19 18	3.8 3.9 3.9	357	7.5			
α Psc	2 02.0	+02 46	3.9 4.3 5.2	269	1.8	268	1.8	930
γ And AB*	2 03.9	+42 20	2.0 2.1 4.8	64	9.8			
γ And BC*	2 03.9	+42 20	4.5 4.8 6.0	103	0.4	103	0.4	64
33 Ori	5 31.2	+03 18	5.5 5.8 6.9	28	1.9			
α CMa*	6 45.1	−16 43	−1.5 −1.5 8.5	117	6.3	111	6.7	50
α Gem	7 34.6	+31 53	1.6 2.0 2.9	61	4.2	61	4.3	445
α CMi*	7 39.3	+5 14	0.4 0.4 10.8	102	3.5	114	3.2	41
ζ Cnc AB*	8 12.2	+17 39	5.0 5.6 6.0	61	0.9	57	1.0	60
ι Cnc	8 46.7	+28 46	3.9 4.0 6.6	307	30.5			
10 UMa*	9 00.6	+41 47	3.9 4.1 6.1	7	0.7	358	0.7	22
σ² UMa	9 10.4	+67 08	4.8 4.9 7.9	352	3.9	352	4.0	1100
ψ Vel	9 30.7	−40 28	3.6 4.0 4.8	328	0.4	8	0.3	34
γ Leo	10 20.0	+19 50	2.3 2.6 3.8	125	4.4	125	4.4	620
ξ UMa*	11 18.2	+31 32	3.8 4.3 4.8	252	1.8	246	1.7	60
α Cru	12 26.6	−63 06	0.2 0.8 1.2	114	4.0			
24 Com*	12 35.1	+18 23	4.8 5.1 6.3	270	20.3			
γ Vir	12 41.7	−1 27	2.7 3.4 3.5	216	0.6	168	0.4	170
ζ UMa*	13 23.9	+54 56	2.0 2.2 3.9	153	14.6			
α Cen*	14 39.6	−60 50	−0.3 0.0 1.3	228	11.3	230	10.6	80
ε Boo	14 45.0	+27 04	2.0 2.3 4.5	346	2.9			
η CrB	15 23.2	+30 17	5.1 5.6 6.1	99	0.5	112	0.5	42
α Sco	16 29.4	−26 26	1.0 1.0 5.4	275	2.4	275	2.3	890
λ Oph*	16 30.9	+01 59	3.6 4.0 5.0	32	1.4	33	1.5	130
ζ Her	16 41.3	+31 36	3.0 3.0 6.5	240	0.8	226	0.9	34
α Her*	17 14.6	+14 23	3.3 3.5 5.4	104	4.6	104	4.6	3600
τ Oph	18 03.1	−8 11	4.8 5.3 5.8	283	1.7	283	1.7	260
70 Oph*	18 05.5	+02 30	3.8 4.0 6.0	140	4.7	138	4.9	88
ε Lyr AB	18 44.3	+39 40	4.7 5.0 6.1	349	2.5	349	2.5	1200
ε Lyr CD	18 44.3	+39 40	4.6 5.2 5.5	81	2.4	80	2.4	720
β Cyg*	19 30.7	+27 58	2.9 3.1 5.1	54	33.7			
16 Cyg	19 41.8	+50 32	5.3 6.0 6.2	133	39.9			
δ Cyg*	19 45.0	+45 08	2.9 2.9 7.9	223	2.6	222	2.6	780
π Aql*	19 48.7	+11 49	5.7 6.1 6.9	105	1.4			
β Cap	20 21.0	−14 47	2.9 3.0 6.1	267	207.			
τ Cyg	21 14.8	+38 03	3.7 3.8 6.3	277	0.7	270	0.7	50
μ Cyg	21 44.1	+28 45	4.4 4.7 6.1	311	1.8	312	1.8	790
ζ Aqr	22 28.8	−0 01	3.7 4.4 4.6	179	2.0	178	2.1	760
δ Cep	22 29.4	+58 25	4.0 4.1 6.3	191	42.1			

*See the preceding note.

VARIABLE STARS

By Janet A. Mattei

Variable stars reveal many stellar properties. Depending upon their type, variables can tell us the mass, radius, temperature, luminosity, internal and external structure, composition, and evolution history of stars. The systematic observation of variable stars is an area in which amateur astronomers can make a valuable contribution to astronomy.

For beginning observers, charts of the fields of four different types of bright variable stars are shown below. On each chart the magnitudes (with decimal point omitted) of several suitable comparison stars are shown. A brightness estimate of the variable is made using two comparison stars, one brighter, one fainter than the variable. The magnitude, date, and time of each observation are recorded. When a number of observations have been made, a graph of magnitude versus date can be plotted. The shape of this "light curve" depends on the type of variable. Further information about variable star observing may be obtained from the American Association of Variable Star Observers (AAVSO), 25 Birch St., Cambridge MA 02138-1205, USA (email: aavso@aavso.org; website: www.aavso.org).

Table 1 is a list of long-period variables, brighter than magnitude 8.0 at maximum and north of −20°. The first column (the Harvard designation of the star) gives the position for the year 1900: the first four characters give the hours and minutes of right ascension, the next three the declination in degrees. The column headed **"Max."** gives the mean maximum magnitude. The period **(Per.)** is in days. **"Epoch"** gives the predicted date of the earliest maximum occurring this year; by adding multiples of the period to this epoch, the dates of subsequent maxima may be found. These variables may reach maximum two or three weeks before or after the epoch and may remain at maximum for several weeks. This table is prepared using the observations of the AAVSO.

Table 2 (on the following page) lists stars that are representative of some other types of variables. The data for the preparation of the predicted epoch of maximum or minimum are taken from the *General Catalogue of Variable Stars,* Vols. I and II, 4th ed., and the data for eclipsing binaries and RR Lyrae variables are from *Rocznik Astronomiczny Obserwatorium Krakowskiego 2001, International Supplement.*

TABLE 1—LONG-PERIOD VARIABLE STARS NORTH OF −20°

Variable		Max. m_v	Per. d	Epoch 2003	Variable		Max. m_v	Per. d	Epoch 2003
0017+55	T Cas	7.8	445	Dec. 8	1425+39	V Boo	7.9	258	May 25??
0018+38	R And	7.0	409	—	1432+27	R Boo	7.2	223	Jun. 14
0211+43A	W And	7.0	397	—	1517+31	S CrB	7.3	361	Oct. 18
0214−03	o Cet	3.4	332	Jul. 3	1546+39	V CrB	7.5	358	Apr. 23
0228−13	U Cet	7.5	235	Mar. 5	1546+15	R Ser	6.9	357	Dec. 13
0231+33	R Tri	6.2	266	Feb. 15	1606+25	RU Her	8.0	484	May 3
0430+65	T Cam	8.0	374	May 25	1621+19	U Her	7.5	406	Apr. 1
0455−14	R Lep	6.8	432	Nov. 30	1621−12	V Oph	7.5	298	Jul. 9
0509+53	R Aur	7.7	459	Feb. 17	1632+66	R Dra	7.6	245	Jan. 8
0549+20A	U Ori	6.3	372	Dec. 21	1647+15	S Her	7.6	307	Mar. 28
0617−02	V Mon	7.0	335	Dec. 5	1702−15	R Oph	7.9	302	Jun. 5
0653+55	R Lyn	7.9	379	Apr. 19	1717+23	RS Her	7.9	219	Jul. 13
0701+22	R Gem	7.1	370	Nov. 26	1805+31	T Her	8.0	165	Mar. 15
0703+10	R CMi	8.0	338	May 10	1811+36	W Lyr	7.9	196	May 16
0727+08	S CMi	7.5	332	Aug. 12	1833+08	X Oph	6.8	334	Jun. 2
0811+12	R Cnc	6.8	362	Oct. 26	1901+08A	R Aql	6.1	270	Jan. 14
0816+17	V Cnc	7.9	272	Apr. 26	1910−17	T Sgr	8.0	392	Jan. 19
0848+03	S Hya	7.8	257	Jun. 5	1910−19	R Sgr	7.3	269	Apr. 30
0850−08	T Hya	7.8	288	Sep. 19	1934+49	R Cyg	7.5	426	Feb. 1
0939+34	R LMi	7.1	372	Oct. 30	1940+48	RT Cyg	7.3	190	May 3
0942+11	R Leo	5.8	313	Sep. 25	1946+32	χ Cyg	5.2	407	Apr. 10
1037+69	R UMa	7.5	302	Jun. 16	2016+47	U Cyg	7.2	465	Oct. 1
1214−18	R Crv	7.5	317	Oct. 30	2044−05	T Aqr	7.7	202	Jul. 13
1220+01	SS Vir	6.8	355	Aug. 31	2108+68	T Cep	6.0	390	Sep. 15
1231+60	T UMa	7.7	257	Jun. 13	2137+53	RU Cyg	8.0	234	Mar. 3??
1233+07	R Vir	6.9	146	Mar. 20	2301+10	R Peg	7.8	378	Nov. 25
1239+61	S UMa	7.8	226	Apr. 12	2307+59	V Cas	7.9	228	Jul. 2
1315+46	V CVn	6.8	192	Mar. 5?	2315+08	S Peg	8.0	319	Jan. 1
1327+06	S Vir	7.0	378	Dec. 31	2338−15	R Aqr	6.5	387	Aug. 15
1344+40	R CVn	7.7	328	May 10	2353+50	R Cas	7.0	431	Jan. 28
1425+84	R Cam	7.9	270	Aug. 19	2357−15	W Cet	7.6	351	Sep. 23

TABLE 2—OTHER TYPES OF VARIABLE STARS

Variable		Max. m_v	Min. m_v	Type	Sp. Cl.	Period d	Epoch 2003 UT
0053+81	U Cep	6.7	9.8	Ecl.	B8 + gG2	2.493 093 7‡	Jan. 2.14*
0258+38	ρ Per	3.3	4.0	Semi R	M4	33–55, 1100	—
0301+40	β Per	2.1	3.3	Ecl.	B8 + G	2.867 315	†
0355+12	λ Tau	3.5	4.0	Ecl.	B3	3.952 952	Jan. 4.79*
0608+22	η Gem	3.1	3.9	Semi R	M3	233.4	—
0619+07	T Mon	5.6	6.6	Cep	F7–K1	27.024 649	Jan. 9.20
0658+20	ζ Gem	3.6	4.2	Cep	F7–G3	10.150 73	Jan. 7.71
1544+28	R CrB	5.8	14.8	R CrB	cFpep		—
1710+14	α Her	3.0	4.0	Semi R	M5	50–130, 6 y	—
1842–05	R Sct	5.0	7.0	RV Tau	G0e–K0p	144	—
1846+33	β Lyr	3.4	4.3	Ecl.	B8	12.940 264‡	Jan. 12.99*
1922+42	RR Lyr	6.9	8.0	RR Lyr	A2–F1	0.566 817 3‡	Jan. 1.18
1947+00	η Aql	3.5	4.3	Cep	F6–G4	7.176 641	Jan. 1.67
2225+57	δ Cep	3.5	4.4	Cep	F5–G2	5.366 341	Jan. 1.84

‡Changing period (period revised for 2003).
*Minimum.
†Algol; predictions for all minima in 2003 are given in THE SKY MONTH BY MONTH section.

DESCRIPTION OF VARIABLE STAR TYPES

Variable stars are divided into four main classes: (1) pulsating and (2) eruptive variables, where variability is intrinsic due to physical changes in the star or stellar system; (3) eclipsing binary and (4) rotating stars, where variability is extrinsic due to an eclipse of one star by another or the effect of stellar rotation. A brief and general description of the major types in each class is given below.

(1) Pulsating Variables

Cepheids are variables that pulsate with periods of 1 to 70 days. They have high luminosity, and the amplitude of light variation ranges from 0.1 to 2 magnitudes. The prototypes of the group are located in open clusters and obey the well-known period–luminosity relation. They are of F spectral class at maximum and G to K at minimum. The later (cooler) the spectral class of a Cepheid, the longer its period. Typical representative: δ Cephei.

RR Lyrae types are pulsating, giant variables with periods ranging from 0.05 to 1.2 days with amplitude of light variation between 1 and 2 magnitudes. They are usually of A spectral class. Typical representative: RR Lyrae.

RV Tauri types are supergiant variables with a characteristic light curve of alternating deep and shallow minima. The periods, defined as the interval between two deep minima, range from 30 to 150 days. The amplitude of light variation may be as much as 3 magnitudes. Many show long-term cyclic variation of 500 to 9000 days. Generally the spectral classes range from G to K. Typical representative: R Scuti.

Long-period—Mira Ceti variables are giant variables that vary with amplitudes from 2.5 to 5 magnitudes or more. They have well-defined periodicity, ranging from 80 to 1000 days. They show characteristic emission spectra of late spectral classes M, C, and S. Typical representative: o Ceti (Mira).

Semiregular variables are giants or supergiants showing appreciable periodicity accompanied by intervals of irregularities of light variation. The periods range from

30 to 1000 days with amplitudes not more than 1 to 2 magnitudes in general. Typical representative: R Ursae Minoris.

Irregular variables are stars that at times show only a trace of periodicity or none at all. Typical representative: RX Leporis.

(2) Eruptive Variables

Novae are close binary systems consisting of a normal star and a white dwarf that increase 7 to 16 magnitudes in brightness in one to several hundred days. After the outburst the star fades slowly until the initial brightness is reached in several years or decades. Near maximum brightness the spectrum is generally similar to A or F giants. Typical representative: CP Puppis (Nova 1942).

Supernovae increase in brightness by 20 or more magnitudes due to a gigantic stellar explosion. The general appearance of the light curve is similar to novae. Typical representative: CM Tauri (Supernova of 1054 AD and the central star of the Crab Nebula).

U Geminorum types are dwarf novae that have long intervals of quiescence at minimum with sudden rises to maximum. Depending upon the star, the amplitude of eruptions ranges from 2 to 6 magnitudes, and the duration between outbursts tens to thousands of days. Most of these stars are spectroscopic binaries with periods of a few hours. Typical representative: SS Cygni.

Z Camelopardalis types are variables similar to U Gem stars in their physical and spectroscopic properties. They show cyclic variations interrupted by intervals of constant brightness ("stillstands") lasting for several cycles, approximately one-third of the way from maximum to minimum. Typical representative: Z Camelopardalis.

SU Ursae Majoris types are dwarf novae similar to U Gem and Z Cam stars in their physical and spectroscopic properties. They have frequent, faint, and narrow eruptions that last from one to a few days, along with infrequent, bright, and long eruptions, "superoutbursts," that last 10 to 20 days. During superoutbursts there are small periodic variations, "superhumps," 2% to 3% longer than the orbital period of the system. Typical representative: SU Ursae Majoris.

R Coronae Borealis types are highly luminous variables that have nonperiodic drops in brightness from 1 to 9 magnitudes due to the formation of "carbon soot" in the stars' atmosphere. The duration of minima varies from a few months to years. Members of this group have F to K and R spectral class. Typical representative: R Coronae Borealis.

(3) Eclipsing Binaries

These are binary stars with the orbital plane lying near the line of sight of the observer. The components periodically eclipse each other, causing a decrease in the apparent brightness of the system. The period of the eclipses coincides with the period of the orbital motion. Typical representative: β Persei (Algol).

(4) Rotating Variables

These are rapidly rotating stars, usually close binary systems that undergo small amplitude changes in light that may be due to dark or bright spots on their surface. Eclipses may also be present in such systems. Typical representative: RS Canum Venaticorum.

BETELGEUSE—AN "URBAN" VARIABLE STAR
BY JOHN R. PERCY AND JANET A. MATTEI

City-bound observers can see very few stars, especially variable stars, but there is one variable star that almost everyone can see: alpha Orionis, or Betelgeuse, the red star that marks the left (as seen by northern observers) shoulder of the great hunter in the sky. It varies between +0.2 and +1.2 in visual magnitude on a time scale of hundreds to thousands of days. Although the variability is slow and may therefore take many months for an observer to detect, you can access earlier measurements on the website of the American Association of Variable Star Observers (AAVSO) to see the "big picture" of the variability and to compare your measurements with other recent ones.

Betelgeuse is a red supergiant star, about 425 light-years away. It is so large that, if it were placed where the Sun is, its atmosphere would stretch to the orbit of Mars, and perhaps beyond. It was the first star, other than the Sun, to have its disk imaged directly. The variability of Betelgeuse was first noticed by Sir John Herschel in 1836; it has been studied both visually and photoelectrically by the AAVSO. The variability is due to pulsation. Given that the star probably has large convection cells in its outer layers, the pulsation is probably more complicated than the usual in-and-out motion. It is classed as a semiregular (SRc) variable. For more information about Betelgeuse, visit the Variable Star of the Month webpage of the AAVSO at:

www.aavso.org/vstar/vsotm/1200.stm

This page also includes a Hubble Space Telescope image of Betelgeuse and a long-term light curve from the AAVSO International Database.

For grade 9 and higher students, measurement of the brightness of Betelgeuse is a realistic project, and it meets many of the expectations of their science and math curricula: understanding the nature and life cycles of stars; using a star chart to locate constellations and stars and distinguish them from planets; observing the positions and motions of objects in the sky; conducting scientific investigations; making measurements; accessing and integrating electronic and print information; organizing and analyzing data; interpreting patterns and trends; making predictions; communicating scientific ideas, procedures, results, and conclusions through tables and graphs; exploring science in many cultures (through constellation myths, for instance); exploring science as a career or hobby.

Orion is visible in the south throughout the winter. **Figure 1** (on the following page) shows Orion and some surrounding constellations, with Betelgeuse and two bright "comparison stars" marked: Aldebaran, with magnitude +0.87, and Procyon, with magnitude +0.41. Observe Betelgeuse when all three stars are well above the horizon. Then you can compare the brightness of Betelgeuse with that of the other two stars: if it is slightly brighter than Procyon, Betelgeuse's magnitude would be about +0.2; if it is midway between Procyon and Aldebaran, its magnitude would be about +0.65; if it is slightly fainter than Aldebaran, its magnitude would be about +1.0. Record your measurement in an observing log. Also record the Julian Date of your observation, to the nearest day, using the instructions on page 41. Continue your measurements over several weeks, in collaboration with other members of your observing group, if you are part of one. You can also plot a "light curve" of the measurements: magnitude plotted vertically (brightest at the top), and Julian Date plotted horizontally. If you are part of an observing group, compare your measurements with those of your fellow observers.

Now you can access and plot other recent measurements from the AAVSO website. Go to

www.aavso.org/ql (quick look) to access the measurements
www.aavso.org/adata/curvegenerator.shtml to plot the observations

and type "alpha ori" in the "Or Name" box. The table of recent measurements includes the calendar and Julian Date, the visual magnitude, and the observer code. Plot a light curve with your measurements and the measurements from the AAVSO, using the data from the above website. Describe the brightness variations in the star. How do your measurements compare with the other recent ones by AAVSO observers?

For more information about the AAVSO and its education project "Hands-On Astrophysics," see the contact information on p. 259.

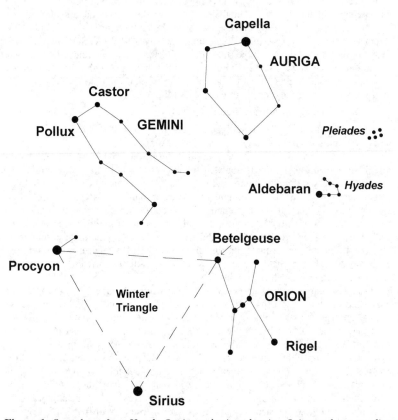

Figure 1: *Star chart, from Hands-On Astrophysics, showing Orion and surrounding constellations relative to the horizon on a midwinter evening, as seen by an observer in North America. Betelgeuse, Procyon (magnitude +0.41), and Aldebaran (magnitude +0.87) are shown. Estimate the magnitude of Betelgeuse, relative to Procyon and Aldebaran.*

STAR CLUSTERS
BY ANTHONY MOFFAT AND PETER JEDICKE

The study of star clusters is crucial to the understanding of stellar structure and evolution. For most purposes, it can be assumed that the stars seen in a given cluster formed nearly simultaneously from the same parent cloud of gas and dust; thus the basic factor that distinguishes one star from another is the quantity of matter each contains. Comparing one cluster with another, it is essentially only the age and the chemical composition of their stars that differ. But what makes one cluster *appear* different from another in the sky is mainly the degree of concentration and regularity, the spread in magnitude and colour of the member stars, all of which vary mainly with age, and the total number of stars. Extremely young clusters are often irregular in shape with clumps of newly formed stars, pervaded by lanes of obscuring dust and bright nebulosity (e.g. the Orion Nebula around the Trapezium Cluster), while the oldest clusters, which have not yet dissipated and have not been torn apart by external forces, tend to be symmetric in shape, with only the slower-burning, low-mass stars remaining visible; the massive stars will have spent their nuclear fuel and passed to the degenerate graveyard of white dwarfs, neutron stars, or black holes, depending on their original mass.

The star clusters in the following lists were selected as the most conspicuous. Two types can be recognized: *open* and *globular*. Open clusters often appear as irregular aggregates of tens to thousands of stars, sometimes barely distinguishable from random fluctuations of the general field; they are concentrated toward the disk of the Milky Way and generally contain stars of chemical abundance like the Sun. They range in age from very young to very old.

Sometimes we observe loose, extended groups of very young stars. When precise methods of photometry, spectroscopy, and kinematics are applied, we see that these stars often have a common, but not necessarily strictly coeval, origin. Such loose concentrations of stars are referred to as *associations*. Dynamically, they are generally unbound over time scales of the order of ten million years, being subject to the strong tidal forces of passing clouds and the background Milky Way Galaxy. Often, they contain subconcentrations of young open clusters (e.g. the double cluster h and χ Persei of slightly different ages despite their proximity, in the association Per OB1, which stretches over some 6° on the sky) with a strong gradient in age as the star formation process rips through them from one edge to another. In view of their sparse nature, we do not consider it appropriate here to list any of the over 100-odd catalogued Milky Way associations.

Globular clusters, on the other hand, are highly symmetric, extremely old and rich agglomerations of up to several million stars, distributed throughout the galactic halo but concentrated toward the centre of the Milky Way Galaxy. Compared to the Sun and other disk stars, they tend to be much less abundant in elements heavier than hydrogen and helium. For the larger and brighter globular clusters, the observer's goal is to see them well enough to distinguish a generous sprinkling of individual stars against a diffuse glowing background. Large telescope apertures and good skies will help resolve globular clusters. Higher powers are helpful for identification of smaller, more distant globular clusters.

The table on the next page includes all well-defined open clusters in the Milky Way Galaxy with diameters greater than 40′ and/or integrated magnitudes brighter than 5.0, as well as the richest clusters and some of special interest. The apparent integrated photographic magnitude (m_{pg}) is from Collinder, the angular diameter (**Diam.**) is generally from Trumpler, and the photographic magnitude of the fifth-brightest star (m_5) is from Shapley, except where in italics, which are new data. The distance (**Dist.**) is mainly from

Becker and Fenkart (*Astr. Astrophys. Suppl. 4,* 241, 1971). The earliest spectral type of cluster stars **(Sp)** is a measure of the age as follows: expressed in millions of years, O5 = 2, B0 = 8, B5 = 70, A0 = 400, A5 = 1000, F0 = 3000, and F5 = 10 000.

OPEN CLUSTERS

NGC/ other†	RA (2000) h m	Dec ° '	Mag. m_{pg}	Diam. '	m_5	Dist. 10^3 ly	Sp	Remarks
188	0 44.0	+85 21	9.3	14	14.6	5.0	F2	Oldest known
752	1 57.8	+37 41	6.6	45	9.6	1.2	A5	
869	2 19.0	+57 10	4.3	30	9.5	7.0	B1	h Per
884	2 22.4	+57 07	4.4	30	9.5	8.1	B0	χ Per, M supergiants
Perseus	3 22	+48 36	2.3	240	5	0.6	B1	Moving cl.; α Per
Pleiades	3 47.1	+24 08	1.6	120	4.2	0.41	B6	M45, best known
Hyades	4 20	+15 38	0.8	400	*3.9*	0.15	A2	Moving cl. **, in Taurus
1912	5 28.6	+35 50	7.0	18	9.7	4.6	B5	M38
1976/80	5 35.4	−5 23	2.5	50	*5.5*	1.3	O5	Trapezium, very young
2099	5 52.4	+32 32	6.2	24	9.7	4.2	B8	M37
2168	6 08.8	+24 21	5.6	29	9.0	2.8	B5	M35
2232	6 26.5	−4 45	4.1	20	7	1.6	B1	
2244	6 32.4	+4 52	5.2	27	*8.0*	5.3	O5	Rosette, very young
2264	6 41.0	+9 53	4.1	30	*8.0*	2.4	O8	S Mon
2287	6 47.1	−20 44	5.0	32	8.8	2.2	B4	M41
2362	7 18.8	−24 56	3.8	7	9.4	5.4	O9	τ CMa
2422	7 35.6	−14 30	4.3	30	9.8	1.6	B3	
2437	7 41.8	−14 49	6.6	27	10.8	5.4	B8	M46
2451	7 45.4	−37 58	3.7	37	6	1.0	B5	
2516	7 58.3	−60 54	3.3	50	10.1	1.2	B8	
2546	8 12.5	−37 39	5.0	45	7	2.7	B0	
2632	8 40.1	+20 00	3.9	90	7.5	0.59	A0	Praesepe, M44
IC2391	8 40.3	−53 03	2.6	45	3.5	0.5	B4	
IC2395	8 41.0	−48 11	4.6	20	10.1	2.9	B2	
2682	8 50.4	+11 50	7.4	18	10.8	2.7	F2	M67, very old
3114	10 02.6	−60 07	4.5	37	7	2.8	B5	
IC2602	10 43.3	−64 23	1.6	65	6	0.5	B1	θ Car
Tr16	10 45.2	−59 42	6.7	10	10	9.6	O3	η Car and Nebula
3532	11 06.4	−58 39	3.4	55	8.1	1.4	B8	
3766	11 36.1	−61 37	4.4	12	8.1	5.8	B1	
Coma	12 25.1	+26 06	2.9	300	5.5	0.3	A1	Very sparse
4755	12 53.6	−60 20	5.2	12	7	6.8	B3	κ Cru, "Jewel Box"
6067	16 13.3	−54 13	6.5	16	10.9	4.7	B3	G, K supergiants
6231	16 54.0	−41 48	3.5	16	7.5	5.8	O9	O supergiants, WR stars
Tr 24	16 57.0	−40 40	3.5	60	*7.3*	5.2	O5	
6405	17 40.1	−32 13	4.6	26	8.3	1.5	B4	M6
IC4665	17 46.7	+5 44	5.4	50	7	1.1	B8	
6475	17 53.9	−34 48	3.3	50	7.4	0.8	B5	M7
6494	17 56.9	−19 01	5.9	27	10.2	1.4	B8	M23
6523	18 03.1	−24 23	5.2	45	7	5.1	O5	M8, Lagoon Nebula
6611	18 18.9	−13 47	6.6	8	10.6	5.5	O7	M16, nebula
IC4725	18 31.7	−19 15	6.2	35	9.3	2.0	B3	M25, Cepheid U Sgr
IC4756	18 39.3	+5 27	5.4	50	8.5	1.4	A3	
6705	18 51.1	−6 17	6.8	12.5	12	5.6	B8	M11, very rich
Mel 227	20 11.2	−79 19	5.2	60	*9*	0.8	B9	
IC1396	21 38.9	+57 30	5.1	60	*8.5*	2.3	O6	Tr 37
7790	23 58.4	+61 13	7.1	4.5	11.7	10.3	B1	Cepheids CEa, CEb and CF Cas

†IC = Index Catalogue; Tr = Trumpler; Mel = Melotte; **Basic for distance determination

The table below includes all the globular clusters in the Messier list and most of the globular clusters with a total apparent visual magnitude brighter than about 8.0. A table of Milky Way globular cluster data is available on the website of W.E. Harris (see **physun.mcmaster.ca/~harris/WEHarris.html**). The apparent diameter (**Diam.**) is from Cragin, Lucyk, and Rappaport (*Deep Sky Field Guide To Uranometria 2000.0*, Willman-Bell, 1993). The concentration class (**Conc.**) is such that I is the most compact, XII the least. The integrated spectral type (**Int. Sp. T.**) varies mainly with the abundances. An observer who can see stars down to the magnitude given in the **V(HB)** ("horizontal-branch" magnitude) column has a good chance of being able to resolve the globular cluster; this information is from Djorgovski and Meylan (*Structure and Dynamics of Globular Clusters*, Astronomical Society of the Pacific, 1993, p. 341).

GLOBULAR CLUSTERS

NGC	M/ other	RA (2000) h m	Dec ° ′	Mag. m_v	Diam. ′	Conc.	Int. Sp.T.	Dist. 10^3 ly	V(HB)
104	47 Tuc	0 24.0	−72 04	3.95	30.9	III	G4	15	14.06
362		1 03.2	−70 50	6.40	12.9	III	F9	28	15.40
1851		5 14.0	−40 02	7.14	11.0	II	F7	46	16.10
1904	79	5 24.1	−24 31	7.73	8.7	V	F5	42	16.20
2808		9 11.9	−64 51	6.20	13.8	I	F7	30	16.19
3201		10 17.6	−46 24	6.75	18.2	X	F6	17	14.75
4590	68	12 39.5	−26 44	7.84	12.0	X	F2	33	15.60
4833		12 59.5	−70 52	6.91	13.5	VIII	F3	20	15.45
5024	53	13 12.9	+18 10	7.61	12.6	V	F6	60	16.94
5139	ω Cen	13 26.8	−47 28	3.68	36.3	VIII	F5	17	14.52
5272	3	13 42.2	+28 22	6.19	16.2	VI	F6	35	15.65
5904	5	15 18.5	+2 04	5.65	17.4	V	F7	26	15.11
6093	80	16 17.0	−22 58	7.33	8.9	II	F6	33	15.86
6121	4	16 23.6	−26 31	5.63	26.3	IX	F8	14	13.35
6171	107	16 32.5	−13 03	7.93	10.0	X	G0	21	15.70
6205	13	16 41.7	+36 27	5.78	16.6	V	F6	21	14.95
6218	12	16 47.1	−1 56	6.70	14.5	IX	F8	24	14.90
6254	10	16 57.1	−4 05	6.60	15.1	VII	F3	20	14.65
6266	62	17 01.2	−30 06	6.45	14.1	IV	F9	22	15.90
6273	19	17 02.6	−26 16	6.77	13.5	VIII	F7	28	16.95
6333	9	17 19.2	−18 30	7.72	9.3	VIII	F5	27	16.10
6341	92	17 17.1	+43 08	6.44	11.2	IV	F2	26	15.05
6388		17 36.3	−44 44	6.72	8.7	III	G2	37	16.90
6397		17 40.7	−53 40	5.73	25.7	IX	F4	9	12.90
6402	14	17 37.6	−3 14	7.59	11.7	VIII	F4	29	17.50
6541		18 08.0	−43 42	6.30	13.1	III	F6	13	15.10
6626	28	18 24.5	−24 52	6.79	11.2	IV	F8	19	15.68
6637	69	18 31.4	−32 20	7.64	7.1	V	G2	28	16.20
6656	22	18 36.3	−23 54	5.10	24.0	VII	F5	10	14.15
6681	70	18 43.2	−32 17	7.87	7.8	V	F5	29	15.60
6715	54	18 55.0	−30 28	7.60	9.1	III	F7	89	17.71
6752		19 10.9	−59 58	5.40	20.4	VI	F4	17	13.85
6779	56	19 16.6	+30 11	8.27	7.1	X	F5	33	16.20
6809	55	19 40.1	−30 57	6.32	19.0	XI	F4	20	14.35
6838	71	19 53.8	+18 46	8.19	7.2	†	G1	13	14.44
6864	75	20 06.0	−21 55	8.52	6.0	I	F9	61	17.45
6981	72	20 53.5	−12 32	9.27	5.9	IX	F7	55	16.99
7078	15	21 30.1	+12 10	6.20	12.3	IV	F3	34	15.86
7089	2	21 33.5	−0 50	6.47	12.9	II	F4	40	16.05
7099	30	21 40.4	−23 10	7.19	11.0	V	F3	26	15.10

†Originally thought to be an open cluster; never assigned a concentration class.

AN EXAMPLE: THE HYADES
THE CLOSEST CLUSTER AND THE FUNDAMENT FOR DISTANCES IN THE UNIVERSE

The Hyades cluster provides the foundation for essentially all distances, both local in our own galaxy and extragalactic, beyond about 300 ly from Earth. Once the distance to the Hyades is determined, the intrinsic brightnesses of its members can be found, leading to a calibration of its Main Sequence (MS) in the Colour–Magnitude diagram. Comparison of this MS with those of other clusters allows one to determine the distances of those clusters. By various methods of "boot-strapping," one obtains distances of globular clusters, Cepheid variable stars, and a host of other objects, eventually leading to the calibration of distances to the far corners of the universe.

At 147 ly, the distance to the centre of the Hyades cluster can now be readily found with very high accuracy using the so-called method of secular parallaxes. This is thanks to the high precision of the astrometric satellite HIPPARCOS proper motions and trigonometric parallaxes, which allow one to fix the distances to individual stars in the Hyades to within an error of about 2%. This in turn leads to a colour–absolute-magnitude diagram that displays an incredibly narrow MS: see the figure below (which is Fig.1 from de Bruijne, Hoogerwerf, and de Zeeuw, *Astrophys. J., 544,* L65, 2000). For the first time, one sees various gaps in the Hyades MS, some of which are intimately related to surface convective properties in the atmospheres of the stars. This in turn provides strong constraints on the stellar models.

Future astrometric satellites, such as ESA's GAIA, will improve the accuracy of such distances by several orders of magnitude, allowing one to study star clusters at much greater distances. This will then allow one to carry out revolutionary tests of the theory of stellar evolution with unprecedented accuracy.

The Hyades can be viewed with the unaided eye from both hemispheres as a loose clump of stars extending over some dozen Moon diameters near the head of Taurus the Bull. It is most conveniently seen, only 15° from the well-known but more distant Pleiades cluster, in the evening hours of January–March. Although the bright giant star Aldebaran is seen in the same direction as the Hyades, it is not a member, being a mere superposition along the line of sight at a different distance.

Colour–absolute-visual-magnitude diagram for 92 single-star members of the Hyades open cluster with high-precision HIPPARCOS secular parallaxes. Four bright member stars are identified, two of which are red giants. The two arrows indicate gaps caused by sudden changes in the properties of the convective atmospheres of the stars there.

AMATEUR SUPERNOVA HUNTING
BY REV. ROBERT EVANS

The first discovery of a supernova by an amateur astronomer was photographic, by G. Romano of Italy (SN 1957B in NGC 4564); the first visual discovery was by J. Bennett of South Africa (SN 1968L in M83). In Australia in 1980, the author began systematic visual searching using a simple 250-mm backyard telescope and made two discoveries the following year. K. Okazaki of Japan, who discovered two supernovae, one each in 1983 and 1984, was one of several Japanese amateurs to mount systematic photographic searches at that time.

By the late 1980s, most of the supernovae brighter than 15th magnitude were being found visually by amateurs. In the early 1990s, professional astronomers started using supernova studies to address major problems in cosmology; at that time, they depended largely upon amateur searches to provide them with the best and brightest supernovae in nearby galaxies. These nearby supernovae provided much of the benchmark information needed for studying supernovae at remote distances, which led to independent estimates for the expansion, age, and fate of the universe.

CCD Supernova Hunting

In the last few years, the cost of charge-coupled devices (CCDs) has fallen to the point where many amateurs can afford to use them on computer-controlled telescopes. Some of these amateurs are hunting supernovae with resounding success. There are a number of advantages to using telescopes with CCDs and computer control:

(1) You can observe in locations with some light pollution or in the presence of fairly strong moonlight.

(2) With a computer to direct the telescope to individual galaxies, it is no longer necessary to know the sky well.

(3) With appropriate computer control of the telescope, you can sit in a warm room facing the computer screen.

(4) If your equipment is good enough, it will find supernovae without your presence.

(5) Stars as faint as 18th or 19th magnitude become accessible, which includes most supernovae in nearby galaxies plus the brighter supernovae in many distant galaxies, out to about 300 million light-years.

Using a CCD brings so many thousands of galaxies within range that you will never have enough time to observe them all! However, you will need reference materials for all the galaxies on your observing list—even if you make the reference images yourself—so that you can tell when a new object appears near a galaxy.

Visual Supernova Hunting

Visual supernova hunting has special requirements, but it has a number of advantages over using a CCD. The requirements are as follows:

(1) A reasonably dark observing site is needed.

(2) Your telescope needs to be easily manageable so that you can locate objects quickly, and the aperture needs to be big enough so that you can see down to about 15th magnitude. You can then observe all the nearby galaxies (out to, say, 100 million light-years). You will then be able to see most supernovae in galaxies out to about 25 million light-years and the brighter supernovae out to 100 million light-years or more. But, naturally, your chances of success decrease with the distance of the galaxy. Fainter supernovae in any given galaxy may be more numerous than the brighter ones, although the latter are the most interesting, scientifically.

(3) As in CCD searches, charts or suitable photographs of all your target galaxies are needed, so that you can tell when a new object appears.

The advantages of visual searching are the following:

(1) The equipment is less expensive than that needed for CCD work.

(2) An experienced visual observer usually knows the location and the normal appearance of many target galaxies and can thus work through observations of galaxies at 10 times the speed of anyone using a CCD on an amateur telescope. Professional-standard CCDs are quicker but are still much more expensive than those used by amateurs.

(3) You become very familiar with the night sky. (Personally, I think this is a great benefit of visual searching.)

(4) Amateurs who rely on computers to find galaxies are deceived by technology into being ignorant of the sky. Thus, when the technology fails (as it does from time to time), the search halts since the observer does not know where to locate target galaxies. A visual observer who knows the sky is immune to this problem.

Verification and Reporting

Verification of any suspected new discovery is vitally important. The first step is to check any suspect against all available photographs, CCD images, or charts of that galaxy. Measure carefully the offset of the new star from the nucleus of the galaxy. Watch the object for any possible movement against nearby stars. Note the time of your discovery (UT). It is necessary to have a team of other observers who can make independent observations of the new object, and who will do so immediately, if asked. These other observers must also have enough galaxy resources so that they can eliminate anything that is not a supernova, and they should be spread out over a number of locations in case bad weather puts any one observer out of action.

The Central Bureau for Astronomical Telegrams has issued instructions describing how much verification is needed about any possible new supernova, and these should be consulted. CCD observers need at least five observations covering 24 hours. A visual observer should have independent observations by people who know what they are doing. And even after the Central Bureau has been notified, spectra will probably need to be obtained through one of the main observatories before the Bureau will finally announce a discovery.

When notifying the Central Bureau, provide full details of all observations of the new object: the name and location of the person making the report, the discoverer's name and location, details of the reference materials consulted, details concerning the equipment used, universal time of all observations, name and position of the galaxy, offset and brightness of the supernova, and similar details about each verifying observation. Observers who are not already known at the Bureau should be especially thorough in detailing and supporting their report. All discoveries can be emailed to the Central Bureau at cbat@cfa.harvard.edu.

Much helpful advice is available in the *AAVSO Supernova Search Manual*, which is available from the AAVSO, 25 Birch Street, Cambridge MA 02138, USA, for the cost of postage only. It can also be downloaded through the Internet at www.aavso.org/supernovatwo.stm (see also www.aavso.org/supernovaone.stm).

Editor's Note: Robert Evans, who made his first supernova discovery in 1981, holds the record for visual discoveries of supernovae: 35. Ten of these were found using a 250-mm telescope, 4 using a 310-mm telescope, 18 with a 410-mm instrument (all "backyard" variety newtonians), and 3 using the 1.02-m telescope at Siding Spring Observatory (Australian National University). In addition, he has discovered 4 supernovae (plus a comet) on U.K. Schmidt films specially exposed by Anglo Australian Observatory staff in a Pro-Am project that Evans shared with Dr. Brian Schmidt of Mount Stromlo Observatory and Robert McNaught for a short period around 1996.

EXPIRED STARS
BY ROY BISHOP

Stars are where the action is, and the action is fuelled by gravitation and thermo-nuclear fusion. Gravitation, the midwife and undertaker, forms a star, heats it to the temperatures necessary to ignite successive stages of fusion reactions, and when nuclear fuel runs out, crushes the ashes of the star into one of three final states: white dwarf, neutron star, or black hole. Thermonuclear fusion merely delays the onset of further collapse and higher temperatures. In the case of our Sun, the first and by far the longest delay, the "hang-up" provided by hydrogen-to-helium fusion, is already half over.

White Dwarfs

Stars comparable to our Sun have insufficient gravity to reach the temperatures necessary to form nuclei heavier than carbon or oxygen. When the thermal support pressure generated by fusion wanes, gravity gradually crushes the central portion of the star. If the mass of this core is less than 1.4 solar masses (a limit discovered by a leading astrophysicist of the 20th century, Subramanyan Chandrasekhar), the collapse halts at a very hot, Earth-sized remnant known as a white dwarf. At this point, the squeeze of gravity is offset by *electron degeneracy pressure,* an intrinsic aspect of the wave–particle nature of matter and the same pressure responsible for the stability and size of an atom. However, in the case of a white dwarf, the pressure is such that the electrons are not tied to individual atomic nuclei but occupy the whole star. In this sense, the star has become a giant atom. In physics jargon: electrons are fermions (i.e. they obey Fermi–Dirac quantum statistics) and, hence, abide by the Pauli Exclusion Principle, which dictates that no two electrons can occupy the same quantum state. This results in an immense pressure, sufficient to prevent further collapse, provided the mass is less than the Chandrasekhar limit. White dwarf diameters are about 1% that of our Sun, which has a nearly water-like average density (1 g/cm^3). Thus a cubic centimetre of white dwarf material has a mass near 100^3 g or one tonne (like a Honda Civic crushed into a sugar cube).

Because of their immense thermal energy and small surface area, white dwarfs cool extremely slowly. The universe is not yet old enough for any white dwarf to have cooled sufficiently to become a "black dwarf." Also, white dwarfs are intrinsically very faint and thus only those close to the solar system can be seen.

Only one white dwarf is easily observable with a small telescope: **omicron 2 Eridani B** (also designated 40 Eridani B), located 16.5 light-years from Earth. Omicron 2 Eridani A, the bright (mag. 4.4) companion to the dim (mag. 9.5) white dwarf, is shown on the JANUARY ALL-SKY CHART on p. 294: o^2 Eri A is the eastern (left-hand) member of the close pair of stars located due west of the word "Rigel." Omicron 2 Eridani B, the white dwarf, is located only 83″ east-southeast of o^2 Eri A (position angle ≈110°). Remarkably, stars A and B are accompanied by a third star, a faint (mag. 11.2) red dwarf star, o^2 Eri C, which resides only 9″ north of B. (There is a brighter and closer white dwarf, the companion of Sirius, α CMa B, but it is usually lost in the glare of Sirius. See THE NEAREST STARS (pp. 251–255) and DOUBLE AND MULTIPLE STARS (pp. 256–258) for more information on both of these stellar systems.)

For the observer with a small telescope, o^2 Eri B is the only Earth-sized object visible in the depths of interstellar space, the only visible object with a mass density far exceeding that of ordinary matter, the only accessible star no longer powered by nuclear reactions, and the only star that has expired and can still be seen.

Neutron Stars

For a large star of about eight or more solar masses, energy-releasing reactions end in its centre with the fusion of silicon nuclei into iron. Iron has the most tightly bound nucleus (per nuclear particle) and, hence, is no good as a fuel for further fusion. Electron degeneracy pressure supports the inert iron core until silicon fusion in a surrounding shell supplies enough additional iron to push the inert core over the Chandrasekhar limit. Gravity then overwhelms electron degeneracy pressure and the core collapses in less than a second. Gravitation-induced temperatures rise past 10^{10} K, sufficient to disassemble heavy nuclei synthesized over the life of the star. This absorbs energy, accelerating the collapse. Also, electrons attain sufficient energy to combine with protons to form neutrons and neutrinos, another energy-absorbing reaction that also removes electrons, further hastening the collapse.

Provided the infalling mass is less than about three solar masses, like a hammer striking an anvil, when the core reaches a diameter of about 20 km the infall is violently arrested by a combination of *neutron* degeneracy pressure and the short-range repulsive nature of the strong nuclear force, the same agents that govern the size and structure of the nuclei of atoms of ordinary matter. With a diameter 500 times smaller than that of a white dwarf, the density at this stage is 500^3 larger, 100 million tonnes per cubic centimetre (like an aircraft carrier crushed to the size of the ball of a ballpoint pen). This is the density of ordinary atomic nuclei. The star's core has effectively become a gigantic nucleus, composed primarily of neutrons.

The abrupt rebound of the nearly rigid central core reverses the infall of the outer layers, turning the implosion into a spectacular explosion, a Type II supernova. The subsequent steps are complex and not yet well understood, but appear to involve interactions with the immense numbers of neutrinos generated in the neutron production. The gravitational energy released in the sudden collapse of the couple of solar masses now locked in the central neutron star is about 10^{46} J. This is far more energy than our Sun will produce in its entire 10-billion-year lifetime.

Over the next several thousand years, the remnants of the outer layers of the star form an expanding, glowing cloud of gas and dust, seeding interstellar space with the heavy chemical elements (oxygen, silicon, iron, uranium, etc.) synthesized in its outer layers both before and during the supernova explosion. The potassium ions moving in the neurons of your brain as you read these words emerged from such a conflagration some 5 billion years ago.

No neutron stars are visible in a small telescope, although one is *indirectly* visible in the **Crab Nebula,** M1. The Crab supernova was a bright, naked-eye star in the skies of Earth in the year 1054 AD, although it had taken 6000 years for the light of the explosion to reach our planet. The nebula we see today is the expanding debris cloud as it was nearly 1000 years after the initial explosion.

The Crab Nebula glows across the electromagnetic spectrum, from radio waves to gamma rays, powered by the energy contained in the gravitational field and the rapid but decreasing spin of the neutron star at its centre. The glow of the debris cloud is like the glow of a red-hot disk brake slowing the spin of a wheel. The visible light from the cloud is *synchrotron radiation* emitted by electrons as they spiral in the tangled magnetic field of the neutron star. Nowhere else in the heavens is such an exotic light visible in a small telescope, polarized light with the brilliance of a thousand suns, emitted not by atoms but by free electrons being flung about by a spinning neutron star. The neutron star itself is known as a *pulsar* because it flashes 30 times per second, in step with its spin. However, even if the Crab pulsar were bright enough to be visible in a small telescope, the flashing would not be apparent because, as in a motion picture or cathode-ray tube monitor, the flicker is too rapid for the eye to follow.

Colour photographs of the Crab Nebula reveal a celestial gift: a package of bluish synchrotron radiation wrapped in the loops of a tattered red ribbon—fragments of the shattered star, fluorescing in hydrogen-alpha light. Unfortunately, the luminance of the fluorescence is below the threshold for retinal cone vision, and rod vision is blind to H-alpha light. Thus all we can see is the ghostly cloud of synchrotron radiation.

The Crab Nebula is located 1° northwest of the star at the tip of the east horn of the constellation Taurus, ζ Tau. In the JANUARY ALL-SKY CHART on p. 294, the nebula is the tiny circle of dots 5 mm to the right of the cross marking the summer solstice (SS). In a telescope the nebula appears merely as a small glowing cloud, but to the knowledgeable observer, this synchrotron radiation brake of a spinning neutron star is an object for profound contemplation.

Black Holes

Stars whose masses are greater than about 20 suns likely retain more than 3 solar masses in their imploding cores. This is sufficient that gravitation will overwhelm not only the degeneracy pressure of electrons, but also the highly incompressible nature of nuclear matter. Within seconds, spacetime itself closes around the imploding stellar core, removing all but the core's gravitational field from the observable universe. The star has become a black hole.

The earliest and best candidate for a stellar black hole is **Cygnus X-1,** one of the strongest galactic X-ray sources in the sky. Cygnus X-1 is the invisible companion of a star that can be seen in a small telescope: HDE 226868, an O9.7Iab star, a very luminous, very hot supergiant located several thousand light-years from the Sun. It orbits its nearby, unseen companion with a 5.6-day period. The mass of the companion is between 10 and 16 solar masses, far too large for it to be a white dwarf or neutron star. X-rays are generated as material from the supergiant falls toward the invisible companion. The X-rays extend to energies of 100 keV and vary on time scales as short as milliseconds, indicative of a very compact companion.

At 9th magnitude, the supergiant HDE 226868 is visible in any small telescope. It is less than half a degree from the 4th magnitude star eta Cygni. Eta Cygni is the star in the neck of the swan, next to the "C" in CYGNUS on the SEPTEMBER ALL-SKY CHART on p. 298. Any low magnification will more than encompass the field shown in the **finder chart** at the left. North is upward, eta Cygni is at the lower right, and HDE 226868 is indicated by the small arrow. The chart magnitude limit is about 13.

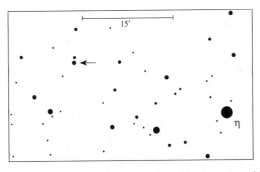

Although HDE 226868 is a blue supergiant, in telescopes of sufficient aperture this star appears orange because of interstellar dust between us and the star.

All that is to be seen is the hot supergiant, but the view will be worth the search if you know that at this same location in the field of your telescope lurks one of the most likely candidates for a black hole, a knot in the fabric of spacetime where a giant star has vanished. No painting, computer simulation, or Hollywood movie can match this observation.

NEBULAE AND GALAXIES

GALACTIC NEBULAE

By William Herbst

The following objects were selected from the brightest and largest of the various classes to illustrate the different types of interactions between stars and interstellar matter in our galaxy. *Emission regions* (HII) are excited by the strong ultraviolet flux of young, hot stars and are characterized by the lines of hydrogen in their spectra. *Reflection nebulae* (Ref) result from the diffusion of starlight by clouds of interstellar dust. At certain stages of their evolution stars become unstable and explode, shedding their outer layers into what becomes a *planetary nebula* (Pl) or a *supernova remnant* (SN). *Protostellar nebulae* (PrS) are objects still poorly understood; they are somewhat similar to the reflection nebulae, but their associated stars, often variable, are very luminous infrared stars that may be in the earliest stages of stellar evolution. Also included in the selection are three *extended complexes* (Comp) of special interest for their rich population of dark and bright nebulosities of various types. In the table S is the optical surface brightness in magnitude per square second of arc of representative regions of the nebula, and m^* is the magnitude of the associated star.

NGC	M	Con	RA (2000) Dec h m	° ′	Type	Size ′	S mag/sq″	m^*	Dist. 10^3 ly	Remarks
1435		Tau	3 47.5	+24 05	Ref	15	20	4	0.4	Merope nebula
1535		Eri	4 14.2	−12 45	Pl	0.5	17	12		
1952	1	Tau	5 34.5	+22 01	SN	5	19	16v	4	"Crab" + pulsar
1976	42	Ori	5 35.3	−5 24	HII	30	18	4	1.5	Orion Nebula
2070		Dor	5 38.6	−69 05	HII	20	—	13	200	Tarantula Nebula
ζ Ori		Ori	5 40.8	−1 56	Comp	2°			1.5	Incl. "Horsehead"
2068	78	Ori	5 46.8	+0 02	Ref	5	20		1.5	
1C443		Gem	6 17.6	+22 36	SN	40			2	
2244		Mon	6 32.4	+4 52	HII	50	21	7	3	Rosette Nebula
2261		Mon	6 39.1	+8 43	PrS	2		12v	4	Hubble's Variable Neb.
2392		Gem	7 29.2	+20 54	Pl	0.3	18	10	10	Clown Face Nebula
2626		Vel	8 35.6	−40 38	Ref	2	—	10	3	
3132		Vel	10 07.0	−40 25	Pl	1	17	10	—	Eight-Burst
3324		Car	10 37.5	−58 38	HII	15	—	8	9	
3372		Car	10 45.1	−59 41	HII	80	—	6v	9	Carina Nebula
3503		Car	11 01.3	−60 43	Ref	3	—	11	9	
3587	97	UMa	11 14.8	+55 01	Pl	3	21	13	12	Owl Nebula
—		Cru	12 51	−63	Dark	6°		—	0.5	Coal Sack
5189		Mus	13 33.8	−66 00	HII	150	—	10	—	
ρ Oph		Oph	16 25.6	−23 27	Comp	4°			0.5	Bright + dark nebula
6514	20	Sgr	18 02.4	−23 02	HII	15	19		3.5	Trifid Nebula
6523	8	Sgr	18 03.6	−24 23	HII	40	18		4.5	Lagoon Nebula
6543		Dra	17 58.6	+66 37	Pl	0.4	15	11	3.5	
6618	17	Sgr	18 20.9	−16 11	HII	20	19		3	Horseshoe Nebula
6720	57	Lyr	18 53.6	+33 03	Pl	1.2	18	15	5	Ring Nebula
6726		CrA	19 01.7	−36 54	PrS	5	—	7	0.5	
6853	27	Vul	19 59.5	+22 43	Pl	7	19	13	3.5	Dumbbell Nebula
6888		Cyg	20 12.3	+38 25	HII	15				
γ Cyg		Cyg	20 22.2	+40 16	Comp	6°				HII + dark nebula
6960/95		Cyg	20 45.6	+30 42	SN	150			2.5	Cygnus loop
7000		Cyg	20 58.9	+44 19	HII	100	22		3.5	North America Nebula
7009		Aqr	21 04.1	−11 23	Pl	0.5	16	12	3	Saturn Nebula
7027		Cyg	21 07.1	+42 14	Pl	0.2	15	13		
7129		Cep	21 43.0	+65 06	Ref	3	21	10	2.5	Small cluster
7293		Aqr	22 29.6	−20 48	Pl	13	22	13		Helix Nebula

THE MESSIER CATALOGUE
BY ALAN DYER

Charles Messier's Catalogue provides a selection of the best and brightest deep-sky wonders for Northern Hemisphere viewers. Messier compiled his list in the late 1700s to aid prospective comet hunters. Some of these objects he discovered himself, some were first seen by other astronomers of the day, while a few (the Pleiades and the Beehive) were known since antiquity. The Messier numbers do not follow an ordered sequence across the sky. Rather, they are numbered in the order he discovered and catalogued them. Although he intended to, Messier never did publish a list with entries renumbered in order of right ascension.

In our version of the Messier Catalogue, we've listed the objects by season *for the evening observer,* grouping the objects within their respective constellations. The constellations are then listed roughly in order of increasing right ascension, that is constellations farther to the east and which rise later in the night are farther down the list. This is to help plan the sequence of an evening's Messier hunt.

The identity of some Messier objects is controversial. There is evidence that M91 and M102 are mistaken observations of M58 and M101, respectively. M104 and M109 were found by a colleague, Pierre Mechain, and reported to Messier for inclusion in his Catalogue. NGC 205, one of the companion galaxies to M31, the Andromeda Galaxy, was apparently found by Messier but never included in his Catalogue. Modern-day observers have dubbed this object M110. In our list, we have included 110 entries, including two objects that some have suggested as alternative candidates for M91 and M102.

Modern-day Messier hunters often wonder what telescopes Messier used. The largest were 190-mm and 200-mm reflectors. However, their speculum metal mirrors would have had the equivalent light gathering power of a modern 80-mm to 100-mm reflector. He also used a number of 90-mm refractors. Today, a dark site and a good 80-mm refractor or 100-mm reflector should be sufficient for completing the entire list. Objects M6 and M7 are the most southerly, while M74 and M76 are often considered the faintest and most difficult. M83's low altitude and diffuse appearance make it a challenge for Canadian observers north of 50° latitude.

The columns contain the Messier number, the object's NGC (New General Catalogue) number, the constellation, the type of object, its epoch 2000 coordinates, visual magnitude m_v, and angular size in minutes of arc (planetary nebula sizes are given in seconds of arc "). Entries marked "**!!**" are showpiece objects. OC = open cluster; GC = globular cluster; PN = planetary nebula; EN = emission nebula; RN = reflection nebula; E/RN = combination of emission and reflection nebula; SNR = supernova remnant; G = galaxy (E = elliptical, I = irregular, SA = normal spiral, SB = barred spiral, S0 = lenticular). Data are taken from *The Deep Sky Field Guide to Uranometria 2000.0* (published by Willmann-Bell, Inc., 1993), compiled by Murray Cragin, James Lucyk, and Barry Rappaport from a variety of contemporary catalogues. Some sizes have been rounded to two significant figures. Also recommended as an excellent guide is *The Messier Objects,* by Stephen James O'Meara (Cambridge University Press, 1998).

> *The RASC offers observing certificates for members who observe the 110 objects in the Messier list or the 110 objects in the Finest NGC list (see pp. 262–264). For beginners or observers using binoculars the Society also offers the "Explore the Universe" Certificate. Contact your local Centre or the RASC National Office (see pp. 8–9) for details.*

NUMERICAL LISTING OF MESSIER OBJECTS

M#	Sky	Con	M#	Sky	Con	M#	Sky	Con	M#	Sky	Con	M#	Sky	Con
1	Win	Tau	23	Sum	Sgr	45	Win	Tau	67	Spr	Cnc	89	Spr	Vir
2	Aut	Aqr	24	Sum	Sgr	46	Win	Pup	68	Spr	Hya	90	Spr	Vir
3	Spr	CVn	25	Sum	Sgr	47	Win	Pup	69	Sum	Sgr	91	Spr	Com
4	Sum	Sco	26	Sum	Sct	48	Win	Hya	70	Sum	Sgr	92	Sum	Her
5	Spr	Ser	27	Sum	Vul	49	Spr	Vir	71	Sum	Sge	93	Win	Pup
6	Sum	Sco	28	Sum	Sgr	50	Win	Mon	72	Aut	Aqr	94	Spr	CVn
7	Sum	Sco	29	Sum	Cyg	51	Spr	CVn	73	Aut	Aqr	95	Spr	Leo
8	Sum	Sgr	30	Aut	Cap	52	Aut	Cas	74	Aut	Psc	96	Spr	Leo
9	Sum	Oph	31	Aut	And	53	Spr	Com	75	Sum	Sgr	97	Spr	UMa
10	Sum	Oph	32	Aut	And	54	Sum	Sgr	76	Aut	Per	98	Spr	Com
11	Sum	Sct	33	Aut	Tri	55	Sum	Sgr	77	Aut	Cet	99	Spr	Com
12	Sum	Oph	34	Aut	Per	56	Sum	Lyr	78	Win	Ori	100	Spr	Com
13	Sum	Her	35	Win	Gem	57	Sum	Lyr	79	Win	Lep	101	Spr	UMa
14	Sum	Oph	36	Win	Aur	58	Spr	Vir	80	Sum	Sco	102	Spr	Dra?
15	Aut	Peg	37	Win	Aur	59	Spr	Vir	81	Spr	UMa	103	Aut	Cas
16	Sum	Ser	38	Win	Aur	60	Spr	Vir	82	Spr	UMa	104	Spr	Vir
17	Sum	Sgr	39	Sum	Cyg	61	Spr	Vir	83	Spr	Hya	105	Spr	Leo
18	Sum	Sgr	40	Spr	UMa	62	Sum	Oph	84	Spr	Vir	106	Spr	CVn
19	Sum	Oph	41	Win	CMa	63	Spr	CVn	85	Spr	Com	107	Sum	Oph
20	Sum	Sgr	42	Win	Ori	64	Spr	Com	86	Spr	Vir	108	Spr	UM
21	Sum	Sgr	43	Win	Ori	65	Spr	Leo	87	Spr	Vir	109	Spr	UMa
22	Sum	Sgr	44	Spr	Cnc	66	Spr	Leo	88	Spr	Com	110	Aut	And

SEASONAL LISTING OF MESSIER OBJECTS

M#	NGC	Con	Type	RA (2000) Dec h m ° ′		m_v	Size ′	Remarks
The Winter Sky								
1	1952	Tau	SNR	5 34.5	+22 01	8.4	6 × 4	!! famous Crab Neb. supernova remnant
45	—	Tau	OC	3 47.0	+24 07	1.2	110	!! Pleiades; look for subtle nebulosity
36	1960	Aur	OC	5 36.1	+34 08	6.0	12	bright but scattered group; use low pow.
37	2099	Aur	OC	5 52.4	+32 33	5.6	20	!! finest of 3 Auriga clusters; very rich
38	1912	Aur	OC	5 28.7	+35 50	6.4	21	look for small cluster NGC 1907 1/2° S
42	1976	Ori	E/RN	5 35.4	−5 27	—	65 × 60	!! Orion Nebula; finest in northern sky
43	1982	Ori	E/RN	5 35.6	−5 16	—	20 × 15	detached part of Orion Nebula
78	2068	Ori	RN	5 46.7	+0 03	—	8 × 6	bright featureless reflection nebula
79	1904	Lep	GC	5 24.5	−24 33	7.8	8.7	200-mm telescope needed to resolve
35	2168	Gem	OC	6 08.9	+24 20	5.1	28	!! look for sm. cluster NGC 2158 1/4° S
41	2287	CMa	OC	6 47.0	−20 44	4.5	38	4° south of Sirius; bright but coarse
50	2323	Mon	OC	7 03.2	−8 20	5.9	16	between Sirius & Procyon; use low mag.
46	2437	Pup	OC	7 41.8	−14 49	6.1	27	!! contains planetary nebula NGC 2438
47	2422	Pup	OC	7 36.6	−14 30	4.4	29	coarse cluster 1.5° west of M46
93	2447	Pup	OC	7 44.6	−23 52	≈6.2	22	compact, bright cluster; fairly rich
48	2548	Hya	OC	8 13.8	−5 48	5.8	54	former "lost" Messier; large, sparse cl.

SEASONAL LISTING OF MESSIER OBJECTS (continued)

M#	NGC	Con	Type	RA (2000) h m	Dec ° ′	m_V	Size ′	Remarks
The Spring Sky								
44	2632	Cnc	OC	8 40.1	+19 59	3.1	95	!! Beehive or Praesepe; use low power
67	2682	Cnc	OC	8 50.4	+11 49	6.9	29	one of the oldest star clusters known
40	—	UMa	2 stars	12 22.4	+58 05	8.0	—	double star Winnecke 4; separation 50″
81	3031	UMa	G-SAab	9 55.6	+69 04	6.9	24 × 13	!! bright spiral visible in binoculars
82	3034	UMa	G-I0	9 55.8	+69 41	8.4	12 × 6	!! the "exploding" galaxy; M81 1/2° S
97	3587	UMa	PN	11 14.8	+55 01	9.9	194″	!! Owl Nebula; distinct grey oval
101	5457	UMa	G-SABcd	14 03.2	+54 21	7.9	26 × 26	!! Pinwheel Gal.; diffuse face-on spiral
108	3556	UMa	G-SBcd	11 11.5	+55 40	10.0	8.1 × 2.1	nearly edge-on; paired with M97 3/4° SE
109	3992	UMa	G-SBbc	11 57.6	+53 23	9.8	7.6 × 4.3	barred spiral near γ UMa
65	3623	Leo	G-SABa	11 18.9	+13 05	9.3	8.7 × 2.2	!! bright elongated spiral
66	3627	Leo	G-SABb	11 20.2	+12 59	8.9	8.2 × 3.9	!! M65 and NGC 3628 in same field
95	3351	Leo	G-SBb	10 44.0	+11 42	9.7	7.8 × 4.6	bright barred spiral
96	3368	Leo	G-SABab	10 46.8	+11 49	9.2	6.9 × 4.6	M95 in same field
105	3379	Leo	G-E1	10 47.8	+12 35	9.3	3.9 × 3.9	bright elliptical near M95 and M96
53	5024	Com	GC	13 12.9	+18 10	7.5	12.6	150-mm telescope needed to resolve
64	4826	Com	G-SAab	12 56.7	+21 41	8.5	9.2 × 4.6	!! Black Eye Gal.; eye needs big scope
85	4382	Com	G-SA0+	12 25.4	+18 11	9.1	7.5 × 5.7	bright elliptical shape
88	4501	Com	G-SAb	12 32.0	+14 25	9.6	6.1 × 2.8	bright multiple-arm spiral
91	4548	Com	G-SBb	12 35.4	+14 30	10.2	5.0 × 4.1	some lists say M91 = M58, not NGC4548
98	4192	Com	G-SABab	12 13.8	+14 54	10.1	9.1 × 2.1	nearly edge-on spiral near star 6 Com. B.
99	4254	Com	G-SAc	12 18.8	+14 25	9.9	4.6 × 4.3	nearly face-on spiral near M98
100	4321	Com	G-SABbc	12 22.9	+15 49	9.3	6.2 × 5.3	face-on spiral with starlike nucleus
49	4472	Vir	G-E2	12 29.8	+8 00	8.4	8.1 × 7.1	very bright elliptical
58	4579	Vir	G-SABb	12 37.7	+11 49	9.7	5.5 × 4.6	bright barred spiral; M59 and M60 1° E
59	4621	Vir	G-E5	12 42.0	+11 39	9.6	4.6 × 3.6	bright elliptical paired with M60
60	4649	Vir	G-E2	12 43.7	+11 33	8.8	7.1 × 6.1	bright elliptical with M59 and NGC 4647
61	4303	Vir	G-SABbc	12 21.9	+4 28	9.7	6.0 × 5.9	face-on two-armed spiral
84	4374	Vir	G-E1	12 25.1	+12 53	9.1	5.1 × 4.1	!! w/ M86 in Markarian's Chain
86	4406	Vir	G-E3	12 26.2	+12 57	8.9	12 × 9	!! w/ many NGC galaxies in Chain
87	4486	Vir	G-E0-1	12 30.8	+12 24	8.6	7.1 × 7.1	the one with famous jet and black hole
89	4552	Vir	G-E	12 35.7	+12 33	9.8	3.4 × 3.4	elliptical; resembles M87 but smaller
90	4569	Vir	G-SABab	12 36.8	+13 10	9.5	10 × 4	bright barred spiral near M89
104	4594	Vir	G-SA	12 40.0	−11 37	8.0	7.1 × 4.4	!! Sombrero Galaxy; look for dust lane
3	5272	CVn	GC	13 42.2	+28 23	5.9	16.2	!! contains many variable stars
51	5194/5	CVn	G-SAbc	13 29.9	+47 12	8.4	8 × 7	!! Whirlpool Galaxy; superb in big scope
63	5055	CVn	G-SAbc	13 15.8	+42 02	8.6	14 × 8	!! Sunflower Galaxy; bright, elongated
94	4736	CVn	G-SAab	12 50.9	+41 07	8.2	13 × 11	very bright and comet-like
106	4258	CVn	G-SABbc	12 19.0	+47 18	8.4	20 × 8	!! superb large, bright spiral
68	4590	Hya	GC	12 39.5	−26 45	7.7	12	150-mm telescope needed to resolve
83	5236	Hya	G-SABc	13 37.0	−29 52	7.6	16 × 13	large and diffuse; superb from far south
102	5866?	Dra	G-SA0+	15 06.5	+55 46	9.9	6.6 × 3.2	or is M102 = M101? (look for 5907)
5	5904	Ser	GC	15 18.6	+2 05	5.7	17.4	!! one of the sky's finest globulars
The Summer Sky								
13	6205	Her	GC	16 41.7	+36 28	5.7	16.6	!! Hercules Cluster; NGC 6207 1/2° NE
92	6341	Her	GC	17 17.1	+43 08	6.4	11.2	9° NE of M13; fine but often overlooked
9	6333	Oph	GC	17 19.2	−18 31	7.6	9.3	smallest of Ophiuchus globulars
10	6254	Oph	GC	16 57.1	−4 06	6.6	15.1	rich globular cluster; M12 is 3° NW
12	6218	Oph	GC	16 47.2	−1 57	6.8	14.5	loose globular cluster near M10
14	6402	Oph	GC	17 37.6	−3 15	7.6	11.7	200-mm telescope needed to resolve
19	6273	Oph	GC	17 02.6	−26 16	6.7	13.5	oblate globular; M62 4° south
62	6266	Oph	GC	17 01.2	−30 07	6.7	14.1	asymmetrical; in rich field

SEASONAL LISTING OF MESSIER OBJECTS (continued)

M#	NGC	Con	Type	RA (2000) h m	Dec ° ′	m_v	Size ′	Remarks
Summer Sky continued…								
107	6171	Oph	GC	16 32.5	−13 03	8.1	10.0	small, faint globular
4	6121	Sco	GC	16 23.6	−26 32	5.8	26.3	bright globular near Antares
6	6405	Sco	OC	17 40.1	−32 13	4.2	33	!! Butterfly Cluster; best at low power
7	6475	Sco	OC	17 53.9	−34 49	3.3	80	!! excellent in binocs or rich-field scope
80	6093	Sco	GC	16 17.0	−22 59	7.3	8.9	very compressed globular
16	6611	Ser	EN + OC	18 18.6	−13 58	—	35 × 28	Eagle Neb. w/ open cl.; use neb. filter
8	6523	Sgr	EN	18 03.8	−24 23	—	45 × 30	!! Lagoon Nebula w/ open cl. NGC 6530
17	6618	Sgr	EN	18 20.8	−16 11	—	20 × 15	!! Swan or Omega Nebula; use neb. filter
18	6613	Sgr	OC	18 19.9	−17 08	6.9	10	sparse cluster; 1° south of M17
20	6514	Sgr	E/RN	18 02.3	−23 02	—	20 × 20	!! Trifid Nebula; look for dark lanes
21	6531	Sgr	OC	18 04.6	−22 30	5.9	13	0.7° NE of M20; sparse cluster
22	6656	Sgr	GC	18 36.4	−23 54	5.1	24	spectacular from southern latitude
23	6494	Sgr	OC	17 56.8	−19 01	5.5	27	bright, loose open cluster
24	—	Sgr	starcloud	18 16.5	−18 50	4.6	95 × 35	rich star cloud; best in big binoculars
25	IC4725	Sgr	OC	18 31.6	−19 15	4.6	32	bright but sparse open cluster
28	6626	Sgr	GC	18 24.5	−24 52	6.8	11.2	compact globular near M22
54	6715	Sgr	GC	18 55.1	−30 29	7.6	9.1	not easily resolved
55	6809	Sgr	GC	19 40.0	−30 58	6.4	19.0	bright, loose globular cluster
69	6637	Sgr	GC	18 31.4	−32 21	7.6	7.1	small, poor globular cluster
70	6681	Sgr	GC	18 43.2	−32 18	8.0	7.8	small globular 2° east of M69
75	6864	Sgr	GC	20 06.1	−21 55	8.5	6	small and distant; 59 000 ly away
11	6705	Sct	OC	18 51.1	−6 16	5.8	13	!! Wild Duck Cl.; the best open cluster?
26	6694	Sct	OC	18 45.2	−9 24	8.0	14	bright, coarse cluster
56	6779	Lyr	GC	19 16.6	+30 11	8.3	7.1	within a rich starfield
57	6720	Lyr	PN	18 53.6	+33 02	8.8	>71″	!! Ring Nebula; an amazing smoke ring
71	6838	Sge	GC	19 53.8	+18 47	8.0	7.2	loose globular; looks like an open cluster
27	6853	Vul	PN	19 59.6	+22 43	7.3	>348″	!! Dumbbell Nebula; a superb object
29	6913	Cyg	OC	20 23.9	+38 32	6.6	6	small, poor open cluster 2° S of γ Cygni
39	7092	Cyg	OC	21 32.2	+48 26	4.6	31	very sparse cluster; use low power
The Autumn Sky								
2	7089	Aqr	GC	21 33.5	−0 49	6.4	12.9	200-mm telescope needed to resolve
72	6981	Aqr	GC	20 53.5	−12 32	9.3	5.9	near the Saturn Nebula, NGC 7009
73	6994	Aqr	OC	20 59.0	−12 38	8.9p	2.8	group of 4 stars only; an "asterism"
15	7078	Peg	GC	21 30.0	+12 10	6.0	12.3	rich, compact globular
30	7099	Cap	GC	21 40.4	−23 11	7.3	11	toughest in 1-night Messier marathon
52	7654	Cas	OC	23 24.2	+61 35	6.9	12	young, rich cl.; faint Bubble Neb. nearby
103	581	Cas	OC	1 33.2	+60 42	7.4	6	three NGC open clusters nearby
31	224	And	G-SAb	0 42.7	+41 16	3.4	185 × 75	!! Andromeda Gal.; look for dust lanes
32	221	And	G-E5 pec	0 42.7	+40 52	8.1	11 × 7	closest companion to M31
110	205	And	G-E3 pec	0 40.4	+41 41	8.1	20 × 12	more distant companion to M31
33	598	Tri	G-SAcd	1 33.9	+30 39	5.7	67 × 42	large, diffuse spiral; requires dark sky
74	628	Psc	G-SAc	1 36.7	+15 47	9.4	11 × 11	faint, elusive spiral; tough in small scope
77	1068	Cet	G-SABab	2 42.7	−0 01	8.9	8.2 × 7.3	a Seyfert galaxy; with starlike nucleus
34	1039	Per	OC	2 42.0	+42 47	5.2	35	best at low power
76	650/51	Per	PN	1 42.4	+51 34	10.1	>65″	Little Dumbbell; faint but distinct

THE FINEST NGC OBJECTS
By Alan Dyer

Those looking for an observing project beyond the Messier Catalogue turn to the New General Catalogue (NGC). The NGC contains 7840 entries and forms the core database of today's computerized backyard telescopes. To match the Messier Catalogue, this list contains 110 of the finest NGC objects visible from midnorthern latitudes. The seasonal order is similar to that used in the Messier list, and there is no overlap. While the brightness of the best NGCs rivals many Messier targets, at least a 200-mm telescope is required to see all 110 objects on this list. Most are easy; a few are challenging.

The NGC was originally published by J.L.E. Dreyer in 1888, a work that expanded upon John Herschel's 1864 "General Catalogue." Supplementary "Index Catalogues" were published by Dreyer in 1895 and 1908. The first IC extends the NGC with another 1529 objects discovered visually between 1888 and 1894. Most are faint, elusive targets. (To provide a flavour of this extension to the NGC, one entry from the first IC is included on this list, IC 289.) The Second Index Catalogue contains 3857 entries, most discovered photographically between 1895 and 1907.

The *Sky Atlas 2000.0,* the sets of index card charts called *AstroCards, The Night Sky Observer's Guide Vol. 1 and 2* by Kepple and Sanner, and the *Uranometria 2000.0* star atlas (the latter two published by Willmann-Bell, Inc.) are recommended finder aids. Most planetarium and deep-sky charting computer programs, as well as computerized telescopes, include all the objects on this list and many more.

Notation below is as in the Messier list. Magnitudes (m_v) are visual, with the exception of those marked "p," which are photographic, or blue, magnitudes. Most galaxies appear smaller than the sizes listed. For open clusters, the number of stars (*) is also given. Data are taken from *The Deep Sky Field Guide to Uranometria 2000.0* (see the introduction to the Messier list), with some sizes rounded to two significant figures.

SEASONAL LISTING OF FINEST NGC OBJECTS

#	NGC	Con	Type	RA (2000) Dec h m ° '	m_v	Size '	Remarks
The Autumn Sky							
1	7009	Aqr	PN	21 04.2 −11 22	8.3p	>25″	!! Saturn Nebula; small bright oval
2	7293	Aqr	PN	22 29.6 −20 48	7.3	>769″	!! Helix Nebula; large, diffuse; use filter
3	7331	Peg	G-SAb	22 37.1 +34 25	9.5	10 × 4	!! large, bright spiral galaxy
4	7635	Cas	EN	23 20.7 +61 12	—	15 × 8	Bubble Neb.; very faint; 1/2° SW of M52
5	7789	Cas	OC	23 57.0 +56 44	6.7	15	!! 300*; faint but very rich cluster
6	185	Cas	G-E3	0 39.0 +48 20	9.2	14 × 12	companion to M31; small and faint
7	281	Cas	EN	0 52.8 +56 37	—	35 × 30	!! large faint nebulosity near η Cas
8	457	Cas	OC	1 19.1 +58 20	6.4	13	80*; rich; one of the best Cas. clusters
9	663	Cas	OC	1 46.0 +61 15	7.1	16	80*; look for NGCs 654 and 659 nearby
10	IC 289	Cas	PN	3 10.3 +61 19	13.3	>34″	dim oval smudge; use nebula filter!
11	7662	And	PN	23 25.9 +42 33	8.3	>12″	!! Blue Snowball; annular at high power
12	891	And	G-SAb	2 22.6 +42 21	9.9	13 × 3	!! faint, classic edge-on with dust lane
13	253	Scl	G-SABc	0 47.6 −25 17	7.6	30 × 7	!! very large and bright but at low altitude
14	772	Ari	G-SAb	1 59.3 +19 01	10.3	7.3 × 4.6	diffuse spiral galaxy
15	246	Cet	PN	0 47.0 −11 53	10.9	225″	large and faint with mottled structure
16	936	Cet	G-SB	2 27.6 −1 09	10.2	5.7 × 4.6	near M77; NGC 941 in the same field

SEASONAL LISTING OF FINEST NGC OBJECTS (continued)

#	NGC	Con	Type	RA (2000) Dec		m_v	Size	Remarks
				h m	° ′		′	
Autumn Sky continued…								
17	869/884	Per	OC	2 21.0	+57 08	≈5	30/30	!! Double Cluster; 315*; use low power
18	1023	Per	G-SB0-	2 40.4	+39 04	9.3	8.6 × 4.2	bright lens-shaped galaxy near M34
19	1491	Per	EN	4 03.4	+51 19	—	25 × 25	visually small and faint emission nebula
20	1501	Cam	PN	4 07.0	+60 55	11.5	52″	faint; dark centre; look for NGC 1502
21	1232	Eri	G-SABc	3 09.8	−20 35	10.0	6.8 × 5.6	face-on spiral; look for NGC 1300 nearby
22	1535	Eri	PN	4 14.2	−12 44	9.6p	>18″	bright planetary with blue-grey disk
The Winter Sky								
23	1514	Tau	PN	4 09.2	+30 47	10.9	>114″	faint glow around 9.4ᵐ central star
24	1931	Aur	E/RN	5 31.4	+34 15	—	4 × 4	haze surrounding four close stars
25	1788	Ori	RN	5 06.9	−3 21	—	5 × 3	fairly bright but diffuse reflection nebula
26	1973+	Ori	E/RN	5 35.1	−4 44	—	≈20 × 10	NGC 1973-5-7 just N. of M42 and M43
27	2022	Ori	PN	5 42.1	+9 05	11.9	>18″	small, faint & distinct with annular form
28	2024	Ori	EN	5 41.9	−1 51	—	30 × 30	bright but masked by glow from ζ Ori
29	2194	Ori	OC	6 13.8	+12 48	8.5	8	80*, fairly rich; look for 2169 nearby
30	2371/2	Gem	PN	7 25.6	+29 29	11.3	>55″	faint double-lobed planetary; use filter
31	2392	Gem	PN	7 29.2	+20 55	9.2	>15″	!! Clown Face or Eskimo Nebula
32	2237+	Mon	EN	6 32.3	+5 03	—	80 × 60	!! Rosette Neb.; very large; use filter
33	2261	Mon	E/RN	6 39.2	+8 44	var	3.5 × 1.5	Hubble's Variable Neb.; comet-shaped
34	2359	CMa	EN	7 18.6	−13 12	—	9 × 6	bright; look for 2360 & 2362 nearby
35	2440	Pup	PN	7 41.9	−18 13	9.4	>14″	almost starlike; irregular at high power
36	2539	Pup	OC	8 10.7	−12 50	6.5	21	50*; rich cluster; near M46 and M47
37	2403	Cam	G-SABc	7 36.9	+65 36	8.5	26 × 13	!! very large & bright; visible in binocs.
38	2655	Cam	G-SAB0	8 55.6	+78 13	10.1	6.0 × 5.3	bright ellipse with starlike nucleus
The Spring Sky								
39	2683	Lyn	G-SAb	8 52.7	+33 25	9.8	8.4 × 2.4	nearly edge-on spiral; very bright
40	2841	UMa	G-SAb	9 22.0	+50 58	9.2	6.8 × 3.3	!! classic elongated spiral; very bright
41	3079	UMa	G-SBc	10 02.2	+55 41	10.9	8.0 × 1.5	edge-on spiral; NGC 2950 nearby
42	3184	UMa	G-SABc	10 18.3	+41 25	9.8	7.8 × 7.2	large, diffuse face-on spiral
43	3877	UMa	G-SAc	11 46.1	+47 30	11.0	5.1 × 1.1	edge-on; same field as χ UMa
44	3941	UMa	G-SB0°	11 52.9	+36 59	10.3	3.7 × 2.6	small, bright and elliptical
45	4026	UMa	G-S0	11 59.4	+50 58	10.8	4.6 × 1.2	lens-shaped edge-on near γ UMa
46	4088	UMa	G-SABbc	12 05.6	+50 33	10.6	5.4 × 2.1	nearly edge-on; NGC 4085 in same field
47	4157	UMa	G-SABb	12 11.1	+50 29	11.3	7.1 × 1.2	a thin sliver; NGC 4026 and 4088 nearby
48	4605	UMa	G-SBcp	12 40.0	+61 37	10.3	6.4 × 2.3	bright, distinct edge-on spiral
49	3115	Sex	G-S0-	10 05.2	−7 43	8.9	8.1 × 2.8	Spindle Galaxy; bright and elongated
50	3242	Hya	PN	10 24.8	−18 38	7.8	>16″	!! Ghost of Jupiter; small but bright
51	3003	LMi	G-Sbc?	9 48.6	+33 25	11.9	5.2 × 1.6	faint elongated streak
52	3344	LMi	G-SABbc	10 43.5	+24 55	9.9	6.9 × 6.4	diffuse face-on barred spiral
53	3432	LMi	G-SBm	10 52.5	+36 37	11.2	6.9 × 1.9	nearly edge-on; faint flat streak
54	2903	Leo	G-SABbc	09 32.2	+21 30	9.0	12 × 6	!! very large, bright elongated spiral
55	3384	Leo	G-SB0-	10 48.3	+12 38	9.9	5.5 × 2.9	same field as M105 and NGC 3389
56	3521	Leo	G-SAb	11 05.8	−0 02	9.0	12 × 6	very large, bright spiral
57	3607	Leo	G-SA0°	11 16.9	+18 03	9.9	4.6 × 4.1	NGC 3605 & 3608 in same field
58	3628	Leo	G-Sb pec	11 20.3	+13 36	9.5	14 × 4	large edge-on; same field as M65 & M66
59	4111	CVn	G-SA0+	12 07.1	+43 04	10.7	4.4 × 0.9	bright lens-shaped edge-on spiral
60	4214	CVn	G-I AB	12 15.6	+36 20	9.8	10 × 8	large irregular galaxy
61	4244	CVn	G-SAcd	12 17.5	+37 49	10.4	17 × 2	!! large distinct edge-on spiral

SEASONAL LISTING OF FINEST NGC OBJECTS (continued)

#	NGC	Con	Type	RA (2000) Dec		m_v	Size	Remarks
				h m	° ′		′	
Spring Sky continued …								
62	4449	CVn	G-I Bm	12 28.2	+44 06	9.6	5.5 × 4.1	bright with odd rectangular shape
63	4490	CVn	G-SBd p	12 30.6	+41 38	9.8	6.4 × 3.3	Cocoon Gal.; bright spiral; 4485 in field
64	4631	CVn	G-SBd	12 42.1	+32 32	9.2	16 × 3	!! large edge-on; with companion 4627
65	4656/7	CVn	G-SBm p	12 44.0	+32 10	10.5	20 × 3	!! in field with 4631; NE end curves up
66	5005	CVn	G-SABbc	13 10.9	+37 03	9.8	5.8 × 2.8	bright elongated spiral near α CVn
67	5033	CVn	G-SAc	13 13.4	+36 36	10.2	10 × 5	large bright spiral near NGC 5005
68	4274	Com	G-SBab	2 19.8	+29 37	10.4	6.7 × 2.5	NGCs 4278/83/86 in same field
69	4414	Com	G-SAc	12 26.4	+31 13	10.1	4.4 × 3.0	bright spiral with starlike nucleus
70	4494	Com	G-E1-2	12 31.4	+25 47	9.8	4.6 × 4.4	small bright elliptical
71	4559	Com	G-SABc	12 36.0	+27 58	10.0	12 × 5	large spiral with coarse structure
72	4565	Com	G-SAb	12 36.3	+25 59	9.6	14 × 2	!! superb edge-on spiral with dust lane
73	4725	Com	G-SABab	12 50.4	+25 30	9.4	10 × 8	very bright, large spiral
74	4038/9	Crv	G-SB/IB	12 01.9	−18 52	≈10.4	≈5 × 3 ea.	"Antennae" interacting galaxies
75	4361	Crv	PN	12 24.5	−18 48	10.9	>45″	small and bright; with 13ᵐ central star
76	4216	Vir	G-SABb	12 15.9	+13 09	10.0	7.8 × 1.6	nearly edge-on; with NGC 4206 and 4222
77	4388	Vir	G-SAb	12 25.8	+12 40	11.0	5.7 × 1.6	with M84 and M86 in Markarian's Chain
78	4438	Vir	G-SA0/a	12 27.8	+13 01	10.2	8.9 × 3.6	paired w/ NGC 4435 to form the "Eyes"
79	4517	Vir	G-Scd	12 32.8	+00 07	10.4	9.9 × 1.4	faint edge-on spiral
80	4526	Vir	G-SAB0°	12 34.0	+07 42	9.7	7.1 × 2.9	between two 7th mag. stars
81	4535	Vir	G-SABc	12 34.3	+8 12	10.0	7.1 × 6.4	near M49 and 3/4° N of NGC 4526
82	4567/8	Vir	G-SABc	12 36.5	+11 15	≈11	≈3 × 2 ea.	"Siamese Twins" interacting galaxies
83	4699	Vir	G-Sab	12 49.0	−8 40	9.5	4.4 × 3.2	small & bright; look for NGC 4697 3° N
84	4762	Vir	G-SB0°?	12 52.9	+11 14	10.3	9.1 × 2.2	flattest galaxy known; 4754 in same field
85	5746	Vir	G-SA?b	14 44.9	+1 57	10.3	6.8 × 1.0	fine edge-on near 109 Virginis
86	5466	Boo	GC	14 05.5	+28 32	9.0	11	loose class XII; like rich open cl.; faint
87	5907	Dra	G-SAc	15 15.9	+56 20	10.3	12 × 2	!! fine edge-on with dust lane; near 5866
88	6503	Dra	G-SAcd	17 49.4	+70 09	10.2	7.3 × 2.4	bright elongated spiral
89	6543	Dra	PN	17 58.6	+66 38	8.1	>18″	Cat's Eye Nebula; with 10.9ᵐ central star
The Summer Sky								
90	6210	Her	PN	16 44.5	+23 49	8.8	>14″	blue starlike planetary
91	6369	Oph	PN	17 29.3	−23 46	11.4	>30″	"Little Ghost"; look for 6309 nearby
92	6572	Oph	PN	18 12.1	+6 51	8.1	8″	tiny bright blue oval
93	6633	Oph	OC	18 27.7	+6 34	4.6	27	sparse wide field cluster; IC 4756 nearby
94	6712	Sct	GC	18 53.1	−8 42	8.2	7.2	small globular; look for IC 1295 in field
95	6781	Aql	PN	19 18.4	+6 33	11.4	>109″	pale version of the Owl Nebula, M97
96	6819	Cyg	OC	19 41.3	+40 11	7.3	9.5	150*; faint but rich cluster in Milky Way
97	6826	Cyg	PN	19 44.8	+50 31	8.8	>25″	!! Blinking Planetary; 10.6ᵐ central star
98	6888	Cyg	EN	20 12.0	+38 21	—	18 × 13	Crescent Nebula; faint; use nebula filter
99a	6960	Cyg	SNR	20 45.7	+30 43	—	70 × 6	!! Veil Nebula west half; use filter!
99b	6992/5	Cyg	SNR	20 56.4	+31 43	—	72 × 8	!! Veil Nebula east half; use filter!
100	7000	Cyg	EN	20 58.8	+44 20	—	120 × 100	!! North America; use filter & low power
101	7027	Cyg	PN	21 07.1	+42 14	8.5	15″	unusual protoplanetary nebula
102	6445	Sgr	PN	17 49.2	−20 01	11.2	>34″	small, bright and annular; near M23
103	6520	Sgr	OC	18 03.4	−27 54	7.6p	6	60*; small; dark nebula B86 in same field
104	6818	Sgr	PN	19 44.0	−14 09	9.3	>17″	"Little Gem"; annular; NGC 6822 0.75° S
105	6802	Vul	OC	19 30.6	+20 16	8.8	3.2	50*, at east end of Brocchi's Cluster
106	6940	Vul	OC	20 34.6	+28 18	6.3	31	60*; fairly rich cluster in Milky Way
107	6939	Cep	OC	20 31.4	+60 38	7.8	7	80*; very rich; NGC 6946 in same field
108	6946	Cep	G-SABcd	20 34.8	+60 09	8.8	13 × 13	faint, diffuse face-on spiral near 6939
109	7129	Cep	RN	21 42.8	+66 06	—	7 × 7	faint reflection neb. around sparse cluster
110	40	Cep	PN	0 13.0	+72 32	12.4	>37″	unusual red planetary; 11.6ᵐ central star

DEEP-SKY CHALLENGE OBJECTS
By Alan Dyer And Alister Ling

For those who wish to get a taste of the unusual, here is a selection of 45 "challenge" targets. Most require a 250- to 450-mm telescope. However, for detecting challenge objects, the quality of sky, quality of the optics, use of an appropriate filter, and the observer's experience are often more important than sheer aperture. Don't be afraid to tackle some of these with a smaller telescope.

Objects are listed in order of right ascension. Abbreviations are the same as in the Messier and NGC lists. Two columns have been added: one lists the page where you'll find that object in the *Uranometria 2000.0;* the last column suggests the minimum aperture in mm needed to see that object. Most data are taken from *Sky Catalogue 2000.0 Vol. 2.* Some visual magnitudes are from other sources.

#	Object	Con	Type	RA (2000) Dec h m ° ′	m_V	Size ′	pg	Min Aperture
1	NGC 7822	Cep	E/RN	0 03.6 +68 37	—	60 × 30	15	300
	large, faint emission neb.; rated "eeF"; also look for E/R nebula Ced 214 (assoc'd with star cluster Berkeley 59) 1° S							
2	IC 59	Cas	E/RN	0 56.7 +61 04	—	10 × 5	36	200–250
	faint emission/reflection nebula paired with IC 63 very close to γ Cas.; requires clean optics; rated as "pF"							
3	NGC 609	Cas	OC	1 37.2 +64 33	11.0	3.0	16	250–300
	faint patch at low power; high power needed to resolve this rich cluster (also look for Trumpler 1 cluster 3° S)							
4	IC 1795	Cas	EN	2 24.7 +61 54	—	27 × 13	17	200
	brightest part of a complex of nebulosity that includes IC 1805 and IC 1848; use a nebula filter							
5	Maffei I	Cas	G–E3	2 36.3 +59 39	≈14	5 × 3	38	300
	heavily reddened galaxy; very faint; requires large aperture and black skies; nearby Maffei II for extremists							
6	NGC 1049	For	GC	2 39.7 −34 29	11.0	0.6	354	250–300
	Class V globular in dwarf "Fornax System" Local Group galaxy 630 000 ly away; galaxy itself invisible?							
7	Abell 426	Per	Gs	3 19.8 +41 31	12–16	≈30′	63	200–400
	Perseus galaxy cluster 300 million ly away; mag. 11.6 NGC 1275 Perseus A at centre; see Webb Vol. 5							
8	NGC 1432/35	Tau	RN	3 46.1 +23 47	—	30 × 30	132	100–150
	Pleiades nebulosity (also includes IC 349); brightest around Merope; requires transparent skies and clean optics							
9	IC 342	Cam	G–SBc	3 46.8 +68 06	≈12	17 × 17	18	200–300
	large and diffuse face–on spiral; member of UMa–Cam cloud (Kemble's Cascade of stars also on this chart)							
10	NGC 1499	Per	EN	4 00.7 +36 37	—	145 × 40	95	80–125 RFT
	California Nebula; very large and faint; use a wide–field telescope or big binoculars plus H–Beta filter							
11	NGC 1554/5	Tau	RN	4 21.8 +19 32	—	var.	133	200?
	Hind's Variable Neb.; small reflect. neb. around 9ᵐ–13ᵐ var. star T Tau; use high power; difficulty varies							
12	IC 405	Aur	E/RN	5 16.2 +34 16	—	30 × 19	97	200
	Flaming Star Neb. assoc'd with runaway star AE Aurigae; see Burnham's Handbook p. 285 (also look for IC 410)							
13	IC 434 / B 33	Ori	E/DN	5 40.9 −2 28	—	60 × 10	226	100–150 in dark sky!
	B33 is the Horsehead Nebula, a dark neb. superimposed on a very faint emission neb. IC 434; use H–Beta filter							
14	Sh 2-276	Ori	EN	5 48 +1 —	—	600 × 30!	226	100–150 RFT
	Barnard's Loop; SNR or interstellar bubble?; difficult to detect due to size; use filter and sweep with wide field							
15	Abell 12	Ori	PN	6 02.4 +9 39	≈13	37″	181	250–300
	also called PK 198 −6.1; faint; not plotted on Uranometria but is on NW edge of μ Orionis; OIII filter required							
16	IC 443	Gem	SNR	6 16.9 +22 47	—	50 × 40	137	250–300
	faint supernova remnant very close to η Gem.; use filter (also look for NGC 2174 and Sh 2–247 on this chart)							
17	J 900	Gem	PN	6 25.9 +17 47	12.2	8″	137	200
	Jonckheere 900; bright starlike planetary; plotted as PK 194 +2.1 in Uranometria; use OIII filter & high power							
18	IC 2177	Mon	E/RN	7 05.1 −10 42	—	120 × 40	273	200–300
	Seagull Nebula; large, faint; contains bright patches Gum 1 (−10°28′), NGC 2327 (−11°18′) & Ced 90 (−12°20′)							
19	PK 205 +14.1	Gem	PN	7 29.0 +13 15	≈13	≈700″	184	200–250
	Medusa Nebula or Abell 21; much larger than plotted in Uranometria; impressive in large aperture w/ OIII filter							
20	PK 164 +31.1	Lyn	PN	7 57.8 +53 25	≈14	400″	43	250
	extremely faint with two small components; use OIII filter; sometimes confused with nearby NGC 2474–75							

DEEP-SKY CHALLENGE OBJECTS (continued)

#	Object	Con	Type	RA (2000) Dec h m ° ′	m_v	Size ′	pg	Min Aperture
21	**Leo I**	Leo	G–E3	10 08.4 +12 18	9.8	10.7 × 8.3	189	300

dwarf elliptical; satellite of Milky Way; very low surface brightness; 0.3° N of Regulus!; requires clean optics

22	**Abell 1367**	Leo	Gs	11 44.0 +19 57	13–16	≈60	147	300–400

cluster of some 30 or more galaxies within a 1 degree field near 93 Leonis; see Webb Handbook Vol. 5, p. 139

23	**NGC 3172**	UMi	G-?	11 50.2 +89 07	13.6	0.7 × 0.7	2	250

"Polarissima Borealis"—closest galaxy to the North Celestial Pole; small, faint and otherwise unremarkable

24	**NGC 4236**	Dra	G-SBb	12 16.7 +69 28	9.6	18.6 × 6.9	25	200–250

very large, dim barred spiral; a diffuse glow (NGC 4395 on Chart #108 a similar large diffuse face-on)

25	**Mrk 205**	Dra	Quasar	12 21.6 +75 18	14.5	stellar	9	300

Markarian 205; a faint star on SW edge of NGC 4319; plotted as a radio source; centre of red-shift controversy

26	**3C 273**	Vir	Quasar	12 29.1 +02 03	12≈13	stellar	238	250–300

at 2 to 3 billon ly away one of the most distant objects visible in amateur telescopes; magnitude variable

27	**NGC 4676**	Com	Gs	12 46.2 +30 44	14.1p	2 × 1	108	250

"The Mice" or VV 224—two classic interacting galaxies; very faint double nature detectable at high power

28	**Abell 1656**	Com	Gs	13 00.1 +27 58	12–16	≈60	149	250–300

Coma Berenices gal. cl.; very rich; 400 million ly away; brightest member NGC 4889; see Webb Vol. 5

29	**NGC 5053**	Com	GC	13 16.4 +17 42	9.8	10.5	150	100–200

faint and very loose globular 1° SE of M53; requires large aperture to resolve; difficult in hazy skies; Class XI

30	**NGC 5897**	Lib	GC	15 17.4 –21 01	8.6	12.6	334	150–200

large, faint and loose globular; mag. 10.9 in Atlas Coeli Catalogue; requires large aperture to resolve; Class XI

31	**Abel 2065**	CrB	Gs	15 22.7 +27 43	≈16	≈30	154	500 in superb sky!

Corona Borealis gal. cluster; perhaps the most difficult object for amateur telescopes; 1.5 billion ly away

32	**NGC 6027**	Ser	Gs	15 59.2 +20 45	≈15	2 × 1	155	400

Seyfert's Sextet (6027 A–F); compact group of 6 small and very faint galaxies; see Burnham's Handbook p. 1793

33	**B 72**	Oph	DN	17 23.5 –23 38	—	30	338	80–125 RFT

Barnard's dark S-Nebula or "The Snake"; opacity of 6/6; 1.5° NNE of θ Ophiuchi; area rich in dark nebulas

34	**NGC 6791**	Lyr	OC	19 20.7 +37 51	9.5	16	118	200–250

large, faint but very rich open cluster with 300 stars; a faint smear in smaller instruments; Type II 3 r

35	**PK 64 +5.l**	Cyg	PN	19 34.8 +30 31	9.6	8″	118	200

Campbell's Hydrogen Star; very bright but very starlike; also catalogued as star BD +30°3639

36	**M 1-92**	Cyg	RN	19 36.3 +29 33	11.0	12″ × 6″	118	250–300

Minkowski 1-92 or Footprint Nebula; bright, starlike reflection neb.; double at high mag.; assoc'd star invisible

37	**NGC 6822**	Sgr	G-Irr	19 44.9 –14 48	≈11	10.2 × 9.5	297	100–150

Barnard's Galaxy; member of the Local Group; large but very low surface brightness; requires transparent skies

38	**Palomar 11**	Aql	GC	19 45.2 –8 00	9.8	3.2′	297	250–300

brightest of 15 heavily reddened GCs found on Sky Survey; magnitude is misleading; 11 Terzan GCs more challenging

39	**IC 4997**	Sge	PN	20 20.2 +16 45	10.9	2″	163	200

bright but starlike planetary; the challenge is to see the disk!; blink the field with and without a nebula filter

40	**IC 1318**	Cyg	EN	20 26.2 +40 30	—	large	84	80–150 RFT

complex of nebulosity around γ Cygni; multitude of patches in rich starfield; use a very wide field plus filter

41	**PK 80 –6.1**	Cyg	PN?	21 02.3 +36 42	13.5	16″	121	250

the "Egg Nebula"; a very small proto-planetary nebula; can owners of large telescopes detect polarization?

42	**IC 1396**	Cep	EN	21 39.1 +57 30	—	170 × 140	57	100–125 RFT

extremely large and diffuse area of emission nebulosity; use nebula filter and very wide field optics in dark sky

43	**IC 5146**	Cyg	E/RN	21 53.5 +47 16	—	12 × 12	86	200–250

Cocoon Nebula; faint and diffuse; use H-Beta filter; at the end of the long filamentary dark nebula Barnard 168

44	**NGC 7317–20**	Peg	Gs	22 36.1 +33 57	13–14	≈1′ ea.	123	250–300

Stephan's Quintet; 0.5° SSW of NGC 7331; easy to pick out 3 or 4 (also look for "companions" to 7331)

45	**Jones 1**	Peg	PN	23 35.9 +30 28	12.1	332″	124	250–300

plotted as PK 104 –29.1 (from Perek & Kohoutek catalogue) in Uranometria; large dim glow; OIII filter required

GALAXIES: BRIGHTEST AND NEAREST
By Barry F. Madore

External galaxies are generally of such low surface brightness that they often prove disappointing objects for the amateur observer. However, it must be remembered that many of these galaxies were discovered with very small telescopes and that the enjoyment of their discovery can be recaptured. In addition, the central concentration of light varies from galaxy to galaxy, making a visual classification of the types possible at the telescope. Indeed, the type of galaxy as listed in **Table 1** is in part based on the fraction of light coming from the central bulge of the galaxy as compared to the contribution from a disk component. Disk galaxies with dominant bulges are classified as Sa; as the nuclear contribution declines, types of Sb, Sc, and Sd are assigned until the nucleus is absent at type Sm. Often the disks of these galaxies show spiral symmetry, the coherence and strength of which is denoted by Roman numerals I through V, smaller numbers indicating well-formed global spiral patterns. Those spirals with central bars are designated SB, while those with only a hint of a disk embedded in the bulge are called SO. A separate class of galaxies that possess no disk component are called ellipticals and can only be further classified numerically by their apparent flattening, EO being apparently round and E7 being the most flattened.

Environment appears to play an important role in determining the types of galaxies we see at the present epoch. Rich clusters of galaxies, such as the system in Coma, are dominated by ellipticals and gas-free SO galaxies. The less dense clusters and groups tend to be dominated by the spiral, disk galaxies. Remarkably, pairs of galaxies are much more frequently of the same Hubble type than random selection would predict. Encounters between disk galaxies may in some cases result in the instabilities necessary to form the spiral structure we often see. M51 (the Whirlpool) and its companion NGC 5195 are an often-cited example of this type of interaction. In the past, when the universe was much more densely packed, interactions and collisions may have been sufficiently frequent that entire galaxies merged to form a single large new system; it has been suggested that some elliptical galaxies formed in this way.

Table 1 lists the 40 brightest galaxies taken from the Revised Shapley-Ames Catalog. As well as their designations, positions, and types, the table also lists the total blue magnitudes, major and minor axis lengths (to the nearest minute of arc), one modern estimate of their distances in kiloparsecs, and their radial velocities corrected for the motion of our Sun about the galactic centre. Although the universe as a whole is in expansion, there are parts that are still bound together (or at very least, held back in their expansion) by gravity. These groups and clusters are, in essence, representative of the largest material structures in the universe. Recently, large-scale flows of material have been reported, far in excess of the velocities expected due to the perturbing presence of other galaxies and clusters of galaxies. Either there are exceedingly large concentrations of matter yet to be discovered just beyond our limited view of the world, or the universe has had a much more interesting history than our present theories indicate. The brightest and nearest galaxies in Table 1 may be moving not only as a result of the universal expansion but also through very complex interactions with distant parts as yet only postulated but not seen.

TABLE 1—THE 40 OPTICALLY BRIGHTEST SHAPLEY-AMES GALAXIES

NGC/IC	Other	RA (2000) Dec h m s	° ′	Type	Mag. B_T	Size ′	Distance kpc	Rad. Vel. km/s
55		0 15 08	−39 13.2	Sc	8.22	25 × 3	3 100	+115
205	M110	0 40 23	+41 41.3	S0/E5pec	8.83	8 × 3	730	+49
221	M32	0 42 41	+40 51.9	E2	9.01	3 × 3	730	+86
224	M31	0 42 45	+41 16.5	Sb I–II	4.38	160 × 40	730	−10
247		0 47 10	−20 45.6	Sc III–IV	9.51	18 × 5	3 100	+604
253		0 47 36	−25 17.4	Sc	8.13	22 × 6	4 200	+504
SMC		0 52 38	−72 48.0	Im IV–V	2.79	216 × 216	60	+359
300		0 54 53	−37 41.2	Sc III	8.70	20 × 10	2 400	+625
598	M33	1 33 53	+30 39.2	Sc II–III	6.26	60 × 40	670	+506
628	M74	1 36 42	+15 47.2	Sc I	9.77	8 × 8	17 000	+507
1068	M77	2 42 41	−0 00.9	Sb II	9.55	3 × 2	25 000	+510
1291		3 17 19	−41 06.5	SBa	9.42	5 × 2	15 000	+512
1313		3 18 16	−66 29.9	SBc III–IV	9.37	5 × 3	5 200	+261
1316	Fornax A	3 22 42	−37 12.5	Sa (pec)	9.60	4 × 3	30 000	+1713
LMC		5 23 36	−69 45.4	SBm III	0.63	432 × 432	50	+34
2403		7 36 54	+65 35.9	Sc III	8.89	16 × 10	3 600	+299
2903		9 32 10	+21 29.9	Sc I–III	9.50	11 × 5	9 400	+472
3031	M81	9 55 34	+69 04.1	SbI–II	7.86	16 × 10	3 600	+124
3034	M82	9 55 54	+69 40.7	Amorphous	9.28	7 × 2	3 600	+409
3521		11 05 49	−0 02.0	Sb II–III	9.64	7 × 2	13 000	+627
3627	M66	11 20 15	+12 59.1	Sb II	9.74	8 × 3	12 000	+593
4258	M106	12 18 57	+47 18.4	Sb II	8.95	20 × 6	10 000	+520
4449		12 28 12	+44 05.8	Sm IV	9.85	5 × 3	5 000	+250
4472	M49	12 29 47	+7 59.8	E1/S0	9.32	5 × 4	22 000	+822
4486	M87	12 30 50	+12 23.6	E0	9.62	3 × 3	22 000	+1136
4594	M104	12 40 00	−11 37.4	Sa/b	9.28	7 × 2	17 000	+873
4631		12 42 05	+32 32.4	Sc	9.84	12 × 1	12 000	+606
4649	M60	12 43 40	+11 33.1	S0	9.83	4 × 3	22 000	+1142
4736	M94	12 50 54	+41 07.1	Sab	8.92	5 × 4	6 900	+345
4826	M64	12 56 45	+21 41.0	Sab II	9.37	8 × 4	7 000	+350
4945		13 05 26	−49 28.0	Sc	9.60	12 × 2	7 000	+275
5055	M63	13 15 50	+42 01.7	Sbc II–III	9.33	8 × 3	11 000	+550
5128	Cen A	13 25 29	−43 01.0	S0 (pec)	7.89	10 × 3	6 900	+251
5194	M51	13 29 53	+47 11.9	Sbc I–II	8.57	12 × 6	11 000	+541
5236	M83	13 37 00	−29 52.0	SBc II	8.51	10 × 8	6 900	+275
5457	M101	14 03 13	+54 21.0	Sc I	8.18	22 × 22	7 600	+372
6744		19 09 46	−63 51.3	Sbc II	9.24	9 × 9	13 000	+663
6822		19 44 57	−14 47.7	Im IV–V	9.35	20 × 10	680	+15
6946		20 34 51	+60 09.4	Sc II	9.68	13 × 9	6 700	+336
7793		23 57 49	−32 35.4	Sd IV	9.65	6 × 4	4 200	+241

The nearest galaxies, listed in **Table 2,** form what is known as the Local Group of Galaxies. Many of the distances are still quite uncertain. However, in the present Hubble Space Telescope era these galaxies are prime targets for a generation of astronomers intent on accurately determining each of their distances to the best possible precision.

TABLE 2—THE NEAREST GALAXIES—OUR LOCAL GROUP

Name	RA (2000.0) Dec h m ° '		Mag. B_T	Type	Distance kpc
M31 = NGC 224	0 42.7	+41 16	4.38	Sb I–II	730
Milky Way Galaxy	—	—	—	Sb/c	—
M33 = NGC 598	1 33.9	+30 39	6.26	Sc II–III	670
LMC	5 23.7	–69 45	0.63	SBm III	50
SMC	0 52.7	–72 49	2.79	Im IV–V	60
NGC 6822	19 45.0	–14 48	9.35	Im IV–V	520
IC 1613	1 04.8	+02 07	10.00	Im V	740
M110 = NGC 205	0 40.4	+41 41	8.83	S0/E5 pec	730
M32 = NGC 221	0 42.7	+40 52	9.01	E2	730
NGC 185	0 38.9	+48 20	10.13	dE3 pec	730
NGC 147	0 33.2	+48 30	10.36	dE5	610
Fornax	2 39.9	–34 32	9.1	dE	130
Sculptor	1 00.2	–33 42	10.5	dE	85
Leo I	10 08.5	+12 19	11.27	dE	230
Leo II	11 13.5	+22 09	12.85	dE	230
Draco	17 20.1	+57 55	—	dE	80
Ursa Minor	15 08.8	+67 12	—	dE	75
Carina	6 41.6	–50 58	—	dE	170
And I	0 45.7	+38 01	13.5	dE	790
And II	1 16.5	+33 26	13.5	dE	730
And III	0 35.3	+36 31	13.5	dE	730
LGS 3	1 03.8	+21 53	—	?	730
Sextans	10 13.0	–1 36	—	dE	85
Antlia	10 04.0	–27 20	—	dE	1200
IC 10	0 20.4	+59 17	11.8	IBm	800

Editor's Notes:

(i) Aside from those famous companions of the Milky Way Galaxy, the Large Magellanic Cloud (LMC) and the Small Magellanic Cloud (SMC), there is only one galaxy beyond our own that is easily visible to unaided human eyes: M31, the Andromeda Galaxy (730 kpc or 2.4 Mly distant). M33, the Triangulum Galaxy, can also be seen, but this is a difficult observation. To locate M31, see the NOVEMBER ALL-SKY MAP on p. 299, where the tiny cluster of six dots above the first "A" of "ANDROMEDA" indicates its location. With modest optical aid (e.g. binoculars) a dozen or more of the galaxies listed in Table 1 can be seen by experienced observers under dark skies. With a 200-mm telescope, the quasar 3C273 at one thousand times the distance of M31 can elicit a noticeable signal in the visual cortex (see the section VARIABLE GALAXIES on p. 292).

(ii) An interesting article by G. Lake entitled "Cosmology of the Local Group" appears in *Sky & Telescope,* December 1992, p. 613.

(iii) The *National Aeronautics and Space Administration/Infrared Processing and Analysis Center* (NASA/IPAC) Extragalactic Database (NED) is a comprehensive compilation of extragalactic data for over 3.7 million distinct extragalactic objects. The database includes most major catalogues and offers references to and abstracts of articles of extragalactic interest that have appeared in most major journals. Also online are over 3.4 million photometric measurements and hundreds of thousands of images. It is possible to search the main NED database for objects selected by catalogue prefix, position, type, or redshift. The database is available at:

nedwww.ipac.caltech.edu

A knowledgebase of review articles and basic information is available at:

nedwww.ipac.caltech.edu/level5

GALAXIES WITH PROPER NAMES
BY BARRY F. MADORE

Below are the catalogue designations and positions of galaxies known to have proper names which usually honour the discoverer (e.g. McLeish's Object), identify the constellation in which the galaxy is found (e.g. Andromeda Galaxy), or describe the galaxy in some easily remembered way (e.g. Whirlpool Galaxy).

Galaxy Name	Other Names / Remarks	RA (2000) h m	Dec ° '
Ambartsumian's Knot	NGC 3561, UGC 06224, ARP 105	11 11.2	+28 42
Andromeda Galaxy	M31, NGC 224, UGC 00454	0 42.7	+41 16
Andromeda I		0 45.7	+38 01
Andromeda II		1 16.5	+33 26
Andromeda III		0 35.3	+36 31
Antennae Galaxy	Ring Tail, NGC 4038/39, ARP 244	12 01.9	–18 52
Antlia Dwarf	AM 1001-270	10 04.0	–27 20
Aquarius Dwarf	DDO 210	20 46.9	–12 51
Arp's Galaxy		11 19.6	+51 30
Atoms For Peace	NGC 7252, ARP 226	22 20.8	–24 41
Baade's Galaxies A & B	MCG+07-02-018/19	0 49.9	+42 35
Barbon's Galaxy	Markarian 328, ZWG 497.042	23 37.7	+30 08
Barnard's Galaxy	NGC 6822, IC 4895, DDO 209	19 44.9	–14 48
Bear's Paw (Claw)	NGC 2537, UGC 04274, ARP 6	8 13.2	+46 00
BL Lacertae		22 02.7	+42 17
Black Eye Galaxy	M64, NGC 4826, UGC 08062	12 56.7	+21 41
Bode's Galaxies	M81/82, NGC 3031/4, UGC 05318/22	9 55.7	+69 23
Burbidge Chain	MCG-04-03-010 to 13	0 47.5	–20 26
BW Tauri	UGC 03087, MCG+01-12-009	4 33.2	+5 21
Carafe Galaxy	Cannon's Carafe, near NGC 1595/98	4 28.0	–47 54
Carina Dwarf		6 41.6	–50 58
Cartwheel Galaxy	Zwicky's Cartwheel, MCG-06-02-022a	0 37.4	–33 44
Centaurus A	NGC 5128, ARP 153	13 25.5	–43 01
Circinus Galaxy		14 13.2	–65 20
Coddington's Nebula	IC 2574, UGC 05666, DDO 81	10 28.4	+68 25
Copeland Septet	MCG+04-28-004/05/07 to 11, UGC 06597, UGC 06602, ARP 320, NGC 3745/46/48/50/51/53/54†	11 37.8	+21 59
Cygnus A	MCG+07-41-003	19 59.4	+40 43
Draco Dwarf	UGC 10822, DDO 208	17 20.2	+57 55
Exclamation Mark Galaxy		0 39.3	–43 06
The Eyes	NGC 4435/8, UGC 07574/5, ARP 120a,b	12 27.7	+13 03
Fath 703	NGC 5892	15 13.7	–15 29
Fornax A	NGC 1316, ARP 154	3 22.7	–37 12
Fornax Dwarf	MCG-06-07-001	2 39.9	–34 32
Fourcade-Figueroa	MCG-07-28-004	13 34.8	–45 33
The Garland	S of NGC 3077 = UGC 05398	10 04.2	+68 40
Grus Quartet	NGC 7552/82/90/99	23 17.8	–42 26
GR 8 (Gibson Reaves)	UGC 08091, DDO 155	12 58.7	+14 13
Hardcastle's Galaxy	MCG-05-31-039	13 13.0	–32 41
Helix Galaxy	NGC 2685, UGC 04666, ARP 336	8 55.6	+58 44
Hercules A	MCG+01-43-006	16 51.2	+4 59
Hoag's Object		15 17.2	+21 35

†Position errors caused these to be historically marked as nonexistent in the NGC and RNGC.

GALAXIES WITH PROPER NAMES (continued)

Galaxy Name	Other Names / Remarks	RA (2000) h m	Dec ° ′
Holmberg I	UGC 05139, DDO 63	9 40.5	+71 11
Holmberg II	UGC 04305, DDO 50, ARP 268	8 19.3	+70 43
Holmberg III	UGC 04841	9 14.6	+74 14
Holmberg IV	UGC 08837, DDO 185	13 54.7	+53 54
Holmberg V	UGC 08658	13 40.6	+54 20
Holmberg VI	NGC 1325a	3 24.9	−21 20
Holmberg VII	UGC 07739, DDO 137	12 34.7	+06 17
Holmberg VIII	UGC 08303, DDO 166	13 13.3	+36 12
Holmberg IX	UGC 05336, DDO 66	9 57.6	+69 03
Horologium Dwarf	Schuster's Spiral	3 59.2	−45 52
Hydra A	MCG-02-24-007	9 18.1	−12 06
Integral Sign Galaxy	UGC 03697, MCG+12-07-028	7 11.4	+71 50
Keenan's System	NGC 5216/16a/18, UGC 08528/9, ARP 104	13 32.2	+62 43
Kowal's Object		19 29.9	−17 41
Large Magellanic Cloud	Nubecula Major	5 23.6	−69 45
Leo I	Regulus Dwarf, UGC 05470, DDO 74, Harrington-Wilson #1	10 08.5	+12 18
Leo II	Leo B, UGC 06253, DDO 93, Harrington-Wilson #2	11 13.4	+22 10
Leo III	Leo A, UGC 05364, DDO 69	9 59.3	+30 45
Lindsay-Shapley Ring	Graham A	6 42.8	−74 15
Lost Galaxy	NGC 4535, UGC 07727	12 34.3	+8 11
McLeish's Object		20 09.7	−66 13
Maffei I	UGCA 34	2 36.3	+59 39
Maffei II	UGCA 39	2 42.0	+59 37
Malin 1		12 37.0	+14 20
Mayall's Object	MCG+07-23-019, ARP 148	11 03.9	+40 50
Mice	NGC 4676a/b, UGC 07938/9, IC 819/20, ARP 242	12 46.1	+30 44
Miniature Spiral	NGC 3928, UGC 06834	11 51.8	+48 41
Minkowski's Object	ARP 133 (NE of NGC 541)	1 25.8	−01 21
Pancake	NGC 2685, UGC 04666, ARP 336	8 55.6	+58 44
Papillon	IC 708, UGC 06549	11 33.9	+49 03
Pegasus Dwarf	UGC 12613, DDO 216	23 28.5	+14 44
Perseus A	NGC 1275/6, UGC 02669	3 19.8	+41 31
Phoenix Dwarf Irr.		1 51.1	−44 26
Pinwheel Galaxy	see also Triangulum Galaxy	1 33.9	+30 39
Pinwheel Galaxy	M99, NGC 4254, UGC 07345	12 18.8	+14 25
Pinwheel Galaxy	M101, NGC 5457, UGC 08981, ARP 26	14 03.3	+54 22
Pisces Cloud	NGC 379/80/82-85, UGC 00682/3/6-9, ARP 331	1 07.5	+32 25
Pisces Dwarf	LGS 3	0 03.8	+21 54
Polarissima Australis	NGC 2573	1 42.0‡	−89 20
Polarissima Borealis	NGC 3172, ZWG 370.002	11 50.3‡	+89 07
Reinmuth 80	NGC 4517a, UGC 07685	12 32.5	+0 23
Reticulum Dwarf	Sersic 040.03	4 36.2	−58 50
Sagittarius Dwarf		19 30.0	−17 41
Sculptor Dwarf	MCG-06-03-015	1 00.2	−33 42
Sculptor Dwarf Irr.		0 08.1	−34 34

‡The high declination of these objects makes the RA particularly uncertain.

GALAXIES WITH PROPER NAMES (continued)

Galaxy Name	Other Names / Remarks	RA (2000) h m	Dec ° ′
Seashell Galaxy	Companion to NGC 5291	13 47.4	−30 23
Sextans A	UGCA 205, MCG-01-26-030, DDO 75	10 11.0	−4 41
Sextans B	UGC 05373, DDO 70	10 00.0	+5 19
Sextans C	UGC 05439	10 05.6	+00 04
Sextans Dwarf		10 13.1	−1 37
Seyfert's Sextet	Serpens Sextet, NGC 6027/6027a-e, UGC 10116	15 59.2	+20 46
Shapley-Ames 1		1 05.1	−6 13
Shapley-Ames 2	NGC 4507	12 35.1	−39 55
Shapley-Ames 3	MCG-02-33-015	12 49.4	−10 07
Shapley-Ames 4	UGC 08041	12 55.2	+0 07
Shapley-Ames 5	MCG-07-42-001	20 24.0	−44 00
Shapley-Ames 6		21 23.2	+45 46
Siamese Twins	NGC 4567/4568	12 36.5	+11 15
Silver Coin	Sculptor Galaxy, NGC 253, UGCA 13	0 47.6	−25 18
Small Magellanic Cloud	Nubecula Minor	0 52.7	−72 50
Sombrero Galaxy	M104, NGC 4594	12 39.9	−11 37
Spider	UGC 05829, DDO 84	10 42.6	+34 27
Spindle Galaxy	NGC 3115	10 05.2	−7 42
Stephan's Quintet	NGC 7317-20, UGC 12099-102, ARP 319	22 36.0	+33 58
Sunflower Galaxy	M63, NGC 5055, UGC 08334	13 15.8	+42 02
Triangulum Galaxy	Pinwheel, M33, NGC 598, UGC 01117	1 33.9	+30 39
Ursa Minor Dwarf	UGC 09749, DDO 199	15 08.8	+67 12
Virgo A	M87, NGC 4486, UGC 07654, ARP 152	12 30.8	+12 23
Whirlpool Galaxy	Rosse's Galaxy, Question Mark Galaxy, M51, NGC 5194/5, UGC 08493/4, ARP 85	13 29.9	+47 12
Wild's Triplet	MCG-01-30-032 to 34, ARP 248	11 46.8	−3 49
Wolf-Lundmark-Melotte	MCG-03-01-015, DDO 221	0 02.0	−15 28
Zwicky #2	UGC 06955, DDO 105	11 58.4	+38 03
Zwicky's Triplet	UGC 10586, ARP 103	16 49.5	+45 30

Catalogues:

AM *Catalogue of Southern Peculiar Galaxies and Associations,* by H.C. Arp and B.F. Madore, Cambridge University Press (1987).

ARP *Atlas of Peculiar Galaxies,* H. Arp, *Ap. J. Suppl. 14,* 1 (1966).

DDO *David Dunlap Observatory Publ.,* S. van den Bergh, II, No. 5, 147 (1959).

IC *Index Catalogue,* J.L.E. Dreyer, *Mem. R.A.S.* (1895–1910).

MCG *Morphological Catalogue of Galaxies,* B.A. Vorontsov-Velyaminovet al., Moscow State University, Moscow (1961–1974).

NGC *New General Catalogue of Nebulae and Clusters of Stars,* J.L.E. Dreyer, *Mem. R.A.S.* (1888).

RNGC *The Revised New General Catalogue of Nonstellar Astronomical Objects,* J.W. Sulentic and W.G. Tifft, University of Arizona Press (1973).

UGC *Uppsala General Catalogue of Galaxies,* P. Nilson, *Nova Acta Regiae Societatis Scientiarum Upsaliensis,* Ser. V: A, Vol. 1, Uppsala, Sweden (1973).

UGCA *Catalogue of Selected Non-UGC Galaxies,* P. Nilson, Uppsala Astronomical Observatory (1974).

ZWG *Catalogue of Galaxies and Clusters of Galaxies,* F. Zwicky et al., Vol. 1–6, California Institute of Technology (1961–1968).

RADIO SOURCES
By Ken Tapping

There are many types of cosmic radio sources, driven by a wide variety of processes. Some are thermal, that is, producing radio emissions through their temperature. Others involve the interaction of high-energy electrons with magnetic fields or complicated interactions of waves with plasmas. There are radio spectral lines from some atoms (such as the 21-cm emission from cosmic hydrogen) and an ever-increasing number of discovered molecular lines originating in cold, dense parts of the interstellar medium.

The list below is not complete; nor does it include only the strongest sources. It is intended to be a representative sampling of the types of sources that have been discovered. Some sources within reach of small (amateur-built) radio telescopes are included. Where possible, the flux densities at 100, 500, and 1000 MHz are given. The unit of flux density used is the jansky (Jy), where 1 Jy = 10^{-26} W·m^{-2}Hz^{-1}. In the Remarks column, m denotes visual magnitude, z redshift, and P period.

For information on radio astronomy, see *Radio Astronomy,* by J.D. Kraus (Cygnus-Quasar Books, Powell, Ohio, 1986). Some maps of the radio sky can be found in *Sky & Telescope, 63,* 230 (1982). Information for amateur radio astronomers can be found in *Astronomy, 5* (12), 50 (1977), in a series of articles in *JRASC, 72,* L5, L22, L38,... (1978), and in *Sky & Telescope, 55,* 385 and 475, and *56,* 28 and 114 (1978). A number of small, simple radio telescopes and some projects to try are described in *Radio Astronomy Projects,* by William Lonc, Radio-Sky Publishing, 1997.

TABLE OF RADIO SOURCES

Source	RA (2000) Dec h m ° ′	Flux Density (Jy) 100, 500, 1000 MHz Remarks
3C10	0 25.3 +64 08	180, 85, 56 Remnant of Tycho's Supernova (1572)
W3	2 25.4 +62 06	—, 80, 150 IC1795; multiple HII region; OH source
Algol	3 07.9 +40 56	* Eclipsing binary star
3C84	3 19.8 +41 32	70, 25, 17 NGC1725; Seyfert gal.; $m = 12.7$, $z = 0.018$
Fornax A	3 20.4 −37 22	900, 160, 110 NGC 1316; galaxy; $m = 10.1$; $z = 0.006$
Pictor A	5 19.9 −45 47	440, 140, 100 Galaxy; $m = 15.8$, $z = 0.034$
V371 Orionis	5 33.7 +1 55	* Red dwarf (flare) star
Taurus A	5 34.5 +22 01	1450, 1250, 1000 Crab Nebula; remnant of 1054 Supernova
NP0532	5 34.5 +22 01	15, 0.5, 1 Crab Pulsar; $P = 0.0331$ s
Orion A	5 35.3 −5 25	90, 200, 360 Orion Nebula; HII region. OH, IR source
3C157	6 17.6 +22 42	360, 195, 180 IC443; supernova remnant
VY CMa	7 23.1 −20 44	* Optical variable start; OH, IR source
Puppis A	8 20.3 −42 48	650, 300, 100 Supernova remnant

TABLE OF RADIO SOURCES (continued)

Source	RA (2000) Dec h m ° ′	Flux Density (Jy) 100, 500, 1000 MHz Remarks
Hydra A	9 18.1 −12 05	390, 110, 65 Galaxy; $m = 14.8$, $z = 0.052$
3C273	12 29.1 +2 03	150, 57, 49 Strongest quasar; $m = 13.0$, $z = 0.158$
Virgo A	12 30.8 +12 23	1950, 450, 300 M87; elliptical galaxy with jet
Centaurus A	13 25.4 −43 02	8500, 2500, 1400 NGC 5128; galaxy; $m = 7.5$, $z = 0.002$
3C295	14 11.4 +52 12	95, 60, 28 Galaxy; $m = 20.5$, $z = 0.461$
OQ172	14 45.3 +9 59	10, 4, 2 Quasar; $m = 18.4$, $z = 3.53$
Scorpius X1	16 19.9 −15 38	* X-ray, radio, and optical variable star
Hercules A	16 51.2 +5 01	800, 120, 65 Galaxy; $m = 18.5$, $z = 0.154$
Galactic Centre	17 42.0 −28 50	4400, 2900, 1800 Strong, diffuse emission
Sagittarius A	17 42.5 −28 55	100, 250, 200 Associated with galactic centre
Sagittarius B2	17 47.3 −28 24	—, 10, 70 Contains many different molecules
SS433	19 11.9 +4 58	* Compact object with high-velocity jets
CP1919	19 21.6 +21 52	0.08, 0.03, 0.005(?) First pulsar discovered; $P = 1.3375$ s
PSR 1937+21	19 39.6 +21 35	5, 0.2(?), 0.04(?) Millisecond pulsar; $P = 0.001\,558$ s
Cygnus A	19 59.5 +40 44	15 500, 4000, 2100 Strong radio galaxy
Cygnus X	20 22.6 +40 23	400, 150, 30 Complex region
BL Lacertae	22 02.7 +42 17	—, 5, 4 Radio galaxy; $m = 14.0$, $z = 0.07$
Cassiopeia A	23 23.4 +58 49	25 000, 4500, 2800 Supernova remnant
Jupiter		Bursts at metre wavelengths
Moon		Thermal source ($\approx$225 K)
Sun		20 000, 300 000, 900 000 Also intense bursts and strong, varying emissions

*Important source, although emission is weak and/or sporadic. Mean flux density less than one jansky.

VARIABLE GALAXIES

Some peculiar galaxies (Seyfert galaxies, BL Lacertae objects, and quasars) have bright, star-like nuclei that vary in brightness by up to several magnitudes on a time scale of months to years. These variations can be studied by amateurs and students, especially using photographic or electronic techniques. The table below lists the brightest variable galaxies. For more information, see *Sky & Telescope, 55,* p. 372 (1978), which gives finder charts and comparison stars for the four brightest Seyfert galaxies (indicated with asterisks in the table).

3C 273, the brightest quasar, was also the first quasar to be identified (in 1963). Charts for finding 3C 273 are at the bottom of this page. Start with the right-hand chart, which shows a "binocular-sized" field of view down to nearly 10th magnitude. The stars η Vir (magnitude 3.9), 16 Vir (5.0), and 17 Vir (6.5) are labelled; η Vir is the star immediately east of the autumnal equinox on the MARCH ALL-SKY MAP on p. 295. The two brightest stars to the west and southwest of the small rectangle are each magnitude 7.6. The area covered by the small rectangle is shown enlarged on the left-hand chart, on which several stars have their visual magnitudes indicated to the nearest tenth of a magnitude (with the decimal point omitted). The position of 3C 273 is indicated by a small cross. With a redshift $z = 0.158$, 3C 273 is receding from us at 44 000 km/s and is probably 2 or 3 billion ly from Earth, making it, by far, the intrinsically brightest (output $\approx 10^{39}$ W), most distant object that can be seen in a small telescope.

Name	Type	RA (2000) Dec		Magnitude
		h m	° ′	
NGC 1275*	Seyfert?	3 19.8	+41 31	11–13
3C 120	Seyfert	4 33.2	+5 21	14–16
OJ 287	BL Lac	8 54.9	+20 07	12–16
NGC 4151*	Seyfert	12 10.5	+39 24	10–12
3C 273	Quasar	12 29.2	+2 03	12–13
3C 345	Quasar	16 43.0	+39 48	14–17
Mkn. 509*	Seyfert	20 44.2	−10 43	12–13
BL Lac	BL Lac	22 02.8	+42 17	14–17
NGC 7469*	Seyfert	23 03.2	+8 52	12–13

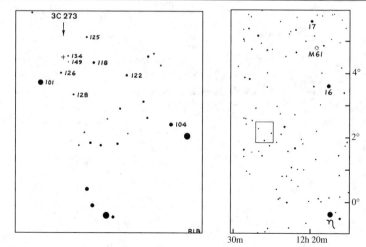

MAPS OF THE NIGHT SKY
By Roy Bishop

The maps on the next seven pages cover the entire sky. Stars are shown down to a magnitude of 4.5 or 5, that is, those that are readily apparent to the unaided eye on a reasonably dark night.

The first six maps are drawn for latitude 45°N but are useful for latitudes several degrees north or south of this. They show the hemisphere of sky visible at various times of year. Because the aspect of the night sky changes continuously with both longitude and time, while time zones change discontinuously with both longitude and time of year, it is not possible to state simply when a particular observer will find that his or her sky fits exactly one of the six maps. The month indicated above each map is the time of year when the map will match the "late evening" sky. On any particular night, successive maps will represent the sky as it appears every four hours later. For example, at 2 a.m. or 3 a.m. on a March night, the May map should be used. Just after dinner on a January night, the November map will be appropriate. The centre of each map is the *zenith,* the point directly overhead; the circumference is the horizon. To identify the stars, hold the map in front of you so that the part of the horizon you are facing (west, for instance) is downward. (The four letters around the periphery of each map indicate compass directions.)

The southern sky map is centred on the south celestial pole and extends to 20°S declination at its periphery. Thus there is considerable overlap with the southern areas of the other maps. Note that the orientation of the various names is generally inverted compared to that on the first six maps. This is in recognition that most users of this Handbook will be residents of the Northern Hemisphere and will make use of the southern sky map when they make trips to the tropics. Thus in "normal" use this map will be read in an area above its centre, unlike the first six maps, which are normally read below their centres. The months indicated around the edge of the map may be used to orient it to each of the preceding six maps and have the same "late evening" significance as explained above. Tick marks around the edge of the map indicate hours of right ascension, with hours 0, 3, 6, etc., labelled. Starting at the centre of the map, the series of small crosses along 0h right ascension indicates southern declinations 90°, 80°, 70°,..., 20°. With the aid of a drawing compass, an observer in the Northern Hemisphere can quickly locate a circle, centred on the south celestial pole, which represents the southern limit of his or her sky.

On all seven maps, stars forming the usual constellation patterns are linked by straight lines, constellation names being given in uppercase letters. Three constellations (Horologium, Mensa, and Microscopium) consist of faint stars; hence no patterns are indicated and the names are placed in parentheses. Small clusters of dots indicate the positions of bright star clusters, nebulae, or galaxies. The pair of wavy dotted lines indicates roughly the borders of the Milky Way. Small asterisks locate the directions of the galactic centre (GC), the north galactic pole (NGP), and the south galactic pole (SGP). LMC, SMC, and CS signify, respectively, the Large Magellanic Cloud, the Small Magellanic Cloud, and the Coal Sack. Two dashed lines appear on each of the first six maps. The one with more dashes is the celestial equator. Tick marks along this indicate hours of right ascension, the odd hours being labelled. The line with fewer dashes is the ecliptic, the apparent annual path of the Sun across the heavens. Letters along this line indicate the approximate position of the Sun at the beginning of each month. Also located along the ecliptic are the Northern Hemisphere vernal equinox (VE), summer solstice (SS), autumnal equinox (AE), and winter solstice (WS).

JANUARY ALL-SKY MAP

Notes:

MARCH ALL-SKY MAP

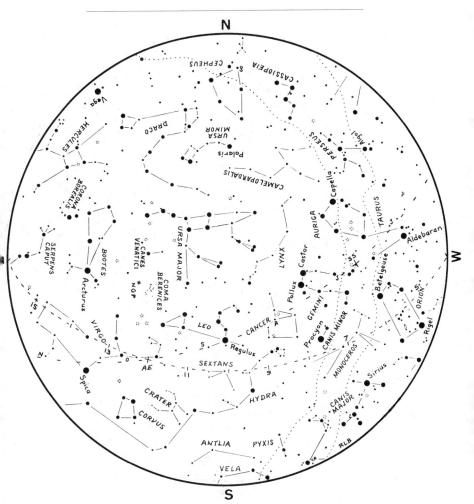

Notes:

MAY ALL-SKY MAP

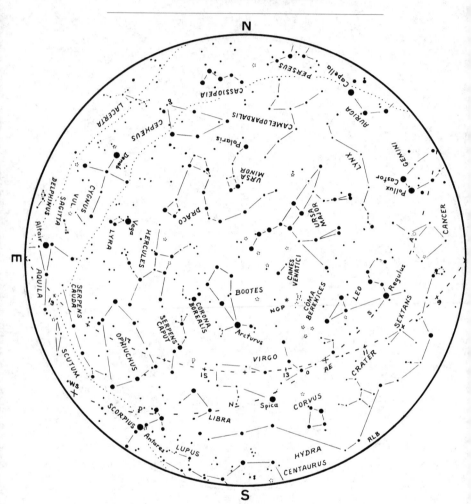

Notes:

JULY ALL-SKY MAP

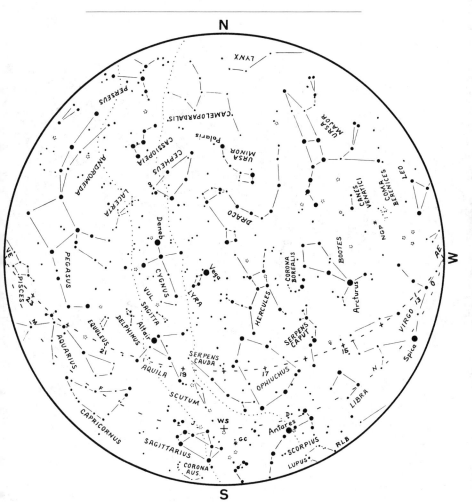

Notes:

SEPTEMBER ALL-SKY MAP

Notes:

NOVEMBER ALL-SKY MAP

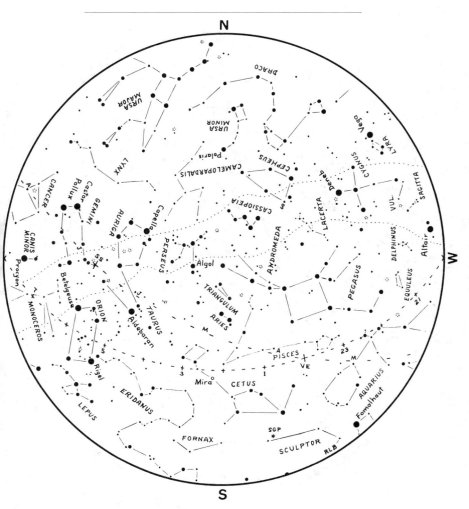

Notes:

THE SOUTHERN SKY

Notes:

OBSERVER'S HANDBOOK 2004
ORDER FORM

(The *Observer's Handbook* for the year 2004 will be available in September 2003.)

Price per copy
Includes shipping and handling

# copies*	Canada†	United States	Elsewhere‡
1–4	$27.77	$25.95 U.S.	$29.95 U.S.

*bulk-order pricing available upon request
†includes GST; GST registration number 119126282
‡shipped via airmail

Please send .... copies of the 2004 *Observer's Handbook*

Name ....

Address ....

....

....

Payment Enclosed $ ....   [ ] Cheque   [ ] Money Order

[ ] VISA   [ ] Mastercard   [ ] Amex

Number...

Name   ....

Expiry .... Signature...

Telephone (.........)...

Email   ....

Order on the Internet using your credit card at **www.store.rasc.ca**

or send this order form to:

The Royal Astronomical Society of Canada
136 Dupont Street
Toronto ON M5R 1V2
Canada

Phone: (416) 924-7973; fax: (416) 924-2911; email: orders@rasc.ca

To order any of the other publications of the RASC, including the award-winning *Observer's Calendar,* please contact the Society or visit **www.store.rasc.ca**.

This page intentionally left blank.

INDEX

SOME HOLIDAYS AND SPECIAL DATES, 2003

New Year's Day..Wed. Jan. 1
Martin Luther King Jr. Day (U.S.)...................Mon. Jan. 20

Chinese New Year ....Sat. Feb. 1
Winter Star Party, Florida Keys ....Mon. Feb. 3 – Sat. Feb. 8
Valentine's Day ....Fri. Feb. 14
President's Day ....Mon. Feb. 17

Islamic New Year ....Tue. Mar. 4

First Day of Passover (Pesach) ....Thu. Apr. 17
Good Friday ....Fri. Apr. 18
Easter Sunday..Sun. Apr. 20
Texas Star Party, Fort Davis, TX.....................Sun. Apr. 27 – Sun. May 4

International Astronomy Day............................Sat. May 10
Mother's Day ....Sun. May 11
Victoria Day (Canada) ....Mon. May 19
Riverside Telescope Makers Conference, CA..Fri. May 24 – Sun. May 25
Memorial Day (U.S.) ....Mon. May 26

Father's Day ....Sun. Jun. 15
St.-Jean-Baptiste Day (Quebec).......................Tue. Jun. 24
RASC General Assembly, Vancouver, BC.......Fri. Jun. 27 – Sun. Jun. 29

Canada Day..Tue. Jul. 1
Independence Day (U.S.)...................................Fri. Jul. 4
Mount Kobau Star Party, BC ....Sat. Jul. 26 – Sun. Aug. 3

Nova East, Smiley's Provincial Park, NS ....Fri. Aug. 1 – Sun. Aug. 3
Stellafane Convention, Springfield, VT ....Fri. Aug. 1 – Sat. Aug. 2
Civic Holiday (Canada) ....Mon. Aug. 4
Starfest, Mount Forest, ON..............................Thu. Aug. 21 – Sun. Aug. 24
Saskatchewan Star Party, Cypress Hills, SK....Fri. Aug. 22 – Sun. Aug. 24

Labour Day ....Mon. Sep. 1
Alberta Star Party, Caroline, AB......................Thu. Sep. 25 – Sun. Sep. 28
Rosh Hashanah..Sat. Sep. 27

Yom Kippur...Mon. Oct. 6
Thanksgiving Day (Canada) ....Mon. Oct. 13
Columbus Day (U.S.)..Mon. Oct. 13
First day of Ramadân ....Mon. Oct. 27
Halloween ....Fri. Oct. 31

Remembrance Day (Canada) ....Tue. Nov. 11
Veteran's Day (U.S.) ....Tue. Nov. 11
Thanksgiving Day (U.S.) ....Thu. Nov. 27

Christmas Day..Thu. Dec. 25
Boxing Day (Canada) ....Fri. Dec. 26